Reforming Family Justice – A Guide to the
Family Court and the Children
and Families Act 2014

Reforming Family Justice – A Guide to the Family Court and the Children and Families Act 2014

Sarah Blackmore

Jacqui Thomas

Family Law

Published by Family Law
A publishing imprint of Jordan Publishing Limited
21 St Thomas Street
Bristol BS1 6JS

British Library Cataloguing-in-Publication Data

A catalogue record for this book is available from the British Library.

ISBN 978 1 84661 890 1

Typeset by Letterpart Limited, Caterham on the Hill, Surrey CR3 5XL

Printed in Great Britain by Hobbs the Printers Limited, Totton, Hampshire SO40 3WX

FOREWORD BY SIR JAMES MUNBY
PRESIDENT OF THE FAMILY DIVISION

Sarah Blackmore and Jacqui Thomas have given us a large and important book that should be on the shelf of every family lawyer.

Reforming Family Justice charts the whole process of the reforms from the work of the Family Justice Review through all the subsequent planning, introduction and implementation, whilst at the same time providing an exemplary analysis of the new law and its subsequent judicial interpretation. This is both an acute work of contemporary legal history, which will be of enduring value, and an accurate guide to the law as it stands. Our authors weave together a wide range of materials to produce a compelling account which puts the new law in its wider historical, social and political context, at the same time as it provides a sure guide for the busy practitioner. They deserve our thanks and our congratulations.

No doubt the continuing processes of reform and the seemingly endless stream of judicial decisions will demand an early second edition. In the meantime, let us take full advantage of the first.

Sir James Munby
September 2014

PREFACE BY LORD JUSTICE RYDER

I am indebted to Sarah Blackmore and Jacqui Thomas for undertaking a task that is integral to the change programme that was envisaged when the recommendations of both the Family Justice Review and the judiciary were accepted. They are right to describe me as an ambassador for change. I am not the originator of change, merely, for a short time, its guardian. Real change is generated out of the good practice of the professionals who work on the ground in the many and difficult cases that come before the family court. It cannot be imposed by others although it can be influenced and led by the judgments of the senior courts, quality leadership and a structure which promotes research based good practice, empirical monitoring of outcomes and the management of priorities and cases within the family justice system. This invaluable book is central to an essential component of change which is education, the dissemination of good practice and the fostering of a co-operative and positive environment in which new and better ideas are allowed to develop.

I hope that the family court that we have created and the leadership and case management principles that have been developed will flourish to the advantage of the children whose futures are influenced by us. Lest it be thought that change places organisational management ahead of the interests of the child, let me be the first to say that in a family justice system the principles of proportionality and good change management must be viewed through the telescope of quality. We must never sacrifice the quality of what we do on the altar of price rationing or cost effectiveness. The quality of the judicial intervention in a child's life should be the object of scrutiny by professionals and public commentators alike. We must continually strive to improve both the quality of evidence and decision-making and this book will help all of us adapt our practices so as to achieve that aim.

I am very grateful to the authors for their careful and detailed consideration of some very important issues.

Sir Ernest Ryder
September 2014

INTRODUCTION

In 2014, the family justice system in England and Wales underwent seismic change. The previous three-tier court system of family proceedings courts, county courts and High Court was replaced by the single family court through the provisions of the Crime and Courts Act 2013, and for the first time statutory time limits were introduced for public law care proceedings through the Children and Families Act 2014 (the 2014 Act).

All areas of family law and family court users were affected, from separating parents to prospective adopters. The 2014 Act places greater emphasis on alternative forms of resolution, particularly mediation, by requiring applicants to attend at a mediation information and assessment meeting (MIAM) before issuing court proceedings in respect of their children or finances.

This book aims to provide an overview to the 2014 Act, with explanations as to the reasons behind the reforms, as well as up-to-date case commentaries.

In chapter 1, the case for change is set out, tracing the history of the family justice review, and the research findings that led to the arguments in favour of reform. The arrangements of the new family court are then explained and the structure of the family court is examined.

The Children and Families Act has a major impact on three main areas; private law, dispute resolution and public law. In chapter 2 the new approach to private law disputes is explored. The effect of the legal aid reforms following the Legal Aid, Sentencing and Punishment of Offenders Act 2012 (LAPSO) cannot be ignored, with the resulting increase in litigants in person appearing before the court.

The reforms to the private law system resulted in an entirely new Child Arrangements Programme (CAP), which aims to simplify and streamline the process, clearly signposting parties to the appropriate services and setting out the stages of court applications. References are provided for links to the up-to-date court forms and draft orders in use at the time of writing.

The Child Arrangements Programme reflects the re-emphasis on dispute resolution services. One unforeseen consequence of the LASPO cuts to legal aid was a vast reduction in the number of couples turning to mediation before going to court, despite public funding remaining available for both the mediation process, and legal advice running alongside mediation. CAP again signposts parties to mediation, and the CFA 2014 makes attendance at a MIAM compulsory prior to a court application. Chapter 3 examines the use of mediation and explains the process, as well as providing draft memorandums of agreement and statements of financial information, the written documents which follow a successful mediation.

Chapter 4 turns attention to the public law reforms and the revisions made to the public law outline. Taryn Lee QC examines the learning curve that took place during the transitional period and the lessons learnt from that time, before the new Public Law Outline and the case management orders are provided by the rest of the chapter. Integral to the reform of the public law system is the introduction of the statutory time limit of 26 weeks for the completion of a care case, unless extended by the court. It is hoped, and research shows, that the accompanying reduction in delay will result in better outcomes for the children that find themselves in the system.

One of the mechanisms used in order to reduce the delays in the care system is the reduction in the reliance on independent experts, which is examined in chapter 5. The Family Procedure Rules 2010, Part 25 has been significantly amended to reduce the number of experts, and to remind all practitioners that the social workers and guardians in a case are often the only experts required by the Court.

The public law system remains the focus of chapter 6 which examines recent policy changes in the field of adoption, and the cases recently decided by the higher courts in that sphere.

The final area considered by the authors is the move towards greater transparency in the family courts and the recent case-law relating to reporting restriction orders.

The appendices to this book include all relevant sections of statute, and the main statutory instruments, as well as the most up-to-date court forms where available.

The law is stated as at 30 June 2014.

Sarah Blackmore
Jacqui Thomas
September 2014

ACKNOWLEDGMENTS

This book grew out of the authors' joint work and research while compiling family law updates on a weekly basis for No 37 Park Square Chambers Family E-lerter service. We are immensely grateful to Sir James Munby P and Lord Justice Ryder for their input into this final version.

We would like to thank everyone who has been behind us, from the initial support and encouragement of our senior clerk, Leigh Royall, who suggested the subject matter in the first place, to everyone who subsequently gave their backing and advice, including Lord Justice McFarlane whose enthusiasm for the written word is infectious. We have also been very kindly assisted by Mr Justice Cobb in relation to the private law reforms. Thanks are also due to His Honour Judge Dowse for his support and enthusiasm for this mammoth task.

We could not have completed this project without the expertise and know-how of Greg Woodgate and his team at Jordan Publishing, who we'd like to thank for all of their help and assistance.

In addition, Gemma Garfoot (Partner at Burton & Dyson Solicitors) has provided invaluable assistance by furnishing us with forms and documents otherwise inaccessible to barristers. As has Sarah Monaghan (Solicitor at North Lincolnshire Council), who together with social workers have allowed us access to and provided input into the balance sheets in chapter 6.

Huge thanks also go to Cafcass for their provision of the example Analysis and Recommendations in chapter 5, in particular the author, Carla Thomson (Family Court Advisor, Hull Locality Team) as well as Maureen Fitzsimmons (Service Manager, Hull & South Humber) and of course Anthony Douglas, Chief Executive.

Finally, we are hugely indebted to our respective families for their patience with us while we took time to write, most notably of course our children, Connie, Nancy, Sophia and Charlie.

CONTENTS

TABLE OF CASES

References are to paragraph numbers.

TABLE OF STATUTES

References are to paragraph numbers.

TABLE OF STATUTORY INSTRUMENTS

References are to paragraph numbers.

CHAPTER 1

THE CASE FOR CHANGE

THE FAMILY JUSTICE REVIEW

1.1   In 2010, David Norgrove, an economist, who had no connection with the family justice system (purposely chosen to enable him to undertake the task independently and objectively, with no preconceptions of how the system operates) was appointed by the Ministry of Justice as Chair of the Family Justice Review Panel. He was assisted in this extensive role by Lord Justice McFarlane, who was to provide an invaluable contribution.

1.2   The family justice system within England and Wales is, and was under strain, with an ever increasing number of cases being brought before the courts, and those cases taking longer and longer to conclude, the need to change was evident.

1.3   The Family Justice Review Panel published its interim report in March 2011, and thereafter, following a consultation which involved over 600 responses, its final report in November that same year. Whilst making some wide reaching recommendations – the initial message; spelt out loud and clear by David Norgrove, was that:[1]

> 'The legal framework of family justice in England and Wales is strong, thanks to the vision of those who constructed the Children Act 1989. Its principles are right, in particular the starting point that the welfare of children must be paramount. And we can be proud of much of what we have done in the past twenty years in terms of processes, institutions and people.'

1.4   Starting with that premise in mind, there were of course many areas in which the family justice system was failing with the most important issue to be tackled for children and families being the question of delay; not only in care cases; which at the time of the final report were taking on average over 60 weeks to reach conclusion, but also in private law disputes, which were taking 32 weeks. On the basis that decisions made by the courts in care cases are some of the toughest that can be made, and that private law cases increasingly involve child protection issues, including serious safeguarding matters it was clear that the damaging consequences of delay in having cases resolved, is concerning not just for the children involved in the individual cases, but for society as a whole.

---

[1]   Interim Report of the Family Justice Review (March 2011), p 3.

The timetable for the child

1.5   It is worth noting at this stage that in response to this Family Justice Review, the Childhood Wellbeing Research Centre (a partnership between the Thomas Coram Research Unit and other centres at the Institute of Education, the Centre for Child and Family Research at Loughborough University and the Personal Social Services Research Unit at the University of Kent) was commissioned by the Department for Education to conduct research into child development, in order to assist understanding amongst those working in the family justice system in areas relating to:[2]

‘•   neuroscience perspectives on children's cognitive, social and emotional development;
•   the implications of maltreatment on childhood and adulthood wellbeing;
•   evidence concerning the outcomes of interventions by the courts and children's social care; and
•   timeframes for intervening and why they are out of kilter with those for children.'

Such is the importance of these issues that no-one involved in family justice should be in any doubt that the child's welfare is their paramount concern.

1.6   One of the overwhelming conclusions of this research is of course, that delay in dealing with cases involving children is against their best interests and further that 'there is a complex interaction between child development timeframes and delayed actions by local authorities and the courts'.[3]

1.7   There have been recent concerns raised by Professor Sue White (Professor of Social Work (Children and Families) at the University of Birmingham) and Professor David Wastell (a cognitive neuro-scientist and current Professor of Information Systems at Nottingham University Business School), in their presentation *The child's timeframe – a neuro scientific perspective* (May 2013) that the DfE research was over-simplified, and that being over-zealous in trying to achieve finality in proceedings too quickly is more damaging to a child than purposeful delay.

1.8   All that said, the length of time proceedings relating to children were taking to conclude seemed to be ever increasing, it needed to be addressed.

The case against delay

1.9   The 'unconscionable delay' that was occurring was being contributed to by the lack of a cohesive system, with the number of organisations and individuals involved in it being too large and disparate. In addition to recommendations regarding legislative changes, the Family Justice Review

---

[2]   *Decision-making within a child's timeframe: An overview of current research evidence for family justice professionals concerning child development and the impact of maltreatment* (October 2012), p 7.
[3]   Ibid, p 87.

recommended the setting up of a Family Justice Service, managed by a Family Justice Board, with the overall aim being:[4]

> 'to drive significant improvements in the performance of the family justice system where performance is defined in terms of how effective (and efficient) the system is in supporting the delivery of the best possible outcomes for children who come into contact with it.'

The Government response to the Family Justice Review: A system with children and families at its heart

1.10 Three months after the final Family Justice Review report, in February 2012, the Government published its response to the recommendations. In accepting the overwhelming majority of them, it was keen to stress that its vision was for a 'system with children's needs at its heart'. Further, it was being guided by eight key principles of reform in coming to its conclusions, namely:[5]

> 'That the welfare of the child remains the paramount consideration in any proceedings determining the upbringing of the child;
>
> That the family is nearly always the best place for bringing up children, except where there is a risk of significant harm;
>
> That in private law, specifically, problems should be resolved out of court, and the courts will only become involved where it is really necessary;
>
> Where the court is the right option, that children deserve a family court in which their needs come first;
>
> That both in public and private law cases children must be given an opportunity to have their voices heard in the decisions that affect them;
>
> That the process must protect vulnerable children, and their families;
>
> That this is a task not limited in responsibility to one organisation or another, but something we must all work on together; and
>
> That judicial independence must be upheld as the system is made more coherent and managed more effectively.'

1.11 It was keen to provide its vision for wider reforms further to its response to the Munro Review in 2011 (commissioned following the tragic Baby P

---

[4]   Family Justice Board *Action Plan to Improve the Performance of the Family Justice System* (January 2013), p 4.
[5]   The Government Response to the Family Justice Review *A system with children and families at its heart* (February 2012), p 8.

case[6]), namely that it recognised that in reforming the court process, in particular tackling delay, that all those involved in safeguarding children must work together with the government:[7]

> 'to build a child protection system where the focus is very firmly on the experience of the child or young person's journey from needing to receiving help.'

1.12   Further that:[8]

> 'what is needed is a fundamental shift in the way the system works, to enable professionals to focus on the needs of children, young people and families and how to give them the best possible help.'

In essence, what the government foresaw was the need for a flexible approach to assessment from social workers and other professionals, which had to include a reduction in bureaucracy.

1.13   The government didn't however accept all the recommendations of the Family Justice Review. The following aspects are worthy of note and were rejected:

(a)   Local authorities should not pay a fee for issuing public law applications – the government stating 'court fees are necessary to ensure that the family courts are properly funded'.[9]

(b)   Appointment of a Vice President of the Family Division and the renaming of Family Division liaison judges to family presiding judges – the government deciding that 'the judiciary will deliver any necessary leadership changes within the existing legislative framework'.[10]

(c)   Extension of a public law case beyond 26 weeks would need agreement of the relevant designated family judge (DFJ) or family liaison judge – the government felt that such '… would encroach on judicial independence and may create further delay'.[11]

1.14   In so far as relates to private law proceedings, the government was keen to reflect and consider further the recommendation that no legislation should be introduced that creates or risks creating the perception that there is a parental right to substantially shared or equal time for both parents:[12]

---

[6]   The serious case review into the death of Baby Peter can be found at http://www.haringeylscb. org/executive_summary_peter_final.pdf.

[7]   The Government Response to the Family Justice Review *A system with children and families at its heart* (February 2012), p 30.

[8]   Ibid.

[9]   Ibid, p 38.

[10]   Ibid, p 40.

[11]   Ibid, p 55.

[12]   Ibid, p 66.

'[The government] believes that legislation may have a role to play in supporting shared parenting and will consider legislative options for encouraging both parents to play as full a role as possible in their children's upbringing.'

1.15 Following this response by the government and (as is clear) the acceptance of the majority of the recommendations made by the Family Justice Review, the Family Justice Board, was created in March 2012, with David Norgrove appointed as its Chair in July that year. In January 2013, the Family Justice Board published its Action Plan for the three years from its creation (up to 2015), indicating that in order to:[13]

'deliver against its high-level aim, that it has particular focus on four key aspects of system performance as follows:

- reducing delay in public law cases and making progress against the proposed six month time limit for care cases;
- resolving private law cases out of court where appropriate;
- building greater cross-agency coherence; and
- tackling variations in local performance.'

1.16 In addition to this national Family Justice Board, there have been established 46 local Boards, aimed at improving and delivering performance at local level – all of which have the over-arching umbrella of the national Board to ensure the much needed cohesive approach.

1.17 Another area of the family justice system that the Family Justice Review identified as lacking cohesion was the judiciary and the court system generally. A clear recommendation was that judicial continuity in dealing with both public and private law cases is vital, that changes are needed to ensure that the ways of working in the different courts and areas of the country become more cohesive, and that strong case management is achieved in every case to ensure the best outcomes for children.

RYDER LJ'S WORK AND THE JUDICIAL PROPOSALS

1.18 On 2 November 2011, Mr Justice Ryder (as he then was) was appointed as Judge-in-Charge of the Modernisation of Family Justice, following the Family Justice Review Panel's final report. His appointment, by the President of the Family Division, with the agreement of the Lord Chief Justice was an obvious one, he having worked alongside Mr Justice Munby (as he then was) and Mr Justice Coleridge in 2003/2004 in the formulation of the original Protocol for Case Management of Public Law Cases, as well as being the architect of the original Private Law Programme in 2004. Thereafter, he was charged with, and devised the Public Law Outline (PLO) and the Experts Practice Direction and led on its revision in the period up to April 2010. He has

---

[13] Family Justice Board *Action Plan to Improve the Performance of the Family Justice System* (January 2013), p 4.

been an ambassador for change, improvement and modernisation of family justice for many years, prior to this appointment.

1.19 His task, over a nine month period was to prepare the judiciary's response to the Review by the end of July 2012. In so doing he engaged with over 5,000 interested parties, and accepted proposals from a plethora of organisations, judges, academics and jurists. He provided updates, under the title *The Family Justice Modernisation Programme* and at the outset made his position clear when he stated:[14]

> 'I am convinced that for further change to be effective, there will need to be a strong consensus and a commitment to a change in culture from all who contribute to the family justice system.'

1.20 Within this first update, he made clear his aim (as well as having agreed proposals in place) to have a plan for their implementation by the end of July 2012, and he identified 10 key areas upon which he would focus, namely:[15]

> '1. Family justice governance
>
> 2. Family management information (including performance and effectiveness)
>
> 3. Judicial and inter-disciplinary training and communication
>
> 4. Unified Family Court
>
> 5. Judicial leadership and management
>
> 6. Judicial deployment (including patterns and listing guidance)
>
> 7. Gatekeeping and allocation (including tracking and continuity)
>
> 8. Case management (including case progression, timetables and deadlines)
>
> 9. Use of experts and assessors
>
> 10. External services including court social work, mediation and ADR, contact services, safeguarding, testing, experts, representation and support in court.'

1.21 Once the government published its response to the Review, on 6 February 2012, work accelerated, and by March 2012, progress was being made within the 10 key areas. The Family Justice Board was under construction and expected to be launched (as it was) in April 2012; it was expected (and it was achieved) that a case management system would be ready for use in a national pilot for collecting data and providing a reporting system; the creation, by statute, of a unified family court was expected within the next year; the judiciary generally had reached consensus about how the new family court

---

[14] *The Family Justice Modernisation Programme: First Update* (January 2012), p 2.
[15] Ibid.

would be managed both nationally and locally, as well as how their roles relating to case management and allocation of work would take shape; as far as case management generally was concerned, Ryder J stated:[16]

> 'The single most important change that I recommend is the creation of standard and exceptional case tracks with guidance in the form of a pathway that describes how some cases can and should be completed within 26 weeks.'

1.22 The use of experts in proceedings was a matter which he described as one of his 'quick wins', (matters which he proposed could and should be implemented without delay and without the need for legislative changes). It has of course resulted in the implementation of the amended Part 25 of the Family Procedure Rules 2010 on 31 January 2013, and work was being done to set out in document form the external services that the new family court would be entitled to expect.

1.23 As indicated above, on 2 April 2012, a new management information system, the case management system, was launched nationally, replacing the varied and often flawed systems that had existed. The system tracks every public law case issued from the beginning of April 2012, and was a pilot for the whole of the financial year 2012/2013. At its commencement, Ryder J described it as:[17]

> '... a major innovation. For the first time the family courts will have a record of baseline information so as to understand where public law cases are allocated and what is the consequence in terms of delay of the case management decisions made ... For the first time we will know why unplanned delay is occurring and we will be able to say so ...'

THE CASE MONITORING SYSTEM (CMS) AND THE TRI-BOROUGH PROJECT

1.24 The intention (and ultimately the reality) being that within a newly centralised system, the importance of case monitoring and management information was fully recognised. The case monitoring system (CMS) was originally introduced in a trial form to a specification written by the judiciary, with particular contribution from the designated family judges. The CMS has introduced pro-forma recitals to orders, which specify clearly the reasons for any adjournments, enabling analysis of the reasons for delay, as well as information about workload, allocation, timelines and the use of experts, more of which below.

1.25 The use of a single court and case management system was first trialled in the Tri-Borough Care Proceedings Pilot, which encompassed the London Boroughs of Kensington and Chelsea, Hammersmith and Fulham and

---

[16] *The Family Justice Modernisation Programme: Third Update* (March 2012), p 3.
[17] *The Family Justice Modernisation Programme: Fourth Update* (April 2012), p 2.

Westminster, working together in the dual aims of improving decision-making for children who are going through care proceedings, and minimising unnecessary delay. The pilot, which was the first of its kind, launched on 1 April 2012 and ran for 12 months. A similar tri-borough experiment took place in Cheshire and Merseyside.

1.26 The project was extremely successful in reducing delay within the system, with the final report showing that the median length of cases had reduced to 26 weeks, although it had been challenging to achieve that, and it wasn't possible in all cases.[18] The Tri-borough Project was swiftly followed by the Bi-borough Project in the London Boroughs of Camden and of Islington, who followed a similar path. It was recognised that for the reforms to work, local authorities across the country needed to demonstrate that they could produce good quality pre-application preparation, as that was the only way that cases could conclude within the 26 week timeframe.

1.27 Following on from the success of the London Boroughs, other regions conducted pilot studies, for example that of West Yorkshire, which began a pilot in February 2013. The aims of the pilot included to reduce the delay in the system, which was widely recognised as detrimental to children. At the beginning of the pilot, the average time for a care case to be concluded across West Yorkshire was 45 weeks. The government timescale introduced in the new Act was 26 weeks, and the local authorities in West Yorkshire set out to achieve that result. The principles of the pilot were set out as follows:[19]

> 'The main purpose of the pilot is to improve outcomes for children;
>
> It is child focused;
>
> It is recognised that timely decision making in Family Proceedings is beneficial to children;
>
> It will seek to work with children and families;
>
> It will be an iterative and reflective process that will identify and implement improvements during the period of the pilot;
>
> Confidentiality will be maintained throughout the pilot. Cases will be identified only, in any documentation used in the pilot, by reference to the case number (and therefore to the originating local authority and court) and not by reference to the child's name or specific judges.
>
> Key stakeholders have agreed a set of commitments for their agency.'[20]

---

[18] See http://www.uea.ac.uk/documents/3437903/0/Triboro-Report.pdf/3ca637 ea-543e-4354-869e-40bef566c021.

[19] Pilot Proposal (25 February 2013).

[20] West Yorkshire Care Proceedings Pilot – Commitment and Expectations of All Stakeholders (25 February 2013).

The West Yorkshire pilot sought to build on the experience and learning of the Tri-Borough Pilots, which identified the following as the main causes of delay.

1.28 *Improving the quality of social work assessments and statements to court.* This was achieved by providing social workers with Best Practice Guidance and briefings; ensuring that, other than in exceptional situations, the same social worker held the case throughout proceedings; employing a case manager to provide support and mentor for social workers presenting in court and to monitor timeliness of statements; ensuring senior managers take a proactive approach to oversight of cases going through court.

1.29 *Judicial continuity and case management of timescales for the child from the court.* The pilot authorities worked with the judiciary and courts to arrange court sittings to promote judicial continuity in the majority of cases during the pilot period. Briefings for the judges helped to encourage tighter case management and the improvements in the quality of assessments and statements from social workers encouraged a reduction in the use of expert assessments.

1.30 Timely and proportionate involvement from Cafcass guardians was agreed. Early direction from the judge in the case ensured focused and directed assessments from the guardian.

1.31 Examination of options for multi-disciplinary assessment provision helped to ensure good decision making early in the process, in relation to the use of expert assessments, so that they were only used to provide additional information that the local authority has been unable to present to the court.

1.32 Critical reflection about pilot cases took place involving key stakeholders and post-case reviews created a learning loop throughout the life of the pilot.

1.33 Tracking of cases and monitoring of timeliness, numbers of hearings, costs and outcomes for children were utilised to promote transparency and to evaluate the success of the pilot. A cumulative running total of the cost of each case within the pilot was used to inform decision making and track progress against the timetable for the child.[21]

1.34 The diagram below provides a summary of the issues to be addressed by the project.

---

[21] Adapted from The Tri-borough: London Borough of Hammersmith and Fulham, Royal Borough of Kensington and Chelsea and City of Westminster *Good decisions for children in court: the Care Proceedings Pilot* (February 2012), Capital Ambition Business Case for Funding Application.

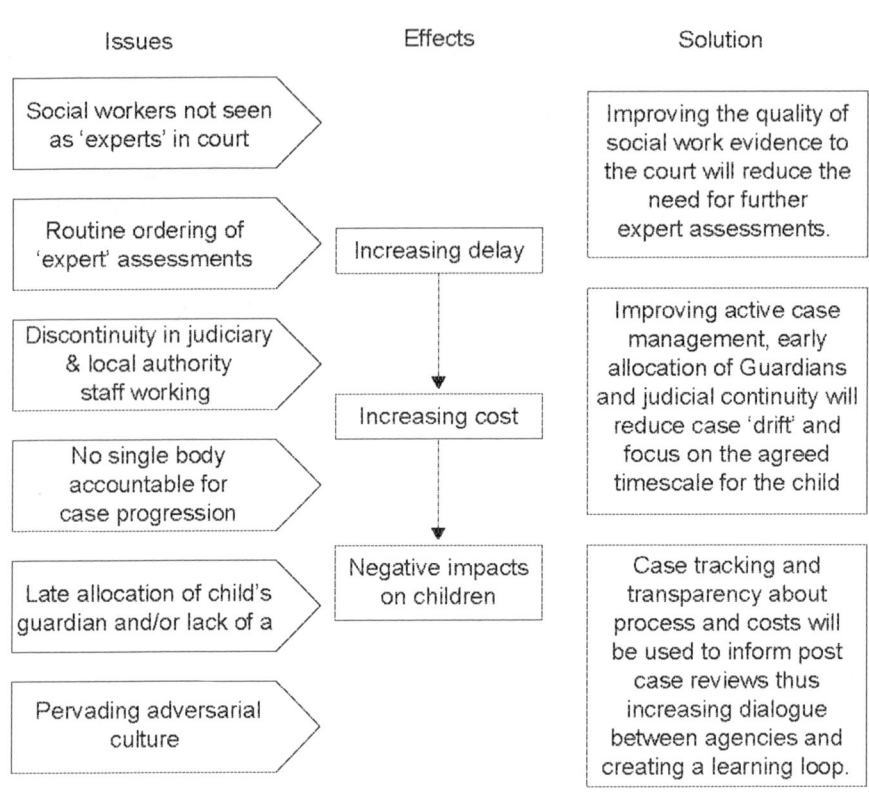

Case monitoring systems

1.35 Integral to the success of the modernisation project was the ability of both individual court centres and the national justice system to be able to monitor the progress of cases, with emphasis on understanding the causes of delay.

1.36 The new care monitoring system is a judicially led management information programme intended to provide accurate ongoing information about case volumes, case progress and allocation. The system will provide the case management information necessary to enable leadership judges and the administration to oversee and manage public law caseloads and the allocation of individual cases in their care centres. The programme will also assist judges, legal advisers and magistrates to focus on avoiding delay for children and will help identify the real causes of delay. CMS has been jointly developed by the judiciary and HMCTS and has been written to a judicial specification which looks at both the real progress of a case through the court and the DFJ's and justices clerks' responsibilities for all cases within their courts.

1.37 The system was piloted nationwide from 2 April 2012 from when all new care and supervision cases were entered on to the system.

1.38 The CMS case summary provided judges/legal advisers/benches with ongoing information updated for every hearing about the ages of the child or children they are dealing with, the length of time a case has been running (measured in weeks), the number of hearings which there have been, any adjournments of hearings and applications for experts.

1.39 Some of the draft forms used by the court in order to achieve this are reproduced in chapter 4. These 'case management systems' were developed locally by the designated family judges in liasion with their court staff, whose responsibility it was to enter the details on the system thereby enabling national statistics to be gathered and analysed.

1.40 A central benefit of information gathering in this way relates to the openness and accountability now inherent in the system, whereby the performance of individual local authorities and court centres can be analysed and compared. The reasons for any adjournment or delay are required to be recorded within the case management system, with the finger firmly pointed at those parties responsible.

1.41 In addition to the formal recording on the system, many DFJ's also adopted a preference for a form of order which named the advocates present on any particular day, and recitals setting out why the case may have departed from the usual timetable of CMC, IRH and final hearing, if that is the situation. Those reasons could include the local authority filing evidence late, the parents responding late, a late application for expert opinion, or a lack of court time. The table below illustrates some of the common reasons recorded on the system:

Evidence	No/poor pre proceedings preparation by Local Authority
	No poor kinship assessments
	No expert instructed by LA
	No/poor parental evidence
	No/poor core assessment (*this includes assessment of parents*)
	No Genogram (*no friends or family identified before hearing*)
	No/poor placement evidence
	No/poor Cafcass analysis
	Disclosure of medical records or materials from other agencies/ proceedings required
Case Management	**No timetable for the child**
	No threshold
	Official Solicitor not instructed/ready (*re adult capacity*)
	Lack of judicial continuity
	No key issue analysis
	Cafcass not allocated/present
	Insufficient time/No courtroom available
	Non compliance with directions
	New party joined
	Lawyers not present or ready
	Interpreter not available
Planned	Consolidation with other proceedings
	New/alternative care plan (*including kinship placement*)
	Parallel proceedings (*including joint directions with crime*)
	New baby/pregnancy

In addition to the 'naming and shaming' approach of tackling delay, wasted costs orders against local authorities or individual advocates also became more likely.

1.42 The President of the Family Division, Sir James Munby had throughout the year-long pilot (and beyond) provided his *View from the President's Chamber*, giving robust guidance to both judges and practitioners alike as to the importance, (amongst other important issues dealt with later in this book) of the success of the CMS, by the issuing of Presidents Guidance documents and by the implementation of the revised Public Law Outline and the piloting of the single family court nationally from 1 July 2013.

1.43 The effect of such an extensive and cohesive case management and practice regime meant the significant amendment of the Family Procedure Rules 2010, in particular *Practice Direction 36C – Pilot Scheme: Care and Supervision Proceedings and other Proceedings under Part 4 of the Children Act 1989*. The launch of the Pilot Scheme within a court area was decided upon by its DFJ, with a choice of either 1 July 2013, 5 August 2013, 2 September 2013 or 7 October 2013, with the purpose of it being:[22]

> '… to assess the use of new practices and procedures to support the 26 week time limit for Part 4 proceedings in the amendments made to s.32 of the Children Act 1989 by clause 14 of the Children and Families Bill, as introduced into Parliament on 4th February 2013.'

1.44 On 10 May 2012, the Crime and Courts Bill was laid before Parliament, and received Royal Assent on 25 April 2013, with the Crime and Courts Act now creating the single family court, which unifies, for the first time the family proceedings court, the family jurisdiction of the county court and the general family work heard by High Court judges. The Family Division of the High Court's supervisory, inherent and international jurisdictions remain separate, as does the Court of Protection. At the same time, it creates a single county court for England and Wales, replacing the 109 local county courts.

THE SINGLE FAMILY COURT

1.45 Central to Ryder J's (as he then was) recommendations was the concept of a unified single court. It was considered vital that this was in place before the other changes came into effect.

1.46 In addition, the Family Justice Review recognised the need for a 'joined up' Family Justice Service,[23] sponsored by the Ministry of Justice, with recognised links to the Department for Education. This represented wholesale

---

[22] *Practice Direction 36C Family Procedure Rules – Pilot Scheme: Care and Supervision Proceedings and other proceedings under Part 4 of the Children Act 1989*, para 4.1.

[23] Family Justice Review, Final Report (November 2011), p 49.

structural change to the court system, on a scale not seen in living history. The core work of the Family Justice Service was described as:

> 'to monitor what was happening in the system, both locally and nationally, to identify best practice and difficulties and to consider how problems could be addressed in a practical way.'

1.47 However, whilst this body relates to the monitoring of the court, it is not responsible for the family judiciary or the operation of the courts. The Review[24] criticised the family court structure that was then in place, and built on the recommendations of the interim report, that there should be a single family court, in place of the previous three-tier system of family proceedings court, county court and High Court. The unified family court has a single point of entry. The full recommendation came following Ryder J's reviews and investigations into the process, (Ryder J's final recommendation):

> 'the single family court will be the vehicle for a significant change of culture characterised by strong judicial leadership and management and evidence-based good practice; a network of local family court centres judicially led and managed by the Designated Family Judges, where all levels of judge and magistrate will sit as Judges of the Family Court.' (final report pg ii).

1.48 All levels of judge and magistrate are members of the single family court, and all sit as judges of the family court. The High Court retains its specialist jurisdiction and it continues with Family Division liaison judges, who are responsible for implementing the change programme in each of the regions, or circuits, of England and Wales.

1.49 Instrumental to the changes is the fact that judges and magistrates sit in the same building wherever possible, which was rarely the case previously. Proceedings commence in the one court, and there is now one administrative system providing listing, case progression and other business support functions. Each regional centre has a designated family judge (DFJ) who is responsible for efficient case management.

1.50 The allocation of cases is now to be dealt with from one centralised office for each region. All matters are therefore issued in the family court, rather than in a particular tier of court. The majority of allocation decisions will be taken daily by a team in each family court comprised of a justices clerk and district judge, with contentious decisions in the event of serious issue being taken by the local DFJ. There will be a detailed allocation schedule for the division of work between the different family court judges – magistrates, district judges (county court and magistrates court), circuit judges and High Court judges. Only work expressly reserved to the High Court will be issued there. Upon allocation, standard directions will then be forthcoming, which will need to be complied with.

---

[24] Ibid, p 72.

THE FAMILY COURT – ITS SHAPE AND ORGANISATION

1.51 The creation of the family court by amendment to Part 1 of the County Courts Act 1984 pursuant to s 17 Crime and Courts Act 2013, namely:

31A Establishment of the family court

(1) There is to be a court in England and Wales, called the family court, for the purpose of exercising the jurisdiction and powers conferred on it –

(a)   by or under this or any other Act, or
(b)   By or under any Act, or Measure, of the National Assembly for Wales.

(2) The family court is to be a court of record and have a seal.

is the basis for the whole of the family justice system. The culmination of the months and years of work to make the aims initially identified by the Family Justice Review a reality.

1.52 The President repeated the four key features of the family court in *View from the President's Chambers (5)*[25] as:

(a)   It deals with ALL family cases with the exception of two classes of case that are reserved for the Family Division (reserved work):
   •   cases invoking the inherent jurisdiction of the High Court, whether in relation to children (wardship) or incapacitated or vulnerable adults (Court of Protection);
   •   international cases (will include cases involving application for relief under either the Hague Convention or Brussels IIR).
(b)   The judiciary of the family court include:
   •   High Court judges;
   •   circuit judges and recorders;
   •   district judges (including district judges of the magistrates' court and district judges of the Principal Registry of the Family Division (now the Central family court);
   •   magistrates.

1.53 Wherever possible all the judges of the family court will sit 'under the same roof':

(a)   The family proceedings court no longer exists, all family work previously dealt with by the county court is now dealt with in the family court. Except for the reserved work of the Family Division, cases that require to be heard by a High Court judge are heard in the family court by a High Court judge (or a s 9 judge). Therefore cases no longer are transferred to the High Court on the grounds of complexity. No transfer of a case from the family court to the High Court will be permitted unless ordered by the

---

[25]   [2013] Fam Law 1137.

President or a High Court judge (not a s 9 judge). One consequence of this is that in future far fewer cases than at present will be issued or heard in the High Court.

(b) England and Wales continues to be divided into geographical areas judicially led and managed by the designated family judge (subject as at present to the Family Division liaison judge and the President of the Family Division).

The local family court

1.54 There are now no longer 'care centres' or 'family hearing centres', the overarching principle for the area for which the designated family judge is responsible being that all the locations at which hearings take place are managed and operated as a single family court. The three key features of the local family court are that:

(a) There is one central location – the designated family centre – where the designated family judge is based and is the principal location at which hearings take place. There may be one or more hearing centres attached to the designated family centre at which hearings can also take place.

(b) There is a 'single point of entry' located at the designated family centre, for the issue of process for the entire local family court.

(c) There is centralised and unified administration, principally based at the designated family centre, for the entire local family court. The key elements of this are:
  - a centralised 'back office';
  - a centralised 'gatekeeping and allocation team'; and
  - centralised listing.[26]

The family court – London

1.55 Because of the complexities involved in the previously huge number of family proceedings and county courts across London, a complete overhaul was necessary to ensure the key features of the local family court could be implemented effectively. The new structure in London has six key elements:[27]

(a) there are three family courts, each with its own DFJ and designated family centre (DFC):
  - The Central Family Court (also includes the Family Drug and Alcohol Court) – First Avenue House (DFC);
  - East London Family Court – Gee Street (as an interim position until Autumn 2014 when other premises in East London will be available) (DFC);
  - West London Family Court – Hatton Cross (DFC);

---

26 Ibid, p 2.
27 Ibid, p 3.

(b) each of the three family courts have a 'single point of entry' and a centralised and unified administration;

(c) each of the three family courts serve a number of local authorities;

(d) each of the three family courts has a number of linked hearing centres;

(e) the hearing of care cases is confined to a limited number of courts;

(f) private law and divorce cases will be handled by all three DFCs and their linked hearing centres, though some specialist jurisdictions may be reserved to the DFCs.

FAMILY DRUG AND ALCOHOL COURT (FDAC)

1.56 This branch of the family court has, since its inception been producing increasingly positive outcomes for children and their families. The President is an enthusiastic supporter of what he describes as 'the FDAC approach' expressing the same in *Re S (A Child)*[28] and stating at paras [35]–[38]:

'The FDAC approach is crucially important. The simple reality is that FDAC works ... FDAC is, it must be, a vital component in the new Family Court.'

1.57 Whilst currently FDAC operates in London only, at the President's Conference in May 2014, Sir James Munby P set every DFJ a challenge – to see FDAC rolled out across the country, as soon as possible. He expects to receive a report from each DFJ at his Conference in May 2015 as to the progress made. He says in his *View from the President's Chambers (12)*[29], he wants to know:

'Is FDAC up and running? If not, are there plans for FDAC? If not, what are the problems?'

1.58 It is recognised that the DFJs cannot achieve this vision on their own. It requires much assistance from local partner agencies, in particular the local authorities and local health and mental health bodies. It is clear that FDAC must go from strength to strength.

LOCATIONS/GEOGRAPHY IN LONDON – PUBLIC LAW

1.59 There are 33 local authorities in London, of which (following on from the original Tri-borough Pilot) 26 have formed themselves into 8 similar groupings to the project, sharing legal services or otherwise co-ordinating their handling of care cases. They are:

- Westminster, Kensington and Chelsea, Hammersmith and Fulham;
- Barnet, Enfield, Haringey;
- Camden, Islington;

---

[28] [2014] EWCC B44 (Fam), [2014] 2 FLR 575.
[29] [2014] Fam Law 978.

- Brent, Ealing, Harrow;
- Richmond, Kingston, Hounslow, Merton, Sutton;
- Lambeth, Southwark, Lewisham, Greenwich;
- Newham, Redbridge, Barking and Dagenham, Waltham Forest, and;
- Bexley, Bromley.

The other seven are involved in aiming to reduce the number of 'un-grouped' authorities.

1.60 The location of the various linked hearing centres therefore needed to take into account these developments. The following table, issued by the President in August 2013 sets out the proposed location for public law hearings in respect of each of the local authorities, which is understood to be largely the position in April 2014.

	Care cases heard at	Present Hearing Centres	Remain	
Central London (569)			Yes	No
City of London (2) Westminster (28) Kensington & C (17) Hammersmith & F (41) Camden (55) Islington (48) Hackney (41) Lewisham (77)* Greenwich (67)* Southwark (91) Lambeth (68) Wandsworth (34)	FAH + Gee St% (569)	FAH (+ GS%) Clerk & S CC% Lambeth CC Wandsworth CC Inner L FPC	X	?X X ?X X
East London (411)				
Tower Hamlets (50) Newham (56) Redbridge (19) Barking & D (61) Waltham Forest (45) Havering (25) Bexley (35) Lewisham* Greenwich*	Exchange Tower (291)	Bow CC Edmonton CC Romford CC Woolwich CC Bexley FPC Stratford FPC	X X	?X X ?X X
Bromley (35) Croydon (54) Sutton (31)	Croydon / Bromley (120)	Bromley CC Croydon CC Bromley FPC Croydon FPC	X X X X	

West London (420)				
Enfield (36) Barnet (44) Haringey (89) Harrow (21)	Barnet (190)	Barnet CC Barnet FPC	X X	
Ealing (63) Brent (49)	Willesden (112)+	Willesden CC Brent FPC	X	?X
Hillingdon (28) Hounslow (37) Kingston (17) Richmond (15) Merton (21)	Kingston (118)+	Brentford CC Kingston CC Uxbridge CC Richmond FPC Uxbridge FPC	X X X	?X X

LOCATIONS/GEOGRAPHY IN LONDON – PRIVATE LAW

1.61 In central London there is no longer a need to continue family hearings in the courts used by Lambeth County Court and Inner London and City Family Proceedings Court is closed. Neither will Clerkenwell and Shoreditch County Court and Wandsworth County Court continue as venues for the family court.

1.62 In East London, Woolwich County Court and Stratford FPC discontinue all family hearings, and consideration is being given by the DFJ for East London as to whether Bow County Court and Bexley FPC should continue.

1.63 In West London all family hearings at Uxbridge FPC discontinue and the DFJ for West London is considering the same for Brent and Richmond FPCs.

1.64 It is right to say that the position is an evolving one, which will take some time to conclude.

THE JUDICIAL PROPOSALS

1.65 By the time of Ryder J's sixth update in July 2012, just prior to the publication of his final report and proposals, he was able to set out the broad timetable for the Family Justice Modernisation Programme. In essence, it was to be in two phases, each one taking approximately a year; Phase One was intended to '... put in place the structures, leadership and management principles to enable the primary legislation which creates the new court to be commenced some time after the summer of 2013'.[30] Running alongside this phase was the 'evidence based good practice pathways and guidance which the family court will use to improve the outcomes for children involved in cases by reducing delay'.[31]

---

[30] *The Family Justice Modernisation Programme: Sixth Update* (July 2012), p 2.
[31] Ibid, p 3.

1.66 At the end of July 2012, Ryder J published *Judicial Proposals for the Modernisation of Family Justice*: the agreed response of the judiciary to the Family Justice Review. In his introduction, he stated, 'It is not the judiciary's purpose to undertake a reform programme for Government. My proposals for change are the judiciary's and are independent of the Government'[32] and further, in the summary of the proposals he indicated that 'The proposals ... are judicial solutions to the problems which are identified in the Family Justice Review'.[33]

1.67 The work that had been going on for the previous 8/9 months culminated in specific headline proposals, underpinned by 2 key elements: (1) strong judicial leadership and management; and (2) robust case management by requirement to have a welfare timetable for each child based on evidence and research.

1.68 The single family court, operationally managed by the Family Business Authority of the HMCTS Board, was set out as:[34]

> 'a network of local Family Court Centres, judicially led and managed by the Designated Family Judges, where all levels of judge and magistrate will sit as Judges of the Family Court.'

1.69 A framework for leadership and management was viewed as essential to ensuring better performance in reducing delay in cases. The implementation and effect of the Case Management System, was instrumental in improving this aspect of the proposals, Ryder J being keen to stress:[35]

> 'Whatever has been the case in the past, it is essential for proper case management that good deployment practices are encouraged. In particular, it is vital that judges, magistrates and legal advisers are given sufficient time to read essential documents and listing practices are in place to ensure that important case management hearings are not compromised by being interposed into part-heard contested cases, thereby damaging the effectiveness of both.'

1.70 A framework of good practice is to be developed, which will provide signposts to rules, practice directions and good practice, which should be used by all those involved in the family justice system, ie: judges, lawyers, self-represented parties, case management staff and childcare professionals, including social workers and members of Cafcass. The materials necessary can be found in the online Family Court Guide at http://www.judiciary.gov.uk/publications-and-reports/FamilyCourtGuide.

1.71 The next necessary ingredient to modernisation, as identified by Ryder LJ, is public law case management, which is dependent on a timetable based on evidence and compliance with that timetable and the directions given

---

[32] *The Judicial Proposals for the Modernisation of Family Justice* (July 2012), p iii.
[33] Ibid, p 1.
[34] Ibid, p 3.
[35] Ibid, p 6.

by the court. In order to achieve this, the *Family Court Guide* describes and explains the pathways, which are 'timetable tracks' as to how to achieve making the best decision for the child within the welfare timetable set for that child. In public law cases there are three pathways; the 'standard pathway' is:[36]

> 'likely to describe a case where the threshold is agreed or is established on a prima facie basis, ie: the filing of further threshold evidence by the Local Authority is not necessary.'

1.72 The 'urgent pathway' describes the process for emergency protection order applications and urgent interim care order applications, where removal of the child from the care of a parent is proposed, and; the 'exceptional pathway' is for cases where it is necessary for the timetable for the child to be set for a period longer than 26 weeks, it being in the interest of the child to do so.

1.73 The private law pathway will 'describe what the court can and cannot do and how it does it, a procedure that helps to identify safeguarding issues, ie: risk and urgent cases and an investigative environment within which most decisions will be made'.[37] As far as pre-proceedings proposals (ie, mediation and ADR) are concerned, the judiciary is clear that it is not responsible for those processes as recommended by the Family Justice Review being implemented and therefore does not make proposals in respect of them. They are however concerned and recognise that post 1 April 2013; the courts will be faced with increasing numbers of litigants in person, and hence the need for a private law pathway that is accessible and understandable for all.

1.74 Financial remedy cases, equally concern the judiciary as to how they will proceed in the single family court, when there will be a significant number of litigants in person. Ryder J stated:[38]

> 'Self-representing litigants will need to be assisted to understand and comply with the procedures which are necessary to achieve fairness in financial remedy cases.'

1.75 The High Court, and its unique jurisdiction, is preserved under the reforms. Ryder J is clear that the leadership offered and provided by the Justices of the Family Division is vital to the success of the single family court. As he says:[39]

> 'their decisions are more likely to influence good practice than any review or rule book and their role both in and out of the Family Court must be acknowledged and strengthened.'

1.76 The voice of the child, a message that came out very clearly from the Family Justice Review, and whilst not directed at the judiciary, is something that

---

[36] Ibid, p 10.
[37] Ibid, p 12.
[38] Ibid, p 13.
[39] Ibid, p 14.

they agree upon and intend to ensure is kept in mind within the family court. Bearing in mind the United Nations Convention on the Rights of the Child 1989, the family court intends to ensure:[40]

'An engagement with children to facilitate their understanding of the process of proceedings where that is coincident with their welfare

The ascertainment of a child's wishes and feelings and an opportunity to be heard, where the child wishes it; and

An explanation for every child of the decision of the court.'

1.77 It has therefore become increasingly recognised that the child at the centre of the dispute has a voice which needs to be heard. Traditionally this has happened through the role of Cafcass, and through potentially the appointment of a children's guardian who instructs a solicitor in court to represent the child and to speak in their perceived best interests.

1.78 The ethos of the voice of the child goes further than that, and requires the court to consider whether the judge should directly speak to the child or children who are the subject of the application.

1.79 There was formerly a perceived presumption against courts hearing from children in evidence, which was expressly disapproved in the case of *Re W*,[41] a decision of the Supreme Court (Lord Walker, Lady Hale, Lord Brown, Lord Mance and Lord Kerr), and has led to courts now routinely having to make considered decisions, balancing:

'the advantages that it will bring to the determination of the truth and the damage it may do to the welfare of this or any other child.'

1.80 Prior to the commencement of the Act, the practice was developing in public law care cases, that where older children were the subject of applications, the judge would see them separately but within the proceedings, usually in the presence of their guardian or solicitor, and try to explain the process and ask about their views directly.

1.81 The reforms to family justice recognised that more direct work and acknowledgement of the voice of the child was needed. Ryder J, in his final recommendations, stated that:

'consideration should always be given to how the voice of the child is to be heard in family proceedings.'

Ryder J found that there should be a demonstrable engagement with children to facilitate their understanding of the process of proceedings where that is

---

40   Ibid, p 15.
41   [2010] 1 FLR 1485.

coincident with their welfare, including an ascertainment of a child's wishes and feelings and an opportunity to be heard, where the child wishes it, and an explanation for every child of the decision of the court.

1.82 In practice, this means that the court has become much more open to the suggestion that the judge should speak to a child, again usually done in private, with a note taken by the child's solicitor. In June 2014 a working party was formed to consider the appropriate steps to be taken when dealing with cases involving children or other vulnerable witnesses giving evidence or meeting the judge.[42] The working party is due to report in July 2014.

THE FAMILY JUSTICE REVIEW'S OVER-ARCHING RECOMMENDATIONS

1.83 The focus had to be, and was, very much on the need for all those involved in the family justice system to work together, with common modes of practice and procedure and the shared single aim of delivering the best possible outcome for children and families.

1.84 Running alongside the structural changes and changes to established working practices are the important recommendations regarding legislative change, which the judiciary and Government have acted upon.

1.85 Within care proceedings, the aim of the recommendations of the Review is clear; the needs of children are to be put first, to achieve that, there must be tighter control on the time it takes for proceedings to reach a conclusion. The court should play a central role in achieving the best outcomes for children, by ensuring that care plans are complete, by considering only the essential components of that plan, those being:[43]

> 'Planned return of the child to their family;
>
> A plan to place (or explore placing) a child with family or friends;
>
> Alternative care arrangements; and
>
> Contact with birth family to the extent of deciding whether it should be regular, limited or none.'

1.86 The more detailed scrutiny by courts goes beyond what is required for a determination of whether a care order is in the best interests of a child. Courts should, by legislative change, be required to trust local authorityies more in their implementation of care plans.

---

[42] *Re KP* [2014] EWCA Civ 554 considered further in chapter 2.
[43] Family Justice Review, Final Report (November 2011), p 14.

1.87 Further, whilst recognising that in a large number of public law cases the court requires evidence from expert witnesses, the Review was concerned that the use of some 'experts' was extending the length of proceedings, as well as increasing the costs in providing evidence that was not necessarily vital for the conclusion of the case. Clear recommendations for the amendment of the Family Procedure Rules were made and were implemented on 31 January 2013 by the amendment of Part 25 Family Procedure Rules 2010 (Parts 25B-25F).

1.88 As far as private law proceedings are concerned, the thrust of the Review's recommendations for legislative change, are aimed at helping more separated parents to sort out their family affairs for themselves, whilst protecting the interests of the children. Parents should be encouraged to seek alternatives to court to resolve their differences, with attempts at mediation, prior to issue of proceedings becoming the norm. There should be a move away from the use of 'loaded' terms such as 'residence' and 'contact', with the development of orders know as child arrangement orders, recognising the importance of supporting shared parental responsibility. The Review was however keen to express its clear recommendation that:[44]

> 'no legislation should be introduced that creates or risks creating the perception that there is a parental right to substantially shared or equal time for both parents.'

1.89 The Children and Families Act 2014[45] provides at s 11:

> (2A) A court, in the circumstances mentioned in subsection (4)(a) or (7), is as respects each parent within subsection (6)(a) to presume, unless the contrary is shown, that involvement of that parent in the life of the child concerned will further the child's welfare.

> (2B) In subsection (2A) "involvement" means involvement of some kind, either direct or indirect, but not any particular division of a child's time.

1.90 The Government clearly having taken on board the note of caution expressed by the Review, and having considered the implications of the failed attempt in Australia to introduce a 'shared time' approach was wanting to:[46]

> 'send a clear signal to separated parents that courts will take account of the principle that both should continue to be involved in their children's lives where that is safe and consistent with the child's welfare, which remains the court's paramount consideration.'

Much debate on this issue and this clause followed the Bill's passage through Parliament, and is discussed further in chapter 2.

---

[44] Ibid, p 21.
[45] Section 11(2) (welfare of the child: parental involvement).
[46] Children and Families Bill, Explanatory Notes, p 4.

CONCLUSION

1.91 Looking back over the many months if not years of hard work by all those involved in the family justice system, it can be seen that the Family Justice Review was the catalyst for dramatic changes to the family justice system, in England and Wales, in the way that practitioners are expected to work and in the service that is delivered to the children whose cases and families come before the court. The result was the Children and Families Act 2014, which received Royal Assent on 13 March 2014, and drew together the various strands of research, review and pilot procedure, with the aim of producing a unified approach to a fitter, leaner and more efficient delivery of justice.

CHAPTER 2

THE AIMS OF THE ACT

PRIVATE LAW DISPUTES

Introduction

'At the time of family breakdown, families often do not break in half, they shatter into little pieces.'[1]

2.1   It was observed within the final report of the Family Justice Review that:[2]

'Parenting after parting is one of the most important, difficult, sensitive and emotive areas of family law.'

2.2   Studies showed that the great majority, approximately 90%,[3] of separating couples agreed the arrangements for the children without going to court. Around 55% settled before proceedings were issued, and 30% did not seek any resolution. That figure includes parents who had walked away from the situation and away from contact. However, of the 10% that went through the court process, they included the most difficult situations, which had multiple problems:[4]

'Private law proceedings range from the most complex family breakdowns, involving intractable disputes and serious safeguarding issues to relatively modest disagreements about contact arrangements' (Ryder J, July 2012 p 12).

2.3   Despite the complexity and difficulty of some of these cases, from 1 April 2013, the system for the provision of legal aid was reformed, and to a large extent the majority of private law disputes between parents, ie those relating to

---

[1]   Cobb J 'Private Law Reform' Family Justice Council (7 February 2014).
[2]   Final Report of the Family Justice Review, para 4.20.
[3]   A Blackwell and F Dawe *Non-resident parent contact* (London, ONS, 2003); Office for National Statistics Omnibus Survey Report No 38 *Non-resident parental contact 2007–2008 A report on research using the National Statistics Omnibus Survey produced on behalf of the Ministry of Justice and the Department for Children, Schools and Families* (London, ONS, 2008).
[4]   Office for National Statistics Omnibus Survey Report No 38 *Non-resident parental contact 2007–2008 A report on research using the National Statistics Omnibus Survey produced on behalf of the Ministry of Justice and the Department for Children, Schools and Families* (London, ONS, 2008); V Peacey, J Hunt *Problematic contact after separation and divorce? A national survey of parents* (One Parent Families/Gingerbread, 2008).

where a child should live or who they should spend time with, are now excluded from eligibility from public funding, irrespective of means or merit.

2.4   Those changes led to a significant increase in litigants in person, as those who can not afford to pay privately for legal representation, have to represent themselves in court, if they choose to pursue the matter in that way. By July 2013, private law cases before the court had increased by 26% from 2012.[5] In May 2014 it was reported that 42% of cases before the family courts did not involve a lawyer, compared to 18% before the April 2013 cuts.[6] This had the contrary effect to that which had been intended when the cost-cutting measures were introduced, as district judges found themselves faced with far more time consuming disputes between unrepresented parties.

2.5   In anticipation of this, Ryder J (as he then was) recognised in his final recommendations,[7] that the courts needed to be ready to assist the volume of unrepresented parents, and that the system had to be open to maintain access to justice for all, as far as ever possible in the light of the funding reforms:[8]

> 'The immediate challenge is to develop effective methods of assisting self-representing litigants in private law cases, while maintaining fairness to all parties.'

2.6   Ryder J identified the likely issues to arise most commonly and cause difficulties for any judge as:[9]

- interpretation facilities;
- capacity to litigate;
- safeguarding issues;
- expert instruction;
- DNA tests;
- drug or alcohol tests.

2.7   All of the above may pose insurmountable problems for the unrepresented parent and the risk faced by the courts is that children of separated parents will lose their relationship with the absent parent, as a result of it becoming too difficult to litigate without the support of lawyers. In cases which would otherwise benefit from the instruction of experts, to consider either paternity or substance misuse, it will often be the case that neither party can afford it. When cases are brought to court, Ryder LJ commented that they will arrive without the benefit of legal advice to identify solutions to their problems, or have had identified to them the issues the court can address.

---

5 Anthony Douglas, Cafcass, 16 July 2013.
6 Cafcass figures.
7 Ryder J *The Family Justice Modernisation Programme: Sixth Update* (July 2012), p 12.
8 Ibid, p 12.
9 Ibid, p 12, para 57.

2.8 By December 2013, the consequences of the cuts were being seen in real terms by the courts. Ryder LJ called for urgent assistance to be given to a scheme to assist litigants in person, and to therefore assist the courts in dealing with their cases in the lead judgment of *C (A Child) & Anor v KH*:[10]

> 'the case presents a salutary lesson to us all to put in place procedures and practices which can accommodate litigants in person who do not know the rules and practice directions of the court.'

C (A Child) & Anor v KH

The facts

2.9 Both parents were litigants in person in the county court. The mother had obtained an order, without notice to the father, prohibiting him from removing his son from the mother's care, or from his primary school, and only allowing for indirect contact. The child was aged 5 at the time of the appeal and the parents had been separated for nearly 2 years. The mother made serious allegations against the father, but the most serious of those came from the Cafcass officer involved in the case. At the time of the appeal, none of the allegations had been heard or proven against the father.

2.10 Following separation, the father had sought direct contact with his son. The mother made a without notice application to the court for prohibited steps and residence orders. An order was made prohibiting the father from removing the child from the mother's care or from his nursery. The mother made allegations of domestic violence against the father, as well as raising concerns that he had threatened to see his son regardless of the mother's consent, and concerns around the father's mental health.

2.11 The case was repeatedly adjourned until a hearing in August 2012, 8 months after the parties' separation. Directions were made, and the prohibited steps order continued. By that time, Cafcass had identified concerns about the father's mental health, the allegations of domestic violence, and the father's allegedly threatening behaviour. A Cafcass report was not ordered until a further hearing. By that time, the father had attended at the former matrimonial home, and at the child's nursery, and Cafcass had decided to treat him as a risk to professionals. He continued to deny the allegations of violence made the mother. He was cautioned by the police for harassing conduct in the form of text messages that he had sent. His behaviour escalated in the form of abusive telephone messages he had with the Cafcass officer, the nursery and the mother, and he was sentenced to a 12 month community order and restraining order in respect of public order offences. The Cafcass officer had been a complainant in that criminal case.

2.12 The court had subsequently held a contested hearing, at which only the Cafcass officer had given evidence. She had filed a detailed schedule of the

---

[10] [2013] EWCA Civ 1412, para 4.

evidence and allegations on the morning of the hearing. The father's application to adjourn was refused. The Cafcass officer gave evidence from behind a screen. The orders made were for contact limited to indirect only, and prohibited steps preventing the child's removal from the mother's care.

The criticisms on appeal and guidance for the future

2.13 Ryder LJ gave the lead judgment, endorsed by the President. He identified a number of procedural irregularities throughout the proceedings which resulted in the decision-making process becoming unjust. These can be summarised as follows:

- The first order made was a 'without notice' order. Evidence adduced orally at that hearing was not recorded anywhere, and was never transcribed or placed into a statement.

- The father's right to set aside or vary the without notice order was limited to being upon 24 hours notice, without explanation for that. He was never served with any evidence to support the without notice application.

- There was no evidence of any exceptional urgency to justify a without notice order.

- The pre-application protocol for mediation was ignored completely, (more of which in chapter 3).

- In relation to Cafcass involvement, a number of criticisms were made.

- Two emails had been sent to the court directly by the Cafcass officer, without copies being served on the parties, and without any discussion, simply as private communications.

- The officer had become a complainant in the criminal proceedings, which was wholly inappropriate.

- The officer's report had contained allegations made by the mother which were not contained in any statement from her directly, and which were accepted as fact by Cafcass without any suggestion of findings of fact needing to be made.

- On the day of the contested hearing, the officer filed and served a chronology of events, which was a detailed schedule of hearsay evidence.

- She then gave evidence from behind a screen, without prior application or notice to the parties.

The appeal was allowed, and the matter returned for a re-hearing with directions given to exclude the problematic evidence and to appoint NYAS to act for the child.

The problems for litigants in person and the courts

2.14 Ryder LJ made a number of comments about the way in which the problems in the case had arisen. Whilst not criticising any individual judge, the case illustrates the complexities that arise when parties are unrepresented and a case repeatedly appears for short appointments in a busy district judge's list.

2.15 Ryder LJ was critical of the court application forms, describing them as containing 'leading' enquiries (para 11), and suggesting that the Family Procedure Rules Committee may wish to consider whether the existing court forms are sufficient to reflect the duty of full and frank disclosure which exists on those seeking to use a without notice procedure.

2.16 In addition, he observed that the magistrates in the family proceedings court and each of the divisions of the High Court have precedent forms of order for use in paper and without notice applications, and which prompt the court to give reasons for the order on the face of the same. Ryder LJ noted that this should be regarded as good practice in all family courts where written reasons or a judgment are not otherwise readily available (para 13).

2.17 Ryder LJ described the court approach to the case, which had not had any judicial continuity, as 'fire fighting, it may have been quality fire fighting, but it was not case management' (para 40). He went on to give the following outline of the way in which such hearings should be conducted in the future:

'47. I have intimated that a more inquisitorial process may help those judges who need to deal with very difficult cases involving litigants in person where emotions can run very high. At the hearing at which the section 7 report was first available there was an opportunity for detailed case management. In less fraught cases this is often a real opportunity for dispute resolution in the same way that an Issues Resolution Hearing provides that facility in public law children proceedings. That was the latest of the various hearings at which the key issues of fact and opinion could have been identified and if not resolved, described on the face of an order so that the parties and the court would have been clear about the purpose of the contested hearing. Directions could have included providing short answers to the key issues identified and up to date materials which would have avoided father's last minute adjournment application and his successful application to this court to adduce additional evidence.

48. At the hearing and given that it would have been clear whether the key issues included the need to make findings of fact, the judge can control the process to ensure that it is fair. Having been sworn, each party can be asked to set out their proposals and to confirm their version of the disputed key facts. They can then be asked by the judge what questions they would like to ask of the other party. Where lawyers are not instructed the judge can then assimilate the issues identified into his or her own questions and ask each party the questions that the judge thinks are relevant to the key issues in the case. It may be appropriate to give the parties the opportunity to give a short reply. In that way the issues can be proportionately and fairly considered.'

2.18 The way forward described above is a more inquisitorial way of conducting hearings, more appropriate where parties lack legal representation, than the traditional adversarial process. Ryder LJ had identified the problems that would arise from the legal aid cuts at a far earlier stage, during his 2012 review, and those proposals will be examined in a moment.

2.19 Before leaving the issue of public funding, and the increase in number of litigants in person, the role of McKenzie friends should be remembered. Anyone involved in a case in which a McKenzie friend appears, or anyone considering using such assistance, should make themselves aware of the Practice Guidance in respect of that role.[11] In 2014, a cross-jurisdictional judicial working group was launched to consider revisions to that guidance, following the controversial growth in the 'professional' McKenzie friend industry.[12] A cross-jurisdictional committee was established in the summer of 2014 under the chairmanship of Asplin J to consider the role of McKenzie friends in the light of the Legal Services Consumer Panel's April 2014 *Report on Fee-charging McKenzie Friends* and to consider what changes may be required to the 2010 Practice Guidance.

From the private law pathway to the Child Arrangements Programme

2.20 When writing his reviews of the family justice system, in an attempt to address the issues that arise from the increase in litigants in person, Ryder LJ suggested the re-development of the Private Law Pathway. That term had been used previously in various guises by the courts, and local practices had developed under that title. Ryder LJ's suggestion included a pathway which would aim to:[13]

> 'describe what the court can and cannot do and how it does it, a procedure that helps to identify safeguarding issues, ie risk and urgent cases and an investigative environment within which most decisions will be made. In a conventional case that may involve restrictions on the right of one party to cross examine another, relying instead on each party having their say, the judge identifying the issues upon which he or she needs further assistance and then the judge asking questions of each party himself of herself.'

2.21 The process described was a far more inquisitorial process than that adopted previously, as it was envisaged that this would be necessary if the court was to obtain the information needed to make the right decision for the children.

2.22 Included within the private law pathway and in keeping with the concept that it is an inquisitorial process, were encouragements to the judiciary to exercise far greater case management powers than previously seen. These include a greater emphasis on judicial control of a hearing, for example by limiting cross examination, and requiring litigants to reduce their questions to

---

[11] See http://www.judiciary.gov.uk/publications/mckenzie-friends/.
[12] See http://www.legalfutures.co.uk/latest-news/probe-growth-professional-mckenzie-friends for more details.
[13] *The Family Justice Modernisation Programme: Sixth Update* (July 2012), p 12, para 55.

the other side to writing, in order to avoid difficult confrontations. Judges were to be encouraged to identify the issues they needed to explore in more depth and cross-examine the parties themselves.

2.23 The private law pathway was intended as a guide for litigants in person, to set out what the court can and cannot do, and how things would be handled and approached by the court. There was also a planned procedure to help identify safeguarding issues and most decisions are now to be made in an inquisitorial manner.

2.24 Ryder LJ's early plans for the adoption of an inquisitorial system in cases involving litigants in person were then demonstrated in the case of *Re C* discussed above, which illustrates the precise need for just such an approach by the courts. Sadly, in *Re C*, nearly two years passed during which there was no direct contact, on the basis of assumptions rather than findings of fact. The impact of that on the child and family as a whole cannot be underestimated.

2.25 In response to Ryder LJ's suggestions, the President of the Family Division, Sir James Munby, set up a Private Law Working Group under the chairmanship of Mr Justic Cobb. It reported in November 2013 and recommended the replacement of the Private Law Programme with an entirely new Child Arrangements Programme (CAP). Before looking at the detail of the CAP, it is necessary to return to the wording of the 2014 Act, to examine the changes that CAP reflects.

Child arrangements orders

2.26 In a change to previous practice, the Children and Families Act 2014 removes the requirement on judges to consider the arrangements for the children when dealing with divorce, or civil partnership (ss 7 and 8 of the 2014 Act). Section 7 is to come into force upon the implementation of secondary legislation, (s 9(2)), and s 8, which repeals previously unimplemented divorce provision within the Family Law Act 1996, will come into force two months following the 2014 Act being passed.

2.27 The rationale behind those reforms lay with the future plans of the legislature to allow for uncontested divorces to be dealt with administratively.

2.28 Instead, the arrangements for the children will now only be looked at upon application to the court by a parent or other family member. They play no part in the actual divorce, and the previous 'statement of arrangements for the children' is no longer necessary.

2.29 In the Family Justice Review, consideration had been given to consolidated hearings to deal with all of the issues of the family breakdown, including the finances and children matters at one hearing:

'The parties should be encouraged to deal with all of the issues related to their separation, including the financial aspects together, whether that be within all issues mediation or by way of consolidated court hearings.'

2.30 Although there is a clear recommendation that 'there should be no link of any kind between contact and maintenance'[14] that was an obvious concern. It was also said that any further risk of delaying decisions for children should be carefully monitored by the court if there is to be a consolidated/all issues hearing. The concept of dealing with 'all issues' together was accepted by the government in its response to the Review, however it was keen to ensure that such matters were certainly explored by couples within family mediation, as a first port of call. Concerns were raised that 'consolidated court hearings should not undermine efforts to encourage settlement of disputes through non-court Dispute Resolution Services'.[15] In the event, this aspect of the Review's recommendations did not form part of the Children and Families Bill and resulting Act.

Applications for orders relating to children

2.31 Part 2 and Sch 1 of the Act reform the law in relation to private law proceedings, which are disputes between parents in relation to the residence of their children, and contact with them. Since the inception of the Children Act 1989, which came into force in 1991, these orders have been described as residence and contact, replacing the previous terms; custody and access. That earlier change in the terms aimed to remove the power imbalance by reflecting in simpler language the factual situation. However, 'residence and contact' did not solve that issue, and the Family Justice Review panel and the consultation process it conducted identified a real problem with the labelling of children's arrangements, with one parent perceiving that they had more control over the other, to the detriment of the child's relationship with both:

'There was widespread but not universal support for the removal of the terms contact and residence:[16]

Eg: On balance, however, we consider that removing the current emphasis on the different labels of residence and contact, implying a winner and a loser, would be helpful as part of a wider and sustained effort to change attitudes and culture. Both residence and contact are in fact about parenting time. Our members report advising clients to forget about the labels and that matters are often easier to resolve if discussions are about co-operative parenting and parenting time in the interests of the child. Otherwise, some cases have been known to fight around the label when there is in fact agreement on parenting time. (Resolution consultation response).'

---

14 Final Report of the Family Justice Review (November 2011), p 25, para 129.
15 The Government Response to the Family Justice Review *A system with children and families at its heart* (February 2012), p 82.
16 Final Report of the Family Justice Review, para 4.55.

2.32 However, other responses to the consultation raised the prospect of confusion, and little benefit in real terms. The Association of Her Majesty's District Judges proposed that residence and contact should be abolished, and replaced by parenting time orders.

2.33 Having considered the totality of the responses, the final recommendation of the Family Justice Review was to develop a 'child arrangements order' to set out the arrangements for the upbringing of the child.[17]

2.34 A child arrangements order may still specify with which parent a child is to live, but there is more emphasis on with whom the child concerned is to spend time, rather than seeming to 'relegate' one parent to contact, whilst elevating the status of the other to residence.

Shared parenting

2.35 The reports of the Family Justice Review considered in detail a 'shared parenting' approach, with a presumption of a child spending equal time with each parent. This followed research into other jurisdictions which have implemented such arrangements, particularly the Swedish and Australian models.

2.36 Calls for a presumption of shared time arose from the perception, often expressed by fathers, that the courts favoured mothers with the result that fathers lost contact. The interim Family Justice Review report referred to the slowness of the system, and the tendency of the courts to uphold the status quo by the time that the hearing took place, resulting in 90% of children typically living with their mother, and only 12% living with their father.[18]

> 'The family justice system is profoundly inefficient and inept – delay, for example, has reached the point where a parent applying for contact can easily have to wait a year before receiving his first order, effectively losing all contact with his child/children during that time. This in turn leads to a status quo which the courts fail to repair.'[19]

2.37 Shared parenting was by no means a new concept, and the courts have used shared residence orders since the implementation of the Children Act 1989. However, steps towards a legislative presumption of equal parenting time had remained controversial, and had been discussed by successive governments. It was considered during the course of the Family Law Bill in 1996, and again in reports during 2004.[20] The Centre for Social Justice considered the issue in 2010 and concluded that a one-size-fits-all formula would not work.

---

[17]   Ibid, para 4.60.
[18]   V Peacey and J Hunt (2008).
[19]   Fathers 4 Justice submission, Interim Report of the Family Justice Review, para 5.49.
[20]   *Parental Seperation: Children's Needs and Parent's Responsibilities* (2004).

2.38 The Family Justice Review considered evidence from cases in England and Wales as well as internationally. Within the Children Act 1989 and the case-law that had developed since its implementation, the courts had started from an assumption that there should be contact with the non-resident parent.[21] There was a fear amongst academics and national support organisations, that to introduce a presumption shifted the focus away from the rights of the child, towards the rights of the adults involved.

International experience

2.39 The evidence considered by the Family Justice review included international experience, from countries such as Sweden, where shared parenting is relatively common.

The Swedish example

2.40 The Swedish Children and Parents Code was amended in 1998 to promote joint custody, although the principle of the child's best interests remained, and if both parents oppose joint custody, the court cannot impose it. In practice, the case-law in Sweden led to a presumption of joint custody. However, the backlash from parents against the reforms, led to another change in the law in 2006, and the Code now explicitly requires the court to take account of any risks to the child, and to pay particular attention to the parents' ability to cooperate before deciding on joint custody. This has limited the use of joint custody where it is not appropriate.

The Australian model

2.41 Whilst the child's best interests are the paramount consideration, in 2006 a presumption was introduced that equal shared parental responsibility is in the best interests of children. The presumption does not apply in cases involving family violence or child abuse, and is capable of rebuttal if it would not be in the child's best interests. When shared parental responsibility is ordered, the court must also consider whether it is in the best interests of the child and reasonably practicable to order equal time or substantial and significant time with both parents. However, the complexity of the law led to a common misunderstanding that the starting point is shared time. The emphasis was found to have shifted to parents' rights, and an increased reluctance to disclose violence and abuse.

2.42 The potential for a legislative presumption of shared parenting time was considered in detail by Belinda Fehlberg et al, in the study *Caring for children after parental separation: would legislation for shared parenting time help children?*[22] The study highlights the difficulties in judicially-imposed arrangements, and observes that whether or not the arrangements work has

---

[21] Dame Elizabeth Butler-Sloss 'Contact and Domestic Violence' [2001] Fam Law, 355–8.

[22] University of Oxford, Department of Social Policy and Intervention (May 2011).

more to do with the characteristics of the family involved, than any legal requirement. In other words, one size will not fit all.

The 2014 Act

2.43 In the light of the consultation responses[23] and the evidence gathered, the Children and Families Act steps back from a presumption of shared time, but it provides as follows:

> **11 Welfare of the child: parental involvement**
>
> (1) Section 1 of the Children Act 1989 (welfare of the child) is amended as follows.
>
> (2) After subsection (2) insert –
>
> > "(2A) A court, in the circumstances mentioned in subsection (4)(a) or (7), is as respects each parent within subsection (6)(a) to presume, unless the contrary is shown, that involvement of that parent in the life of the child concerned will further the child's welfare.
> >
> > (2B) In subsection (2A) 'involvement' means involvement of some kind, either direct or indirect, but not any particular division of a child's time."
>
> (3) After subsection (5) insert –
>
> > "(6) In subsection (2A) 'parent' means parent of the child concerned; and, for the purposes of that subsection, a parent of the child concerned –
> >
> > > (a) is within this paragraph if that parent can be involved in the child's life in a way that does not put the child at risk of suffering harm; and
> > >
> > > (b) is to be treated as being within paragraph (a) unless there is some evidence before the court in the particular proceedings to suggest that involvement of that parent in the child's life would put the child at risk of suffering harm whatever the form of the involvement.
> >
> > (7) The circumstances referred to are that the court is considering whether to make an order under section 4(1)(c) or (2A) or 4ZA(1)(c) or (5) (parental responsibility of parent other than mother)."

2.44 Therefore, the only presumption is that involvement of that parent in the life of the child concerned will further the child's welfare. That is no more than is already stated in established case-law, and is the starting point for the court in any event.

2.45 However, concerns remain about the message sent out to parents by such a statutory presumption, and the potential for misunderstanding that exists. The Act **does not** provide any presumption that a non-resident parent should have contact, nor does it provide grounds for a particular division of time, it merely means that the applicant should be involved in the child's life.

---

[23] Consultation – 'Co-operative Parenting Following Family Separation: Proposed Legislation on the Involvement of Both Parents in a Child's Life'.

Involvement can take many forms, ranging from substantial and significant time, to indirect contact, or involvement at arm's length.

2.46 Section 11(2), which inserts sub-s (2B) into s 1 of the Children Act 1989, was a late Lords amendment to the 2014 Act, and is designed to deal expressly with the concern that the presumption would be perceived by many, including the media and litigants in person as grounds for an equal division of time.

2.47 The presumption is then followed by significant caveats, namely;

(a) they can be involved in a way that does not put the child at risk of suffering harm;

(b) and para (a) will be considered, if there is evidence to **suggest** that involvement would put the child at risk of suffering harm.

2.48 Therefore, if a respondent to an application for a child arrangements order, can put evidence before the court that **suggests** the involvement would put the risk of suffering harm, the presumption is capable of being displaced.

2.49 Section 11 needs to be considered in any application under:

•   section 8 of the Children Act 1989, or a special guardianship, and for variation or discharge of such orders (s 1(4) CA 1989);

•   an unmarried father's application to the court for parental responsibility (s 4(1)(c) CA 1989);

•   an application for removal of parental responsibility granted under s 4(1) CA 1989 (s 1(2A) CA 1989);

•   an application by an unmarried second female parent for parental responsibility (these types of case arise out of lesbian couples undergoing IVF) (s 4ZA(1)(c) CA 1989); and

•   an application for removal of parental responsibility granted under s 4ZA(1)(c) (s 4ZA(5) CA 1989).

What is meant by 'suggests?'

2.50 The threshold set by the Act is very low. The usual standard of proof in family proceedings is whether or not a fact is proven on the balance of probabilities. The Act does not go on to say whether the court will be required to consider the evidence and adjudge whether or not the risk of harm exists. It would follow that there may have to be hearings to decide whether or not the presumption can apply. It may be that evidence which suggests that someone is a risk, is not capable of proof to the requisite standard, for example if police intelligence suggests a risk of harm, but is not capable of proof. A risk of harm may be suggested by a wide-ranging number of factors, for example drug use, alcohol reliance, aggressive or violent tendencies. It may be argued that it is not for a respondent to prove the substance of the evidence on the usual balance of probabilities, but only to establish that the evidence *suggests* a risk. Once the court is so satisfied, the presumption will be displaced and the court will have to look at involvement that can be managed safely.

2.51 The way forward appears therefore to be that the court's starting point will be a presumption of parental involvement, unless one parent is able to provide evidence which suggests that such involvement would expose the child to a risk of harm. Once that is established, no guidance is given within the Act as to how to decide the appropriate level of parental involvement, but when going on to consider the arrangements for the child, the welfare checklist at s 1 of the Children Act 1989 will be applied as before. That checklist, set out below, includes any risk of harm that the child may suffer at para (e):

(a) the ascertainable wishes and feelings of the child concerned (considered in the light of his age and understanding);

(b) his physical, emotional and educational needs;

(c) the likely effect on him of any change in his circumstances;

(d) his age, sex, background and any characteristics of his which the court considers relevant;

(e) any harm which he has suffered or is at risk of suffering;

(f) how capable each of his parents, and any other person in relation to whom the court considers the question to be relevant, is of meeting his needs;

(g) the range of powers available to the court under this Act in the proceedings in question.

2.52 It may be therefore that the 2014 Act results in little change in the operation of the courts, as the welfare checklist will continue to govern the judge's consideration of the competing factors.[24]

Child arrangements order

2.53 As described above, the Act abolishes the terms residence and contact,[25] and instead provides for the court to make child arrangements orders, within s 12.

2.54 A child arrangements order is defined as:[26]

> an order regulating arrangements relating to any of the following –
>
> a) With whom a child is to live, spend time or otherwise have contact, and
> b) When a child is to live, spend time or otherwise have contact with any person.

---

[24] As suggested in *Children and Families Bill 2013: Contextual Information and Responses to Pre-Legislative Scrutiny.*

[25] Children and Families Act 2014, s 2.

[26] Section 2(3).

Grandparents and other family members

2.55 Despite lobbying from pressure groups at the consultation stage, to simplify and improve the court process for grandparents and other family members, they still need leave to apply for a child arrangements order. Entitlement to apply mirrors the entitlement in the Children Act 1989, s 10(9). This means that grandparents will still need leave to apply for an order, which was strongly argued against by lobbying groups during the consultation process.

2.56 Section 10(9) reads as follows;

> Where the person applying for leave to make an application for a section 8 order is not the child concerned, the court shall, in deciding whether or not to grant leave, have particular regard to –
>
> (a)   the nature of the proposed application for the section 8 order;
> (b)   the applicant's connection with the child;
> (c)   any risk there might be of that proposed application disrupting the child's life to such an extent that he would be harmed by it; and
> (d)   where the child is being looked after by a local authority –
>   (i)   the authority's plans for the child's future; and
>   (ii)   the wishes and feelings of the child's parents.

2.57 If a resident carer is not a relative, then the child needs to have lived with them for three years out of the preceding five years, for that carer to be entitled to apply, s 10(5)(b) 1989 Act.

2.58 It had been hoped by supporters of relative carers, and in particular grandparents, for example through the Grandparents Association, that the reforms of the 2014 Act would include an introduction of a legal right of grandparents to have contact with their grandchildren, and that it would become easier for kinship carers to formalise the arrangements under a residence order. Grandparents do not have access to legal aid, and therefore if they want to go to court to seek residence or contact orders they are faced with doing it themselves without representation. The additional hurdle of seeking leave is viewed by many as an added and potentially unnecessary burden:[27]

> 'We were disappointed to see the Review did not propose removing the requirement for a grandparent to seek leave of the court before applying for a contact order ... A grandparent's relationship to a child is different and special but the law treats them like any other adult when they are trying to establish contact with their grandchildren. We believe this should change and do not accept the argument that the court system would be overrun with applications if this requirement were removed.'

---

[27]   Grandparents Plus consultation response to the Interim Report, Final Report of the Family Justice Review, para 4.43.

2.59   The Government has long since argued that the leave requirement acts as an 'early filter' for those applications that were in the best interests of the child, and was not aimed to make it unnecessarily for grandparents to gain contact:[28]

'We have no immediate plans to commission research on the role of parents in governing grandparent/grandchild relations. We believe that parents are usually best placed to make decisions about their children's relationships with grandparents and other relatives.'

2.60   However, in 2010, the Government announced a policy review, stating that it intended to:[29]

'Remove the requirement for grandparents to obtain the leave of the Court before making an application for a contact order.'

2.61   Accordingly the position was reviewed by Norgrove in the Family Justice Review. In his final report he concluded that:

4.45 We recognise the importance to children of relationships with their grandparents and recommend that this be emphasised in the process to come to an agreement about their future care. However we continue to feel that the requirement for grandparents to seek leave of the court before making an application is not overly burdensome and should remain.

4.46 As a matter of principle we agree with the many in the call for evidence who argued that just as contact is a right of the child not of the parents so also grandparents do not have a "right" to contact. We noted in our interim report research showing that grandparents are unlikely to lose contact with a grandchild if they had meaningful contact whilst the parental relationship was still in being and if they resist taking sides after the separation.[30] We do not believe that courts refuse leave unreasonably or that seeking leave is slow or expensive for grandparents. Rather, the requirement to seek leave prevents hopeless or vexatious applications that are not in the interests of the child.'

And therefore the leave requirement has remained, much to the opposition from those lobbying on behalf of kinship carers.

OTHER AMENDMENTS TO THE PRIVATE LAW REGIME

2.62   Schedule 1 of the 2014 Act largely provides amendments in terminology within the Children Act 1989, replacing residence and contact with child arrangements.

---

[28]   Kevin Brennan MP in answer to a Parliamentary question, HC Deb 29th January 2003 cc 913–4W.

[29]   Support for all: Families and Relationships Green Paper, DCSF January 2010 cm 7787.

[30]   Ferguson et al *Grandparenting in Divorced Families* (2004, Bristol Policy Press). For example, some grandparents may display greater animosity towards their son or daughter's ex-partner than the separated parties themselves. At times grandparents can express these negative feelings in front of their grandchildren.

Parental responsibility

2.63 A further significant change to the Children Act, and one which goes beyond the terminology, is Sch 1, para 21(4) of the 2014 Act which introduces a new s 12(2A) to the Children Act 1989, creating a power of the court to give parental responsibility to a person who is not a child's parent or guardian, in cases where the child arrangements order provides for the child concerned to spend time with, or other have contact (but not live) with that person. There is also a new provision for any person with whom the child is to live on an interim basis, to have parental responsibility for the duration of the order.

Child Arrangements Programme

> 'The CAP will be a legal instrument ... drafted not for a legal readership but for an audience of litigants in person. In this respect, we believe that our work has been unique. This has shaped one important feature of the design, to create a scheme which covers the life of the case from "start" to "finish". The language of the document has been accordingly modified. The title of the Programme (CAP) takes us away from inherently court-based processes. We speak of the post-separation period, rather than pre-proceedings, in an endeavour to encourage parties not to view dispute resolution by reference to court process. The CAP is designed to put the child's welfare at the centre of dispute resolution.'[31]

2.64 In November 2013, the working group led by Cobb J published its report and recommendations for the establishment of a Child Arrangements Programme (CAP).

2.65 In its interim report,[32] it considered:

(a) The launch of the family court, (dealt with elsewhere in this book).

(b) The increased emphasis on dispute resolution outside the court process, (dealt with in chapter 3).

(c) The impact of the changes in public funding, (as illustrated in the discussion at the start of this chapter).

(d) The likely change in terminology for private law orders.

2.66 In order of priority, the working group considered that the emphasis on mediation and out-of-court dispute resolution came first, followed by the preservation and development of those aspects of the current court system which were believed to work well, and finally to find a system to meet the needs of the high number of litigants in person. It was stressed that the 'child' is the focus of the scheme, as reflected in the title, rather than the previous pre-application protocol or private law programme, which refer to the court process itself. The key principles of all private law children disputes underpin all of the working groups' suggestions, namely that:

---

[31]   Ibid, per Cobb J.
[32]   See http://www.judiciary.gov.uk/publications-and-reports/FamilyCourtGuide.

(a)   the child's welfare is the paramount consideration;

(b)   delay is likely to be prejudicial to the welfare of the child; and

(c)   a court order should only be made if it positively promotes the best interests of the child.

2.67 The CAP aimed to combine the previous pre-proceedings protocol, contained within PD3A FPR 2010, and the private law programme at FPR 2010, PD12B. The working group's report set out the objective as finding a 'supportive, clear, process for private law cases', giving a greater profile to the pre-proceedings phase than previous programmes.

2.68   In summary, CAP is designed to be more:

(a)   *Comprehensive* – it includes all aspects of the private law process end-to-end.

(b)   *Accessible* – for litigants in person and judges – the whole scheme contained in one document.

(c)   *Versatile* – in encouraging and reinforcing determination of disputes out of the court system both before and during proceedings.

Litigants in person

2.69   In response to calls to assist litigants in person (LIP) to navigate their way through the process, the language of the CAP was simplified in the final draft, and a glossary of terms is now included.[33]

2.70   In addition, where the case has to proceed to a contested hearing, either finding of fact or welfare hearing, the court service agreed to prepare the trial bundle, if so directed by the court. This is anticipated to be a significant assistance to the judges as well as the parties. The documents to be included will have to be the subject of judicial case management.

2.71   Further assistance given to LIPs is agreement by the court service to serve the C100 application form on respondents, rather than the applicant doing so, as was previously the case. This should reduce the number of cases in which the applicant fails to properly serve the respondent, resulting in delays and adjournments. There is also published assistance for LIPs in the *Guide to Urgent and Without Notice Hearings* available on the HMCTS website,[34] as well as witness statement templates for use by litigants in person.[35]

---

[33]   Final report and CAP Annex.

[34]   Drafted by the Private law working group, along with a guide on Capacity issues, available from the Family Justice Council.

[35]   Announced by the President in his *View from the President's Chambers (12)* [2014] Fam Law 978 and to be issued by HMCTS.

The court process – hearings and evidence

Allocation and gatekeeping – CAP para 9 and Practice Guidance

2.72 The CAP provides a clear guide for litigants to the court process. The first court hearing will be directed on paper by the court at the gatekeeping stage as set out at para 9. In addition, Practice Guidance has been issued by the President which is available in Appendix 7. In summary:

- an application for a CAO will be considered by a nominated legal adviser and/or nominated district judge within one day of the date of receipt;

- it will be allocated in accordance with the guidance;

- in determining allocation, judicial continuity is an important consideration and the President's Guidance on Judicial Continuity and Deployment (Private Law) is to be followed;

- it is envisaged that all relevant family applications will be heard by lay justices unless they are estimated to take more than 3 days, or in the circumstances set out in the schedule to the guidance;

- the directions on issue on Form CAP 01 will then be given, as set out below.

In the Family Court   Case No ....

Sitting at [*Place*]

The Children Act 1989

THE CHILDREN

Names	Girl /Boy	Dob.

<u>Order – Directions at Gatekeeping/Allocation</u>

Child Arrangements Programme (CAP 01)

1. THE PARTIES

The applicant (mother/father/as appropriate) is [*name*]

The [first] respondent (father/mother/as appropriate) is [*name*]

2.   The child/ren is/are living with ....

THE COURT ORDERS

3.   The First Hearing Dispute Resolution Appointment (FHDRA) shall take place
      (a)   on [*date*]
      (b)   at [*time*]
      (c)   at [*name and address of relevant Family Court*]
4.   In advance of the FHDRA, the [applicant] / [the parties] shall attend a Mediation Information and Assessment Meeting (MIAM), and shall deliver to the court evidence (in a Form FM1 or otherwise) of attendance at the MIAM (the Court finding on the material supplied that the MIAM exemption has not been validly claimed).
5.   [*Where the application is for enforcement of a Child Arrangements Order, and more than three months have passed since the making of the order*] Cafcass / CAFCASS Cymru shall, within 17 working days of receipt of this order, send to the court a safeguarding letter in respect of the parties.
6.   [*other directions as appropriate*]

7. COMPLIANCE

(a) No document other than a document specified in this order or sent/ delivered in accordance with the Rules or any Practice Direction shall be sent/delivered by any party without the court's permission.

(b) Any application to vary this order or for any other order is to be made to the allocated judge on notice to [   ] / all parties.

(c) In the event of non-compliance by any person with any order or direction made today, each party shall be responsible for notifying the court of the same, in order to avoid delay.

THESE DIRECTIONS ON ISSUE WERE MADE BY [DISTRICT JUDGE/JUSTICES CLERK [NAME]]

Dated

Court address: for filing/communication:

2.73 The first hearing dispute resolution appointment (FHDRA) will be dealt with by week 5–6 of the case. There will then be directions for a finding of fact hearing if necessary, and a dispute resolution appointment, followed by a final welfare hearing.

2.74 The aim of the FHDRA continues to be to resolve the case completely where possible by way of final order through agreement. This raises difficulties on occasion where the hearing is conducted by a legal advisor to lay magistrates sitting without a bench. Following consideration and consultation the working group recommended that in those areas in which legal advisors have already been undertaking this function, they could continue, provided that they could make arrangements for a bench to sit to approve any agreed orders on the same day that the agreement is reached, and if the designated family judge for the area agrees. In those areas in which the practice wasn't already in place, it should not be able to start without the agreement of the liaison judge.[36]

Without notice applications – CAP para 12

2.75 One area of law that has caused particular concern, and is likely to be a continuing theme in the new regime where far more parents are representing themselves, is the increase in applications made to the court without notice having been given to the other parent. That was the way in which the mother made her first application in the case of *Re C* examined above.

2.76 During 2013, there were a number of cases in which senior judges reminded practitioners of the appropriate steps to be taken in order to ensure good practice when applications are made without notice, and most notably the principles were summarised by Mostyn J (with the authority of the President) in *UL v BK (Freezing Orders: Safeguards: Standard Examples).*[37] The case itself concerns freezing orders, but the following guidance was given at para 35 of the judgment onwards:

- Without notice applications must be confined to cases of exceptional urgency. The respondent must be given short, informal notice unless it is essential he is not made aware of the application.

- Without notice, or short notice applications impose on the applicant a high duty of candour. Breach of that duty will likely lead to the discharge of the order.

- All the safeguards must be applied on short / no notice applications. The applicant must draw the court's attention to any variation of the safeguards and justify them.

- A failure to comply with the principles may lead to either a refusal to make the order sought, or a wasted costs order against the solicitors involved.

---

[36] See also the forthcoming Justices Clerks Rules 2014 which will enlarge the scope of the legal advisors' powers.

[37] [2013] EWHC 1735 (Fam).

2.77 The CAP working group were concerned to find during the course of their research,[38] that litigants in person were issuing without notice applications on the grounds of urgency, and therefore bypassing all pre-proceedings steps. Whilst it recognised that for any unrepresented parent, proceedings concerning their child are urgent, the working group report reminded the court that such orders should only be made exceptionally and that:[39]

> 'except in cases where it is essential that the respondent must not be aware of the application, the applicant should take steps to notify the respondent informally of the application.'

2.78 The following guidance is given within the CAP itself at para 12.3 onwards:

(a)   If the applicant had given notice to the respondent this would have enabled the respondent to take steps to defeat the purpose of the injunction; cases where the application is brought without notice in order to conceal the step from the respondent are very rare indeed.

(b)   The case is one of exceptional urgency; that is to say, that there has been literally no time to give notice before the injunction is required to prevent the threatened wrongful act.

(c)   If the applicant had given notice to the respondent, this would be likely to expose the applicant or relevant child to risk of physical or emotional harm.

2.79 The final version of the CAP included the additional requirement that any order made 'without notice' should specify:

(a)   the reasons why the order was made without notice;

(b)   the outline facts alleged against the respondent which were relied upon by the court (unless this is already clear from the statement in support of the application).

The private law working group went onto publish a guide to urgent and without notice hearings[40] to assist litigants in person and judges involved in private law cases.

Timeframes

2.80 Unlike public law proceedings (see chapter 4) there continues to be no specific time-limit for the resolution of private law cases. This was a considered approach (for example see final report of the working group at para 16),[41] on

---

[38]   Working Group Report, para 39.
[39]   FPR 2010, PD20A, paras 4.3–4.5.
[40]   To be published by HMCTS as CB8.
[41]   See http://www.judiciary.gov.uk/Resources/JCO/Documents/family-court-guide/private-law/pfd-report-private-law-working-group.pdf.

the basis that private law can encompass a vast range of issues, and judges' need to have access to the widest spectrum of procedure. However, the working group observed that only a limited number of cases should proceed to a final hearing, with the majority being resolved at either the first hearing dispute resolution appointment, or the later dispute resolution appointment. The emphasis on the resolution of cases without delay remains however, and guidance is given to avoid the micro management of private law cases that can sometimes exist long after the key issues themselves have been decided, as parents become dependent on the court to make decisions for them rather than communicating with each other.

2.81 To try to tackle that problem, the following recommendations were made:

(a) Courts should not retain involvement by ordering a review, or ongoing reviews of a final order, unless it was both necessary and in the interests of the child (CAP, para 15.3).

(b) If a report pursuant to the Children Act 1989, s 7 is ordered, Cafcass should, where possible, recommend a stepped phasing-in of arrangements, so that there is no need to return to court at each stage (CAP, para 15.4).

(c) Where ongoing professional oversight or involvement is felt to be needed, the court may consider making either a Cafcass monitoring order under the Children Act 1989, s 11H, or a family assistance order under s 16 of the 1989 Act, subject to the agreement of the parties and the local authority (CAP, para 15.5).

2.82 The FHDRA continues to be listed within 5–6 weeks of issue of the application. During development of the programme there were calls for that timetable to be reduced, but this was not considered to be realistic taking into account the time needed for safeguarding checks to be done. The timetable thereafter will be fixed by the court, but should be referable to key events in the child's life.

2.83 However, the recommendations above are expressly not intended to deter the courts from making interim orders in specific cases, if that is what is necessary.

The child in the dispute

2.84 CAP is expressly supportive of the right of children to have their voices heard in the decision making process, at which they are at the very heart, and the final version of the programme includes a specific section to address this at paras 14–15. Over the years preceding the 2014 Act, it had become increasingly recognised that the child at the centre of the dispute has a voice which needs to be heard. Traditionally that had happened through the role of Cafcass, and potentially the appointment of a children's guardian who instructs a solicitor in court to represent the child and to speak in their perceived best interests.

2.85   The ethos of the voice of the child goes further than that, and requires the court to consider whether the judge should directly speak to the child or children who are the subject of the application.

2.86   There was formerly a perceived presumption against courts hearing from children in evidence, arising from the case of *LM v Medway Council, RM and YM*,[42] which was expressly disapproved in the case of *Re W* discussed below. Prior to the commencement of the Act, the practice was developing in public law care cases, that where older children were the subject of applications, the judge would see them separately but within the proceedings, usually in the presence of their guardian or solicitor, and try to explain the process and ask about their views directly.

2.87   The reforms to family justice recognised that more direct work and acknowledgement of the voice of the child was needed. In its response to the Family Justice Review, the Office of the Children's Commissioner conducted its own consultation[43] with 35 children aged between 3 and 17 years, and found that they wanted the following improvements to the family justice system:

- adults should understand all the pressures children face at every stage of the family justice process;
- information should be in child-friendly language and formats; and
- every child and young person should have their own plan detailing how they would like to be supported and have their voice heard.

2.88   Ryder J, in his final recommendations, stated that:

> 'consideration should always be given to how the voice of the child is to be heard in family proceedings.'

2.89   Ryder J found that there should be a demonstrable engagement with children to facilitate their understanding of the process of proceedings where that is coincident with their welfare, including an ascertainment of a child's wishes and feelings and an opportunity to be heard, where the child wishes it, and an explanation for every child of the decision of the court.

2.90   In practice, this means that the court has become much more open to the suggestion that the judge should speak to a child, again usually done in private, with a note taken by the child's solicitor.[44] It has also become more common for applications to be made for children to give evidence, since the Supreme Court decision in *Re W (Children) (Rev 2)*,[45] which expressly disapproved the approach in Medway, finding that:[46]

---

[42]   [2007] EWCA Civ 9.
[43]   See http://www.childrenscommissioner.gov.uk/content/publications/content_514.
[44]   See for example the approach taken in the case of *P-S (Children)* [2013] EWCA Civ 223.
[45]   [2010] UKSC 12.
[46]   Per Lady Hale, para 22.

'The existing law erects a presumption against a child giving evidence which requires to be rebutted by anyone seeking to put questions to the child. That cannot be reconciled with the approach of the European Court of Human Rights, which always aims to strike a fair balance between competing Convention rights. Article 6 requires that the proceedings overall be fair and this normally entails an opportunity to challenge the evidence presented by the other side. But even in criminal proceedings account must be taken of the article 8 rights of the perceived victim: see *SN v Sweden*, App no 34209/96, 2 July 2002, BAILII: [2002] ECHR 551. Striking that balance in care proceedings may well mean that the child should not be called to give evidence in the great majority of cases, but that is a result and not a presumption or even a starting point.'

2.91 However, Lady Hale went onto make the following comments, which are relevant to the private law arena:[47]

'In principle, the approach in private family proceedings between parents should be the same as the approach in care proceedings. However, there are specific risks to which the court must be alive. Allegations of abuse are not being made by a neutral and expert local authority which has nothing to gain by making them, but by a parent who is seeking to gain an advantage in the battle against the other parent. This does not mean that they are false but it does increase the risk of misinterpretation, exaggeration or downright fabrication. On the other hand, the child will not routinely have the protection and support of a Cafcass guardian. There are also many more litigants in person in private proceedings. So if the court does reach the conclusion that justice cannot be done unless the child gives evidence, it will have to take very careful precautions to ensure that the child is not harmed by this.'

2.92 The implications of this decision are that whilst more applications may now be made by litigants for the child to either be called, or at least spoken to directly by the judge, careful consideration is still required, and the courts often look to find ways in which the child's voice can be heard, without necessarily involving them directly in the court arena.

2.93 In June 2014, the President announced the formation of a working group to review the April 2010 guidelines on judges meeting children and the *Guidance on Children Giving Evidence*.[48] The working group will also look at issues arising from evidence given by children and other vulnerable witnesses,[49] particularly following the decision of the Court of Appeal in *Re KP*,[50] and that of the Supreme Court in *Re LC*.[51]

---

[47] At para 29.
[48] [2012] Fam Law 79.
[49] *View from the President's Chambers (12)* [2014] Fam Law 978.
[50] [2014] EWCA Civ 554.
[51] [2014] UKSC 1.

Re KP – the facts

2.94 The 13-year-old child had been wrongfully removed from Malta by her mother and relocated in England. The father sought her return. The mother relied on the child's objections as grounds for refusing to return.

The issues

2.95 The judge at first instance met with the child, and asked her a series of 87 questions in a meeting which took over an hour. Whilst it is common practice for the views of the subject child to be sought in international cases,[52] and this is sometimes carried out by Cafcass, and sometimes by the judge, the question in this case was whether the judge had gone too far.

The outcome and implications

2.96 The Court of Appeal found that Parker J had. By asking so many questions, the judge had strayed into the process of gathering evidence, not simply seeking her views. By reference to the 2010 guidelines, the purpose of such a meeting is to enable the child to gain some understanding of what is going on, and to be reassured that the judge has understood her. Parker J had characterised the meeting in her judgment as hearing the child's representations, and asking her to expand and explain. That should not be the purpose of such a meeting. By seeking to probe the child's answers, and by asking her so many questions in a lengthy meeting, the judge had strayed over the line. The appeal was allowed and the case remitted to be reheard before a different court.

Re LC – the facts

2.97 The other significant case in this area is that of *Re LC*.[53] The case involved four children, who had been found by the High Court to be habitually resident in Spain and to have been wrongfully retained by their father in England. Whilst the eldest child objected, he should be returned to Spain, along with his younger siblings. The Court of Appeal reversed the return of the eldest child, and remitted the matter for the strain of separating the siblings to be considered. The three eldest children, including the eldest who was aged 13, appealed against the refusal to make them parties to the applications

The issues

2.98 The central issues on appeal concerned the question of habitual residence, which is not relevant here. The subsidiary question however of the child's appeal against the refusal of party status, is relevant at this stage. The Court noted that an older child in particular may be able to contribute relevant evidence not easily obtainable from either parent, about their state of mind (para 49 of judgment).

---

[52] *Re T (Abduction: Child's Objections to Return)* [2000] 2 FLR 192; *Re D (A Child) (Abduction: Rights of Custody)* [2006] UKHL 51.

[53] [2014] UKSC 14.

The outcome and implications

2.99 The appeal against the refusal of party status was allowed, although it was noted that the court is left with a wide discretion as to what extent the child should then play in the proceedings. In *LC*, it was said to be probably appropriate for the child to give a witness statement, for the parents to be cross-examined on the basis of that, and for submissions to be made. However, the possibility of the child being cross-examined by Counsel away from the court room is also mooted, and it seems clear that in the future the courts and practitioners will be expected to be increasingly creative when considering how best to hear the child's voice.

2.100 The recent pilot of video recorded cross-examination in criminal proceedings raises the possibility of that as a way forward in cases involving children's evidence and vulnerable witnesses, and no doubt issues of that sort will be considered by the working group in due course.

2.101 Once party status has been granted, it follows that a child's guardian is appointed, pursuant to the FPR 2010, r 16.4. This also has the additional benefit that public funding remains available for a child to be represented in an appropriate case. In an appropriate case, as defined by the FPR, r 16.4, the child can still be made a party to the proceedings, and be appointed a guardian from Cafcass, and a solicitor to represent them. Rule 16.2(1) provides that a child may be made a party to the proceedings, if the court considers it to be in the child's best interests to do so. Once the child is a party, the court must appoint a guardian under r 16.4. FPR 2010 Practice Direction 16A provides the following guidance:

> '7.1 Making the child a party to the proceedings is a step that will be taken only in cases which involve an issue of significant difficulty and consequently will occur in only a minority of cases.
>
> 7.2 The decision to make the child a party will always be exclusively that of the court, made in the light of the facts and circumstances of the particular case. The following are offered, solely by way of guidance, as circumstances which may justify the making of such an order –
>
> (a)   where an officer of the Service or Welsh family proceedings officer has notified the court that in the opinion of that officer the child should be made a party;
>
> (b)   where the child has a standpoint or interest which is inconsistent with or incapable of being represented by any of the adult parties;
>
> (c)   where there is an intractable dispute over residence or contact, including where all contact has ceased, or where there is irrational but implacable hostility to contact or where the child may be suffering harm associated with the contact dispute;
>
> (d)   where the views and wishes of the child cannot be adequately met by a report to the court;
>
> (e)   where an older child is opposing a proposed course of action;

(f)   where there are complex medical or mental health issues to be determined or there are other unusually complex issues that necessitate separate representation of the child;

(g)   where there are international complications outside child abduction, in particular where it may be necessary for there to be discussions with overseas authorities or a foreign court;

(h)   where there are serious allegations of physical, sexual or other abuse in relation to the child or there are allegations of domestic violence not capable of being resolved with the help of an officer of the Service or Welsh family proceedings officer;

(i)   where the proceedings concern more than one child and the welfare of the children is in conflict or one child is in a particularly disadvantaged position;

(j)   where there is a contested issue about scientific testing.'

2.102 The Practice Direction expressly recognises that the separate representation of a child may result in delay in the proceedings. However, the CAP working group expressed concern to find that the average length of a case in which a guardian had been appointed is 96 weeks. Of that time, on average the case had been proceeding for approximately 50 weeks before the appointment was ordered. It was suggested that earlier involvement of guardians may have prevented the parties' attitudes becoming too entrenched.

The role of Cafcass

2.103 Within its contribution to the development of the CAP, Cafcass identified the following functions as being principal to its role:

- safeguard and promote the welfare of the children;

- give advice to the court about any application made to it in such proceedings;

- make provision for the children to be represented;

- provide information, advice and other support for the children and their families[54]; and

- when a Cafcass officer is given cause to suspect that a child who is a subject of proceedings is at risk of harm he/she has a duty to undertake a risk assessment and to provide it to the court.[55]

2.104 In a private law case, the role of Cafcass is seen in two main ways, firstly the provision of safeguarding information in the form of a letter and attendance at the first hearing dispute resolution appointment, and secondly if further work is required, in the preparation of a report pursuant to s 7 of the 1989 Act.

2.105 It is important that all safeguarding checks are carried out prior to the first hearing dispute resolution appointment. These include a check of all

---

[54]   Criminal Justice and Court Services Act 2000, s 12(1).
[55]   Children Act 1989, s 16A.

information held on the police national computer, and a check with the local authority children's services. In addition, they will attempt to speak to the parties by telephone, but do not initiate contact with the child at that stage. Cafcass and CAFCASS Cymru have agreed that provided they receive the application notice, including dates of birth of the parties and addresses, on the day of issue, then they will endeavour to provide the safeguarding checks by Day 17.

2.106 At the first hearing dispute resolution appointment (FHDRA), the Cafcass officer will speak separately to each party, and assists the court by providing advice about the potential for resolving the issues, and whether or not it would be appropriate for the parties to attend at a separated parenting information programme.

2.107 Following the FHDRA, Cafcass will prepare the s 7 report if so directed, and address those issues identified by the court. If a recommendation is made for supervised contact, Cafcass is not able to provide that service directly, but is able, if the court so orders, to commission resources to facilitate contact without cost to the parties.[56]

2.108 The procedure to be followed at the FHDRA is set out at para 14 of the CAP. Two forms of draft orders following the FHDRA have been approved by the President. The full version is set out below.[57]

---

[56] Commissioning and Partnerships Service – referred to in Cafcass commentary to CAP.

[57] See also CAP 02 lite, available from the FLBA website, which was drafted and approved by the President following concerns that the FDRA form CAP 02 was unwieldy and difficult to use.

In the Family Court   Case No ....
Sitting at [*Place*]

The Children Act 1989

THE CHILDREN

Names	Girl /Boy	Dob.

Order – First Hearing Dispute Resolution Appointment (FHDRA)/directions (CAP 02)

[*Sequential number in these proceedings*]

HHJ/DJ/AJC [*NAME OF JUDGE*]   **SITTING IN OPEN COURT/ PRIVATE ON** [*DATE*]

1. THE PARTIES

The applicant (mother/father/as appropriate) is [*name*]
The [first] respondent (father/mother/as appropriate) is [*name*]
[The second respondent (child(ren) through their children's guardian) [*name*]]

2. The child/ren is/are living with ....

3. NOTICE

Today's hearing is on notice/not on notice/on short notice [*give details*]

4. REPRESENTATION AT THIS HEARING

The parties appeared before the court as follows:

Party/Name	In Person	Counsel/Solicitor/ Advocate	Contact telephone and email address
Applicant			
Respondent(s)			
(1)			
(2)			
Other (specify)			

The names of the children set out in the heading to this Order and the names of the persons set out in paragraphs 3 are not to be disclosed in public without the permission of the court.

5. ALLOCATION / TRANSFER

The proceedings are today/continue to be allocated to be heard by [lay justices/District Judge/Circuit Judge/High Court Judge] and are reserved to [   ]

This application is transferred to the [Family Court sitting at]

6. Cafcass/CAFCASS Cymru

The court has decided that a Cafcass/CAFCASS Cymru investigation and report is not required in this case

or The Court has appointed a Cafcass/CAFCASS Cymru officer.

If the identity of the Cafcass/CAFCASS Cymru officer is known at this stage:

The Cafcass/CAFCASS Cymru officer is:-

Name

Professional address

Date of appointment

7. THE APPLICATION(S)

(a) The applicant has applied for a Child Arrangements Order/Specific Issue Order/Prohibited Steps Order other Part II order [*delete as appropriate or specify*] [*today/on date*]

(b) [*If there are other applications add as follows or delete*]

(c) The [mother/father/as appropriate] has applied for [   ] [*today/on date*]

8. SAFEGUARDING CHECKS

(a) The safeguarding checks by Cafcass/CAFCASS Cymru are/are not complete

(b) The safeguarding checks show no safety issues/that the safety issues are ..../that the safety issues are not yet known [*delete as appropriate or specify*]

9. TODAY'S HEARING

(a) Today's hearing is listed as a *[FHDRA/directions hearing]*

(b) Today's hearing has been [EFFECTIVE AS THE FINAL HEARING] [EFFECTIVE AS THE FHDRA] [EFFECTIVE AS A DIRECTIONS HEARING] [CANCELLED] [ADJOURNED]

(c) The reason why the hearing has been adjourned is: *[specify]*

10. TIMETABLE FOR THE CHILD(REN)

The key dates and events in the timetable for the child are [   ].

11. KEY ISSUES

A. The issues about which the parties are agreed are:-

a)	
b)	
c)	
d)	

B. The issues which remain to be resolved are:-

a)	
b)	
c)	
d)	

C. The steps planned to resolve the issues are:-

[where the parties intend to refer themselves to mediation or other form of non-court dispute resolution if appropriate]

a)	
b)	
c)	
d)	

12. FACT-FINDING

Having considered the documents, received the representations of the parties, and the safeguarding report, a separate fact-finding hearing is not necessary in this case because the nature of the allegations [and/or admissions] are such that the court does not require such a hearing in order to be able to decide whether to make the orders sought.

Or

Having considered the documents, received the representations of the parties, and the safeguarding report, a fact-finding hearing is necessary in this case because ....

[delete/complete as appropriate]

The issues to be determined are

a)	
b)	
c)	
d)	

13. AGREED [INTERIM] ARRANGEMENTS FOR THE CHILDREN

If determined at this hearing, specify, such as:-

- [Between now and [date/the final hearing] the agreed arrangements for the child[ren] will be [as set out in the schedule to this order *(if extensive)* / as follows ....].
- [Between now and [date/the final hearing]] the child[ren] will live with the [mother/father].
- [Between now and [date/the final hearing]] the children will live with the mother and the father.
- [Between now and [date/the final hearing]], the child[ren] will spend time or otherwise have contact with the [mother/father] as follows/ as set out in the schedule to this order *(if extensive)*.
- [Between now and [date/the final hearing]], the child[ren] will have indirect contact as [follows/ as set out in the schedule to this order *(if extensive)*}.

14. UNDERTAKINGS

Record as appropriate

THE COURT ORDERS:

15. JOINDER OF CHILD[REN]/OTHER PARTIES/INTERVENERS

(a) The child[ren] *[name]* shall forthwith be made [a party/parties] to the proceedings and pursuant to rule 16.4 and PD16A, Part 4 FPR 2010 an officer of Cafcass/ CAFCASS Cymru shall be appointed to act as [his/her/their] children's guardian.

(b) A copy of this order shall be faxed/e-mailed to the Cafcass/CAFCASS Cymru office and a hard copy of this order shall be sent within two working days of this order.

(c) The service manager [is requested / has agreed to] allocate an officer as children's guardian as promptly as possible following receipt of this order, and to notify the court within 7 days of such allocation.

(d) It is recorded that there are [no] reasons why the Cafcass officer / WFPO dealing with the case should not continue to deal with it as guardian.

(e) In the event that Cafcass/CAFCASS Cymru is unable to provide a children's guardian to act within [28 days] they shall notify the court forthwith, to enable the court to consider the appointment of another person.

16. CHILD ARRANGEMENTS

[if made at this hearing, specify as appropriate]

Such as:

• It is ordered [by consent] that [between the date of this order and ..../the date of the next hearing/final disposal of the applications] the arrangements for the child[ren] shall be [as set out in the schedule to this order *(if extensive)*/as follows .... *[specify]*: e.g. the child[ren] shall live with / spend time / indirect contact with [name] by way of [Skype/Facetime/telephone etc]]

• It is ordered that [a warning notice will be endorsed][by consent] [that between the date of this order and [the next hearing/final disposal of the applications] the [father/mother] shall make the child[ren] available to [spend time] / [have indirect contact] with the [father/mother] as set out in the schedule to this order *(if extensive)*/as follows .... *[specify]*

A warning notice directed to the [father/mother] shall attach to paragraph [   ] of this order.

17. PARENTAL RESPONSIBILITY

Further to the Child Arrangements Order made [today/date], which provides that the child is to live with [the father, who does not currently have parental responsibility] / [*woman* who is a parent of the child by virtue of section 43 of the Human Fertilisation and Embryology Act 2008, without parental responsibility], the court grants parental responsibility to [the father] / [the woman].

Further to the Child Arrangements Order made [*today/date*], which provides that the child is to spend time or otherwise have contact (but not live) with [the father, who does not currently have parental responsibility] / [*woman* who is a parent of the child by virtue of section 43 of the Human Fertilisation and Embryology Act 2008, without parental responsibility], the court grants parental responsibility to [the father] / [*the woman*].

Further to the Child Arrangements Order made [*today/date*], which provides that the child is to live with [*a person who is not the parent or guardian of the child concerned is named in the order as a person with whom the child is to spend time or otherwise have contact but not live*] the court grants parental responsibility for the child for as long as the order is in place.

Further to the Child Arrangements Order made [*today/date*], which provides that the child is to spend time or otherwise have contact (but not live) with [*a person who is not the parent or guardian of the child concerned is named in the order as a person with whom the child is to spend time or otherwise have contact but not live*] the court grants parental responsibility for the child for as long as the order is in place.

18. ACTIVITY DIRECTIONS/CONDITIONS

[*if made at this hearing, specify as appropriate*]

Such as:-

The [father/mother] [other party] is directed to take part in:

Set out any order for Activity Direction/Condition [e.g. Separated Parents Information Programme/ Mediation Information and Assessment Meeting]

on such dates and times as are specified by .... [the provider]

The Court shall forthwith send this order to the provider.

The provider shall notify the Court whether the parties attended at the conclusion of the Separated Parents Information Programme/mediation directed.

19. CASE MANAGEMENT AND OTHER ORDERS/DIRECTIONS

(a) **Safeguarding incomplete:** Cafcass / CAFCASS Cymru must write to the court by [*date*] with the outcome of safeguarding checks / the case is adjourned to [date] (the parties' attendance is excused) when the court will either make an order in the terms agreed by the parties or list the case for further consideration.

(b) **Sending and delivering of evidence**
   (i) [specify what is to be sent and delivered by each party]
   (ii) With this order, the mother/father will be provided with a witness statement template relevant for a case concerning:
   - allegations of domestic abuse;
   - allegations of child harm;
   - where the child is to live and who the child is to see (and when);
   - schooling issues;
   - temporary or permanent relocation from the jurisdiction.

(iii) By 16:00hs on [   ], the Applicant shall file in court and serve on all parties (and Cafcass / CAFCASS Cymru / Local Authority) his/her concise witness statement/s which are signed and contain a statement of truth.

(iv) By 16:00hs on [   ], the Respondent shall file in court and serve on all parties (and Cafcass / CAFCASS Cymru / Local Authority) his/her concise witness statement/s which are signed and contain a statement of truth

(v) The statements shall only contain evidence relevant to the issue/s to be determined and shall set out the terms of any Order they invite the court to make and their reasons for it.

(c) **Fact finding Schedules**
   (i) The parties have prepared, with the assistance of the court at this hearing, a document setting out the concise schedule of the allegations on which the [mother/father] relies, and [the father/mother]'s answers to the allegations, for the purposes of the fact finding hearing;
   (ii) The [mother/father] shall, by 16:00 on [date], send/deliver to the [father/mother] and to the court a concise schedule of allegations on which [s]he relies for the purpose of the fact finding hearing.
   (iii) The [father/mother] shall, by 16:00 on [date] send/deliver to the [mother/father] and to the court a concise schedule of the answer(s) to the allegations relied on for the purpose of the fact finding hearing.

(d) **Disclosure from Police / Medical records**
   (i) Cafcass/CAFCASS Cymru are requested to initiate enhanced checks of the relevant local police force, in particular in respect of their investigation into [incident] on [date] and shall send/deliver any relevant information that is received to the [father or mother] and the court.
   (ii) The [solicitor for the] [mother/father] shall seek disclosure of any Force Wide Incident Notices/Sleuth Reports (FWINs) in respect of the parties for the following addresses and for the following periods in accordance with the Police Protocol:

From [   ] to [   ] at the address:

From [   ] to [   ] at the address:

and shall send/deliver the resulting disclosure to the [father/mother] and the court on receipt.

(iii) The [solicitor for the] [mother/father] shall seek disclosure from the police of any statements / reports / notes of interview relevant to their investigation into [incident] on [date], in accordance with the Police Protocol and shall send/deliver the resulting disclosure to the [father/mother] and the court on receipt.

(iv) The Court considering it both necessary and proportionate so to order for there to be a proper determination of the (preliminary) issues, the applicant/respondent has permission to rely on a report/statement from [*Hospital, GP*] which must be filed at court and a copy served on the other party by 16:00hs on [ ].

(v) Permission is granted to [the solicitor for] the applicant/respondent to disclose this order to the record holder. The costs of obtaining the report shall be divided equally between the parties and shall be a proper charge upon the funding certificates of the publicly funded parties.

(e) **Cafcass / CAFCASS Cymru / Local Authority s.7 Reports / s.37 investigation and report.**

A [Cafcass / CAFCASS Cymru officer / local authority social worker] is directed to prepare a section 7 report on:

Specify as appropriate, such as:-

- The ascertainable wishes and feelings of the children.
- It is recorded that the [mother/father] alleges that the children have expressed a wish that [*specify*]
- The home conditions and suitability of the accommodation of the [mother/father]
- The concerns of the [mother/father] with regard to [*specify*]
- Whether or not the children's physical/emotional/educational needs are being met by the [mother/father]
- How the children will be affected by the proposed change of [*specify*]
- Whether or not it appears that the children have suffered or at risk of suffering the harm alleged by the [mother/father]
- The parenting capacity of the [mother/father] having regard to the allegations that [*specify*]
- Whether [*Specify*] local authority should be requested to report under section 37 Children Act 1989.

A [*named local authority*] is directed to prepare a section 37 report in respect of the child(ren), the Court being of the view that it may be appropriate for a care or supervision order to be made with respect to the child(ren). The authority shall, when advising the court, consider whether they should apply for a care or supervision order, or provide services or assistance to the child(ren), and/or take any further action.

In the event that the Local Authority considers that it is unable to comply with this direction, it shall no later than 16:00hs 3 days after service of this order upon it provide to the court in writing its reasons for holding that view. A copy shall at the same time be sent by email to [*insert email address*]

Permission is given for the Court to release [and send to the Local Authority] the safeguarding screening report by Cafcass to the Department, together with all the applications, statements and orders.

[Cafcass / CAFCASS Cymru / the local authority] shall send the report to the court by 16:00 on [date] and at the same time deliver a copy of the report to each of the parties and, if applicable, to their solicitors.

(f) **Disclosure of documents**

The following documents are to be disclosed (by sending or delivering such documents) by the mother/father to [Cafcass / CAFCASS Cymru / the local authority with children's services functions of [local authority as appropriate][*list documents to be disclosed*].

(g) **Experts**

Drug and alcohol testing

The Court considering it both necessary and proportionate so to order for there to be a proper determination of the (preliminary) issues, the [Mother] [and] [Father]/ shall co-operate with scientific hair strand testing for

(a)   [all prohibited substances]/ [for the following prohibited substances ..... for the ..... months immediately preceding this order.

(b)   [and] [for excessive alcohol consumption (by FAEE/CDT and EtG testing)] for a ..... month period of assessment.

(c)   It is recorded that the ..... has been advised that any future tests should be carried out on hair from his/her head if at all possible and it is in his/her interests to ensure that it is of sufficient length to enable an effective test to be carried out.

(d)   a written report as to the results of the tests shall be sent to the court and the parties by 16:00hs on .....

(e)   the costs of the testing shall be shared equally by the parties and shall be a proper charge of the funding certificates of the publicly funded parties.

DNA Paternity Testing

The Court considering it both necessary and proportionate so to order for there to be a proper determination of the (preliminary) issues, and pursuant to Section 20 (1) of the Family Law Reform Act 1969, the solicitor for the children may instruct [   ] to conduct scientific tests to ascertain whether [   ] is or is not the father of [   ] and the following directions shall apply:-

a.   for that purpose bodily samples be taken on or before [   ] from the following persons:

i.   the child:

ii.   the mother:

iii. the putative father:

b.   The person appearing to the court to have care and control of the child is: [   ].

c. Arrangements for the provision of samples shall be made by the solicitor for the children;

d. The report regarding the paternity of [   ] shall be served on all other parties by the solicitor for the children by 16:00hs on the   ; and

e. The reasonable fees for the paternity testing shall be divided equally between the parties and shall be a proper charge of the funding certificates of the publicly funded parties.

Adult psychiatrist

The Court considering it both necessary and proportionate so to order for there to be a proper determination of the (preliminary) issues, permission is granted to the [   ] solicitor as nominated lead solicitor to disclose the case papers and relevant medical records to and to instruct [   ] to undertake a psychiatric assessment of the [   ].

a. The report shall by filed by the lead Solicitor no later than 16:00hs on the [   ] and shall address the following issues:

b. The lead solicitor shall forthwith send an electronic copy of this order to the expert instructed

c. The approved letter of instruction and the bundle of documents shall be delivered to the expert by not later than 4.00pm on the [   ]

d. The reasonable costs incurred in the preparation of this report shall be divided equally between the parties and shall be deemed a reasonable disbursement upon the publicly funded parties' public funding certificates.

Adult psychologist

The Court considering it both necessary and proportionate so to order for there to be a proper determination of the (preliminary) issues, permission is granted to the [   ] solicitor as nominated lead solicitor to disclose the case papers and relevant medical records to and to instruct [   ] to undertake a psychological assessment of the [   ].

a. The report shall by filed by the lead Solicitor no later than 4.00pm on the [ ] and shall address the following issues:

b. The lead solicitor shall forthwith send an electronic copy of this order to the expert instructed

c. The approved letter of instruction and the bundle of documents shall be delivered to the expert by not later than 16:00hs on the [ ]

d. The reasonable costs incurred in the preparation of this report shall be divided equally between the parties and shall be deemed a reasonable disbursement upon the publicly funded parties' public funding certificates.

General

For the avoidance of doubt, the expert directed above [shall/shall not] have permission to examine and assess the child[ren].

(h) **Special arrangements for witnesses**

[The following special arrangements for witnesses shall apply to the evidence of [name of witness] *[specify]*: *or* the court will determine at the hearing on [date] whether and, if so, which special arrangements shall apply in the case of [name witness]].

20. CONTACT CENTRE DIRECTION

The order for supported contact at the [   ] contact centre is subject to the following conditions for its operation and effect:-

a.   The [parties/ solicitors for the [Mother/Father][   ] shall inform the centre co-ordinator of the contents of this order as soon as practicable.

b.   The [parties/ solicitors for the parties] shall jointly be responsible for
     i.   completing a referral form for the centre co-ordinator and
     ii.   providing a copy of this order and any subsisting injunction orders involving the parties to the co-ordinator as soon as practicable and in any event within 2 days of today.

c.   Confirmation from the centre co-ordinator that:
     i.   the centre is an accredited member of NACCC;
     ii.   the referral has been accepted following completion of a preparation for contact interview (which interview is a compulsory requirement of all NACCC centres);
     iii. a vacancy is available or the parties have been allocated a place upon a waiting list (the order for supported contact is suspended during any waiting period until a place is available).

d.   The parties and any person permitted to accompany them to the centre shall abide by the rules of the centre.

e.   The parties must attend a preparation for contact meeting with the centre co-ordinator (the parties' solicitors, if acting, must take responsibility for ensuring that information about the meeting is passed to the parties).

f.   The [Mother/Father] [   ] agrees to take the child(ren) for a pre-contact introductory visit to the centre.

g.   The child(ren) will be informed of the contact arrangements by [Mother/ Father] [   ]

           The following arrangements for the contact sessions shall apply:-
     i.   The child(ren) shall be taken to the centre by [   ]
     ii.   The child(ren) shall be collected at the conclusion of contact by [   ]
     iii. The [Father/Mother] [   ] may [not] be accompanied during the contact session [by]
     iv.   The [Father/Mother] [   ] may [not] remain in the same room as the child(ren) during the contact session
     v.   After [   ] sessions of contact, the [Father/Mother] [   ] shall not remain in the same room as the child(ren) but may remain in the confines of the centre.
     vi.   [Other agreements about contact at the centre]

i.   The [parties/ the parties' solicitors] shall jointly be responsible for informing the centre co-ordinator when the place is no longer required.

21. FURTHER HEARINGS

Directions as appropriate, such as:-

(a) [This/These] application[s] shall be listed for [fact-finding hearing/Dispute Resolution Appointment/other directions hearing/final hearing] before [Legal Advisor/Lay Justices/District Judge/Circuit Judge/High Court Judge] [reserved to . . .] on [date] with a time estimate of [specify] and for final hearing on [date] with a time estimate of [specify].

(b) The author of the [section 7] report [shall not] [shall] be required to attend the Dispute Resolution Appointment;

(c) The author of the [section 7] [section 37] report shall attend the [final/as appropriate] hearing on [date] unless all parties have confirmed to him/her no less than five days in advance of the hearing date that [his/her] attendance is not required.

(d) The [mother/father] shall by 16:00 on [date] deliver to the court a paginated and indexed trial bundle [and provide a copy to [party/Cafcass/CAFCASS Cymru].

(e) The parties **MUST** arrive at court at least [30 45 60] minutes before any future hearings.

22. COSTS

No order as to costs *or*

Costs in the application *or*

Costs reserved *or*

Funded services assessment of the costs of *[specify]or*

Other *[specify]*

23. COMPLIANCE

(a) No document other than a document specified in this order or delivered in accordance with the Rules or any Practice Direction shall be delivered by any party without the court's permission.

(b) Any application to vary this order or for any other order is to be made to the allocated judge on notice to [   ] / all parties.

(c) In the event of non-compliance by any person with any order or direction made today, each party shall be responsible for notifying the court of the same, in order to avoid delay.

Dated

Court address: for filing/communication:

The dispute resolution appointment – CAP para 19

2.109 The DRA is to be listed following the preparation of the s 7 report or any other expert report considered to be necessary. The author of the report will attend if ordered to do so. The court will consider the key issues, and whether the DRA can be used as a final hearing. It is able to hear evidence to resolve the issues, and to give further directions for a final hearing or a fact-finding hearing.

In the Family Court
Sitting at [*Place*]

Case No ....

The Children Act 1989 - Child Arrangements Programme

THE CHILDREN

Names	Girl /Boy	Dob.

Order - Dispute Resolution Appointment – Child Arrangements Programme (CAP03)

HHJ/DJ/AJC [*NAME OF JUDGE*]   **SITTING IN OPEN COURT / PRIVATE ON** [*DATE*]

1. THE PARTIES

The applicant [mother/father/as appropriate] is [*name*]
The [first] respondent [father/mother/as appropriate] is [*name*]
The second respondent [children through their children's guardian] [*name*]
[The first intervener [*state relationship to child(ren) or other party*] *is* [*name*]]

2. The child/ren is/are living with ....

3. REPRESENTATION AT THIS HEARING

The parties appeared before the Court as follows:

Party/Name	In Person	Counsel/Solicitor/ Advocate	Contact telephone and email address
Applicant			
respondents: (1) (2) (3)			
Other (specify)			

The names set out in paragraph 3 are not to be disclosed in public without the permission of the court.

4. Cafcass / CAFCASS Cymru / Local Authority *[if appropriate]*

Name [welfare officer / children's guardian]

Professional address

Date of appointment (if children's guardian):

Date of order of [section 7] [section 37] report

5. THE APPLICATIONS

The applicant has applied for a Child Arrangements Order / Specific Issue Order/Prohibited Steps Order/ other Part 2 order *[delete as appropriate or specify] [today / on date]*

[If there are other applications add as follows or delete]

The [mother/father/as appropriate] has applied for [   ] *[today / on date]*

6. TODAY'S HEARING

a.   Today's hearing has been [EFFECTIVE AS A DISPUTE RESOLUTION APPOINTMENT/ DIRECTIONS][CANCELLED] [ADJOURNED]
b.   The reason why the hearing has been adjourned is: *[specify]*.

The next hearing is [final hearing or as appropriate] on [date and time   ] at [court] with a time estimate of [   ].

7. EVIDENCE

The court heard the evidence of the following witnesses:-

Witness	Party calling	Issue

8. KEY ISSUES

A. The following issues have been resolved

a)	
b)	
c)	
d)	

B. It remains necessary to decide the following remaining issues in order to determine [the applications that have been made/the application for ....]:-

a)	
b)	
c)	
d)	

9. AGREED [INTERIM] ARRANGEMENTS FOR THE CHILDREN

Specify if these are different to those in place previously, such as:-

a. [Between now and [date/the final hearing]] the child[ren] will live with the [mother/father].

b. [Between now and [date/the final hearing]] the child[ren] will live with the mother and the father.

c. [Between now and [date/the final hearing]], the child[ren] will spend time or otherwise have contact with the [mother/father] as follows/ as set out in the schedule to this order *(if extensive)* to this order.

d. Between now and [date/the final hearing]], the child[ren] will have indirect contact as follows/ as set out in the schedule to this order *(if extensive)*.

10. OTHER AGREEMENTS REACHED BETWEEN THE PARTIES

Record as appropriate

11. UNDERTAKINGS

Record as appropriate

THE COURT ORDERS:

12. CHILD ARRANGEMENTS

[if made at this hearing, specify as appropriate]

Such as:

- [By consent,] [between the date of this order and . . ./the date of the next hearing/final disposal of the applications] the child[ren] shall live with the mother and the father [as set out in the schedule to this order *(if extensive)*/as follows .... *[specify]*].
- [By consent,] [between the date of this order and [the next hearing/final disposal of the applications] the arrangements for the child[ren] shall be that [the child[ren] shall live with the [mother/father] and spend time with / have indirect contact with the [father/mother] by way of [telephone/Skype/Facetime etc].
- [a contact warning notice will be endorsed][by consent] that [between the date of this order and [the next hearing/final disposal of the applications] the [father/mother] shall make the child[ren] available to spend time with the [father/mother] as set out in the schedule to this order *(if extensive)*/as follows .... *[specify]*

A warning notice directed to the [father/mother] shall attach to paragraph [   ] of this order.

13. PARENTAL RESPONSIBILITY

Further to the Child Arrangements Order made [today/date], which provides that the child is to live with [the father, who does not currently have parental responsibility] / [*woman* who is a parent of the child by virtue of section 43 of the Human Fertilisation and Embryology Act 2008, without parental responsibility], the court grants parental responsibility to [the father] / [*the woman*].

Further to the Child Arrangements Order made [*today/date*], which provides that the child is to spend time or otherwise have contact (but not live) with [the father, who does not currently have parental responsibility] / [*woman* who is a parent of the child by virtue of section 43 of the Human Fertilisation and

Embryology Act 2008, without parental responsibility], the court grants parental responsibility to [the father] / [*the woman*].

Further to the Child Arrangements Order made [*today/date*], which provides that the child is to live with [*a person who is not the parent or guardian of the child concerned is named in the order as a person with whom the child is to spend time or otherwise have contact but not live*] the court grants parental responsibility for the child for as long as the order is in place.

Further to the Child Arrangements Order made [*today/date*], which provides that the child is to spend time or otherwise have contact (but not live) with [*a person who is not the parent or guardian of the child concerned is named in the order as a person with whom the child is to spend time or otherwise have contact but not live*] the court grants parental responsibility for the child for as long as the order is in place.

14. ACTIVITY DIRECTIONS/CONDITIONS

[*if made at this hearing, specify as appropriate*]

Such as:-

The [father/mother] [other party] is directed to take part in:

Set out any order for Activity Direction/Condition [e.g. Separated Parents Information Programme/ Mediation Information and Assessment Meeting]

on such dates and times as are specified by .... [the provider]

The Court shall forthwith send this order to the provider.

15. SPECIFIC ISSUES

Such as:

The [mother/father] is permitted to take all necessary steps to ensure that a place is available for the [child[ren] at [x] school, starting in [y] term. This shall include causing the [child/ren] to attend the open day on [date] and the entrance examination on [date]. The [father/mother] shall take all steps which are necessary on his part to secure the said place.

16. PROHIBITED STEPS

Such as:

Pending the final hearing of [this/these] applications, the [mother/father] shall not cause the [child[ren]] to live at any address other than [*specify*] or to attend any school other than [*specify*].

17. OTHER ORDERS/DIRECTIONS

(a) **Cafcass / CAFCASS Cymru / Local Authority**
Specify any directions required/not dealt with at the FHDRA

(b) **Delivering of evidence**
[specify what is to be sent and delivered by each party]

(c) **Fact finding Schedules**
   (i) The [mother/father] shall, by 16:00 on [date] send/deliver to the [father/mother] and the court a concise schedule of allegations on which [s]he relies for the purpose of the fact finding hearing.
   (ii) The [father/mother] shall by 16:00 on [date] send/deliver to the [mother/father] and the court a concise schedule of the answer(s) to the allegations relied on for the purpose of the fact finding hearing.
   (iii) Cafcass/CAFCASS Cymru are requested to initiate enhanced checks of the relevant local police force, in particular in respect of their investigation into [incident] on [date] and shall send/deliver any relevant information that is received to the [father or mother] and the court.
   (iv) The [solicitor for the] [mother/father] shall seek disclosure from the police of any statements / reports / notes of interview relevant to their investigation into [incident] on [date], in accordance with the ACPO Protocol and shall send/deliver the resulting disclosure to the [father/mother] and the court on receipt.
   (v) The [insert party] shall have permission to rely on a [report/ statement] from *[e.g. hospital, GP]* which must be delivered/sent to the court and a copy delivered/sent to the other party by 16:00 on [date].
   (vi) Permission is granted for the solicitor for the applicant/respondent to disclose this order to the record holder.

(d) **Disclosure of documents**
The following documents are to be disclosed by the mother/father to [Cafcass /CAFCASS Cymru / the local authority with children's services functions of [local authority as appropriate] *[list documents to be disclosed]*

(e) **Special arrangements for witnesses.**
[The following special arrangements shall apply to the evidence of [name of witness] *[specify]*: *or* the court will determine at the hearing on [date] whether and, if so, which special arrangements shall apply in the case of [*name witness*]].

18. FURTHER HEARING[S]

Directions as appropriate, such as:

(a) [this/these] application[s] be listed for [fact finding/final hearing] before [Lay Justices / District   Judge/Circuit Judge/High Court Judge] [reserved to ....] on [date] with a time estimate of [specify] and for final hearing on [date] with a time estimate of [specify].

(b) The author of the [section 7] [section 37] report shall attend the [review/final/as appropriate] hearing on [date] unless all parties have confirmed no less than five days before the hearing date that [his/her] attendance is not required.

(c) The [mother/father] shall by 16.00 on [date] lodge a paginated and indexed trial bundle [and send/deliver a copy to [party/Cafcass / CAFCASS Cymru].

19. COSTS

No order as to costs *or*

Costs in the application *or*

Costs reserved *or*

Funded services assessment of the costs of *[specify]or*

Other *[specify]*

20. COMPLIANCE

(a) No document other than a document specified in this order or sent in accordance with the Rules or any Practice Direction shall be delivered by any party without the court's permission.

(b) Any application to vary this order or for any other order is to be made to the allocated judge on notice to [ ] / all parties.

(c) In the event of non-compliance by any person with any order or direction made today, each party shall be responsible for notifying the court of the same, in order to avoid delay.

Dated

Court address: for filing/communication:

Fact finding hearings – CAP para 20

2.110 The working group proposed amendments to Practice Direction 12J of the Family Procedure Rules 2010, dealing with the need for finding of fact hearings in cases of domestic abuse and harm. The Practice Direction is available in full in Appendix 4.

2.111 Important points to note in relation to the new practice direction include:

- the definition of domestic violence includes any incident or pattern of incidents of controlling, coercive or threatening behaviour, violence or abuse, including but not limited to psychological, physical, sexual, financial or emotional abuse;
- controlling behaviour is further defined as acts designed to make a person subordinate or dependant, and coercive is abuse used to harm, punish or frighten the victim;
- the court at the FHDRA consider whether domestic violence is raised as an issue;
- the court should determine as soon as possible whether it is necessary to conduct a fact-finding hearing;
- the PD goes onto provide guidance as to the conduct of fact-finding hearings, which can be inquisitorial or adversarial as the situation demands.

2.112 In making the amendments, the recommendations of Ryder LJ in the case of *Re C (A Child)* were taken into account, as discussed above.[58]

Capacity – CAP para 16

2.113 The CAP working group went on to consider the issues raised by LIPs who lack capacity. This is dealt with at para 16 of the CAP and refers judges who have to deal with a case in which they become concerned about capacity to Practice Direction 15B.

Enforcement – CAP para 21

2.114 The working group made specific recommendations about enforcement, including that district judges should have the power to deal with committal applications. Where an application to enforce is made more than three months after the final order, the safeguarding checks will need to be renewed. The CAP now provides at para 21 which factors shall be considered by the court on an application for enforcement, and directs that the case should be returned to the previously allocated judge (where possible) within 20 days of issue.

---

[58] [2013] EWCA Civ 1412, para 47.

In the Family Court   Case No ....

Sitting at [*Place*]

The Children Act 1989 - Child Arrangements Programme

THE CHILDREN

Names	Girl /Boy	Dob.

Final Order (CAP 04)

MR/MRS JUSTICE/HHJ[S.9]/DJ/AJC [*NAME OF JUDGE*] **SITTING IN OPEN COURT / PRIVATE ON** [*DATE*]

1. THE PARTIES

The applicant (mother/father/as appropriate) is [*name*]
The first respondent (father/mother/as appropriate) is [*name*]
The second respondent (child/father of/as appropriate) is [*name*]
[The third respondent(s) is/are (the children) by their children's guardian [*name*]]
[The first intervener [*state relationship to child(ren) or other party*] *is* [*name*]]

2. The child/ren is/are living with ....

3. REPRESENTATION AT THIS HEARING

The parties appeared before the court as follows:

Party/Name	In Person	Counsel/Solicitor/ Advocate	Contact telephone and email address
Applicant			
Respondent(s) (1) (2)			
Other (specify)			

The names set out in paragraph 3 are not to be disclosed in public without the permission of the court.

4. Cafcass / CAFCASS Cymru / Local Authority *[if appointed]*

Name

Professional address

Date of appointment (if children's guardian):

Date of order of [section 7] [section 37] report

5. THE APPLICATIONS

The applicant has applied for a Child Arrangements Order/Specific Issue Order/Prohibited Steps Order/ other Part 2 order *[delete as appropriate or specify]* *[today / on date]*

[If there are other applications add as follows or delete]

The *[specify party]* has applied for [ ] *[today / on date]*

6. THE HEARING

a. Today's case was listed for: [*]
b. Today's hearing has been [EFFECTIVE AS THE FINAL HEARING] [EFFECTIVE] [CANCELLED] [ADJOURNED]
c. The reason why the hearing has been adjourned is: [*]

The next hearing is a [*] on *[date and time   ]* at *[court]* with a time estimate of [ ] [this matter is part heard]

7. AGREEMENTS/AGREED ARRANGEMENTS FOR THE CHILDREN

Such as:-

*   The child[ren] will live with the [mother/father/mother and father] as set out in the schedule to this order *(if extensive)*/as follows ....]
*   The [mother/father] agrees to make the child[ren] available to visit/stay with/have indirect contact with the [mother/father] [as set out in the schedule to this order *(if extensive)*/as follows...]

The [mother/father] may remove the child[ren] from England and Wales [for the purposes of a holiday to *[specify]*][to live in]. The details of the arrangements for the [holiday/removal from the jurisdiction] are to be [as follows ..../ as set out in the schedule to this order *(if extensive)*.

8. UNDERTAKINGS

The [mother/father] gave undertakings to the court [as set out on the [undertaking form] signed by [her/him] on [date] a copy of which is annexed to this order *or* the [mother/father] gave the following undertakings to the court *[specify]*

9. KEY ISSUES [*only if adjourned*]

The issues which remain to be determined are as follows:-

a)	
b)	
c)	
d)	

10. After reading the materials provided to the court.

The court heard no oral evidence

or

After hearing the evidence of the following witnesses:-

Name of witness	Called by

THE COURT ORDERS:

11. CHILD ARRANGEMENTS

Such as

- [By consent,] that the arrangements for the children shall be [as set out in the schedule to this order *(if extensive)*/as follows *[specify]*]
- [a contact warning notice will be endorsed][by consent] that the [father/mother] shall make the child[ren] available to spend time with /

have [indirect] contact with] the [father/mother] as set out in the schedule to this order *(if extensive)*/as follows .... *[specify]*

12. PARENTAL RESPONSIBILITY

Further to the Child Arrangements Order made [today/date], which provides that the child is to live with [the father, who does not currently have parental responsibility] / [*woman* who is a parent of the child by virtue of section 43 of the Human Fertilisation and Embryology Act 2008, without parental responsibility], the court grants parental responsibility to [the father] / [*the woman*].

Further to the Child Arrangements Order made [*today/date*], which provides that the child is to spend time or otherwise have contact (but not live) with [the father, who does not currently have parental responsibility] / [*woman* who is a parent of the child by virtue of section 43 of the Human Fertilisation and Embryology Act 2008, without parental responsibility], the court grants parental responsibility to [the father] / [*the woman*].

Further to the Child Arrangements Order made [*today/date*], which provides that the child is to live with [*a person who is not the parent or guardian of the child concerned is named in the order as a person with whom the child is to spend time or otherwise have contact but not live*] the court grants parental responsibility for the child for as long as the order is in place.

Further to the Child Arrangements Order made [*today/date*], which provides that the child is to spend time or otherwise have contact (but not live) with [*a person who is not the parent or guardian of the child concerned is named in the order as a person with whom the child is to spend time or otherwise have contact but not live*] the court grants parental responsibility for the child for as long as the order is in place.

13.ACTIVITY CONDITIONS

[if made at this hearing, specify as appropriate]

Such as:-

The [father/mother] [other party] is directed to take part in:

Set out any order for Activity Direction/Condition [e.g. Separated Parents Information Programme] such dates and times as are specified by .... [the provider]

The court shall forthwith send this order to the provider.

14. PROHIBITED STEPS

Specify as appropriate, such as:-

- The [mother/father] shall not cause or permit [name child[ren] to [cease to attend ....*name school*] [live at an address other than *[specify]*] [come into contact with *[specify]*] without the prior written agreement of the [father/mother] or an order of the court.

- The [mother/father] shall not remove [name child/ren] from England and Wales without the prior written agreement of [father/mother] or an order of the court [except .... *[specify]*].

15. SPECIFIC ISSUE – REMOVAL FROM THE JURISDICTION

(a) The [mother/father] is permitted to remove [name of child(ren)] from England and Wales on or after [date] to live permanently in [as appropriate].

(b) *[for example]* Before the removal of the [name child[ren] from the jurisdiction, the [mother/father] shall obtain, and then deliver and send to the court and to the other parties, an order from [court] an order reflecting the terms of this order insofar as they relate to the child arrangements [or as appropriate].

16. SPECIFIC ISSUE – SCHOOLING

From [date/the start of the ....term ....] [name child[ren]] shall attend [name and address of school].

[set out any ancillary provisions re schooling e.g. provision of information, fees etc.]

17. SPECIFIC ISSUE – OTHER STEPS

Specify as appropriate

18. CONTACT CENTRE DIRECTION

The order for supported contact at the [ ] contact centre is subject to the following conditions for its operation and effect:-

(a) The [parties/ solicitors for the [Mother/Father][ ] shall inform the centre co-ordinator of the contents of this order as soon as practicable.

(b) The [parties/ solicitors for the parties] shall jointly be responsible for
    i. completing a referral form for the centre co-ordinator and
    ii. providing a copy of this order and any subsisting injunction orders involving the parties to the co-ordinator as soon as practicable and in any event within 2 days of today.

(c) Confirmation from the centre co-ordinator that:
  i.   the centre is an accredited member of NACCC;
  ii.   the referral has been accepted following completion of a preparation for contact interview (which interview is a compulsory requirement of all NACCC centres);
  iii. a vacancy is available or the parties have been allocated a place upon a waiting list (the order for supported contact is suspended during any waiting period until a place is available).

(d) The parties and any person permitted to accompany them to the centre shall abide by the rules of the centre.

(e) The parties must attend a preparation for contact meeting with the centre co-ordinator (the parties' solicitors, if acting, must take responsibility for ensuring that information about the meeting is passed to the parties).

(f) The [Mother/Father] [ ] agrees to take the child(ren) for a pre-contact introductory visit to the centre.

(g) The child(ren) will be informed of the contact arrangements by [Mother/ Father] [ ]

(h) The following arrangements for the contact sessions shall apply:-
  i.   The child(ren) shall be taken to the centre by [   ].
  ii.   The child(ren) shall be collected at the conclusion of contact by [   ].
  iii. The [Father/Mother] [ ] may [not] be accompanied during the contact session [by]
  iv.   The [Father/Mother] [ ] may [not] remain in the same room as the child(ren) during the contact session.
  v.   After [ ] sessions of contact, the [Father/Mother] [ ] shall not remain in the same room as the child(ren) but may remain in the confines of the centre.
  vi.   [Other agreements about contact at the centre].

(i) The [parties/ the parties' solicitors] shall jointly be responsible for informing the centre co-ordinator when the place is no longer required.

19. MONITORING CONTACT ORDER

(a) Cafcass/CAFCASS Cymru shall, pursuant to s 11H Children Act 1989, make an officer available to monitor whether the person required to allow the contact, or the person having contact with the child[ren] complies with the contact order;

(b) The contact monitoring order shall remain in force until [ ][up to 12 mths];

(c) The [mother / father / person having contact] shall co-operate with the Cafcass officer / WFPO [in particular by ....] so that the officer can comply with the order to monitor the contact;

(d) The Cafcass officer / WFPO is directed to prepare a report for the Court (and provide a copy to the parties) if he/she considers that the order is not being complied with; the report shall include any information which the

Cafcass officer / WFPO considers relevant to the issue of compliance and shall specifically advise on the question of whether the order should be varied or discharged.

20. FAMILY ASSISTANCE ORDER

(a) Cafcass/CAFCASS Cymru/[ ] Local Authority shall, pursuant to s 16 Children Act 1989, make an Officer available to advise assist and (where appropriate) befriend the following persons who have (save for a named child) today consented to the making of this Order:

(b) The Family Assistance Order shall remain in force until [ ][up to 12 mths].

(c) The Officer is directed to give advice and assistance as regards establishing, improving and maintaining contact to those identified above.

(d) The Officer is directed to report to the Court by 16:00hs on [ ] on the following matters (*including but limited to the question of whether the s 8 order should be varied or discharged*):

(e) It is recorded for the purpose of this Order that
    a. the opinion of the appropriate officer has been obtained and
    b. all relevant persons have been given the opportunity to comment on that opinion prior to the making of this order pursuant to PD12M FPR 2010.

(f) The Local Authority/Cafcass/CAFCASS Cymru may send representations to the Court and the other parties on or before [14 days from service] as to the making of the Family Assistance Order pursuant to PD12M FPR 2010. Any party wishing to respond to those representations must do so within 7 days of receipt.

21. COSTS

No order as to costs *or*
Costs in the application *or*
Costs reserved *or*
Funded services assessment of the costs of *[specify] or*
Other *[specify]*
Dated
Court address: for sending documents/communication:

2.115 See also the Child Arrangments Progamme below:

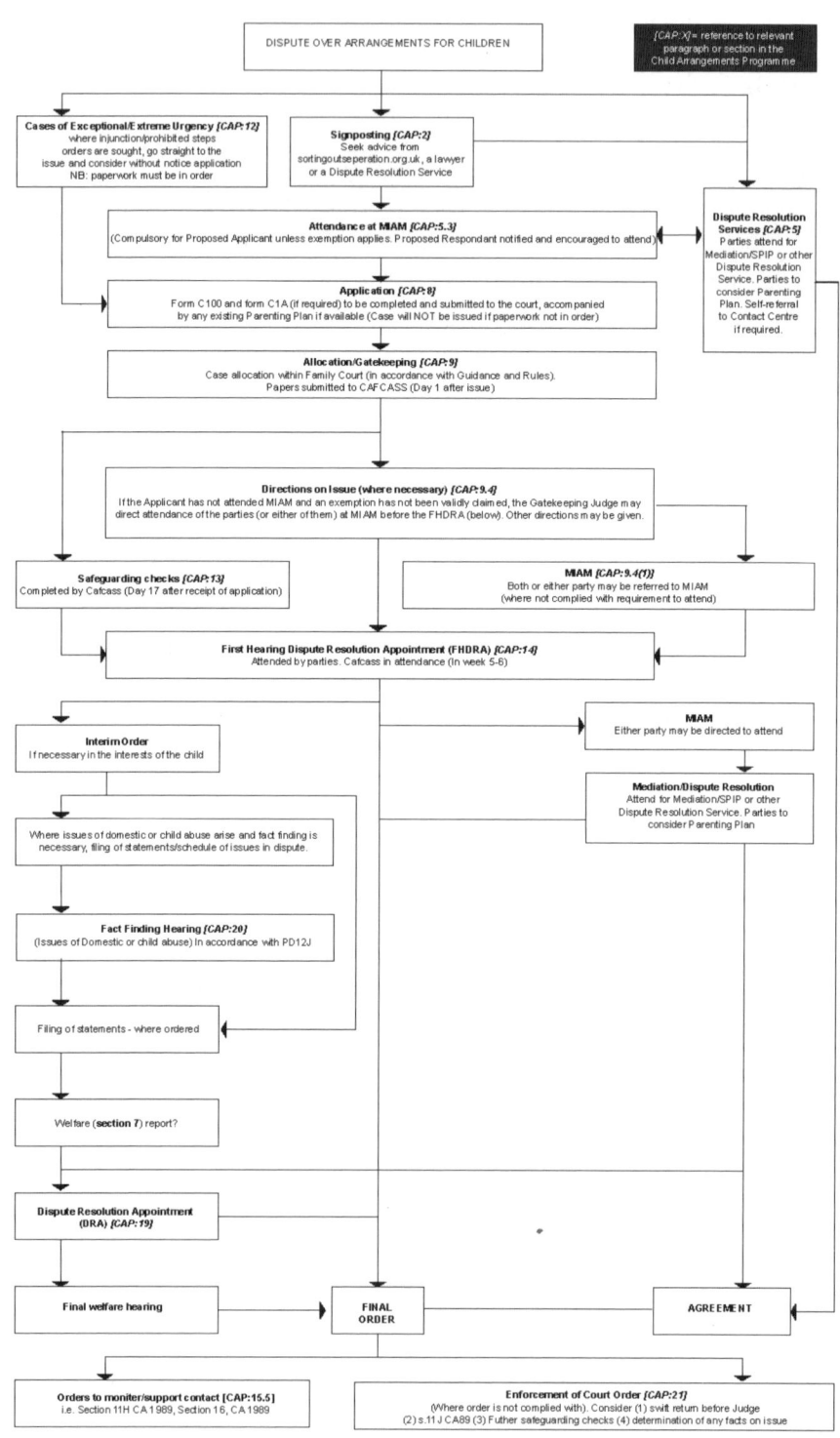

FREQUENTLY ASKED QUESTIONS

'I'm in court tomorrow at a final hearing in an old style "residence" case which was issued pre-April 2014. What should the order be, in the old form or the new?'

2.116 The transitional provisions are found in the Children and Families Act 2014 (Transitional Provisions) Order 2014.[59] Article 6 of the SI deems contact orders and residence orders that were made under s 8 of the 1989 Act as child arrangements orders, and also deems applications for such orders made before 22 April, but still ongoing post-22 April as applications for child arrangements orders, and therefore the new orders should be used.

'How do I know which level of judge in the family court my case will be listed before?'

2.117 The Family Court (Composition and Distribution of Business) Rules 2014[60] set out the procedure to be followed for allocation. The schedules provide details of the type of work to be dealt with by the different levels of judiciary.

'I need to appeal against the decision of the district judge in the family court, where does my appeal go to now?'

2.118 The previous routes of appeal against decisions of judges and magistrates in family proceedings reflected the three-tier structure of the old court. Upon implementation of the Crime and Courts Act 2013, technically all appeals from the new family court lay to the Court of Appeal, which was clearly unworkable as a position. The Access to Justice Act 1999 (Destination of Appeal) (Family Proceedings) Order 2014 therefore makes the necessary provision to maintain the previous position that appeals against the decisions made at district judge level and below in family proceedings will be routed away from the Court of Appeal. Generally, appeals within the family court will be dealt with by a circuit judge or High Court judge.

2.119 The procedure for appeals is set out in the amended FPR 2010 r 30 and accompanying practice direction, which can be found at the conclusion of this book.

2.120 The allocation of appeals is dealt with in the Family Court (Composition and Distribution of Business) Rules 2014,[61] rr 5–7. Appeals from a district judge shall be heard by the family court composed of a judge of circuit judge level, or a judge of High Court level, where there is a need.

---

[59] SI 2014/1042.
[60] SI 2014/840.
[61] Ibid.

'Under the old scheme, the holder of a residence order could remove the child from the jurisdiction for up to 28 days. What are the rules now?'

2.121   Schedule 2 of the 2014 Act, para 22(3) amends s 13 to read that the person named in a child arrangements order as the person with whom the child is to live can remove the child for the same periods as before. Schedule 2 provides all other amendments necessary to implement the new regime.

'Is the presumption of parental involvement in force now?'

2.122   The sections of the Act in force as at 22 April 2014 are:

- s 9 (contact: post adoption);[62]
- s 10 (family mediation information and assessment meetings);
- s 12 (child arrangements orders);
- s 13 (control of expert evidence and of assessments in children proceedings);
- s 14 (care, supervision and other family proceedings: time limits and timetables;
- s 15(1) and (3) (care plans);
- s 16 (care proceedings and care plans);
- s 17 (repeal of restrictions on divorce and dissolution where there are children);[63]
- Sch 2 (child arrangements orders: amendments).

2.123   On 13 May 2014, the following provisions came into force:

- s 4 (recruitment, assessment and approval of prospective adopters);
- s 7 (Adoption and Children Act register);
- Sch 1 (Adoption and Children Act register).

2.124   The following came into force on 25 July 2014:

- s 1 (England only) (contact between prescribed persons and adopted person's relatives);
- ss 2–3 (placement of looked after children with prospective adopters and repeal of ethnicity requirement);
- s 6 (adoption support services);
- s 8 (contact: children in care of local authorities).

In answer to the question therefore, the presumption of parental involvement is not yet in force at the time of writing.

---

[62]   Children and Families Act 2014 (Commencement No 2) Order 2014, SI 2014/889.
[63]   Children and Families Act 2014 (Commencement No 1) Order 2014, SI 2014/793.

'My committal proceedings for enforcement of a child arrangements order have been listed before a district judge in the family court, what are their powers?'

2.125 The new Part 37 of FPR 2010 sets out a stand-alone procedure for contempt matters in the family court. In addition, the powers of the Court have been defined and refined through statutory instruments:[64]

- The maximum committal powers available to judges of the family court are the powers previously available in the High Court.
- A judge of district judge level is limited when dealing with contempt in the face of the court to a maximum period of one month (reg 3).
- Lay justices are limited when dealing with breach of judgment to a maximum period of two months (reg 4).
- Lay justices are also limited when dealing with contempt in the face of the court to a maximum period of one month (reg 4);
- All judges, other than those of High Court level, are limited when considering fines to an amount not exceeding level 5 on the standard scale (reg 5).

'How have the powers of the justices' clerks and assistants changed in the new Court?'

2.126 Their powers are now set out in the Justices' Clerks and Assistances Rules 2014[65] and the Schedule attached.

'To what extent have the FPR 2010 changed?'

2.127 The following are the main points to note:

- new Part 37 deals with contempt and committal;
- Part 30 has been amended to adjust the appeals rules;
- full amendments can be found in the statutory instruments.[66]

Financial remedy proceedings

2.128 In his *View from the President's Chamber (12)*, Sir James Munby P explained that Mostyn J and Cobb J had been invited to chair a new Financial Remedies Working Group, with a two-fold task, to explore ways of improving the accessibility of the system for litigants in person, and to identify ways of further improving good practice in financial remedy cases. The objective was to produce something analogous to CAP: the Money Arrangements Programme, (MAP).

---

[64] Family Court (Contempt of Court) (Powers) Regulations 2014, SI 2014/833, see http://www.legislation.gov.uk/uksi/2014/833/contents/made.

[65] See http://www.legislation.gov.uk/uksi/2014/603/contents/made.

[66] See http://www.legislation.gov.uk/uksi/2014/667/contents/made and http://www.legislation.gov.uk/uksi/2014/843/contents/made.

2.129 These recommendations were in line with the February 2014 Law Commission report *Matrimonial Property, Needs and Agreements*, which recommended[67] that guidance should be produced in plain English and made widely available to the public.

2.130 As noted above, there had been a suggestion in the Family Justice Review that Children Act applications should be dealt with alongside financial remedy applications at a composite hearing. This did not find its way into the Act, and the general scheme for financial remedy applications remains largely unchanged by the reforms, and is outside the scope of the 2014 Act.

2.131 However, the formation of the single family court has impacted on financial applications within London, with the conversion of the Principal registry to the 'Central Family Court' at First Avenue House. The central family court is hoped to become the flagship of excellence for high value and complex financial remedy litigation. In September 2013, the 'Financial Remedies Unit' commenced work, and the financial remedies officer was appointed. The unit commenced hearing cases from 2 January 2014.[68] With a familiar emphasis on the reduction of delay within the system, there are new policies and procedures within the financial remedies unit to be followed with a view to reducing listing times, and the introduction of a special accelerated first appointment procedure to be used where directions are not controversial. At the time of writing, this is a pilot procedure to be used when attendance at the first appointment can be avoided.[69]

2.132 The FRU is intended to focus on a more efficient and effective hearing of financial cases, through the application of key policies, to speed up listing and improve the smooth operation of the court.

2.133 The review announced in June 2014 was confined to practice and procedure, not substantive law. It was aimed at improving the process for litigants in person, and encouraging out of court methods of dispute resolution. This is looked at further in chapter 3. The working group is to report by 31 July 2014.

Draft orders in financial remedy applications

2.134 In his *View from the President's Chambers (4)*[70], Sir James Munby P said that:

> 'Inordinate amounts of time and money are spent – wasted – in the process of drafting orders that could, and therefore should, be standardised. I have appointed

---

[67]   At para 3.89.

[68]   For further details of the workings of the FRU see HHJ O'Dwyer and DJ Hess 'The Financial Remedies Unit at the Central Family Court' [2014] Fam Law 344.

[69]   The full procedure can be found at http://www.justice.gov.uk/courts/rcj-rolls-building/principal-registry, and at [2014] Fam Law 887.

[70]   [2014] Fam Law 344.

a small drafting group under the determined leadership of Mostyn J to provide us with a comprehensive set of orders the use of which will in due course become mandatory in the Family Court and the Family Division.'

2.135 At the end of November 2013, Mostyn J released the first batch of proposed standard orders. In respect of financial remedy applications, there are two orders, one to deal with the directions stage of proceedings, and one to deal with final orders. The full text of the orders is set out Appendix 11 and Appendix 12 to this book.[71]

---

[71] As updated following the Report of the Financial Remedies Working Group in August 2014.

CHAPTER 3

DISPUTE RESOLUTION SERVICES

3.1   The Children and Families Act 2014, combined with the changes brought about by Legal Aid, Sentencing and Punishment of Offenders Act 2012, have both brought renewed focus to methods of alternative dispute resolution in family law, and the process of mediation in particular. At the second reading of the bill in the House of Commons on 25 February 2013, the Minister explained the Government's view that:

'simply too many children are involved in private proceedings.'

3.2   Statistics showed that just over 56,000 children were the subject of new contact and residence cases in 2011–12. The starting point of the private law reforms were that separated parents should resolve their disputes out of court whenever possible, in recognition of the fact that an adversarial court process is not always best-suited to the resolution of family disputes.

3.3   Before moving to look at the process of mediation specifically, the other important forms of ADR must be considered, namely collaborative law and arbitration.

COLLABORATIVE LAW

3.4   Under the collaborative law process, each party to the separation has their own solicitor, who attends meetings with them and the other side, commonly known as four-way meetings. They work together to reach an agreement which avoids going to court. If the matter does proceed to court, those lawyers cannot represent the parties, having been part of the collaborative process. The negotiations conducted during the collaborative meetings are often far more wide-ranging than would be possible in court, and can result in comprehensive agreements which can then be placed before the court for approval. The process has had the approval of the judiciary for a number of years.[1]

---

[1]   See for example *S v P (Settlement by Collaborative Law Process)* [2008] 2 FLR 2040, Coleridge J.

ARBITRATION

3.5   In cases involving the division of financial assets, whether on divorce, dissolution or separation, it is possible for parties to turn to arbitration for a solution. At an arbitration, the parties may be represented and the case if fully argued before an independent arbitrator, who then makes the decision. Sometimes referred to as a form of 'private judging' the system has the benefit of working to a timetable to suit the clients, at hours to suit their convenience. It also carries the notable advantage of guaranteed privacy.[2] In the case of *S v S*,[3] Sir James Munby P endorsed the suggestion of a streamlined approach to the approval of an arbitral award, in line with Coleridge J's suggestions in *S v P* referred above. He went on to observe:

> '21. Where the consent order which the judge is being asked to approve is founded on an arbitral award under the IFLA Scheme or something similar (and the judge will, of course, need to check that the order does indeed give effect to the arbitral award and is workable) the judge's role will be simple. The judge will not need to play the detective unless something leaps off the page to indicate that something has gone so seriously wrong in the arbitral process as fundamentally to vitiate the arbitral award. Although recognising that the judge is not a rubber stamp, the combination of (a) the fact that the parties have agreed to be bound by the arbitral award, (b) the fact of the arbitral award (which the judge will of course be able to study) and (c) the fact that the parties are putting the matter before the court by consent, means that it can only be in the rarest of cases that it will be appropriate for the judge to do other than approve the order. With a process as sophisticated as that embodied in the IFLA Scheme it is difficult to contemplate such a case.'

3.6   In his *View from the President's Chambers (12)*, Sir James Munby P continued to support a simplified approach to arbitral awards. As part of the Financial Remedies Working Group's review, he sought to increase the ease with which out of court agreements can be implemented. At the time of writing, in June 2014, the President stated an intention to issue a draft rule change to the FPR 2010, to enable the relevant applications under the Arbitration Act 1996 to be made in the Family Division rather than just the Commercial Court as previously, and also to issue draft guidance to cover procedural matters raised by *S v S*.[4]

MEDIATION IN 2014

3.7   Although the grass roots of family mediation in England and Wales date back to the 1970's, with the first ever mediation service starting in Bristol in 1978, family mediation first rose in profile and prominence following the enactment of the Family Law Act 1996, s 29, which required most applicants for public funding to have first attended a mediation information and assessment meeting (MIAM) meeting with an LSC competence-assessed

---

2   *W v M (TOLATA Proceedings; Anonymity)* [2012] EWHC 1679 (Fam).
3   [2014] EWHC 7 (Fam).
4   Ibid.

mediator. If one party refused to attend the meeting, then the other was not required to do so, which was known as the willingness test. At the very least however, mediation had to be considered by the parties and their representative. If mediation followed, further public funding was made available for the subsequent mediation, and if the meeting did not lead to mediation then public funding was made available for a court application.

3.8 The next inroad to proceedings by mediation came in the form of Practice Direction 3A to the Family Procedure Rules 2010, which set out the court's expectation that applicants would comply with the pre-application protocol for MIAMs, and would expect all respondents to have attended a MIAM if invited to do so:[5]

> 'parties will be expected to explore the scope for resolving their dispute through mediation before embarking on the court process.'

3.9 The aim was to ensure as far as possible that all parties have considered mediation as an alternative means of resolving their dispute. If court proceedings followed, the court was entitled to take account of any failure to comply with the pre-action protocol and could refer the parties to a meeting with a mediator before the proceedings continued further. The private law programme, set out in Practice Direction 12B, provided for a first hearing dispute resolution appointment, when the court would actively manage the case, discuss the nature of the dispute, and whether it could be resolved through ADR, including mediation. The Family Procedure Rules 2010, r 3.2, imposes a duty on the court to consider, at every stage in proceedings, whether alternative dispute resolution is appropriate, and goes on at r 3.3 to provide for proceedings to be adjourned to enable ADR to take place.

The Family Justice Review

3.10 The Family Justice Review, published in 2010, found that 'long and complicated legal processes are emotionally and financially draining for parents and distressing for children'. As such, one of the aims of the review was to produce a system using family mediation as far as possible to support individuals themselves to reach agreements.

3.11 In the final report published in November 2011, the Family Justice Review recommended:

> '4.85 We recommend all applicants should be required to attend a MIAM prior to making a court application. We cannot compel respondents to attend, but they should be encouraged to do so. Judges will retain the power to order attendance at a MIAM and the expectation is that this power should be exercised as much as possible where respondents have not considered mediation. Judges could be powerful advocates to encourage an expectation that other means of reaching agreement will be tried before an application to court.'

---

[5] Paragraph 3.5.

3.12   Following the MIAMs, the review further recommended that;

> '4.87 After the MIAM the parties should be referred to a Separated Parents Information Programme (PIP).'

3.13   The requirement on an applicant to attend at a PIP was not included in either the Bill or the final 2014 Act as it was presented to Parliament. The FJR intended that that be dealt with after the MIAMs but before substantive mediation. That recommendation was based on research conducted after the interim report:

> '4.90 Assessment for suitability for PIPs is currently carried out as part of the court process but should in future form part of the mediation assessment as happens in Australia. We do not believe it would be necessary or perhaps even appropriate for Cafcass to carry out safeguarding checks before attendance at PIPs. But mediators will need training to identify risks as an element in the training needed to carry out MIAMs.'

3.14   The ability of the court to direct parties to attend at PIPs remains in the FPR. It has not however become part of the mediation process at the early stage prior to proceedings as suggested in the review.

3.15   The FJR recommendations were summarised as follows;

'Final recommendations

- "Alternative dispute resolution" should be rebranded as "Dispute Resolution Services", in order to minimise a deterrent to its use.
- Where intervention is necessary, separating parents should be expected to attend a session with a mediator, trained and accredited to a high professional standard who should:
  - assess the most appropriate intervention, including mediation and collaborative law, or whether the risks of domestic violence, imbalance between the parties or child protection issues require immediate referral to the family court; and
  - provide information on local Dispute Resolution Services and how they could support parties to resolve disputes.
- The mediator tasked with the initial assessment (Mediation Information and Assessment Meeting) would need to be the key practitioner until an application to court is made.
- The regime would allow for emergency applications to court and the exemptions should be as in the Pre-Application Protocol.
- Those parents who were still unable to agree should next attend a Separated Parents Information Programme and thereafter if necessary mediation or other dispute resolution service.
- Attendance at a Mediation Information and Assessment Meeting and Separated Parent Information Programme should be required of anyone wishing to make a court application. This cannot be required, but should be expected, of respondents.

- Judges should retain the power to order parties to attend a mediation information session and Separated Parents Information Programmes, and may make cost orders where it is felt that one party has behaved unreasonably.
- Where agreement could not be reached, having been given a certificate by the mediator, one or both of the parties would be able to apply to court.
- Mediators should at least meet the current requirements set by the Legal Services Commission. These standards should themselves be reviewed in the light of the new responsibilities being laid on mediators. Mediators who do not currently meet those standards should be given a specified period in which to achieve them.
- Government should closely watch and review the progress of the Family Mediation Council to assess its effectiveness in maintaining and reinforcing high standards. The Family Mediation Council should if necessary be replaced by an independent regulator.'

3.16 The Government's response to the FJR recommendations accepted the value of mediation, and the need for specialist parenting programmes to be strengthened. It did not however adopt the recommendations to include the PIP course within the pre application process.

Child Arrangements Programme

3.17 When the CAP was developed, all of the recommendations of the FJR were taken into account and the working group highlighted the urgent need for more people to be guided down the appropriate route to resolve their disputes, away from the court system.

3.18 It was recommended that there should be better co-ordination of information about dispute resolution, in accordance with the suggestion of an online information hub specifically recommended by the Family Justice Review, and a greater support for and signposting of MIAMs and mediation services.

3.19 The CAP commences with information aimed at encouraging and supporting separated parents through the mediation process (para 1):

'1.1 The Child Arrangements Programme (the 'CAP') applies where a dispute arises between separated parents and/or families about arrangements concerning children.

1.2 The CAP is designed to assist families to reach safe and child-focused agreements for their child, where possible out of the court setting. If parents / families are unable to reach agreement, and a court application is made, the CAP encourages swift resolution of the dispute through the court.

1.3 It is well-recognised that negotiated agreements between adults generally enhance long-term co-operation, and are better for the child concerned. Therefore, separated parents and families are strongly encouraged to attempt to resolve their disputes concerning the child outside of the court system. This may also be quicker and cheaper.'

CAP then includes a specific section on 'Signposting Services for Families' at para 2, which refers to family mediation and how to find a mediator.

3.20 Paragraph 5 of CAP sets out the steps to be followed when involved with 'non-court resolution of disputed arrangements for children'. It states that dispute resolution services, including mediation, should be actively considered and attempted where it is safe and appropriate to do so.

3.21 Pursuant to the CAP, the court is specifically required at the FHDRA to consider whether the parties, and in particular any reluctant respondent, should be required to attend at a MIAM appointment. The rules currently only compel the applicant, not the respondent. In addition, whether or not the applicant has attempted to use mediation by attending at the MIAM will be checked at the point of issue of any application, at the gatekeeping stage, and again at the FHDRA. The FM1 form which used to be completed by mediators to confirm attendance or otherwise, has now been incorporated into a new C100, the application form used for court appointments.

3.22 Part 5 of the CAP provides the requirements in detail.[6] Anyone who is considering making an application to the court must attend at a family MIAM. A prospective respondent is *expected* to do so. There are some exceptions, in which cases MIAMs and mediation itself is not considered to be appropriate, including domestic violence, or cases where alcohol or drug abuse render the process unsafe.

Parenting plans

3.23 Parenting plans have been used by mediators to set out the agreed arrangements for children, and following their endorsement by the Family Justice Review, are now for the first time formally recognised within the Child Arrangements Programme.

3.24 The working group placed emphasis[7] on parents working together to produce 'parenting plans', designed to help separated parents and their families to work out the best possible arrangements for children in a consistent and reliable way:[8]

> '26. "Parenting Plans" can be a useful resource to support parents as they make arrangements for their children. We specifically recommend use of the Parenting Plan published by Cafcass to parties, mediators and other dispute resolution services.

---

[6]   PD 12 (B) CAP.
[7]   Paragraph 26.
[8]   See http://www.cafcass.gov.uk/PDF/FINAL%20web%20version%20251108.pdf which provides information and guidance on parenting plans.

27. The FJR recommended the consideration of Parenting Plans at a FHDRA;[9] while this may potentially be a useful discussion document at such a hearing, we do not believe that time will permit for taking parties through a Parenting Plan at a court appointment.

28. Consideration may in due course need to be given to the weight (if any) to be attached to a Parenting Plan in the event of a court dispute. It is suggested that any such Plan should be admissible in any subsequent proceedings to establish what the couple had considered a reasonable arrangement at the time.'

3.25 Cafcass have provided guidance[10] as to the things to be considered by parents when trying to work together to agree the day-to-day arrangements for children, and includes headings such as:

- where will the children live;
- when will they spend time with each parent;
- how will they be told about the arrangements;
- how will any arrangements be changed;
- will anyone else help with child care;
- will there be telephone calls;
- what routine will be maintained;
- what are the holiday arrangements;
- what will school or nursery be told;
- what arrangements will be made for religious beliefs;
- what are the arrangements for medical appointments.

3.26 In its final report, the working group stated an expectation that parenting plans reached during mediation should be open documents, and if a parenting plan is in place at the time that a court application is made, a copy should be attached to the C100 application form.

Mediation as ongoing process

3.27 As the CAP makes clear 'Mediation should not be seen as a "once and for all" exercise'.[11] The court is required, pursuant to CAP para 6.1, to consider at every stage whether alternative dispute resolution is appropriate, even if proceedings are issued and ongoing. The proceedings can then be adjourned to enable ADR to take place.

3.28 With a view to encouraging this process, an increasing number of 'at court' mediation services have developed, which enables the judge to stand matters down, or adjourn, for further discussion to take place with a trained mediator. However, concern about mediators being drawn inappropriately into

---

9   FJR 2011, p 163, para 4.
10 See leaflet above, p 10.
11 Working group report, para 29.

the court process led to the development of 'suggested good practice Guidelines' being drawn up by the Family Mediation Council, specifically to deal with at-court mediation.[12] In particular the following guidance is given:

'Before Mediators see Parties

C2. The Mediator is to take an active role with Cafcass and the gatekeeper for the day (District Judge or Legal Advisor) in case triage (ie reviewing the cases in the list for the day and determining which may be suitable for mediation) at the beginning of each list. Cafcass safeguarding information must be available at this stage.

C3. The District Judge/Legal Adviser introduces the Parties and their representatives to the Mediator/s.

C4. The District Judge/Legal Adviser is positive about the mediation assessment/mediation process which may take a minimum of an uninterrupted hour.

After Mediators have seen parties

C5. After seeing parties, and subject to parties consenting to break mediation privilege and confidentiality, Mediators may feedback (whether orally or in written format) the outcomes/decisions from their at-court meetings with parties to:-

• Advocates; and then to
• District Judge/Legal Adviser and Cafcass as appropriate

C6. Mediators will not enter into dialogue or discussion when giving feedback to advocates, Cafcass and/or judiciary.

C7. Mediators must clearly establish with parties whether or not parties wish for their mediated outcomes to be converted into consent orders at court following any in-court mediation.

C8. Mediators and those involved in the administration of the mediation process may not be compelled to give evidence regarding information arising out of or in connection with any mediation except by reference to overriding public policy considerations (eg child protection or to prevent harm) or where disclosure of the content of the agreement resulting from any mediation is necessary in order to implement or enforce that agreement.'

The above guidance, if followed, ensures that mediation remains a voluntary and impartial service, and does not become a substitute for Cafcass or court decision making.

---

[12] See Family Mediation Council *In Court Mediation Suggested Good Practice Guidelines* (approved by the Council 15 February 2011).

The 2014 Act and mediation

3.29 The requirement for parties to a relevant family application to attend a MIAM is set out at s 10 of the Act.

The new provisions

3.30 The 2014 Act provides:

10 Family mediation information and assessment meetings

(1) Before making a relevant family application, a person must attend a family mediation information and assessment meeting.

(2) Family Procedure Rules –

- (a) may provide for subsection (1) not to apply in circumstances specified in the Rules,
- (b) may make provision about convening a family mediation information and assessment meeting, or about the conduct of such a meeting,
- (c) may make provision for the court not to issue, or otherwise deal with, an application if, in contravention of subsection (1), the applicant has not attended a family mediation information and assessment meeting, and
- (d) may provide for a determination as to whether an applicant has contravened subsection (1) to be made after considering only evidence of a description specified in the Rules.

(3) In this section –

"the court" means the High Court or the family court;
"family mediation information and assessment meeting", in relation to a relevant family application, means a meeting held for the purpose of enabling information to be provided about –
- (a) mediation of disputes of the kinds to which relevant family applications relate,
- (b) ways in which disputes of those kinds may be resolved otherwise than by the court, and
- (c) the suitability of mediation, or of any such other way of resolving disputes, for trying to resolve any dispute to which the particular application relates;

"family proceedings" has the same meaning as in section 75 of the Courts Act 2003;
"relevant family application" means an application that –
(a) is made to the court in, or to initiate, family proceedings, and
(b) is of a description specified in Family Procedure Rules.

3.31 The effect of the section is to make it compulsory that the applicant at the very least attends at the assessment stage of mediation. Clearly, no further compulsion in a process that is by its very nature voluntary would be appropriate, but the aim is that those cases in which mediation may be appropriate proceed in that way rather than by application to the court.

3.32 The effectiveness of the new provisions will be dependent on the court staff who check for the FM1/C100 at the time of issue, and the judiciary enforcing the need to attend at a MIAM. However, with the removal of public funding for most private law proceedings via the implementation of the Legal Aid, Sentencing and Punishment of Offenders Act in April 2013, mediation remains funded by legal aid, and therefore will be the only option to many parents who would have previously applied to court.

3.33 A 'relevant family application' is defined as:

> an application that is made to the court in, or to initiate, family proceedings, and is of a description specified in the Family Procedure Rules.

Provision is made at s 10(2)(c) for the court to refuse to issue or otherwise deal with an application if the applicant has not attended a MIAM.

Mediation information and assessment session – what is it?

3.34 The mediation information and assessment session, or MIAM, is not mediation itself. Instead, it is a short session, usually around 40 minutes, conducted by the mediator either with the parties individually or jointly, to assess their suitability for fuller mediation.

3.35 At the session, the mediator can facilitate the identification of the issues that need to be resolved between the parties, whether children, finances or both. The options for dispute resolution are then discussed and explained to the parties, and screening is carried out for domestic violence or child protection issues that may make the case unsuitable for mediation.

3.36 In addition, the mediator will explain the principles under which they work, namely:

- *Impartiality* – the mediator is not 'on either side'.
- *Voluntary* – the process can be ended at any time by either party or the mediator.
- *Confidentiality* – with some exceptions for issues of child protection, criminal activity.

3.37 Once the process is fully explained, and if the mediator deems the situation suitable for mediation, then the parties can choose to engage in it. If they do not wish to do so, or the mediator does not consider that the matter can progress, then he or she will sign the FM1, which can be filed with any application to the court to confirm that the session has been attended.

3.38 The mediation information and assessment meeting can only be conducted by a qualified mediator who is accredited to deal with mediation at that preliminary stage. The MIAM is an opportunity for the parties to receive information about the process, the benefits of mediation as opposed to court proceedings, and the different routes to settlement. It also gives the mediator the important chance to assess the parties and their situation, as it is not appropriate for some cases. These can include those involving allegations of domestic violence, although that is a matter of risk assessment for the mediator, and allegations are not an automatic bar. Other situations that do not lend themselves to mediation are those involving police or social services investigations, or child protection concerns, extreme power imbalances, mental illness, mental disability, substance misuse, or evidence of deceit.

3.39 Where an application to court follows, the applicant is required under the pre-action protocol to file a completed MIAM form, (FM1, or the amended C100), confirming attendance at the meeting, or giving the reasons for not attending. In any of the circumstances described above, the mediator will be able to complete the form giving the reasons for their assessment that the case is not suitable.[13] In addition, where the applicant's solicitor has contacted three mediation organisations within 15 miles of the applicant's home, and none are available to conduct a MIAM within 15 days of the date of contact, then the applicant is not required to attend at an appointment.[14]

LASPO and mediation

3.40 Legal aid for mediation survived the reforms of the Legal Aid, Sentencing and Punishment of Offenders Act 2012. In addition, in its response to the Family Justice Review, the government pledged an increase in funding from £10m to £25m a year. In addition, legal aid continues to be available for legal advice to support mediation, which was recognised as valuable during the FJR process:[15]

> 'Legal advice is required alongside mediation in all financial cases to ensure that agreements which are reached are fair and are capable of being made into an enforceable court order. Legal advice is desirable alongside mediation in relation to matters pertaining to children, if the issue is more complex than simply the quantum of contact.'

Legal aid funding

3.41 The reforms of the 2012 Act were implemented in April 2013, and were dramatic in the breadth and depth of the cuts made. On 1 April 2013 the Legal Services Commission was abolished and replaced with the Legal Aid Agency. Schedule 1 of the Act sets out the areas in which public funding remains for the provision of civil legal services. In relation specifically to mediation, the provisions are set out below:

14 Mediation in family disputes

(1) Mediation provided in relation to family disputes.

---

[13] See also the annex to the CAP.
[14] Annex, ibid.
[15] Family Justice Council, consultation response.

(2) Civil legal services provided in connection with the mediation of family disputes.

Definitions

(7) For the purposes of this paragraph –

(a)   a dispute is a family dispute if it is a dispute between individuals about a matter arising out of a family relationship between the individuals,

(b)   there is a family relationship between two individuals if they are associated with each other, and

(c)   "associated" has the same meaning as in Part 4 of the Family Law Act 1996 (see section 62 of that Act).

(8) For the purposes of this paragraph –

(a)   matters arising out of a family relationship include matters arising under a family enactment, and

(b)   (subject to paragraph (a)) the Lord Chancellor may by regulations make provision about when matters arise out of a family relationship.

(9) In this paragraph –

"child" means a person under the age of 18;
"family enactment" has the meaning given in paragraph 12.

3.42 As noted in the CAP, where one party is eligible for legal aid, the legal aid agency will fund both parties to attend at a MIAM, in order that the respondent can consider using the mediation process without incurring any cost:

'3.3 For public funding issues, note that the Legal Aid Agency (LAA) will provide funding for Mediation Information and Assessment Meetings (MIAMs) and family mediation for all those who are eligible.

3.3.1 Where at least one party is eligible, the LAA will cover the costs of both MIAMs to encourage any non-eligible client to find out about the benefits and suitability of mediation without incurring any costs.

3.3.2 Eligible parties who participate in family mediation may also receive independent legal advice connected to the mediation process and where a settlement is reached can receive legal advice to draft and issue proceedings to obtain a consent order.

3.3.3 Parties may find out if they are likely to be eligible for legal aid at the following link: https://www.gov.uk/check-legal-aid.

3.3.4 To find the nearest publicly funded mediation service a client can use the find a legal advisor or family mediator justice website at the following link: http://find-legal-advice.justice.gov.uk/.'

3.43 However, from April 2013 to December 2013, prior to the implementation of the 2014 Act, but following the implementation of LASPO, the Family Mediation Association reported that private law applications had increased substantially, whilst publicly funded referrals to family mediation had dropped substantially, a reduction of 48.5% according to the Legal Aid Agency. Privately funded mediation services also complained of a reduction in work, up to as much as 75% in some geographical areas.[16] This was likely to be due to a loss in solicitor referrals to mediation services as they withdrew from the arena of private law, and a lack of knowledge and understanding of the process by the general public. Therefore unfortunately, in the months following the introduction of LASPO, but prior to the implementation of the 2014 Act, litigants in person were resorting to the court process at the first opportunity, rather than making use of mediation. A number of reasons were anecdotally given for this, including a lack of good communication to the public about the availability of public funding for mediation, and a lack of faith in the mediation process. It seemed that without lawyers to advise them about the mediation process, most separating parents viewed the first step as an application to court.

Process of mediation

3.44 Clearly, the aims of the legislation are not only that separating couples attend at a MIAM session, but that they go on to resolve their dispute through full mediation. The benefits of this system are clear. Whilst the court process can only determine a dispute in the fairest way at a fixed moment in time, separated parents need to be able to resolve problems and disagreements throughout the child's minority. Mediation provides for far greater flexibility and reflects an agreement reached between the parents voluntarily, rather than an arrangement imposed on them by the court.

3.45 Mediation can resolve children matters or financial disputes, or both. The mediator facilitates discussion between the parties, and provides information, but not advice. It can take as long as the parties want it to, but generally sessions last for around 1½ hours, and arrangements for children can usually be resolved in 4–6 sessions.

3.46 If financial matters need to be resolved, then the parties are asked to provide full financial disclosure, which must be completely open, and is shared between the parties. This opens up discussion as to the needs and wishes of the parties, in terms of housing, employment etc.

3.47 If agreement can be reached then the mediator can draw up a memorandum of understanding and statement of financial information. This is not a binding document, but can be used by a lawyer to convert the parties' agreement into a court order, which can then be put before a judge for approval.

3.48 Where agreement has not been possible, but financial disclosure has been completed, the mediator can still draft a statement of information. This is an open document, which records the financial position of the parties and can be used by them in future negotiations or court proceedings.

---

[16] FMA (November 2013).

3.49 An example memorandum of understanding, and example statement of financial information are given at the conclusion of this chapter.

The limits of mediation

3.50

- Mediation does not create a binding agreement which is capable of enforcement through the courts.
- It has to be voluntary, and a reluctant respondent cannot be compelled to engage with the process.
- It requires discussion and constructive dialogue between the parties.

Benefits of mediation

3.51

- It is cheaper than an application to court, even where public funding is not available to the parties. The general position is that each party will pay their share of the mediation, on a session by session basis.
- It is quicker than an application to the court, and the speed of the process is set by the parties' and mediator's availability, rather than the court timetable.
- The parties retain control over the process and the outcome, as the whole point is to reach an agreement, rather than have to abide by an order that neither party wanted or thinks is fair.
- It can deal with all issues arising from a separation, rather than requiring separate applications and processes for children and money.

The child's voice in mediation

3.52 Just as it is recognised elsewhere within the family justice system that children should be given the opportunity to be heard and to participate in the decision-making process, it is also seen in the mediation setting that there are real long term benefits to a child-inclusive approach.

3.53 The child's voice can be heard within the mediation setting through specialist mediators who are trained as child consultants, and who can speak directly to children about their wishes and feelings, before returning to the parents to convey their views (with the child's permission), and encourage parents to see the situation from the viewpoint of their child. That can be invaluable, particularly where older children are involved in painful separations of the family, although some research has shown that children as young as three years old can participate effectively in appropriately conducted conversations about what is happening.[17]

3.54 However, as is perhaps the case within the court process, the use of child-inclusive mediation in the UK has been described as patchy.[18] Where used, research[19] has shown that the long term benefits, (measured over four years), indicated that child-inclusive mediation:

- gave children a safe avenue to express their views;
- led to a higher level of repair in the parental relationship and improved attachment;
- improved the emotional availability of parents to their children;
- produced developmentally sensitive agreements which were sustained over time;
- improved the parental alliance;
- improved father-child relationships;
- helped fathers to recover confidence in the co-parental relationship;
- upheld children's rights to be heard and to participate.

3.55 As ever, this type of mediation will not be right for every family, and it is a question of assessment of suitability for the mediator at the time. However, it provides an important dynamic which should always remain under consideration, if the focus is truly to be on the interests of the child, rather than the perceived rights of the parents.[20]

---

[17] C Aubrey and S Dahl 'Children's Voices: The views of vulnerable children on their service providers and the relevance of the services they receive' (2006) *British Journal of Social Work* 21–39.

[18] J Walker 'How can we ensure children's voices are heard in mediation?' [2013] Fam Law 191.

[19] (2008) 46(1) *Family Court Review* 105–124; J McKintosh, B Smyth, M Kelaher, Y Wells, and C Long 'Post-separation parenting arrangements: Patterns of developmental outcomes' (2011) *Family Matters No 86, AIFS journal*).

[20] See also Barton and Pugsley 'The voice of the child: Are mediators listening?' [2014] Fam Law 357.

3.56

Example of a memorandum of understanding

CONFIDENTIAL

MEMORANDUM OF UNDERSTANDING

(Privileged Summary of Proposals)

Mr Homer Pilkington
Of Flat 11, 13 Redwine Grove, Lincolnshire
and Mrs Marge Jennifer Pilkington
of Flat 2B, Letchworth, Storyville

Prepared by
Miss Mediator

THIS DOCUMENT IS LEGALLY PRIVILEGED

Memorandum of Understanding

(Privileged Summary of Proposals)

Homer Pilkington and Marge Pilkington have been in mediation with Miss Mediator, with regard to various issues concerning themselves, their children and the financial issues consequent on their separation. This memorandum is a summary of the outcome of the mediation and of the proposals reached.

This memorandum/summary is legally privileged and 'without prejudice'. It does not record or create a binding agreement between Homer Pilkington and Marge Pilkington and any proposals set out in this memorandum/summary have not been set out with the intention of creating legal relations by the creation of this document. It is intended to facilitate each of them obtaining independent professional advice which the mediator has recommended them to do before they take any steps to enter into an agreement whether through solicitors or informally between themselves. Unless and until they decide to enter into a binding agreement, no such binding agreement exists between them.

Mr Homer Pilkington and Mrs Marge Pilkington have signed an open summary of the information disclosed by each of them. They understand that this may be produced to the court, (unlike this memorandum/summary) and have had the necessity for full and complete disclosure explained to them and recorded to them in writing. The Memorandum of Understanding (summary of proposals) may, of course, be produced to legal advisers upon the basis that it is and remains a privileged document.

The mediation was carried out in accordance with the professional requirements and the Code of Practice of ADR. The mediation was carried out over 6 sessions on the 22nd, 23rd and 24th of June and 6th, 7th and 8th of July 2012.

1. Background information.

- Homer and Marge were married on 22nd June 2003, and separated on 30th May 2012. Homer is aged 43 years old, (b. 22/08/69), and Marge is aged 41 years old, (b. 15/06/71).

- They have two children Ross Anthony Pilkington, aged 8, (b. 14/09/03) and Emma Dawn Pilkington, aged 5, (b. 21/01/07). The children live mainly with their mother in the former family home. The property is in the joint names of the parties.

- Homer lives in a rented flat, with his new partner.

- Both Homer and Marge are employed. Homer is a district manager for ToysRUS, and Marge has recently started work on a part-time basis as an administrative assistant.

2. Arrangements by Homer and Marge, parents, for their children Ross Anthony Pilkington and Emma Dawn Pilkington.

The arrangements for Ross and Emma are of the utmost importance to Homer and Marge as parents, and they are in agreement that consultation and good communication between them on children's matters is essential.

Arrangements for parenting time

Homer and Marge have decided that Ross and Emma will live primarily with Marge, and will spend time with their father every weekend, including overnight stays on each Saturday night. Homer will collect and deliver the children to and from Marge's address on Saturday afternoon and return them at Sunday tea time. The children will spend half of the school holidays with Homer and half with Marge. Homer and Marge will make arrangements to ensure that the children spend time with both of them on important days such as Christmas and birthdays.

3. Child Maintenance

Homer and Marge have decided that Homer will pay £200 pcm directly into Marge's bank account by standing order, for the benefit of Ross and Emma. After the family home is sold, this will increase to £450 pcm, as Homer will no longer be paying the mortgage and will be able to afford to pay the increased level to Marge, to help her with her outgoings. The money will be paid on the 5th of the month as Homer is paid on the 3rd. If there are any one-off expenses needed by the children, such as school trips or holiday money, Homer and

Marge will communicate with each other about the contributions they can both afford to make, to ensure that the children's needs are met by them jointly.

4. Separation/Divorce

Homer and Marge have discussed the legal framework for their separation and have both received independent financial advice. They have decided that Marge will instruct her solicitors to issue an application for divorce on the grounds of Homer's unreasonable behaviour. Homer has decided to allow this to proceed on an uncontested basis. They have decided to share the costs of the divorce.

Available assets

The family home is valued at £395,000 and has a mortgage outstanding of £100,000. Homer and Marge agree that the net equity is approximately £283,150 after the costs of the estate agents have been paid. Both Homer and Marge would like to purchase new properties and each need a home that can comfortably accommodate the children.

Homer has a total of £5,500 held in an ISA and a deposit account. Marge has a total of £10,000 held between two bank accounts. Homer and Marge each have £1,950 in shares. Marge has a savings account with a balance of £150. Each of them have their own cars.

5. Family Home

Homer and Marge have decided that the former family home will be sold. The market value is £395,000 and it will be placed on the market at that figure for at least 2 months and then the price will be reviewed by both parties. It will be marketed through Wrigley Clayden estate agents, and both Marge and Homer will take their advice as to pricing and marketing options. As Marge is currently living in the property, she will take primary responsibility for liaising with the agents, arranging views and practical steps.

Division of the proceeds of sale

It is anticipated that the net equity is £283,150 after costs of sale and redemption of the mortgage. Homer and Marge have decided that Marge will received £260,000 to purchase a home for her and the children. Neither parent wants the children to have to change schools and therefore the new property will be in a location that enables them to continue at school.

Homer will receive the balance of the proceeds of sale to use as a deposit on a new property.

These decisions have been taken on the basis of a sale price of £360,000 or more being achieved. In the event that the property sells for less than £360,000, they both wish to renegotiate the position.

6. Capital and other assets

Homer and Marge have decided that they will each retain any savings, current accounts, ISAs, shares and cars that they currently hold in their sole names.

Marge will retain:

(a)   Monies held in Barclays deposit account 84321
(b)   Monies held in HSBC Current account 8324189
(c)   Shares; Abbey National (300) British Gas (150) and Energis (300)
(d)   National Savings 482929
(e)   Fiesta Car

Homer will retain:

(a)   Abbey National ISA
(b)   Monies held in Halifax Deposit account 12376768
(c)   Monies held in HSBC current account 124879
(d)   Shares; Abbey National (300) British Gas (150) and Energis (300)
(e)   Megane Car

The joint savings plan and endowment policies will be surrendered or closed, and the proceeds divided equally between Marge and Homer.

7. Debts and Liabilities

Homer and Marge have decided that they will remain responsible for any liabilities in their sole names.

8. Financial support

Marge and Homer have decided that there is no need for Marge to receive financial support from Homer at the present time, (other than the child maintenance which has been agreed above). Marge is currently employed and feels able to support herself. However, she is anxious about the future and therefore wants to take legal advice about a nominal order which would allow the position to be reviewed in the future. Homer will also take advice about that option and they will then discuss it further. Homer and Marge have discussed, and have received neutral information about, the principles of a clean break or nominal maintenance but both feel that they would prefer to have their own independent advice in respect of this. Marge does not seek anything above a nominal order to preserve her position for the future and both Homer and Marge propose a clean break in relation to all of the other assets.

9. Pensions

Homer and Marge have decided that Homer will retain his pension, as Marge is receiving a greater share of the equity from the house.

10. Inheritance

The matter of inheritance was raised by the mediator. Neither Marge nor Homer have any immediate prospects of inheritance.

11. Wills

The effect of divorce on existing wills was discussed in mediation with Marge and Homer. They both understand the importance of making new wills. They are aware that any independent legal advice they obtain will be able to assist them regarding the drafting of new wills.

12. Tax

Homer and Marge understand that each of them remains liable for their own tax liabilities. Should they wish to take advice in respect of this, they have been encouraged to contact a tax advisor.

13. Contents/Personal Possessions

It was decided that Marge would retain the contents of 10 The High Grove for herself and for the benefit of the children. It was acknowledged that Homer had taken his personal possessions and items he required when he left the family home.

14. Welfare benefits

In mediation the issue of welfare benefits has been raised with Homer and Marge. It has been recommended that they each check their entitlement to new benefits or ensure that they have told their local Benefits Agency Office of their change in circumstances, particularly as Marge has started employment and is in receipt of child maintenance.

15. Other issues

Homer has a life assurance policy with Abbey Life. This is detailed in the open financial summary and has no value to it. Homer intends to continue making the monthly payments. Homer and Marge have decided he will assign the death benefits under this policy to Marge for the benefit of the two children.

Annex 1

Summary of Proposals and Timetable

The former family home will be sold through Wrigley Claydon estate agents. Marge will take the lead in arrangements with the agents and for viewings. The initial market price will be £395,000;

Upon sale, Marge will receive £260,000 and Homer will receive the balance after redemption of the mortgage and the costs of sale. In the event that the property sells for £360,000 or less, the parties will look to renegotiate this division;

The children's primary home will be with their mother and they will continue at their present school. They will spend time with their father at the weekends and there will be shared parenting during the school holidays;

Homer will pay to Marge £200pcm for the benefit of the children, to be increased to £450pcm following sale of the house;

Homer and Marge will each retain any assets or debts in their sole names, including pensions;

The benefits of the continuing life assurance policy held by Homer will be assigned to Marge for the benefit of the children equally;

Both Homer and Marge will seek legal advice about the nominal maintenance order and will discuss that further.

Signed .... Signed ....

Mediator .... Mediator ....

Date .... Date ....

3.57

Example of a statement of financial information

CONFIDENTIAL

OPEN SUMMARY/STATEMENT OF FINANCIAL INFORMATION

Mr Homer Pilkington
and Mrs Marge Jennifer Pilkington

Prepared by
Miss Mediator

This Document is provided on an open basis to record the Financial Information disclosed by Homer Pilkington and Marge Pilkington.

This open summary records on a formal and open basis the financial information disclosed by each of us and which has formed the basis of our discussions in mediation and any proposals that have resulted from such discussions. The need for full financial disclosure has been explained and supporting documents produced where practical and where requested. It is acknowledged that no independent verification has been undertaken by the mediator as to accuracy or completeness, other than referred to specifically in the summary.

Both parties confirm that their financial disclosure is complete. We have agreed to value our assets as at the 5th July 2012 and that the values should form the basis of any proposal for financial settlement.

A separate memorandum relating to the discussions in the mediation, the outcome and any proposals made which are 'without prejudice' and which is legally privileged has also been provided.

1. Background Information

Homer Pilkington and Marge Pilkington are in mediation, with the aim of settling issues surrounding the breakdown of their marriage, including the question of financial settlement.

- Homer and Marge were married on 22nd June 2003, and separated on 30th May 2012. Homer is aged 43 years old, (b. 22/08/69), and Marge is aged 41 years old, (b. 15/06/71).
- They have two children Ross Anthony Pilkington, aged 8, (b. 14/09/03) and Emma Dawn Pilkington, aged 5, (b. 21/01/07). The children live with their mother in the former family home. The property is in the joint names of the parties.

- Homer lives in a rented flat. He is living with his new partner, Jacky.
- Both parties are employed. Homer is a district manager for ToysRUS, and Marge has recently started work on a part-time basis as an administrative assistant.

2. Schedule of Assets

Description	Joint	Homer	Marge
Family home – £395,000 Mtg – £100,000, (acc no. 6543) NCS – £11,850 (3%)	Equity – £283,150		
Sun Alliance End policy – (5644)	£4,500		
Abbey Life End policy – (8484)	£5,250		
Abbey National savings	£2,000		
Abbey National Cash ISA		£2,000	
Halifax deposit acc (6768)		£3,500	
Barclays (4321)			£5,000
HSBC (4189)			£5,000
HSBC (4879)		£25	
Shares – Abbey National		£750	£750
Shares – British Gas		£450	£450
Shares – Energis		£750	£750
National Savings acc (2929)			£150
Cars		£5,000	£500
Subtotals	£294,900	£12,475	£12,600
Grand total	£319,975		
Pension CETV		Greenshires BS £118,855	

3. Debts and Liabilities

Description	Joint	Homer	Marge
Debenhams Store Card			£500

4. Income

	Joint	Homer	Marge
		£2,543 pcm (net salary)	£1,000 pcm (net salary) £596 pcm benefits £450 pcm child maintenance Total £2,046
Total joint income	£4,139		

NOTE.

The income detailed above at point 4 does not include any income from Homer's partner, as she is not currently contributing.

6. Expenditure

Homer	Item	Marge	Homer to Marge
£1,014	Property	£423	
£348	Financial	£120	
£175	Housekeeping	£525	
£146	Personnel	£204	
£132	Car	£152	
£117	Leisure	£157	
£200	Children	£496	£450
£2,132	Sub total	£2077	
£39	Deficit	£31	

NOTE

It should be noted that the above expenditure reflects the current, interim situation as detailed in Homer and Marge's Financial Disclosure Forms, which were completed and submitted to the Mediators at the start of the Mediation process.

ANNEX 1

The following original documents have been produced in Mediation.

Documents produced by Homer

(a)   Mortgage Statement from the Abbey National, for 10 High Grove, dated 1.7.2012

(b)   CETV Greenshires Staff Retirement Benefits Scheme date 30.6.2012

(c)   Share Certificates for Abbey National, British Gas and Energis

(d)   Surrender Quotation for Sun Alliance Endowment 555644 dated 1.7.2012

(e)   Surrender Quotation for Abbey Life Endowment 148484 dated 1.7.2012

(f)   Surrender Quotation for Abbey National Savings plan dated 30.6.2012

(g)   Statement for Abbey Cash ISA dated 30.6.2012

(h)   Statements for Halifax Deposit Account 12376768 for preceding 6 months up to 30.6.2012

(i)   Statements for HSBC Current Account 124879 for preceding 12 months up to 1.6.2012

(j)   Copy Pay slips and last P60

Documents produced by Marge

(a)   Share certificates for Abbey National, British Gas, and Energis

(b)   Statement for Barclays Deposit Account 84321 dated 1.7.12 and for preceding 12 months

(c)   Statement for HSBC Current account 8324189 dated 1.7.2012 and for preceding 12 months

(d)   Valuation of 10 the High Grove provided by Hart Estate Agents dated 15.6.2012

(e)   Copy Payslip dated 30.6.2012

(f)   Benefit assessment forms and award statements

(g)   Debenhams Store card statements dated 30.6.2012 and preceding 12 months

(h)   National Savings certificate 482929

Copies of these documents, plus copies of the Financial Disclosure Forms as completed by Homer and Marge are attached.

This documents was drafted on 1.8.2012

Signed ....   Signed ....

Homer Pilkington   *Marge Jennifer Pilkington*

Date   Date

CHAPTER 4

PUBLIC LAW

THE INTERIM POSITION – A LEARNING CURVE

4.1   Every professional around the country has a view and an opinion about the revised Public Law Outline (PLO) and its success or otherwise. It is ineluctable that every professional working within the family justice system would wish to see a reduction in the timeframe within which decisions for children are made. Concerns have been raised as to whether justice for the child and the parents can be met when the 26-week timeframe is so short.

4.2   As will be discussed in this section there appears to be little evidence in support of that fear and practitioners will no doubt draw reassurance from the words of the President in his seventh view[1] and reiterated in his recent judgment in the case of *Re S*:[2] 'It is not, and must never be allowed to become a straight-jacket, least of all if rigorous adherence to an inflexible timetable risks putting justice in jeopardy'. Similarly Mrs Justice Pauffley stated in the case of *Re NL*, 'Justice must never be sacrificed on the altar of speed'.[3]

4.3   As with any proposed change there has been a degree of both reluctance and indeed cynicism as to whether the reforms imposed would achieve the desired objectives. The early results of the research into the pilot scheme provides solid evidence that with the right conditions and input of resources, drastic reductions in the timeframes for making decisions for children can be achieved.

4.4   The use of a single court and case management system was first trialled in the Tri-Borough Care Proceedings Pilot, which encompassed the London Boroughs of Kensington and Chelsea, Hammersmith and Fulham and Westminster, which tracked 90 cases with commencement dates between 1 April 2012 and 31 March 2013.

4.5   The findings of the pilot scheme, which tracked 65 of the 90 cases, were published in a report by the University of East Anglia in July 2013 and are set

---

[1]   *View from the President's Chambers (7)* [2013] Fam Law 1394.
[2]   *Re S (A Child)* [2014] 2 FLR 575, at para 28.
[3]   *Re NL* [2014] EWHC 270 (Fam), para 40, [2014] 1 FLR 1384.

out in chapter 1.[4] They published a further report *Concluding Care Proceedings Within 26 Weeks* in September 2013[5] in which they incorporate all of their findings from the March report but go on to highlight the key features of the pilot, which contributed to its success:

(a)   The appointment of a 'case manager'.

(b)   Timely and more selective use of assessments.

(c)   Agreements with providers of independent assessments and the fostering and adoption service undertaking assessments more quickly.

(d)   A dedicated team of four children's guardians/early appointment of children's guardians.

(e)   A commitment from the courts to try to ensure judicial continuity and robust case management.

(f)   Social worker confidence.

(g)   Focus and commitment from everyone involved.

(h)   Quarterly 'post-case reviews' to identify and share learning points and Overall leadership.

4.6   It is important to look at these key features when considering what factors might affect the longer-term sustainability and transferability of the new way of working. It is to be remembered that the Tri-Borough Project had dedicated teams and services put in place in order to give this pilot the best prospect of success. The reality of replicating that across the country, particularly in relation to the courts and judicial continuity, may not prove to be so easy.

Strong and robust leadership

4.7   It is apparent from the research produced, but common sense also tells us, that it is possible to achieve far more when strong and robust leadership and support is available. It is clear that the need for this strength of leadership is not just required from within the local authorities but from every person and agency involved within the family justice system, if the success of the pilot scheme is to be replicated nationally and sustained.

4.8   Certainly, we venture to suggest that it is going to be necessary for most, if not all, local authorities to engage in some internal restructuring and reorganisation in order to meet the demands of; (i) the pre-proceedings work (ii) the need for quality assessments in much shorter timeframes, and (iii) robust

---

[4]   *Evaluation of the Tri-borough Care Proceedings Pilot*: Report for the Tri-borough Care Proceedings Steering Group (Centre for Research on Families, University of East Anglia, July 2013).

[5]   *Concluding Care Proceedings Within 26 Weeks*: Report of the Evaluation of the Tri-borough Care Proceedings Pilot (Centre for Research on Children & Families, University of East Anglia, September 2013), pp 2 and 18.

support and guidance for social workers preparing their statements for the court. A view supported by the Ipsos Mori research.[6]

The 'case manager' role

4.9　The Tri-Borough initiative provided a 'case manager' who was based at Hammersmith and Fulham. The case manager was a social work team manager who was seconded to the post for a year. The role of the case manager was to have an overview of the cases being considered for and brought to court, to advise social workers on the quality of their assessments and statements, support social workers during proceedings, liaise with the courts and 'troubleshoot' if cases did appear to be losing momentum.[7]

4.10　Certainly the findings overall were that the case manager helped to drive up standards and was able to guide the social workers to provide more focused and analytical statements, as opposed to statements that reproduced lots of information in a chronological format but provided no focus on the key evidence and no analysis.

4.11　In training that we have provided to local authorities we have explored the case manager role with them and they are open to seeing if they can replicate the role either within their own organisation or by joining up with neighbouring local authorities.

4.12　Our own experience over recent years tends to illustrate the fact that social workers have lost confidence in their own abilities and expertise. As the President has commented:[8]

> 'One of the problems is that in recent years too many social workers have come to feel undervalued, disempowered and de-skilled. In part at least this is an unhappy consequence of the way in which care proceedings have come to be dealt with by the courts.'

4.13　There is a general consensus amongst practitioners that there has been an overuse and overreliance on experts in areas that really are the province of the social worker. In addition social workers' own experiences in court and in the witness box have played their part in undermining confidence. Undoubtedly the often long and unfocused statements of social workers have played a large part in that experience, but arguably those statements have grown over the years because of social workers feeling they have had their 'fingers burnt' by being accused of not including all the information.[9] Thus a case manager dedicated to

---

[6]　*Action research to explore the implementation and early impacts of the revised Public Law Outline (PLO)* Ipsos Mori, Ministry of Justice Analytical Series 2014, p 27.

[7]　Concluding Care Proceedings in 26 Weeks, ibid, p 2.

[8]　*View from the President's Chambers (2)* [2013] Fam Law 680, p 683.

[9]　Ipsos Mori Research, p 20

supporting them through the court process, which would very much include the production of succinct, focused and analytical statements would provide a huge confidence boost to social workers.

Timely and more selective use of assessments and agreements with providers

4.14 The evidence of the Tri-Borough Project is that special arrangements and agreements were reached to ensure that any assessments that were required were completed in a much shorter timeframe than would ordinarily have been the case.

4.15 The evidence provided from one social worker was that the connected persons assessments were being done in 10 weeks as opposed to the usual 16 weeks. In addition a review was conducted at 6 weeks and if the assessment was looking negative then a decision was taken to end it at that point, rather than proceeding to the end and building in unnecessary delay.[10]

4.16 There was certainly an overwhelming consensus that the pilot had managed to achieve both a reduction in the number of assessments and the time taken for them to be completed. There was a clear view that the assessments were more focused.

4.17 It is not entirely apparent, from the evidence available, what pressure was placed on both resources and finances to ensure these assessments were undertaken so quickly and comprehensively and although it is too early in the process to see whether savings will be made in the longer-term, the evidence, so far, would suggest that savings were made and are likely to continue to be made for local authorities in the form of reduced legal costs arising from fewer court hearings and the proceedings progressing more swiftly.[11]

4.18 Inevitably there is likely to be some short-term pressure on costs, for most local authorities, in obtaining the necessary assessments in shorter timeframes and there did indeed appear to be evidence within the report that the fostering and adoption team were placed under pressure, which led to delays in children being moved on to final placements, and additional temporary staff needing to be recruited to cover this work.[12] However, it was thought likely, at least within the report, that the need for temporary staff would be a short-term requirement whilst local authorities settle into the new regime.

4.19 The report did highlight some concerns that if more assessments are carried out pre-proceedings, in order to reduce the length of the proceedings themselves, then the costs to the local authority could actually rise because

---

[10]   Concluding Care Proceedings in 26 Weeks, ibid, p 18.
[11]   Ibid, pp 38 and 40.
[12]   Ibid, p 38.

unlike assessments within proceedings, the costs of which tend to be shared equally between the parties, the local authority would be solely responsible for the costs incurred for all assessments undertaken pre-proceedings.

4.20 This may prove to be a disincentive to pro-active work and it almost certainly will be if the judiciary and courts fail to be robust and reject the assessments and go on to order further assessments within the proceedings.[13]

4.21 Obviously the assessments, undertaken in the pre-proceedings period, will need to be comprehensive, focused and appropriately analytical if they are to be accepted as solid by the courts, this will be particularly so in cases were adoption is the ultimate plan for the child or children.

4.22 The report did highlight that the Tri-Borough authorities were relatively affluent and well resourced, which would therefore have an impact on both the quality of preventative work they are able to do, as well as the court work.[14]

4.23 As one participant noted:[15]

> 'It is like a classroom full of kids where a teacher puts high expectations on three and they are the brightest kids in the class and there is an expectation that the kids live up to that expectation.'

The picture is therefore likely to be very different across the country, particularly for those authorities that are less affluent and who have much larger geographical areas to service that are experiencing high levels of social deprivation.

The early appointment of children's guardians

4.24 The Tri-Borough initiative enjoyed the luxury of having four dedicated guardians assigned to the pilot. It was clear that the guardians' focused input from the outset was seen as a huge benefit to the efficient and smooth progress of cases through the court.

4.25 The requirement for guardians to file an initial case summary and analysis at the outset assisted in focusing the minds of all parties on the key issues to be addressed. It was certainly viewed as one of the prime drivers in enabling timeframes to be so drastically reduced.[16]

---

13 Ibid, p 42.
14 Ibid, p 35.
15 Ibid, p 47.
16 Ibid, p 20; Ipsos Mori research, p 26.

4.26 The guardians who took part in the pilot did not think their workload had increased mainly because proportionate working had been in place prior to the pilot. There was a perception that they were spending less time on cases as a result of the changes.[17]

4.27 There was evidence that the local authority had taken steps to notify Cafcass of the existence of a case prior to issue and this had allowed Cafcass valuable additional time in which to allocate the case and had even led to focused discussions taking place between the guardian and the local authority prior to issue.

4.28 If that experience were to be replicated nationwide then it would be hoped that the pressure overall on Cafcass would be reduced. However, concerns were raised in the research commissioned on behalf of the Ministry of Justice by Ipsos Mori[18] that the allocation of a guardian by Day Two could prove problematic if the court did not notify Cafcass in a timely way or if that particular Cafcass office/region was facing resourcing difficulties.

4.29 The reality is that many Cafcass offices are facing those very problems and unless they are addressed the situation is likely to become worse as cases continue to be issued and require allocation. In view of the fact that the early appointment of guardians was seen to be a pivotal factor in drastically reducing the timeframe for proceedings this is an aspect that will need to be urgently addressed in those regions that have resource issues if it is not to impact on the effective operation of the PLO.

Judicial continuity and robust case management

4.30 There was a clear commitment from the courts to try and ensure judicial continuity for the Tri-Borough cases. In addition court days were specifically set aside to deal with the Tri-Borough cases.[19]

4.31 It is undoubtedly the case that this commitment brought with it huge benefits in the way the pilot cases progressed through the court.

4.32 The judges involved were firmly assigned to the cases and they were provided with dedicated time to deal with the hearings and applications. This allowed the judges involved to be fully 'au fait' with the cases and the key issues and they were able, as a result, to drive the case and make robust case management decisions.

4.33 The families involved received clear and consistent messages from the judge hearing their case as to what the expectations were and what the consequences would be if they did not follow through on those expectations.

---

[17] *Concluding Care Cases within 26 weeks*, p 45.
[18] *Action research to explore the implementation and early impacts of the revised Public Law Outline (PLO)* Ipsos Mori, Ministry of Justice Analytical Series 2014, pp 34–35.
[19] *Concluding Care Cases in 26 weeks*, p 20.

The judges were described as 'tough but fair'. It is not difficult to see how the families in that situation have a much clearer picture and receive much clearer messages from the judge whom they see each time they attend court and who they know clearly understands every aspect of their case.

4.34 Those involved in the pilot cases described how beneficial it had been and it had allowed so much to be achieved with having both dedicated judges and dedicated court time. As one solicitor pointed out she was able to deal with four cases in one morning as they had all been listed on the assigned court day before a dedicated judge – so much was achieved.[20]

4.35 Experience and history has shown, time and again, that the inevitable consequences of a lack of judicial continuity are delay and often poor or inconsistent decision-making. The results of the pilot show what can be achieved with judicial continuity and favourable listing of cases.

4.36 The reality is of course that these conditions were largely artificial and it is likely to be extremely difficult, if not nigh on impossible to provide dedicated judges and court days across the country. There are many busy court centres that have only one family judge sitting at any one time trying to manage very full court lists.

4.37 To provide an example, in one busy court centre on the North Eastern circuit there is one, possibly two family judges sitting at any one time. Four local authorities feed into that court, one of those local authorities is responsible for some of the largest and most deprived housing areas in the country. Frequently the family judges who sit have to juggle criminal and civil cases in amongst their family lists. It would be expecting something of a miracle, perhaps, to expect that they can provide the luxury of dedicated judges and court days to provide the same commitment and focus that was afforded to the Tri-Borough cases.

4.38 This was noted by one of the solicitors who took part in the Tri-Borough Pilot who highlighted the potential problem created by the Ministry of Justice trying to make large savings in terms of judicial sittings and the appointments of full-time judges (and the issue therefore arising as to whether the courts will actually be able to deliver on the early hearing dates to ensure the smooth running of the PLO). Even if great efforts are made by the courts at the outset, the real issue arises as to whether that situation is sustainable in the longer-term without further investment.[21]

Social worker confidence

4.39 The report identifies that there was a consensus of view that social workers' confidence had increased over the course of the pilot period. It is

---

[20] Ibid, p 20.
[21] Ibid, pp 46-47.

perhaps self-evident that if a professional feels that reliance is being placed upon their professional assessments and opinions and the courts are openly expressing their view that the social workers are experts in their field, then their confidence will build.

4.40 In turn the social workers will come to have more confidence in their own professional judgement. Once they have been through the court process and experienced respect for the work they have produced they are likely to be far more confident in moving on to their next case. More importantly they are likely to feel more able to provide support and guidance to their colleagues and to younger colleagues entering into the profession.

4.41 Sadly, as the President has rightly acknowledged, a culture has developed over recent years whereby 'experts' have been instructed to undertake the work that really falls within the remit and expertise of the social worker. This has had the effect of de-skilling social workers causing them to lack confidence in their own professional assessment and judgment and created an unhelpful cycle of producing what have been described, quite properly, as anodyne and inadequate assessments and statements that do not address the heart of the matter which is central to the case. A 'sloppy practice' which must now stop.[22]

4.42 Personal experience shows that many social workers do not enjoy the court aspect of their role and when they have had a poor experience of court this can and does build into a huge amount of stress and anxiety leading to sickness, absence from work and even greater pressure on other colleagues.

4.43 In the recent training sessions that we have undertaken with social workers they have expressed considerable anxiety about whether, even if they do provide the more focused and analytical assessments and statements, the judges will respect and follow their opinions in the event applications are made by parents' advocates for independent assessments.

4.44 It is inevitable that it will take time to rebuild the skills and the confidence of social workers that has been eroded over a number of years and the judiciary has a significant role to play in ensuring that happens by providing the focused and robust case management that is required. In order to achieve that, the courts need to be provided with the appropriate level of resources to ensure they can meet the inevitable increased demands on the time they will need to take with these cases within a much tighter timeframe.

4.45 The stark reality at this point in time is that there are, sadly, a number of local authorities at crisis point were morale is so low that social workers leave in 'groups' and so children's social care services, in some areas, are being provided by agency workers, who cost far more to employ and who have little investment in the local community and thus can and do leave when the problems get tough. It is going to be very difficult for some local authorities to

---

[22] *Re B-S (Children)* [2013] EWCA Civ 1146; per the President, para 40.

break out of that cycle when they are coping with a huge drain on their resources by social workers having left or being on long-term sickness absence and the consequent employment of numerous agency workers.

4.46 However, it is the authors' view that a huge in-road into that difficulty can be provided by the judiciary making robust case management decisions which support the local authority plans and recommendations, thereby providing the social workers with confidence and allowing pride in their role and profession to be re-built.

Focus and commitment

4.47 The report highlighted the fact that 'focus' was a key theme, not only in respect of, what was perceived to be, a re-focusing back onto the child but also on the aims and objectives that the pilot scheme promoted. The report indicated that there was a greater focus by the professionals at the outset of the case, which was necessary in order to identify the key issues and determine what would need to be done if the timeframes were to be met. Everybody was focused upon case management issues, ensuring that assessments would be completed more quickly and social workers were reporting that they were focusing on their analysis of the cases in a way they had not done previously.[23]

4.48 It is without question that every professional within the family justice system would want to see better outcomes and less delay in decision-making for children and families. There is no shortage of commitment from every involved professional to make the revised PLO work, the question will be whether the necessary resources within the local authorities and the courts will be available to ensure that the commitment can be matched.[24]

Quarterly 'post-case reviews' to identify and share learning points and overall leadership

4.49 During the pilot all the professionals involved, including all the agencies and private practice solicitors, would meet each quarter to identify and share learning points. Although the report does not detail any of the learning points raised it is evident that the focused and collaborative approach of all of those involved in the family justice process contributed to the success of the pilot in dramatically reducing the timeframes for completing cases.

4.50 Similarly, it was clear that the success of the pilot was also due to the strategic planning and decision-making by those within the local authorities who are not part of the 'front line' management of the cases for court but who took steps to ensure that the local authority could for example accommodate the need for assessments to be completed quickly. The inescapable message is

---

[23] *Concluding Care Proceedings Within 26 Weeks*, above, p 45.
[24] Ibid, p 46; *Action Research to explore the implementation and early impacts of the revised PLO* Ipsos Mori, above, p 5.

that strong and robust leadership needs to be in place from the top to the bottom. If that is put in place now, in local authorities across the country, as they gear themselves up for meeting the demands of the revised PLO then arguably there is a much greater prospect of the changes and improvements observed during the pilot being transferred and sustained in the longer-term.

4.51 The Tri-Borough initiative has clearly illustrated that with the right resources in place along with the commitment and focus from all those involved, timeframes for the completion of cases can be dramatically reduced in the vast majority of cases.

4.52 These factors were echoed in the Ipsos Mori research alongside other factors such as protocols being agreed with the police, local authorities implementing their own 'application tracker systems' and case management officers.[25]

Concerns

4.53 Inevitably, as with all proposed change, many professionals expressed concern, not just within the report but also nationally within meetings and in articles, about issues such as:

(a) Thoroughness of assessments and use of experts.

(b) Thoroughness of hearings.

(c) Justice for children and parents.

(d) Delays being incurred pre- or post-proceedings.

(e) The case management orders and case management hearings.

(f) Extensions to the 26-week timeframe.

(g) Sustainability in the longer-term.

Thoroughness of assessments and use of experts

4.54 The authors' experience has been that there has been fairly widespread general concern regarding whether appropriately comprehensive assessments can be completed within the much shorter timeframes directed by the court. Certainly any fears that may have been held during the Tri-Borough Pilot period were dispelled on the basis that the assessments proved to be far more focused and analytical than had previously been the case.

4.55 Undoubtedly, strong leadership providing the right support and guidance from the outset, a role to a large part provided by the 'case manager', played a huge part in ensuring that statements and assessments proceeded on the right track. Similarly, undertaking parallel planning was seen as essential, even though it was a greater drain on resources. One case cited involved a mother and baby being placed in a residential assessment unit whilst an assessment of a

---

[25] Ibid, p 50.

family member was being undertaken at the same time. When the residential assessment broke down the local authority were in a position to place the child with the family member under a special guardianship order.[26]

4.56 Obviously there may have been an unnecessary cost incurred in undertaking the family assessment if the residential assessment had proved successful. By contrast, the local authority would undoubtedly have saved money in this example by being able to place the child quickly within a family placement and conclude the proceedings. It is entirely probable that what would have been more likely to have happened, pre-pilot, is that the family assessment would have taken place sequentially, with the net effect being that the court proceedings would have continued and further expense would have been incurred on unnecessary hearings.

4.57 There will clearly need to be a balancing exercise conducted by local authorities in respect of each case because concerns have been raised that time and expense may be devoted to assessments when the case may not go into proceedings at all.[27] Overall however, it is more likely that proactive working is likely to bring financial savings in the longer-term and will permit informed decisions to be made about a child's long-term placement much more quickly, to the undoubted benefit of the child concerned.

4.58 One of the other concerns raised was that the shorter timeframes for completing the assessments may mean that they lost the benefit of providing that additional time to work with the families to help them understand and make the required changes and in addition for other family members to realise the seriousness of the situation and make the mental and practical adjustments to enable them to put themselves forward sooner.

4.59 Again the contrary argument was raised that in fact because everybody was operating in a much more focused way this message was getting across to families much quicker and the general impression was that the families knew they had to 'pull things together' if they wanted to retain the care of their children within the family.[28]

4.60 The Ipsos Mori research suggested that a minority of the participants (including members of the judiciary) expressed the fear that 'the pendulum may have swung too far the other way' in considering the reduction and restriction in the use of experts.[29]

Thoroughness of hearings

4.61 Similarly, there was a general concern being expressed by practitioners that the court would not give the degree of scrutiny to assessments, which may

---

[26] *Concluding Care Proceedings Within 26 Weeks*, above at p 25.
[27] Ipsos Mori research, p 29.
[28] Ibid, p 26.
[29] Ipsos Mori research, p 23.

previously have been the position, in the need to meet the 26-week deadline. That the robust case management required from the judiciary would lead to applications for independent assessments on behalf of parents being routinely refused.

4.62 Social workers, as discussed above, were equally concerned that their assessments would be routinely overlooked in favour of independent assessments without any real consideration of whether any such further assessment was warranted.

4.63 The report indicates that these concerns were unfounded in respect of applications for further independent assessments being refused. Ultimately, participants were satisfied that the court's role was to provide independent scrutiny of the evidence before them and if they were unhappy with any aspect of the assessments before them then they would order a further assessment.

4.64 Although one of the judges spoken to indicated that she was being far more robust about not allowing further assessments some of the social workers felt that the judges were not being robust enough and they believed that this was not because the further assessment was needed but because the judges were concerned about an appeal if it were refused.

4.65 Despite some participants' perceptions that the way the court was dealing with things 'had not really changed' the evidence from the pilot suggested otherwise with reduced numbers of assessments and court hearings.

4.66 It is of course essential that all assessments fulfill the criteria set by the revised PLO and the line of cas- law requiring full but succinct, focused and analytical assessments that explore the central issues in the case and provide clear evidence-based recommendations for the court.[30]

4.67 A steep learning curve awaits all in producing assessments of the required quality, quickly, and the courts will need to be scrupulous and robust in deciding whether a further assessment is necessary to assist the court to resolve the proceedings justly.[31]

Justice for children and parents

4.68 Despite concerns that the 26-week timeframe would lead to hasty and unjust decisions the evidence provided in the report indicated that extra time was granted in cases that needed it to allow the parent to make the changes necessary but that this was only happening in cases where the parents were positively engaging with the process.

---

[30] *Concluding Care Proceedings Within 26 Weeks*, above, p 35.
[31] Section 13(6) of the Children and Families Act 2014.

4.69 It was apparent that none of the participants felt that parents' rights had been ridden over rough-shod but more that the rights of the child had been brought to the forefront of everyone's attention and the focus was no longer on the parents' rights to assessments unless they were positively engaging with the process and the extra time was then permitted to allow the parent to make the necessary changes.[32]

Delays being incurred pre- or post-proceedings

4.70 The report looked at whether delay for the child had been increased pre-proceedings but the early results seemed to indicate that decision-making in the pre-proceedings stage had also become more focused and had speeded up, although the caveat was given that this was a provisional view and would need to be re-visited when more information became available. In addition some of the participants' perceptions, contrary to the actual evidence, was that the pre-proceedings requirements had slowed cases down. This was a concern that was also echoed in the Ipsos Mori research.[33]

4.71 Similarly it was too early in the process to say whether the drive to get proceedings completed within 26 weeks created delay for the children post-proceedings. Again that is a matter that will need to be re-visited.[34]

The timing of the case management hearing and the case management order

4.72 The Ipsos Mori research highlighted the difficulties with the requirement to have the CMH by Day 12 and how this impacted on the ability of the solicitor to take full instructions from the parent or even to get them to engage. There was the clear desire to be able to become involved earlier in the hope that they may be able to provide greater assistance to the parents.[35] Obviously the problem being that there would be no funding available for solicitors to assist the parents at that stage.

4.73 There was a body of opinion that supported the introduction of greater flexibility in the listing of the CMH. This was taken on board when the final version of the PLO (PD 12A) was published, as it now requires the CMH to be listed not before Day 12 but no later than Day 18.[36] In addition a further CMH may take place, if required in a complex case, no later than Day 25.

---

[32] *Concluding Care Proceedings Within 26 Weeks*, above, pp 28-29.
[33] Ipsos Mori Research, pp 2, 3-4, 15 and 28.
[34] *Concluding Care Pare Proceedings Within 26 Weeks*, above, p 33; Ipsos Mori Research, pp 33, 41-43.
[35] Ipsos Mori Research, pp 3-4, 16, 18 and 27.
[36] Ibid, p 4.

4.74 In addition the CMO was found to be too long, unwieldy and unnecessarily repetitive and the CMO is now being revised to take into account the observations from using the form in practice.[37]

4.75 In our training there has been concern expressed by some local authorities that a practice appears to have developed in some courts, of the court clerks completing the final page of the CMO which details the reason for the cause of any delay incurred in the case. Obviously this information is of importance and the authors agree that the detail in this form needs to be completed by the advocates and the allocated judge for the case on each occasion so that the information is both accurate and preferably the consensus view of all those involved in the case. Where the advocates are not in agreement as to the reason for the delay then it should be determined by the allocated judge and duly recorded.

Extensions to the 26-week timeframe

4.76 Participants in the Ipsos Mori research expressed concerns about the need for guidance as to what type of cases might be considered as appropriate for extending beyond the 26-week timeframe.[38]

4.77 That request has been responded to by the President, Sir James Munby, who provided guidance in the recent judgment of *Re S*.[39] The types of case identified were as follows:

(a)   very heavy cases involving the most complex medical evidence, and requiring a split hearing;

(b)   FDAC type cases;

(c)   cases with an international element where investigation/assessment abroad is necessary;

(d)   parental disabilities requiring specialist assessments or measures.

4.78 Despite robust judicial case management something emerges unexpectedly to change the nature of the proceedings:

(a)   allegations of sexual harm surface;

(b)   the death, serious illness or imprisonment of a proposed carer;

(c)   a realistic alternative family carer emerges late in the day.

The final type of case that may fall outside the 26-week timetable are those where litigation failure on the part of one or more of the parties makes it impossible to complete the case justly within 26 weeks.

---

[37]   Ibid, p 48.
[38]   Ibid, pp 46-48.
[39]   *Re S (A Child)* [2014] 2 FLR 575, para 28.

Sustainability in the longer-term

4.79 The report highlighted the concerns of participants that firstly, the Tri-Borough initiative had been a 'special case' well-organised, relatively prosperous authorities, they benefitted from special treatment during the pilot year, which could not be sustained when the pilot was launched nationally. Secondly, that only half the cases were completed within the 26-week timeframe, a significant improvement, but a long way short of the requirement that all but 'exceptional' cases will complete within this timescale.

4.80 However, the very clear positive conclusion of the report is that timeframes can be reduced without compromising fairness or the quality of the decisions by eradicating unnecessary delay. The key drivers were: (i) having better-prepared cases; (ii) quicker and more focused assessments; (iii) timelier and proportionate working by children's guardians; and (iv) stronger judicial case management (notably a more robust approach to ordering further assessments, ensuring that all parties comply with court directions and more effective timetabling).[40] These are all important and achievable messages for the national implementation.

THE REVISED PUBLIC LAW OUTLINE (PLO)

4.81 In readiness for 22 April 2014 and the now statutory 26-week time limit[41] the President introduced the final version of the Revised PLO known as the Public Law Outline 2014. Following the national pilot, which began in July 2013, feedback was received and a targeted consultation undertaken in November and December 2013 by the Family Procedure Rule Committee, resulting in the following amendments:

(a) At the issue and allocation stage the court is to give consideration as to whether an urgent, preliminary case management hearing (CMH) or urgent contested interim care order hearing may be necessary.

(b) The CMH is to take place within a window of 'not before Day 12 and not later than Day 18' instead of the fixed 'by Day 12'. In the event that a further case management hearing (FCMH) is necessary, this pushes the listing of that hearing back to 'no later than Day 25' instead of Day 20.

(c) The meaning of 'Day' has been clarified in the *Interpretation* section of the PLO. It means 'business day'. 'Day 1' is the day of issue and 'Day 2' is the next business day following the day of issue of proceedings. 'Day 12', Day 18' and 'Day 25' respectively are the 11th, 17th and 24th business days after 'Day 1'. In addition, '26 weeks' means 26 calendar weeks beginning on the day of issue of proceedings ('Day 1').

---

40 *Concluding Care Proceedings Within 26 Weeks*, p 52.
41 Children and Families Act 2014, s 14.

(d) In Part 1 *Key Stages of the PLO,* amendments have been made to assist the court in identifying cases with an international element. Such issues now form part of the considerations at:

(i)   The advocates' meeting;

(ii)   The CMH;

(iii) On any occasion when the court may wish to exercise its flexible powers in relation to an urgent hearing;[42] and

(iv)   When identifying the timetable for the child.[43]

(e) In Part 1, *Key Stages of the PLO* further amendments have been made in relation to protected parties and others with a disability, where it is made clear that directions in relation to litigation capacity now form part of the Case Management Directions at CMH stage. Within the *Interpretation* section, a new aspect relating to parenting capability is now included.

4.82 The amendments in respect of cases with an international element and cases requiring an urgent hearing are included in an updated version of the C110A application form, as are any factors affecting litigation capacity. It is important to note that whilst previously, the threshold statement and allocation proposal form, were annex documents, these have now been incorporated into the form.

4.83 The revised C110A should be used for all applications for care or supervision or other Part 4 orders and for emergency protection orders (EPOs). It is important to note that it is now possible to issue Part 4 (care or supervision order applications) and EPO proceedings on the same form and **at the same time**. EPOs are provided for within the C110A due to the need for the court to identify cases for urgent hearing at the outset. All such applications should therefore be filed using C110A and not C1 and supplemental C11.

---

[42] Public Law Outline 2014, para 2.4.
[43] Ibid, para 5.6.

C110A

Application for a care or supervision order and other orders under Part 4 of the Children Act 1989 or an Emergency Protection Order under section 44 of the Children Act 1989

To be completed by the court	
The family court sitting at	
Date issued	Case number
Child(ren)'s name(s)	Child(ren)'s number(s)
Fee charged	

Name of applicant	X Local Authority
Name of respondent(s)	M & A (a child)

Nature of application

What order(s) are you applying for? (tick all which apply)

✓ Care and supervision or other Part 4

- ✓ Care
- ☐ Supervision
- ✓ Interim care order
- ☐ Interim supervision order
- ☐ Other *(please specify)*

✓ Emergency Protection Order

- ☐ information on the whereabouts of the child[ren] (Section 48(1) Children Act 1989).
- ☐ authorisation for entry of premises (Section 48(3) Children Act 1989).
- ☐ authorisation to search for another child on the premises (Section 48(4) Children Act 1989).
- ☐ Other *(please specify)*

Is the Local Authority considering adoption?

✓ Yes ☐ No

If Yes, please complete Section 7b

Additional information required

			If Yes, complete
Is an urgent hearing required?	✓ Yes	☐ No	If Yes, complete Section 1
Is a without notice hearing required?	☐ Yes	✓ No	If Yes, complete Section 2
Are there previous or ongoing proceedings for the child(ren)?	☐ Yes	✓ No	If Yes, complete Section 3
Are there factors affecting litigation capacity?	✓ Yes	☐ No	If Yes, complete Section 4
Is this a case with an international element?	✓ Yes	☐ No	If Yes, complete Section 5

Summary of children's details

Child 1 - Name of child	Date of birth	Order(s) applied for (including interim orders)
	0 1 / 0 5 / 2 0 1 4	
	Is the child accommodated?	☐ Yes ☑ No
	If Yes, from what date?	

Name of mother	Name of father	Parental Responsibility
M	Unknown	☐ Yes ☑ No

1. Is the application for urgent consideration?

Complete this section if you have ticked the relevant box on the front of the form

Is the urgent hearing for:
(tick as required)

☐ Contested ICO

✓ EPO

☐ urgent preliminary Case Management Hearing

Part A - All applications

Set out the order(s)/ directions sought

(1) Emergency Protection Order
(2) Psychiatric Assessment of M as to litigation capacity

Set out the reasons for urgency

M is a French National, who came to the UK only a few weeks ago. She presented to Anytown hospital in labour on 30 April 2014 and A was born on 1 May 2014. The medical professionals have significant concerns as to M's mental health and capacity. A is currently showing signs of withdrawing from heroin as is M.

Proposed timetable

The application should be considered within   24   hours

If consideration is sought within 48 hours, you must complete the section below

What efforts have been made to put each respondent on notice of the application?

M and A remain inpatients at Anytown Hospital. Social Workers and the Midwives have informed her of this application, but due to the concerns about her mental health and capacity it is unknown whether she understands what is sought.

If the application is for an Emergency Protection Order only, please complete B, C and D as appropriate

B - The grounds are

Any applicant

✓ that there is reasonable cause to believe that this child is likely to suffer significant harm if

or ☐ the child[ren] [is] [are] not removed to accommodation provided by or on behalf of this applicant

or ✓ the child does not remain in the place where the child is currently being accommodated.

Local authority applicants

☐ that enquiries are being made about the welfare of the child[ren] under Section 47(1)(b) of Children Act 1989 and those enquiries are being frustrated by access to the child[ren] being unreasonably refused to someone who is authorised to seek access and there is reasonable cause to believe that access to the child[ren] is required as a matter of urgency.

Authorised person applicants

☐ that there is reasonable cause to suspect that the child[ren] [is] [are] suffering, or [is] [are] likely to suffer, significant harm and enquiries are being made with respect to the welfare of the child[ren] and those enquiries are being frustrated by access to the child[ren] being unreasonably refused to someone who is authorised to seek access and there is reasonable cause to believe that access to the child[ren] is required as a matter of urgency.

C - The additional order(s) applied for

☐ information on the whereabouts of the child[ren] (Section 48(1) Children Act 1989).

☐ authorisation for entry of premises (Section 48(3) Children Act 1989).

authorisation to search for another child on the premises (Section 48(4) Children Act 1989).

D - The direction(s) sought

contact with any named person (Section 44(6)(a) Children Act 1989).

a medical or psychiatric examination or other assessment of the child[ren] (Section 44(6)(b) Children Act 1989).

to be accompanied by a registered medical practitioner, registered nurse or registered midwife (Section 45(12) Children Act 1989).

an exclusion requirement (Section 44A(1) Children Act 1989).

2. Is the application for a without notice hearing?

Complete this section if you have ticked the relevant box on the front of the form

Set out the order/ directions sought

Set out the reasons for the application to be considered without notice. (This information is a requirement, a without notice hearing will **not** be directed without reason)

Do you require a without notice hearing because it is not possible to give notice including abridged or informal notice?

Yes   No

If Yes, please set out reasons below

Do you require a without notice hearing because notice to a respondent will frustrate the order that is being applied for?

Yes   No

If Yes, please set out reasons below

Other *(please specify)*

3. Previous or ongoing proceedings

Complete this section if you have ticked the relevant box on the front of this form.

Please give details (include name of child(ren), case no., date(s) of application, dates proceedings concluded, order made)

Please also provide the name of any children's guardian who has been involved in any previous or ongoing proceedings involving a child of one or both respondents

Is continuity of the children's guardian required?   Yes   No

If No, why not?

4. Factors affecting ability to participate in proceedings

Complete this section if you have ticked the relevant box on the front of this form.

Please give details of any factors affecting litigation capacity

Medical professionals caring for M and A are concerned that: (1) M is a heroin addict, (2) M is incapable of understanding the position she and A are in; (3) M is not caring for A, and appears unable to do so (4) M is unable to provide a coherent history of her background

Provide details of any referral to or assessment by the Adult Learning Disability team, and/or any adult health service, where known, together with the outcome

M is unknown to Health and Children's Services in the UK, she being a French National having only arrived in the UK a few weeks ago. M has been seen briefly on the post natal ward by the hospital psychiatric team. They require a further 24 hours to consider M's mental health fully and provide an assessment of her condition

Are you aware of any other factors which may affect the ability of the person concerned to take part in the proceedings?

No - M is able to speak English well

5. Cases with an international element

Complete this section if you have ticked the relevant box on the front of this form.

Do you have any reason to believe that any child, parent or potentially significant adult in the child's life may be habitually resident in another state?

✓ Yes   No

If Yes, please give details

M arrived in the UK on 9 April 2014 at Dover Seaport. She travelled on a French Passport and she has indicated to medical professionals that she lives in Paris

Do you have any reason to believe that there may be an issue as to jurisdiction in this case (for example under Brussels 2 revised)?	✓ Yes No
	If Yes, please give details
	M is a French National, habitually resident in Paris. Whilst it is not yet clear, due to concerns about M's mental health, it is considered likely that M is not intending to remain long-term in the UK, and would wish to return to France with A.

Has a request been made or should a request be made to a Central Authority or other competent authority in a foreign state or a consular authority in England and Wales?	✓ Yes No
	If Yes, please give details
	A request has been made, today 2 May 2014, of the French Central Authority seeking its position in respect of jurisdiction

6. Grounds for the application

The grounds for the application are that the child(ren) is suffering or is likely to suffer, significant harm and the harm or likelihood of harm is because the child is:

✓ not receiving care that would be reasonably expected from a parent

☐ beyond parental control

Set out in not more than the two following pages the threshold criteria relied upon

7. Plans for the child(ren)

7a. Please give a brief summary of the plans for the child(ren).

The summary must include any contact arrangements that are in place or are proposed.

What is the local authority's proposal including placement and support services and are there any requirements which the local authority wish the court to impose under Part 1 of Schedule 3 Children Act 1989?

It is not sufficient just to refer to or repeat the Care Plan.

7b. Having regard to s. 22 Adoption and Children Act 2002 is the local authority considering adoption?

✓ Yes   ☐ No

Does the application for a placement order(s) accompany this application?

☐ Yes   ✓ No

If not, why not and when will it be submitted?

Have you notified the relevant Central Authority or the competent authority in the foreign state in cases to which section 5 of this form applies?

✓ Yes   ☐ No

8. Timetable for the child(ren)

The timetable for the child will be set by the court to take account of dates of the significant steps in the child's life that are likely to take place during the proceedings. Those steps include not only legal steps, but also social, care, health, education and developmental steps and any timetable for a case with an international element.

Please give any relevant dates/events in relation to the child(ren)
  • it may be necessary to give different dates for each child.

Are you aware of any significant event in the timetable, before which the case should be concluded?

☐ Yes   ✓ No

If Yes, please give a date

and give your reasons

By what date should the child(ren) be placed on a permanent basis?	Name of child
	A 2 8 / 1 1 / 2 0 1 4
Please give your reasons	

9. Attending the court

If an interpreter will be required, you must tell the court now so that one can be arranged.

Are you aware of whether an interpreter will be required?

☐ Yes   ✓ No

If Yes, please specify the language and dialect:

Are you aware of whether an intermediary will be required?

✓ Yes   ☐ No

If Yes, please give details

If attending the court, do any of the parties involved have a disability for which special assistance or special facilities would be required?

☐ Yes   ✓ No

If Yes, please specify what the needs are:

Please state whether the court needs to make any special arrangements for the parties attending court (e.g. providing a separate waiting room or other security requirements).

Court staff may get in contact with you about the requirements

10. Allocation proposal

Part 1 (To be completed by the applicant
Local Authority on issue)

Judicial continuity
Please give the following details of other
proceedings:

Case number	
Name of Judge	
Date of last relevant order	
Are proceedings finished or outstanding?	☐ Finished ☐ Outstanding

Applicant's allocation proposal

☐ Lay justices

✓ District Judge level

☐ Circuit Judge level

☐ DFJ/Section 9 sitting as a Judge of the High Court

☐ High Court Judge level

Set out the applicable paragraphs of the
schedule to the President's Guidance on
the distribution of business

Part 2 (To be completed by the Court)

**Allocation decision in
accordance with the Allocation
Rules and the President's
Guidance on the distribution
of business**

☐ Lay justices

☐ District Judge level

☐ Circuit Judge level

☐ High Court Judge level

**Listed for Case
Management Hearing**

Time	_____ D D \ M M \ Y Y Y Y
Location of court	
or	
Name of Judge	

Allocated by	District Judge	
	Legal Adviser	
	Date	D D \ M M \ Y Y Y Y

11. Signature

Print full name   A N Other

Your role/position held   Solicitor

The facts in this application are true to the best of my knowledge and belief and the opinions set out are my own.

Signed

Applicant

Date   0 2 0 5 2 0 1 4

Details of parties - please complete this section in full

The applicant

Name of applicant (local authority or authorised person)	
Name of contact	
Job title	
Address	
Postcode	
Contact telephone number	
Mobile telephone number	
Fax number	
Email	
DX number	

Solicitor's details

Solicitor's name	
Address	
Postcode	
Telephone number	
Mobile telephone number	
Fax number	
Email	
DX number	
Solicitor's Reference	

If there are more than two respondents please continue on a separate sheet.

The respondents

Respondent 1

Respondent's first name	
Middle name(s)	
Surname	

Date of birth: D D \ M M \ Y Y Y Y   Gender: Male   ✓ Female

Place of birth (town/county/country, if known)	
Current address	
Postcode	
Telephone number	

Relationship to the child(ren)

Name of child(ren)	Relationship	Parental Responsibility
		✓ Yes No

The child(ren)

Please give details of the child(ren) and the order(s) you are applying for.

Child 1

Child's full name	A

Date of birth: 0 1 / 0 5 / 2 0 1 4   Gender: ✓ Male   Female

Name of Social worker and telephone number	Miss V Helpful
If the child is not accommodated, who does the child live with?	Currently an inpatient at Anytown Hospital
At which address does the child live?	No known address in the UK
Postcode	

Others who should be given notice

Person 1

Person's full name	

Date of birth		Gender	Male	Female

Address	
Postcode	

Relationship to the child(ren)

Name of child	Relationship	Parental Responsibility
		Yes No

Relationship to the respondents

Name of respondent	Relationship

Annex

This annex must be completed by the applicant with any application for a care order or supervision order.
The documents specified in this annex must be filed with the application if available.
If any relevant document is not filed with the application, the reason and any expected date of filing must be stated.
All documents filed with the application must be clearly marked with their title and numbered consecutively.

1. Social Work Chronology   ✓ attached   to follow

   (A succinct summary)   If **to follow** please give reasons why not included and the date when the
document will be sent to the court.

2. Social Work Statement and genogram   ✓ attached   to follow

If **to follow** please give reasons why not included and the date when the
document will be sent to the court.

3. The current assessment relating to the   attached   ✓ to follow
child and/or the family and friends of the
child to which the Social Work Statement   If **to follow** please give reasons why not included and the date when the
refers and on which the local authority   document will be sent to the court.
relies
M and A have only been known to Children's Services since 30 April
2014. The Social Worker is undertaking investigations into M's history,
and in relation to family and friends in France and any in the UK. Those
investigations are to be completed by 9 May 2014 and thereafter
assessment plans filed with the court by 12 May 2014

4. Care Plan   ✓ attached   to follow

If **to follow** please give reasons why not included and the date when the
document will be sent to the court.

5. Index of checklist documents   ✓ attached   to follow

If **to follow** please give reasons why not included and the date when the
document will be sent to the court.

What to do once you have completed this form

Ensure that you have:

   ✓ attached copies of any **annex** documents.

   ✓ signed the form at Section 11.

   ✓ provided a **copy** of the application and attached documents for each of the respondents, and for Cafcass or
CAFCASS CYMRU.

   given details of the additional children if there are more than four.

given details of the additional respondents if there are more than two.

✓ the correct fee.

It is good practice to inform Cafcass or CAFCASS CYMRU that you are making this application. The court will expect the local authority to have informed Cafcass or CAFCASS CYMRU that proceedings are being issued.

Have you notified Cafcass - Children and Family Court Advisory and Support Service (for England)
or
CAFCASS CYMRU - Children and Family Court Advisory and Support Service Wales.

✓ Yes   No

If Yes, please give the date of notification

D	D	\	M	M	\	Y	Y	Y	Y

Now take or send your application with the correct fee and four copies to the court.

Please refer to the Family Proceedings Fees Order for the correct fee in respect of your application.

26 week timetable

4.84 Section 14 of the Children and Families Act 2014 amends s 32 Children Act 1989 as follows:[44]

(2) In section 32(1)(a) (timetable for dealing with application for care or supervision order) for "disposing of the application without delay; and" substitute "disposing of the application –

    (i)   Without delay, and

    (ii)   In any event within twenty-six weeks beginning with the day on which the application was issued.".

4.85 The 26 weeks may be extended, but only if the court determines that such extension is necessary for it to resolve the proceedings justly and in any event for not more than 8 weeks per extension:[45]

S 32(5) A court in which an application under this Part is proceeding may extend the period that is for the time being allowed under subsection 1(a)(ii) in the case of the application, but may do so only if the court considers that the extension is necessary to enable the court to resolve the proceedings justly.

(6) When deciding whether to grant an extension under subsection (5), a court must in particular have regard to –

    (a)   the impact which any ensuing timetable revision would have on the welfare of the child to whom the application relates, and

    (b)   the impact which any ensuing timetable revision would have on the duration and conduct of the proceedings ...

(8) Each separate extension under subsection (5) is to end no more than eight weeks after the later of –

    (a)   the end of the period being extended; and

    (b)   The end of the day on which the extension is granted.

The Act provides that extensions are not to be granted routinely and are to be seen as requiring specific justification.[46]

4.86 In addition the PLO 2014 provides guidance on extensions to the timetable at section 6, and the President has recently gone further in:

Re S (A Child) [2014] EWCC B44 (Fam), [2014] 2 FLR 575

4.87 On 16 April 2014, in his above judgment in care proceedings, in which the mother had applied for an assessment under s 38(6) of the Children Act 1989 the President gives consideration to the amended Children Act 1989, s 38(7A) and (7B) and the scope for extending the 26-week time limit. His guidance is useful particularly in light of s 14(7) Children and Families Act 2014.

---

[44] Children and Families Act 2014, s 14(2).
[45] Ibid, s 14(3).
[46] Children Act 1989, s 32(7).

The facts

4.88 S was the mother's fourth child; her elder three siblings had been removed from the mother's care a number of years ago. She is a vulnerable woman with a history of street prostitution and drug-taking, who struggles to care for herself, has mental health problems, and a low IQ.

4.89 S was born in October 2013. By the time of the final hearing, care proceedings had been running for approximately five months. The court had the benefit of a local authority parenting assessment in respect of the mother and also a psychiatric assessment from an independently instructed expert. The local authority plan, supported by the guardian, was to place the child with an extended family member with a view to a special guardianship order being made following a trial placement.

4.90 The mother was opposed to such a placement and made an application for residential assessment pursuant to s 38(6) of the Children Act 1989. Ultimately that application was dismissed on the grounds that it was not necessary in order to resolve the proceedings justly. In fact in this case the President concluded:[47]

> 'Far from this being a case where the child's welfare demands an extension of the 26 weeks time limit, S's needs point if anything in the other direction.'

For the purposes of this chapter, the guidance given in respect of extension to the time limit generally is the most pertinent.

Scope to extend care proceedings beyond 26 weeks

4.91 The timescale of proceedings had already taken five months. Regarding the new statutory framework he made a number of points:

- The 26-week time limit is a mandatory limit which must be complied with, subject to the statutory exception set out in the new s 32(5) Children Act 1989. He reiterated his message that deadlines can and must be met.

- However, he approved of Pauffley J's judgment in *Re NL*[48] that 'justice must never be sacrificed upon the altar of speed'.

- The President in *Re B-S*[49] had dealt with the possibility of extension beyond 26 weeks in a potential adoption case if the court was not properly equipped to make decisions. In this judgment he said at para 27:

> 'That approach, which is entirely compatible with the requirements of section 32, applies not just in the particular context under consideration in *Re B-S* but more generally.'

---

[47] *Re S (a child)* [2014] EWCC B44 (Fam), [2014] 2 FLR 575 para 44.
[48] *Re NL (A Child) (Appeal: Interim Care Order: Facts and Reasons)* [2014] EWHC 270 (Fam).
[49] [2013] EWCA Civ 1146.

- Whether a case would warrant a s 32(5) extension must be determined on a case-by-case basis, but by way of illustration, it may be appropriate in drug abuse/alcohol abuse cases or cases involving parental mental ill-health to consider an extension beyond 26 weeks to see if a parent can make changes within the child's timescales. However, extensions should not be granted in the hope that something may turn up, but rather:[50]

> 'Typically three questions will have to be addressed. First, is there some solid, evidence based, reason to believe that the parent is committed to making the necessary changes? If so, secondly, is there some solid, evidence based, reason to believe that the parent will be able to maintain that commitment? If so, thirdly, is there some solid, evidence based, reason to believe that the parent will be able to make the necessary changes within the child's timescale?'

Interim care orders

4.92 In addition to the amendments to s 38 Children Act 1989 in respect of the general timetable of the case, s 14(4) Children and Families Act 2014 states:

In section 38 (interim care and supervision orders) –

(a)   in subsection (4) (duration of interim order) omit –
    (i)   Paragraph (a) (order may not last longer than 8 weeks), and
    (ii) Paragraph (b) (subsequent order generally may not last longer than 4 weeks ...

The consequence of this amendment is that every interim care or supervision order made on or after 22 April 2014 is now made for the duration of the proceedings. There is no longer any requirement for such orders to be reviewed initially after 8 weeks and then every 28 days thereafter.

Practice Direction 27A – court bundles

4.93 Within section 1 of the PLO 2014, it is made clear that:[51]

'In applying the provisions of FPR Part 12 and the Public Law Outline the court and the parties must also have regard to:

(1)   all other relevant rules and Practice Directions and in particular –
- FPR Part 1 (Overriding Objective);
- FPR Part 4 (General Case Management Powers);
- FPR Part 15 (Representation of Protected Parties) and Practice Direction 15B (Adults Who May Be Protected Parties and Children Who May Become Protected Parties in Family Proceedings);
- FPR Part 18 (Procedure for Other Applications in Proceedings);
- FPR Part 22 (Evidence);
- FPR Part 24 (Witnesses, depositions generally and taking of evidence in Member States of the European Union);

---

[50] *Re S (a child)* [2014] EWCC B44 (Fam), [2014] 2 FLR 575, para 38.
[51] Practice Direction 12A Care, Supervision and other Part 4 Proceedings: Guide to Case Management, para 1.3(1).

- FPR Part 25 (Experts) and the Experts Practice Directions;
- FPR 27.6 and Practice Direction 27A (Court Bundles);
- FPR 30 (Appeals) and Practice Direction 30A Appeals ...'

4.94 At this stage, more detailed consideration is being given to the requirements of PD27A, it being of significant importance for the successful implementation of the PLO 2014:[52]

> 'Failure to comply with any part of this practice direction may result in the judge removing the case from the list or putting the case further back in the list and may also result in a "wasted costs" order or some other adverse costs order.'

and of significant practical importance for the parties to proceedings in the family court generally!

4.95 This Practice Direction is in force from 22 April 2014 and applies to:

- All hearings before a judge sitting in the Family Division of the High Court, wherever the court may be sitting; AND all hearings in the family court.[53]
- 'Hearing' includes all appearances before the court, whether with or without notice to other parties and whether for directions or substantive hearing, although if the hearing is of an urgent nature, such that it would be impossible to comply with PD27A, in those circumstances only, it will not so apply.[54]

Preliminary documents

4.96 To assist the court in meeting its case management obligations, it is vital that the information available to it is in a format that is easily accessible, and that each party's respective position and the issues to be determined are easily identifiable. Whilst it is the responsibility of the applicant (in public law proceedings, usually the local authority) to prepare the bundle[55] and to lodge the preliminary documents, each party has an obligation in respect of these important matters, with agreement in relation to the case summary, statement of issues, chronology and reading list being necessary,[56] as well as each party being required to file a position statement for each hearing.[57]

---

[52] Practice Direction 27A Family Proceedings: Court Bundles (Universal practice to be applied in the High Court and Family Court), para 12.1.
[53] Ibid, para 2.1.
[54] Ibid, paras 2.2 and 2.4.
[55] Ibid, para 3.1.
[56] Ibid, para 4.6.
[57] Ibid, para 4.3(c).

Table showing preliminary documents required

Case summary – summary of background to hearing, if possible limited to four A4 pages.[58]	NB: When hearing is before magistrates the case summary to be anonymised, leaving out the names and identifying information of every person referred to other than the legal representatives.[59]
Statement of issues to be determined (1) at that hearing and (2) at the final hearing.[60]	
Position statements from each party, to include a summary of the orders sought by that party (1) at that hearing and (2) at the final hearing.[61]	
Up to date **chronology** – if a final hearing OR if case summary is insufficient.[62]	
Skeleton arguments, if appropriate.[63]	
List of essential reading for that hearing.[64]	
The time estimate.[65]	This document must specify: (1) t/e for judicial pre-reading, (2) t/e for hearing all evidence and submissions, and (3) t/e for preparing and delivering judgment, taking into account any need for interpreters or intermediaries and on the basis all witnesses will have read all relevant material before giving evidence.[66]
Each of the above documents shall be 'as short and succinct as possible'.[67]	All documents, save the reading list and time estimate shall be 'cross-referenced to the relevant pages of the bundle'.[68]

---

58 Ibid, para 4.3 (a).
59 Ibid, para 4.4.
60 Ibid, para 4.3 (b).
61 Ibid, para 4.3(c).
62 Ibid, para 4.3(d).
63 Ibid, para 4.3(e).
64 Ibid, para 4.3(f).
65 Ibid, para 4.3(g).
66 Ibid, para 10.1.
67 Ibid, para 4.4.
68 Ibid, para 4.5.

Documents 1, 2, 4 and 6 above shall for a final hearing (and so far as practicable for any other hearing) consist of a single AGREED document.	Where the parties disagree as to content the 'fact of their disagreement and their differing contentions shall be set out at the appropriate places in the document'.[69]

Example of a local authority case summary

4.97 It is right to say that the designated family judges throughout England and Wales are at liberty to issue their own guidance as to the format of the case summary, but it seems to the authors that a consensus of style is emerging across the country.

---

[69]   Ibid, para 4.6.

IN THE FAMILY COURT
<u>(sitting at Anytown Combined Court Centre)</u>   Case No: DG13C00071

X LOCAL AUTHORITY v M, F
and C

<u>CASE SUMMARY</u>

ISSUES RESOLUTION HEARING

22 April 2014

1. The Child

1.1 C, a girl born on 15 December 2011, now aged 2 years 3 months.

2. Parties

2.1 The Applicant is X Local Authority represented by Mr L of Counsel. The key social worker is Verity Caring.

2.2 The mother of the child is **M** represented by Miss W (Solicitor).

2.3 The father of the child is **F** represented by Mrs J (Solicitor). Mrs A takes her instructions from the **Official Solicitor**, he having agreed to act for F, due to his lack of capacity to instruct.

2.4 The child is represented by Mrs C and Guardian **Ms Geraldine Cotton.**

3. Applications

3.1 The application before the court is the Local Authority's application for a care order which was issued on 5 December 2013.

3.2 The Local Authority having filed its final care plan (dated 20 February 2014 – **C9-20**) now invites the Court to make a Special Guardianship Order in favour of C's maternal grandparents, **Pat and Bob Barlow.**

4. Previous or concurrent proceedings

4.1 None.

5. Chronology of Proceedings

5.1 <u>Allocation</u> – The proceedings are allocated to District Judge T for case management and hearing.

5.2 <u>Timetable</u> – The proceedings are allocated to the standard track of 26 weeks (that date being **5 June 2014**).

5.3 Hearings to date

- A Case Management Hearing took place on **17 December 2013** when an interim care order was made, a psychological report of the parents was ordered, other directions were made and the matter listed for Final Hearing on 27 May 2014 t/e 4 days before District Judge T.

- A further Case Management Hearing took place on **3 January 2014** where applications for capacity assessment of both parties were granted and other directions were made by District Judge T.

- A further Case Management Hearing, was necessary in the light of the capacity assessments and took place on **18 January 2014**, when District Judge Lord determined that a parenting assessment by a PAMS trained Independent Social Worker (**Chris Taylor**) of both parents was necessary in this case, and directed that a report be filed by **28 February 2014**, in addition the Official Solicitor was appointed to act on behalf of F and thereafter timetabling directions were made and the matter was listed for an Issues Resolution Hearing at 2pm on **22 April 2014**.

5.4 Proceedings are listed today for an **Issues Resolution Hearing.**

6. Key issues in the case

6.1 Neglect.

6.2 Home conditions.

6.3 The parents' learning difficulties.

7. Summary of Events leading to Proceedings

Referrals were received in May, August, September 2012 and January 2013 in relation to allegations that the parents were failing to meet C's needs and that she was suffering from neglect. A core assessment was completed and C was placed on the child protection register. Visits from family support from Spring 2013 until November 2013 reported that the house was in a terrible state with dirt and debris everywhere and rubbish was overflowing. C did not gain her expected weight and she was frequently seen in dirty clothes. She slept in her buggy rather than a cot. The parents separated following allegations by the mother that the father had been violent towards her. The mother continued to leave C with other adults despite being asked not to by the support workers involved. The home conditions worsened during the time that the Local Authority has been involved despite the attempts to put support in place. The parents have not shown any understanding of the concerns and have not demonstrated any change.

8. Current position

8.1 The child is residing with her maternal grandparents (**Pat and Bob Barlow**) pursuant to an interim care order. Supervised contact is offered to the parents 3 times per week for 1 hour.

8.2 A viability assessment of the Paternal Grandmother (**Bet Lynch**) dated **21 December 2013** has been filed and served which is negative.

8.3 The Local Authority has completed an SGO assessment of the Maternal Grandparents (**Pat and Bob Barlow**), which is positive. It now recommends the making of a Special Guardianship Order in favour of them. The Local Authority has also filed and served a Special Guardianship Support Plan, together with a Contact Plan for contact between C and each of her parents in the event a Special Guardianship Order is made.

8.4 **Chris Taylor** (Independent Social Worker) has undertaken a parenting assessment of the parents. He is unable to recommend that C return to either or both of their care.

9. Parties response to key issues

9.1 The Local Authority recommends the Court make a Special Guardianship Order in favour of the Maternal Grandparents (**Pat and Bob Barlow**). It further recommends that contact between C and each of her parents should gradually reduce and continue at the rate of once per month in the long-term. Such contact will be supervised by Mr and Mrs Barlow.

9.2 The Mother supports the making of a Special Guardianship Order in favour of her parents. She seeks contact at the level of once per week in the long-term.

9.3 The Official Solicitor on behalf of the Father does not oppose the making of a Special Guardianship Order in favour of Mr and Mrs Barlow. He seeks contact at the level of once per week in the long-term.

9.4 The Children's Guardian supports the making of a Special Guardianship Order in favour of Mr and Mrs Barlow, and she further supports the recommendation that contact between C and each of her parents take place at the level of once per month in the long term. She however, recommends that supervision of that contact remain the responsibility of the Local Authority for a longer period than anticipated in the Contact Plan. Rather than the Maternal Grandparents supervising contact within a couple of months of the final hearing, she envisages a period of 12 months or so being more realistic. She invites the Local Authority to amend its final care plan to set out how it will support the family in managing contact in the foreseeable future.

10. Issues for Determination at hearing today

10.1 Whether the final hearing needs a four day time estimate, or whether all issues can be determined in one day (namely 27 May 2014).

10.2 The issues to be determined at the final hearing relate to contact; the level for each parent and the question of how long such contact should continue to be supervised by the Local Authority.

11. Recommended Reading list

11.1 Second Statement and Chronology of Verity Caring, Social Worker, dated 11 March 2014 [B60-B74].

11.2 Statement of the First Respondent, Mother, dated 25 March 2014 [B75-B76].

11.3 Final Care Plan [C9-C20].

11.4 Report of Chris Taylor, Independent Social Worker, dated 28 February 2014 [D55-D110].

11.5 SGO assessment, Pat and Bob Barlow, dated 31 January 2014, [E48-E129].

11.6 Special Guardianship Support Plan dated 10 April 2014.

11.7 Contact Plan dated 10 April 2014.

11.8 Children's Guardian's Final Analysis & Recommendations.

11.9 Statement of the Deputy Official Solicitor dated 16 April 2014.

Dated 17 April 2014

Mr L of Counsel

Barristers' Chambers, Leeds

Counsel for the Local Authority

Format and contents of the bundle

4.98 With effect from 31 July 2014:[70]

'Unless the court has specifically directed otherwise, being satisfied that such direction is necessary to enable the proceedings to be disposed of justly, the bundle shall be contained in one A4 size ring binder or lever arch file limited to no more than 350 sheets of A4 paper and 350 sides of text.'

4.99 To assist in achieving the reduction in voluminous paperwork, the contents of the bundle is now limited to sections divided as follows:

- The preliminary documents, (and any other case management documents required by any other practice direction).
- Applications and orders.
- Statements and affidavits.
- Care plans (where appropriate).
- Experts' reports and other reports (including those of a guardian, children's guardian or litigation friend).
- Other documents, divided into further sections as may be appropriate.[71]

4.100 Certain classes of documents are now specifically excluded from the bundle, with a mandatory instruction that they must not be included unless specifically directed by the court. Those documents are as follows:

- Correspondence (including letters of instruction to experts).
- Medical records (including hospital, GP and health visitor records).
- Bank and credit card statements and other financial records.
- Notes of contact visits.
- Foster carer logs.
- Social services files (with the exception of any assessment being relied on by any of the parties).
- Police disclosure.[72]

That said, despite specific exclusion, if specific documents are to be referred to at the hearing and it is necessary for the court to read them then they are not prevented from being included.

---

[70] Ibid, para 5.1.
[71] Ibid, para 4.2.
[72] Ibid, para 4.1.

Timetable for lodging of the bundle and preliminary documents

4.101

- The applicant to the proceedings is usually the party responsible for preparing and lodging the bundle. If however that party is a litigant in person, then the first listed respondent who is not a litigant in person is so responsible. In the event that all the parties are litigants in person none of them shall be obliged to provide a bundle, but if they choose to then it must be prepared so as to comply with the Practice Direction.[73]

- Not less than 4 working days before the hearing, the party preparing the bundle shall provide a paginated index to the parties (whether or not it is agreed).[74]

- Not less than 3 working days before the hearing, any counsel instructed should be provided with a paginated bundle by the person instructing that counsel.[75]

- Not less than 2 working days before the hearing (minus the preliminary documents if they are as yet unavailable) the bundle must be lodged with the court.[76]

- No later than 11am on the day before the hearing, all preliminary documents must be lodged with the court and (where the matter is being heard by a named High Court judge) be e-mailed to the judge's clerk.[77]

Additional requirements are in place in respect of cases being heard at the Royal Courts of Justice.[78]

A flowchart for the Public Law Outline (2014) is set out below.

---

[73] Ibid, para 3.1.
[74] Ibid, para 6.1.
[75] Ibid, para 6.2.
[76] Ibid, para 6.3.
[77] Ibid, para 6.4.
[78] Ibid, para 8.

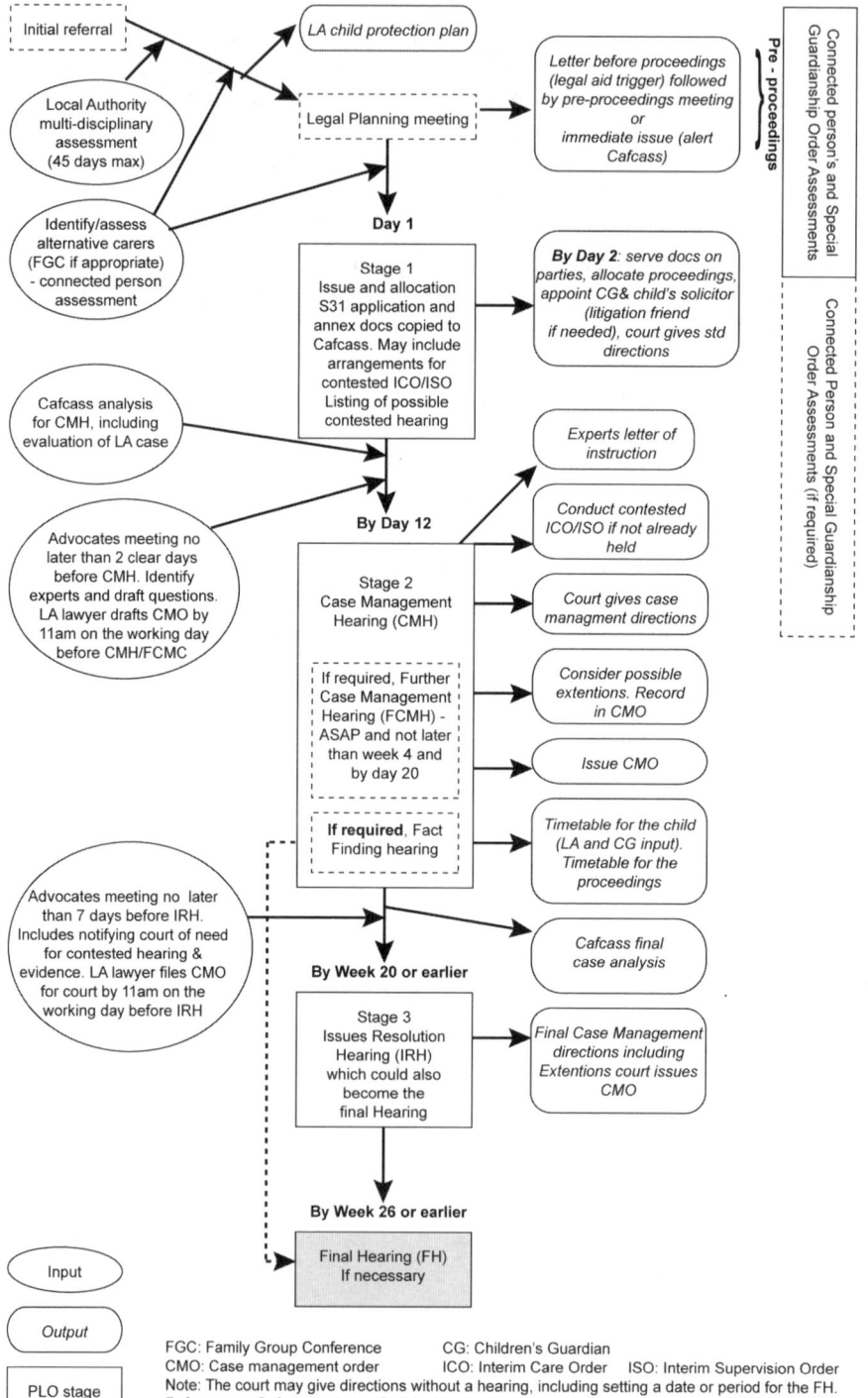

FGC: Family Group Conference   CG: Children's Guardian
CMO: Case management order   ICO: Interim Care Order   ISO: Interim Supervision Order
Note: The court may give directions without a hearing, including setting a date or period for the FH.
Reference to Cafcass includes CAFCASS CYMRU

Stage 1: Issue and allocation

4.102 On 'Day 2' the following standard directions are given:

- Ensuring compliance by the local authority with the pre-proceedings checklist.
- Appointment of children's guardian (to be allocated by Cafcass/CAFCASS CYMRU.
- Appointment of solicitor for the child only if necessary.
- Appointment (if person to be appointed consents) of any litigation friend, including the Official Solicitor where appropriate.
- Ensuring compliance with rules relating to cases with an international element.
- Timetabling the filing of the following:
  — local authority case summary;
  — case analysis by the children's guardian;
  — parents' response;
  — any Part 25 application (see chapter 5).
- Requesting disclosure to (for example) the police or health service body.
- Requiring the solicitor for the child(ren) to arrange an advocates' meeting no later than 2 business days before the CMH.
- Listing the CMH.[79]

Stage 2: The advocates' meeting

4.103 Such meetings must include any litigants in person, and are aimed at identifying the issues to enable the Local Authority advocate to draft a Case Management Order, which must be filed with court by 11 am on the business day before the CMH and/or FCMH.

4.104 On 23 May 2014, the final versions of the Standard Directions on Issue and Case Management Orders were issued. On that day the President said the following:

'Please find attached the final public law prescribed orders in word format: the CMO and SDO. These are updated in line with the new PLO (PLO 2014). The CMO template permits locally agreed standard directions for any of the suggested headings (and more, as appropriate) but the mandatory headings should always be used unless there is a reasoned basis for their exclusion. The CMS material referred to in the template must always be completed but please note that expert code G was a replication which has now been removed. The templates have been altered to be compatible with the new Act and the Rules. It is an obligation to complete the timetable for proceedings and jurisdiction paragraphs. Where reasons are to be specified that is because there is a legal obligation to do so. When considering any

---

[79] Practice Direction 12A *Care, Supervision and other Part 4 Proceedings: Guide to Case Management*, p 4.

extension of time beyond 26 weeks please choose and complete the relevant sub-paragraph by reference to the guidance given in Re S (A Child) [2014] EWCC 16 April.'

4.105 The following example of a draft case management order involves a case, which is expected to conclude within 26 weeks. For assistance to practitioners, the guidance in respect of the reasons required in the event an extension to the timetable is necessary have been left in, as has the guidance in respect of jurisidictional issues.

The Family Court

Sitting at Anytown Combined Court Centre   Case No: AN14C00215

The Children Act 1989

THE CHILDREN

Please add a separate sheet if more than 4 children

| Child A | gender | [female] | **d.o.b** | [21.10.12] |
| Child B | gender | [female] | **d.o.b** | [25.02.14] |

DRAFT CASE MANAGEMENT ORDER NO 1 (12 May 2014)

1. THE PARTIES

The Applicant local authority is X Local Authority
The first respondent (mother) is M
The second respondent (father) is F
The third respondent(s) are (the children) by their children's guardian, Sally Fisher

2. THE CHILD(REN) ARE LIVING WITH

Local Authority approved foster carers, together [Placement 5].

3. THE REPRESENTATIVES AT THIS HEARING

The parties are represented as follows:

(a) The applicant is represented by Miss A N Other (Counsel), their contact details being 01234 456789/another@chambers.co.uk.

(b) The 1st respondent is represented by Mr L Barrister (Counsel), their contact details being 01234 098765/lbarrister@legal.co.uk.

(c) The 2nd respondent is represented by Mrs S Lawyer (Counsel), their contact details being 01234 675489/sl@lawyer.co.uk.

(d) The 3rd respondent is represented by Miss V Caring (Solicitor), their contact details being 01234/876945/vcaring@solicitors.co.uk.

The identity of the children and those named in paragraphs 1 and 2 are not to be disclosed in public without the permission of the court.

4. ALLOCATION

The proceedings are today allocated to HHJ Fairminded.

5. THE APPLICATION(S)

The local authority has applied for care orders on 22 April 2014.

6. JURISDICTION

The court is satisfied that it has jurisdiction in relation to the children as both they and their parents are habitually resident in England.

[*or*]

(a) There is an issue as to jurisdiction in respect of the children and consideration needs to be given to this issue [*and the application of Council Regulation (EC) No 2201/2003 (Brussels 2 Revised)*] to these proceedings by the parties as a matter of urgency; and

(b) The local authority shall liaise with the [*identify country*] consular authority in England and Wales or other competent authority in [*name of foreign state*] in relation to the proceedings or make a request to the Central Authority of [*identify country*] for such information as may be relevant to determine issues of jurisdiction.

7. TODAY'S HEARING

(a) Today's case was listed for: CMH.
(b) Today's hearing has been EFFECTIVE, although a FCMH is required.

8. THE TIMETABLE FOR THE PROCEEDINGS

[see in the matter of *Re S* (*a Child*) 16 April 2014]

The timetable for the proceedings is 26 weeks.

([or]

The proceedings cannot be completed within 26 weeks, but are to be completed within [ ] weeks or by [date] for the following reason [tick one]

☐   (i) It is necessary to extend the timetable for the proceedings beyond 26 weeks in order to resolve the proceedings justly because: [*specify reason, eg. very heavy cases involving the most complex medical evidence where a separate fact-finding hearing is directed, FDAC type case, cases with an international element where investigations or assessments have to be carried out abroad, cases where the parent's disabilities require recourse to special assessments or measures.*]

☐ (ii) Despite robust and vigorous case management, the nature of the proceedings has changed and it is necessary to extend the timetable for the proceedings for one or more of the children in order to resolve the proceedings justly because: [*specify reason, eg cases proceeding on allegations of neglect or emotional harm where allegations of sexual abuse subsequently surface, cases which are unexpectedly 'derailed' because of the death, serious illness or imprisonment of the proposed carer, cases where a realistic alternative family carer emerges late in the day*]

☐ (iii) The progress of the case has been delayed because of the litigation failure on behalf of one or more of the parties and it is necessary to extend the timetable for the proceedings in order to resolve the proceedings justly because: [*specify reason:*])

AND in each of the above cases, the impact on the welfare of the children of extending the proceedings is [*state impact*]

The next hearing is a FCMH on 9 June 2014 at 10 am at Anytown Combined Court Centre with a time estimate of 1 hour. Parties to attend at 9 am.

9. TIMETABLE FOR THE CHILD(REN)

The key dates and events in the Timetable for the Child(ren) are:

The Child	Event/permanent placement	Dates
A	Decision as to A's long term placement	21.10.14
B	Decision as to whether a parent or another person has caused injuries to her Decision as to B's long term placement	21.10.14

10. THRESHOLD

The s 31 threshold for the making of orders is in dispute, but not opposed on an interim basis. The Local Authority is not yet in a position to draft a perfected Schedule of Findings Sought in satisfaction of the s 31 Children Act threshold criteria until medical evidence and further disclosure is received.

An interim, unopposed, threshold document is at A2-3.

11. THE KEY ISSUES IN THE CASE ARE:

(a) Whether B has been injured on one or more occasion by the deliberate or neglectful act of either or both parents or by another person caring for her, causing a bruise and a fracture to her arm by the age of 7 weeks.

(b) Whether the children have been neglected or are at risk of neglect and/or domestic violence.

(c)   Placement in the interim and long-term.

(d)   Whether there are any viable alternative family carers if the children cannot be returned to their parents.

12. THE PARTIES' POSITIONS:

(a)   The Local Authority invites the Court to make interim care orders to allow it to share parental responsibility during on-going assessments.

(b)   The Mother denies neglect and does not know how the injuries to B were caused. She wishes to care for the children together with the Father. She neither consents to nor opposes the making of interim care orders.

(c)   The Father denies neglect and does not know how the injuries to B were caused. He admits past domestic violence but says there has been none since about May 2013. He wishes to care for the children together with the Mother. He neither consents to nor opposes the making of interim care orders.

(d)   The Children's Guardian supports the position of the Local Authority, as proposed and discussed at the Advocates Meeting on 7 May 2014. She supports the making of interim care orders.

13. IDENTIFICATION OF PERSON(S) TO BE ASSESSED AS POTENTIAL ALTERNATIVE CARER(S)

(a)   The parents have identified all family members they wish to be assessed and the court has explained to them that any persons identified by them in the future may not be assessed due to the delay not being consistent with the timetable for the child.

(b)   The person(s) identified by the mother and by the father are Susan and Anthony Fowler.

14. EVIDENCE

After reading the materials filed, which are described in an index/record of hearing.

PREAMBLE

Upon it being recorded, in the light of the recent decision of *Re S* that this is not a single issue or otherwise exceptional case to justify a fact finding hearing to determine the causation of B's injuries;

AND upon it being recorded that the only paediatric radiologist who will report at the current legal aid rate of £108 per hour requires in excess of 12 weeks to report, the Local Authority will pay the hourly difference between the old rate of £135 per hour required by most qualified experts and the current rate, if not met by the Legal Aid Agency.

15. THE COURT ORDERS

16. EXPERTS

(a) An application was today made for the instruction of an expert.

(b) The application was granted.

(c) The type of expert whose instruction was allowed by the court: B.

(d) The date by which the report is due is: 23 June 2014.

(e) The report of an expert is necessary to assist the court to resolve the proceedings because the nature, age and mechanism of causation of B's fracture is material to whether she was injured by one of the parents or as a result of their care.

(f) Leave to the parties to instruct Dr Boney, (Paediatric Radiologist), to report on B's x-rays and medical history to determine the nature of any fracture, timing and likely method of causation. The Solicitor for the Children shall take the lead in the letter of instruction, the parameters of the same having been agreed by the Court. The costs of the instruction shall be shared equally between the parties, the Court declaring that such costs are both a reasonable and necessary disbursement on the certificates of the publicly-funded parties.

The Court further orders:

(i) The proposed assessment and report by Dr Boney is vital to the resolution of the case.

(ii) The case is exceptional on its facts.

(iii) The costs to be incurred in the preparation of such report are wholly necessary, reasonable, proportionate disbursements on the funding certificates of the publicly funded parties.

(iv) The Court considers Dr Boney's hourly rate of £135 plus VAT and the estimated costs of the assessment report to be reasonable in the context of his qualifications, experience and expertise.

(v) The field in which Dr Boney practices and the particular expertise which he brings to bear on paediatric radiology is highly specialised. There is no realistic prospect of finding an alternative expert with the necessary expertise at a lower fee, who will report within the child's timescales.

(vi) The Court considers that any delay in order to give the LAA the opportunity to consider an application for prior authority to incur the costs of the proposed report would be entirely outside the children's timescales.

17. OTHER ORDERS

Local Authority

(i) The Local Authority shall file and serve:

(a) Parenting assessment in respect of M and F by 18 July 2014;

(b) Viability assessment in respect of Susan and Anthony Fowler by 6 June 2014, and full assessment (if viability is positive), on a date to be fixed at the FCMH. Permission to the Local Authority to disclose to Mr and Mrs Fowler a copy of the assessment(s);

1st and 2nd Respondents

(ii) The parents, shall each, by 23 May 2014, file and serve a factual statement setting out:
- details of any person who has had care of B since birth or who may otherwise be implicated in her injuries;
- their account of involvement with B in the days preceding discovery of the bruise;
- their relationship generally, and;
- a factual response to the issues raised in the interim threshold document, statement of the HV and statement of Dr P Daetrician;

(iii) The Mother shall obtain, file and serve her obstetric records in respect of both children;

Disclosure

(iv) The Chief Constable for Anytown shall by 28 May 2014 serve on the Local Authority for the purposes of filing herein:

(a) PNC details for M (dob: 30.08.95) and for F (dob: 14.09.94);

(b) Details of any call-outs by or in respect of either of the above or to any addresses occupied by them – in particular relating to the assault by F on M on or about 22.12.12;

(c) All statements, copies of interview, reports and/or logs in connection with the investigation into injuries sustained by B (dob: 25.02.14);

(d) Permission to the Local Authority to serve a copy of this order on the police and permission to the police to apply to vary or discharge this order on notice to all parties and to the Court;

(v) The Solicitor for the Children shall, by 28 May 2014 obtain, file and serve all primary health records for the children to include GP, health visitor and hospital;

General Case Management

(vi) There shall be a FCMH at 10 am on 9 June 2014 before HHJ Fairminded, with a time estimate of 1 hour. Parties to attend at 9 am, when the Court will specifically consider

(a) Whether any person/s shall be invited to intervene in the proceedings for the purposes of establishing causation of B's injuries;

(b) Further case management and timetabling to IRH;

(c) Any police or medical disclosure issues;

(vii) No further hearings are listed beyond FCMH at this stage, but the IRH will be fixed at the next hearing on 9 June 2014.

18. COMPLIANCE

No document other than a document specified in this order or filed in accordance with the Rules or any Practice Direction shall be filed by any party without the court's permission.

19. Any application to vary this order or for any other order is to be made to the allocated judge on notice to all parties.

20. All parties must immediately inform the allocated judge and the court if any party or person fails to comply with any part of this order.

21. CASE OUTCOME [*to be completed only if proceedings are finally disposed of at a Case Management/Issues Resolution Hearing*]

Court address: for filing/communication

1. Type of Placement [for paragraph 2]

Type of Placement for children	
1.	Not removed – At home
2.	Not removed – In RPaCA placement (*a residential assessment with parent*)
3.	Not removed – In community placement
4.	Removed – To kinship placement
5.	Removed – To foster care
6.	Removed – To potential adoptive placement
7.	Reunification – Assessment placement with parent
8.	Reunification – Assessment placement with kinship placement
9.	Complex needs – In a specialist placement including hospital

2. Type of Hearing [for paragraph 7 and paragraph 8]

PLO Stage	
Urgent Case Management Hearing	
Case Management Hearing (CMH)	Other – Fact-Finding
Further Case Management Hearing (FCMH)	Other – Directions not part of PLO
Issues Resolution Hearing (IRH)	Other – Contested Interim Care Hearing
Final Hearing (FH)	Other – s 38(6)

3. Reasons for Adjournment [for paragraph 7]

Please list the **ONE** reason which best explains why the hearing has been adjourned.

Reason for Adjourned Hearing	
Local Authority	LA1 – No/poor pre-proceedings preparation by LA, other than (core) social work assessment of the family
	LA2 – No friends/family identified before the hearing by LA
	LA3 – No/poor kinship assessments by LA
	LA4 – No expert instructed by LA
	LA5 – No/poor/late (core) social work assessment of the family by LA
	LA6 – New social work report/assessment required following a change in circumstances
	LA7 – No timetable for the child LA8 – New/alternative care plan
	LA8 – No/poor/late/new/care plan
	LA9 – Placement order proceedings delay
	LA10 – No/poor placement evidence by LA
	LA11 – No threshold document
Cafcass	CA1 – Cafcass not allocated/present
	CA2 – No/poor Cafcass analysis

Reason for Adjourned Hearing	
Other parties	LW1 – Lawyers not instructed, present or ready, party or witness fail to attend
	LW2 – No key issue analysis
	LW3 – No/poor parental evidence
HMCTS	HM1 – No courtroom available
	HM2 – No special measures
	HM3 – Interpreter not available
Judiciary	JU1 – Lack of judicial continuity
	JU2 – Insufficient time listed or to complete hearing
LAA	LS1 – Prior authority from LSC not available
	LS2 – Other legal aid
Official Solicitor	OS1 – Official Solicitor not instructed/ready
Experts	EX1 – Late expert report/assessment/ Poor expert report/assessment
	EX2 – New expert report/assessment required following a change in circumstances
Health	HE1 – No/poor medical records etc from other agency
Crime	CR1 – Police disclosure/documents incomplete/not available
Other	OT1 – Case transferred
	OT2 – Need for an interim contested hearing
	OT3 – Other non-compliance with directions
	OT4 – Consolidation with other family proceedings
	OT5 – Parallel proceedings
	OT6 – New baby/pregnancy
	OT7 – New Party joined
	OT8 – Immigration and international difficulties
	OT9 – Severe weather
	OT10 – Industrial action

4. Instruction of Expert

Please list all that apply.

Expert Code
A – Paediatric
B – Paediatric Radiologist
C – Other Medical Report
Family Centre Assessment (Parenting Skills): D1 – Residential D2 – Non-Residential
E – Multi-Disciplinary Assessment
F – Independent Social Worker
G – Paediatrician
Psychiatric Report: H1 – Parent(s) alone H2 – Child(ren) and Parent(s) / carer(s) H3 – Child(ren) alone
Psychological Report J1 – Clinical – Child(ren) only J2 – Educational – Child(ren) only J3 – Parent(s) only J4 – Parent(s) and Child(ren)
K – Other Expert Report

Stage 3: Issues resolution hearing

4.106 With robust and flexible case management by the court at Stage 2,[80] and an active role in monitoring the progress of compliance with directions by all the parties to ensure that the timetable for the child and the timetable for proceedings[81] does not slip, then the final stage of the PLO 2014 can be comfortably met.

4.107 It is only necessary therefore for there to be two advocates' meetings in the course of a 26-week case, with the second one (no later than 7 business days before the IRH) being decisive as to identifying the advocates' views of:

- The remaining key issues and how the issues may be resolved or narrowed, including by the making of final orders.
- Any further evidence which is required to enable the key issues to be resolved or narrowed.
- Which evidence is relevant and which witnesses are required at the final hearing.
- The need for a contested hearing and/or time for oral evidence to be given at the IRH.[82]

4.108 It is then the responsibility of the local authority advocate to notify the court immediately of the outcome of the discussion at the meeting and to file a further draft CMO by 11 am on the business day before the IRH.

4.109 The IRH shall be on a date 'as directed by the court, in accordance with the timetable for the proceedings'[83] at which the court:

- Identifies the key issue(s) (if any) to be determined and the extent to which those issues can be resolved or narrowed.
- Considers whether final orders can be made.
- Resolves or narrows issues by hearing evidence.
- Identifies the evidence needed to be heard to resolve remaining issues at the final hearing.
- Gives final case management directions to ensure effective final hearing takes place within the timetable of the proceedings which has been set before or at the IRH.[84]

---

[80] Ibid, section 2, p 8.
[81] Ibid, section 5, p 10.
[82] Ibid, p 7.
[83] Ibid.
[84] Ibid.

CHAPTER 5

EXPERTS

THE NEED FOR REFORM

5.1 Prior to 31 January 2013, the court had a duty to restrict expert evidence '… to that which is reasonably required to resolve the proceedings'.[1] Over time it became common practice for judges dealing with cases relating to children, (primarily within public law proceedings, but increasingly in the private law sphere), to allow the parties to routinely instruct experts simply because they all agreed such instruction was required. This led to a proliferation in the number of experts used in what were often straight forward cases. Those experts were producing longer and longer reports (not infrequently them being 200 pages in length), both of these factors of course serving to lengthen the hearing times needed for the issues to be determined and thus the length of the proceedings themselves.

THE CHANGE IN CULTURE

5.2 In his *View from the President's Chambers (3)*,[2] Sir James Munby, President of the Family Division made it clear that the problem of excessive use of experts did not lie with the experts themselves, but in the way the courts used them.

5.3 Three things were required:

(a) a reduction in the use of experts;

(b) a more focused approach in cases where experts are still needed, and;

(c) a reduction in the length of reports.

5.4 Part 25 of the Family Procedure Rules 2010, was amended, and came into force on 31 January 2013. The new test for the court is:[3]

> 'Expert evidence will be restricted to that which in the opinion of the court is necessary to assist the court to resolve the proceedings.'

---

[1] Family Procedure Rules 2010, r 25.1.

[2] *View from the President's Chambers (3) The process of reform: expert evidence* [2013] Fam Law 816.

[3] Family Procedure Rules 2010, r 25.1 (as amended).

5.5   The aim being to stop the immediate reaction of many legal representatives and judges faced with care proceedings or difficult private law proceedings that 'an independent expert will be required!' Of particular note is the following extract of evidence given by the President on 5 March 2013, to the House of Commons Public Bill Committee, which was considering the Children and Families Bill:

> 'Social Workers are experts. In just the same way, CAFCASS officers are experts. What has gone wrong with the system is that we have at least two experts in every care case – a social worker and a guardian – and yet we have grown up with the culture of believing that they are not really experts and we therefore need experts with a capital E. Much of the time we do not.'

5.6   The Government was already conscious of the importance of high quality expert evidence being available to the family courts and on 18 January 2013 in an impact assessment set out policy objectives and intended effects as being '... to ensure experts providing evidence to the family courts in proceedings relating to children have a level of qualifications, skills and experience consistent with the provision of good quality advice to the court ...'. In the light of this proposed policy, between 16 May and 18 July 2013 the Ministry of Justice and the Family Justice Council undertook a consultation entitled *Standards for Expert Witnesses in the Family Courts in England and Wales*. It specifically looked to:

> 'Expert witnesses supporting the family courts in England and Wales, particularly in proceedings relating to children, representative and regulatory bodies for the professions from which experts are drawn, including the health and social care sectors; Royal Colleges; members of the judiciary; family solicitors and barristers; local authority children services; expert witness training providers; academics; and others with an interest in the provision of expert evidence to the family courts.'

5.7   On 8 November 2013, following a successful consultation period, the joint response of the Ministry of Justice and the Family Justice Council was published; it recognised that change was vital. In any event the courts' and family justice professionals' approach to the use of expert evidence changed.

'NECESSARY'

5.8   To ensure there is no doubt as to the meaning of the new test, Sir James Munby P in June 2013, in the case of *Re H-L (A Child)*[4] stated:

> 'The short answer is that "necessary", means necessary. It is after all, an ordinary English word. It is a familiar expression nowadays in family law, not least because of the central role it plays, for example, in Article 8 of the European Convention and the wider Strasbourg jurisprudence. If elaboration is required, what precisely does it mean? That was a question considered, albeit in a rather different context, in *Re P (Placement Orders: Parental Consent)* [2008] EWCA Civ 535, [2008]

---

[4]   [2013] EWCA Civ 655, para 3.

2 FLR 625, paras [120], [125]. This court said it "has a meaning lying somewhere between 'indispensable' on the one hand and 'useful', 'reasonable' or 'desirable' on the other hand" having "the connotation of the imperative, what is demanded rather than what is merely optional or reasonable or desirable." In my judgment, that is the meaning, the connotation the word "necessary" has in rule 25.1.'

5.9   The President suggests that the case management judge's approach, when faced with an application for permission to instruct an expert, should be 'give me three good reasons why you say this expert is necessary'.[5] He goes on to express the view that there are two aspects to this central question of whether an expert is necessary:

(a)   Whether what the expert will tell the court is something which is already familiar to all family justice professionals;

(b)   If it is, then the court must go on to consider whether it is 'necessary' to have as an expert someone other than the social worker or Cafcass officer. If such professionals can provide the relevant expertise then the employment of some other expert will not be necessary.[6]

The Children and Families Act 2014

5.10   All of the above has now been enshrined in statute by virtue of s 13 of the Children and Families Act 2014 (control of expert evidence, and of assessments, in children proceedings). It is interesting to note that the Act states:

13(6) The court may give permission as mentioned in subsection (1), (3) or (5) only if the court is of the opinion that the expert evidence is necessary to assist the court to resolve the proceedings justly.

which, refines the 'necessary test' by simply reasserting the overriding objective in the Family Procedure Rules 2010.

5.11   It is also important to note that the 2014 Act has added a refinement to s 38 Children Act 1989:

13(11) In section 38 of the Children Act 1989 (court's power to make interim care and supervision orders, and to give directions as to medical examination etc of children) after subsection (7) insert –

"(7A) A direction under subsection (6) to the effect that there is to be a medical or psychiatric examination or other assessment of the child may be given only if the court is of the opinion that the examination or other assessment is necessary to assist the court to resolve the proceedings justly.

(7B)   When deciding whether to give a direction under subsection (6) to that effect the court is to have regard in particular to –

5   *View from the President's Chambers (1) The process of reform: April 2013* [2013] Fam Law 548.
6   *View from the President's Chambers (3) The process of reform: expert evidence* [2013] Fam Law 816.

(a)   any impact which any examination or other assessment would be likely to have on the welfare of the child, and any other impact which giving the direction would be likely to have on the welfare of the child,

(b)   the issues with which the examination or other assessment would assist the court,

(c)   the questions which the examination or other assessment would enable the court to answer,

(d)   the evidence otherwise available,

(e)   the impact which the direction would be likely to have on the timetable, duration and conduct of the proceedings

(f)   the cost of the examination or other assessment, and

(g)   any matters prescribed by Family Procedure Rules."

'ROBUST CASE MANAGEMENT'

5.12   The Revised Public Law Outline came into effect on 1 July 2013, which together with the amendments to the Family Procedure Rules 2010 and of course the Children and Families Act 2014 have all paved the way for there being no excuse for the 'ways of the past' to continue.

5.13   The overriding objective of the Rules is to enable '... the court to deal with cases justly, having regard to any welfare issues involved'.[7] Dealing with cases justly, includes 'ensuring that it is dealt with expeditiously and fairly'.[8] The court must further the overriding objective by actively managing cases,[9] where active case management includes 'controlling the use of expert evidence'.[10]

5.14   The President has been very clear that both judges and the parties, through their legal representatives, within the auspices of the Revised PLO, must have a much more focused approach to all issues of case management, which includes the use of expert evidence.[11] When the court is considering an application for permission to instruct an expert, it can expect to hear the views of each party stated robustly as to whether such an expert is necessary. There is to be no more 'sitting on the fence' or adopting a position of simple neutrality. If a party feels that a particular expert is not necessary then they should say so, and explain why. In addition the case management judge, with their duty to manage cases robustly, cannot absolve themselves of their personal responsibility for deciding whether or not an expert is indeed necessary, just because all the parties are of the view that it is. It is no ground of appeal if a judge in such a situation decides that it is not necessary.[12]

---

[7]   Family Procedure Rules 2010 (as amended), r 1.1(1).
[8]   Ibid, r 1.1(2)(a).
[9]   Ibid, r 1.4(1).
[10]   Ibid, r 1.4(2)(e).
[11]   *View from the President's Chambers (3) The process of reform: expert evidence* [2013] Fam Law 816.
[12]   *Re F (A Child)* [2013] EWCA Civ 656.

TIMETABLE FOR AN APPLICATION

5.15 The importance of the first hearing in care proceedings, (the case management hearing or CMH) cannot be under-estimated. In order for cases to be dealt with expeditiously, fairly and justly and within the 26 week timescale, parties and the court must 'grasp the nettle' and apply their minds very early on as to whether permission is to be sought to instruct an expert and thereafter whether such permission is to be granted.

5.16 The local authority when seeking to issue the proceedings, is required by the revised PLO to set out its thinking about whether any additional expert evidence or assessment is necessary, and set out what it says is required (or not) in the social worker's statement.[13] It may be that consideration and even instruction of experts has happened prior to the issue of proceedings, which should have been compliant with Practice Direction 25A, para 3. In any event, permission of the court will be required for any such expert evidence to be admitted into the proceedings.

5.17 Thereafter, and when issuing the proceedings, the court will consider allocation of the case and give standard directions, including directions for the filing and service of any application for permission relating to experts, which must be a date prior to the advocates' meeting fixed in readiness for the CMH.[14] This advocates' meeting must be no later than two clear days before the CMH, with one of the issues to be dealt with being the identification of proposed experts and drafting of the questions to be posed.[15]

5.18 It is worth noting and remembering at this stage that applications for the use of an expert in all other family proceedings, is similarly under scrutiny, and that if a party to private law children proceedings, adoption and placement proceedings, proceedings for a financial remedy or defended divorce or dissolution of civil partnership proceedings seeks permission to instruct such an expert, the same rules apply as within care proceedings, and application must be made in private law proceedings no later than the first hearing dispute resolution appointment,[16] in adoption and placement proceedings no later than the first directions hearing,[17] in proceedings for a financial remedy, no later than the first appointment[18] and in defended divorce or dissolution of civil partnership proceedings by no later than any case management hearing directed by the court.[19] All applications must be in the same format.

5.19 That format is by way of a notice, which must state:

(a)   the field in which the expert evidence is required;

---

[13]   Annex to Practice Direction 36C, Pilot Practice Direction 12A, para 7.1.
[14]   Ibid, Public Law Outline.
[15]   Ibid.
[16]   Family Procedure Rules 2010, Part 25.6(b).
[17]   Ibid, Part 25.6(c).
[18]   Ibid, r 25.6(d).
[19]   Ibid, r 25.6(e).

(b) where practicable, the name of the proposed expert;

(c) the issues to which the expert evidence is to relate;

(d) whether the expert evidence could be obtained from a single joint expert;

(e) the other matters set out in Practice Direction 25C or 25D, as the case may be.[20]

5.20 In addition, the application for permission must also state:

(a) the discipline, qualifications and expertise of the expert (by way of CV where possible);

(b) the expert's availability to undertake the work;

(c) the timetable for the report;

(d) the responsibility for instruction;

(e) whether the expert evidence can properly be obtained by only one party (for example, on behalf of the child);

(f) why the expert evidence proposed cannot properly be given by an officer of the service, Welsh family proceedings officer or the local authority (social services undertaking a core assessment) in accordance with their respective statutory duties or any other party to the proceedings or an expert already instructed in the proceedings;

(g) the likely cost of the report on an hourly or other charging basis;

(h) the proposed apportionment (at least in the first instance) of any jointly instructed expert's fee; when it is to be paid; and, if applicable, whether public funding has been approved.[21]

5.21 The parties must not forget that the notice is only part of the application; that in addition the court must be provided with a draft order setting out the following:

(a) the issues in the proceedings to which the expert evidence is to relate and which the court is to identify;

(b) the questions relating to the issues in the case which the expert is to answer and which the court is to approve ensuring that they:
   (i)   are within the ambit of the expert's area of expertise;
   (ii) do not contain unnecessary or irrelevant detail;
   (iii) are kept to a manageable number and are clear, focused and direct;

(c) the party who is responsible for drafting the letter of instruction and providing the documents to the expert;

(d) the timetable within which the report is to be prepared, filed and served;

(e) the disclosure of the report to the parties and to any other expert;

---

[20] Ibid, r 25.7(2)(a).

[21] Practice Direction 25C – *Children Proceedings – The use of single joint experts and the process leading to an expert being instructed or expert evidence being put before the court*, para 3.10.

(f) the organisation of, preparation for and conduct of any experts' discussion;

(g) the preparation of a statement of agreement and disagreement by the experts following an experts' discussion;

(h) making available to the court at an early opportunity the expert reports in electronic form;

(i) the attendance of the expert at court to give oral evidence (alternatively, the expert giving his or her evidence in writing or remotely by video link), whether at or for the final hearing or another hearing; unless agreement about the opinions given by the expert is reached at or before the issues resolution hearing or, if no IRH is to be held, by a date specified by the court prior to the hearing at which the expert is to give oral evidence.[22]

5.22 The aim of course, with all the required detail being provided to the court at the first productive case management hearing, is to ensure that the proceedings are completed within the 26-week period, (wherever possible) in care proceedings, and without any unnecessary delay in other family proceedings. Provided practitioners comply with these rigorous requirements and the court robustly and with a 'hands-on' approach deals with applications for expert evidence, cases can be dealt with fairly, but without the extensive delays of the past.

5.23 A salutary note of extreme caution was issued by the President when he said:[23]

'If these requirements are met, the CMH will be effective. If they are not, the CMH will not be effective and the timetable may be irretrievably prejudiced. The case management judge must be rigorous in ensuring that parties comply with the PLO, with FPR Part 25 and with PD25C. If they have not, the case management judge must ensure that any non-compliance is noted at the end of the CMH in the Case Management Order and recorded on the court's electronic Care Monitoring System. Non-compliance which necessitates a Further Case Management Hearing is a serious matter. It may, where appropriate, be penalised in costs.'

5.24 A flowchart to show timetable of an application for use of expert evidence can be seen below.

---

[22] Ibid, para 3.11.
[23] *View from the President's Chambers (3) The process of reform: expert evidence* [2013] Fam Law 816.

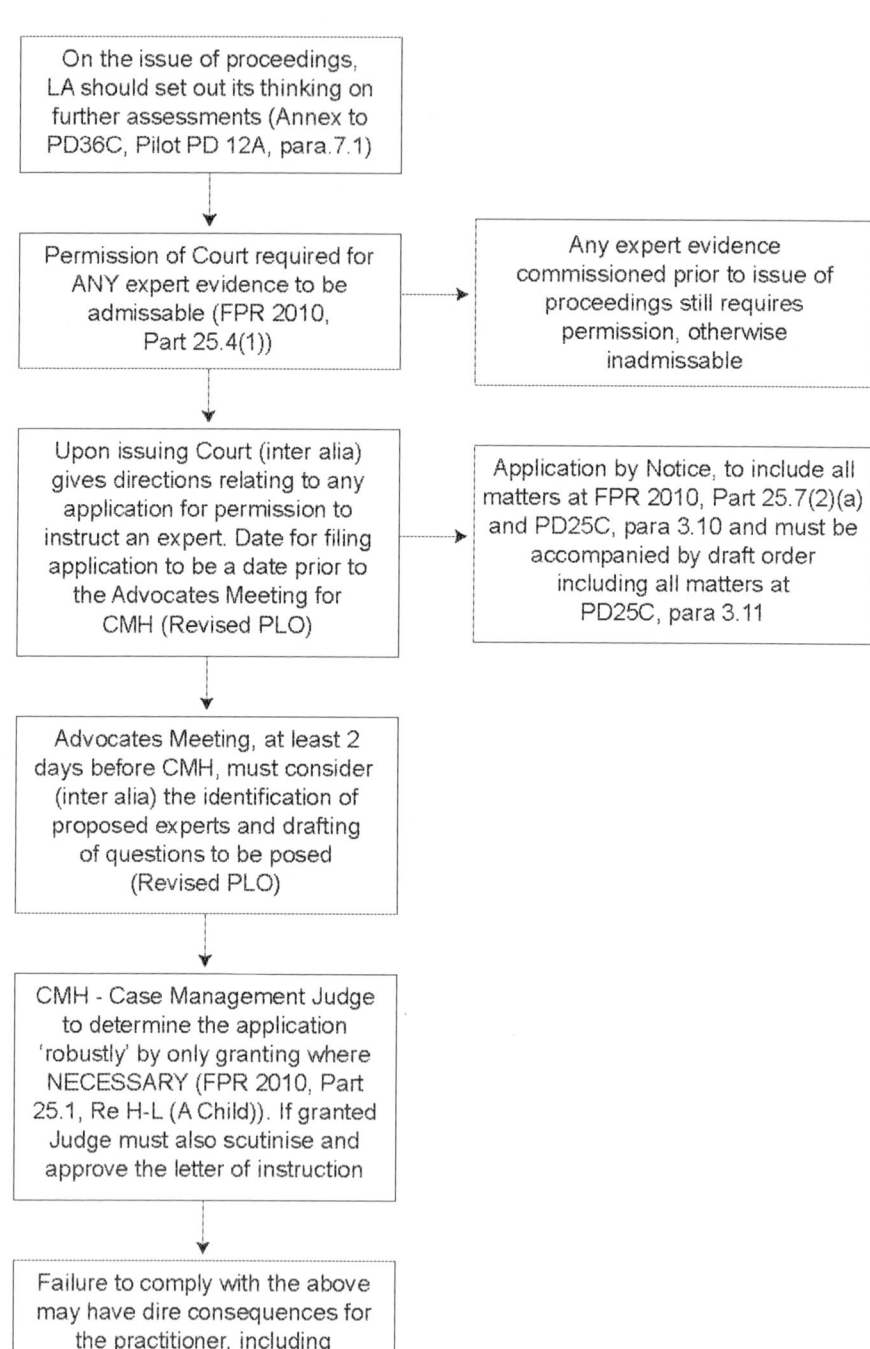

Case study: *X Local Authority v A, B and C*

Background

5.25   X Local Authority issued applications for care orders in respect of 3 children (A, B and C), then aged 6, 2 and 14 months, on 2 September 2013, there having been Children's Services involvement with the family for some years.

5.26   The mother (M) has a history of committing violent offences including convictions in 2005 for battery, arson and common assault. Following the birth of A there was concern about M's parenting skills, in particular relating to her ability to budget and to provide for A's basic needs; that she was suffering from post-natal depression; that the home was untidy and dirty and that she was seen to handle A roughly.

5.27   M and the father (F) of B and C commenced their relationship in 2010, and it was a violent one. Concerns for A and ultimately B and C were at such a level which meant that in 2010 and again in 2012 the children were the subjects of Child In Need Plans following Children's Services receiving referrals regarding domestic violence and neglect. In addition the police were called to the family home on a number of occasions in the Spring/Summer of 2013 following reports of domestic abuse.

5.28   In June 2013 A suffered bruising to her back. Both A and M alleged that it was caused by F hitting her. M made efforts to leave F and assistance was obtained to move her and the children into a women's refuge outside of X Local Authority's area.

5.29   Notwithstanding the separation, on 25 July 2013 M admitted to a social worker that she and the children had stayed away from the refuge the previous night with F. B was observed to have a significant bruise and lump to her forehead and M gave three different explanations for the cause of those injuries. M was arrested for assault and the children were taken into Police Protection and placed with foster carers the same day.

5.30   On 26 July 2013 A and B underwent a child protection medical. A was found to have a yellow bruise to her right hip. She told the paediatrician who undertook the examination that 'daddy did it, he smacked me eight times'. A also had another large bruise to her buttock – she alleged 'my dad punched me really hard'. As a consequence the doctor concluded that there were significant concerns that the injuries were non-accidental in nature. The youngest child, C suffered from cystic fibrosis. There are concerns that her condition is not managed well (or at all) by the parents.

5.31   X Local Authority completed a core assessment of the family between 16 July and 13 August 2013, prior to the commencement of proceedings. At the conclusion of that assessment the social worker identified that:

(a) A full parenting assessment of both parents' ability to provide good enough care for the children was required, which would be undertaken by Children's Social Care.

(b) A psychological assessment of M, (whose current presentation and worrying past history suggested a psychological problem), was necessary as a social worker was not qualified to make any diagnosis.

(c) An opinion from an independent consultant paediatrician, looking at the most likely cause of the injuries to A and B, as well as providing a full overview of all three children's health, (in particular as to C's medical condition) was also required, this information again not being within a social worker's area of expertise.

5.32 Upon issue of the care proceedings, both the solicitor for the children and children's guardian, having reviewed the work of the local authority, concur that input from both a psychologist and from a consultant paediatrician are necessary, and agree that application for permission to instruct these experts should be made. Ultimately, it is agreed that it should be the children's guardian who makes the application.

5.33 The court, upon issue of the proceedings directs that any application for permission to instruct an expert be filed by 10 September 2013, and listed the CMH on 17 September 2013.

C2	**Application**	To be completed by the court

- For permission to start proceedings
- For an order or directions in existing proceedings
- To be joined as, or cease to be, a party in existing family proceedings under the Children Act 1989

To be completed by the court
Name of court
Date issued
Case number

Before completing this form please read the leaflet `**CB1 - Making an application - Children and the Family Courts'**. You can get a copy of from your local court or at www.justice.gov.uk.

- Failure to complete every question or state if it does not apply, could delay the case, as the court will have to ask you to provide the additional information required.
- If there is not enough space please attach separate sheets.
- Cafcass/CAFCASS CYMRU will carry out checks as it considers necessary. See Section J of leaflet CB1 for more information about Cafcass and CAFCASS CYMRU.

1. Summary of application

Your name (the applicant(s))	Messrs Lovely & Co, Solicitors
The respondent's name(s) See Sections G and H of the booklet CB1.	X Local Authority, M & F

Some people need permission to apply - See Section C of the leaflet CB1

Are you applying for permission to issue an application?

- [ ] Yes, and I attach a completed form C100
- [✓] Permission not required
- [ ] Permission already granted

If you are making an application in existing proceedings, please give the existing case number(s).

AB13C001234

Please list the name(s) of the child(ren) and the type(s) of order you are applying for, starting with the oldest. To understand which order to apply for read the booklet CB1 Section D.

Child 1 - Full name of child	Date of birth	Gender	Order(s) applied for
A	1 3 / 0 7 / 2 0 0 7	☐ Male ☐ Female	Part 25 FPR 2010 & PD25C
Relationship to applicant(s)	**Relationship to respondent(s)**		
Child Client	Local Authority/Mother/Father		

Child 2 - Full name of child	Date of birth	Gender	Order(s) applied for
B	2 0 / 0 6 / 2 0 1 1	☐ Male ☐ Female	Part 25 FPR 2010 & PD25C
Relationship to applicant(s)	**Relationship to respondent(s)**		
Child Client	Local Authority/Mother/Father		

Child 3 - Full name of child	Date of birth	Gender	Order(s) applied for
C	2 8 / 0 8 / 2 0 1 2	☐ Male ☐ Female	Part 25 FPR 2010 & PD25C
Relationship to applicant(s)	Relationship to respondent(s)		
Child Client	Local Authority/Mother/Father		

2. About you (the applicant(s)

	Applicant 1 (You)	**Applicant 2 (if applicable)**
Full names	Messrs Lovely & Co, Solicitors	
Previous names (if any)	n/a	
Gender	☐ Male ☐ Female	☐ Male ☐ Female
Date of birth (If under 18 read section R of leaflet CB1)		
Place of birth (town/county/country)	n/a	

If you do not wish your address to be made known to the respondent, leave the details below blank and complete Confidential contact details Form C8.

Address	1-2 High Street Anytown	
	Postcode A B 1 2 C D	Postcode
Home telephone number	01234 567890	
Mobile telephone number		
Email address	lovelyandco@solicitors.co.uk	
Have you lived at this address for more than 5 years?	☐ Yes ☐ No	☐ Yes ☐ No

If No, please provide details of all previous addresses you have lived at for the last 5 years.

If you do not wish your contact details to be made known to the Respondent, leave the details blank and complete Confidential contact details Form C8		

3. The respondents

Sections G and H of the the booklet **'CB1 - Making an application - Children and the Family Courts'** explain who a respondent is.

	RESPONDENT 1	**RESPONDENT 2**
Full names	M	F
Previous names (if known)		
Gender	☐ Male ☑ Female	☑ Male ☐ Female
Date of birth (If party under 18 read section R of leaflet CB1)		
Place of birth (town/county/country)		
Address (to which documents relating to this application should be sent)	c/o: Care Solicitors 4-5 High Street Anytown	c/o: Longstanding Lawyers 7-8 High Street Anytown
	Postcode A B 1 3 C D	Postcode A B 1 4 C D
Home telephone number	01234 987654	01234 246810
Mobile telephone number		
Email address	care@solicitors.co.uk	longstanding@lawyers.co.uk
Have they lived at this address for more than 5 years?	☐ Yes ☐ No ☐ Don't know	☐ Yes ☐ No ☐ Don't know

If No, please provide details of all previous addresses for the last 5 years below (if known, including the dates and starting with the most recent)

	RESPONDENT 3	**RESPONDENT 4**
Full names	X Local Authority	
Previous names (if known)		
Gender	☐ Male ☐ Female	☐ Male ☐ Female
Date of birth (If party under 18 read section R of leaflet CB1)		
Place of birth (town/county/country)	n/a	
Address (to which documents relating to this application should be sent)	Legal Services County Hall Anytown	
	Postcode A B 1 7 X Y	Postcode
Home telephone number	01234 906050	
Mobile telephone number		
Email address	xlocalauthority@careproceedings.com	
Have they lived at this address for more than 5 years?	☐ Yes ☐ No ☐ Don't know	☐ Yes ☐ No ☐ Don't know

If No, please provide details of all previous addresses for the last 5 years below (if known, including the dates and starting with the most recent)

4. Others who should be given notice

There may be other people who should be notified of your application, for example, someone who cares for the child but is not a parent. Sections G and I of the the booklet **'CB1 - Making an application - Children and the Family Courts'** explain who others are.

	PERSON 1	**PERSON 2**
Full names		
Previous names (if known)		
Gender	☐ Male ☐ Female	☐ Male ☐ Female
Date of birth		
Address		
	Postcode	Postcode
Please state their relationship to the children listed on page 1. If their relationship is not the same to each child please state their relationship to each child.		

5. Solicitors details

Do you have a solicitor acting for you? ☑ Yes ☐ No   If No, see section R of leaflet CB1 for more information

If Yes, please give the following details

Your solicitor's name: Miss S Lovely

Name of firm: Lovely & Co

Address: 1-2 High Street
Anytown

Postcode: A B 1 | 2 C D

Telephone number: 01234 567890

Fax number: 01234 567891

DX number: 123 ANYTOWN

Solicitor's Reference: SL/AB

Email address: lovelyandco@solicitors.co.uk

6. Details of application

Please give brief details about what you are applying for and your reasons for making the application.

1. Permission to instruct a psychologist to undertake an assessment of M to ascertain the extent of M's psychological difficulties and how they may impact on her ability to parent her children - full details to be provided in the Notice which is to be filed by 11 am on 16 September 2013

2. Permission to instruct a Consultant Paediatrician to provide an opinion as to the likely cause of bruising to Client Children A & B, as well as providing an opinion as to the overall health of all three children - full details to be provided in the Notice which is to be filed by 11 am on 16 September 2013

7. Attending the court

Section N of the the booklet **'CB1 - Making an application - Children and the Family Courts'** provides information about attending court.

If you require an interpreter, you must tell the court now so that one can be arranged.

Do you or any of the parties
need an interpreter at court?
☐ Yes   ☑ No

If Yes, please specify the language and dialect:

If attending the court, do you or
any of the parties involved have
a disability for which you require
special assistance or special
facilities?
☐ Yes   ☑ No

If Yes, please say what the needs are

Please say whether the court
needs to make any special
arrangements for you to attend
court (e.g. providing you with a
separate waiting room from the
respondent or other security
provisions).

Court staff may get in touch with you about the requirements

8. Statement of truth

The applicant believes that the facts stated in this application are true.

*delete
as appropriate

*I am duly authorised by the applicant to sign this statement.

Print full name | Miss S Lovely

Name of applicant solicitors firm | Lovely & Co

Signed

Dated | 1 0 / 0 9 / 2 0 1 3

(Applicant) (Applicant's solicitor)
(Respondent)(Respondent's solicitor)

Position or office held
(If signing on behalf of firm or
company)

**Proceedings for contempt of court may be brought against a person who
makes or causes to be made, a false statement in a document verified by a
statement of truth.**

What to do now

If you are applying for permission to issue an application

☐ Check you have attached copies of the form C100 application and form C1A if appropriate

☐ Check any necessary documents are attached to the form C100 application

For all applications

☐ Check you have completed and signed Section 8 of this form

☐ Check you have attached the correct fee. The leaflet `EX50 County court fees' provides information about court fees you will have to pay.

Now take or send your application with the correct fee and correct number of copies (one copy for the court, one copy for Cafcass/CAFCASS CYMRU and one for each party or other person) to the court.

Court fees

You may be exempt from paying all or part of the fee. The combined booklet and application form `EX160A Court Fees - Do you have to pay them' gives more information. You can get a copy from the court or download a copy from our website at www.justice.gov.uk

5.34 An advocates' meeting takes place on 12 September 2013, the children's solicitor having circulated the CVs of three paediatricians and two psychologists. The paediatricians are all able to provide their reports within 7–8 weeks of receiving a letter of instruction and the case papers. The psychologists can provide their reports within 4–6 weeks of instruction. They each indicate that they are prepared to accept instructions at the Legal Aid Agency current rates. Their availability to attend court to give evidence, either in person or via video-link, is also obtained.

5.35 The following notice (including a list of the proposed questions for the experts) is lodged with the court by 11 am the day before the CMH, namely 16 September 2013.

On Behalf of: The Children (3rd, 4th and 5th Respondents)

THE ANYTOWN FAMILY COURT   Case No: AB13C001234

BETWEEN

A LOCAL AUTHORITY   Applicant

And

M   1st Respondent

And

F   2nd Respondent

And

A, B and C   3rd, 4th and 5th
Respondents

(by their Children's Guardian)

**NOTICE OF APPLICATION FOR PERMISSION TO INSTRUCT EXPERTS
ON BEHALF OF THE CHILDREN**
(Dated 16 September 2013)

THE NECESSITY FOR ASSESSMENT(S): The Law

1.   The leading case in relation to directions under s 38(6) Children Act 1989 is that of *Re S (A Child)* [2011] EWCA Civ 812. In that case Black LJ stated that there is no automatic right for a parent who is facing permanent removal of their child to have the assessment of their choice. In essence the relevant question was whether the assessment in question would assist the judge in reaching the right conclusion at a final hearing.

2.   The Court of Appeal in this case referred to the case of *Re C (Interim Care Order: Residential Assessment)* [1997] 1 FLR 1 in which Lord Brown Wilkinson stated that the purpose of s 38(6) is to enable the court to obtain information necessary for its own decision notwithstanding the control over the child which in all other aspects rests with the Local Authority.

3.   In considering a review of the case-law, the Court of Appeal also considered the case of *Re G (Interim Care Order: Residential Assessment)*

[2005] UKHL 68 and endorsed comments of Baroness Hale (as she then was) in respect of s 38(6) applications as follows:

> 'the purpose of those provisions is, therefore, not only to enable the court to obtain information that it needs but also to enable the court to control the information gathering activities of others, but the emphasis is always on obtaining information.'

4. Later on in her judgment, Baroness Hale comments that the court must think early and clearly about what assessments are necessary to decide a case and that furthermore in many cases:

> 'the Local Authority should be able to make its own core assessments and the Child's Guardian to make an independent assessment in the interests of the child. Further or other assessments should only be commissioned if they can bring something important to the case which neither the Local Authority nor the Guardian is able to bring.'

5. In *Re L (A Child) and H (A Child)* [2010] EWCA Civ 213 Lord Justice Wall stated what is equally important is that the hearing of proceedings should be fair and that the court should have before it all of the relevant evidence necessary for the decision. Further:

> 'as I see the case it is manifestly in the interests M to see if his parents are able to care for him and it is a responsibility of the court to ensure that it has the best evidence of which to reach a conclusion about his welfare.'

It is also:

> 'procedurally fair for his parents to be given the opportunity to demonstrate that they can overcome the manifest difficulties and care for him and it would in my judgment be unfair were they to be denied that opportunity.'

6. Part 25 of the Family Procedure Rules 2010 (as amended) is clear:

> 'Expert evidence will be restricted to that which in the opinion of the court is **necessary** to assist the court to resolve the proceedings.'

7. The President of the Family Division, Sir James Munby, has determined the meaning of 'necessary' in the case of *Re H-L (A Child)* [2013] EWCA Civ 655 as follows:

> 'The short answer is that 'necessary, means necessary. It is after all, an ordinary English word. It is a familiar expression nowadays in family law, not least because of the central role it plays, for example, in Article 8 of the European Convention and the wider Strasbourg jurisprudence. If elaboration is required, what precisely does it mean? That was a question considered, albeit in a rather different context, *in Re P (Placement Orders: Parental Consent)* [2008] EWCA Civ 535, [2008] 2 FLR 625, paras [120], [125]. This court said it "has a meaning lying somewhere between 'indispensable' on the

one hand and 'useful', 'reasonable' or 'desirable' on the other hand" having "the connotation of the imperative, what is demanded rather than what is merely optional or reasonable or desirable." In my judgment, that is the meaning, the connotation the word "necessary" has in rule 25.1.'

TYPE OF EXPERT SOUGHT

1. Consultant Paediatrician to provide:
    (a) an opinion as to the likely cause of bruising to A & B, and;
    (b) a full overview of all three children's medical position

EXPERT(S) PROPOSED:

Name	Availability/Filing date	Fees	CV
Dr AM Kindly	File report within 8 weeks of instruction Available to attend court (either in person or via videolink) to give evidence on Mondays & Wednesdays in January & February 2014	£2500 + vat (estimate) £135 hourly rate	Attached
Dr V Scary	File report within 7–8 weeks of instruction Available to attend court to give evidence (by videolink) on Fridays only, from March onwards	£2750 + vat (estimate) £130 hourly rate	Attached
Dr U Dunnit	File report within 8 weeks of instruction Available to attend court to give evidence (either in person or via videolink) any day from 17 March 2014 onwards	£2500 + vat (estimate) £135 hourly rate	Attached

RELEVANCE/PURPOSE OF ASSESSMENT:

1. A and B have sustained suspected non-accidental injuries. An opinion from this type of expert is necessary to assist the court in determining whether the injuries are in fact non-accidental.

2. The extent of C's condition and the prognosis for her future is not known.

3. A paediatric overview will clarify the extent of all the children's health needs.

SUGGESTED QUESTIONS:

1. Please provide a paediatric overview of the medical notes and records of the children.

2. Please provide an opinion as to the likely cause of the injuries (bruising) to A & B.

3. Please consider what illnesses (if any) the children may suffer from and provide your opinion as to the long-term prognosis and what support (if any) that will be required.

4. Please advise whether you recommend the instruction of any further experts.

RESPONSIBILITY FOR INSTRUCTION:

Solicitor for the Children, Messrs Lovely & Co

BASIS OF INSTRUCTIONS AND FEE APPORTIONMENT:

It is proposed that the expert will be instructed jointly with the costs being shared equally between all the parties.

1. **Clinical Psychologist** to undertake a psychological assessment of M and provide an opinion as to diagnosis, prognosis and impact on her capacity to parent

EXPERT(S) PROPOSED:

Name	Availability/Filing date	Fees	CV
Miss V Understanding	Filing date: 4-5 weeks from receipt of letter of instruction and case papers Available to attend court to give evidence in person, on most days of the week, if given 4 weeks' notice of date required	£1220–£1440 £110 hourly rate	Attached
Mr Del Ecate	4–5 weeks from letter of instruction & receiving full bundle. Available to attend court (either in person or via videolink) on Mondays or Tuesdays if given 4 weeks' notice of date required	£2410.50 + vat £117 hourly rate	Attached

RELEVANCE/PURPOSE OF ASSESSMENT:

1. M has a history of violent behaviour and alleges that she is also a victim of domestic violence. An investigation into whether these issues are caused by her psychological make-up and/or mental well-being is required.

2. M has suffered/is suffering from post-natal depression.

3. In the light of the above an expert opinion as to the impact of these issues on M's ability to safely parent her children is also necessary.

SUGGESTED QUESTIONS:

1. Please carry out a full psychological assessment in relation to M.
2. Please consider whether M suffers from any learning difficulty, mental illness or disability.
3. Please consider whether domestic violence has impacted upon her emotionally.
4. Staff at the refuge have indicated that M on occasion seems depressed. Please consider whether she is suffering from depression and if so, what treatment/therapy she requires.
5. Please consider M's relationship with A.
6. Please consider whether M can prioritise the needs of her children over her own needs.
7. Please consider whether M understands the concerns of the Local Authority, and whether she is capable of engaging with the Local Authority.
8. Please provide any other information that you feel is relevant.

RESPONSIBILITY FOR INSTRUCTION:

Solicitor for the Children, Messrs Lovely & Co.

BASIS OF INSTRUCTIONS AND FEE APPORTIONMENT:

It is proposed that the expert will be instructed jointly with the costs being shared equally between all the parties.

MISS S LOVELY
Messrs Lovely & Co
Solicitors for the Children
16 September 2013

AT THE CASE MANAGEMENT HEARING

5.36 With all of the information before it, namely:

(a) The type of experts requested, including their names, CVs and availability for both filing their reports and attending to give evidence;

(b) The succinct reasons why those experts were necessary, including providing an analysis of the legal position, and;

(c) A list of the proposed questions to be asked of the experts, which could be simply scrutinised

the case management judge was able to determine the applications quickly and carefully. Indeed such careful preparation by the children's solicitor allowed the parents to analyse their positions on the instruction of these experts, and they too formed the view that their reports were indeed necessary.

5.37 The judge being persuaded that the reports were necessary and determining that questions were appropriate (and not voluminous or repetitive), the letters of instruction, together with all the case papers were dispatched to the experts on 20 September 2013.

5.38 The proceedings having been issued on 2 September 2013 meant that the 26 week date for concluding the case was 3 March 2014. By instructing the experts at the first CMH, their reports were all completed by 15 November 2013, which then allowed for careful consideration of their conclusions by all the parties, but in particular the Local Authority and the children's guardian. All issues could be dealt with within a composite hearing, and whilst both M and F sought to persuade the court that the children should return to their individual care, and both vehemently denied that the injuries to A and B were anything other than accidental, because robust case management decisions had been taken at the outset of the case, and the judge had been greatly assisted by the presentation of the applications for permission to instruct expert evidence by the lawyers, a fair and final hearing of 5 days was able to conclude the proceedings for the children, enabling permanent long-term plans for them to be put in place by 31 January 2014 – 20 weeks after issue.

THE QUALITY AND LENGTH OF EXPERT REPORTS

5.39 The use of independent experts, is by no means a thing of the past, and there is and will continue to be a need for them to assist the court. In those cases, it is important that the reports received are sufficiently focussed and concise to ensure that pages and pages of repetitive information are no longer commonplace, lengthening the amount of judicial reading time, and thus inevitably, the length of the proceedings themselves.

5.40 The President expressed his view as to why too many expert reports were unnecessarily and unhelpfully long, again within his *View from the President's Chambers (3)*.[24] He gave two reasons:

(a) too many questions are asked, which are either unnecessary or repetitive or both; and

(b) the reports are simply too long, because they contain too much history and too much factual narrative.

5.41 The first problem was not the fault of the experts, but rather the court and the parties in producing unwieldy letters of instruction. He was clear that the responsibility for putting a stop to this practice rests with the case management judge. Practice Direction 25C sets out the obligations on all the parties in this regard and to ensure compliance, if the form of the letter of instruction and the formulation of the questions has not been fixed by the end of the CMH, the President encourages the case management judge to '... direct that the parties' legal representatives are not to leave the court precincts until they have prepared a final draft which has been approved by the judge'.[25]

5.42 As far as the quality and length of reports is concerned, the President was clear:[26]

> 'Expert reports can in many cases be much shorter than hitherto, and they should be more focused on analysis and opinion than on history and narrative. In short, expert reports must be succinct, focused and analytical. But they must also of course be evidence-based.'

5.43 It is the duty of the case management judge to take appropriate steps to encourage compliance by experts with the requirements of Practice Direction 25B, and the judge should not be afraid to set limits on the length of the report, nor to remind the expert that they should:

(a) '... confine the opinion to matters material to the issues in the case and in relation only to the questions that are within the expert's expertise (skill and experience)';[27]

(b) 'include a statement identifying the document(s) containing the material instructions and the substance of any oral instructions and, as far as necessary to explain any opinions or conclusions expressed in the report, summarising the facts and instructions which are material to the conclusions and opinions expressed';[28] and

(c) 'contain a summary of the expert's conclusions and opinions'.[29]

---

[24] *View from the President's Chambers (3) The process of reform: expert evidence*, [2013] Fam Law 816.

[25] Ibid.

[26] Ibid, p 10.

[27] Practice Direction 25B, para 4.1(e).

[28] Ibid, para 9.1(b).

[29] Ibid, para 9.1(h).

5.44 Equally, it is suggested that it is incumbent upon practitioners to be proactive in reminding case management judges of the importance of directing instructed experts in this way. Judges do (when necessary) and should set limits on the length of statements they receive in evidence, as well as restricting advocates in the length of skeleton arguments, case summaries and the like. They shouldn't be afraid to deal with experts in the same way!

THE FINAL RECOMMENDED STANDARDS

5.45 The Ministry of Justice and Family Justice Council have now concluded their recommendations and finalised the standards expected of expert witnesses in children's cases – they bear repeating, (and remembering):[30]

'Subject to any order made by the court, expert witnesses involved in family proceedings (involving children) in England and Wales, whatever their field of practice or country of origin, must comply with the standards (1–11)

1. The expert's area of competence is appropriate to the issue(s) upon which the court has identified that an opinion is required, and relevant experience is evidenced in their CV.

2. The expert has been active in the area of work or practice, (as a practitioner or an academic who is subject to peer appraisal), has sufficient experience of the issues relevant to the instant case, and is familiar with the breadth of current practice or opinion.

3. The expert has working knowledge of the social, developmental, cultural norms and accepted legal principles applicable to the case presented at initial enquiry, and has the cultural competence skills to deal with the circumstances of the case.

4. The expert is up-to-date with Continuing Professional Development appropriate to their discipline and expertise, and is in continued engagement with accepted supervisory mechanisms relevant to their practice.

5. If the expert's current professional practice is regulated by a UK statutory body, they are in possession of a current licence to practise or equivalent.

6. If the expert's area of professional practice is not subject to statutory registration (eg: child psychotherapy, systemic family therapy, mediation, and experts in exclusively academic appointments) the expert should demonstrate appropriate qualifications and/or registration with a relevant professional body on a case by case basis. Registering bodies usually provide a code of conduct and professional standards and should be accredited by the Professional Standards Authority for Health and Social Care. If the expertise is academic in nature (eg: regarding evidence of cultural influences) then no statutory registration is required (even if this includes direct contact or interviews with individuals) but consideration should be given to appropriate professional accountability.

7. The expert is compliant with any necessary safeguarding requirements, information security expectations, and carries professional indemnity insurance.

---

[30] Joint Ministry of Justice and Family Justice Council Response: *Standards for Expert Witnesses in Children's Proceedings in the Family Courts* (8 November 2013), pp 35–36.

8.   If the expert's current professional practice is outside the UK they can demonstrate that they are compliant with FJC 'Guidelines for the instruction of medical experts from overseas in family cases' (December 2011).

9.   The expert has undertaken appropriate training, updating or quality assurance activity – including actively seeking feedback from cases in which they have provided evidence – relevant to the role of the expert in the family courts in England and Wales within the last year.

10.   The expert has a working knowledge of, and complies with, the requirements of Practice Directions relevant to providing reports for and giving evidence to the family courts in England and Wales. This includes compliance with the requirement to identify where their opinion on the instant case lies in relation to other accepted mainstream views and the overall spectrum of opinion in the UK.

Expectations in relation to experts' fees

11.   The expert should state their hourly rate in advance of agreeing to accept instruction, and give an estimate of the number of hours the report is likely to take. This will assist the legal representative to apply expeditiously to the Legal Aid Agency if prior authority is to be sought in a publicly funded case.'

5.46 Provided the standards set both by Practice Direction 25B and these recommended by the MOJ and FJC, experts reports can and should be much more streamlined, analytical and ultimately helpful to the court in determining the important issues.

FUNDING OF INDEPENDENT EXPERT EVIDENCE – THE LEGAL AID AGENCY

5.47 In addition to the Final Recommended Standards for independent experts, came a review of their remuneration by the Legal Aid Agency, culminating on 2 December 2013 in a reduction in the rates payable to them in cases where the parties are publicly funded. The Legal Aid Agency's published guidance states:[31]

'The Legal Aid Agency (LAA) will not pay fees or rates in excess of those listed in the Remuneration Regulations unless we consider it reasonable in exceptional circumstances and have granted prior authority to exceed the fees or rates.

Exceptional circumstances are where the expert's evidence is key to the client's case and either –

(a)   the complexity of the material is such that an expert with a high level of seniority is required; or

(b)   the material is of such a specialised and unusual nature that only very few experts are available to provide the necessary evidence

---

[31]   Guidance on the Remuneration of Expert Witnesses – Version 2: November 2013.

Where a rate set out in the Remuneration Regulations has been exceeded and no authority to exceed the rates has previously been granted the LAA will disallow any fees exceeding the maximum rates.'[32]

5.48 Both the implementation of the final recommended standards for experts and the reduction in the fees payable led to concerns being raised as to the impact on the quality (and quantity) of suitable experts able to provide 'necessary' evidence to the court.

5.49 By example, prior to 2 December 2013 the LAA rate for a child psychiatrist was £135 per hour. This is now reduced to £108 per hour, and is subject to a maximum of 25 hours being allowed.

5.50 On Monday 9 December 2013 BBC Newsnight broadcast its investigation into the changes[33] taking into account and referencing the results of a survey of its members undertaken by the Consortium of Expert Witnesses to the Family Courts, which showed that 27% had stopped family court work altogether because of the changes, with a further 9% saying that they planned to stop and 19% saying that they would not work at the lower rate, (and so would continue to charge at the 'old rate', necessitating an increase in applications for prior authority). The head of the Consortium, Dr Judith Freedman (Child Psychiatrist) told Newsnight:

> 'Expert rates were cut significantly in October 2011, we never thought that they needed to be cut any further, some people said they were unable to work at the cut rate, but most people found a way to continue working, but it is the further cut we think is destructive.'

5.51 In view of this position, it is right that there is a diminishing pool of experts willing to work at the reduced fee levels[34] with the authors' own experience in practice being that in an increasing number of cases (particularly those involving non-accidental injury allegations, and thus the instruction of radiologists/neuro-radiologists/paediatricians) prior authority from the Legal Aid Agency is having to be sought. Such applications can take up to 4–5 weeks to reach a decision, which of course bites significantly into the 26-week timetable, and by no means encompasses the ethos of the new regime. In many cases prior authority is being refused, the LAA finding that it is not 'reasonable in exceptional circumstances' and Local Authorities are being asked to 'pick up the shortfall' between the old and new rates. It remains to be seen for how much longer Local Authorities will continue to be prepared to meet this funding gap. It is anticipated that sooner or later, they will seek to challenge the LAA, but in the meantime there will continue to be difficulties and pressures in securing funding to provide the evidence which the court has determined is 'necessary' for it to make decisions in a case.

---

[32] Ibid, p 3.
[33] See http://www.familylaw.co.uk/articles/New-cuts-to-experts-fees-compromises -care-cases-101213-654.
[34] Guidance on the Remuneration of Expert Witnesses – Version 2: November 2013, Annex 1 (The Civil Legal Aid (Remuneration)(Amendment) Regulations 2013: Experts' fees and rates.

5.52 In cases without local authority involvement, and in cases where one party is 'privately paying' and the other is funded by Legal Aid, the issue is even more stark, and in an increasing number of cases the court is having to determine the issues without evidence it has decided is 'necessary'.

Re R (Children: *Temporary Leave to Remove from Jurisdiction*)[35]

5.53 In this case, HHJ Clifford Bellamy, sitting as a Deputy Judge of the High Court, Leicester District Registry made heavy criticism of the LAA, describing it as 'wasteful and inefficient' in dealing with an application for funding an expert in Indian family law.

5.54 The court had determined that a report from such an expert, costing up to £2,500 was necessary for it to determine an application by the mother of four children to take them to her birth home in India. The father, from whom the mother is separated, opposed the application as he feared that the mother would not bring the children back to England.

5.55 HHJ Bellamy had directed that the costs of the expert opinion should be borne by the mother and the Children's Guardian, and as they are publicly funded therefore as a disbursement on each public funding certificate.

5.56 Application was made to the LAA for prior authority, which was refused on the basis that it determined the costs should be 'equally shared'.

5.57 Subsequent to this decision, the case came before Mrs Justice Eleanor King for further case management, where she determined:

> 'And upon the Court observing that:
>
> a.   the expert's report directed at paragraph 1 of this order is absolutely necessary for the proper determination of this case; this is both the view of the learned Judge and represents settled authority from the Court of Appeal; the case cannot be fairly decided without the expert;
> b.   the report is appropriately the instruction of the mother and the Children's Guardian; it is not properly the instruction of the father who has already filed evidence in relation to the disputed international legal issue; the proposed report does not, accordingly, 'support' the father's case; rather it is obtained by the mother to meet the case brought by the father, and is necessary for the Children's Guardian, in order that she can advise the court from a position of informed neutrality.'

Notwithstanding this, the further application by the mother's solicitor for authority to the LAA was met with refusal.

---

[35]   [2014] EWHC 643 (Fam).

5.58 In Judge Bellamy's judgment he said that it was 'simply unacceptable' that King J's case management directions were 'effectively over ridden' by the LAA. He was concerned about the 'negative, costly and unhelpful impact' of the LAA's actions in the case, and added; 'if this case is at all illustrative of the way the LAA normally discharges its responsibilities then that is deeply troubling.'

5.59 Without the expert evidence which the court had determined on more than one occasion was 'necessary' for it to decide the issues the only order it could make was that the mother should not be allowed to take the children to India as there were not sufficient safeguarding measures in place.

5.60 In light of the criticisms, the judge directed that the solicitor for the children forward a copy of the judgment to the Chief Executive of the LAA, with an order that he respond to it, in writing, within 28 days. The LAA indicated that it would so respond, as directed.

JG v The Lord Chancellor & others[36]

5.61 The decision of the Court of Appeal in this case was handed down on 21 May 2014. Lady Justice Black gave the leading judgment. The child's appeal against the decision of Ryder J (as he then was) reported at [2013] 2 FLR 1174 was allowed. In place of Ryder J's dismissal of the child's judicial review claim the Court of Appeal substituted a declaration that the Legal Services Commission's (now Legal Aid Agency's) decision not to meet the whole of the cost of the expert's report was unlawful.

5.62 This is a welcome decision but it is important to keep in mind that the appeal was decided on the basis that the children's guardian had initiated the application for an expert assessment and the order was not a device to get round the inability of the parents to share the cost of the assessment.

SOCIAL WORKERS AND CAFCASS OFFICERS – ALREADY INSTRUCTED EXPERTS

5.63 The President has from the inception of the reforms relating to expert evidence, made it very clear that the court must not forget that within care proceedings, there are already two experts instructed – the social workers involved in the case and most likely those who instigated the proceedings and the independent 'eyes and ears of the court' – the children's guardian, whose own experience and ultimate analysis of the issues are invaluable to the court in determining the case and making the right decisions in the best interests of the children.

---

[36] [2014] EWCA Civ 656.

5.64 There has been much collaboration between Cafcass and the Association of Directors of Children's Services (ADCS), together with the Association of Directors of Adult Social Services (ADASS) culminating in the production of *Good Practice Guidance for Social Work Practised in the Family Courts*. The aim being to ensure that the evidence and analysis being provided to the court is of such quality that in a large number of cases it will not be 'necessary' to obtain any further expert evidence.

GOOD PRACTICE GUIDANCE FOR SOCIAL WORK PRACTISED IN THE FAMILY COURTS

5.65 It is right to say that this Guidance can only work effectively if the Social Workers involved are familiar with the relevant legislation, Practice Directions and Regulations, and the authors of the Guidance (Anthony Douglas CBE, Chief Executive of Cafcass, Andrew Webb, Vice President of ADCS and Sarah Pickup, President of ADASS) make it clear that this is the starting point.

5.66 The Guidance operates during the pre-proceedings, the care proceedings and the post-proceedings stages of a family court case. It states:[37]

'These stages can encompass the child's entire time in care, so can also be seen as three stages of the child's journey through the care system.'

Pre-proceedings

'A short period in care can help a family stay together. If it is made available at a time of crisis or great need and if the period in care is accompanied by support to overcome the crisis or risk the child faces.'[38]

5.67 It is vital therefore that during this time the social worker is beginning to analyse the position, undertake an assessment of need, and put together a short care plan. This will form a strong base from which to go further if it becomes clear that it is not possible to safely manage the concerns about the child within a child protection plan, and that care proceedings are required.[39]

'At this stage of a case, the evidence base for the level of harm should be reviewed within the local authority and brought together in the form of a threshold analysis. This includes all necessary assessments, including specialist health assessments.'

5.68 The Guidance recommends that to ensure this is as complete as possible (as well as being given the best chance of successfully assisting the court, if that becomes necessary) that at this early stage pre-proceedings meetings with parents take place and are fully minuted. This is important as it allows for the parents to be legally represented, with funding available from the Legal Aid

---

[37] *Good Practice Guidance for Social Work Practised in the Family Courts*, para 1.4, p 1.
[38] Ibid, para 2.1, p 2.
[39] Ibid, para 2.2, p 2.

Agency for this purpose, and very importantly it also allows for the joint instruction of external, independent experts, if the case requires it. If these simple steps are taken, with early co-operation and information-sharing between the local authority and the parents' legal representatives, it can and should avoid contests in court once proceedings are issued.

The threshold analysis

5.69 The Guidance provides:[40]

> 'A threshold analysis is based upon the following areas of social work practice:

- An analysis of the child's life to date, including the trend in risk/s to the child, the trend in child development/health/wellbeing and the impact on the child of parental behaviour e.g signs of hidden (and usually cumulative) harm such as anxiety and hyper-vigilance as a result of living in a neglectful or dangerous household.
- An analysis of local authority intervention/support and its impact and also the impact of other interventions.
- A chronology of key events and incidents in the child's life, with an interpretation of that chronology built into the case analysis. Taxonomies of exposure to risk, neglect and domestic violence, for example, can be useful to include.
- Analysis of the parenting capacity gap, with the reasons for professional pessimism if the judgment is that the gap either cannot be bridged at all, or cannot be bridged in the child's timescale.
- The plan for the child flows directly from the evidence base in the threshold analysis. The plan also has to consider the viability of the local care system to effectively support a particular child. Such a viability analysis is crucial to which of the five early permanence options for a child in care are proposed, namely:-
  1. Safe reunification at home, assumed to be permanent
  2. Permanence away from home with approved (under the requisite regulations) relatives
  3. Permanence with foster parent/s
  4. Permanence with a special guardian/s
  5. Permanence with adoptive parent/s.'

5.70 It is recommended by the Guidance that a social worker from Cafcass become involved in the case to advise the local authority at this stage, giving an early independent view on behalf of the child, and assisting in the formulation of future plans, (which should be parallel plans), unless it is obvious that early permanence demands a 'single proposition' plan. The aim always being of having as much work done as possible before the case comes before a court ('front loading'), but that work being an evidence-based analysis aimed at assisting the court in making the important decisions needed, within the 26-week period.

---

[40] Ibid, para 2.4, pp 2–3.

5.71 To ensure timely intervention and action throughout the process, the pre-proceedings stage is envisaged to last no longer than 3 months.

The care proceedings

5.72 A highly effective social worker, who will assist the court without the need for further expert evidence, needs the following core skills to be able to support the judge in their active case management role:[41]

> '•   A strong grounding in child development and the impact of parental difficulties on that development
> •   An understanding of effective, evidence-based interventions and how they can be used with families, with progress effectively monitored and recorded
> •   Assessment and analytical skills, so that the key issues are analysed, as this supports robust judicial decision-making
> •   Producing high quality social work statements, chronologies and court reports
> •   Giving evidence in court
> •   Discussing and negotiating issues with parties to the case so as to move the case on as quickly as possible within the child's timescale
> •   Refining the case analysis if new information comes to light.'

5.73 Getting all of this right (together with a strong case analysis from the children's guardian) will give the court confidence that the decisions it makes, will be implemented positively for the child, in particular that the care plan will be followed through – even if circumstances mean that it has to be changed at some point in the future.

Post-proceedings

5.74 The Guidance makes it clear, that whilst the 'role of the court and the role of officers of the court, such as Cafcass practitioners, ends when the case ends'[42] the role of the local authority continues, with support being provided to the child for as long as is needed. There should also be a continual monitoring of the 'child's journey' with as much care as was taken in both the pre and care proceedings stages, and 'just as all steps should be taken to prevent a child coming into care, so all steps should be taken to discharge a child from care into permanent family support, unless remaining in care is a positive care plan in its own right for good reasons'.[43]

5.75 In addition and crucially, the Guidance advises very strongly that support and continued engagement with parents who have ultimately been unable to care for their children be provided by social workers. It is well known that a significant number of parents in care proceedings go on to have more children, who often become the subject of pre-birth concerns and assessments. Looking

---

[41]   Ibid, para 3.1, p 4.
[42]   Ibid, para 4.1, p 5.
[43]   Ibid, para 4.2, p 5.

to the future and either looking to avoid further care proceedings, or if those proceedings are inevitable it is vital that 'a care plan for the child and a care plan for the parent [are put in place] to ensure as far as possible that the next child born to a parent judged as being having a hard-to-bridge parenting capacity gap, has the best possible chance of being born and looked after safely at home'.[44]

THE INDEPENDENT SOCIAL WORKER ASSESSMENT

5.76 In essence – a good social worker, supported by an effective local authority and overseen by the children's guardian, will obviate the need for applications for independent social worker assessments. If however the Guidance is not implemented and 'front loading' analysis and assessment by the social worker on the ground is not available to the court, it is almost inevitable that such applications will be made on behalf of parents.

5.77 A study published by Oxford University[45] in September 2013, canvassed the views of 23 family court judges in England and Wales, and found that many judges felt independent social workers (ISWs) made up for deficiencies in the quality and timeliness of local authority assessments. Most of the judges questioned said ISWs were usually called when local authorities had failed to deliver an assessment, had produced inadequate assessments, lacked the necessary expertise or could not meet the court's timescales.

5.78 It remains to be seen whether, in the light of the Guidance, local authority employed social workers can consistently provide the high quality evidence in the form of analysis and assessment, which the family judges obviously need to make the critically important decisions in respect of children subject to care proceedings. Clearly, to enable those decisions to be made without delay, it is vital that they do.

THE CHILDREN'S GUARDIAN

5.79 Not that prior to the Revised PLO coming into force, children's guardians were not an extremely influential cog in the care proceedings wheel. The courts quite rightly taking on board advice and recommendations from these independent 'eyes and ears of the court'; most of whom have a wealth of experience in dealing with children and families involved in care proceedings; but with the coming into force of the new regime, there came a need for a more streamlined approach to placing their evidence-based analysis before the court, thus enabling judges to understand the overall picture of the case, and continuing to be able to rely upon the guardian's judgment.

---

[44] Ibid, para 4.4, p 6.
[45] Dr Julia Brophy, Judith Sidaway, Dr Jagbir Jhutti-Johal and Charlie Owen *Neither Fear Nor Favour, Affection or Ill Will: Modernisation of Proceedings and the Use and Value of Independent Social Work Expertise to Senior Judges* (University of Oxford).

5.80 Through the *Good Practice Guidance for Social Work Practised in the Family Courts,* greater than ever was the drive towards more involvement at an early stage from Cafcass practitioners, geared at making sure as much evidence-based analysis is available in the very early days of the care proceedings.

5.81 This Guidance is supplemented for guardians in *The Revised PLO: Guidance for Cafcass* prepared by Anthony Douglas, Chief Executive of Cafcass. Its aim being to help guardians provide clear, focussed and analytical reports for the court.

The analysis and recommendations report

5.82 The format of the guardian's report has changed, with the template covering five areas requiring expert analysis, namely:

(a)   Threshold analysis.

(b)   Analysis of parenting capacity.

(c)   Child impact analysis.

(d)   Early permanence analysis including the proposed placement and contact framework.

(e)   Case management analysis and advice.

Threshold analysis

5.83 From the guardian's perspective, the threshold analysis is:[46]

'the guardian's analysis of what the child is likely to face without a protective court order. The starting point of a guardian's threshold analysis is a root cause analysis of why a child's needs are not being met, of the significant harm this is causing or is likely to cause, and whether the parenting capacity gap can be bridged or not.'

Analysis of parenting capacity

5.84 It is the guardian's job to appraise the position taken by the local authority and to scrutinise whether the level of care being provided by a parent is demonstrably 'good enough'. The analysis here 'needs to be clear about whether, in the view of the guardian, the parent can bridge any "capacity gap" between what they are providing to the child and what the child needs'.[47] The court must be assisted in deciding the issues in the case by an analysis of parenting capacity which focusses on '... whether the care plan for the child (the "what happens next") will provide physical, emotional and psychological permanence for the child'.[48]

---

[46]   Anthony Douglas *The Revised PLO: Guidance for Cafcass* (August 2013), para 13, p 3.
[47]   Ibid, para 17, p 4.
[48]   Ibid.

Child impact analysis

5.85 The child impact analysis is at the heart of the guardian's case analysis – it should include:

(a) The child's wishes and feelings.

(b) Analysis of the impact of the anticipated court process and all related administrative timetables on the child's needs.

(c) Analysis of the impact of poor parenting.

(d) The quality of the interim care being provided.[49]

Early permanence analysis including the proposed placement and contact framework

5.86 The guardian must assist the court in considering all of the different placement options:

'The early permanence options (for physical, emotional and psychological permanence) are:

- Safe reunification with one or both parents/and respective partners
- Kinship care
- Long-term (permanent) fostering
- Special guardianship
- Adoption
- Residential care.'[50]

5.87 To re-iterate, as the 'eyes and ears of the court' it is imperative that this care plan analysis:[51]

'consider[s] the evidence base for the proposed care plan including the placement, the support plan, and the health care and education plans, if the child needs additional support. The proposed contact framework should also be analysed, particularly in relation to how it fits with the early permanence proposal ... Guardians must liaise with Independent Reviewing Officers to agree the key issues in the child's care plan to support after the care proceedings have concluded'.

5.88 It is only with this strong evidence-based analysis that the court can be properly assisted in reaching the right decisions for the child.

Case management analysis and advice

5.89 The responsibility for case management lies with all professionals involved in the family justice system. In so far as children's guardians are concerned their case management advice 'should concentrate on two main

---

49   Ibid, para 18, p 4.
50   Ibid, para 19, p 5.
51   Ibid, paras 21 and 22, p 5.

issues: gaps in evidence, including where an additional or specialist assessment might be needed ... and advice on behalf of the child about what might be needed and by when'.[52] The Guidance for Cafcass also makes it clear that to make this type of analysis effective 'the guardian should be scrutinising and challenging the local authority's work to ensure a "culture of urgency" is being applied to the child's situation by all key professionals'.[53] The guardian must also apply this level of scrutiny to their own work.

5.90 By streamlining guardians' reports in this way, they too as experts are providing their advice and recommendations to the court in the most effective and focussed way. In order for the 26-week timetable to be able to be kept to in the majority of cases, the court needs such assistance. The days of voluminous, repetitive reports of the past have gone!

---

[52]   Ibid, para 24, p 6.
[53]   Ibid.

5.91

Example of revised PLO Cafcass case analysis

Date of Application:	02.09.2013
Court:	
Court Case Number:	XX14C00001
Cafcass CMS Number:	123456
Application Type:	Interim Care Orders
Hearing Type:	Issues Resolution Hearing
Hearing Date:	Week of 27 January 2014
Children's Guardian:	Carla Thomson
Office Address:	The Deep Business Centre, The Deep, Hull, East Yorkshire, HU1 2SA
Date Report Completed:	13.09.13
Initial Analysis Filing Date:	13.09.13
Current Update Filing Date:	24.01.14
Child's solicitor (where applicable):	Solicitor for the Children, Messrs Lovely & Co
Details of any current orders:	

Name of child/ren	Date of birth	M/F	Ethnic origin
A	Aged 6	F	White British
B	Aged 2	F	White British
C	Aged 14 months	F	White British

Name of parties (and other important adults)	Relationship to child	Date of birth	M/F	Ethnic Origin
M	Mother		F	White British
F	Father of B and C		M	White British
F	Father of A		M	White British

Key agencies involved	*(Give brief details of their involvement)*
XX Local Authority	Social work team, role as determined by the care proceedings currently before the Court. Independent Reviewing Officer, to ensure that the needs of A, B and C are being met. Fostering Services, supporting the foster carer in the placement of A, B and C. Contact provision, supervision of mother's contact with the three children.
Statutory Educational provision	Offering statutory role to A, B and C
Statutory Health provision	Offering statutory role to A, B and C

In compiling this report I have had regard to the welfare checklists set out in section 1(3)(a) to (f) of the Children Act 1989.

SIGNIFICANT HARM THRESHOLD ANALYSIS	
<u>Risk analysis</u>	<u>Strengths in the family system</u>
Evidence base: The family have been known to the Local Authority, since the birth of A six years ago with long-standing concerns regarding the mother's parenting capacity in terms of finance, basic care, rough handling, poor home conditions, physical harm to A by B and C's Father and Mother. The mother has a history of committing violent offences including convictions in 2005 for battery, arson and common assault. C suffers from Cystic Fibrosis and her condition is not managed well by her parents. The mother is vulnerable due to suffering from post-natal depression and depression may remain an issue for mother. Mother and Father's relationship is subject to repeated occasions of domestic violence, resulting in a number of police call-outs. Mother is unable to separate from Father. Within the evidence before the Court at this time there is little known about A's birth father.	*Evidence base:* The Local Authority has provided a significant package of support to the family in an attempt to maintain the children within their family. Protective measures were taken and the children are considered safe within Local Authority Foster Placements. Mother has made attempts to separate from Father, however has been unable to sustain this.

ANALYSIS OF PARENTING CAPACITY TO MEET THE CHILD'S NEEDS
— — —

Evidence base:

1. The following analysis in respect of Mother and Father's parenting capacity is formed from the information contained within the papers before the Court, discussions with the Independent Reviewing Officer and allocated Social Worker, visits to the three children on 6th September 2013, interview with Mother on 9th September 2013 and Father on 10th September 2013.

2. Mother's choices and actions have placed A, B and C at risk of harm whilst in her care, as detailed within the Local Authority Chronology of involvement and detailed within the section above of this report. It is my view that there is cause for concern in relation to Mother and Father's

parenting ability to safely and consistently care for the three children. The evidence before the Court depicts a situation where the father is violent to the mother and has physically harmed two of the children on at least one occasion.

3.   The Local Authority evidence within their initial Statement, dated 30th September 2013, significant Children's Services involvement and the level of concern in recent years can be summarised as A, B and C becoming subject to Child In Need plans in 2010 and again in 2012. On 25th July 2013, following medical opinion being that injuries to A and B where non-accidental, Mother was arrested for assault and the children were taken into Police Protection and placed with foster carers the same day. It is reasonable to conclude from the period of substantial Local Authority intervention that the situation for the children has become more concerning.

4.   The Local Authority evidence extensive support packages over extended periods in order to maintain the children within their family. When considering this level of intervention with Mother and Father, it is of concern that they appear to have very little understanding of the concerns and the needs of their children at this time. It is positive to note that Mother and Father both accept that there is need for further assessment of them.

5.   The issue of domestic violence has to also be considered alongside the Police logs filed by the Local Authority, which records serious and violent crimes having been committed by Mother in the past, all of which remain unaddressed by the mother. This indicates further risk factors for the children.

6.   It should be noted that both Mother and Father remain firm that neither has physically harmed the children. It is concerning as the older two children have been clear with professionals that these events have taken place, this may raise anxiety for these two children in terms of being believed.

7.   Mother can be viewed as vulnerable in her own right due to her fluctuating mental health and being the victim of domestic violence. This has to be born in mind when considering her as a sole carer for A, B and C. Mother appears to be dependent upon her relationship with Father, despite the relationship being an abusive one. This does not depict a safe situation for the future when considering rehabilitation of the children to her care.

8.   It is of significant concern that neither Mother nor Father have been able to protect the children from harm, in the form of physical and emtional harm and neglect. A and B have sustained injuries, which are subject to investigation within these proceedings, medical opinion is that these have been non-accidental injuries. It is also of concern that neither parent has maintained sufficient engagement with medical professions in terms of C's significant health needs.

9. Based upon all of the information available and the issues highlighted within this report it is my view that neither Mother nor Father are in a position to jointly or solely care for the children at this time. There are a number of significant gaps within their parenting capacity that requires further assessments, within the timescales of the children.

10. There are no other family members who have been positively assessed by the Local Authority.

CHILD IMPACT ANALYSIS (How the child is affected)
— — —

Evidence Base:

11. These proceedings can be viewed as having positive and negative implications for A, B and C. It is not known what emotional effect the removal from their mother, and their father, will have had upon them in the longer term. A, B and C's parenting experience has been their mother as their main carer, they also have experience of being parented by their mother and father jointly, albeit intermittently. That said, the action of the Local Authority in taking protective measures, and the Police removing the children via Police Protection, were appropriate at the time due to level of safeguarding concerns.

12. It is my view that the Local Authority have gone to great lengths to try to maintain A, B and C in their mother's and father's care, offering advice and support and ensuring that appropriate services have been in place. However this has not been effective.

13. The chronology of Local Authority intervention with the three children depicts a very worrying situation for them over a prolonged period of time. I am quite concerned for the children's emotional wellbeing due to the events they are known to have experienced. I have a level of concern that there may be further distressing events that the children have witnessed that we are not aware of, this has to be held in mind by all professionals working with the children.

14. It is of concern that A has on two occasions reported to professionals that she has suffered physical harm by her mother and B and C's father, she was not afforded safe care following the first incident, exposing her to further harm. It is reasonable to conclude that A will have an awareness that her and her siblings' needs have not been met sufficiently and consistently. There is, in my view, a risk that A may have taken on caring tasks for her siblings.

15. Child A will have a greater understanding and memory of the poor parenting she has received due to her age. It is reasonable to conclude that the children will have learnt how to respond to their parents in order to

have their needs met. This is likely to have been unpredictable parenting resulting in all three children having distorted attachments to their parents. Consideration will also need to be given to all three children's developmental progress as this is also likely to have been impacted upon.

16. Mother and Father have failed to understand the serious nature of C's health needs having been diagnosed with Cystic Fibrosis. This is a condition which is life-limiting and requires daily commitment to providing medication and physical care, and a good level of understanding from the child's carer to ensure their health remains stable. Failure to do so can result in complications. I am very concerned that Mother and Father have not ensured C's medical needs are met consistently.

17. The children's Independent Reviewing Officer has raised with myself that she is very concerned in terms of Mother and Father's ability to safely care for the three children, sharing a view that the matter has to conclude within the children's timeframes.

18. I have to express concern on the children's behalf in terms of delay, this is a view shared by the children's Independent Reviewing Officer. The children have been known to the Local Authority periodically for six years and the matter has only just come to the Court's attention. The issue of delay for the children has to be noted, and the effects for them in terms of longer-term decision-making.

19. It is noted within the evidence that A's father is unknown. This will remain an important factor for A as she grows and develops in terms of her identity and self-esteem. I would ask Mother to consider this from A's perspective and to provide the Local Authority with any information to assist in locating him.

EARLY PERMANENCE ANALYSIS, INCLUDING AN ANALYSIS OF THE PROPOSED PLACEMENT AND CONTACT FRAMEWORK	
Safe reunification	Due to the evidence before the Court this is viewed as an unsafe option for A, B and C at this time.
Kinship care	There are no extended family members positivity assessed to consider for this.
Permanent (long-term) fostering	This is not appropriate due to A, B and C's ages.
Adoption	This is not appropriate at this stage as Mother and Father are to be further assessed, this may be an option to the Court at final conclusion of the case.
Special guardianship	There are no extended family members positivity assessed to consider for this.
Residential care	This is not appropriate due to A, B and C's ages.

Evidence base:

20. There is a need for legal Orders to be granted to secure A, B and C's care needs in the short to longer term. It is my view that further assessment is required before any final decisions can be made on the children's behalf.

CASE MANAGEMENT REQUIREMENTS
— — —

Evidence base:

21. Both Mother and Father need to demonstrate to the Court that; i) they can commit to A, B and C via contact, ii) Mother access the support of and engage with Women's Aid and attend the Freedom Programme, iii) consider how her adult relationships impact upon A, B and C, iv) Mother and Father to work openly and honestly with all professionals, v) Mother access support services in terms of her mental health needs, vi) Father access services to address anger management issues vii) Mother and Father find information about parenting groups within their local area and attend groups viii) Mother to share any further details of males whom she considers might be A's father as she has a right to know her identity.

22. It is my view that Mother and Father should be given a six-week period to demonstrate that they have undertaken everything possible to start the process of change in the areas set out above and any further areas raised by other parties.

23. I am of the view that it would be beneficial to A, B and C if Mother and Father were to file statements in five weeks' time addressing what they have each done to address the points above, then the Local Authority were to file an updating statement a week after this in terms of what if any progress Mother and Father have made, for myself to then file a position statement the same week as the Local Authority statement, then the matter be listed the week after for a review hearing. This in effect could determine and narrow the issues, provide further information for any expert instructed should the Court deem this necessary, and enable a swift resolution to the case.

24. Due to concerns that have been raised via comments of the children and their foster carers it would assist if the Local Authority were to serve contact notes on a regular basis. This will serve to provide an informed position for reviewing contact proposals in the short and longer term.

25. As a result of the allegations of non-accidental injury and additional health needs the Court needs to consider an expert Consultant Paediatrician to be instructed to review all of the children's medical records. It is my view that

this is necessary and proportionate to the case in order for the Court to conclude the matter as the Court will need to determine how A and B came to sustain injuries.

26. In addition there are indications that Mother has mental health needs. In light of this I invite the Court to consider the need for an expert Clinical Psychologist to undertake a psychological assessment and provide an opinion as to diagnosis, prognosis and impact on her capacity to parent. It is my view that this is also necessary and proportionate to the case in order for the Court to conclude the matter.

27. Mother and Father need to provide details of any extended family members they wish to be assessed as alternative carers within 7 days of the next hearing.

28. Clarity by the Local Authority as to what extent attempts have been made to locate A's birth father, within an addendum report within 7 days of the next hearing.

29. I can confirm that I will undertake work required to reach conclusion in this matter within a 26-week timeframe.

UPDATE SINCE LAST FILED CASE ANALYSIS
— — —

Evidence Base:

Update provided on 24.01.14

30. I have considered the evidence before the Court and undertaken the following in order to form final recommendations; Ongoing liaison with the Social Worker, Social Work manager, and the allocated Independent Reviewing Officer and the children's foster carer, attendance at most Court hearings, attended a Child Looked After Review for all three children, observation of contact on 17th December 2013, direct work with the children on 15th January 2014, home visit and interview with Mother and Father on 20th January 2014.

31. As the Court and parties will be aware there have been further two expert assessments within the proceedings. The Consultant Paediatrician has concluded that the site of the bruising is not consistent with non-accidental injury and states that '*on balance of probabilities*' it is accidental. Therefore the Local Authority do not seek any findings relating to this.

32. The Clinical Psychologist concluded the following in relation to Mother, that she has a borderline personality disorder. The Clinical Psychologist is not confident that Mother will engage with CBT which is what is

recommended, the timescale for such work would be 12–18 months, this is viewed by the Local Authority and myself to be outside of the children's timeframes.

33. The Local Authority has now filed its final evidence and Care Plans. Their assessment of Father is positive assessment, he has acknowledged within that assessment and my meeting with him that the relationship between himself and Mother was volatile and that he did not deal with the effects of Mother's personality issues. Father, in my view, now needs to take responsibility for his part and access services in order to support his understanding of her needs, and how he manages himself when in stressful situations, detailed further in the next point of this report. That said, despite the allegation of physical harm his relationship with all three children is observed by all professionals as good, he has committed well to contact with them. Father wishes to care for all three children. Whilst there has been a positive assessment of him there is some concern in that he lives in a shared house with another male who doesn't have any children and is in arrears with his rent. The Local Authority has indicated that they will support him to find alternative, appropriate housing. Mother, albeit reluctantly, accepts that she cannot care for the children at this time. A's father is unknown, the Local Authority have made all possible attempts to locate him, therefore no consideration of him or his extended family can be given.

34. The evidence is that the parents' relationship has ended which is a positive step for them and their children as this demonstrates acceptance that the situation was not conducive to the needs of their children. Credit should be given to each parent having made the difficult decision.

35. The Local Authority supports the making of Residence Orders in favour of Father, this is supported by Mother, and the Local Authority also seeks a Supervision Order for twelve months, to address facilitating supporting re-housing and to assist the children with contact to Mother. The children's Independent Reviewing Officer has expressed a view that in light of the progress Father has made that they support the Local Authority Care Plans as detailed above, and would welcome consideration of the further work I have identified in terms of the father. I invite the Local Authority to also explore with Father what work can be undertaken to enhance his understanding of domestic violence and the impact upon children, for Father to attend parenting groups within the community to further assist him in parenting three children.

36. Based upon all of the evidence before the Court and from the information I have gained within the course of my work I support the Orders sought by the Local Authority. I invite the Local Authority to consider the suggestions I make above in terms of further work for Father to undertake. Due to the history this case is set in I agree that the Local Authority require a twelve month Supervision Order, serious consideration will need to be given at the time these Orders are due to expire as to if they require a further role under this remit of the Children Act 1989.

37. I also invite the Court and Local Authority to consider the need for a Contact Order to define what contact the Mother is expected to commit to. It is my view, given the therapy that she requires and the duration of this work to have any impact for her, that the contact should be school holidays only, equating to six times per year for two hours per contact and consideration for this to be activity based. It is my view that this contact needs to be supervised due to the potential risks. This will also allow the children time to adjust when seeing their mother without impacting upon their educational attainment.

RECOMMENDATIONS

—

Final Recommendations

38. I support the making of Residence Orders in favour of Father, in respect of A, B and C. I also support the Local Authority in seeking a twelve month Supervision Order in respect of A, B and C.

39. As set out in the body of this report, I invite the Court and Local Authority to consider the benefits for the children in having a defined Contact Order in relation to their Mother, as set out at paragraph 36 of this report.

Signed:

Name:

Cafcass Role: Children's Guardian

Date: 24.01.14

CHAPTER 6

ADOPTION REFORM

6.1 The compulsory adoption of a child against the wishes of their parents is the most serious step that the family court can take. It impacts upon the parents' lives, and that of the child, and the repercussions of the decision will be felt by all concerned for the rest of their lives. An adoption order severs all parental responsibility between the birth parents and child, and effectively gives the child a new identity. The steps taken alongside an adoption, which can include the end of all contact with birth parents and any siblings who may act as a conduit of information as well as a refusal of any exchange of photographs in the future, remain extremely controversial. Imposing adoption without parental consent is a step not taken by many other jurisdictions worldwide.

6.2 In 2012, 5,206 children in total were the subject of adoption orders in England and Wales.[1] Of these, 2,574 were girls and 2,632 were boys. The number of children approved for adoption but waiting for a family to be found was 5,750 as at 31 March 2012.[2] That figure only reflects those children known to Local Authorities, and known children or private arrangements may be higher. In 2013 the Department of Education released adoption 'maps' showing the differences between Local Authority areas in England, to assist prospective adopters with their decision-making. In addition, 'Adoption Scorecards' were released, which show the length of time that children wait in care.[3] On average, between 2009 and 2012, a child entering the care system waited 625 days before moving in with its adoptive parents, nearly 2 years.

6.3 Part 1 of the Act addresses concerns arising from those delays. Sections 1–9 of the Act amends the Children Act 1989 and Adoption and Children Act 2002, in relation to the placement of children with prospective adopters, the recruitment, assessment and approval of prospective adopters, removes the requirement to consider ethnicity when placing children for adoption, and provides increased support for adoption.

6.4 In 2013/14, BAAF matched a record number of children with adoptive families, 1,023, for the first time in 34 years of work. This was described as a

[1] See http://www.ons.gov.uk/ons/search/index.html?content-type=Dataset&content-type=Reference+table&newquery=adoption&pagetype=&display=data.

[2] See http://webarchive.nationalarchives.gov.uk/20130922141720/http://www.education.gov.uk/childrenandyoungpeople/families/adoption/a00219985/adoption-map.

[3] See http://webarchive.nationalarchives.gov.uk/20130922141720/http://www.education.gov.uk/childrenandyoungpeople/families/adoption/a00208817/adoption-scorecards.

significant increase, reflecting, said BAAF, both the rise in the number of children waiting to be adopted as well as the continued improvement throughout the UK's adoption services, including more creative matching processes and more effective recruitment and approval of prospective adopters. Barbara Hutchinson, Interim Chief Executive, BAAF said:

> 'This is tremendous news for the children whose lives will be turned around by moving into stable, loving adoptive families. BAAF is proud to have been able to play a major part in bringing this about.'

THE BACKGROUND TO REFORM

6.5 The position prior to the Act was governed by a combination of the Children Act 1989 and the Adoption and Children Act 2002. Ordinarily, a local authority would seek care orders, and upon finalising a plan of adoption, would then seek a placement order under s 21 of the 2002 Act. Prior to that application being made to the court, under the previous regulations, the plan had to be approved by an Adoption Panel, and that decision ratified by the decision-maker within the local authority. Once those steps had been completed, the plan could be presented to court, and the order sought.

6.6 The process of family finding and matching did not ordinarily commence until the court had made the orders, therefore causing considerable delay.

6.7 Following the *Narey Report* published in July 2011, Sir Martin Narey, former head of Barnardo's, was appointed as chief Government Advisor on Adoption, and led the way to adoption reaching the top of the political agenda. Building on his work, the Department for Education published *An Action Plan for Adoption: Tackling Delay* in March 2012. Michael Gove MP, Secretary of State for Education, stated that the Government would:

- legislate to reduce the number of adoptions delayed in order to achieve a perfect or near ethnic match between adoptive parents and the adoptive child;
- require swifter use of the national Adoption Register in order to find the right adopters for a child wherever they might live;
- encourage all local authorities to seek to place children with their potential adopters in anticipation of the court's placement order;
- radically speed up the adopter assessment process so that two months are spent in training and information gathering – a pre-qualification phase – followed by four months of full assessment;
- introduce a 'fast-track' process for those who have adopted before or who are foster carers wanting to adopt a child in their care; and
- develop the concept of a 'national Gateway to adoption' as a consistent source of advice and information for those thinking about adoption.

6.8   Given the need to improve timescales for children in the care system, the action plan highlighted the detrimental impact on children of waiting in the system before an adoptive match can be found, identifying that children often waited 2 or 3 years (para 31). The Family Justice Review had identified that there was duplication in cases before the court, which also had to obtain approval from the Adoption Panel that adoption was appropriate. That requirement was removed from 1 September 2012, although local authorities still have to seek the approval of an agency decision-maker, and follow the statutory guidance.[4]

THE CAUSES OF DELAY

6.9   The Department for Education action plan identified certain trigger points for delay, including the length of time taken before they are brought into care, the involvement of the court process, and the matching stage, which caused particular delay for certain groups of children:[5]

'One of the primary reasons why children miss out on adoption altogether, or spend most of their early childhood waiting to be matched with a family, is the mismatch between children in need of adoption and the families approved to adopt them. Disabled children, sibling groups, children with severe emotional and behavioural difficulties, older children and black children all currently wait longer than average.'

6.10   It was found that it could take up to a year longer for a black child to be matched with a family, when compared with white or Asian children, (action plan para 50). The study, *An investigation of family finding and matching in adoption* had found that attempts to find families of similar ethnicity were a cause of delay for 70% of the black and minority ethnic children who had been delayed in the system.[6]

THE IMPORTANCE OF ETHNICITY

6.11   The study referred to above considered 149 children's files, and also interviewed social workers and the adoptive parents where possible. A third, (31%) of the sample were black or minority ethnic children. 29% of those children were ultimately placed with families whose characteristics did not match their ethnicity, often in order to secure a placement for children with complex needs, where the need to place was considered more important than finding an 'ideal' match.

---

[4]   See http://webarchive.nationalarchives.gov.uk/20130401151655/http://media.education.gov.uk/assets/files/pdf/s/master%20version%2021%20february%202011%.
[5]   At para 17.
[6]   E Farmer, C Dance, J Beecham, E Bonin and D Ouwejan *An investigation of family finding and matching in adoption: Briefing Paper* (DfE-RBX-10–05, 2010).

6.12 BME children were not alone in being difficult to place, as those who are older or have significant health or developmental problems often also experienced the highest level of delays.

6.13 In the earlier study, *Pathways to Permanence for Black, Asian and Mixed Ethnicity Children: Dilemmas, Decision-Making and Outcomes* (October 2008),[7] it was found that the sub-sample of black children, came to the notice of Children's Services when they were older than the sample of white, Asian or mixed ethnicity children, making it harder for them to be placed, and the child's age was found to be the most important predictive factor in whether or not the child was adopted. However, the plans for 64% of the children moved away from adoption, which the authors of the study found may have arisen through an overly narrow approach to matching. It was found that the wish for a 'same race' placement dominated descriptions of the child's identified needs, and their ethnicity was focussed upon as being the difficulty in finding a placement, rather than the child's age or other potential problems. Most social workers hoped to find a two-parent adoptive family who already had children and to match exactly by ethnic category.

6.14 The placement outcomes for this group of children were described as disheartening. Despite the difficulties, the major source of professional disagreement were requests by white foster carers to adopt minority ethnic children who they had cared for since birth, as issues of 'same race' placements were then raised. Interestingly, where those issues resulted in hearings before the court, the judgment in those cases in the study, went in favour of the foster carers, despite the arguments raised in relation to the child's mental health and identity needing an ethnic match.

6.15 The statutory guidance for local authorities drew on the 2008 research and stated that:

'Ethnicity and culture of children and prospective adopters

6. The structure of white, black and minority ethnic groups is often complex and their heritage diverse, where the race, religion, language and culture of each community has varying degrees of importance in the daily lives of individuals. It is important that social workers avoid "labelling" a child and ignoring some elements in their background, or placing the child's ethnicity above all else when looking for an adoptive family for the child.

7. A prospective adopter can be matched with a child with whom they do not share the same ethnicity, provided they can meet the child's other identified needs. The core issue is what qualities, experiences and attributes the prospective adopter can draw on and their level of understanding of the discrimination and racism the child may be confronted with when growing up. This applies equally whether a child is placed with a black or minority ethnic family, a white family, or a family which includes members of different ethnic origins.

---

[7] See http://www.adoptionresearchinitiative.org.uk/briefs/DCSF-RBX-13–08.pdf.

8. All families should help children placed with them to understand and appreciate their background and culture. Where the child and prospective adopter do not share the same background, the prospective adopter will need flexible and creative support to be given by their agency. This should be in the form of education and training, not just simplistic advice, provided in a vacuum, on learning their children's cultural traditions or about the food/cooking from their birth heritage. The support plan should consider how the child's understanding of their background and origin might be enhanced. This can include providing opportunities for children to meet others from similar backgrounds, and to practise their religion – both in a formal place of worship and in the home. Maintaining continuity of the heritage of their birth family is important to most children; it is a means of retaining knowledge of their identity and feeling that although they have left their birth family they have not abandoned important cultural, religious or linguistic values of their community. This will be of particular significance as they reach adulthood.'

6.16 In the Action Plan for Adoption, the Department for Education stated that:

'a review of research on transracial adoption by the Evan B. Donaldson Institute concluded that adoption across ethnic boundaries does not in itself produce psychological or behavioural problems in children. However, where a child is adopted across ethnic boundaries, they and their families can face a range of challenges. The manner in which parents handle these challenges, particularly their sensitivity and approach to racism, facilitates or hinders children's development. The authors conclude that these challenges need to be addressed when matching children with families and in preparing families to meet their children's needs. A recent review of international evidence on matching in adoptions from care has also shown that adoptions across ethnic boundaries are at no greater risk of disruption.[8]

52. That is not to say that ethnicity can never be a consideration. Where there are two sets of suitable parents available then those with a similar ethnicity to the child may be the better match for the child. Sometimes an ethnic match will be in a child's best interests, for example where an older child expresses strong wishes. However, it is not in the best interests of children for social workers to introduce any delay at all into the adoption process in the search for a perfect or even partial ethnic match when parents who are otherwise suitable are available and able to provide a loving and caring home for the child.

53. Similarly, there are approved adopters who are ready and able to offer loving homes but who are too readily disregarded because they are single, or considered too old. These can, of course, be relevant factors, but we know that in most cases delay and the instability associated with it will be the greater potential cause of damage to the child.

54. The Government will bring forward primary legislation at the next available opportunity to address these issues. The overriding principle in finding a match for a child will remain what is in the child's best interests throughout their life.'

---

[8] D Quinton *Matching In Adoptions From Care: A Conceptual And Research Review* (British Association for Adoption and Fostering, 2012).

6.17 Section 2 of the 2014 Act removes s 1(5) of the Adoption and Children Act 2002, which previously read that:

> (5) In placing the child for adoption, the adoption agency must give due consideration to the child's religious persuasion, racial origin and cultural and linguistic background.

Therefore removing the requirement for religious or racial background to be considered. It will however remain a factor when considering placement, as set out above, but with far less weight than previously.

EARLY PERMANENCE

6.18 The Act introduces formally the concept of early permanence, through s 1 which amends s 22C of the Children Act 1989 by inserting a new sub-s (9A) and (9B):

> **1 Placement of looked after children with prospective adopters**
>
> (1) Section 22C of the Children Act 1989 is amended as follows.
>
> (2) In subsection (7), after "subject to" insert "subsection (9B) and".
>
> (3) After subsection (9) insert –
>
> "(9A) Subsection (9B) applies (subject to subsection (9C)) where the local authority are a local authority in England and –
>> (a)   are considering adoption for C, or
>> (b)   are satisfied that C ought to be placed for adoption but are not authorised under section 19 of the Adoption and Children Act 2002 (placement with parental consent) or by virtue of section 21 of that Act (placement orders) to place C for adoption.
>
> (9B) Where this subsection applies –
>> (a)   subsections (7) to (9) do not apply to the local authority,
>> (b)   the local authority must consider placing C with an individual within subsection (6)(a), and
>> (c)   where the local authority decide that a placement with such an individual is not the most appropriate placement for C, the local authority must consider placing C with a local authority foster parent who has been approved as a prospective adopter.
>
> (9C) Subsection (9B) does not apply where the local authority have applied for a placement order under section 21 of the Adoption and Children Act 2002 in respect of C and the application has been refused."

6.19 The effect of the amendment is to require a local authority, when they are satisfied that a child should be placed for adoption, but they do not have parental consent, or a placement order, to consider placing the child with an individual who is a relative, friend or other person connected with the child (s 22C(9B)(c) Children Act 1989) and where such a connected person placement is not the most appropriate, the local authority **must** consider placing the child with a local authority foster parent who has also been approved as a prospective adopter. The requirement to place a child in the most appropriate placement available still remains, and the local authority are still required to act in the child's best interests.

6.20 Where the court has refused an application for a placement order, the new provisions do not apply, as to do otherwise would be to effectively ignore the court's decision. However, where the plan is one of adoption, the local authority no longer has to ensure that the considerations set out in s 8 of the 2002 Act are applied, namely:

(a)   the placement allows the child to live near home;

(b)   does not disrupt their education; or

(c)   allows siblings to be placed together.

6.21 Those considerations remain relevant in cases other than those of adoption, but the new sub-s (9B) disapplies s 8 of the Act, and enables local authorities to move a child straight to a 'fostering for adoption' placement, without specifically considering sibling placement or location, (although the need to act in the child's best interests will still play an important part).

6.22 The need to make it possible for early placements to become permanent was identified in the action plan for adoption. Whilst it was acknowledged that there can be no question of pre-empting the court's decision, the Department for Education referred to the practice of 'concurrent planning' which was already in use in some local authorities, and meant that adults bore the risk of disruption, rather than the children.[9]

6.23 Importantly, the local authority still have to consider placement with parents, and only if that cannot be arranged in a way that is reasonably practicable and consistent with the child's welfare, it should then give preference to placement with a relative, friend or other connected person. Where a kinship placement is not possible, then the new fostering for adoption provisions will apply.

6.24 In the first instance decision of *Re P (A Child: Assessment of Kinship Carers)*,[10] the factors which the court should consider when evaluation an application for further assessment of kinship carers were set out, when such an assessment would extend the court timetable beyond the statutory 26-week limit:

> '140. I have already referred to the statutory requirement in s 32(1) Children Act 1989 to complete care cases within 26 weeks. An extension may be granted if it is "necessary to enable the court to resolve the proceedings justly". As Pauffley J has said, justice must never be sacrificed upon the altar of speed. If the court does not have the evidence to enable it to undertake a global, holistic evaluation or if a party is able to satisfy the court that one of the indicative criteria for granting an

---

9   Action Plan for Adoption, para 61.
10   [2014] EWFC B73.

extension set out at paragraph 33 of the President's judgment in *Re S (A Child)* is made out, then the court should be prepared to extend the timetable.

141. It does not follow from all of this that the prejudicial impact of delay should be ignored. The general principle that delay is likely to be prejudicial to a child's welfare is enshrined in statute. The potential for delay to seriously prejudice a child's welfare has been highlighted by the recent report Beyond the Adoption Order: challenges, interventions and adoption disruption which states (page 272) that,

> "Three-quarters of children who experienced a disruption were more than 4 years old at placement with their adoptive family. Children who were 4 years old or older at placement were 13 times more likely to disrupt than those who were placed as infants …This much larger dataset highlights the impact of delay."

142. Having made that point, I am entirely clear that if, in this case, I am satisfied that Mr Dodds' assessment is inadequate and that further evidence by way of an independent social work assessment is necessary in order to enable the court to resolve these proceedings justly, then I must adjourn this hearing and give the permission sought by the mother.'

6.25 The Coram Centre for Early Permanence commissioned Practice Guidance[11] for the fostering for adoption scheme. The guidance was written by the British Association for Adoption and Fostering, and sets out the challenges present in the new system.

6.26 The guidance identifies the following scenarios as typical ones where fostering for adoption may be appropriate:[12]

- Where parents have had one or more children previously placed for adoption or other forms of permanent placement and the evidence strongly suggests that their circumstances have not changed and pose the same risks as they did to the previous child/ren. The local authority does not have a proactive plan to rehabilitate the child as the circumstances of the parents are such to pose a serious on-going risk.
- Where this is the first child, the circumstances of the parents and the risks to the child are such that there is no proactive plan to return the child to the birth parents or to other family members.
- Where parents have indicated that they may want their child adopted, but have not formally consented. (s 52(3) Adoption and Children Act 2002).
- There are other circumstances where placement with a dually approved carer may be in the best interests of the child. Concurrent planning is the clearest example.

6.27 The guidance emphasises the need to move away from the sequential approach in care planning, and to avoid the assumption that 'because the child

---

11   See   http://www.coram.org.uk/sites/default/files/resource_files/46%20Fostering%20for%20 Adoption%20Guidance_2013.pdf.

12   Fostering for Adoption: Practice Guidance, p 7.

is placed with temporary foster carers, all is well'. The impact on the child's attachment processes of their separation from their birth parents, and subsequent separation from foster carers, who may have cared for the child for over a year, can be devastating. Under concurrent planning, or fostering for adoption, if rehabilitation to the family is the ultimate agreement or court-ordered outcome, there will be disruption to the placement, but where the placement order is approved, the child can continue to build relationships without disturbance.

6.28 The parents should be informed, and where possible, their cooperation obtained, of the local authority plan, meaning that the position of the foster carers as dually approved carers cannot be concealed from the parents. The Care Planning, Placement and Case Review Statutory Guidance notes[13] that:

> 'As part of the assessment process, it is essential when planning a placement to consult all those concerned with the child. The need for consultation should be explained to the parents and the child. The responsible authority should coordinate the involvement of all relevant agencies and all the individuals who are significant in the child's life. Before making any decision with respect to a child whom they are looking after or propose to look after, section 22(4) provides that the responsible authority should, as far as is reasonably practicable ascertain the wishes and feeling of:
>
> - the child;
> - his parents;
> - any person who is not a parent of his but
> - had parental responsibility for him; and
> - any other person whose wishes and feelings the authority consider to be relevant;
>
> regarding the matters to be decided.'

6.29 In addition to the removal of the requirement for the adoption panel to approve the plan of adoption, matters have been further simplified by the introduction of reg 25A to the 2010 Regulations.[14] This enables approved adopters to be temporarily approved as foster carers by the local authority, without having to first be referred to a fostering panel:

Amendment of the Care Planning, Placement and Case Review (England) Regulations 2010

2. The Care Planning, Placement and Case Review (England) Regulations 2010(c) are amended as follows.

3. After regulation 25 insert –

---

[13] (2010), para 2.13.
[14] Care Planning, Placement and Case Review Regulations 2010, reg 25A in force from 1 July 2013.

"25A Temporary approval of prospective adopter as foster parent

(1) Where the responsible authority is satisfied that –

- (a) the most appropriate placement for C is with a person who is not approved as a local authority foster parent, but who is an approved prospective adopter, and (b) it is in C's best interests to be placed with that person,
- (b) the responsible authority may approve that person as a local authority foster parent in relation to C for a temporary period ("temporary approval period") provided that the responsible authority first comply with the requirements of paragraph (2).

(2) Before approving an approved prospective adopter as a local authority foster parent under paragraph (1), the responsible authority must –

- (a) assess the suitability of that person to care for C as a foster parent, and
- (b) consider whether, in all the circumstances and taking into account the services to be provided by the responsible authority, the proposed arrangements will safeguard and promote C's welfare and meet C's needs set out in the care plan.

(3) The temporary approval period expires –

- (a) on C's placement with the approved prospective adopter being terminated by the responsible authority,
- (b) on the approved prospective adopter's approval as a prospective adopter being terminated,
- (c) on the approved prospective adopter being approved as a foster parent in accordance with the Fostering Services Regulations,
- (d) if the approved prospective adopter gives written notice to the responsible authority that they no longer wish to be temporarily approved as a foster parent in relation to C, with effect from 28 days from the date on which the notice is received by the responsible authority, or
- (e) on C being placed for adoption with the approved prospective adopter in accordance with the Adoption and Children Act 2002(a).

(4) In this regulation "approved prospective adopter" means a person who has been approved as suitable to adopt a child under the Adoption Agencies Regulations 2005(b) and whose approval has not been terminated.".

6.30 The requirements of s 42 of the 2002 Act still apply, and therefore whilst placement may have been expedited, the child will need to have been placed with those foster parents for the period of one year preceding the application for an adoption order.

6.31 The policy of fostering for adoption (Ffa) is not without controversy. It risks being perceived by the birth family that the outcome of the case has already been decided upon and that the making of a placement order is a 'done deal'.[15] However, as seen in the authorities below, the question for the court is firstly whether the child can be rehabilitated to the birth family, or whether long term removal by the state is in his best interests. Only after the court has

---

[15]   Ibid.

found that long term removal is necessary, will the competing plans of long term fostering over adoption be considered. It is not a question of birth family as opposed to adoption.

THE APPROACH OF THE COURTS

6.32 The Court of Appeal considered the tension between the child's need for a speedier care and adoption system, and the need to consider the parents and child's right to a family life in a number of judgments delivered in 2013. In the leading authority of *Re B-S (Children)*,[16] the President of the Family Division reviewed the case-law, and emphasised that the severance of family ties by an adoption without parental consent is the most draconian step a court can take. The President identified a number of concerns held by the Court of Appeal in relation to the way in which the first instance courts dealt with applications for placement orders, as well as applications for permission to oppose an adoption order.

6.33 The statutory framework following the making of a placement order remains that set out in the Adoption and Children Act 2002. Once the court has authorised the placing of a child for adoption by making an order under s 21 of the Act, the birth parents may seek leave to apply for revocation of the order (s 24(2)(a)). The test at that stage is:[17]

> 'whether in all the circumstances, including the mother's prospect of success in securing revocation of the placement order and T's interests, leave should be given.'

6.34 Once the child is placed for adoption, the parental right to apply for leave to revoke the placement order comes to an end (s 24(2)(b)).[18] Once the requirements of s 42 have been satisfied, the adoptive parents may then apply for an adoption order pursuant to s 50 or s 51. In the case of placement by a local authority or other adoption agency, the child must have lived with the applicant for at least 10 weeks prior to the application (s 42). The birth parents are given notice of the application, and are asked in writing whether or not they consent to the adoption. If they object, the matter is listed for a hearing at which the parents must seek the leave of the court to object to the making of the order, pursuant to s 47(3) or (5). If leave is refused, the court can dispense with the parents' consent (s 47(2)(c)).

6.35 Upon the order being made, the parental responsibility of the birth parents is extinguished (s 46). In addition, the court must consider whether there should be any ongoing contact with any person, such as birth family or siblings (s 46(6)).

---

[16] [2013] EWCA Civ 1146.

[17] *NS-H v Kingston upon Hull City Council and MC* [2008] EWCA Civ 493.

[18] *M v Warwickshire County Council* [2007] EWCA Civ 1084, [2008] 1 FLR 1093; *Re F (Placement Order)* [2008] EWCA Civ 439, [2008] 2 FLR 550.

Re B-S – the need for full analysis

6.36 The statutory test to be applied when a parent sought leave to oppose an order is set out at s 47(7):

> (7) The court cannot give leave under subsection (3) or (5) unless satisfied that there has been a change in circumstances since the consent of the parent or guardian was given or, as the case may be, the placement order was made.

6.37 In *W (A Child)*,[19] the mother had been granted leave to oppose an order following an error in the service of the adoption application. The order had been set aside. On appeal by the adopters, Thorpe LJ held that:[20]

> 'it cannot be too strongly emphasised that that is an absolute last ditch opportunity and it will only be in exceptionally rare circumstances that adoption orders will be set aside after the making of the care order, the making of the placement order, the placement of the child, and the issue of the adoption order application.'

6.38 Following the decision of the Supreme Court in *Re B (A Child) (Care Proceedings: Threshold Criteria)*,[21] it was considered appropriate to look again at the judgment in *Re W*. In *Re B*, three key points were made as set out at para 27 of *Re B-S*:

- that although the child's interests are paramount, these interests include being brought up by his/her natural family;
- that the relevant statutes impose a requirement that the court 'must' consider all available options when coming to a decision;
- that the court's assessment of the parents' capacity to care for the child should include consideration of support that the authorities could offer them in doing so.

6.39 The President drew on the language of *Re B* at para 22 of *Re B-S*.

> '22. The language used in *Re B* is striking. Different words and phrases are used, but the message is clear. Orders contemplating non-consensual adoption – care orders with a plan for adoption, placement orders and adoption orders – are "a very extreme thing, a last resort", only to be made where "nothing else will do", where "no other course [is] possible in [the child's] interests", they are "the most extreme option", a "last resort – when all else fails", to be made "only in exceptional circumstances and where motivated by *overriding requirements* pertaining to the child's welfare, in short, where nothing else will do": see *Re B* paras 74, 76, 77, 82, 104, 130, 135, 145, 198, 215.'

---

[19]   [2010] EWCA Civ 1535.

[20]   At para 17.

[21]   [2013] UKSC 33.

Re B-S – The facts

6.40 *B-S* considered the issue of whether or not leave should be given to birth parents to object to an adoption order, and specifically whether the approach set out above in the case of *Re W* still applied in the light of the Supreme Court judgment in *Re B*.

6.41 The mother had 'turned her life around' since the making of the placement order. The Court had been perfectly satisfied that there had been a change, although at first instance Parker J had noted the identified risk that the mother might not be able to cope if the care order was discharged and that 'there was a long road to travel'.

The outcome

6.42 The Court held that the reference in *Re W* to 'exceptionally rare circumstances' and 'stringent' tests, were misleading and conveyed the wrong message. Section 47(5) was intended to afford a parent a meaningful remedy and care must be taken to ensure that it remained effective as a remedy and not merely illusory. There are two questions for the Court, has there been a change in circumstances, and if so should leave to oppose be given?

6.43 When considering the second question, the court had to consider all the circumstances, including the parent's ultimate prospect of success of opposing the adoption order if leave is given, and the impact on the child if leave is given. The child's welfare throughout his life is paramount. The court set out in detail at para 74 the considerations to be applied in leave applications:

'(i)   Prospect of success here relates to the prospect of resisting the making of an adoption order, *not*, we emphasise, the prospect of ultimately having the child restored to the parent's care.

(ii)   For purposes of exposition and analysis we treat as two separate issues the questions of whether there has been a change in circumstances and whether the parent has solid grounds for seeking leave. Almost invariably, however, they will be intertwined; in many cases the one may very well follow from the other.

(iii) Once he or she has got to the point of concluding that there has been a change of circumstances and that the parent has solid grounds for seeking leave, the judge must consider very carefully indeed whether the child's welfare really does necessitate the refusal of leave. The judge must keep at the forefront of his mind the teaching of *Re B*, in particular that adoption is the "last resort" and only permissible if "nothing else will do" and that, as Lord Neuberger emphasised, the child's interests include being brought up by the parents or wider family unless the overriding requirements of the child's welfare make that not possible. That said, the child's the overriding requirements of the child's welfare make that not possible. That said, the child's welfare is paramount.

(iv)   At this, as at all other stages in the adoption process, the judicial evaluation of the child's welfare must take into account *all* the negatives and the positives, *all* the pros and cons, of *each* of the two options, that is, either giving or refusing the parent leave to oppose. Here again, as elsewhere, the use of Thorpe LJ's "balance sheet" is to be encouraged.

(v)   This close focus on the circumstances requires that the court has proper evidence. But this does not mean that judges will always need to hear oral evidence and cross-examination before coming to a conclusion. Sometimes, though we suspect not very often, the judge will be assisted by oral evidence. Typically, however, an application for leave under section 47(5) can fairly and should appropriately be dealt with on the basis of written evidence and submissions: see *Re P* paras 53–54.

(vi)   As a general proposition, the greater the change in circumstances (assuming, of course, that the change is positive) and the more solid the parent's grounds for seeking leave to oppose, the more cogent and compelling the arguments based on the child's welfare must be if leave to oppose is to be refused.

(vii)   The mere fact that the child has been placed with prospective adopters cannot be determinative, nor can the mere passage of time. On the other hand, the older the child and the longer the child has been placed the greater the adverse impacts of disturbing the arrangements are likely to be.

(viii) The judge must always bear in mind that what is paramount in every adoption case is the welfare of the child "throughout his life". Given modern expectation of life, this means that, with a young child, one is looking far ahead into a very distant future – upwards of eighty or even ninety years. Against this perspective, judges must be careful not to attach undue weight to the short term consequences for the child if leave to oppose is given. In this as in other contexts, judges should be guided by what Sir Thomas Bingham MR said in *Re O (Contact: Imposition of Conditions)* [1995] 2 FLR 124, 129, that "the court should take a medium-term and long-term view of the child's development and not accord excessive weight to what appear likely to be short-term or transient problems". That was said in the context of contact but it has a much wider resonance: *Re G (Education: Religious Upbringing)*,[22] para 26.

(ix)   Almost invariably the judge will be pressed with the argument that leave to oppose should be refused, amongst other reasons, because of the adverse impact on the prospective adopters, and thus on the child, of their having to pursue a contested adoption application. We do not seek to trivialise an argument which may in some cases have considerable force, particularly perhaps in a case where the child is old enough to have some awareness of what is going on. But judges must be careful not to attach undue weight to the argument. After all, what from the perspective of the proposed adopters was the smoothness of the process which they no doubt anticipated when issuing their application with the assurance of a placement order, will already have been disturbed by the unwelcome making of the application for leave to oppose. And the disruptive effects of an order giving a parent leave to oppose can be minimised by firm judicial case management *before* the hearing of the application for leave. If appropriate directions are given, in particular in relation to the expert and other evidence to be adduced on behalf of the parent, *as soon as* the application for leave is issued and *before* the question of leave has been determined, it ought to be possible to direct either that the application for leave is to be listed with the substantive adoption application to follow immediately, whether or not leave is given, or, if that is not feasible,

---

[22]   [2012] EWCA Civ 1233, [2013] 1 FLR 677.

to direct that the substantive application is to be listed, whether or not leave has been given, very shortly after the leave hearing.

(x) We urge judges always to bear in mind the wise and humane words of Wall LJ in *Re P*, para 32. We have already quoted them but they bear repetition: "the test should not be set too high, because … parents … should not be discouraged either from bettering themselves or from seeking to prevent the adoption of their child by the imposition of a test which is unachievable".'

In the present case, Parker J's findings and conclusions were found to be right and the appeal was dismissed.

6.44 The court went on to outline the serious concerns that had arisen from a number of first instance decisions in respect of adoption and set out the correct approach to be taken by the courts, local authorities and guardians when considering an application for a placement order.

Adoption essentials

(i) Proper evidence from the local authority and guardian addressing **all** the options which are realistically possible and must contain an analysis of the arguments for and against each option.

(ii) Adequately reasoned judgments, which acknowledge that adoption is a last resort and sets out the justification for it:

'We emphasise the words "global, holistic evaluation". This point is crucial. The judicial task is to evaluate all the options, undertaking a global, holistic and multi-faceted evaluation of the child's welfare which takes into account all the negatives and the positives, all the pros and cons, of each option.' [para 44]

6.45 The Court of Appeal took the opportunity in *Re B-S* to outline concerns regarding the approach taken to adoption cases by first instance judges:[23]

'We have real concerns, shared by other judges, about the recurrent inadequacy of the analysis and reasoning put forward in support of the case for adoption, both in the materials put before the court by local authorities and guardians and also in too many judgments. This is nothing new. But it is time to call a halt.'

6.46 The court went on to outline the serious concerns that had arisen from a number of first instance decisions in respect of adoption and set out the correct approach to be taken by the courts, local authorities and guardians when considering an application for a placement order.

---

[23] At para 30.

Re B-S in the context of the modernisation reforms

6.47 Sir James Munby P considered the need for proper analysis in the context of the other wider reforms at para 47 onwards of the judgment:

> '49. We do not envisage that proper compliance with what we are demanding, which may well impose a more onerous burden on practitioners and judges, will conflict with the requirement, soon to be imposed by statute, that care cases are to be concluded within a maximum of 26 weeks. Critical to the success of the reforms is robust judicial case management from the outset of every care case. Case management judges must be astute to ensure that the directions they give are apt to the task and also to ensure that their directions are complied with. Never is this more important than in cases where the local authority's plan envisages adoption. If, despite all, the court does not have the kind of evidence we have identified, and is therefore not properly equipped to decide these issues, then an adjournment must be directed, even if this takes the case over 26 weeks. Where the proposal before the court is for non-consensual adoption, the issues are too grave, the stakes for all are too high, for the outcome to be determined by rigorous adherence to an inflexible timetable and justice thereby potentially denied.'

Therefore it is vital that the local authority and guardian conduct the proper analysis if cases are to be completed within the statutory time limit.

Application of *Re B-S*

6.48 The approach of the Court of Appeal has been applied, confirmed and approved in further judgments, notably *Re W (A Child); Re H (Children)*,[24] and the recent case of *Re S*.[25]

Re W (A Child); Re H (Children)[26]

> 'The Court of Appeal will expect, and be entitled to expect, that from now on judgments will reflect and give effect to the approach which *Re B-S* requires. Judgments that do not clearly do so are likely to be subject to anxious scrutiny and critical comment.'[27]

6.49 This case confirms that the guidance in *Re B-S* is to be applied by the lower courts whenever an application for leave to oppose the making of an adoption order is before the court in the future. In relation to any cases decided shortly before *Re B-S*, the Court held that:[28]

> 'Plainly, in the case of judgments given before the decision in *Re B-S* the Court of Appeal must have regard to and make appropriate allowance for that fact. The focus must be on substance rather than form. Does the judge's approach as it appears from the judgment engage with the essence? Can it be said, on a fair

---

[24]   [2013] EWCA Civ 1177.
[25]   [2014] EWCA 135.
[26]   [2013] EWCA Civ 1177.
[27]   Sir James Munby P, para 15.
[28]   At para 16.

reading of the judgment taken as a whole – a fair and sensible reading, not a pedantic or nit-picking reading – that the judge has directed his mind to and has provided answers to the key questions?'

6.50 The Court went on to to reiterate the two stage test to be considered in leave to oppose applications, namely has there been a change in circumstances, and if so, should leave to oppose be given? When considering whether leave to oppose should be given, the court has to analyse the prospects of success, and then the effect on the child's welfare:[29]

'Once he or she has got to the point of concluding that there has been a change of circumstances and that the parent has solid grounds for seeking leave, the judge must consider very carefully indeed whether the child's welfare really does necessitate the refusal of leave. The judge must keep at the forefront of his mind the teaching of *Re B*, in particular that adoption is the "last resort" and only permissible if "nothing else will do".'

6.51 In relation to the procedure of the court to deal with a parent's application for leave, and if dismissed, to go on to make the adoption order straight away, the President held that:[30]

'I can understand the pragmatic and very human (and humane) grounds on which judges have come to adopt the current practice, and I can see no reason why the hearing of the adoption application, if the judge thinks this appropriate, should not immediately follow the dismissal of the parent's application (see *Re B-S*, para 74(ix)). Nor do I see any problem if the judge then and there announces his decision that there should be an adoption order. The problem arises if the judge proceeds then and there to make the formal adoption order. For the future, judges should postpone both the making of the formal adoption order and the holding of the celebratory event until after the parent's time for applying to this court for permission to appeal has expired. (This will necessitate some adjustment to para 12 of President's Guidance: Listing Final Hearings in Adoption Cases, 3 October 2008, set out in the 2013 Family Court Practice, 2958. Until new Guidance is issued, para 12 of the existing Guidance should be applied in a manner consistent with this judgment.) It would also be prudent for judges, when dismissing an application under section 47(5), to ask the parent whether an appeal is proposed and, even if told that an appeal is not in mind, to make clear to the parent that the time for doing so is strictly limited.'

Re S (A Child)[31]

6.52 The central issue in this case on appeal was whether or not the judgment of the first instance judge was compliant with the guidance in *Re B-S*. Applying *Re W* above, it was held that the judgment did not engage the essence of *Re B-S*, and the appeal was allowed.

---

29   At para 22.
30   At para 31.
31   [2014] EWCA 135.

Re G (Care Proceedings: Welfare Evaluation);[32] *Re C (Appeal from Care and Placement Orders)*[33]

6.53 These cases give clear guidance as to the holistic approach to be followed, as opposed to linear, and McFarlane LJ explains in his judgments that sequential elimination risks leaving adoption, the most draconian option, as the only outcome remaining. There has to be a global, holistic evaluation of each welfare option available.

6.54 One example of a clear change in circumstances, but relating to the prospective adopters rather than the birth family can be found in *Re L (Leave to Oppose Making of Adoption Order)*[34] where in fact, the prospective adoptive parents had separated and Mrs X was no longer part of the household nor looking after the child.

6.55 If leave to oppose the order is given, the considerations set out in *Borough of Poole v W and another* apply:[35]

> '11. First, would SR survive the rehabilitation process? If yes, secondly, would the parents survive the rehabilitation process? If yes, thirdly, would they produce parenting consistent with the needs of SR over the balance of her childhood?'

The balance sheet

6.56 *Re B-S* refers to the usefulness of a 'balance sheet' approach and the need for full analysis of the 'pros and cons' of each potential course of action open to the court. The cases which have followed and have been analysed above underline the necessity of such an approach. In summary therefore:

- Local authorities and guardians should provide the necessary information/ 'proper evidence' to the court which addresses ALL options realistically available and must contain an analysis of the arguments *for* and *against* each option.[36]
- A balance sheet analysis should be provided with reference to the specific/relevant welfare checklist depending upon the orders being sought. (Namely s 1(3) CA 1989 and s 1(4) ACA 2002). An analysis of the 'pros and cons' and a 'fully reasoned recommendation' should be provided.[37]
- The 'balance sheet analysis' document should be annexed to the final statements/care plans and perhaps provided to the Agency Decision Maker (ADM) alongside all the usual documents provided.

---

[32]   [2013] EWCA Civ 965.
[33]   [2013] EWCA Civ 1257.
[34]   [2013] EWCA Civ 1481.
[35]   [2014] EWHC 1777 (Fam), per Hedley J.
[36]   *Re B-S (Children)* [2013] EWCA Civ 1146, para 34.
[37]   *Re B-S* above, para 36.

- Adequately reasoned judgments are essential – the judge must grapple with the factors at play in the particular case and give 'proper focussed attention to the specifics'.[38]

- The court should be alerted to the dangers of engaging in a linear process of analysis and should be reminded of the need to undertake a 'global, holistic, evaluation of each of the options available …'.[39]

- The use of the words/phrases 'exceptionally rare circumstances', 'stringent' and 'entirely improbable' to define the test to be applied under s 47(5) ACA 2002, should cease and no longer be referred to.[40]

- There is a two-stage process when considering applications under s 47(5) – The court has to ask itself two questions: Has there been a change in circumstances, within s 47(7)? If so, should leave to oppose be given?[41]

- In relation to the second question – if there has been a change in circumstances, should leave to oppose be given? – the court will need to consider all of the circumstances. The court will have to consider two inter-related questions: one, the parent's ultimate prospect of success if given leave to oppose; the other, the impact on the child if the parent is, or is not, given leave to oppose, always remembering, that at this stage the child's welfare is paramount. The court should then be referred to the guidance in relation to the evaluation, the weighing and balancing of the factors.[42]

- A parent will need to demonstrate that their prospects of success are more than just fanciful and must be solid.[43]

- It will be prudent for judges, when dismissing an application under section 47(5), to ask the parent whether an appeal is proposed and, even if told that an appeal is not in mind, to make clear to the parent that the time for doing so is strictly limited.[44]

- In future judges should postpone *both* the making of the formal adoption order and the holding of the celebratory event until after the parent's time for applying for permission to appeal has expired.[45]

---

[38] *Re B-S*, para 42.
[39] *Re G (A Child)* [2013] EWCA Civ 965, paras 49–50 and *Re B-S*, para 44.
[40] *Re B-S*, paras 68–69.
[41] *Re B-S*, para 73.
[42] *Re B-S*, para 74 (i)–(x).
[43] *Re B-S*, para 59.
[44] *Re W (A Child)* [2013] EWCA Civ 1177, para 31.
[45] *Re W* above.

Balance sheet regarding benefits/disadvantages of adoption for L

6.57

Benefits of adoption for L	Disadvantages of adoption for L
Safety Expert assessments have concluded that neither of L's parents can care for her safely. An adoptive placement would enable L to have the opportunity to be cared for by adoptive parents who will not place her at risk of harm.	Sibling relationships If L is placed for adoption, she will not have any direct contact with her siblings. L currently has regular contact (three times per week) with her siblings and so it could impact on L significantly if she were not to see her siblings.
Parental responsibility Adopters will have full parental responsibility for L and so birth family members will not have any role in the care afforded to and the decisions made in respect of L. This will ensure that L is not put at risk of harm. Adoption is the only care plan that will enable L's new carers to have full parental responsibility for her for life.	Birth parent relationships If L is placed for adoption she will not have any direct contact with her birth parents. This will be a change in routine for L as she currently has three sessions per week of contact with her birth parents/family members. L is observed to have an attachment to both of her parents and will have significant memories of them. This will become confusing if placed for adoption with no direct contact.
Confidentiality The adoption placement will be kept confidential and so this will eliminate the possibility of birth family members undermining L's carers or putting her at risk from harm.	Identity If L is placed for adoption, out of area adoption placements will need to be considered and this could result in L moving from North Lincolnshire; the area where her birth parents originate and her siblings have lived for a significant time. As L grows and develops and learns of her adoption, she may have feelings of confusion, rejection and upset over why she could not be cared for by her birth family. This will especially be the case when there are family members suitable and willing to care for L.
Stability	Opportunity for change It is recognised that adoption is a draconian measure that should only be explored as a last option for any child. It is understood that Mrs and Mr X feel that they can care for L (separately) with the assistance of family members/parenting classes/therapeutic support. A plan of adoption would not allow the possibility for change. Whilst the Local Authority does not support a future restoration to parents' care for L, she will benefit from some form of relationship/contact with them in future.

Matching	Social relationships
Adoptive parents go through a rigorous assessment process. This will ensure that L is cared for by parents whom are safe (verified through thorough checks and references), knowledgeable (developed through training) and skilled in meeting her needs. The adoption family finder/Match Panel will ensure that adopters are carefully matched to L in order to ensure that her needs will be met to a high standard by parents who are committed to her.	L is a sociable and friendly child who has developed many friendships with her family members and children at nursery. L could experience significant loss if adopted and moved away from these peer relationships.
Professional	**Children Act 1989**
Due to the nature of the confidential adoption, adopters will not have a pre-existing relationship with L's birth family. This will therefore eliminate any potential for collusion with birth family members, ensuring that they always act in L's best interests.	The ethos of the Children Act 1989 states that Children should be cared for within their families, where it is safe to do so. If L were adopted, this care plan would not support the ethos of the Children Act 1989 due to their being suitable family members willing to care for L. This is particularly important when considering recent case law *Re B-S*.
Monitored Contact	**Development**
Indirect letterbox contact set up through adoption will ensure that effective safeguards can be put in place for L when receiving information from her birth family. This is more difficult to manage in connected person placements where the risk of birth family attending the placement, is higher.	An adoption placement for L could provide her with confused attachments due to having to adapt to different primary caregivers over a short period of time. L will have to develop a completely new relationship with adopters and this may be difficult for her, given her understanding of who her birth family are.
Motivation	**Understanding**
Adoptive parents are motivated to adopt children as they wish for them to be cared for as one of their own family members. It is more difficult to assess the motivation of connected persons and ensure that they are fully committed to the child and not colluding with birth family.	Although adopted children have a life story book and letter for later life. L's current understanding of her situation and who her birth family are may confuse her considerably if moving to an adoptive placement. Family members may be better suited in L's case, to explain to her why she cannot return to her parents' care and will be able to ease her anxiety due to their familiarity and pre-existing relationship with her.

Conclusions on adoption

Birth parents have been given ample opportunity to modify their parenting in order to provide L with a placement in their care but this has not been achieved and so L cannot be expected to be placed at risk in order to meet their needs.

However, it is recognised through the undertaking of this balance sheet that through the adoption of L she will lose direct contact and links with her birth family and the area in which she was born. This disadvantage affects both L and her siblings. This could have a significant impact on L due to her having such a good awareness of her family for her current age. It is of concern that if adopted, L will be very confused about her identity. L needs and deserves a consistent, loving, caring and safe placement. Adoption is the only care plan that will enable carers to have full parental responsibility for L. However, there are family members willing and able to care for L and so this must be explored in order to promote L's human rights and her identified needs under the Children Act 1989.

Balance sheet regarding benefits/disadvantages of a connected persons/family placement for L

6.58

Benefits of L being placed with connected person/family member	Disadvantages of L being placed with connected person/family member
Paternal Family A family member assessment was completed in regards to Mr and Mrs M (paternal aunt and uncle). They wished only to provide care for L and are being considered as long-term carers for her. Mr and Mrs M have been identified as having a number of strengths in their ability to safeguard L from harm potentially caused by her birth parents.	Burden of placement with Parents As outlined within the Final Statement filed with this report the risks to L should she be placed with her parents either together or separately are excessive. The Local Authority has drawn this conclusion from the extensive assessments filed by the Local Authority and through the court appointed expert assessments.
Identity By being cared for by a connected person, L will have more direct links to her birth family. Timescales L could be placed with a connected person more quickly than she could with adoptive parents and contact will commence shortly for her transition.	Burden of placement with Family Members *Maternal Grandfather* Mr D was assessed in September 2013 as a potential carer for L. The Local Authority would not view this as a viable safe option for L. The assessment filed within these proceedings indicates the extent of these concerns and that Mr D is not able to see the risks that L's birth mother presents and as such this raises significant concerns in regards to his ability to protect.
Contact It is more likely that L would have direct contact or a higher frequency of contact with her birth family if placed with connected persons than adoption.	*Maternal Grandmother* Extensive assessments have been undertaken with Ms W who originally expressed a desire to care for C, K and L when initially assessed in September 2013.

Belonging

If L was placed with connected persons she may have fewer feelings of rejection as she grows up and learns about her background. A connected person may be able to provide L with reassurance that she was wanted and loved by relative/friends of her birth family.

Sibling relationships

If L is placed for adoption, she will not have any direct contact with her siblings. L currently has regular contact (three times per week) with her siblings and so it could impact on L significantly if she were not to see her siblings.

Birth parent relationships

If L is placed for adoption she will not have any direct contact with her birth parents. This will be a change in routine for L as she currently has three sessions per week of contact with her birth parents/family members. L is observed to have an attachment to both of her parents and will have significant memories of them. This will become confusing if placed for adoption with no direct contact.

Identity

If L is placed for adoption, out of area adoption placements will need to be considered and this could result in L moving from North Lincolnshire; the area where her birth parents originate and her siblings have lived for a significant time. As L grows and develops and learns of her adoption, she may have feelings of confusion, rejection and upset over why she could not be cared for by her birth family. This will especially be the case when there are family members suitable and willing to care for L.

Opportunity for change

Whilst the Local Authority does not support a future restoration to parents' care for L, she will benefit from some form of relationship/contact with them in future.

However, since being included in the expert assessments and gaining increased understanding into the children's needs and the risk posed by SL, Ms W wishes to care for C and K only. Ms W states that she loves all of her grandchildren but recognises that she has a stronger attachment to C and K due to them living with her previously. Although saddened by this, Ms W does not feel able to offer care to L.

Maternal Aunt

An assessment is available to the court within these proceedings which outlines that Miss N feels unable to offer L a permanent placement with her. Miss N has her own two children who require a lot of time and attention due to their own needs. She feels that this would not be in L's best interests.

Connected Person – L's previous childminders

A Connected person assessment of Mr and Mrs W has been completed. Mr and Mrs W had a lot of skills in regards to caring for children. However, they presented as overly confident to the point of minimising the risk posed by SL to the children and the instability that SL's risk would cause to the children. Concerns were also raised in regard to how much time could be offered to L and E due to Mr and Mrs W running a full-time business from their home. Mr and Mrs W again minimised the relevance of this.

The assessment concluded that Mr and Mrs W wanted to adopt L and E and treat them as their own; concerns were raised that Mr and Mrs W'S motivation was to bypass the mainstream assessment of foster carers/adopters and that their claiming of the children would cause conflict between themselves and SL. It was felt that SL had nominated Mr and Mrs W in the knowledge they may be approved to care for the children; allowing her access to them. This would cause major instability and insecurity for L and so a placement with Mr and Mrs W would not be suitable to meet her needs.

Stability

Due to parents' knowing the address of a connected person's placement, there is a risk that Mr and Mrs L could attempt to see L outside of agreed contact times.

A placement with a connected person will enable Mr and Mrs L to receive support for their parenting in order to make contact with L of a better quality.	This could cause instability to the placement and L.

Social relationships

L is a sociable and friendly child who has developed many friendships with her family members and children at nursery. L will be able to maintain these relationships if placed with Mr and Mrs M.

Children Act 1989

The ethos of the Children Act 1989 states that children should be cared for within their families, where it is safe to do so. If L was cared for by her paternal aunt and uncle, this care plan would support the ethos of the Children Act 1989 due to their being suitable family members willing to care for L. This is particularly important when considering recent case-law *Re B-S*.

Human Rights Act 1998

Under Article 8, 'Right to respect for private and family life' the Act states that:

1. Everyone has the right to respect for his private and family life, his home and his correspondence.

2. There shall be no interference by a public authority with the exercise of this right except such as is in accordance with the law and is necessary in a democratic society in the interests of national security, public safety or the economic well-being of the country, for the prevention of disorder or crime, for the protection of health or morals, or for the protection of the rights and freedoms of others.

A placement for L with her family members would promote her and her birth family's human rights in a safe way.

The Convention on the Rights of the Child

The convention states that 'Children have the right to live with their parent(s), unless it is bad for them.

Children whose parents do not live together have the right to stay in contact with both parents, unless this might hurt the child.' Placement with her family members would promote direct contact for L and may advocate her rights in this respect. Development L has a pre-existing relationship with Mr and Mrs M and so she will not be required to start a new relationship with primary care givers, rather she will be able to develop her pre-existing attachment to them. This will promote L's emotional health and wellbeing. Understanding Family members may be better suited in L's case, to explain to her why she cannot return to her parents' care and will be able to ease her anxiety due to their familiarity and pre-existing relationship with her.	

Conclusions on connected person/family member placement

When examining the benefits of a connected person placement, there are many benefits and strengths to considering L being cared for by family members. The fact that birth parents will know the identity of a connected person placement places L at increased risk of harm and instability. However, Mr and Ms M have had a thorough assessment and L could be placed with them on an Interim Care Order initially, in order to provide support and supervision to the placement. The benefits of a family member placement are felt to outweigh the risks for L. Her identity needs and need for direct contact with her siblings are very important for her at her current age and understanding. As there are family members suitable and willing to care for L; she must be given this chance to be cared for within her family. This is to meet L's needs and act in her best interest; not her parents'. Should the safety of L be jeopardised by birth family members, the Local Authority would seek legal advice to protect L from such risk.

6.59 As a postscript to these example balance sheets, it should be noted that the type of support and services which could be made available to parents if they were to have the care of their child/ren in the long-term should be set out, including an analysis of why that would not meet the child's particular needs. The case-law is clear in saying that just because a local authority pursues a plan of adoption and doesn't feel that placement with parents with support is viable, it cannot avoid its obligations to lay out what could be made available and then go on to analyse why it would not meet the child/ren's needs.

6.60 The information to go into the balance sheet will be specific to the services and support providers available in the local area where the family lives, and be tailored to the particular facts of the case as to the risk that the local authority will be trying to manage and how the needs of the children for safety and protection will or will not be met. Although this information is likely to form part of the local authority's final statement to the court, it should also be included in the balance sheet exercise.

CONTACT POST-ADOPTION

6.61 The benefits to a child of maintaining contact with their birth family after they have been adopted have been the subject of research and remain debatable. Whilst in some cases it can help the child's development, and enable them to understand their history and identity, in others it can have negative consequences and destabilise their placement. One study found that the proportion of children suffering negative consequences from contact after adoption was twice the proportion for those whom contact had a positive effect.[46]

6.62 In order to try to better support adoptive parents who may face unsolicited contact from the birth family therefore, the 2014 Act introduces a 'no contact' order specifically aimed at adoption situations. Whilst s 8 of the CA 1989 provides similar safeguards, the Government wanted to specifically support adoption by introducing a form of order which can be made at the time that an adoption order is granted, or any time thereafter.

6.63 The 2014 Act therefore inserts a new s 51A to the 2002 Act, to apply where an adoption order is granted. The relevant provisions are as follows:

> (2) When making the adoption order or at any time afterwards, the court may make an order under this section –
>
> (a) requiring the person in whose favour the adoption order is or has been made to allow the child to visit or stay with the person named in the order under this section, or for the person named in that order and the child otherwise to have contact with each other, or
>
> (b) prohibiting the person named in the order under this section from having contact with the child.

6.64 The individuals who can be specifically named in the order include any birth relative, any former guardian or anyone who had parental responsibility for the child prior to the adoption order being made, as well as any other person with whom the child has previously lived for at least one year.

6.65 Section 51A orders can be made on the court's own initiative as well as by application by the adopters, or other individual with leave of the court.[47]

6.66 Once a s 51A order has been made, s 8 CA 1989 orders cannot be made in relation to the same named individuals and the child, (2014 Act s 8(8)).

---

[46] Catherine MacAskill *Safe Contact: Children in Permanent Placement and their Birth Relatives* (2002).

[47] 2014 Act s 8(4) and (6).

Instead, it can be varied or revoked by the court on an application by the child, the adoptive parents or the person named in the order (s 51B).

6.67 The order can have conditions attached, and the court may give directions about how it is to be carried into effect, pursuant to s 51B.

SUPPORT FOR ADOPTERS – DUTIES OF LOCAL AUTHORITIES

6.68 The final significant changes introduced by the 2014 Act relate to an increase in support for adopters through the Adoption Support Services (Amendment) Regulations 2014.[48] Following the Department for Education Action Plan, the Government published a follow-up document entitled *Further Action on Adoption: Finding More Loving Homes*,[49] which focussed on the need to recruit more adopters. It was considered that more than 600 additional adopters were needed, on top of the 2,000–3,000 that were approved annually, in order to keep up with the growing number of children waiting to be adopted. At the end of March 2012, there were over 4,600 children with a placement order waiting to move in with a new family[50] and the lack of adopters was identified as a major cause of delay. The Government proposed systemic change, as well as short-term improvements in the processes.

6.69 Sections 3–5 of the 2014 Act attempt to address this issue by making further provision for the recruitment, assessment and approval of prospective adopters, as well as improving the support services available. One identified issue was the level of information given to prospective adopters about their entitlement to support and assessment under s 4 of the 2002 Act,[51] which requires a local authority to carry out an assessment of needs for adoption support when requested.

6.70 Section 6 of the 2014 Act inserts a new s 4B into the 2002 Act, which places a duty on local authorities to inform potential adopters of their entitlements to adoption support. The information must be provided to any person who has contacted the local authority to request information about adoption, or has stated that they wish to adopt. The emphasis is on the local authority being proactive and offering information, rather than reacting to requests.

---

[48] See https://www.gov.uk/government/uploads/system/uploads/attachment_data/file/285714/The_Adoption_Support_Services__Amendment__Regulations_2014_-_Consultatio …pdf.

[49] See https://www.gov.uk/government/uploads/system/uploads/attachment_data/file/219661/Further_20Action_20on_20Adoption.pdf.

[50] Paragraph 12.

[51] Adoption UK survey 2012 – 64% of 455 adoptive parents were not informed by their adoption agency about their right to an assessment. 38% of respondents to the same survey did know about their entitlements.

6.71 Updated statutory guidance for social workers was consulted upon in early 2014, to consider professionals' views on the proposed new regulations.[52]

---

[52] See https://www.gov.uk/government/uploads/system/uploads/attachment_data/file/285749/Adoption_consultation_document.pdf.

CHAPTER 7

TRANSPARENCY AND REPORTING RESTRICTION ORDERS – THE NEW ETHOS

7.1 On 16 January 2014, Sir James Munby P, issued Practice Guidance to take effect from 3 February 2014, dealing with the publication of judgments in the family courts as they then were. At that stage, the guidance was limited to the judgments of the High Court and circuit judges, although the intention was expressed to expand this to include lay justices in the family proceedings court and district judges.

7.2 The Guidance can be found in full at the conclusion of this chapter. The key principles and cases will be referred to below. Whilst this guide to the principles is not the appropriate forum to debate the pros and cons of the new guidance, it is right to acknowledge that it has attracted considerable debate from legal commentators, who have expressed concerns about issues of clarity as to what may or may not amount to a breach of the guidance, as well as the reality of jigsaw identification, particularly in the light of ever-advancing technology.

7.3 To return to the Guidance itself, which must now be followed by practitioners, the President identified two different types of cases, namely those in which the court **must** ordinarily allow the judgment to be published, and those that **may** be published.

7.4 It is important to remember that the court hearing the case retains the discretion to refuse to publish the judgment notwithstanding the Guidance, (see para 13). The judge also has the discretion to control the terms on which publication may be permitted, and to set out those terms in the rubric at the beginning of the judgment. The standard rubric, which is deemed to be included in a judgment, even if not expressly set out, reminds readers that the judgment has been published on the condition that the identity of the children and family members shall remain anonymous. This rubric may be amended or added to by the court at the time that judgment is delivered.

7.5 Concerns have been raised as to the legal standing of the rubric, and whether or not it can form the basis of committal proceedings, as it is not a term of an order, but a recording at the outset of the judgment. At the time of writing, no committal proceedings have tested this point, but it may be that a challenge arises in due course.

7.6 The publication or otherwise of a judgment remains a matter for the court, regardless of whether or not an application is made by the media or a party. If the court concludes that publication would be in the public interest, then permission to publish should always be given (para 16).

7.7 The Guidance sets out at para 17 those matters in which permission to publish should always be given, unless there are compelling reasons why the judgment should not be published. It is likely therefore that future cases will focus on what amounts to 'compelling reasons' not to publish.

7.8 Schedule 1 of the Guidance deals with cases in the family courts in which judgments should be published:

(i)   a substantial contested fact-finding hearing at which serious allegations, for example allegations of significant physical, emotional or sexual harm, have been determined;

(ii)   the making or refusal of a final care order or supervision order under Part 4 of the Children Act 1989, or any order for the discharge of any such order, except where the order is made with the consent of all participating parties;

(iii)   the making or refusal of a placement order or adoption order under the Adoption and Children Act 2002, or any order for the discharge of any such order, except where the order is made with the consent of all participating parties;

(iv)   the making or refusal of any declaration or order authorising a deprivation of liberty, including an order for a secure accommodation order under s 25 of the Children Act 1989;

(v)   any application for an order involving the giving or withholding of serious medical treatment;

(vi)   any application for an order involving a restraint on publication of information relating to the proceedings.

In all other cases, the starting point is that permission may be given on the application of a party or the media.

THE CALL FOR TRANSPARENCY

7.9 There are long-standing and well-established 'automatic restraints' on the publication of information relating to proceedings under the Children Act 1989. Section 97 of that Act provides that:

> (2) No person shall publish to the public at large or any section of the public any material which is intended, or likely, to identify –

(a)   any child as being involved in any proceedings before the High Court, a county court or a magistrates' court in which any power under this Act or the Adoption and Children Act 2002 may be exercised by the court with respect to that or any other child; or

(b)   an address or school as being that of a child involved in any such proceedings.

(3) In any proceedings for an offence under this section it shall be a defence for the accused to prove that he did not know, and had no reason to suspect, that the published material was intended, or likely, to identify the child.

(4) The court or the Lord Chancellor may, if satisfied that the welfare of the child requires it and, in the case of the Lord Chancellor, if the Lord Chief Justice agrees, by order dispense with the requirements of subsection (2) to such extent as may be specified in the order.

(6) Any person who contravenes this section shall be guilty of an offence and liable, on summary conviction, to a fine not exceeding level 4 on the standard scale.

7.10   However, the effects of that section come to an end once the proceedings have been concluded,[1] although it can be extended by appropriate injunctions. An appropriate injunction can also protect the identity of other individuals involved in the process, an expert, a social worker or a local authority for example.

7.11   The other statutory protection afforded by s 12 of the Administration of Justice Act 1960 is as follows:

12 Publication of information relating to proceedings in private

(1) The publication of information relating to proceedings before any court sitting in private shall not of itself be contempt of court except in the following cases, that is to say –

(a)   where the proceedings –
   (i)   relate to the exercise of the inherent jurisdiction of the High Court with respect to minors;
   (ii)   are brought under the Children Act 1989; or
   (iii) otherwise relate wholly or mainly to the maintenance or upbringing of a minor.

7.12   These provisions do not protect individuals, simply the information relating to the proceedings, such as the substance of the case or the evidence. It does not offer any protection to any party or witness in a case, or to the child.

7.13   The automatic restraint on the publication of family proceedings has given rise over recent years to accusations that the family court was operating as a 'secret' court, with something to hide. This perception was furthered by the

---

[1]   *Clayton v Clayton* [2006] EWCA Civ 878.

inference that parents had been prevented from telling their story in the media, and the court was seen as potentially protecting the system and local authorities.

7.14 Sir James Munby P held the view that 'sunlight is the best disinfectant'[2] and that the best way to counter the suggestion of secrecy was to publish more judgments and therefore open the family courts up to the appropriate public scrutiny:[3]

> 'There is a pressing need for more transparency, indeed for much more transparency, in the family justice system. There are a number of aspects to this.
>
> 27. One is the right of the public to know, the need for the public to be confronted with, what is being done in its name. Nowhere is this more necessary than in relation to care and adoption cases. Such cases, by definition, involve interference, intrusion, by the state, by local authorities and by the court, into family life. In this context the arguments in favour of publicity – in favour of openness, public scrutiny and public accountability – are particularly compelling. The public generally, and not just the professional readers of law reports or similar publications, have a legitimate, indeed a compelling, interest in knowing how the family courts exercise their care jurisdiction: *Re X; London Borough of Barnet v Y and X* [2006] 2 FLR 998, para [166].
>
> 28. I have said this many times in the past but it must never be forgotten that, with the state's abandonment of the right to impose capital sentences, orders of the kind which family judges are typically invited to make in public law proceedings are amongst the most drastic that any judge in any jurisdiction is ever empowered to make.'[4]

7.15 The second aspect of the need for transparency identified by the President in *Re J* is the need to avoid miscarriages of justice:[5]

> 'We must have the humility to recognise – and to acknowledge – that public debate, and the jealous vigilance of an informed media, have an important role to play in exposing past miscarriages of justice and in preventing possible future miscarriages of justice.'

7.16 The final aspect discussed by the President was that of public confidence:[6]

> 'It is vital that public confidence in the family justice system is maintained or, if eroded, restored. There is a clear and obvious public interest in maintaining the confidence of the public at large in the courts. It is vitally important, if the administration of justice is to be promoted and public confidence in the courts maintained, that justice be administered in public – or at least in a manner which

---

2   US Supreme Court Justice Louis Brandeis.
3   *Re J (A Child)* [2013] EWHC 2694 (Fam).
4   Ibid, para 27.
5   At para 29.
6   At para 32.

enables its workings to be properly scrutinised – so that the judges and other participants in the process remain visible and amenable to comment and criticism. This principle, as the Strasbourg court has repeatedly reiterated, is protected by both Article 6 and Article 10 of the Convention. It is a principle of particular importance in the context of care and other public law cases.'

7.17   A clear conflict arises between the rights of the family members and the child to a private life, and the need for transparency, and numerous authorities have grappled with this issue in recent times. Before looking at the case-law, it is important to set out the correct procedure which must be applied when obtaining any reporting restriction order.

PROCEDURE

7.18   Practice Direction 12I – *Applications for Reporting Restriction Orders* is still the applicable procedural guide and should be followed in all cases. It relates to any application in the family court which is founded on Convention rights for an order restricting publication of information about children or incapacitated adults.

7.19   Service of the application is a vital step, and one that too often causes difficulties for practitioners. The court cannot make the RRO unless it is satisfied that:

(a)   the applicant has taken all practicable steps to notify the respondent; or

(b)   there are compelling reasons why the respondent should not be notified.

7.20   Service on subscribing national newspapers can be effected via the Press Association's CopyDirect service. However, there needs to be a note of caution in simply relying on the service as not all newspapers and media organisations subscribe to CopyDirect, and it does not deal with the local press, which is often the first newspaper to take an interest in a case at the local County Court. Neither does it serve applications on magazines, and therefore doesn't assist in a case where a magazine has taken an interest in publishing information, or where a family member has contacted a magazine seeking to sell their story.

7.21   Importantly, CopyDirect only deals with applications, not the court order that may subsequently be made. Court orders need to be served by the traditional postal method or they risk being unenforceable.

Service outside of the jurisdiction – the Facebook problem

7.22   Increasingly, family members turn to social media to complain publicly about the handling of their cases and their perceived injustices. From posting daily updates about the witnesses, to publishing the judge's comments online, Facebook in particular has become a regular feature in court cases. In 2011, Facebook estimated that it had 30 million users in England and Wales.

However, Facebook has no legal entity in the jurisdiction of England and Wales; it is physically based in California, with offices also at Austin, Texas, Dublin, and Hyderabad.

7.23 The question then arises how to go about forcing the removal of contemptive posts, and preventing the posting of material on the website.

7.24 In *Re J*, the President reviewed the authorities in respect of injunctive relief against legal entities based outside of the jurisdiction of England and Wales:[7]

> 'It is plain that this Court has jurisdiction to order a person in this country to perform an act abroad; but it is said that this Court has no jurisdiction to make an order requiring a person resident abroad to do an act there. Notwithstanding the strenuous argument of Mr Archer it appears to me that his proposition is wholly untenable. The moment a person is properly served under the provisions of Order XI that person, so far as the jurisdiction of this Court is concerned, is precisely in the same position as a person who is in this country.'

7.25 It is therefore established law that for injunctive purposes, a defendant is within the reach of the court if properly served in accordance with the relevant rules of the court. Whilst the Civil Procedure Rules require the permission of the court before service can be effected out of the jurisdiction, the Family Procedure Rules provide as follows:[8]

> Any document to be served for the purposes of these rules may be served out of the jurisdiction without the permission of the court.

7.26 Methods of service for international service are dealt with at FPR 6.43(3):

> Where the applicant wishes to serve an application form, or other document, on a respondent out of the United Kingdom, it may be served by any method –
>
> (a) provided for by –
>   (i) rule 6.44 (service in accordance with the Service Regulation);
>   (ii) rule 6.45 (service through foreign governments, judicial authorities and British Consular authorities); or
> (b) permitted by the law of the country in which it is to be served.

7.27 Where, as in the case of *Re J*, service has been effected on international entities by post and emails, the court will need to have evidence that service by those methods is permitted by the law of the relevant foreign country. Secondly, the President held in *Re J*, that evidence would also be needed as to:[9]

> 'the applicable law and practice in the foreign court, evidence as to the nature of any proposed proceedings to be commenced in the foreign jurisdiction, and evidence as to whether the foreign court would be likely to enforce the injunction:

---

[7] *In re Liddell's Settlement Trusts* [1936] Ch 365.
[8] FPR 2010, r 6.41.
[9] *Re J*, para 63.

compare *Dadourian Group International Inc v Simms and others (Practice Note)* [2006] EWCA Civ 399, [2006] 1 WLR 2499. Where the injunction, as here, engages freedom of speech, the evidence will also have to detail the foreign jurisdiction's approach to such matters. Given the First Amendment, this is obviously particularly important in the case of the United States of America: cf the comments of His Honour Judge Parkes QC in *Davison v Habeeb and others* [2011] EWHC 3031 (QB), para [69].'

7.28 In relation to injunctions in contra mundum, where the injunction is against the world at large, and not a named defendant, the guidance given in *Re J* confirms that it is appropriate to adopt the procedure followed in worldwide freezing orders, as set out in the annex to CPR PD 25A, whereby the applicant undertakes not to seek to enforce the order in any country outside of England and Wales without the prior permission of the court.

Open justice – The case-law

7.29 In the Supreme Court decision *A (Respondent) v British Broadcasting Corporation (Appellant)*[10] the Court considered the appeal by the BBC against an order preventing the publication of the name and identity of a convicted sex offender. The court identified the following questions:

'(i)   Whether the court possesses any power at common law to protect the anonymity of a party to proceedings before it, where the Convention rights set out in Schedule 1 to the Human Rights Act 1998 are engaged. It is argued on behalf of the BBC that any common law power which might previously have been exercised in such circumstances has been superseded by the Convention rights.

(ii)   Whether the court acted compatibly with the BBC's rights under article 10 of the European Convention for the Protection of Human Rights and Fundamental Freedoms (ECHR), as given effect by the Human Rights Act, in making the order complained of, both in relation to the substance of its decision and in relation to the procedure which it followed.

(iii) Whether the order fell within the scope of section 12 of the Human Rights Act, with the consequence that the BBC should have been notified and given an opportunity to make representations before any order was made.'

Re A

The facts

7.30 The defendant was a foreign national who arrived in the UK as a visitor in 1991, and subsequently married and had a child. He was granted indefinite leave to remain in the UK. In 1996 he was convicted of sexual offences against his step-child and was sentenced to 4 years' imprisonment. In 1998, a notice of intention to make a deportation order was served. Having been divorced from his first wife, he re-married in 2000 and went on to have more children.

---

[10]   [2014] UKSC 25.

7.31 In 2011, the first-tier tribunal hearing A's appeal in relation to the immigration matters, gave a direction that no report of the proceedings should directly or indirectly identify A. That was later superseded by an order in 2012 during judicial review proceedings 'prohibiting the publication of the name of the petitioner, or any particulars or details calculated to lead to the identification of the petitioner' and directing that 'no picture shall be published or broadcast of the petitioner in connection with these proceedings'.

7.32 The BBC became aware of that order and applied for it to be set aside. The anonymity and the issues around the deportation were inextricably linked, it being A's case that he faced risks of persecution if he were returned to his country of origin and his offences became known.

The principles of open justice

7.33 The Supreme Court made the following observations about the principles of law in this important area:

> '23. It is a general principle of our constitutional law that justice is administered by the courts in public, and is therefore open to public scrutiny. The principle is an aspect of the rule of law in a democracy. As Toulson LJ explained in *R (Guardian News & Media Ltd) v City of Westminster Magistrates' Court (Article 19 intervening)* [2012] EWCA Civ 420; [2013] QB 618, para 1, society depends on the courts to act as guardians of the rule of law. Sed quis custodiet ipsos custodes? Who is to guard the guardians? In a democracy, where the exercise of public authority depends on the consent of the people governed, the answer must lie in the openness of the courts to public scrutiny.
>
> 24. The significance of the principle of open justice is illustrated by the fact that it was one of the matters covered by the constitutional legislation enacted following the accession of William and Mary. The Court of Session Act 1693, which remains in force, provides:
>
> > "That in all time coming, all bills, reports, debates, probations and others relating to processes shall be considered, reasoned, advised and voted by the Lords of Session with open doors, where parties, procurators and all others are hereby allowed to be present, as they used to be formerly in time of debates, but with this restriction, that in some special cases the said Lords shall be allowed to cause remove all persons, except the parties and their procurators."
>
> The corresponding Act "Anent Advising Criminal Processes with Open Doors", passed on the same date, made similar provision for the High Court of Justiciary. As Lord Shaw of Dunfermline commented in *Scott v Scott* [1913] AC 417, 475, the two Acts formed part of the Revolution Settlement, and bore testimony to a determination to secure civil liberties against judges as well as against the Crown.
>
> 25. The principle that courts should sit in public has important implications for the publishing of reports of court proceedings. In *Sloan v B* 1991 SC 412, 442, Lord President Hope, delivering the opinion of the court, explained that it is by an application of the same principle that it has long been recognised that proceedings

in open court may be reported in the press and by other methods of broadcasting in the media. "The principle on which this rule is founded seems to be that, as courts of justice are open to the public, anything that takes place before a judge or judges is thereby necessarily and legitimately made public, and, being once made legitimately public property, may be republished" (*Richardson v Wilson* (1879) 7 R 237, 241 per Lord President Inglis).

26. The connection between the principle of open justice and the reporting of court proceedings is not however merely functional. Since the rationale of the principle is that justice should be open to public scrutiny, and the media are the conduit through which most members of the public receive information about court proceedings, it follows that the principle of open justice is inextricably linked to the freedom of the media to report on court proceedings.'

7.34 However, the courts clearly have discretion within the inherent jurisdiction to decide how the principle of open justice should be applied. The Supreme Court went on to review the authorities in which the principle has been disapplied, commenting that:

'Whether a departure from the principle of open justice was justified in any particular case would depend on the facts of that case. As Lord Toulson observed in *Kennedy v The Charity Commission* [2014] UKSC 20, para 113, the court has to carry out a balancing exercise which will be fact-specific. Central to the court's evaluation will be the purpose of the open justice principle, the potential value of the information in question in advancing that purpose and, conversely, any risk of harm which its disclosure may cause to the maintenance of an effective judicial process or to the legitimate interests of others.'

7.35 In the present case, the Court went on to find that the appeal was dismissed, and that;

'75. In these circumstances, it was plainly necessary in the interests of justice, and in order to protect the safety of a party to the proceedings, to depart from the general principle of open justice to the extent involved in the making of the orders made by Lord Boyd. It follows that, subject to any issue arising under the Convention, the order allowing A to withhold his identity in the proceedings was in accordance with the common law, and the section 11 order was made in accordance with the power conferred by that provision.

76. It also follows that the section 11 order was not incompatible with the Convention rights of the BBC. The interference with its freedom of expression was necessary to maintain the authority and impartiality of the judiciary, since its publication of A's identity in connection with the proposed deportation would have completely undermined the judicial review proceedings. In these circumstances, where the publication of A's identity in connection with the proceedings might well have rendered those proceedings pointless, the interference with the BBC's article 10 rights was unavoidable if the authority and impartiality of the judiciary, within the meaning of article 10(2), were to be maintained. Put shortly, the order had to be made if the court was to do its job, notwithstanding the resulting restriction upon the BBC's capacity to do its job. The interference with the BBC's article 10 rights was also necessary for the protection of the rights

of others, namely the right of A not to be subjected to violent attack. As Lord Rodger observed in *In re Guardian News and Media Ltd* [2010] UKSC 1; [2010] 2 AC 697, para 27, the media do not have the right to publish information at the known potential cost of an individual being killed or maimed.

77. Although the BBC was not represented before Lord Boyd, it was able to apply to the court promptly for the recall of the order. As I have explained, that application was due to be heard by the court on 9 November 2012, only two days after the order had been made. With the BBC's agreement, that hearing was postponed until 14 November 2012, when Lord Glennie heard the BBC's application over the course of two days. He concluded that the order was justified and should not be recalled. For the reasons I have explained, that decision was correct. The procedure that was followed in my opinion satisfied the BBC's entitlement under the Convention to an effective remedy.'

7.36 The BBC case provides a thorough review of both English and Scottish jurisprudence, as well as a review of the European authorities and should be the starting point for any practitioner considering these arguments. The following cases deal specifically with the principle of open justice as they applied to the family law context.

Re J (A Child)[11]

The facts

7.37 The father of four children, all of whom had been the subject of care proceedings, had posted a lot of material about the children, the proceedings and the social workers involved on Facebook. The proceedings in respect of the eldest three children had concluded but the case was still ongoing in relation to the youngest child, J. The father's internet postings had included photographs of the social worker at hospital at the time of removal, and letters written to him by the local authority. His comments and language used against the social worker were offensive and insulting. A reporting restriction order was made against him. The father had then posted a film of the execution of the emergency protection order in respect of J, referring to J by name. It was published via the website UK Column Live, YouTube and shared on Facebook.

7.38 Following an application by the local authority, the father pleaded guilty to breaches of the order and was sentenced to six weeks' imprisonment for each breach, suspended on the condition that he complied with various orders and undertakings.

The issue

7.39 The issue for the court was whether or not there was justification for extending J's anonymity beyond the point at which s 97 of the 1989 Act ceased to bite.

---

[11] [2013] EWHC 2694 (Fam).

The conclusions

7.40   The court agreed that in J's specific case, an order contra mundum was required, although the President limited the terms of the order sought. The only justification for the order was to protect J's Art 8 rights, not because of the abusive attacks on the professionals involved. The court drew a distinction between the publication of J's name, and his image via the video footage that had been published:[12]

> '81. There is, however, in my judgment, a crucial difference in a case such as this, where we are concerned with a baby a day old (though the same point will no doubt apply to somewhat older children), between restraining publication of the child's name and restraining publication of visual images of the child. There are three reasons for this. First, the reality is that although anyone can identify a baby by its name it is almost impossible, unless you are the parent, to distinguish between photographs of children of that age who have the same general appearance. Second, the reality, at least with current domestic technology where searches of the internet are by word (name) and not image, is that unless you have a name, or a mass of other identifying details, it is going to be very difficult, if not impossible, to locate anonymous postings about an individual. Third, in a case such as this, although there may be a powerful argument for asserting that the baby who features in a filmed episode should not be named, there are at least as powerful arguments for asserting that the publication on the internet of film such as I am concerned with here, commenting on the operation of the care system and conveying a no doubt powerful and disturbing message, should not be prevented merely because it includes images of the baby.

> 82. Assessing these three factors together, there is, it seems to me, a very powerful argument that the balance between the public interest in discussing the workings of the system and the personal privacy and welfare interests of the child is best and most proportionately struck by restraining the naming of the child while not restraining the publication of images of the child. The effect of this is that (a) the essential vice – the identification of the child – is in large measure prevented, (b) internet searches are most unlikely to provide any meaningful 'link' in the searcher's mind with the particular child, and (c) the public debate is enabled to continue with the public having access to the footage albeit not knowing who the anonymous child is whose image is on view.'

7.41   The order was therefore made, but no protection was offered to the professionals and social workers in the case, and the restriction was firmly against the publication of J's name, not his image. The judgment caused some controversy amongst local authorities and social workers, and it has been argued by some commentators that as technology improves, identification via facial recognition will become more likely. In addition, there potentially remains the risk of identification via the identity of other professionals, and the geographical area.

---

[12]   At paras 81–82.

Re P (A Child)[13]

7.42 Following the decision in *Re J* above, the President dealt with an application arising from Court of Protection and associated Children Act proceedings, *Re P (A Child)*.[14] The local authority involved sought a reporting restriction order to protect the child's identity following widespread reporting worldwide, much of it sadly inaccurate as to the facts. The case was controversial and attracted public attention as it dealt with a Court of Protection application for the performance of a caeseraen section, with the use of restraint if necessary, the mother having been found to lack capacity to make decisions as to treatment.

7.43 Following the baby's birth, care proceedings commenced and a care and placement order were made. The mother pursued proceedings in Italy, where she was from, but did not appeal against the orders in England. The baby was subsequently adopted.

7.44 There had subsequently been extensive reporting in the national press about the case. Most of it was factually incorrect:

'21. The media coverage of all this has been very extensive. It is neither necessary nor appropriate for me to attempt even to list let alone analyse this in any detail. For present purposes it suffices to say that the coverage in this country (I say nothing about the foreign media) has had four principal themes.

22. The first, and most substantial, is comment about, and in some instances criticisms of, the various orders made by the English courts. Much of this has been strident and some of it has been inaccurate. The initial coverage on 1 and 2 December 2013 appeared under such headlines as "Operate on this mother so that we can take her baby", "Woman's baby taken from womb by social services" and "Social workers took baby into care after forcing her mother to have a Caesarean". In fact, as we now know, the application to the Court of Protection was made by the relevant NHS Trust, not the local authority. In relation to all this there is interesting comment by various legal commentators on the blogosphere, including suggestions that some of the orders made might be vulnerable to legal challenge. Since these matters may yet require judicial determination I say nothing more.

23. The second consists of reports of what is being said by and interviews with the mother and, more recently, her own father.

24. The third consists of comments about and criticisms of the lack of transparency in the court process, the fact that the hearing in the Court of Protection was in "secret" and the delay in publication of the judgments – hence the comment in a national newspaper on 2 December 2013 that "no information concerning any element of our treatment of the Italian mother has been made public by the courts".

---

[13] [2013] EWHC 4048 (Fam).
[14] [2013] EWHC 4048 (Fam).

25. The fourth, though largely confined to legal commentators on the blogosphere, relates to criticisms, some expressed in strong terms, of the way in which the case has been reported by the media.'

7.45 In relation to inaccurate reporting, the President repeated his earlier comments at paras 37–39 of *Re J*:[15]

'First, that "It is not the role of the judge to seek to exercise any kind of editorial control over the manner in which the media reports information which it is entitled to publish". Second, that "Comment and criticism may be ill-informed and based, it may be, on misunderstanding or misrepresentation of the facts [but the] fear of such criticism, however justified that fear may be, and however unjustified the criticism, is ... not of itself a justification for prior restraint by injunction of the kind being sought here, even if the criticism is expressed in vigorous, trenchant or outspoken terms ... or even in language which is crude, insulting and vulgar". Third, that "It is no part of the function of the court exercising the jurisdiction I am being asked to apply to prevent the dissemination of material because it is defamatory ... If what is published is defamatory, the remedy is an action for defamation, not an application in the Family Division for an injunction".'

7.46 In considering the application for a RRO, the President found that:

'35. The public has an interest in knowing and discussing what has been done in this case, both in the Court of Protection and in the Chelmsford County Court. Given the circumstances of the case and the extreme gravity of the issues which here confronted the courts – whether to order an involuntary caesarean section and whether to place a child for adoption despite the protests of the mother – it is hard to imagine a case which more obviously and compellingly requires that public debate be free and unrestricted.

36. The mother has an equally obvious and compelling claim to be allowed to tell her story to the world. I repeat what I have on previous occasions (see most recently *Re J*, para 36) about the importance in a free society of parents who feel aggrieved at their experiences of the family justice system being able to express their views publicly about what they conceive to be failings on the part of individual judges or failings in the judicial system and likewise being able to criticise local authorities and others. I repeat what I said last week (*Re P* [2013] EWHC 4037 (Fam), para 4):

"The mother wishes to complain publicly about the way in which the courts in this country have handled her and her daughter. The court should be very slow indeed before preventing a parent doing what the mother wishes to do in the present case."

If ever there was a case in which that right should not be curtailed it is surely this case. To deny this mother in the circumstances of this case the right to speak out – and, I emphasise, to speak out, if this is her wish, using her own name and displaying her own image – would be affront not merely to the law but also, surely, to any remotely acceptable concept of human dignity and, indeed, humanity itself.

---

[15] *Re P*, para 26.

37. P also, it should go without saying, has an equally compelling claim to privacy and anonymity.'

7.47   The court went on to balance the competing interests and held that the child's welfare demanded that neither she nor her carers should be identified. However, the President declined to go further and prohibit identification of either the mother or father, and did not prevent the mother identifying herself by her first name or maiden name. The strength of the President's views are shown at para 45 of the judgment:

> 'This case must surely stand as final, stark and irrefutable demonstration of the pressing need for radical changes in the way in which both the family courts and the Court of Protection approach what for shorthand I will refer to as transparency. We simply cannot go on as hitherto. Many more judgments must be published. And, as this case so very clearly demonstrates, that applies not merely to the judgments of High Court Judges; it applies also to the judgments of Circuit Judges.'

The President went onto publish the terms of the order, which is reproduced at the conclusion of this chapter.

FAMILY AND CRIMINAL PROCEEDINGS – THE OVERLAP

7.48   Other than those cases in which aggrieved parents want to volunteer information to the media in order to publicly complain, the other category of cases in which there is often a public interest are those involving criminality where criminal trials are due to take place, or have already done so. In these cases, the starting point is to consider any automatic reporting restrictions which are provided for through the criminal justice legislation.

7.49   Automatic reporting restrictions apply to proceedings in the Youth Court, (whether it be defendant, witness, address or school), and to victims of sexual offences,[16] whether children or not. The most commonly referred to restriction on reporting arising through criminal cases is found in s 39 of the Children and Young Person's Act 1933 (CYPA). Section 39 permits a criminal court to prohibit publication by the media of the name, address, school or any information calculated to lead to the identification of any child or young person concerned in criminal proceedings before that court. The power extends to pictures of the child or young person but only applies to the proceedings in the court by which it was made, and is discretionary, not automatic:

39 Power to prohibit publication of certain matter in newspapers

(1) In relation to any proceedings in any court ... the court may direct that –

    (a)   no newspaper report of the proceedings shall reveal the name, address or school, or include any particulars calculated to lead to the identification, of any child or young person concerned in the proceedings, either as

---

[16]   Sexual Offences (Amendment) Act 1992.

being the person by or against or in respect of whom the proceedings are taken, or as being a witness therein:

(b)   no picture shall be published in any newspaper as being or including a picture of any child or young person so concerned in the proceedings as aforesaid;

except in so far (if at all) as may be permitted by the direction of the court.

(2) Any person who publishes any matter in contravention of any such direction shall on summary conviction be liable in respect of each offence to a fine not exceeding level 5 on the standard scale.

7.50   However, s 39 doesn't always provide the protection that parties to family proceedings would like against identification, as scenarios commonly arise whereby the reporting of a defendant's name will result in the identification of children involved in the case, whether as witnesses or victims. The courts have to scrutinise the practice of the publication of a defendants' identity, balancing the competing rights under Art 8 and 10 ECHR.[17] The starting point is that it is in the public interest to know the identity of those accused of criminal acts, particularly after they have been charged and are proceeding through court. It is often said that the identification of defendants may lead to other victims coming forward, and serves to protect the public:

'The need to be vigilant arises from the natural tendency for the general principle to be eroded and for exceptions to grow by accretion as the exceptions are applied by analogy to existing cases. This is the reason it is so important not to forget why proceedings are required to be subjected to the full glare of a public hearing. It is necessary because the public nature of the proceedings deters inappropriate behaviour on the part of the court. It also maintains the public's confidence in the administration of justice. It enables the public to know that justice is being administered impartially. It can result in evidence becoming available which would not become available if the proceedings were conducted behind closed doors or with one or more of the parties' or witnesses' identity concealed. It makes uninformed and inaccurate comment about the proceedings less likely ... Any interference with the public nature of court proceedings is therefore to be avoided unless justice requires it. However Parliament has recognised there are situations where interference is necessary.'[18]

'A criminal trial is a public event. The principle of open justice puts, as has often been said, the judge and all who participate in the trial under intense scrutiny. The glare of contemporaneous publicity ensures that trials are properly conducted. It is a valuable check on the criminal process. Moreover, the public interest may be as much involved in the circumstances of a remarkable acquittal as in a surprising conviction. Informed public debate is necessary about all such matters. Full contemporaneous reporting of criminal trials in progress promotes public confidence in the administration of justice. It promotes the values of the rule of law.'[19]

---

[17]   *Re S (A Child) (Identification: Restriction on Publication)* [2005] 1 AC 593.
[18]   *R v Legal Aid Board ex parte Kaim Todner (A Firm)* [1999] QB 966 at 977 per Lord Woolf MR.
[19]   *Re S*, para 30.

7.51   However, where that defendant is a parent or family member, and their identification will inevitably lead to the identification of a child in care proceedings, it may become necessary to seek a reporting restriction order from the High Court. The definitive statement of principle about how these issues should be approached is found in the decision of the House of Lords in *Re S (A Child) Identification: Restriction on Publication)*:[20]

> 'By section 12(4) of the Human Rights Act 1998 Parliament made special provision regarding freedom of expression. It provides that when considering whether to grant relief which, if granted, might affect the exercise of the Convention right to freedom of expression the court must have particular regard to the importance of the right.
>
> The interplay between articles 8 and 10 has been illuminated by the opinions in the House of Lords in *Campbell v MGN Ltd* [2004] 2 WLR 1232. For present purposes the decision of the House on the facts of Campbell and the differences between the majority and the minority are not material. What does, however, emerge clearly from the opinions are four propositions. First, neither article has as such precedence over the other. Secondly, where the values under the two articles are in conflict, an intense focus on the comparative importance of the specific rights being claimed in the individual case is necessary. Thirdly, the justifications for interfering with or restricting each right must be taken into account. Finally, the proportionality test must be applied to each. For convenience I will call this the ultimate balancing test. This is how I will approach the present case.'

7.52   *Re S* was relied upon by Jackson J in the recent case of *A Council v M & Ors (Judgment 3: Reporting Restrictions)*,[21] in which the court prevented the reporting of the mother's name, despite her being the defendant in criminal proceedings. That step had only been taken once before.[22] It was further applied in *Z & Ors v News Group Newspapers Ltd & Ors (Judgment 1)*,[23] and remains the test to be considered in each case. In *Z & Ors*, the identification of the mother was only prevented until her conviction, at which point Cobb J concluded that the balance fell in favour of reporting and Art 10 rights:

> '27. The inevitable yet highly unfortunate consequence of naming the defendant (in the event of her conviction) is that there will be opportunity for those who wish, and are able, to do so to identify the children who were involved in the defendant's (in this scenario, proven) fraudulent activities; the children were, as I earlier indicated, innocent instruments of the alleged fraud. I regret that by involving the children in any proven crime, the mother herself must take significant responsibility for the public acquiring knowledge of her exploitation of them ...
>
> 31. In my judgment, those who cheat the over-stretched resources of the welfare state can neither generally nor reasonably expect to escape the proper reporting of their wrongdoing, or hope to achieve the concealment of their identities. It is with considerable regret that in varying the Reporting Restriction Order in the event of

---

[20]   [2005] 1 AC 593, paras 16–17.
[21]   [2012] EWHC 2038 (Fam).
[22]   *A Local Authority v W* [2005] EWHC 1564 (Fam).
[23]   [2013] EWHC 1150 (Fam).

a conviction, I will expose the children of Mrs Z to the risk of identification. A guilty verdict would reflect the jury's satisfaction that Mrs Z had improperly used her children as innocent instruments of her crime; if this is the outcome of the criminal process, then it is she alone who has unhappily heaped upon her family the misery, shame and disadvantage, which is the inevitable consequence of her offending.'

7.53 The acute balancing exercise was most recently considered in *Surrey CC v ME* and others,[24] in which Keehan J refused an application for an RRO in circumstances where two of the young people were facing trial for the murder of their father/stepfather:

> '69. As Sir Mark Potter P observed in *A Local Authority v PD*, the facts of this case are "unusual and sensational" but they are not exceptional. The facts of this case are "far from sufficient to outweigh the plain and substantial interference with the right of [media organisations]" to indentify JE and the parents and to report the current criminal proceedings.'

The court went on to refuse the application for the RRO.

TRANSPARENCY – THE FUTURE

7.54 At the time of writing, the next stage in the transparency agenda is the consideration of provision of court documents to the media. This step highlights issues that require careful scrutiny, raising as it does data protection implications. It is likely that a pilot scheme will be trialled in the High Court in 2014, and further consultation is expected.

---

[24] [2014] EWHC 489 (Fam).

7.55

DRAFT ORDER

Before the President

IN THE MATTER OF CHILD P [A GIRL, D.O.B. 24.08.2012]

IN THE MATTER OF THE ADMINISTRATION OF JUSTICE ACT 1960
AND IN THE MATTER OF THE CHILDREN ACT 1989
AND IN THE MATTER OF THE HUMAN RIGHTS ACT 1998

After hearing Mr R Howling QC who appeared on behalf of the local authority

And upon reading confirmation from Associated Newspapers Limited that they consent to the terms of this order

REPORTING RESTRICTION ORDER MADE BY THE PRESIDENT ON 13 DECEMBER 2013 SITTING IN OPEN COURT.

IMPORTANT WARNING: ANY PERSON OR BODY WHO KNOWS OF THIS ORDER AND DOES ANYTHING TO BREACH ITS TERMS MAY BE HELD TO BE IN CONTEMPT OF COURT AND MAY BE IMPRISONED, FINED OR HAVE THEIR ASSETS SEIZED.

IF YOU ARE SERVED WITH THIS ORDER YOU SHOULD READ IT EXTREMELY CAREFULLY AND ARE ADVISED TO CONSULT A SOLICITOR AS SOON AS POSSIBLE. YOU HAVE THE RIGHT TO ASK THE COURT TO VARY OR DISCHARGE THE ORDER.

The parties

1 The Applicant is Essex County Council ('the Local Authority')
The First Respondent is B ('The Mother').
The Second Respondent is C ('The Father').
The Third Respondent is P ('The Child').

2 The lead lawyer employed by the Local Authority is … , whose direct telephone number is … and email address is … , and to whom all enquiries about the scope and effect of this order should be addressed.

Recitals

3 On 13 December 2013 the Court considered an application for a reporting restriction order.

4 This order was made at a hearing with notice having been given to the Press Association. Both the First and Second Respondent had also been given notice of this hearing by email.

5 The Judge read the following documents: the Application, a draft Order, a chronology and position statement prepared by Essex County Council, together with a statement from a social worker employed by Essex County Council, and was informed that the child had been placed for adoption.

6 Schedule 1 to this order [omitted] is an explanatory note in plain English. It forms part of this order. The note must always be supplied to any person affected by this order but otherwise is not to be published.

7 At present the address of the child and the names and address of her carers are not public knowledge. Those names and address are therefore not set out in this order. Those details must remain strictly confidential.

8 Subject to the following paragraph, this order binds all persons and all companies or unincorporated bodies (whether acting by their directors, employees or in any other way) who know that the order has been made.

Territorial limitation

9 In respect of persons outside England and Wales:

(i)   Except as provided in sub-paragraph (ii) below, the terms of this order do not affect or concern anyone outside the jurisdiction of this court.

(ii) The terms of this order will bind the following persons in a country, territory or state outside the jurisdiction of this court:
  (a)   the First and Second Respondents or their agents;
  (b)   any person who is subject to the jurisdiction of this court;
  (c)   any person who has been given written notice of this order at his residence or place of business within the jurisdiction of this court;
  (d)   any person who is able to prevent acts or omissions outside the jurisdiction of this court which constitute or assist in a breach of the terms of this order; and
  (e)   any other person, only to the extent that this order is declared enforceable by or is enforced by a court in that country or state.

Undertakings to the court

10 If the court later finds that this order has caused loss to a Respondent or to a third party and decides that such Respondent or third party should be compensated for that loss, the Applicant shall comply with any order the court may make.

11 The Applicant will not, without permission of the Court, seek to enforce this order in any country, state or territory outside England and Wales.

IT IS ORDERED THAT:

12 The Applicant is granted permission pursuant to the Children Act 1989 s 100 to apply for an order in the exercise of the Court's inherent jurisdiction.

Prohibited publications

13 Subject to the 'territorial limitation' above, this order prohibits the Respondents from facilitating or permitting the publishing or broadcasting in any newspaper, magazine, public computer network, internet website, social networking website, sound or television broadcast or cable or satellite program service any information, including the mother's married surname, that reveals the identity or name or address or whereabouts of the child (whose details are set out in Schedule 1), or the identity or name or address or whereabouts of her carers, or any pictures of the child or her carers if, but only if, such publication is likely, whether directly or indirectly, to lead to the identification of the child as being:

(a)   A child who is or has been subject of proceedings under the Children Act 1989 or the Adoption and Children Act 2002; and/or

(b)   A child who has been removed from the care of her parents; and/or

(c)   A child whose contact with her parents has been prohibited or restricted.

Provided that nothing in this order prevents the publication of the mother's first and maiden names.

14 No publication of the text or summary of this order or the supporting documents (except as provided for below under 'service of this order') shall include any of the matters referred to in the preceding paragraph.

Permitted publications

15 Nothing in this order shall prevent any person from:

(a)   publishing information relating to any part of a hearing in a court in England and Wales (including a coroner's court) in which the court was sitting in public and did not itself make any order restricting publication;

(b)   seeking or publishing information which is not restricted by the section 'prohibited publications' above;

(c)   enquiring whether a person or place falls within the section 'prohibited publications' above;

(d)   seeking information relating to the child while acting in a manner authorised by statute or by any court in England and Wales;

(e)   seeking information from the lead solicitor acting for the local authority, whose details are set out under 'the parties' above, or from any press officer employed by the local authority;

(f) seeking or receiving information from anyone who before making of this order had previously approached that person with the purpose of volunteering information (but this paragraph will not make lawful the provision or receipt of private information which would otherwise be unlawful).

Duration of this order

16 Subject to any different order made in the meantime, this order shall have effect until 6pm on 24 August 2030, save in the event that the child is returned to the care of the mother in which case this order shall thereupon cease to have effect.

The right to apply for variation or discharge of this order

17 The parties and any person affected by any of the restrictions in the section 'prohibited publications' above of this order may make application to vary or discharge it to a judge of the High Court on no less than two working hours' notice to the Applicant and the Press Association and, if practicable, to the other parties. Any such application shall be supported by a witness statement endorsed with a statement of truth.

Service of this order

18 Without prejudice to the terms of the 'territorial limitation' above, copies of this order (which is endorsed with the notice warning of the consequences of disobedience) shall be served by the Applicant (and may be served by any other parties to the proceedings):

(a) by service on such newspaper and sound or television broadcasting or cable satellite or programme services as they see fit, by fax or first class post addressed to the editor (in the case of a newspaper) or senior news editor (in the case of a broadcasting, cable or satellite programme service) or website administrator (in the case of an internet website) and/or to their respective legal departments; and/or

(b) on such other persons as the parties may think fit, by personal service.

Costs

19 There shall be no order as to costs.

7.56

PRESIDENT'S GUIDANCE

TRANSPARENCY IN THE FAMILY COURTS

PUBLICATION OF JUDGMENTS

PRACTICE GUIDANCE issued on 16 January 2014 by SIR JAMES MUNBY, PRESIDENT OF THE FAMILY DIVISION

The purpose of this Guidance

1 This Guidance (together with similar Guidance issued at the same time for the Court of Protection) is intended to bring about an immediate and significant change in practice in relation to the publication of judgments in family courts and the Court of Protection.

2 In both courts there is a need for greater transparency in order to improve public understanding of the court process and confidence in the court system. At present too few judgments are made available to the public, which has a legitimate interest in being able to read what is being done by the judges in its name. The Guidance will have the effect of increasing the number of judgments available for publication (even if they will often need to be published in appropriately anonymised form).

3 In July 2011 Sir Nicholas Wall P issued, jointly with Bob Satchwell, Executive Director of the Society of Editors, a paper, *The Family Courts: Media Access & Reporting* (Media Access & Reporting), setting out a statement of the current state of the law. In their preface they recognised that the debate on increased transparency and public confidence in the family courts would move forward and that future consideration of this difficult and sensitive area would need to include the questions of access to and reporting of proceedings by the media, whilst maintaining the privacy of the families involved. The paper is to be found at:

http://www.judiciary.gov.uk/Resources/JCO/Documents/Guidance/family-courts-media-july2011.pdf

4 In April 2013 I issued a statement, *View from the President's Chambers: the Process of Reform*, [2013] Fam Law 548, in which I identified transparency as one of the three strands in the reforms which the family justice system is currently undergoing. I said:

> "I am determined to take steps to improve access to and reporting of family proceedings. I am determined that the new Family Court should not be saddled, as the family courts are at present, with the charge that we are a system of secret and

unaccountable justice. Work, commenced by my predecessor, is well underway. I hope to be in a position to make important announcements in the near future."

5 That applies just as much to the issue of transparency in the Court of Protection.

6 Very similar issues arise in both the Family Court (as it will be from April 2014) and the Court of Protection in relation to the need to protect the personal privacy of children and vulnerable adults. The applicable rules differ, however, and this is something that needs attention. My starting point is that so far as possible the same rules and principles should apply in both the family courts (in due course the Family Court) and the Court of Protection.

7 I propose to adopt an incremental approach. Initially I am issuing this Guidance. This will be followed by further Guidance and in due course more formal Practice Directions and changes to the Rules (the Court of Protection Rules 2007 and the Family Procedure Rules 2010). Changes to primary legislation are unlikely in the near future.

8 As provided in paragraph 14 below, this Guidance applies only to judgments delivered by certain judges. In due course, following the introduction of the Family Court, consideration will be given to extending it to judgments delivered by other judges (including lay justices).

The legal framework

9 The effect of section 12 of the Administration of Justice Act 1960 is that it is a contempt of court to publish a judgment in a family court case involving children unless either the judgment has been delivered in public or, where delivered in private, the judge has authorised publication. In the latter case, the judge normally gives permission for the judgment to be published on condition that the published version protects the anonymity of the children and members of their family.

10 In every case the terms on which publication is permitted are a matter for the judge and will be set out by the judge in a rubric at the start of the judgment.

11 The normal terms as described in paragraph 9 may be appropriate in a case where no-one wishes to discuss the proceedings otherwise than anonymously. But they may be inappropriate, for example, where parents who have been exonerated in care proceedings wish to discuss their experiences in public, identifying themselves and making use of the judgment. Equally, they may be inappropriate in cases where findings have been made against a person and someone else contends and/or the judge concludes that it is in the public interest for that person to be identified in any published version of the judgment.

12 If any party wishes to identify himself or herself, or any other party or person, as being a person referred to in any published version of the judgment, their remedy is to seek an order of the court and a suitable modification of the rubric: Media Access & Reporting, para 82; *Re RB (Adult) (No 4)* [2011] EWHC 3017 (Fam), [2012] 1 FLR 466, paras [17], [19].

13 Nothing in this Guidance affects the exercise by the judge in any particular case of whatever powers would otherwise be available to regulate the publication of material relating to the proceedings. For example, where a judgment is likely to be used in a way that would defeat the purpose of any anonymisation, it is open to the judge to refuse to publish the judgment or to make an order restricting its use.

Guidance

14 This Guidance takes effect from 3 February 2014. It applies

(i)   in the family courts (and in due course in the Family Court), to judgments delivered by Circuit Judges, High Court Judges and persons sitting as judges of the High Court; and

(ii) to all judgments delivered by High Court Judges (and persons sitting as judges of the High Court) exercising the inherent jurisdiction to make orders in respect of children and incapacitated or vulnerable adults.

15 The following paragraphs of this Guidance distinguish between two classes of judgment:

(i)   those that the judge *must* ordinarily allow to be published (paragraphs 16 and 17); and

(ii) those that *may* be published (paragraph 18).

16 Permission to publish a judgment should always be given whenever the judge concludes that publication would be in the public interest and whether or not a request has been made by a party or the media.

17 Where a judgment relates to matters set out in Schedule 1 or 2 below and a written judgment already exists in a publishable form or the judge has already ordered that the judgment be transcribed, the starting point is that permission should be given for the judgment to be published unless there are compelling reasons why the judgment should not be published.

SCHEDULE 1

In the family courts (and in due course in the Family Court), including in proceedings under the inherent jurisdiction of the High Court relating to children, judgments arising from:

(i)   a substantial contested fact-finding hearing at which serious allegations, for example allegations of significant physical, emotional or sexual harm, have been determined;

(ii)   the making or refusal of a final care order or supervision order under Part 4 of the Children Act 1989, or any order for the discharge of any such order, except where the order is made with the consent of all participating parties;

(iii) the making or refusal of a placement order or adoption order under the Adoption and Children Act 2002, or any order for the discharge of any such order, except where the order is made with the consent of all participating parties;

(iv)   the making or refusal of any declaration or order authorising a deprivation of liberty, including an order for a secure accommodation order under section 25 of the Children Act 1989;

(v)   any application for an order involving the giving or withholding of serious medical treatment;

(vi)   any application for an order involving a restraint on publication of information relating to the proceedings.

SCHEDULE 2

In proceedings under the inherent jurisdiction of the High Court relating to incapacitated or vulnerable adults, judgments arising from:

(i)   any application for a declaration or order involving a deprivation or possible deprivation of liberty;

(ii)   any application for an order involving the giving or withholding of serious medical treatment;

(iii) any application for an order that an incapacitated or vulnerable adult be moved into or out of a residential establishment or other institution;

(iv)   any application for a declaration as to capacity to marry or to consent to sexual relations;

(v)   any application for an order involving a restraint on publication of information relating to the proceedings.

18 In all other cases, the starting point is that permission may be given for the judgment to be published whenever a party or an accredited member of the media applies for an order permitting publication, and the judge concludes that permission for the judgment to be published should be given.

19 In deciding whether and if so when to publish a judgment, the judge shall have regard to all the circumstances, the rights arising under any relevant provision of the European Convention on Human Rights, including Articles 6 (right to a fair hearing), 8 (respect for private and family life) and 10 (freedom of expression), and the effect of publication upon any current or potential criminal proceedings.

20 In all cases where a judge gives permission for a judgment to be published:

(i) public authorities and expert witnesses should be named in the judgment approved for publication, unless there are compelling reasons why they should not be so named;

(ii) the children who are the subject of the proceedings in the family courts, and other members of their family, and the person who is the subject of proceedings under the inherent jurisdiction of the High Court relating to incapacitated or vulnerable adults, and other members of their family, should not normally be named in the judgment approved for publication unless the judge otherwise orders;

(iii) anonymity in the judgment as published should not normally extend beyond protecting the privacy of the children and adults who are the subject of the proceedings and other members of their families, unless there are compelling reasons to do so.

21 Unless the judgment is already in anonymised form or the judge otherwise orders, any necessary anonymisation of the judgment shall be carried out, in the case of judgments being published pursuant to paragraphs 16 and 17 above, by the solicitor for the applicant in the proceedings and, in the case of a judgment being published pursuant to paragraph 18 above, by the solicitor for the party or person applying for publication of the judgment. The anonymised version of the judgment must be submitted to the judge within a period specified by the judge for approval. The version approved for publication will contain such rubric as the judge specifies. Unless the rubric specified by the judge provides expressly to the contrary every published judgment shall be deemed to contain the following rubric:

> "This judgment was delivered in private. The judge has given leave for this version of the judgment to be published on condition that (irrespective of what is contained in the judgment) in any published version of the judgment the anonymity of the children and members of their family must be strictly preserved. All persons, including representatives of the media, must ensure that this condition is strictly complied with. Failure to do so will be a contempt of court."

22 The judge will need to consider who should be ordered to bear the cost of transcribing the judgment. Unless the judge otherwise orders:

(i) in cases falling under paragraph 16 the cost of transcribing the judgment is to be at public expense;

(ii) subject to (i), in cases falling under paragraph 17 the cost of transcribing the judgment shall be borne equally by the parties to the proceedings;

(iii) in cases falling under paragraph 18, the cost of transcribing the judgment shall be borne by the party or person applying for publication of the judgment.

23 In all cases where permission is given for a judgment to be published, the version of the judgment approved for publication shall be made available, upon

payment of any appropriate charge that may be required, to any person who requests a copy. Where a judgment to which paragraph 16 or 17 applies is approved for publication, it shall as soon as reasonably practicable be placed by the court on the BAILII website. Where a judgment to which paragraph 18 applies is approved for publication, the judge shall consider whether it should be placed on the BAILII website and, if so, it shall as soon as reasonably practicable be placed by the court on the BAILII website.

APPENDIX 1

CHILDREN AND FAMILIES ACT 2014, PT 1

PART 1
ADOPTION AND CONTACT

Adoption

1 Contact between prescribed persons and adopted person's relatives

(1) In section 98 of the Adoption and Children Act 2002 (pre-commencement adoptions: information), after subsection (1) insert—

"(1A) Regulations under section 9 may make provision for the purpose of facilitating contact between persons with a prescribed relationship to a person adopted before the appointed day and that person's relatives."

(2) In each of subsections (2) and (3) of that section, for "that purpose" substitute

"a purpose within subsection (1) or (1A)".

(3) In subsection (7) of that section, after the definition of "appointed day" insert—
""prescribed" means prescribed by regulations under section 9;".

2 Placement of looked after children with prospective adopters

(1) Section 22C of the Children Act 1989 is amended as follows.

(2) In subsection (7), after "subject to" insert "subsection (9B) and".

(3) After subsection (9) insert—

"(9A) Subsection (9B) applies (subject to subsection (9C)) where the local authority are a local authority in England and—

    (a)   are considering adoption for C, or

    (b)   are satisfied that C ought to be placed for adoption but are not authorised under section 19 of the Adoption and Children Act 2002 (placement with parental consent) or by virtue of section 21 of that Act (placement orders) to place C for adoption.

(9B) Where this subsection applies—

    (a)   subsections (7) to (9) do not apply to the local authority,

    (b)   the local authority must consider placing C with an individual within subsection (6)(a), and

    (c)   where the local authority decide that a placement with such an individual is not the most appropriate placement for C, the local authority must consider placing C with a local authority foster parent who has been approved as a prospective adopter.

(9C) Subsection (9B) does not apply where the local authority have applied for a placement order under section 21 of the Adoption and Children Act 2002 in respect of C and the application has been refused."

3 Repeal of requirement to give due consideration to ethnicity: England

(1) Section 1 of the Adoption and Children Act 2002 (considerations applying when making decisions about the adoption of a child) is amended as follows.

(2) In subsection (5) (due consideration to be given to religious persuasion, racial origin and cultural and linguistic background), for "In placing the child for adoption, the adoption agency" substitute "In placing a child for adoption, an adoption agency in Wales".

(3) In consequence of the amendment made by subsection (2)—

(a)   in subsection (1), for "This section applies" substitute "Subsections (2) to (4) apply";

(b)   in subsection (6), for "The court or adoption agency" substitute "In coming to a decision relating to the adoption of a child, a court or adoption agency";

(c)   after subsection (8) insert—

"(9) In this section "adoption agency in Wales" means an adoption agency that is—

(a)   a local authority in Wales, or

(b)   a registered adoption society whose principal office is in Wales."

4 Recruitment, assessment and approval of prospective adopters

(1) In Chapter 2 of Part 1 of the Adoption and Children Act 2002 (the Adoption Service) after section 3 insert—

"3A Recruitment, assessment and approval of prospective adopters

(1) The Secretary of State may give directions requiring one or more named local authorities in England, or one or more descriptions of local authority in England, to make arrangements for all or any of their functions within subsection (3) to be carried out on their behalf by one or more other adoption agencies.

(2) The Secretary of State may by order require all local authorities in England to make arrangements for all or any of their functions within subsection (3) to be carried out on their behalf by one or more other adoption agencies.

(3) The functions are their functions in relation to—

(a)   the recruitment of persons as prospective adopters;

(b)   the assessment of prospective adopters' suitability to adopt a child;

(c)   the approval of prospective adopters as suitable to adopt a child."

(2) In section 140(3) of that Act (statutory instruments containing subordinate legislation that are subject to the affirmative procedure), before paragraph (a) insert—

"(za) under section 3A(2),".

(3) The Secretary of State may not make an order under subsection (2) of section 3A of the Adoption and Children Act 2002 (as inserted by subsection (1)) before 1 March 2015.

5 Adoption support services: personal budgets

In Chapter 2 of Part 1 of the Adoption and Children Act 2002 (the Adoption Service) after section 4 insert—

"4A Adoption support services: personal budgets

(1) This section applies where—

    (a)   after carrying out an assessment under section 4, a local authority in England decide to provide any adoption support services to a person ("the recipient"), and

    (b)   the recipient is an adopted person or the parent of an adopted person.

(2) The local authority must prepare a personal budget for the recipient if asked to do so by the recipient or (in prescribed circumstances) a person of a prescribed description.

(3) The authority prepare a "personal budget" for the recipient if they identify an amount as available to secure the adoption support services that they have decided to provide, with a view to the recipient being involved in securing those services.

(4) Regulations may make provision about personal budgets, in particular—

    (a)   about requests for personal budgets;

    (b)   about the amount of a personal budget;

    (c)   about the sources of the funds making up a personal budget;

    (d)   for payments ("direct payments") representing all or part of a personal budget to be made to the recipient, or (in prescribed circumstances) a person of a prescribed description, in order to secure any adoption support services to which the budget relates;

    (e)   about the description of adoption support services to which personal budgets and direct payments may (and may not) relate;

    (f)   for a personal budget or direct payment to cover the agreed cost of the adoption support services to which the budget or payment relates;

    (g)   about when, how, to whom and on what conditions direct payments may (and may not) be made;

    (h)   about when direct payments may be required to be repaid and the recovery of unpaid sums;

    (i)   about conditions with which a person or body making direct payments must comply before, after or at the time of making a direct payment;

    (j)   about arrangements for providing information, advice or support in connection with personal budgets and direct payments.

(5) If the regulations include provision authorising direct payments, they must—

    (a)   require the consent of the recipient, or (in prescribed circumstances) a person of a prescribed description, to be obtained before direct payments are made;

    (b)   require the authority to stop making direct payments where the required consent is withdrawn.

(6) Any adoption support services secured by means of direct payments made by a local authority are to be treated as adoption support services provided by the authority for all purposes, subject to any prescribed conditions or exceptions.

(7) On the occasion of the first exercise of the power to make regulations under this section—

    (a)   the statutory instrument containing the regulations is not to be made unless a draft of the instrument has been laid before, and approved by a resolution of, each House of Parliament, and

    (b)   accordingly section 140(2) does not apply to the instrument.

(8) In this section "prescribed" means prescribed by regulations."

6 Adoption support services: duty to provide information

In Chapter 2 of Part 1 of the Adoption and Children Act 2002 (the Adoption Service) after section 4A (as inserted by section 5) insert—

"4B Adoption support services: duty to provide information

(1) Except in circumstances prescribed by regulations, a local authority in England must provide the information specified in subsection (2) to—

    (a)   any person who has contacted the authority to request information about adopting a child,

    (b)   any person who has informed the authority that he or she wishes to adopt a child,

    (c)   any person within the authority's area who the authority are aware is a parent of an adopted child, and

    (d)   any person within the authority's area who is a parent of an adopted child and has contacted the authority to request any of the information specified in subsection (2).

(2) The information is—

    (a)   information about the adoption support services available to people in the authority's area;

    (b)   information about the right to request an assessment under section 4 (assessments etc for adoption support services), and the authority's duties under that section and regulations made under it;

    (c)   information about the authority's duties under section 4A (adoption support services: personal budgets) and regulations made under it;

    (d)   any other information prescribed by regulations."

7 The Adoption and Children Act Register

(1) The Adoption and Children Act 2002 is amended as follows.

(2) In section 125 (Adoption and Children Act Register)—

    (a)   in subsection (1)(a), after "children who are suitable for adoption" insert ", children for whom a local authority in England are considering adoption";

    (b)   in subsection (3), after "search" insert "(subject to regulations under section 128A)".

(3) In section 128 (supply of information for the register), in subsection (4)(b), after "children suitable for adoption" insert "or for whom a local authority in England are considering adoption".

(4) After section 128 insert—

"128A Search and inspection of the register by prospective adopters

(1) Regulations may make provision enabling prospective adopters who are suitable to adopt a child to search and inspect the register, for the purposes of assisting them to find a child for whom they would be appropriate adopters.

(2) Regulations under subsection (1) may make provision enabling prospective adopters to search and inspect only prescribed parts of the register, or prescribed content on the register.

(3) Access to the register for the purpose of searching and inspecting it may be granted on any prescribed terms and conditions.

(4) Regulations may prescribe the steps to be taken by prospective adopters in respect of information received by them as a result of searching or inspecting the register.

(5) Regulations may make provision requiring prospective adopters, in prescribed circumstances, to pay a prescribed fee to the Secretary of State or the registration organisation in respect of searching or inspecting the register.

(6) On the occasion of the first exercise of the power to make regulations under this section—

(a) the statutory instrument containing the regulations is not to be made unless a draft of the instrument has been laid before, and approved by a resolution of, each House of Parliament, and

(b) accordingly section 140(2) does not apply to the instrument."

(5) In section 129 (disclosure of information), in subsection (2)(a) after "suitable for adoption" insert "or for whom a local authority in England is considering adoption".

(6) In section 140(7) (power for subordinate legislation to make different provision for different purposes) after "purposes" insert "or areas".

(7) In section 97 of the Children Act 1989 (privacy for children involved in certain proceedings), after subsection (6) insert—

"(6A) It is not a contravention of this section to—

(a) enter material in the Adoption and Children Act Register (established under section 125 of the Adoption and Children Act 2002), or

(b) permit persons to search and inspect that register pursuant to regulations made under section 128A of that Act."

(8) Schedule 1 (amendments to the Adoption and Children Act 2002 to provide for the Adoption and Children Act Register not to apply to Wales and Scotland and to remove the requirement to make provision for that register by Order in Council, and other related amendments) has effect.

Contact

8 Contact: children in care of local authorities

(1) Section 34 of the Children Act 1989 (parental contact etc with children in care) is amended as follows.

(2) In subsection (1), after "subject to the provisions of this section" insert "and their duty under section 22(3)(a)".

(3) After subsection (6) insert—

"(6A) Where (by virtue of an order under this section, or because subsection (6) applies) a local authority in England are authorised to refuse to allow contact between the child and a person mentioned in any of paragraphs (a) to (c) of paragraph 15(1) of Schedule 2, paragraph 15(1) of that Schedule does not require the authority to endeavour to promote contact between the child and that person."

(4) In subsection (8), before paragraph (a) insert—

"(za) what a local authority in England must have regard to in considering whether contact between a child and a person mentioned in any of paragraphs (a) to (d) of subsection (1) is consistent with safeguarding and promoting the child's welfare;".

(5) In subsection (11) after "Before" insert "making, varying or discharging an order under this section or".

9 Contact: post-adoption

(1) After section 51 of the Adoption and Children Act 2002 insert—

"Post-adoption contact

51A Post-adoption contact

(1) This section applies where—

(a)   an adoption agency has placed or was authorised to place a child for adoption, and

(b)   the court is making or has made an adoption order in respect of the child.

(2) When making the adoption order or at any time afterwards, the court may make an order under this section—

(a)   requiring the person in whose favour the adoption order is or has been made to allow the child to visit or stay with the person named in the order under this section, or for the person named in that order and the child otherwise to have contact with each other, or

(b)   prohibiting the person named in the order under this section from having contact with the child.

(3) The following people may be named in an order under this section—

(a)   any person who (but for the child's adoption) would be related to the child by blood (including half-blood), marriage or civil partnership;

(b)   any former guardian of the child;

(c)   any person who had parental responsibility for the child immediately before the making of the adoption order;

(d)   any person who was entitled to make an application for an order under section 26 in respect of the child (contact with children placed or to be placed for adoption) by virtue of subsection (3)(c), (d) or (e) of that section;

(e)   any person with whom the child has lived for a period of at least one year.

(4) An application for an order under this section may be made by—

(a)   a person who has applied for the adoption order or in whose favour the adoption order is or has been made,

(b)   the child, or

(c)   any person who has obtained the court's leave to make the application.

(5) In deciding whether to grant leave under subsection (4)(c), the court must consider—

(a)   any risk there might be of the proposed application disrupting the child's life to such an extent that he or she would be harmed by it (within the meaning of the 1989 Act),

(b)   the applicant's connection with the child, and

(c)   any representations made to the court by—

(i)   the child, or

(ii)   a person who has applied for the adoption order or in whose favour the adoption order is or has been made.

(6) When making an adoption order, the court may on its own initiative make an order of the type mentioned in subsection (2)(b).

(7) The period of one year mentioned in subsection (3)(e) need not be continuous but must not have begun more than five years before the making of the application.

(8) Where this section applies, an order under section 8 of the 1989 Act may not make provision about contact between the child and any person who may be named in an order under this section.

51B Orders under section 51A: supplementary

(1) An order under section 51A—

(a)   may contain directions about how it is to be carried into effect,

(b)   may be made subject to any conditions the court thinks appropriate,

(c)   may be varied or revoked by the court on an application by the child, a person in whose favour the adoption order was made or a person named in the order, and

(d)   has effect until the child's 18th birthday, unless revoked.

(2) Subsection (3) applies to proceedings—

    (a) on an application for an adoption order in which—
        (i) an application is made for an order under section 51A, or
        (ii) the court indicates that it is considering making such an order on its own initiative;
    (b) on an application for an order under section 51A;
    (c) on an application for such an order to be varied or revoked.

(3) The court must (in the light of any rules made by virtue of subsection (4))—

    (a) draw up a timetable with a view to determining without delay whether to make, (or as the case may be) vary or revoke an order under section 51A, and
    (b) give directions for the purpose of ensuring, so far as is reasonably practicable, that that timetable is adhered to.

(4) Rules of court may—

    (a) specify periods within which specified steps must be taken in relation to proceedings to which subsection (3) applies, and
    (b) make other provision with respect to such proceedings for the purpose of ensuring, so far as is reasonably practicable, that the court makes determinations about orders under section 51A without delay."

(2) In section 1 of the Adoption and Children Act 2002 (considerations applying to the exercise of powers relating to the adoption of a child), in subsection (7)(a) after "section 26" insert "or 51A".

(3) In section 26 of that Act (children placed, or authorised to be placed, for adoption: contact), omit subsection (5).

(4) In section 96(3) of that Act (section 95 does not prohibit payment of legal or medical expenses in connection with applications under section 26 etc) after "26" insert ", 51A".

(5) In section 1(1) of the Family Law Act 1986 (orders which are Part 1 orders) after paragraph (ab) insert—

    "(ac) an order made under section 51A of the Adoption and Children Act 2002 (post-adoption contact), other than an order varying or revoking such an order;".

(6) In section 2 of that Act (jurisdiction of courts in England and Wales to make Part 1 orders: pre-conditions) after subsection (2B) insert—

    "(2C) A court in England and Wales shall not have jurisdiction to make an order under section 51A of the Adoption and Children Act 2002 unless—

    (a) it has jurisdiction under the Council Regulation or the Hague Convention, or
    (b) neither the Council Regulation nor the Hague Convention applies but the condition in section 3 of this Act is satisfied."

(7) In section 9 of the Children Act 1989, in subsection (5)(a) (restrictions on making certain orders with respect to children) after "order" insert "or an order under section 51A of the Adoption and Children Act 2002 (post-adoption contact)".

(8) In section 17(4) of the Armed Forces Act 1991 (persons to be given notice of application for service family child assessment order) before paragraph (e) insert—

    "(db) any person in whose favour an order under section 51A of the Adoption and Children Act 2002 (post-adoption contact) is in force with respect to the child;".

(9) In section 18(7) of that Act (persons who may apply to vary or discharge a service family child assessment order) before paragraph (e) insert—

"(db) any person in whose favour an order under section 51A of the Adoption and Children Act 2002 (post-adoption contact) is in force with respect to the child;".

(10) In section 20(8) of that Act (persons who are to be allowed reasonable contact with a child subject to a protection order) before paragraph (d) insert—

"(cb) any person in whose favour an order under section 51A of the Adoption and Children Act 2002 (post-adoption contact) is in force with respect to the child;".

(11) In section 22A(7) of that Act (persons who are to be allowed reasonable contact with a child in service police protection) before paragraph (d) insert—

"(cb) any person in whose favour an order under section 51A of the Adoption and Children Act 2002 (post-adoption contact) is in force with respect to the child,".

(12) In Part 1 of Schedule 1 to the Legal Aid, Sentencing and Punishment of Offenders Act 2012 (civil legal services)—

(a) in paragraph 12(9) (victims of domestic violence and family matters), in the definition of "family enactment" after paragraph (o) insert—

"(p) section 51A of the Adoption and Children Act 2002 (post-adoption contact orders).", and

(b) in paragraph 13(1) (protection of children and family matters) after paragraph (f) insert—

"(g) orders under section 51A of the Adoption and Children Act 2002 (post-adoption contact)."

APPENDIX 2

PRACTICE DIRECTION 12A – CARE, SUPERVISION AND OTHER PART 4 PROCEEDINGS: GUIDE TO CASE MANAGEMENT

This Practice Direction supplements FPR Part 12

1 The key stages of the court process

1.1 The Public Law Outline set out in the Table below contains an outline of –

(1)   the order of the different stages of the process;
(2)   the matters to be considered at the main case management hearings;
(3)   the latest timescales within which the main stages of the process should take place in order to resolve the proceedings within 26 weeks.

1.2 In the Public Law Outline –

(1)   "CMH" means the Case Management Hearing;
(2)   "FCMH" means Further Case Management Hearing;
(3)   "ICO" means interim care order;
(4)   "IRH" means the Issues Resolution Hearing;
(5)   "LA" means the Local Authority which is applying for a care or supervision order or a final order in other Part 4 proceedings;
(6)   "OS" means the Official Solicitor.

1.3 In applying the provisions of FPR Part 12 and the Public Law Outline the court and the parties must also have regard to –

(1)   all other relevant rules and Practice Directions and in particular –
  •   FPR Part 1 (Overriding Objective);
  •   FPR Part 4 (General Case Management Powers);
  •   FPR Part 15 (Representation of Protected Parties) and Practice Direction 15B (Adults Who May Be Protected Parties and Children Who May Become Protected Parties in Family Proceedings);
  •   FPR Part 18 (Procedure for Other Applications in Proceedings);
  •   FPR Part 22 (Evidence);
  •   FPR Part 24 (Witnesses, depositions generally and taking of evidence in Member States of the European Union);
  •   FPR Part 25 (Experts) and the Experts Practice Directions;
  •   FPR 27.6 and Practice Direction 27A (Court Bundles);
  •   FPR 30 (Appeals) and Practice Direction 30A (Appeals);
(2)   the Allocation Rules;
(3)   the Justices' Clerks Rules;

(4)   President's Guidance issued from time to time on
- Distribution of business of the family court;
- Judicial continuity and deployment;
- Prescribed templates and orders;

(5)   International instruments
- The Council Regulation (EC) No 2201/2003 (Brussels 2 revised);
- The 1996 Hague Convention;

(6)   Guidance relating to protected parties and others with a disability –
- Protected Parties in Family Proceedings: Checklist For the Appointment of a Litigation Friend (including the Official Solicitor) (published in Family Law (January 2014);
- The Mental Capacity Act 2005 (Transfer of Proceedings) Order 2007 SI 2007/1899, relating to young people over 16 where they are likely to lack decision-making capacity at age 18.

Public Law Outline

PRE-PROCEEDINGS
PRE-PROCEEDINGS CHECKLIST

<u>Annex Documents</u> are the documents specified in the Annex to the Application Form which are to be attached to that form and filed with the court:	<u>Checklist documents</u> (already existing on the LA's files) are –
	(a) Evidential documents including –
• Social Work Chronology • Social Work Statement and Genogram • The current assessments relating to the child and/or the family and friends of the child to which the Social Work Statement refers and on which the LA relies • Care Plan • Index of Checklist Documents	• Previous court orders including foreign orders and judgments/reasons
	• Any assessment materials relevant to the key issues including capacity to litigate, section 7 and 37 reports
	• Single, joint or inter-agency materials (e.g., health and education/Home Office and Immigration Tribunal documents);
	(b) Decision-making records including –
	• Records of key discussions with the family
	• Key LA minutes and records for the child
	• Pre-existing care plans (e.g., child in need plan, looked after child plan and child protection plan)
	• Letters Before Proceedings
	Only Checklist documents in *(a) are to be served* with the application form
	Checklist Documents in *(b) are to be disclosed on request* by any party
	Checklist documents are *not* to be –
	• filed with the court unless the court directs otherwise; and
	• older than 2 years before the date of issue of the proceedings unless reliance is placed on the same in the LA's evidence

STAGE 1 – ISSUE AND ALLOCATION
DAY 1 AND DAY 2 (see interpretation section)

On Day 1 (Day of issue):

• The LA files the Application Form and Annex Documents and sends copies to Cafcass/CAFCASS Cymru

• The LA notifies the court of the need for an urgent preliminary case management hearing or an urgent contested ICO hearing where this is known or expected

• Court officer issues application

Within a day of issue (Day 2):

• Court considers jurisdiction in a case with an international element

• Court considers initial allocation to specified level of judge, in accordance with the Allocation Rules and any President's Guidance on the distribution of business

• LA serves the Application Form, Annex Documents and evidential Checklist Documents on the parties together with the notice of date and time of CMH and any urgent hearing

• Court gives standard directions on Issue and Allocation including:

– Checking compliance with Pre-Proceedings Checklist including service of any missing Annex Documents

– Appointing Children's Guardian (to be allocated by Cafcass/CAFCASS Cymru)

– Appointing solicitor for the child only if necessary

– Appointing (if the person to be appointed consents) a litigation friend for any protected party or any non-subject child who is a party, including the OS where appropriate

– Identifying whether a request has been made or should be made to a Central Authority or other competent authority in a foreign state or a consular authority in England and Wales in a case with an international element

– Filing and service of a LA Case Summary

– Filing and service of a Case Analysis by the Children's Guardian

– Filing and Serving the Parents' Response

– Sending a request for disclosure to, e.g., the police or health service body

– Filing and serving an application for permission relating to experts under Part 25 on a date prior to the advocates meeting for the CMH

– Directing the solicitor for the child to arrange an advocates' meeting no later than 2 business days before the CMH

– Listing the CMH

• Court considers any request for an urgent preliminary case management hearing or an urgent contested ICO hearing and where necessary lists the hearing and gives additional directions.

• Court officer sends copy Notice of Hearing of the CMH and any urgent hearing by email to Cafcass/CAFCASS Cymru.

STAGE 2 – CASE MANAGEMENT HEARING	
ADVOCATES' MEETING (including any litigants in person)	**CASE MANAGEMENT HEARING**
No later than 2 business days before CMH (or FCMH if it is necessary)	CMH: Not before day 12 and not later than day 18 A FCMH is to be held only if necessary, it is to be listed as soon as possible and in any event no later than day 25
• Consider information on the Application Form and Annex documents, the LA Case Summary, and the Case Analysis • Identify the parties' positions to be recited in the draft Case Management Order • Identify the parties' positions about jurisdiction, in particular arising out of any international element • If necessary, identify proposed experts and draft questions in accordance with Part 25 and the Experts Practice Directions • Identify any disclosure that in the advocates' views is necessary • Immediately notify the court of the need for a contested ICO hearing and any issue about allocation • LA advocate to file a draft Case Management Order in prescribed form with court by 11a.m. on the business day before the CMH and/or FCMH	• Court gives detailed case management directions, including: – Considering jurisdiction in a case with an international element; – Confirming allocation – Drawing up the timetable for the child and the timetable for the proceedings and considering if an extension is necessary – Identifying additional parties, intervenors and representation (including confirming that Cafcass/CAFCASS Cymru have allocated a Children's Guardian and that a litigation friend is appointed for any protected party or non-subject child) – Giving directions for the determination of any disputed issue about litigation capacity – Identifying the key issues – Identifying the evidence necessary to enable the court to resolve the key issues – Deciding whether there is a real issue about threshold to be resolved – Determining any application made under Part 25 and otherwise ensuring compliance with Part 25 where it is necessary for expert(s) to be instructed

STAGE 2 – CASE MANAGEMENT HEARING	
ADVOCATES' MEETING (including any litigants in person)	**CASE MANAGEMENT HEARING**
	– Identifying any necessary disclosure and if appropriate giving directions – Giving directions for any concurrent or proposed placement order proceedings – Ensuring compliance with the court's directions – If a FCMH is necessary, directing an advocates' meeting and Case Analysis if required – Directing filing of any threshold agreement, final evidence and Care Plan and responses to those documents for the IRH – Directing a Case Analysis for the IRH – Directing an advocates' meeting for the IRH – Listing (any FCMH) IRH, Final Hearing (including early Final Hearing), as appropriate – Giving directions for special measures and/or interpreters and intermediaries – Issuing the Case Management Order

STAGE 3 – ISSUES RESOLUTION HEARING	
ADVOCATES' MEETING (including any litigants in person)	**IRH**
No later than 7 business days before the IRH	As directed by the court, in accordance with the timetable for the proceedings
• Review evidence and the positions of the parties • Identify the advocates' views of – – the remaining key issues and how the issues may be resolved or narrowed at the IRH including by the making of final orders – the further evidence which is required to be heard to enable the key issues to be resolved or narrowed at the IRH – the evidence that is relevant and the witnesses that are required at the final hearing – the need for a contested hearing and/or time for oral evidence to be given at the IRH • LA advocate to – – notify the court immediately of the outcome of the discussion at the meeting – file a draft Case Management Order with the court by 11a.m. on the business day before the IRH	• Court identifies the key issue(s) (if any) to be determined and the extent to which those issues can be resolved or narrowed at the IRH • Court considers whether the IRH can be used as a final hearing • Court resolves or narrows the issues by hearing evidence • Court identifies the evidence to be heard on the issues which remain to be resolved at the final hearing • Court gives final case management directions including: – Any extension of the timetable for the proceedings which is necessary – Filing of the threshold agreement or a statement of facts/issues remaining to be determined – Filing of: o Final evidence and Care Plan o Case Analysis for Final Hearing (if required) o Witness templates o Skeleton arguments – Judicial reading list/reading time, including time estimate and an estimate for judgment writing time – Ensuring Compliance with PD27A (the Bundles Practice Direction) – Listing the Final Hearing • Court issues Case Management Order

2 Flexible powers of the court

2.1 Attention is drawn to the flexible powers of the court either following the issue of the application or at any other stage in the proceedings.

2.2 The court may give directions without a hearing including setting a date for the Final Hearing or a period within which the Final Hearing will take place. The steps, which the court will ordinarily take at the various stages of the proceedings provided for in the Public Law Outline, may be taken by the court at another stage in the proceedings if the circumstances of the case merit this approach.

2.3 The flexible powers of the court include the ability for the court to cancel or repeat a particular hearing. For example, if the issue on which the case turns can with reasonable practicability be crystallised and resolved by taking evidence at an IRH then such a flexible approach must be taken in accordance with the overriding objective and to secure compliance with section 1(2) of the 1989 Act and resolving the proceedings within 26 weeks or the period for the time being specified by the court.

2.4 Where a party has requested an urgent hearing a) to enable the court to give immediate directions or orders to facilitate any case management issue which is to be considered at the CMH, or b) to decide whether an ICO is necessary, the court may list such a hearing at any appropriate time before the CMH and give directions for that hearing. It is anticipated that an urgent preliminary case management hearing will only be necessary to consider issues such as jurisdiction, parentage, party status, capacity to litigate, disclosure and whether there is, or should be, a request to a Central Authority or other competent authority in a foreign state or consular authority in England and Wales in an international case. It is not intended that any urgent hearing will delay the CMH.

2.5 Where it is anticipated that oral evidence may be required at the CMH, FCMH or IRH, the court must be notified in accordance with Stages 2 and 3 of the Public Law Outline well in advance and directions sought for the conduct of the hearing.

2.6 It is expected that full case management will take place at the CMH. It follows that the parties must be prepared to deal with all relevant case management issues, as identified in Stage 2 of the Public Law Outline. A FCMH should only be directed where necessary and must not be regarded as a routine step in proceedings.

3 Compliance with pre-proceedings checklist

3.1 It is recognised that in a small minority of cases the circumstances are such that the safety and welfare of the child may be jeopardised if the start of proceedings is delayed until all of the documents appropriate to the case and referred to in the Pre-proceedings Checklist are available. The safety and welfare of the child should never be put in jeopardy by delaying issuing proceedings whether because of lack of documentation or otherwise. (Nothing in this Practice Direction affects an application for an emergency protection order under section 44 of the 1989 Act). Also, where an application for an interim order is urgent, then the hearing of that application is NOT expected to be postponed until the Case Management Hearing. The Case Management Hearing is still to be held not before day 12 and not later than day 18 in accordance with the Public Law Outline and guidance in this Practice Direction. If an urgent preliminary Case Management Hearing or an urgent contested ICO hearing is held before the CMH, the court should not dispense with the CMH unless all of the parties have been sufficiently prepared and the court has been able to deal with all case management issues which would have come before it at the CMH.

3.2 The court recognises that preparation may need to be varied to suit the circumstances of the case. In cases where any of the Annex Documents required to be attached to the Application Form are not available at the time of issue of the application, the court will consider making directions on issue about when any missing documentation is to be filed. The expectation is that there must be a good reason why one or more of the documents are not available. Further directions relating to any missing documentation will also be made at the Case Management Hearing.

4 Allocation

4.1 The court considers the allocation of proceedings in accordance with the Allocation Rules and any Guidance issued by the President on distribution of business of the family court. The justices' clerk or assistant justices' clerk (with responsibility for gatekeeping and allocation of proceedings) will discuss initial allocation with a district judge (with responsibility for allocation and gatekeeping of proceedings) as provided for in any Guidance issued by the President on distribution of business of the family court. The expectation is that, wherever possible, any question relating to allocation of the proceedings will be considered at the CMH.

5 The timetable for the child and the timetable for proceedings

5.1 The timetable for the proceedings:

(1)   The court will draw up a timetable for the proceedings with a view to disposing of the application –
(a)   without delay; and
(b)   in any event within 26 weeks beginning with the day on which the application was issued in accordance with section 32(1)(a)(ii) of the Children Act 1989.

(2)   The court, when drawing up or revising a timetable under paragraph (1), will in particular have regard to –
(a)   the impact which the timetable or any revised timetable would have on the welfare of the child to whom the application relates; and
(b)   the impact which the timetable or any revised timetable would have on the duration and conduct of the proceedings.

5.2 The impact which the timetable for the proceedings, any revision or extension of that timetable would have on the welfare of the child to whom the application relates are matters to which the court is to have particular regard. The court will use the Timetable for the Child to assess the impact of these matters on the welfare of the child and to draw up and revise the timetable for the proceedings.

5.3 The "Timetable for the Child" is the timetable set by the court which takes into account dates which are important to the child's welfare and development.

5.4 The timetable for the proceedings is set having particular regard to the Timetable for the Child and the Timetable for the Child needs to be reviewed regularly. Where adjustments are made to the Timetable for the Child, the timetable for the proceedings will have to be reviewed consistently with resolving the proceedings within 26 weeks or the period for the time being specified by the court.

5.5 Examples of the dates the court will record and take into account when setting the Timetable for the Child are the dates of –

(1)   any formal review by the Local Authority of the case of a looked after child (within the meaning of section 22(1) of the 1989 Act);

(2) any significant educational steps, including the child taking up a place at a new school and, where applicable, any review by the Local Authority of a statement of the child's special educational needs;

(3) any health care steps, including assessment by a paediatrician or other specialist;

(4) any review of Local Authority plans for the child, including any plans for permanence through adoption, Special Guardianship or placement with parents or relatives;

(5) any change or proposed change of the child's placement;

(6) any significant change in the child's social or family circumstances; or

(7) any timetable for the determination of an issue in a case with an international element.

5.6 To identify the Timetable for the Child, the applicant is required to provide the information needed about the significant steps in the child's life in the Application Form and the Social Work Statement and to update this information regularly taking into account information received from others involved in the child's life such as the parties, members of the child's family, the person who is caring for the child, the children's guardian, the Independent Reviewing Officer, the child's key social worker and any Central Authority or competent authority in a foreign state or a consular authority in England and Wales in a case with an international element.

5.7 Where more than one child is the subject of the proceedings, the court should consider and will set a Timetable for the Child for each child. The children may not all have the same timetable, and the court will consider the appropriate progress of the proceedings in relation to each child.

5.8 Where there are parallel care proceedings and criminal proceedings against a person connected with the child for a serious offence against the child, linked directions hearings should where practicable take place as the case progresses. The timing of the proceedings in a linked care and criminal case should appear in the Timetable for the Child. The time limit of resolving the proceedings within 26 weeks applies unless a longer timetable has been set by the court in order to resolve the proceedings justly in accordance with section 32(1)(a)(ii) and (5) of the 1989 Act. Early disclosure and listing of hearings is necessary in proceedings in a linked care and criminal case.

6 Extensions to the timetable for proceedings

6.1 The court is required to draw up a timetable for proceedings with a view to disposing of the application without delay and in any event within 26 weeks. If proceedings can be resolved earlier, then they should be. A standard timetable and process is expected to be followed in respect of the giving of standard directions on issue and allocation and other matters which should be carried out by the court on issue, including setting and giving directions for the Case Management Hearing.

6.2 Having regard to the circumstances of the particular case, the court may consider that it is necessary to extend the time by which the proceedings are to be resolved beyond 26 weeks to enable the court to resolve the proceedings justly (see section 32(5) of the 1989 Act). When making this decision, the court is to take account of the guidance that extensions are not to be granted routinely and are to be seen as requiring specific justification (see section 32(7) of the 1989 Act). The decision and reason(s) for extending a case should be recorded in writing (in the Case Management Order) and orally stated in court, so that all parties are aware of the reasons for delay in the case (see FPR 12.26C). The Case Management Order must contain a record of this information, as well as the impact of the court's decision on the welfare of the child.

6.3 The court may extend the period within which proceedings are intended to be resolved on its own initiative or on application. Applications for an extension should, wherever possible, only be made so that they are considered at any hearing for which a date has been fixed or for which a date is about to be fixed. Where a date for a hearing has been fixed, a party who wishes to make an application at that hearing but does not have sufficient time to file an application notice should as soon as possible inform the court (if possible in writing) and, if possible, the other parties of the nature of the application and the reason for it. The party should then make the application orally at the hearing.

6.4 If the court agrees an extension is necessary, an initial extension to the time limit may be granted for up to eight weeks (or less if directed) in order to resolve the case justly (see section 32(8) of the 1989 Act). If more time is necessary, in order to resolve the proceedings justly, a further extension of up to eight weeks may be agreed by the court. There is no limit on the number of extensions that may be granted in a particular case.

6.5 If the court considers that the timetable for the proceedings will require an extension beyond the next eight week period in order to resolve the proceedings justly, the Case Management Order should –

(1)   state the reason(s) why it is necessary to have a further extension;
(2)   fix the date of the next effective hearing (which might be in a period shorter than a further eight weeks); and
(3)   indicate whether it is appropriate for the next application for an extension of the timetable to be considered on paper.

6.6 The expectation is that, subject to paragraph 6.5, extensions should be considered at a hearing and that a court will not approve proposals for the management of a case under FPR 12.15 where the consequence of those proposals is that the case is unlikely to be resolved within 26 weeks or other period for the time being allowed for resolution of the proceedings. In accordance with FPR 4.1(3)(e), the court may hold a hearing and receive evidence by telephone or by using any other method of direct oral communication. When deciding whether to extend the timetable, the court must have regard to the impact of any ensuing timetable revision on the welfare of the child (see section 32(6) of the 1989 Act).

7 Interpretation

7.1 In this Practice Direction –

"Allocation Rules" mean any rules relating to composition of the court and distribution of business made under section 31D of the Matrimonial and Family Proceedings Act 1984;

"Care Plan" is a separate document from the evidence that is filed by the local authority. It is a "section 31A plan" referred to in section 31A of the 1989 Act which complies with guidance as to content issued by the Secretary of State;

"Case Analysis" means a written or, if there is insufficient time for a written, an oral outline of the case from the perspective of the child's guardian or Welsh family proceedings officer for the CMH or FCMH (where one is necessary) and IRH or as otherwise directed by the court, incorporating an analysis of the key issues that need to be resolved in the case including –
(a)   a threshold analysis;

(b)   a case management analysis, including an analysis of the timetable for the proceedings, an analysis of the Timetable for the Child and the evidence which any party proposes is necessary to resolve the issues;

(c)   a parenting capability analysis;

(d)   a child impact analysis, including an analysis of the ascertainable wishes and feelings of the child and the impact on the welfare of the child of any application to adjourn a hearing or extend the timetable for the proceedings;

(e)   an early permanence analysis including an analysis of the proposed placements and contact framework; by reference to a welfare and proportionality analysis;

(f)   whether and if so what communication it is proposed there should be during the proceedings with the child by the court;

"Case Management Order" is the prescribed form of order referred to in any Guidance issued by the President from time to time on prescribed templates and orders;

"Day" means "business day". "Day 1" is the day of issue and "Day 2" is the next business day following the day of issue of proceedings. "Day 12", "Day 18" and "Day 25" are respectively the 11th, 17th and the 24th business days after the day of issue of proceedings (Day 1). "26 weeks" means 26 calendar weeks beginning on the day of issue of proceedings (Day 1);

"Experts Practice Directions" mean –

(a)   Practice Direction 25A (Experts – Emergencies and Pre Proceedings Instructions);

(b)   Practice Direction 25B (The Duties of An Expert, The Expert's Report and Arrangements For An Expert To Attend Court);

(c)   Practice Direction 25C (Children's Proceedings – The Use Of Single Joint Experts and The Process Leading to An Expert Being Instructed or Expert Evidence Being Put Before the Court);

(d)   Practice Direction 25E (Discussions Between Experts in Family Proceedings);

"Genogram" means a family tree, setting out in diagrammatic form the child's family and extended family members and their relationship with the child;

"Index of Checklist Documents" means a list of Checklist Documents referred to in the Public Law Outline Pre-Proceedings Checklist which is divided into two parts with Part A being the documents referred to in column 2, paragraph (a) of the Pre-Proceedings Checklist and Part B being those referred to in column 2, paragraph (b) of the Pre-proceedings Checklist;

"International instruments"

"the Council Regulation (EC) No 2201/2003 (Brussels 2 revised)" means Council Regulation (EC) No 2201/2003" of 27 November 2003 on jurisdiction and the recognition and enforcement of judgments in matrimonial matters and in matters of parental responsibility;

"The 1996 Hague Convention" means the Convention on Jurisdiction, Applicable Law, Recognition, Enforcement and Co-operation in Respect of Parental Responsibility and Measures for the Protection of Children;

"Justices' Clerks Rules" means any rules made under section 310 of the Matrimonial and Family Proceedings Act 1984 enabling functions of the family court or judge of that court to be carried out by a justices' clerk or assistant to a justices' clerk;

"Letter Before Proceedings" means any letter from the Local Authority containing written notification to the parents and others with parental responsibility for the child of the Local Authority's likely intention to apply to court for a care or supervision order and any related subsequent correspondence confirming the Local Authority's position;

"Local Authority Case Summary" means a document prepared by the Local Authority legal representative for each case management hearing in the form referred to in any Guidance issued by the President from time to time on prescribed templates and orders;

"Parents' Response" means a document from either or both of the parents containing

(a)   in no more than two pages, the parents' response to the Threshold Statement, and

(b)   the parents' placement proposals including the identity and whereabouts of all relatives and friends they propose be considered by the court;

(c)   Information which may be relevant to a person's capacity to litigate including information about any referrals to mental health services and adult services;

"Section 7 report" means any report under section 7 of the 1989 Act;

"Section 37 report" means any report by the Local Authority to the court as a result of a direction under section 37 of the 1989 Act;

"Social Work Chronology" means a schedule containing –

(a)   a succinct summary of the length of involvement of the local authority with the family and in particular with the child;

(b)   a succinct summary of the significant dates and events in the child's life in chronological order – i.e. a running record up to the issue of the proceedings; providing such information under the following headings –

(i)   serial number;

(ii)   date;

(iii)   event-detail;

(iv)   witness or document reference (where applicable);

"Social Work Statement" means a statement prepared by the Local Authority limited to the following evidence –

Summary

(a)   The order sought;

(b)   Succinct summary of reasons with reference as appropriate to the Welfare Checklist;

Family

(c)   Family members and relationships especially the primary carers and significant adults/other children;

(d)   Genogram;

Threshold

(e)   Precipitating events;

(f)   Background circumstances;

(i)   summary of children's services involvement cross-referenced to the chronology;

(ii)   previous court orders and emergency steps;

(iii)   previous assessments;

(g)   Summary of significant harm and or likelihood of significant harm which the LA will seek to establish by evidence or concession;

Parenting capability

(h)   Assessment of child's needs;

(i)   Assessment of parental capability to meet needs;
(j)   Analysis of why there is a gap between parental capability and the child's needs;
(k)   Assessment of other significant adults who may be carers;

Child impact
(l)   Wishes and feelings of the child(ren);
(m)   Timetable for the Child;
(n)   Delay and timetable for the proceedings;

Permanence and contact
(o)   Parallel planning;
(p)   Realistic placement options by reference to a welfare and proportionality analysis;
(q)   Contact framework;

Case Management
(r)   Evidence and assessments necessary and outstanding;
(s)   Any information about any person's litigation capacity, mental health issues, disabilities or vulnerabilities that is relevant to their capability to participate in the proceedings; and
(t)   Case management proposals.

"Standard Directions on Issue and Allocation" means directions given by the court on issue and upon allocation in the prescribed form referred to in any Guidance issued by the President from time to time on prescribed templates and orders;

"Threshold Statement" means a written outline by the legal representative of the LA in the application form of the facts which the LA will seek to establish by evidence or concession to satisfy the threshold criteria under s 31(2) of the 1989 Act limited to no more than 2 pages;

"Welfare Checklist" means the list of matters which is set out in section 1(3) of the 1989 Act and to which the court is to have particular regard in accordance with section (1)(3) and (4).

Amendments—FPR Update 12.

APPENDIX 3

PRACTICE DIRECTION 12B –
CHILD ARRANGEMENTS PROGRAMME

1. When does the Child Arrangements Programme Apply?

1.1 The Child Arrangements Programme (the 'CAP') applies where a dispute arises between separated parents and/or families about arrangements concerning children.

1.2 The CAP is designed to assist families to reach safe and child-focused agreements for their child, where possible out of the court setting. If parents/families are unable to reach agreement, and a court application is made, the CAP encourages swift resolution of the dispute through the court.

1.3 It is well-recognised that negotiated agreements between adults generally enhance long-term co-operation, and are better for the child concerned. Therefore, separated parents and families are strongly encouraged to attempt to resolve their disputes concerning the child outside of the court system. This may also be quicker and cheaper.

2. Signposting Services, Parenting Plans, & Public Funding

2.1 **Services**: Where a dispute arises in relation to a child, or children, parents and families are encouraged to obtain advice and support as soon as possible.

2.2 There are many services available for such families, who seek advice about resolving disputes concerning their child.

2.3 The following services are recommended:

(1)   For more information about family mediation and to find the nearest mediation service (including those providing a MIAM): www. familymediationcouncil.org.uk;

(2)   For a Guide about children and the family courts for separating parents (including representing yourself in court): the form 'CB7': http://www.cafcass. gov.uk/media/168195/cb7-eng.pdf;

(3)   For Cafcass (England): www.cafcass.gov.uk;

(4)   For CAFCASS Cymru (Wales): www.wales.gov.uk/cafcasscymru;

(5)   To find a legal adviser or family mediator: http://find-legaladvice. justice.gov.uk;

(6)   To check whether you can get financial help (legal aid) to pay for non-court dispute resolution, &/or advice and representation at court, and to find a legal aid solicitor or mediator: https://www.gov.uk/check-legal-aid;

(7)   For general advice about sorting out arrangements for children, the use of post-separation mediation, &/or going to court: http://www.advicenow.org.uk; http://www.advicenow.org.uk/advicenow-guides/family/sortingout-arrangements-for-your-children/;

(8)   For general advice on separation services and options for resolving disputes: www.sortingoutseparation.org.uk;

(9)   For general advice about sorting out arrangements for children: http://
       theparentconnection.org.uk/;
(10)   For advice about Contact Centres, which are neutral places where children of
       separated families can enjoy contact with their nonresident parents and
       sometimes other family members, in a comfortable and safe environment; and
       information about where they are: www.naccc.org.uk;
(11)   For the form to apply for a child arrangements order: https://www.gov.uk/
       looking-after-children-divorce/apply-for-court-order;
(12)   For help with taking a case to court without a lawyer, the Personal Support
       Unit: http://thepsu.org/;
(13)   For guidance on representing yourself at court, including a list of commonly
       used terms that you may come across: http://www.barcouncil.org.uk/
       instructing-a-barrister/representing-yourself-in-court/;
(14)   For advice about finding and using a family law solicitor see: Law Society
       http://www.lawsociety.org.uk, and Resolution (family law solicitors): http://
       www.resolution.org.uk;
(15)   For advice about finding using a family law barrister: see http://www.
       barcouncil.org.uk/about-the-bar/find-a-barrister/, and for arrangements for
       using a barrister directly see http://www.barcouncil.org.uk/instructing-a-
       barrister/publicaccess/.

2.4 **Parenting Plan**: A Parenting Plan is widely recognised as being a useful tool for
separated parents to identify, agree and set out in writing arrangements for their
children; such a plan could appropriately be used as the basis for discussion about a
dispute which has arisen. It is likely to be useful in any event for assisting arrangements
between separated parents.

2.5 The Parenting Plan should cover all practical aspects of care for the child, and
should reflect a shared commitment to the child and his/her future, with particular
emphasis on parental communication (learning how to deal with differences), living
arrangements, money, religion, education, health care and emotional well-being.

2.6 A Parenting Plan is designed to help separated parents (and their families) to work
out the best possible arrangements for the child; the plan should be understood by
everyone, including (where the child is of an appropriate age and understanding) the
child concerned.

2.7 For help on preparing a Parenting Plan, see:

(1)   Cafcass "Putting Your Children First: A Guide for Separated Parents" (see also
       paragraph 4 below);
(2)   A draft of a Parenting Plan for parents or families to complete:
       http://www.cafcass.gov.uk/media/190788/parenting_plan_final_web.pdf.

2.8 Publicly funded mediation and/or legal advice: If parents need access to mediation,
and legal advice in support of that mediation, they may be eligible for public funding.
The Legal Aid Agency (LAA) will provide funding for Mediation Information and
Assessment Meetings (MIAMs) and family mediation for all those who are eligible:

(1)   Where at least one party is eligible, the LAA will cover the costs of both parties
       to attend a MIAM to encourage any non-eligible client to find out about the
       benefits and suitability of mediation without incurring any costs.
(2)   The LAA will provide public funding for eligible parties to participate in family
       mediation and they may also receive some independent legal advice connected
       to the mediation process and where a settlement is reached can receive legal
       assistance to draft and issue proceedings to obtain a consent order.

(3)   Parties may find out if they are likely to be eligible for legal aid at the following link: https://www.gov.uk/check-legal-aid.

(4)   To find the nearest publicly funded mediation service a client can use the search at familymediationcouncil.org.uk. Publicly funded legal advisors can be found at: https://www.gov.uk/check-legalaid.

2.9 Public funding for legal advice and/or representation at court is available in limited circumstances. Further information can be found here: http://www.justice.gov.uk/legal-aid-for-private-family-matters.

3. Explanation of terms

3.1 Some of the terms used in this document, and in the websites referred to above, may not be familiar to those who seek help and support.

3.2 A guide to some of the relevant terms is attached in the Annex at the end of this document.

4. The child in the dispute

4.1 In making any arrangements with respect to a child, the child's welfare must be the highest priority.

4.2 Children and young people should be at the centre of all decision-making. This accords with the Family Justice Young People's Board Charter (https://www.cafcass.gov.uk/media/179714/fjypb_national_charter_1013. pdf).

4.3 The child or young person should feel that their needs, wishes and feelings have been considered in the arrangements which are made for them.

4.4 Children should be involved, to the extent which is appropriate given their age and level of understanding, in making the arrangements which affect them. This is just as relevant where

(1)   the parties are making arrangements between themselves (which may be recorded in a Parenting Plan), as when:

(2)   arrangements are made in the context of dispute resolution outside away from the court, and/or

(3)   the court is required to make a decision about the arrangements for the child.

4.5 If an application for a court order has been issued, the judge may want to know the child's view. This may be communicated to the judge in one of a number of ways:

(1)   By a Cafcass officer (in Wales, a Welsh Family Proceedings Officer (WFPO)) providing a report to the court which sets out the child's wishes and feelings;

(2)   By the child being encouraged (by the Cafcass officer or WFPO, or a parent or relative) to write a letter to the court;

(3)   In the limited circumstances described in paragraph 18 below, by the child being a party to the proceedings; and/or:

(4)   By the judge meeting with the child, in accordance with approved Guidance (currently the FJC Guidelines for Judges Meeting Children subject to Family Proceedings (April 2010)). http://www.judiciary.gov.uk/JCO%2fDocuments%2fFJC%2fvoc%2 fGuidelines_+Judges_seeing_+Children.pdf.

5. Non-court resolution of disputed arrangements for children

5.1 Dispute resolution services, including mediation, are available to provide opportunities for parents and families to work in a positive and constructive way, and should be actively considered and attempted where it is safe and appropriate to do so. Information about mediation and other non-court dispute resolution is available widely (see 'Signposting Services for Families' – paragraph 2 above).

5.2 It is not expected that those who are the victims of domestic violence should attempt to mediate or otherwise participate in forms of non-court dispute resolution. It is also recognised that drug and/or alcohol misuse and/or mental illness are likely to prevent couples from making safe use of mediation or similar services; these risk factors (which can be discussed at a MIAM – see below, paragraph 5.3) are likely to have an impact on arrangements for the child. Court Orders, including those made by consent, must be scrutinised to ensure that they are safe and take account of any risk factors, in accordance with Practice Direction 12J FPR.

5.3 **Attendance at Mediation Information and Assessment Meeting ("MIAM")**: Subject to paragraph 5.6 (below), before making a family application to the court (a 'relevant family application' as defined in paragraph 23 below), the person who is considering making such application must attend a family MIAM. A prospective respondent is expected to attend a MIAM – whether this is a separate MIAM or the same MIAM attended by the prospective applicant. At the MIAM, information will be provided about mediation of disputes of the kind to which the application relates, ways in which the dispute may be resolved otherwise than by the court, and the suitability of mediation (or any other way of resolving the dispute) for trying to resolve the dispute. The mediator will also assess whether there has been, or is a risk of,

(1)　domestic violence, and/or
(2)　harm by a prospective party to a child that would be the subject of the application.

5.4 It is the responsibility of the prospective applicant (or that person's legal representative) to contact a family mediator to arrange attendance at a MIAM.

5.5 Only an authorised family mediator can carry out a MIAM. An authorised family mediator means a mediator who is a member of a mediation organisation affiliated to the Family Mediation Council (and is therefore subject to the Family Mediation Council's Code of Conduct), and is authorised to undertake MIAMs by the professional practice consultant supervising the mediator's practice.

5.6 A prospective applicant is not required to attend a MIAM where one of the circumstances set out in rule 3.8(1) or 3.8(2) FPR applies.

5.7 Information on how to find a family mediator may be obtained from www.familymediationcouncil.org.uk website which hosts the "find a local family mediator" database (see also 'Signposting Services for Families' – paragraph 2 above).

5.8 The prospective applicant (or the prospective applicant's legal representative) should provide the mediator with contact details for the other party or parties to the dispute ('the prospective respondent(s)'), so that the mediator can contact the prospective respondent(s) to discuss their willingness and availability to attend a MIAM.

5.9 The prospective applicant and, where they agree to do so, the prospective respondent(s), should then attend a MIAM arranged by the mediator. If the parties are willing to attend together and where it is assessed by the mediator to be safe, the meeting may be conducted jointly; otherwise, separate meetings will be held.

5.10 The Family Mediation Council sets the requirements for mediators who conduct MIAMs. In summary, a mediator who arranges a MIAM with one or more parties to a dispute should consider any risk factors present and how these should be managed, and should also consider with the party or parties concerned whether public funding may be available to meet the cost of the meeting and any subsequent mediation. Where neither of the parties is eligible for, or wishes to seek, public funding, any charge made by the mediator for the MIAM will be the responsibility of the party or parties attending, in accordance with any agreement made with the mediator.

5.11 Mediation is a confidential process; none of the parties to the mediation may provide information to the court as to the content of any discussions held in mediation and/or the reasons why agreement was not reached. Similarly, the mediator may not provide such information, unless the mediator considers that a safeguarding issue arises.

5.12 However, it is important that the parties, or either of them, introduce at the MIAM (or any subsequent court application) any other evidence of attempts to resolve a dispute and to focus on the needs of the child.

6. Resolution of disputed arrangements for children through the Court

6.1 The judge is obliged to consider, at every stage of court proceedings, whether non-court dispute resolution is appropriate.

6.2 The parties should also actively consider non-court dispute resolution even if proceedings are issued and are ongoing.

6.3 If the court considers that another form of dispute resolution is appropriate, the court may direct that the proceedings, or a hearing in the proceedings, be adjourned for such specified period as it considers appropriate:

   (1)   to enable the parties to obtain information and advice about non-court dispute resolution; and
   (2)   where the parties agree, to enable non-court dispute resolution to take place.

6.4 Where the court adjourns proceedings, it shall give directions about the timing and method by which the parties must tell the court if any of the issues in the proceedings have been resolved.

6.5 It is to be noted that some courts operate an at-court mediation scheme, and at-court MIAMs, with providers contracted to the Legal Aid Agency. Some mediators may prefer to conduct mediation outside of the court premises. A mediation assessment may be possible at court; alternatively, the court may help in making an appointment with a local mediator for a MIAM or for mediation. Information about mediation arrangements should be advertised in the local court.

7. Local Good Practice

7.1 The CAP is designed to provide a framework for a consistent approach to the resolution of the issues in private family law in England & Wales.

7.2 Local practices and initiatives can be operated in addition to, and within, the framework.

8. Application to court

8.1 Unless one of the MIAM exemptions applies (see rule 3.8 FPR), an application to court for determination of most issues concerning a child (see the definition of 'relevant family application' in rule 3.6 FPR and paragraphs 11 and 12 of PD3A) can be made only after a MIAM has taken place (at which meeting mediation and other forms of non-court dispute resolution will have been considered). One of the exemptions may be that the case is urgent, in which case see 'Urgent and Without Notice Applications' in paragraph 12 below. The grounds for urgency are defined in rule 3.8(c) FPR.

8.2 The application for a child arrangements order or other Children Act 1989 private law order shall be made on the relevant prescribed form.

8.3 For section 8 Children Act 1989 applications, the applicant will be required, on the form C100, to confirm attendance at a MIAM or specify that an exemption applies **unless** the application is for a consent order, or if the application concerns a child who is the subject of ongoing emergency proceedings, care proceedings or supervision proceedings, or if the child concerned is already the subject of an emergency protection order, care order or supervision order (see paragraphs 11 and 12 of PD3A).

8.4 The relevant part of the form C100 must be completed showing that either:

(1)   the applicant has attended a MIAM; or

(2)   the applicant has not attended a MIAM and claims one of the exemptions (rule 3.8(1) FPR) – exemptions include (but are not limited to) evidence of domestic violence, child protection concerns, urgency, previous MIAM attendance or exemption; or (3) an authorised family mediator confirms in the form that he or she is satisfied that

    (a)   mediation is not suitable because the respondents is (if more than one respondent, any one of them is) unwilling to attend a MIAM;

    (b)   mediation is not suitable as a means of resolving the dispute because the respondent (if more than one, any of them) failed without good reason to attend a MIAM; or

    (c)   mediation is otherwise not suitable as a means of resolving the dispute.

8.5 The C100 form may be obtained from the Family Court or from www.gov.uk.

8.6 If the parties have previously prepared a Parenting Plan, this shall be attached to the Form C100.

8.7 If possible at the time of issue, and in any event by no later than one working day after issue, or in courts where applications are first considered on paper by no later than two working days after issue, the court shall send or hand to the Applicant the following:

i)   A copy of the application form C100 (together with the Supplemental Information Form C1A),

ii)   The Notice of Hearing;

iii)   The Acknowledgment Form C7;

iv)   A blank Form C1A, (if required);

v)   Information leaflets for the parties (which must include the CB7 leaflet).

8.8 Unless the applicant requests to do so, or the court directs the applicant to do so, the Court will serve the respondent(s) with:

i.   A copy of the application form C100 (together with Supplemental Information Form C1A)(if provided);

ii.   The Notice of Hearing;

iii.   The Acknowledgement Form C7;

iv.   A blank form C1A;

v.   Information leaflet for the parties (which must include the CB7 leaflet).

8.9 The court shall send to Cafcass/CAFCASS Cymru a copy of the Form C100 (and the form C1A, if supplied), and the C6 Notice of Hearing no later than 2 working days after the date of issue. This will be in electronic format where possible.

8.10 The court shall not send to Cafcass/CAFCASS Cymru any other application under the Children Act 1989, or any other private law application, unless the Court has made a specific direction requesting the assistance of Cafcass/CAFCASS Cymru. Therefore, any application which is not in Form C100 or which does not contain a direction to Cafcass/CAFCASS Cymru will be returned to the court at which the application has been issued.

9. Allocation and Gatekeeping

9.1 It is important that the form C100 is fully completed (including the provision of telephone numbers of the relevant parties), otherwise there may be a delay in processing the application; where the form is not fully completed, the court staff may request further information before the application form is accepted for issue.

9.2 The application shall be considered by a nominated Legal Adviser &/or nominated District Judge ("the Gatekeeper(s)") within one working day of the date of receipt in accordance with the appropriate Rules of Procedure.

9.3 An application for a relevant family order shall be allocated to a level of judge in the Family Court in accordance with the Guidance issued by the President on "Allocation and Gatekeeping for Proceedings under Part II of the Children Act 1989 (Private Law Proceedings) and the Family Court (Composition and Distribution of Business) Rules 2014, together with the Allocation Schedule.

9.4 Gatekeepers shall be able to issue Directions on Issue (on Form CAP01) in the following circumstances:

(1)   where, on the basis of information provided on the application form and any additional information provided on a C1A Supplemental Information Form, the Gatekeeper finds that the exemption from attending a MIAM has not been validly been claimed, the Gatekeeper will direct the applicant, or direct the parties to attend a MIAM before the FHDRA, unless the Gatekeeper considers that in all the circumstances of the case the MIAM requirement should not apply to the application in question; the Gatekeeper will have particular regard to the matters set out in rule 3.10(3) FPR when making this decision;

(2)   where it appears that an urgent issue requires determination, the Gatekeeper may give directions for an accelerated hearing;

(3)   exceptionally, where it appears that directions need to be given for the service and filing of evidence, he/she may give directions for the filing of evidence.

10. Judicial continuity

10.1 All private law cases will be allocated to a level of judge within the Family Court upon issue.

10.2 Continuity of Judicial involvement in the conduct of proceedings from the FHDRA to the making of a final order should be the objective in all cases.

10.3 Where the case has been allocated to be heard before lay justices, the expectation of judicial continuity should apply where

(1)   There has been a hearing to determine findings of fact,

(2)   A decision yet to be made in the interests of a child by a court depends upon
       rulings or judicial assessments already made in the proceedings, in which case,
       wherever possible, the hearing shall be listed before the same lay justices;
       alternatively, it shall be listed before the same the legal adviser and at least one
       lay justice (preferably the chairman) to provide that continuity. Where a case is
       adjourned part-heard the court which resumes the hearing shall, wherever
       possible, be composed of the same lay justices as dealt with the previous part of
       the hearing (see rule 8 of the Family Court (Composition and Distribution of
       Business) Rules 2014).

11. Key welfare principles

11.1 Section 1 of the Children Act 1989 applies to all applications for orders concerning
the upbringing of children. This means that:

(1)   the child's welfare is the court's paramount consideration;
(2)   delay is likely to be prejudicial to the welfare of the child, and
(3)   a court order shall not be made unless the court considers that making an order
       would be better for the child than making no order at all.

11.2 Parties, and the court, must also have regard to the FPR in particular the following:

(1)   FPR Rule 1. The 'overriding objective' will apply, so that the court will deal
       with a case justly, having regard to the welfare issues involved and specifically
       will
       (a)   Ensure that the case is dealt with expeditiously and fairly;
       (b)   Deal with the case in ways which are proportionate to the nature,
              importance and complexity of the issues;
       (c)   Ensure that the parties are on an equal footing;
       (d)   Save expense;
       (e)   Allot to each case an appropriate share of the court's resources, while
              taking account of the need to allot resources to other cases.
(2)   Rule 3, and Practice Direction 3A;
(3)   FPR Part 4 'General Case Management Powers';
(4)   FPR Part 15 (Representation of Protected Parties) and Practice Direction 15B
       (Adults Who May Be Protected Parties and Children Who May Become
       Protected Parties in Family Proceedings);
(5)   FPR Part 16 (Representation of Children) (and see also paragraph 18 below);
(6)   FPR Part 18 (procedure for Other Applications in proceedings);
(7)   FPR Part 22 (Evidence);
(8)   FPR Part 24 (Witnesses, depositions generally and taking of evidence in
       Member States of the European Union);
(9)   FPR Part 25 (Experts) and the Experts Practice Directions;
(10)   FPR 27.6 and Practice Direction 27A (Court Bundles).

11.3 Where a fact-finding hearing is required, this shall take place in accordance with
revised Practice Direction 12J FPR.

11.4 The court shall exercise its powers flexibly. The flexible powers of the court include
the ability for the court to cancel or repeat a particular hearing.

12. Urgent and Without Notice Applications

12.1 **Urgent**: Where an order is sought as a matter of urgency, an application may be
made to the Court for an emergency order without the requirement for the Applicant to

have attended at a MIAM. The categories of urgent application justifying such an exemption are set out in rule 3.8(c) FPR and include cases in which:

(1) There is a risk to the life, liberty, or the physical safety of the prospective applicant or his or her family, or his or her home;

(2) Any delay caused by attending a MIAM would cause:

    (1) A risk of harm to the child;

    (2) A risk of unlawful removal of a child from the United Kingdom or a risk of unlawful retention of a child who is currently outside England and Wales;

    (3) A significant risk of a miscarriage of justice;

    (4) Unreasonable hardship to the prospective applicant;

    (5) Irretrievable problems in dealing with the dispute (including the irretrievable loss of significant evidence).

(3) There is a significant risk that in the period necessary to schedule and attend a MIAM, proceedings relating to the dispute will be brought in another state in which a valid claim to jurisdiction may exist, such that a court in that other State would be seised of the dispute before a court in England and Wales.

12.2 **'Without Notice'**: Applications to court made 'Without Notice' to the respondent(s) shall be allocated in accordance with the Family Court (Composition and Distribution of Business) Rules 2014, and determined by reference to the provisions of Practice Direction 18A, paragraph 5.1, with further regard to the principles set out in Practice Direction 20A, paragraph 4.3-4.5 FPR (noting particularly paragraph 4.3(c)).

12.3 Without Notice Orders should be made only exceptionally, and where:

(1) If the applicant were to give notice to the respondent(s) this would enable the respondent(s) to take steps to defeat the purpose of the injunction; cases where the application is brought without notice in order to conceal the step from the respondent(s) are very rare indeed; or

(2) The case is one of exceptional urgency; that is to say, that there has been literally no time to give notice (either by telephone, text or e-mail or otherwise) before the injunction is required to prevent the threatened wrongful act; or

(3) If the applicant gives notice to the respondent(s), this would be likely to expose the applicant or relevant child to unnecessary risk of physical or emotional harm.

12.4 Any Order which follows an emergency 'without notice' hearing should specify:

(1) the reason(s) why the order has been made without notice to the respondent(s),

(2) the outline facts alleged which have been relied upon by the court in making the order, unless the facts are clearly contained in the statement in support; and

(3) the right of the respondent(s) to apply to vary or discharge the order.

12.5 **Gatekeeping decisions**: Following any urgent or 'without notice' hearing, unless all issues have been determined or the application has been dismissed without any further directions given, the judge may make gatekeeping decisions, including allocation and venue of future hearing, (and if so, shall notify the Gatekeeping team responsible for the area in which the child resides), or shall refer the application to the relevant Gatekeeping team for a decision on allocation and venue of future hearing; in either event, a copy of the C100 shall be sent to Cafcass for safeguarding checks, and (depending on the Gatekeeping decision) the file shall be sent to the court where future hearings will take place (if at a different court centre from the court where the urgent hearing occurred).

13. Safeguarding

13.1 Where an application is made for a child arrangements order (but not necessarily for specific issue or prohibited steps orders), before the FHDRA (see paragraph 14 below) Cafcass/CAFCASS Cymru shall identify any safety issues by the steps outlined below.

13.2 Such steps shall be confined to matters of safety. The Cafcass Officer or (in Wales) the Welsh Family Proceedings Officer (WFPO) shall not discuss with either party before the FHDRA any matter other than one which relates to safety. The parties will not be invited to talk about other issues, for example relating to the substance of applications or replies or about issues concerning matters of welfare or the prospects of resolution. If such issues are raised by either party, they will be advised that such matters will be deferred to the FHDRA when there is equality between the parties and full discussion can take place which will be a time when any safety issues that have been identified can also be taken into account.

13.3 In order to inform the court of possible risks of harm to the child Cafcass/CAFCASS Cymru will carry out safeguarding enquiries. For all child arrangements orders this will include seeking information from local authorities, and carrying out police checks on the parties. For all other applications received from the court on the form C100, Cafcass/CAFCASS Cymru will carry out a screening process and will undertake those checks if in the professional judgment of the Cafcass officer, or the WFPO in Wales, such checks are necessary.

13.4 Cafcass/CAFCASS Cymru will, if possible, undertake telephone risk identification interviews with the parties and if risks of harm are identified, may invite parties to meet separately with the Cafcass Officer, or WFPO in Wales, before the FHDRA to clarify any safety issue.

13.5 Cafcass/CAFCASS Cymru shall record and outline any safety issues for the court, in the form of a Safeguarding letter (in Wales, this is called a 'Safeguarding report').

13.6 The Cafcass officer, or WFPO, will not initiate contact with the child prior to the FHDRA. If contacted by a child, discussions relating to the issues in the case will be postponed to the day of the hearing or after when the Cafcass officer or WFPO will have more knowledge of the issues.

13.7 Within 17 working days of receipt by Cafcass/CAFCASS Cymru of the application, and at least 3 working days before the hearing, the Cafcass Officer or WFPO shall report to the court, in a Safeguarding letter/report, the outcome of the risk identification work which has been undertaken.

13.8 Further, Cafcass and CAFCASS Cymru are required, under section 16A Children Act 1989, to undertake (and to provide to the court) risk assessments where an officer of the Service ('Cafcass Officer' or WFPO) suspects that a child is at risk of harm.

14. First Hearing Dispute Resolution Appointment (FHDRA)

14.1 The FHDRA may (where time for service on the respondent(s) has been abridged) take place within 4 weeks, but should ordinarily take place in week 5 following the issuing of the application; at the latest it will take place in week 6 following the issuing of the application.

14.2 The respondent(s) shall have at least 10 working days' notice of the hearing where practicable, but the court may abridge this time.

14.3 The respondent(s) should file a response on the Forms C7/C1A no later than 10 working days before the hearing, unless the court has abridged this time.

14.4 Unless the court otherwise directs, any party to proceedings, and any litigation friend of the parties must attend this (and any other) hearing. If a child is a party and represented by a children's guardian, the children's guardian need not attend directions hearings if represented.

14.5 A party may choose to be accompanied at this (or any) hearing by a McKenzie Friend to support them (a McKenzie Friend is someone who can provide moral support at court for the party; take notes; help with case papers; quietly give advice on any aspect of the conduct of the case). If so, the McKenzie Friend must comply with the relevant Guidance (currently set out in the Practice Guidance: McKenzie Friends (Civil and Family Courts): July 2010: http://www.judiciary.gov.uk/Resources/JCO/Documents/ Guidance/mcken zie-friends-practice-guidance-july-2010.pdf).

14.6 A Cafcass Officer or WFPO shall attend this hearing. A mediator may attend where available.

14.7 The Cafcass Officer or WFPO shall, where practicable, speak separately to each party at court before the hearing in particular where it has not been possible to conduct a risk identification interview with either party.

14.8 The FHDRA provides an opportunity for the parties to be helped to an understanding of the issues which divide them, and to reach agreement. If agreement is reached,

    (1)   The Court will be able to make an order (which in many cases will be a final order) reflecting that agreement;

    (2)   The Court will assist the parties (so far as it is able) in putting into effect the agreement/order in a co-operative way.

14.9 The FHDRA is not privileged. That is to say that what is said at the FHDRA may be referred to at later court hearings.

14.10 By the time of the hearing, the Court should have the following documents:

    (a)   C100 application, and C1A (if any);
    (b)   Notice of Hearing;
    (c)   C7 response and C1A (if any);
    (d)   Cafcass/CAFCASS Cymru safeguarding letter/report.

14.11 At the FHDRA the judge, working with the Cafcass Officer, or WFPO, will seek to assist the parties in conciliation and in resolution of all or any of the issues between them. Any remaining issues will be identified, the Cafcass Officer or WFPO will advise the court of any recommended means of resolving such issues, and directions will be given for the future resolution of such issues. At all times the decisions of the Court and the work of the Cafcass Officer or WFPO will take account of any risk or safeguarding issues that have been identified.

14.12 The court should have information obtained through safeguarding checks carried out by Cafcass/CAFCASS Cymru, to ensure that any agreement between the parties, or any dispute resolution process selected, is in the interests of the child and safe for all concerned.

14.13 The FHDRA will be conducted in the most appropriate way in the interests of the child. In particular the court shall consider the following matters:

Safeguarding, in this respect:

(a) The court shall inform the parties of the content of the safeguarding letter/report provided by Cafcass/CAFCASS Cymru, where it has not already been sent by Cafcass/CAFCASS Cymru to the parties, unless it considers that to do so would create a risk of harm to a party or the child. The court may need to consider whether, and if so how, any information contained in the checks should be disclosed to the parties if Cafcass/CAFCASS Cymru have not disclosed the letter/report.

The court will further consider:

(b) Whether a fact finding hearing is needed to determine allegations which are not accepted, and whose resolution is likely to affect the decision of the court.

(c) Risk identification followed by active case management including risk assessment, and compliance with the Practice Direction 12J.

Further:

(d) If the safeguarding information is (contrary to the arrangements set out in the CAP) not available at the FHDRA, the court should adjourn the application until the safeguarding checks are available. Interim orders (unless to protect the safety of a child) should not be made in the absence of safeguarding checks.

And further:

(e) Where the court so directs, a safeguarding letter/report ought to be attached to any referral to a supported or supervised child contact centre in the event the court directs supported or supervised contact.

MIAM, specifically:

(a) Whether, if a MIAM exemption has been claimed, the Applicant has validly claimed the exemption;

(b) Whether the Respondent has attended a MIAM;

(c) If the court finds that a MIAM exemption has not been validly claimed the court will direct the applicant or direct the parties to attend a MIAM and if necessary adjourn the proceedings to enable a MIAM to take place, unless the court considers that in all the circumstances of the case, the MIAM requirement should not apply to the application in question; when making the decision the court will have particular regard to the matters contained in rule 3.10(3) FPR.

Mediation, At-Court Mediation assessment, and other Dispute Resolution: allowing the parties the time and opportunity to engage in noncourt dispute resolution.

(a) At the FHDRA, the judge will specifically consider whether, and the extent to which, the parties can safely resolve some or all of the issues with the assistance of the Cafcass Officer, WFPO, or a mediator.

(b) There will be, at every FHDRA, a period in which the Cafcass Officer, or WFPO, will seek to conciliate and explore with the parties the resolution of all or some of the issues between them if safe to do so. The procedure to be followed in this connection at the hearing will be determined by local arrangements between the Cafcass manager, or equivalent in Wales, and the Designated Family Judge or the Justices' Clerk where appropriate.

The court will further consider:

(c)   What is the result of any such meeting at Court?

(d)   What other options there are for resolution e.g. may the case be suitable for further intervention by Cafcass/CAFCASS Cymru; Should a referral for mediation be made? Is collaborative law appropriate? Should the parties be advised to complete a Parenting Plan?

(e)   Would the parties be assisted by attendance at an Activity Separated Parents Information Programme, (or in Wales, Working Together For Children (WT4C)) or other Activity or intervention, whether by formal statutory provision under section 11 Children Act 1989 or otherwise;

(f)   An at-court assessment of the suitability of the parties for mediation.

Consent Orders:

(a)   Where agreement is reached at any hearing or submitted in writing to the court, no order will be made without scrutiny by the court.

(b)   Where safeguarding checks or risk assessment work remain outstanding, the making of a final order may be deferred for such work. In such circumstances the court shall adjourn the case for no longer than 28 days to a fixed date. A written notification of this work is to be provided by Cafcass/CAFCASS Cymru in the form of an updating Safeguarding letter/report, or if deemed relevant by Cafcass/CAFCASS Cymru, a section 16A risk assessment in accordance with the timescale specified by the court. If satisfactory information is then available, the order may be made at the adjourned hearing in the agreed terms without the need for attendance by the parties. If satisfactory information is not available, the order will not be made, and the case will be adjourned for further consideration with an opportunity for the parties to make further representations

Reports:

(a)   Reports may be ordered where there are welfare issues or other specific considerations which should be addressed in a report by Cafcass/CAFCASS Cymru or the Local Authority. Before a report is ordered, the court should consider alternative ways of working with the parties such as are referred to in paragraph 5 ('non-court resolution of disputed arrangements') above.

(b)   If a report is ordered in accordance with section 7 of the Children Act 1989, the Court should direct which specific matters relating to the welfare of the child are to be addressed. Welfare reports will generally only be ordered in cases where there is a dispute as to with whom the child should live, spend time, or otherwise have contact with. A report can also be ordered:

   i.   If there is an issue concerning the child's wishes, and/or

   ii.   If there is an alleged risk to the child, and/or

   iii. Where information and advice is needed which the court considers to be necessary before a decision can be reached in the case.

(c)   General requests for a report on an application should be avoided; the Court should state on the face of the Order the specific factual and/or other issue which is to be addressed in the focused report.

(d)   In determining whether a request for a report should be directed to the relevant local authority or to Cafcass/CAFCASS Cymru, the court should consider such information as Cafcass/CAFCASS Cymru has provided about the extent and nature of the local authority's current or recent involvement with the subject of the application and the parties, and any relevant protocol between Cafcass and the Association of Directors of Children's Services.

(e)   The court may further consider whether there is a need for an investigation under section 37 Children Act 1989.

(f)   A copy of the Order requesting the report and any relevant court documents are to be sent to Cafcass/CAFCASS Cymru or, in the case of the Local Authority to the Legal Adviser to the Director of the Local Authority Children's Services and, where known, to the allocated social worker by the court forthwith.

(g)   Is any expert evidence required? If so, section 13 Children and Families Act 2014, and Part 25 of the FPR must be complied with. This is the latest point at which consideration should be given to the instruction of an expert in accordance with Rule 25.6(b) of the FPR; the court will need to consider carefully the future conduct of proceedings where the preparation of an expert report is necessary but where the parties are unrepresented and are unable to fund the preparation of such a report.

Wishes and feelings of the child:

(a)   In line with the Family Justice Young People's Board Charter, children and young people should be at the centre of all proceedings.

(b)   The child or young person should feel that their needs, wishes and feelings have been considered in the court process.

(c)   Each decision should be assessed on its impact on the child.

(d)   The court must consider the wishes and feelings of the child, ascertainable so far as is possible in light of the child's age and understanding and circumstances. Specifically, the Court should ask:

i.   Is the child aware of the proceedings?

ii.   Are the wishes and feelings of the child available, and/or to be ascertained (if at all)?

iii.   How is the child to be involved in the proceedings, and if so, how; for example, should they meet the judge/lay justices? Should they be encouraged to write to the court, or have their views reported by Cafcass/CAFCASS Cymru or by a local authority?

iv.   Who will inform the child of the outcome of the case, where appropriate?

Case Management:

(a)   What, if any, issues are agreed and what are the key issues to be determined?

(b)   Should the matter be listed for a fact-finding hearing?

(c)   Are there any interim orders which can usefully be made (e.g. indirect, supported or supervised contact) pending Dispute Resolution Appointment or final hearing?

(d)   What directions are required to ensure the application is ready for a Dispute Resolution Appointment or final hearing – statements, reports etc?

(e)   Should the application be listed for a Dispute Resolution Appointment (it is envisaged that most cases will be so listed)?

(f)   Should the application be listed straightaway for a final hearing?

(g)   Judicial continuity should be actively considered (especially if there has been or is to be a fact finding hearing or a contested interim hearing).

Allocation:

(a)   The Allocation decision will be considered by the Court;

(b)   If it is necessary to transfer the case to another court within the DFJ area or another area, or re-allocate it, the court shall state the reasons for transfer/re-allocation, and shall specifically make directions for the next hearing in the court.

Order (other than a final order): Where no final agreement is reached, and the court is required to give case management directions, the following shall be included on the order [CAP02]:

(a)   The issues about which the parties are agreed;

(b)   The issues that remain to be resolved;

(c)   The steps that are planned to resolve the issues;

(d)   Any interim arrangements pending such resolution, including arrangements for the involvement of children;

(e)   The timetable for such steps and, where this involves further hearings, the date of such hearings;

(f)   A statement as to any facts relating to risk or safety; in so far as they are resolved the result will be stated and, in so far as not resolved, the steps to be taken to resolve them will be state;

(g)   Whether the parties are to be assisted by participation in mediation, Separated Parents Information Programme, WT4C, or other types of parenting intervention, and to detail any activity directions or conditions imposed by the court;

(h)   The date, time and venue of the next hearing;

(i)   Whether the author of any section 7 report is required to attend the hearing, in order to give oral evidence. A direction for the Cafcass officer or WFPO to attend court will not be made without first considering the reason why attendance is necessary, and upon what issues the Cafcass officer or WFPO will be providing evidence;

(j)   Where both parties are Litigants in Person, the court may direct HMCTS to produce a Litigant in Person bundle;

(k)   The judge will, as far as possible, provide a copy of the order to both parties before they leave the courtroom, and will, if necessary, go through and explain the contents of the order to ensure they are clearly understood by both parties. The parties should know the date, time and venue of any further hearing before they leave the court.

15. Timetable for the child

15.1 Court proceedings should be timetabled so that the dispute can be resolved as soon as safe and possible in the interests of the child.

15.2 The judge shall, at all times during the proceedings, have regard to the impact which the court timetable will have on the welfare and development of the child to whom the application relates. The judge and the parties shall pay particular attention to the child's age, and important landmarks in the immediate life of the child, including:

(a)   the child's birthday;

(b)   the start of nursery/schooling;

(c)   the start/end of a school term/year;

(d)   any proposed change of school; and/or

(e)   any significant change in the child's family, or social, circumstances.

15.3 While it is acknowledged that an interim order may be appropriate at an early stage of court proceedings, cases should not be adjourned for a review (or reviews) of contact or other orders/arrangements, &/or for addendum section 7 report, unless such a hearing is necessary and for a clear purpose that is consistent with the timetable for the child and in the child's best interests.

15.4 When preparing a section 7 report, Cafcass/CAFCASS Cymru (or, where appropriate, the local authority) is encouraged to make recommendations for the stepped phasing-in of child arrangements (i.e. recommendations for the medium and longer term future for the child) insofar as they are able to do so safely in the interests of the child concerned;

15.5 Where active involvement or monitoring is needed, the court may consider making:

(1)   An order under section 11H Children Act 1989 (Monitoring);
(2)   A Family Assistance Order under section 16 Children Act 1989 (in accordance with the Practice Direction 12M FPR), and if all the named adults in the order agree to the making of such an order and if the order is directed to a local authority, the child lives (or will live) within that local authority area or the local authority consents to the making of the order.

16. Capacity of Litigants

16.1 In the event that the judge has concerns about the capacity of a litigant before the court, the judge shall consider:

(1)   the Guidance issued by the Family Justice Council in relation to assessing the capacity of litigants;
(2)   Practice Direction 15B (Adults Who May Be Protected Parties and Children Who May Become Protected Parties In Family Proceedings).

17. Evidence

17.1 No evidence shall be filed in relation to an application until after the FHDRA unless:

(1)   It has been filed in support of a without notice application
(2)   It has been directed by the Court by the Directions on Issue (CAP01);
(3)   It has been directed by the Court for the purposes of determining an interim application.

18. Rule 16.4 children's guardians

18.1 The Court should be vigilant to identify the cases where a rule 16.4 children's guardian should be appointed. This should be considered initially at the FHDRA.

18.2 Where the court is considering the appointment of a children's guardian from Cafcass/CAFCASS Cymru, it should first ensure that enquiries have been made of the appropriate Cafcass/CAFCASS Cymru manager in accordance with paragraph 7.4, Part 4 of the Practice Direction 16A. This should either be in writing before the hearing or by way of case discussion with the relevant Cafcass service manager; for cases in Wales, the 'hotline' protocol agreed with CAFCASS Cymru will ensure that such a discussion can take place. The court should consult with Cafcass/CAFCASS Cymru, so as to consider any advice in connection with the prospective appointment, and the timescale involved.

18.3 When the court decides to appoint a children's guardian, consideration should first be given to appointing an Officer of the Service or WFPO. If Cafcass/CAFCASS Cymru is unable to provide a children's guardian without delay, or if there is some other reason why the appointment of a Cafcass officer is not appropriate, the court should (further to rule 16.24 of the FPR) appoint a person other than the Official Solicitor, unless the Official Solicitor expressly consents.

18.4 In considering whether to make such an appointment the Court shall take account of the demands on the resources of Cafcass/CAFCASS Cymru that such an appointment would make. The court should also make clear on the face of any order the purpose of the appointment and the timetable of any work to be undertaken.

19. Dispute Resolution Appointment (DRA)

19.1 The Court shall list the application for a Dispute Resolution Appointment ('DRA') to follow the preparation of section 7 or other expert report, or Separated Parenting Information Programme (SPIP) (or WT4C in Wales), if this is considered likely to be helpful in the interests of the child.

19.2 The author of the section 7 report will only attend this hearing if directed to do so by the Court.

19.3 At the DRA the Court will:

(1) Identify the key issue(s) (if any) to be determined and the extent to which those issues can be resolved or narrowed at the DRA;
(2) Consider whether the DRA can be used as a final hearing;
(3) Resolve or narrow the issues by hearing evidence;
(4) Identify the evidence to be heard on the issues which remain to be resolved at the final hearing;
(5) Give final case management directions including:
  (a) Filing of further evidence;
  (b) Filing of a statement of facts/issues remaining to be determined;
  (c) Filing of a witness template and/or skeleton arguments;
  (d) Ensuring Compliance with Practice Direction 27A (the Bundles Practice Direction);
  (e) Listing the Final Hearing.

20. Fact-finding hearing

20.1 If the court considers that a fact-finding hearing is necessary it shall conduct that hearing in accordance with revised Practice Direction 12J.

21. Enforcement of Child Arrangements

21.1 On any application for enforcement of a child arrangements order, the court shall:

- consider whether the facts relevant to the alleged non-compliance are agreed, or whether it is necessary to conduct a hearing to establish the facts;
- consider the reasons for any non-compliance;
- consider how the wishes and feelings of the child are to be ascertained;
- consider whether advice is required from Cafcass/CAFCASS Cymru on the appropriate way forward;
- assess and manage any risks of making further or other child arrangements order;
- consider whether a SPIP or referral for dispute resolution is appropriate;
- consider whether an enforcement order may be appropriate, and
- consider the welfare checklist.

21.2 The Gatekeepers shall list any application for enforcement of a child arrangements order for hearing, before the previously allocated judge if possible, within 20 working days of issue. Enforcement cases should be concluded without delay.

21.3 An application made within existing proceedings in the family court shall be allocated to the level of judge in accordance with rule 17 of the Family Court (Composition and Distribution of Business) Rules 2014.

21.4 The Gatekeepers shall, if considered necessary, direct that further safeguarding checks are required from Cafcass/CAFCASS Cymru. On any application for enforcement issued more than three months after the order which is the subject of the enforcement, safeguarding checks shall be ordered.

21.5 The court has a wide range of powers in the event of a breach of a child arrangements order without reasonable excuse.

21.6 This range of powers includes (but is not limited to):

(a) referral of the parents to a SPIP, or in Wales a WT4C, or mediation;
(b) variation of the child arrangements order (which could include a more defined order and/or reconsidering the contact provision or the living arrangements of the child);
(c) a contact enforcement order or suspended enforcement order under section 11J Children Act 1989 ('Enforcement order' for unpaid work), (see paragraph 21.7 below);
(d) an order for compensation for financial loss (under section 11O Children Act 1989);
(e) committal to prison; or
(f) a fine.

21.7 In the event that the court is considering an enforcement order for alleged non-compliance with a court order (under section 11J Children Act 1989) or considering a Compensation order in respect of financial loss (under section 11O Children Act 1989), the court shall (in the absence of agreement between the parties about the relevant facts) determine the facts in order to establish the cause of the alleged failure to comply.

21.8 Section 11L Children Act 1989 provides that if the court finds that a breach has occurred without reasonable excuse it may order the non-compliant party to undertake unpaid work if that is necessary to secure compliance, and if the effect on the non-compliant party is proportionate to the seriousness of the breach. The court must also consider whether unpaid work is available in the locality and the likely effect on the non-compliant party. It is good practice to ask Cafcass/CAFCASS Cymru to report on the suitability of this order. Section 11L(7) also requires the court to take into account the welfare of the child who is the subject of the order for contact.

22. Court timetable

22.1 Working Day 1: Paperwork received. Court office checks whether the revised form C100 has been completed correctly. The application will not be issued unless the form has been completed correctly.

22.2 Working Day 2: Case considered by Gatekeeping team. Case allocated by Gatekeepers in accordance with the President's Guidance on allocation and the Family Court (Composition and Distribution) Rules 2014.

The Gatekeeper(s) undertaking allocation to check whether form C100 has been completed. If there has been no MIAM, and there are reasons to believe that the applicant should have attended a MIAM, the Gatekeeping judge can direct that a MIAM should take place before the FHDRA.

22.3 17 working days from the date of its receipt of the application Cafcass/CAFCASS Cymru will provide the safeguarding letter/report to the Court (20 working days in the area of CAFCASS Cymru).

22.4 Week 5 (or latest, week 6): Case listed for FHDRA (before week 5 if requirements of notice have been abridged).

22.5 Thereafter, case may be listed for fact-finding hearing, DRA &/or final hearing.

23. Relevant Family Application (definition)

23.1 A relevant family application for the purposes of the CAP is an application that

(1)   Is made to the court in, or to initiate, family proceedings, and
(2)   Is of a description specified in the Family Procedure Rules.

Annex: Explanation of terms

Abuse	Any behaviour which causes harm.
Adjourn/Adjournment	Where the case, or a hearing, is directed to take place or continue at a later time (which might be on the same day or another day).
Allegation	A claim that someone has done something wrong.
Applicant	The name given to someone who is asking the court for a court order.
Application	How a person asks the court to do something.
Cafcass	Cafcass stands for the 'Children and Family Court Advisory and Support Service'. Cafcass is independent of the courts, social services, education and health authorities and all similar agencies. Cafcass workers (sometimes called 'Family Court Advisers' or 'officers') are specialist social workers who help the court by making safeguarding checks, helping parties at the FHDRA to consider solutions, and if necessary writing reports for the court &/or monitoring arrangements after court.
CAFCASS Cymru	This is Cafcass in Wales. CAFCASS Cymru is part of the Department of Health and Social Services in the Welsh Government.
Child Arrangements Order	This is an order which will set out arrangements relating to (a) *with whom* a child is to live, spend time or otherwise have contact, and (b) *when* a child is to live, spend time or otherwise have contact with any other person.
Collaborative law	One of the ways of trying to sort out disputes away from court; each party appoints their own lawyer, and you and your lawyers all meet together to work things out face to face.
Consent order	When you have reached an agreement with the other parent, which resolves the dispute, the judge may agree to make that agreement into an order called a consent order.

Contact centre	A place for a parent to see their child in a neutral and 'safe' environment. 'Supervised' contact centres provide a safe and neutral place for contact. 'Supported' contact centres, which are often run by volunteers, offer a neutral place for contact in cases where no safety concerns exist.
Designated Family Judge	This is the judge who has responsibility to provide leadership to the family judiciary within the court centre or group of courts.
Dispute Resolution	The method of solving disagreements.
Domestic violence	This phrase is used to describe a wide range of behaviours including any incident or pattern of incidents of controlling, coercive or threatening behaviour, violence or abuse between those aged 16 or over who are or have been intimate partners or family members regardless of gender or sexuality. This can encompass, but is not limited to, the following types of abuse: psychological, physical, sexual, financial, or emotional. Controlling behaviour is: a range of acts designed to make a person subordinate and/or dependent by isolating them from sources of support, exploiting their resources and capacities for personal gain, depriving them of the means needed for independence, resistance and escape and regulating their everyday behaviour. Coercive behaviour is: an act or a pattern of acts of assault, threats, humiliation and intimidation or other abuse that is used to harm, punish, or frighten their victim.
DRA Dispute Resolution Appointment.	This is a court hearing which takes place towards the end of the court's involvement, and is another opportunity to see if the dispute can be sorted out with the help of a judge.
Enforcement	Making sure that an order is complied with.
Expert evidence	Evidence and opinions provided by someone with special skills and knowledge (but, for these purposes, does not refer to a social worker employed by, and giving evidence on behalf of, a local authority who is a party to the case).
Fact finding hearing	A court hearing set up for the court to decide on issues of fact or allegations which are in dispute.
Family Assistance order	An order of the court which allows Cafcass or local authorities to provide social-work support to help parties to establish contact arrangements which might otherwise fail.
FHDRA	First Hearing Dispute Resolution Appointment. This is a court hearing which takes place at the beginning of the court's involvement.
File	This means to send/deliver to the court office.
FPR	Family Procedure Rules 2010; the rules of court which govern family cases.
Gatekeeper(s)	The nominated District Judge and/or nominated Legal Adviser responsible for deciding which level of judge in the family court should initially deal with an application.
Hearing	The name given to a meeting or court appointment with a judge.
Indirect contact	Any contact which is not face-to-face (for example, letters, birthday cards, phone calls).

Interim contact	Contact that takes place between the first court hearing and the final hearing.
Investigation under section 37	Where it appears to a judge that a child is or may be at risk of significant harm and it may be appropriate for local authority children's services to apply for a court order giving them responsibilities towards a family, the judge can direct the local authority to investigate the child's circumstances.
Judge	Where the term 'Judge' is used, this refers to any judge of the Family Court including lay justices (magistrates) and judges of the High Court.
Judgment	The decision of the Judge, and the reasons why the decision has been made.
LAA	Legal Aid Agency; this is the body responsible for providing public funding for legal representation.
Litigant in Person or LiP	This is the name given to a person in court proceedings who does not have a lawyer.
Litigant in Person Bundle	A bundle of court documents, contained in a file, which contains the following: Section A: Applications, Section B: Orders, Section C: Statements, Section D: Cafcass safeguarding letter, analyses and any expert reports, and Section E: Police, medical, other documents.
McKenzie Friend	A friend or other person who can help you prepare your case and go to court with you to give you support and take notes MIAM Mediation Information and Assessment Meeting. At this meeting, a trained mediator will explain what mediation is and how it works, explain the benefits of mediation and the likely costs, answer questions, assess whether the person is eligible for legal aid for mediation, assess whether mediation is suitable in the case. A MIAM should be held within 15 working days of contacting the mediator.
NACCC	National Association of Child Contact Centres: NACCC has in its membership about 350 child contact centres and services throughout England (including the Channel Isles), Wales and Northern Ireland. Child contact centres and services are neutral places where children of separated families can enjoy contact with the parent with whom the child does not live and sometimes with other family members, in a comfortable and safe environment.
Parental responsibility	All the legal rights and responsibilities normally associated with being a parent.
Part-heard	Means a hearing which has started but which has not been finished within the day, and then continues on another day.
Party	Someone involved in the court proceedings – either the person who has made the application, or the person(s) against whom the application has been made.
Practice Direction	This is a document which sets out good practice in supporting the FPR (Family Procedure Rules) or other Rules (see above) and/or may contain provisions which could otherwise be contained in rules of court and have same effect as rules.
Private family law/private law	Family disputes between individuals about arrangements for children.

Respondent(s)	This is the name given to the person or people who receive the court application.
Review	To look at something again.
Rule 16.4 children's guardian	A person (usually a specialist social worker) appointed by the court to look after the interests of a child in the case.
Safeguarding	Making sure that people are safe.
Serve	Delivery of court documents.
SPIP	Separated Parents Information Programme; this is available across England, and is for both parents and for grandparents.
Statement or Witness Statement	A document setting out what you want to say to the Judge about the case. You should sign it and date it. What you say in the statement must be true.
Undertaking	A solemn promise to the court to do, or not do, something.
WFPO	Welsh Family Proceedings Officer. A Cafcass officer in Wales.
WT4C	The Working Together For Children programme which runs in Wales – and is the equivalent of the SPIP (see above).

APPENDIX 4

PRACTICE DIRECTION 12J – CHILD ARRANGEMENTS & CONTACT ORDER: DOMESTIC VIOLENCE AND HARM

This Practice Direction supplements FPR Part 12, and incorporates and supersedes the President's Guidance in Relation to Split Hearings (May 2010) as it applies to proceedings for child arrangements orders.

1. This Practice Direction applies to any family proceedings in the Family Court under the relevant parts of the Children Act 1989 or the relevant parts of the Adoption and Children Act 2002 ('the 2002 Act') in which an application is made for a child arrangements order, or in which any question arises about where a child should live, or about contact between a child and a parent or other family member, where the court considers that an order should be made.

2. The purpose of this Practice Direction is to set out what the Family Court should do in any case in which it is alleged or admitted, or there is other reason to believe, that the child or a party has experienced domestic violence or abuse perpetrated by another party or that there is a risk of such violence or abuse.

3. For the purpose of this Practice Direction, the term 'domestic violence' includes any incident or pattern of incidents of controlling, coercive or threatening behaviour, violence or abuse between those aged 16 or over who are or have been intimate partners or family members regardless of gender or sexuality. This can encompass, but is not limited to, psychological, physical, sexual, financial, or emotional abuse.

> 'Controlling behaviour' means an act or pattern of acts designed to make a person subordinate and/or dependent by isolating them from sources of support, exploiting their resources and capacities for personal gain, depriving them of the means needed for independence, resistance and escape and regulating their everyday behaviour.
> 'Coercive behaviour' means an act or a pattern of acts of assault, threats, humiliation and intimidation or other abuse that is used to harm, punish, or frighten the victim.

General principles

4. The Family Court presumes that the involvement of a parent in a child's life will further the child's welfare, so long as the parent can be involved in a way that does not put the child or other parent at risk of suffering harm.

5. Domestic violence and abuse is harmful to children, and/or puts children at risk of harm, whether they are subjected to violence or abuse, or witness one of their parents

being violent or abusive to the other parent, or live in a home in which violence or abuse is perpetrated (even if the child is too young to be conscious of the behaviour). Children may suffer direct physical, psychological and/or emotional harm from living with violence or abuse, and may also suffer harm indirectly where the violence or abuse impairs the parenting capacity of either or both of their parents.

6. The court must, at all stages of the proceedings, and specifically at the First Hearing Dispute Resolution Appointment ('FHDRA'), consider whether domestic violence is raised as an issue, either by the parties or by Cafcass or CAFCASS Cymru or otherwise, and if so must:

- identify at the earliest opportunity (usually at the FHDRA) the factual and welfare issues involved;
- consider the nature of any allegation, admission or evidence of domestic violence or abuse, and the extent to which it would be likely to be relevant in deciding whether to make a child arrangements order and, if so, in what terms;
- give directions to enable contested relevant factual and welfare issues to be tried as soon as possible and fairly;
- ensure that where violence or abuse is admitted or proven, that any child arrangements order in place protects the safety and wellbeing of the child and the parent with whom the child is living, and does not expose them to the risk of further harm. In particular, the court must be satisfied that any contact ordered with a parent who has perpetrated violence or abuse is safe and in the best interests of the child;
- ensure that any interim child arrangements order (i.e. considered by the court before determination of the facts, and in the absence of admission) is only made having followed the guidance in paragraphs 25–27 below.

7. In all cases it is for the court to decide whether a child arrangements order accords with Section 1(1) of the Children Act 1989; any proposed child arrangements order, whether to be made by agreement between the parties or otherwise must be scrutinised by the court accordingly. The court shall not make a child arrangements order by consent or give permission for an application for a child arrangements order to be withdrawn, unless the parties are present in court, all initial safeguarding checks have been obtained by the court, and an officer of Cafcass or CAFCASS Cymru has spoken to the parties separately, except where it is satisfied that there is no risk of harm to the child in so doing.

8. In considering, on an application for a child arrangements order by consent, whether there is any risk of harm to the child, the court shall consider all the evidence and information available. The court may direct a report under Section 7 of the Children Act 1989, to be provided either orally or in writing, before it makes its decision; in such a case, the court may ask for information about any advice given by the officer preparing the report to the parties and whether they, or the child, have been referred to any other agency, including local authority children's services. If the report is not in writing, the court shall make a note of its substance on the court file.

Before the FHDRA

9. Where any information provided to the court before the FHDRA or other first hearing (whether as a result of initial safeguarding enquiries by Cafcass or CAFCASS Cymru or on form C1A or otherwise) indicates that there are issues of domestic violence or abuse which may be relevant to the court's determination, the court must ensure that the issues are addressed at the hearing, and that the parties are not expected to engage in conciliation or other forms of dispute resolution which are not suitable.

10. If at any stage the court is advised by the applicant, by Cafcass or CAFCASS Cymru or otherwise that there is a need for special arrangements to secure the safety of any party or child attending any hearing, the court shall ensure that appropriate arrangements are made for the hearing and for all subsequent hearings in the case, unless it considers that these are no longer necessary.

First hearing/FHDRA

11. At the FHDRA, if the parties have not been provided with the safeguarding letter/report by Cafcass/CAFCASS Cymru, the court shall inform the parties of the content of any safeguarding letter or report or other information which has been provided by Cafcass or CAFCASS Cymru, unless it considers that to do so would create a risk of harm to a party or the child.

12. Where the results of Cafcass or CAFCASS Cymru safeguarding checks are not available at the FHDRA, and no other reliable safeguarding information is available, the court shall adjourn the FHDRA until the results of safeguarding checks are available. The court shall not generally make an interim child arrangements order, or orders for contact, in the absence of safeguarding information, unless it is to protect the safety of the child.

13. There is a continuing duty on the Cafcass Officer/Welsh FPO which requires them to provide a risk assessment for the court under section 16A Children Act 1989 if they are given cause to suspect that the child concerned is at risk of harm. Specific provision about service of a risk assessment under section 16A of the 1989 Act is made by rule 12.34 of the FPR 2010.

14. The court must ascertain at the earliest opportunity whether domestic violence or abuse is raised as an issue of risk of harm to the child which is likely to be relevant to any decision of the court relating to the welfare of the child, and specifically on the making of any child arrangements order.

Admissions

15. Where at any hearing an admission of domestic violence or abuse toward another person or the child is made by a party, the admission should be recorded in writing and retained on the court file. A copy of any record of admissions must be made available as soon as possible to any Cafcass officer or officer of CAFCASS Cymru or local authority officer preparing a report under section 7 of the Children Act 1989.

Directions for a fact-finding hearing

16. The court should determine as soon as possible whether it is necessary to conduct a fact-finding hearing in relation to any disputed allegation of domestic violence or abuse:

    (a)   in order to provide a factual basis for any welfare report or for assessment of the factors set out in paragraphs 36 and 37 (below);

    (b)   in order to provide a basis for an accurate assessment of risk; or

    (c)   before it can consider any final welfare-based order(s) in relation to child arrangements, or

    (d)   before it considers the need for a domestic violence-related Activity (such as a Domestic Violence Perpetrator Programme (DVPP)).

17. In determining whether it is necessary to conduct a fact-finding hearing, the court should consider:

(a)   the views of the parties and of Cafcass or CAFCASS Cymru;

(b)   whether there are admissions by a party which provide a sufficient factual basis on which to proceed;

(c)   if a party is in receipt of legal aid, whether the evidence required to be provided to obtain legal aid provides a sufficient factual basis on which to proceed;

(d)   whether there is other evidence available to the court that provides a sufficient factual basis on which to proceed;

(e)   whether the factors set out in paragraphs 36 and 37 below can be determined without a fact-finding hearing;

(f)   the nature of the evidence required to resolve disputed allegations;

(g)   whether the nature and extent of the allegations, if proved, would be relevant to the issue before the court;

(h)   whether a separate fact-finding hearing would be necessary and proportionate in all the circumstances of the case.

18. Where the court determines that a finding of fact hearing is not necessary, the order shall record the reasons for that decision.

19. Where the court considers that a fact-finding hearing is necessary, it must give directions as to how the proceedings are to be conducted to ensure that the matters in issue are determined as soon as possible, fairly and proportionately, and within the capabilities of the parties. In particular it should consider:

(a)   what are the key facts in dispute;

(b)   whether it is necessary for the fact-finding to take place at a separate (and earlier) hearing than the welfare hearing;

(c)   whether the key facts in dispute can be contained in a schedule or a table (known as a Scott Schedule) which sets out what the applicant complains of or alleges, what the respondent says in relation to each individual allegation or complaint; the allegations in the schedule should be focused on the factual issues to be tried; and if so, whether it is practicable for this schedule to be completed at the first hearing, with the assistance of the judge;

(d)   what evidence is required in order to determine the existence of a pattern of coercive, controlling or threatening behaviour, violence or abuse;

(e)   directing the parties to file written statements giving details of such behaviour and of any response;

(f)   whether documents are required from third parties such as the police or health services and giving directions for those documents to be obtained;

(g)   whether oral evidence may be required from third parties and if so, giving directions for the filing of written statements from such third parties;

(h)   whether any other evidence is required to enable the court to decide the key issues and giving directions for that evidence to be provided;

(i)   what evidence the alleged victim of violence is able to give and what support the alleged victim may require at the fact-finding hearing in order to give that evidence;

(j)   what support the alleged perpetrator may need in order to have a reasonable opportunity to challenge the evidence;

(k)   whether a pre-hearing review would be useful prior to the fact-finding hearing to ensure directions have been complied with and all the required evidence is available.

20. Where the court fixes a fact-finding hearing, it must at the same time fix a Dispute Resolution Appointment to follow. Subject to the exception in paragraph 31 below, the hearings should be arranged in such a way that they are conducted by the same judge or,

wherever possible, by the same panel of lay justices; where it is not possible to assemble the same panel of justices, the resumed hearing should be listed before at least the same chairperson of the lay justices. Judicial continuity is important.

Reports under Section 7

21. In any case where a risk of harm to a child resulting from domestic violence or abuse is raised as an issue, the court should consider directing that a report on the question of contact, or any other matters relating to the welfare of the child, be prepared under section 7 of the Children Act 1989 by an Officer of Cafcass or a Welsh family proceedings officer (or local authority officer if appropriate), unless the court is satisfied that it is not necessary to do so in order to safeguard the child's interests.

22. If the court directs that there shall be a fact-finding hearing on the issue of domestic violence or abuse, the court will not usually request a section 7 report until after that hearing. In that event, the court should direct that any judgment is provided to Cafcass/CAFCASS Cymru; if there is no transcribed judgment, an agreed list of findings should be provided.

23. Any request for a section 7 report should set out clearly the matters the court considers need to be addressed.

Representation of the child

24. Subject to the seriousness of the allegations made and the difficulty of the case, the court shall consider whether it is appropriate for the child who is the subject of the application to be made a party to the proceedings and be separately represented. If the court considers that the child should be so represented, it shall review the allocation decision so that it is satisfied that the case proceeds before the correct level of judge in the Family Court.

Interim orders before determination of relevant facts

25. Where the court gives directions for a fact-finding hearing, the court should consider whether an interim child arrangements order is in the interests of the child; and in particular whether the safety of the child and (bearing in mind the impact which domestic violence against a parent can have on the emotional well-being of the child) the parent who has made the allegation and is at any time caring for the child can be secured before, during and after any contact.

26. In deciding any interim child arrangements question pending a full hearing the court should:

    (a)   take into account the matters set out in section 1(3) of the Children Act 1989 or section 1(4) of the Adoption and Children Act 2002 ('the welfare check-list'), as appropriate;

    (b)   give particular consideration to the likely effect on the child, and on the care given to the child by the parent who has made the allegation of domestic violence, of any contact and any risk of harm, whether physical, emotional or psychological, which the child and that parent is likely to suffer as a consequence of making or declining to make an order.

27. Where the court is considering whether to make an order for interim contact, it should in addition consider:

(a)   the arrangements required to ensure, as far as possible, that any risk of harm to
       the child and the parent who is at any time caring for the child is minimised
       and that the safety of the child and the parties is secured; and in particular:
       i.   whether the contact should be supervised or supported, and if so, where
             and by whom; and
       ii.   the availability of appropriate facilities for that purpose;
(b)   if direct contact is not appropriate, whether it is in the best interests of the child
       to make an order for indirect contact; and
(c)   whether contact will be beneficial for the child.

The fact-finding hearing

28. While ensuring that the allegations are properly put and responded to, the
fact-finding hearing can be an inquisitorial (or investigative) process, which at all times
must protect the interests of all involved. At the fact-finding hearing:

- Each party can be asked to identify what questions they wish to ask of the
  other party, and to set out or confirm in sworn evidence their version of the
  disputed key facts.
- The judge or lay justices should be prepared where necessary and appropriate
  to conduct the questioning of the witnesses on behalf of the parties, focusing
  on the key issues in the case.

Victims of violence are likely to find direct cross-examination by their alleged abuser
frightening and intimidating, and thus it may be particularly appropriate for the judge or
lay justices to conduct the questioning on behalf of the other party in these
circumstances, in order to ensure both parties are able to give their best evidence.

29. The court should, wherever practicable, make findings of fact as to the nature and
degree of any domestic violence or abuse which is established and its effect on the child,
the child's parents and any other relevant person. The court shall record its findings in
writing, and shall serve a copy on the parties. A copy of any record of findings of fact or
of admissions must be sent to any officer preparing a report under section 7 of the 1989
Act.

30. At the conclusion of any fact-finding hearing, the court shall consider,
notwithstanding any earlier direction for a section 7 report, whether it is in the best
interests of the child for the court to give further directions about the preparation or
scope of any report under section 7; where necessary, it may adjourn the proceedings for
a brief period to enable the officer to make representations about the preparation or
scope of any further enquiries. The court should also consider whether it would be
assisted by any social work, psychiatric, psychological or other assessment of any party
or the child (such as an expert risk assessment), and if so (subject to any necessary
consent) make directions for such assessment to be undertaken and for the filing of any
consequent report. Any section 7 or other report should address the factors set out in
paragraphs 36 and 37, unless the court directs otherwise.

31. Where the court has made findings of fact on disputed allegations, any subsequent
hearing in the proceedings should be conducted by the same judge or by at least the
same chairperson of the justices. Exceptions may be made only where observing this
requirement would result in delay to the planned timetable and the judge or chairperson
is satisfied, for reasons recorded in writing, that the detriment to the welfare of the child
would outweigh the detriment to the fair trial of the proceedings. In all cases where
domestic violence or abuse has occurred.

32. The court should take steps to obtain (or direct the parties or an Officer of Cafcass or a Welsh family proceedings officer to obtain) information about the facilities available locally to assist any party or the child in cases where domestic violence or abuse has occurred.

33. Following any determination of the nature and extent of domestic violence or abuse, whether or not following a fact-finding hearing, the court should consider whether any party should seek advice, treatment or other intervention as a precondition to any child arrangements order being made or as a means of assisting the court in ascertaining the likely risk of harm to the child and to the parent with whom the child is living from that person, and may (with the consent of that party) give directions for such attendance and the filing of any consequent report.

34. Further or as an alternative to the advice, treatment or other intervention referred to in paragraph 33 above, the court may make an Activity Direction under section 11A and 11B Children Act 1989. Any intervention directed pursuant to this provision should be one commissioned and approved by Cafcass. It is acknowledged that acceptance on a DVPP is subject to a suitability assessment by the service provider, and that completion of a DVPP will take time in order to achieve the aim of risk reduction for the long-term benefit of the child and the parent with whom the child is living.

Factors to be taken into account when determining whether to make child arrangements orders in all cases where domestic violence or abuse has occurred.

35. When deciding the issue of child arrangements the court should ensure that any order for contact will be safe and in the best interests of the child.

36. In the light of any findings of fact the court should apply the individual matters in the welfare checklist with reference to those findings; in particular, where relevant findings of domestic violence or abuse have been made, the court should in every case consider any harm which the child and the parent with whom the child is living has suffered as a consequence of that violence or abuse, and any harm which the child and the parent with whom the child is living, is at risk of suffering if a child arrangements order is made. The court should only make an order for contact if it can be satisfied that the physical and emotional safety of the child and the parent with whom the child is living can, as far as possible, be secured before during and after contact, and that the parent with whom the child is living will not be subjected to further controlling or coercive behaviour by the other parent.

37. In every case where a finding of domestic violence or abuse is made, the court should consider the conduct of both parents towards each other and towards the child; in particular, the court should consider:

(a) the effect of the domestic violence or abuse on the child and on the arrangements for where the child is living;

(b) the effect of the domestic violence or abuse on the child and its effect on the child's relationship with the parents;

(c) whether the applicant parent is motivated by a desire to promote the best interests of the child or is using the process to continue a process of violence, abuse, intimidation or harassment or controlling or coercive behaviour against the other parent;

(d) the likely behaviour during contact of the parent against whom findings are made and its effect on the child;

(e) the capacity of the parents to appreciate the effect of past violence or abuse and the potential for future violence or abuse.

Directions as to how contact is to proceed

38. Where the court has made findings of domestic violence or abuse but, having applied the welfare checklist, nonetheless considers that direct contact is safe and beneficial for the child, the court should consider what, if any, directions or conditions are required to enable the order to be carried into effect and in particular should consider:

(a) whether or not contact should be supervised, and if so, where and by whom;

(b) whether to impose any conditions to be complied with by the party in whose favour the order for contact has been made and if so, the nature of those conditions, for example by way of seeking intervention (subject to any necessary consent);

(c) whether such contact should be for a specified period or should contain provisions which are to have effect for a specified period;

(d) whether it will be necessary, in the child's best interests, to review the operation of the order; if so the court should set a date for the review consistent with the timetable for the child, and shall give directions to ensure that at the review the court has full information about the operation of the order.

39. Where the court does not consider direct contact to be appropriate, it shall consider whether it is safe and beneficial for the child to make an order for indirect contact.

The reasons of the court

40. In its judgment or reasons the court should always make clear how its findings on the issue of domestic violence or abuse have influenced its decision on the issue of arrangements for the child. In particular, where the court has found domestic violence or abuse proved but nonetheless makes an order which results in the child having future contact with the perpetrator of domestic violence or abuse, the court should always explain, whether by way of reference to the welfare checklist the factors in paragraphs 36 and 37 or otherwise, why it takes the view that the order which it has made is safe and beneficial for the child.

This Practice Direction is issued by the President of the Family Division, as the nominee of the Lord Chief Justice, with the agreement of the Lord Chancellor.

FAMILY PROCEDURE RULES 2010, PART 25

PART 25
EXPERTS AND ASSESSORS

Amendments—FPR 2010, Pt 25 substituted by SI 2012/3061.

25.1 *(revoked)*

25.2 Interpretation

(1) In this Part –

...

"children proceedings" means –

    (a)   proceedings referred to in rules 12.1 and 14.1 and any other proceedings which relate wholly or mainly to the maintenance or upbringing of a minor;

    (b)   applications for permission to start proceedings mentioned in paragraph (a); and

    (c)   applications made in the course of proceedings mentioned in paragraph (a);

"expert" means a person who provides expert evidence for use in proceedings;

(Section 13(8) of the 2014 Act provides for what is not included in reference to providing expert evidence or putting expert evidence before the court in children proceedings)

...

"single joint expert" means a person who provides expert evidence for use in proceedings on behalf of two or more of the parties (including the applicant) to the proceedings.

(2) The meaning of "children proceedings" in paragraph (1) is the prescribed meaning for the purposes of section 13(9) of the 2014 Act.

(Regulation 3 of the Restriction on the Preparation of Adoption Reports Regulations 2005 (SI 2005/1711) sets out which persons are within a prescribed description for the purposes of section 94(1) of the 2002 Act.)

Amendments—SI 2014/843.

25.3 Experts – overriding duty to the court

(1) It is the duty of experts to help the court on matters within their expertise.

(2) This duty overrides any obligation to the person from whom experts have received instructions or by whom they are paid.

(Particular duties of an expert are set out in Practice Direction 25B (The Duties of an Expert, the Expert's Report and Arrangements for an Expert to Attend Court.)

25.4 Control of expert evidence in proceedings other than children proceedings

(1) This rule applies to proceedings other than children proceedings.

(2) A person may not without the permission of the court put expert evidence (in any form) before the court.

(3) The court may give permission as mentioned in paragraph (2) only if the court is of the opinion that the expert evidence is necessary to assist the court to resolve the proceedings.

> (Provision relating to the control of expert evidence in children proceedings is contained in section 13 of the 2014 Act.)

Amendments—Substituted by SI 2014/843.

25.5 Further provisions about the court's power to restrict expert evidence

(1) When deciding whether to give permission as mentioned in section 13(1), (3) or (5) of the 2014 Act or to give a direction under 38(6) of the 1989 Act in children proceedings, the court is to have regard in particular to any failure to comply with rule 25.6 or any direction of the court about expert evidence.

(1A) The matter referred to in paragraph (1) is a prescribed matter for the purposes of section 13(7)(h) of the 2014 Act and section 38(7B) of the 1989 Act.

(2) When deciding whether to give permission as mentioned in rule 25.4(1) in proceedings other than children proceedings, the court is to have regard in particular to –

(a) the issues to which the expert evidence would relate;
(b) the questions which the court would require the expert to answer;
(c) the impact which giving permission would be likely to have on the timetable, duration and conduct of the proceedings;
(d) any failure to comply with rule 25.6 or any direction of the court about expert evidence; and
(e) the cost of the expert evidence.

Amendments—SI 2014/843.

25.6 When to apply for the court's permission

Unless the court directs otherwise, parties must apply for the court's permission as mentioned in section 13(1), (3) or (5) of the 2014 Act or rule 25.4(2) as soon as possible and –

(a) in Part 4 proceedings referred to in rule 12.2 and in so far as practicable other public law proceedings referred to in that rule, no later than a Case Management Hearing;
(b) in private law proceedings referred to in rule 12.2, no later than the First Hearing Dispute Resolution Appointment;
(c) in adoption proceedings and placement proceedings, no later than the first directions hearing;
(d) in proceedings for a financial remedy, no later than the first appointment; and
(e) in a defended case referred to in rule 7.1(3), no later than any Case Management Hearing directed by the court under rule 7.20.

Amendments—Substituted by SI 2014/843.

25.7 What an application notice requesting the court's permission must include

(1) Part 18 applies to an application for the court's permission as mentioned in section 13(1), (3) or (5) of the 2014 Act or rule 25.4(2).

(2) In any proceedings –

(a) the application notice requesting the court's permission as mentioned in section 13(1), (3) or (5) of the 2014 Act or rule 25.4(2) must state –
  (i) the field in which the expert evidence is required;
  (ii) where practicable, the name of the proposed expert;
  (iii) the issues to which the expert evidence is to relate;
  (iv) whether the expert evidence could be obtained from a single joint expert;
  (v) the other matters set out in Practice Direction 25C or 25D, as the case may be; and
(b) a draft of the order sought is to be attached to the application notice requesting the court's permission and that draft order must set out the matters specified in Practice Direction 25C or 25D, as the case may be.

(3) In children proceedings, an application notice requesting the court's permission as mentioned in section 13(1), (3) or (5) of the 2014 Act must, in addition to the matters specified in paragraph (2)(a), state the questions which the expert is to be required to answer.

Amendments—SI 2014/843.

25.8 Where permission is granted

(1) In any proceedings, where the court grants permission as mentioned in section 13(1), (3) or (5) of the 2014 Act or rule 25.4(2) –

(a) it will grant permission only in relation to the expert named or the field identified in the application notice requesting the court's permission; and
(b) the court will give directions specifying the date by which the expert is to provide a written report.

(2) In children proceedings, in addition to the directions in paragraph (1)(b), the court will give directions –

(a) approving the questions which the expert is required to answer;
(b) specifying the date by which the expert is to receive the letter of instruction.

Amendments—SI 2014/843.

25.9 General requirement for expert evidence to be given in a written report

(1) Expert evidence is to be given in a written report unless the court directs otherwise.

(2) The court will not direct an expert to attend a hearing unless it is necessary to do so in the interests of justice.

25.10 Written questions to experts

(1) A party may put written questions about an expert's report to –

(a) an expert instructed by another party; or
(b) a single joint expert appointed under rule 25.11.

(2) Unless the court directs otherwise or a practice direction provides otherwise, written questions under paragraph (1) –

(a)   must be proportionate;

(b)   may be put once only;

(c)   must be put within 10 days beginning with the date on which the expert's report was served;

(d)   must be for the purpose only of clarification of the report; and

(e)   must be copied and sent to the other parties at the same time as they are sent to the expert.

(3) An expert's answers to questions put in accordance with paragraph (1) –

(a)   must be given within the timetable specified by the court; and

(b)   are treated as part of the expert's report.

(4) Where –

(a)   a party has put a written question to an expert instructed by another party; and

(b)   the expert does not answer that question,

the court may make one or both of the following orders in relation to the party who instructed the expert –

(i)   that the party may not rely on the evidence of that expert; or

(ii)   that the party may not recover the fees and expenses of that expert from any other party.

25.11 Court's power to direct that evidence is to be given by a single joint expert

(1) Where two or more parties wish to put expert evidence before the court on a particular issue, the court may direct that the evidence on that issue is to be given by a single joint expert.

(2) Where the parties who wish to put expert evidence before the court ("the relevant parties") cannot agree who should be the single joint expert, the court may –

(a)   select the expert from a list prepared or identified by the relevant parties; or

(b)   direct that the expert be selected in such other manner as the court may direct.

25.12 Instructions to a single joint expert

(1) Where the court gives a direction under rule 25.11(1) for a single joint expert to be used, the instructions are to be contained in a jointly agreed letter unless the court directs otherwise.

(2) Where the instructions are to be contained in a jointly agreed letter, in default of agreement the instructions may be determined by the court on the written request of any relevant party copied to the other relevant parties.

(3) Where the court permits the relevant parties to give separate instructions to a single joint expert, each instructing party must, when giving instructions to the expert, at the same time send a copy of the instructions to the other relevant parties.

(4) The court may give directions about –

(a)   the payment of the expert's fees and expenses; and

(b)   any inspection, examination or assessments which the expert wishes to carry out.

(5) The court may, before an expert is instructed, limit the amount that can be paid by way of fees and expenses to the expert.

(6) Unless the court directs otherwise, the relevant parties are jointly and severally liable for the payment of the expert's fees and expenses.

25.13 Power of court to direct a party to provide information

(1) Subject to paragraph (2), where a party has access to information which is not reasonably available to another party, the court may direct the party who has access to the information to –

(a)   prepare and file a document recording the information; and
(b)   serve a copy of that document on the other party.

(2) In proceedings under Part 14 (procedure for applications in adoption, placement and related proceedings), a court officer will send a copy of the document recording the information to the other party.

25.14 Contents of report

(1) An expert's report must comply with the requirements set out in Practice Direction 25B.

(2) At the end of an expert's report there must be a statement that the expert understands and has complied with the expert's duty to the court.

(3) The instructions to the expert are not privileged against disclosure.

(Rule 21.1 explains what is meant by disclosure.)

25.15 Use by one party of expert's report disclosed by another

Where a party has disclosed an expert's report, any party may use that expert's report as evidence at any hearing where an issue to which the report relates is being considered.

25.16 Discussions between experts

(1) The court may, at any stage, direct a discussion between experts for the purpose of requiring the experts to –

(a)   identify and discuss the expert issues in the proceedings; and
(b)   where possible, reach an agreed opinion on those issues.

(2) The court may specify the issues which the experts must discuss.

(3) The court may direct that following a discussion between the experts they must prepare a statement for the court setting out those issues on which –

(a)   they agree; and
(b)   they disagree, with a summary of their reasons for disagreeing.

25.17 Expert's right to ask court for directions

(1) Experts may file written requests for directions for the purpose of assisting them in carrying out their functions.

(2) Experts must, unless the court directs otherwise, provide copies of the proposed requests for directions under paragraph (1) –

(a)   to the party instructing them, at least 7 days before they file the requests; and

(b)   to all other parties, at least 4 days before they file them.

(3) The court, when it gives directions, may also direct that a party be served with a copy of the directions.

25.18 Copies of orders and other documents

Unless the court directs otherwise, a copy of any order or other document affecting an expert filed with the court after the expert has been instructed, must be served on the expert by the party who instructed the expert or, in the case of a single joint expert, the party who was responsible for instructing the expert, within 2 days of that party receiving the order or other document.

25.19 Action after final hearing

(1) Within 10 business days after the final hearing, the party who instructed the expert or, in the case of a single joint expert, the party who was responsible for instructing the expert, must inform the expert in writing about the court's determination and the use made by the court of the expert's evidence.

(2) Unless the court directs otherwise, the party who instructed the expert or, in the case of the single joint expert, the party who was responsible for instructing the expert, must send to the expert a copy of the court's final order, any transcript or written record of the court's decision, and its reasons for reaching its decision, within 10 business days from the date when the party received the order and any such transcript or record.

Amendments—SI 2014/843.

25.20 Assessors

(1) This rule applies where the court appoints one or more persons under section 70 of the Senior Courts Act 1981 as an assessor.

(2) An assessor will assist the court in dealing with a matter in which the assessor has skill and experience.

(3) The assessor will take such part in the proceedings as the court may direct and in particular the court may direct an assessor to –

(a) prepare a report for the court on any matter at issue in the proceedings; and

(b) attend the whole or any part of the hearing to advise the court on any such matter.

(4) If the assessor prepares a report for the court before the hearing has begun –

(a)   the court will send a copy to each of the parties; and

(b)   the parties may use it at the hearing.

(5) Unless the court directs otherwise, an assessor will be paid at the daily rate payable for the time being to a fee-paid deputy district judge of the principal registry and an assessor's fees will form part of the costs of the proceedings.

(6) The court may order any party to deposit in the court office a specified sum in respect of an assessor's fees and, where it does so, the assessor will not be asked to act until the sum has been deposited.

(7) Paragraphs (5) and (6) do not apply where the remuneration of the assessor is to be paid out of money provided by Parliament.

Amendments—SI 2014/667.

APPENDIX 6

PRACTICE DIRECTION 25C – CHILDREN PROCEEDINGS – THE USE OF SINGLE JOINT EXPERTS AND THE PROCESS LEADING TO AN EXPERT BEING INSTRUCTED OR EXPERT EVIDENCE BEING PUT BEFORE THE COURT

This Practice Direction supplements FPR Part 25

Amendments—FPR Update 6.

Scope of this Practice Direction

1.1 This Practice Direction applies to children proceedings and contains guidance on –

(a) the use of single joint experts;

(b) how to prepare for the hearing at which the court will consider whether to give permission for an expert to be instructed, a child to be medically or psychiatrically examined or otherwise assessed for the purposes of provision of expert evidence in the proceedings or for putting expert evidence (in any form) before the court including –

   (i) preliminary enquiries of experts;

   (ii) the content of an application for the court's permission in addition to matters mentioned in FPR 25.7;

   (iii) matters to be set out in the draft order to be attached to the application for permission; and

(c) the letter of instruction to the expert.

1.2 "Children proceedings" includes proceedings under Schedule 1 to the 1989 Act as those proceedings are proceedings which relate wholly or mainly to the maintenance or upbringing of a minor referred to in FPR 25.2(1).

Single joint experts

2.1 Section 13(1), (3) and (5) of the 2014 Act applies to a single joint expert ("SJE") in addition to an expert instructed by one party. This means that the court's permission is required to put expert evidence from an SJE (in any form) before the court (section 13(5) of the 2014 Act). The court's permission is also required to instruct an SJE and for a child to be medically or psychiatrically examined or otherwise assessed for the purposes of provision of evidence from an SJE (section 13(1) and (3) of the 2014 Act). Wherever possible, expert evidence should be obtained from an SJE instructed by both or all the parties. To that end, a party wishing to instruct an expert should as soon as possible after the start of the proceedings first give the other party or parties a list of the names of one or more experts in the relevant speciality whom they consider suitable to be instructed.

2.2 **Within 5 business days after receipt of the list of proposed experts,** the other party or parties should indicate any objection to one or more of the named experts and, if so, supply the name(s) of one or more experts whom they consider suitable.

2.3 Each party should disclose whether they have already consulted any of the proposed experts about the issue(s) in question.

2.4 Where the parties cannot agree on the identity of the expert, each party should think carefully before seeking the permission of the court to instruct their own expert because of the costs implications. Disagreements about the use and identity of an expert may be better managed by the court in the context of the application for the court's permission to instruct the expert and for directions for the use of an SJE (see paragraph 2.6 below).

Instructing separate experts

2.5 If the parties seek the permission of the court to instruct separate experts –

(a) they should agree in advance that the reports will be disclosed; and
(b) the instructions to each expert should comply, so far as appropriate, with paragraphs 4.1 and 6.1 below (Letter of instruction).

Where two or more parties wish to instruct an SJE

2.6 If two or more parties wish to instruct an SJE, before applying to the court for permission and directions for the use of an SJE, the parties should –

(a) so far as appropriate, comply with the guidance in paragraphs 3.2 (Preliminary enquiries of the expert) and paragraphs 3.10 and 3.11 below;
(b) receive the expert's confirmation in response to preliminary enquiries referred to in paragraph 8.1 of Practice Direction 25B;
(c) have agreed in what proportion the SJE's fee is to be shared between them (at least in the first instance) and when it is to be paid; and
(d) if applicable, have obtained agreement for public funding.

2.7 The instructions to the SJE should comply, so far as appropriate, with paragraphs 4.1 and 6.1 below (Letter of instruction).

Amendments—FPR Update 12.

Preparation for the permission hearing

3.1 Paragraphs 3.2 to 3.11 give guidance on how to prepare for the hearing at which the court will consider whether to give permission for an expert to be instructed, a child to be examined or otherwise assessed or expert evidence to be put before the court. The purpose of the preparation is to ensure that the court has the information required to enable it to exercise its powers under section 13(1), (3), (5) and (7) of the 2014 Act and FPR 25.5.

Preliminary enquiries of the expert

3.2 In good time for the information requested to be available for the hearing at which the court will consider whether to give permission for an expert to be instructed, a child to be examined or otherwise assessed or expert evidence to be put before the court or for the advocates' meeting or discussion where one takes place before that hearing, the party or parties intending to instruct the expert shall approach the expert with the following information –

(a)   the nature of the proceedings and the issues likely to require determination by the court;

(b)   the issues in the proceedings to which the expert evidence is to relate;

(c)   the questions about which the expert is to be asked to give an opinion (including any ethnic, cultural, religious or linguistic contexts) and which relate to the issues in the case;

(d)   the date when the court is to be asked to give permission for the instruction (or if – unusually – permission has already been given, the date and details of that permission);

(e)   whether permission is to be asked of the court for the instruction of another expert in the same or any related field (that is, to give an opinion on the same or related questions);

(f)   the volume of reading which the expert will need to undertake;

(g)   whether or not permission has been applied for or given for the expert to examine the child;

(h)   whether or not it will be necessary for the expert to conduct interviews – and, if so, with whom;

(i)   the likely timetable of legal and social work steps;

(j)   in care and supervision proceedings, any dates in the Timetable for the Child which would be relevant to the proposed timetable for the assessment;

(k)   when the expert's report is likely to be required;

(l)   whether and, if so, what date has been fixed by the court for any hearing at which the expert may be required to give evidence (in particular the Final Hearing); and whether it may be possible for the expert to give evidence by telephone conference or video link: see paragraphs 10.1 and 10.2 (Arrangements for experts to give evidence) of Practice Direction 25B;

(m)   the possibility of making, through their instructing solicitors, representations to the court about being named or otherwise identified in any public judgment given by the court;

(n)   whether the instructing party has public funding and the legal aid rates of payment which are applicable.

Confidentiality of children proceedings and making preliminary enquiries of an expert

3.3 For the purposes of the law of contempt of court, information relating to children proceedings (whether or not contained in a document filed with the court or recorded in any form) may be communicated only to an expert whose instruction by a party has been permitted by the court (see FPR 12.73(1)(a)(vii) and 14.14(c)(vii)) as children proceedings are confidential.

3.4 Before permission is obtained from the court to instruct an expert in children proceedings, the party seeking permission needs to make the enquiries of the expert referred to above in order to provide the court with information to enable it to decide whether to give permission. In practice, enquiries may need to be made of more than one expert for this purpose. This will in turn require each expert to be given sufficient information about the case to decide whether or not he or she is in a position to accept instructions. Such preliminary enquiries, and the disclosure of information about the case which is a necessary part of such enquiries, will not require the court's permission and will not amount to a contempt of court.

Expert's response to preliminary enquiries

3.5 In good time for the hearing at which the court will consider whether to give permission for an expert to be instructed, a child to be examined or otherwise assessed or expert evidence to be put before the court, **the party or parties** intending to instruct the expert must obtain the confirmations from the expert referred to in paragraph 8.1 of Practice Direction 25B. These confirmations include that the work is within the expert's expertise, the expert is available to do the work within the relevant timescale and the expert's costs.

3.6 Where the parties **cannot agree who should be the single joint expert** before the hearing at which the court will consider whether to give permission for an expert to be instructed, a child to be examined or otherwise assessed or expert evidence to be put before the court, they should obtain the above confirmations in respect of all experts whom they intend to put to the court for the purposes of FPR 25.11(2)(a) as candidates for the appointment.

The application for the court's permission mentioned in section 13(1), (3) and (5) of the 2014 Act

Timing and oral applications for the court's permission mentioned in FPR 25.4

3.7 An application for the court's permission for an expert to be instructed, a child to be examined or otherwise assessed or expert evidence to be put before the court should be made as soon as it becomes apparent that it is necessary to make it. FPR 25.6 makes provision about the time by which applications for the court's permission should be made.

3.8 Applications should, wherever possible, be made so that they are considered at any directions hearing or other hearing for which a date has been fixed or for which a date is about to be fixed. It should be noted that one application notice can be used by a party to make more than one application for an order or direction at a hearing held during the course of proceedings. An application for the court's permission for an expert to be instructed, a child to be examined or otherwise assessed or expert evidence to be put before the court may therefore be included in an application notice requesting other orders to be made at such a hearing.

3.9 Where a date for a hearing has been fixed, a party who wishes to make an application at that hearing but does not have sufficient time to file an application notice should as soon as possible inform the court (if possible in writing) and, if possible, the other parties of the nature of the application and the reason for it. The party should provide the court and the other party with as much as possible of the information referred to in FPR 25.7 and paragraph 3.10 below. That party should then make the application orally at the hearing. An oral application of this kind should be the exception and reserved for genuine cases where circumstances are such that it has only become apparent shortly before the hearing that an expert opinion is necessary.

The application

3.10 In addition to the matters specified in FPR 25.7(2)(a) and (3), an application for the court's permission for an expert to be instructed, a child to be examined or otherwise assessed or expert evidence to be put before the court, must state –

    (a)   the discipline, qualifications and expertise of the expert (by way of C.V. where possible);

    (b)   the expert's availability to undertake the work;

(c)   the timetable for the report;

(d)   the responsibility for instruction;

(e)   whether the expert evidence can properly be obtained by only one party (for example, on behalf of the child);

(f)   why the expert evidence proposed cannot properly be given by an officer of the service, Welsh family proceedings officer or the local authority (social services undertaking a core assessment) in accordance with their respective statutory duties or any other party to the proceedings or an expert already instructed in the proceedings;

(g)   the likely cost of the report on an hourly or other charging basis;

(h)   the proposed apportionment (at least in the first instance) of any jointly instructed expert's fee; when it is to be paid; and, if applicable, whether public funding has been approved.

The terms of the draft order to be attached to the application for the court's permission

3.11 FPR 25.7(2)(b) provides that a draft of the order giving the court's permission as mentioned in section 13(1), (3) and (5) of the 2014 Act is to be attached to the application for the court's permission. That draft order must set out the following matters –

(a)   the issues in the proceedings to which the expert evidence is to relate and which the court is to identify;

(b)   the questions relating to the issues in the case which the expert is to answer and which the court is to approve ensuring that they
   (i)   are within the ambit of the expert's area of expertise;
   (ii)   do not contain unnecessary or irrelevant detail;
   (iii) are kept to a manageable number and are clear, focused and direct;

(c)   the party who is responsible for drafting the letter of instruction and providing the documents to the expert;

(d)   the timetable within which the report is to be prepared, filed and served;

(e)   the disclosure of the report to the parties and to any other expert;

(f)   the organisation of, preparation for and conduct of any experts' discussion (see Practice Direction 25E – Discussions between Experts in Family Proceedings);

(g)   the preparation of a statement of agreement and disagreement by the experts following an experts' discussion;

(h)   making available to the court at an early opportunity the expert reports in electronic form;

(i)   the attendance of the expert at court to give oral evidence (alternatively, the expert giving his or her evidence in writing or remotely by video link), whether at or for the Final Hearing or another hearing; unless agreement about the opinions given by the expert is reached at or before the Issues Resolution Hearing ("IRH") or, if no IRH is to be held, by a date specified by the court prior to the hearing at which the expert is to give oral evidence.

Amendments—FPR Update 12.

Letter of instruction

4.1 The party responsible for instructing the expert shall prepare (in agreement with the other parties where appropriate), a letter of instruction to the expert and shall –

(a)   set out the context in which the expert's opinion is sought (including any ethnic, cultural, religious or linguistic contexts);

(b)   set out the questions approved by the court and which the expert is required to answer and any other linked questions ensuring that they –
   (i)   are within the ambit of the expert's area of expertise;
   (ii)   do not contain unnecessary or irrelevant detail;
   (iii) are kept to a manageable number and are clear, focused and direct; and
   (iv)   reflect what the expert has been requested to do by the court;

(Annex A to this Practice Direction sets out suggested questions in letters of instruction to (1) child mental health professionals or paediatricians, and (2) adult psychiatrists and applied psychologists, in Children Act 1989 proceedings);

(c)   list the documentation provided, or provide for the expert an indexed and paginated bundle which shall include –
   (i)   an agreed list of essential reading; and
   (ii)   a copy of this Practice Direction and Practice Directions 25B and E and where appropriate Practice Direction 15B;

(d)   identify any materials provided to the expert which have not been produced either as original medical (or other professional) records or in response to an instruction from a party, and state the source of that material (such materials may contain an assumption as to the standard of proof, the admissibility or otherwise of hearsay evidence, and other important procedural and substantive questions relating to the different purposes of other enquiries, for example, criminal or disciplinary proceedings);

(e)   identify all requests to third parties for disclosure and their responses in order to avoid partial disclosure, which tends only to prove a case rather than give full and frank information;

(f)   identify the relevant people concerned with the proceedings (for example, the treating clinicians) and inform the expert of his or her right to talk to them provided that an accurate record is made of the discussions;

(g)   identify any other expert instructed in the proceedings and advise the expert of their right to talk to the other experts provided that an accurate record is made of the discussions;

(h)   subject to any public funding requirement for prior authority, define the contractual basis upon which the expert is retained and in particular the funding mechanism including how much the expert will be paid (an hourly rate and overall estimate should already have been obtained), when the expert will be paid, and what limitation there might be on the amount the expert can charge for the work which they will have to do. In cases where the parties are publicly funded, there may also be a brief explanation of the costs and expenses excluded from public funding by Funding Code criterion 1.3 and the detailed assessment process.

Adult who is a protected party

5.1 Where the adult is a protected party, that party's representative shall be involved in any instruction of an expert, including the instruction of an expert to assess whether the adult, although a protected party, is competent to give evidence (see Practice Direction 15B – *Adults Who May Be Protected Parties and Children Who May Become Protected Parties in Family Proceedings*).

Asking the court to settle the letter of instruction to a single joint expert

6.1 Where possible, the written request for the court to consider the letter of instruction referred to in rule 25.12(2) should be set out in an e-mail to the court and copied by e-mail to the other instructing parties. The request should be sent to the relevant court or (by prior arrangement only) directly to the judge dealing with the proceedings. Where a legal adviser has been appointed as the case manager, the request should also be sent to the appointed legal adviser. The court will settle the letter of instruction, usually without a hearing to avoid delay; and will send (where practicable, by e-mail) the settled letter to the lead solicitor for transmission forthwith to the expert, and copy it to the other instructing parties for information.

Amendments—FPR Update 9.

ANNEX A

(drafted by the Family Justice Council)

Suggested questions in letters of instruction to child mental health professional or paediatrician in Children Act 1989 proceedings

A. The Child(ren)

1. Please describe the child(ren)'s current health, development and functioning (according to your area of expertise), and identify the nature of any significant changes which have occurred

- Behavioural
- Emotional
- Attachment organisation
- Social/peer/sibling relationships
- Cognitive/educational
- Physical
    - Growth, eating, sleep
    - Non-organic physical problems (including wetting and soiling)
    - Injuries
    - Paediatric conditions

2. Please comment on the likely explanation for/aetiology of the child(ren)'s problems/difficulties/injuries

- History/experiences (including intrauterine influences, and abuse and neglect)
- Genetic/innate/developmental difficulties
- Paediatric/psychiatric disorders

3. Please provide a prognosis and risk if difficulties not addressed above.

4. Please describe the child(ren)'s needs in the light of the above

- Nature of care-giving
- Education
- Treatment

in the short and long term (subject, where appropriate, to further assessment later).

B. The parents/primary carers

5. Please describe the factors and mechanisms which would explain the parents' (or primary carers) harmful or neglectful interactions with the child(ren) (if relevant).

6. What interventions have been tried and what has been the result?

7. Please assess the ability of the parents or primary carers to fulfil the child(ren)'s identified needs now.

8. What other assessments of the parents or primary carers are indicated?

- Adult mental health assessment
- Forensic risk assessment
- Physical assessment
- Cognitive assessment

9. What, if anything, is needed to assist the parents or primary carers now, within the child(ren)'s time scales and what is the prognosis for change?

- Parenting work
- Support
- Treatment/therapy

C. Alternatives

10. Please consider the alternative possibilities for the fulfilment of the child(ren)'s needs

- What sort of placement
- Contact arrangements

Please consider the advantages, disadvantages and implications of each for the child(ren).

Suggested questions in letters of instruction to adult psychiatrists and applied psychologists in Children Act 1989 proceedings

1. Does the parent/adult have – whether in his/her history or presentation – a mental illness/disorder (including substance abuse) or other psychological/emotional difficulty and, if so, what is the diagnosis?

2. How do any/all of the above (and their current treatment if applicable) affect his/her functioning, including interpersonal relationships?

3. If the answer to Q1 is yes, are there any features of either the mental illness or psychological/emotional difficulty or personality disorder which could be associated with risk to others, based on the available evidence base (whether published studies or evidence from clinical experience)?

4. What are the experiences/antecedents/aetiology which would explain his/her difficulties, if any, (taking into account any available evidence base or other clinical experience)?

5. What treatment is indicated, what is its nature and the likely duration?

6. What is his/her capacity to engage in/partake of the treatment/therapy?

7. Are you able to indicate the prognosis for, time scales for achieving, and likely durability of, change?

8. What other factors might indicate positive change?

> (It is assumed that this opinion will be based on collateral information as well as interviewing the adult).

APPENDIX 7

PRESIDENT'S GUIDANCE ON ALLOCATION AND GATEKEEPING FOR PROCEEDINGS UNDER PART II OF THE CHILDREN ACT 1989 (PRIVATE LAW)

Issued in accordance with rule 21 of the Family Court (Composition and Distribution of Business) Rules 2014

Introduction

1. This Guidance is issued by the President of the Family Division and applies to all private law proceedings under Part II of the Children Act 1989 (hereinafter referred to as 'private law proceedings') from 22 April 2014. It is issued following consultation with, and where applicable with the agreement of, the Lord Chancellor, in accordance with rule 21 of the Family Court (Composition and Distribution of Business) Rules 2014, and is to be read with those Rules and PD 12B FPR (CAP 2014)).

2. The purpose of the Guidance is to ensure that all new private law proceedings are allocated to the appropriate level of judge and, where appropriate to a named case management judge (or case manager in those cases allocated to lay justices) who shall provide continuity for the proceedings in accordance with the President's Guidance on Judicial Continuity and Deployment (Private Law).

3. This Guidance applies to the allocation of all relevant proceedings to all judges of the Family Court (including lay justices sitting with assistant justices' clerks (referred to in this Guidance as legal advisers). During the implementation and consolidation of arrangements for the Family Court, this includes allocation to legal advisers conducting FHDRAs in court centres where:

(i)   there is agreement between the Designated Family Judge ('DFJ'), HMCTS Head of CFT, the justices' clerk and the relevant Panel Chair(s) that available judicial resources locally require that FHDRAs continue to be listed before the legal advisers; or

(ii)   in areas where the practice does not currently take place, where there is agreement between the DFJ, HMCTS Head of CFT, the justices' clerk and the relevant Panel Chair(s), and specific permission granted from the President of the Family Division and the HMCTS Director for Civil Family and Tribunals, that it be extended to facilitate the appropriate allocation of cases;

And in any event

(iii)   provided that such allocation does not restrict the court's ability to make substantive orders on the day of the hearing (i.e. by using parallel or back-to-back lists, so that lay justices or judges are available to consider the case and, where appropriate, make a substantive order).

Allocation and Resources

4. In some DFJ's areas, full implementation of this guidance may result in a significant shift of caseload between levels of the judiciary. Before implementation it will therefore be necessary for the DFJ in consultation with the local judiciary, the justices' clerk, and HMCTS to review the available resources, in terms of courtrooms, court staff and judiciary including lay justices and legal advisers. The extent and timescale of implementation of the guidance should take these factors into account alongside any shift in allocation of public law cases following the implementation of the President's Guidance on Allocation Gatekeeping for Care Supervision and other Proceedings under Part IV of the Children Act 1989 (Public Law). The overarching intention should be to avoid delay in all children's proceedings wherever possible.

Allocation and listing schedules

5. The DFJ in consultation with the judiciary, the justices' clerk and HMCTS should review the family listing schedules in place within the DFJ's area taking into account the plans for the implementation of the Family Court. Where feasible and practical, consideration should be given to arranging listing schedules so that First Hearing Dispute Resolution Appointments (FHDRAs) are taking place in parallel lists (i.e. on the same day and ideally in the same building) before District Judges and lay justices (sitting with a legal adviser), or where appropriate (in accordance with paragraph 3 above) before legal advisers sitting alone. This will allow for reallocation to be considered up to and including the date of the hearing of the case, so that an alternative judicial level to that selected by the Gatekeeper(s) (see paragraph 6 below) can be arranged if necessary (in particular, should receipt of the Cafcass Safeguarding checks or interview with the parties raise matters of particular significance which justify a revised allocation decision).

Gatekeeping teams

6. Each DFJ will lead a gatekeeping team responsible for private law gatekeeping in each of the Family Hearing Centres that are nominated by the President to be Designated Family Centres. The team will consist of the DFJ and the justices' clerk with as many legal advisers and District Judges as the DFJ considers necessary to carry out the gatekeeping role depending on local demand and conditions. The DFJ in consultation with the District Judges and the justices' clerk will determine whether gatekeeping decisions are to be made by the District Judges or legal advisers acting alone, or together. The District Judge and legal advisers when making gatekeeping and allocation decisions are referred to as 'the Gatekeeper(s)' in this guidance.

7. All applications for private law orders which are received by 4.00 pm will be issued by HMCTS and placed before the Gatekeeper(s) for their consideration on the next working day, except where they are (or have been) dealt with as an urgent application. The Gatekeeper(s) should consider the application on the basis of the information provided in the application, and shall determine the appropriate level of judiciary in accordance with this guidance, and the requirements of the Family Court (Composition and Distribution of Business) Rules 2014, based on consideration of the relative significance of:

    (a)   The need to make the most effective and efficient use of the local judicial resources that is appropriate, given the nature and type of application;

(b)   The need to avoid delay;

(c)   The need for judicial continuity;

(d)   The location of the parties or of any child relevant to the proceedings; and

(e)   Complexity.

8. The judiciary including lay justices and legal advisers have an ongoing duty to keep allocation decisions under review particularly:

(a)   when any response to the application is received;

(b)   the safeguarding checks are received; and

(c)   at the FHDRA when further information has been ascertained from the parties and Cafcass or CAFCASS Cymru at court.

9. When making an allocation decision the Gatekeepers will enquire into whether a MIAM exemption has been validly claimed, to the extent possible at this stage. If the MIAM exemption has not been validly claimed, the Gatekeepers shall give directions in accordance with rule 3.10(2)/(3) FPR 2010.

10. Prior to making an allocation decision the Gatekeeper(s) shall consider whether to allocate the application to a different location for hearing within the DFJ area, or to transfer the application to another DFJ area, where it appears that the parties, and/or the child(ren) who are the subject of the application, reside(s) in an area other than that covered by the DFJ.

11. Gatekeeper(s) are to be made available for a period of time on each weekday to allocate all private law proceedings which have been issued. Gatekeeper(s) will consider the file in each new application which has been issued on the preceding day and any urgent applications which are outstanding, and determine to which level of judge the proceedings should be allocated, i.e. to lay justices, a judge at District Judge level, a judge at Circuit Judge level or judge at High Court level sitting in the Family Court:

(a)   Based on consideration of the relative significance of the matters set out in paragraph 7 (a)-(e) (above), and

(b)   When considering complexity, by reference to the schedule to this guidance.

The Gatekeeper(s) will record their allocation decision and reasons on the case papers and make any appropriate arrangements for transfer (between courts) as necessary. In addition, where it appears that a case needs an urgent listing, the Gatekeeper(s) will ensure that the case is listed as a matter of urgency, and will give directions to abridge time for service if necessary.

12. The DFJ shall make arrangements to ensure the swift allocation of all cases within the Family Court to a named case manager so that it can be listed (in accordance with this Guidance and the Family Court (Composition and Distribution of Business) Rules 2014) in week 5 or 6 after issue, for an FHDRA, or sooner if an FHDRA is not appropriate.

13. If any Gatekeeper requires further guidance on a particular case, they should refer the allocation decision to the DFJ or his nominated deputy.

14. An allocation decision made by the Gatekeepers does not prevent a party to the proceedings applying for a review of the decision

15. The DFJ shall monitor the allocation and gatekeeping practices in the DFJ area to ensure that there is consistency of allocation, effective use of resources and the capacity to list cases at the earliest opportunity to avoid delay. He/she may issue local guidance to the Gatekeepers from time to time to reflect local circumstances and ensure the best use

of resources. The allocation of work between the Circuit Bench, the District Bench, the lay justices and, where appropriate and agreed, the legal advisers may be subject to local directions by the DFJ.

Directions on Issue

16. Gatekeepers shall be able to issue Directions on Issue on Form CAP01 in the following circumstances:

(a)   where the Gatekeeper finds on the basis of the information provided that the exemption from attending a MIAM has not validly been claimed, the Gatekeeper will direct the applicant, or will direct the parties, to attend a MIAM before the FHDRA, unless the Gatekeeper considers that in all the circumstances of the case the MIAM requirement should not apply to the application in question; the Gatekeeper will have regard to the matters set out in rule 3.10(3) FPR when making this decision;

(b)   where it appears that an urgent issue requires determination, the Gatekeeper may give directions for an accelerated hearing;

(c)   exceptionally, where it appears that directions need to be given for the service and filing of evidence, he/she may give directions for the filing of evidence.

Principles of Allocation

17. Allocation decisions must be made in accordance with the Family Court (Composition and Distribution of Business) Rules 2014.

18. This Guidance identifies criteria which are intended to be consistent with the Family Court (Composition and Distribution of Business) Rules 2014, and the decisions of superior courts.

19. In determining allocation, judicial continuity is an important consideration and the President's Guidance on Judicial Continuity and Deployment (Private Law) is to be followed.

20. In determining allocation consideration must be given to the matters set out in paragraph 7(a)–(e) above, in particular the need to avoid delay and provide the earliest possible hearing dates consistent with the welfare of the subject child(ren).

21. No distinction is to be drawn between proceedings which may be heard by District Judges and District Judges (Magistrates' Courts). There is an expectation that District Judges will assume personal responsibility for all case management hearings in proceedings allocated to them in accordance with the President's Guidance on Judicial Continuity and Deployment (Private Law).

Allocation Guidance

22. Subject to the guidance given below, all private law proceedings may be heard by any judge who has been authorised or nominated to conduct such proceedings, and may be case managed by the same judge or legal adviser.

23. When considering specifically the complexity of a case (see paragraph 7(e) above), it is envisaged that all relevant family applications (as defined in CAP paragraph 23) will be heard by lay justices (or at the FHDRA by legal advisers) unless they are of the type set out in the Schedule to this Guidance (see paragraphs 25 and 26 below). Additionally, a relevant family application may:

(a) be allocated to be heard by lay justices where specifically approved by the justices' clerk (or his nominated deputy) in consultation with the DFJ, or

(b) be re-allocated to be heard by lay justices where, at FHDRA or other hearing, it appears to the judge that the case does not fall, or no longer falls, within the Schedule.

24. There is an expectation that lay justices will not hear any contested private law application where the estimated length of the hearing is in excess of 3 days without the same having been approved by the justices' clerk in consultation with the DFJ.

25. When considering specifically the complexity of a case (see paragraph 7(e) above), it is envisaged that:

(c) proceedings described in Part 1 of the schedule to this Guidance will be allocated to a District Judge, or a District Judge (Magistrates' Court). If, on allocation it appears to the District Judge that the particular circumstances of the individual case justify allocation to a Circuit Judge, the District Judge shall so allocate it.

(d) subject to paragraph 27 (below), proceedings described in Part 2 of the schedule to this Guidance will be allocated to either a District Judge, District Judge (Magistrates' Court) or to a Circuit Judge or a High Court Judge.

26. Where the Gatekeeper allocates proceedings described in Part 2 of the schedule to a Circuit Judge or to a High Court Judge sitting in the Family Court, the FHDRA for that case shall be listed before a District Judge or District Judge (Magistrates' Court) unless the Gatekeeper considers (in discussion with the DFJ) that the FHDRA should be conducted by the Circuit Judge or High Court Judge (as appropriate).

27. Proceedings described in Part 3 of the schedule to this Guidance are to be issued in the High Court, not the Family Court. If they are received in the Family Court, then they must be identified and transferred to the Family Division of the High Court.

28. Where it appears to a Court that the issues in a case have developed from the point of initial allocation in such a way as to justify re-allocation, the court shall consider re-allocation in accordance with this Guidance and Schedule, having regard to the matters set out in paragraph 7(a)–(e) above, and taking account to the extent appropriate the principle of judicial continuity, and the need to avoid delay.

Urgent hearings

29. Urgent applications are those in which the applicant for a private law family order invites the court by application C2 either to (a) list the application for a hearing without notice to the respondent, or (b) reduce the normal (14 days) time-limit for service of an application and list a hearing at short notice.

30. If the application is considered by the Gatekeeper(s), they are to have regard generally to the guidance in paragraph 12.1–12.5 of the CAP in relation to the making of without notice orders when considering how to allocate an application that is presented for allocation as 'urgent'.

31. When presented with an application said to be urgent, the Gatekeeper(s) shall upon receipt:

(a) allocate the application to the appropriate level of judiciary in accordance with rule 16 of the Family Court (Composition and Distribution of Business) Rules 2014, and

(b) determine whether the application requires:

(i)   a hearing on that day, or

(ii)   requires an early hearing in advance of the FHDRA, with a reduced time for service of the application.

If an application for an urgent hearing is refused, reasons shall be given in writing and the application listed for FHDRA; the Gatekeeper may issue further directions in accordance with paragraph 16 above.

Schedule to the Allocation and Gatekeeping Guidance – Private Law
NOTE THAT
When, on allocation, Gatekeepers are considering specifically the issue of complexity, it is envisaged that they will allocate all relevant family applications (as defined in the Child Arrangements Programme paragraph 23) to the lay justices (or at the FHDRA by legal advisers) UNLESS they are of the type set out in this Schedule (below)
(See paragraph 23 Guidance on Allocation & Gatekeeping for Proceedings under Part II of the Children Act 1989 (Private Law Proceedings))

Part 1 – District Judge (unless in the opinion of the allocated District Judge, the particular characteristics of the individual case justify transfer to a Circuit Judge	Part 2 – District Judge but may be by Circuit Judge (or at most serious level by High Court Judge)	Part 3 – High Court and Inherent Jurisdiction
Allegations of significant physical, emotional or sexual abuse, or behaviours which have caused, or are at risk of causing, significant harm to the relevant child. Cases where significant factual matters are in issue (including substance misuse, domestic abuse, paternity, physical and/or mental health of relevant adults or children) such that a factfinding hearing lasting more than one day is likely and the necessity for expert evidence (i.e. beyond the expertise of CAFCASS and/or social worker) is likely to arise.	Cases involving significant factual disputes (including allegations of abuse, violence, alleged or proven criminal activity, gravely inappropriate behaviours, sexual abuse, complex physical and/or mental health issues in relation to relevant adults or children) particularly where a fact finding hearing of 3 days or more is a real possibility and/or where it is likely that more than one expert (not including CAFCASS and/or social worker) will be involved.	Inherent jurisdiction of the court relating to minors. Application to make a child a ward of court, or to bring such an order to an end. Proceedings under the Child Abduction & Custody Act 1985, and other international abduction cases Proceedings with an international element relating to or enforcement of Orders, conflict or comity of laws which have exceptional immigration/asylum status issues. Declarations of incompatibility under the Human Rights Act 1998 Applications for Declaratory Relief
Cases where the capacity of one of the parents is, or is likely to be, raised as an issue. Cases where there is a real possibility that the child will have to be joined as a party (see guidelines under *rule 16.4 FPR 2010*) &/or may be called to give evidence.	Cases where there are particularly difficult and unusual immigration or jurisdictional issues. Cases involving leave to remove (permanently or temporarily) from the jurisdiction to Hague Convention and/or EU countries which are factually or legally complex.	Registration of foreign judgments under Part 1 of the Foreign Judgments (Reciprocal Enforcement) Act 1920 Registration of judgments given in a different part of the UK under Part 2 of the Civil Jurisdiction and Judgments Act 1982

Part 1 – District Judge (unless in the opinion of the allocated District Judge, the particular characteristics of the individual case justify transfer to a Circuit Judge	Part 2 – District Judge but may be by Circuit Judge (or at most serious level by High Court Judge)	Part 3 – High Court and Inherent Jurisdiction
Cases where there is, or is likely to be, a significant issue in relation to disclosure of documents to or from third parties or outside agencies. Cases where immigration issues are likely to be relevant and significant Cases involving leave to remove children (permanently or temporarily) from the jurisdiction to Hague Convention and/or EU countries.	Cases which appear to involve, or have the potential to involve, intractable opposition to contact. Cases seeking enforcement of existing Orders made by a Circuit Judge or Recorder or in cases where a Circuit Judge or Recorder has previously made orders in relation to the same parties. Allocation should be to the same Circuit Judge or Recorder where practicable.	Registration of custody (Part 1) orders made in a court in another part of the UK under the Family Law Act 1986, section 32(1) Parental Responsibility order prior to adoption abroad (Adoption and Children Act 2002, section 84(1)) Application for direction that section 67(3) of the Adoption and Children Act 2002 (status conferred by adoption) does not apply.
Cases which involve significant issues to be determined in relation to the disclosure of information to one or other of the parties (e.g. where the Cafcass officer seeks to withhold information contained in a Safeguarding letter). Cases involving the enforcement of existing orders made by a District Judge or cases where a District Judge has previously made orders in relation to the same parties. Allocation should be to the same District Judge where practicable.	Circuit Judge (not District Judge): Cases seeking leave to remove from the jurisdiction [permanently or temporarily] outside of the Hague Convention/the EU. Where there are particular factual or legal complexities, the cases should ordinarily be allocated to the High Court following consultation with the DFJ.	Application for annulment of overseas or Convention adoption under Adoption and Children Act 2002, section 89 Issuance of letter of request for person to be examined out of the jurisdiction. Applications under Article 15 of the 2201/2003 Council Regulation and Article 9 of the 1996 Hague Convention (request for transfer of jurisdiction). Applications under Article 16 of the 1996 Hague Convention for a declaration as to the extent or existence of parental responsibility
Cases where there is a real possibility that Public Law Orders will be required, where the issues arising are of a type described in Part 1 or Part 2 of the Schedule to the President's Guidance on Allocation and Gatekeeping for Care, Supervision and other Part 4 proceedings.		Applications under Part 31 of the FPR (registration of orders under the 2201/2003 Council Regulation, the 1996 Hague Convention and the Civil Partnership (Jurisdiction and Recognition of Judgments) Regulations 2005). Cases which require the jurisdiction of the Administrative Court to be invoked

APPENDIX 8

PRESIDENT'S GUIDANCE ON ALLOCATION AND GATEKEEPING FOR CARE, SUPERVISION AND OTHER PROCEEDINGS UNDER PART IV OF THE CHILDREN ACT 1989 (PUBLIC LAW)

Issued in accordance with rule 21 of the Family Court (Composition and Distribution of Business) Rules 2014

Introduction

1. This Guidance is issued by the President of the Family Division and applies to all care, supervision and other Part IV proceedings commencing on and after 22 April 2014. It is issued following consultation with, and where applicable the agreement of, the Lord Chancellor, in accordance with rule 21 of the Family Court (Composition and Distribution of Business) Rules 2014, and is to be read with those Rules and PD12A (PLO 2014).

2. This Guidance applies to the allocation of all relevant proceedings to judges of the Family Court, including allocation to lay justices working with Justices' Clerks or Assistant Justices' Clerks (referred to in this guidance as "legal advisers"). The purpose of the Guidance is to ensure that all new care, supervision and other Part IV proceedings are allocated to the appropriate level of judge and, where appropriate, to a named case management judge (or case manager) who shall provide continuity for the proceedings in accordance with the President's Guidance on Judicial Continuity and Deployment (Public Law).

Gatekeeping teams

3. Each Designated Family Judge (DFJ) will lead a gatekeeping team in each Designated Family Centre. A gatekeeping team will consist of the Designated Family Judge, his nominated deputy, the Justices' Clerk (or his nominated legal adviser) and an equal number of District Judges nominated by the Designated Family Judge, and legal advisers who will be identified by the Justices' Clerk in agreement with the Designated Family Judge. The number of legal advisers and District Judges is to be consistent with the needs of the business and the expertise of those who are available. Members of the gatekeeping team are referred to in this guidance as "gatekeepers".

4. All applications for care, supervision and other Part IV orders which are received for issue by 4.00 pm will be issued by HMCTS and placed before gatekeepers for their joint consideration on the next working day. Applications that are considered urgent will be allocated to the first available judge of the Family Court (in accordance with rule 16 of the Family Court (Composition and Distribution of Business) Rules 2014).

5. Local Authority applicants are to complete the Allocation Proposal section of the C110A application form when issuing proceedings. The Allocation Proposal section is to be used by the gatekeepers to record their allocation decision.

6. Members of the gatekeeping team are to be available at fixed times on each weekday to allocate jointly all relevant proceedings that have been issued. It is recommended that if they do not sit together at a fixed time in a court list for this purpose, they have a listed time for discussion between each other, for example, an hour at the beginning of the day. The gatekeepers will have access to information about existing allocated case volumes in the family court to help inform allocation decisions, as well as information about when and where Case Management Hearings can be listed. They will consider the file in each new application that has been issued on the preceding day and any outstanding applications and determine, in accordance with the Family Court (Composition and Distribution of Business) Rules 2014 and this guidance, the level of judge, and where possible the identity of the judge to which the proceedings are to be allocated. They will record their allocation decision on the Allocation Proposal section of the C110A application form.

7. When the allocation decision has been made, the case management judge or case manager will issue the Standard Directions on Issue and Allocation (SDO) in accordance with PD12A (PLO 2014) together with any appropriate Notice of Hearing. Court staff will notify by e-mail the relevant local authority of the date, time, location and identity of the allocated case management judge (or case manager) for the case management hearing and will list the case management hearing before an identified case management judge or case manager in accordance with the guidance of the DFJ and the allocation decision that has been made.

8. If the gatekeepers cannot agree on an allocation decision or they require further guidance, they must refer the allocation decision to the Designated Family Judge or his nominated deputy.

9. An allocation decision made by the gatekeepers does not prevent the possibility of a party to the proceedings making a subsequent application for a review of the decision.

10. If a care or supervision application is issued by a local authority as "urgent" with a request for an early hearing to authorise the removal of a child and permission to abridge time to serve the parties, the application for expedition and any consequential directions will be considered by the gatekeepers. These are exceptional cases which may include newborn babies who are about to be discharged from hospital where the issue of care and supervision order applications is part of planned pre-proceedings involvement with the family. In

all other cases where there is an identified real and immediate safety risk to the child, the expectation is that an application will be made for an Emergency Protection Order. This Guidance does not affect the existing procedures for dealing with Emergency Protection Order applications.

11. The Designated Family Judge shall monitor the allocation and gatekeeping process with a consultation group comprising: a Circuit Judge, a District Judge, a District Judge (Magistrates Court), the Justices' Clerk or his nominated deputy, a legal adviser and two members of the administration in the Designated Family Centre. The consultation group will meet at least once a month to identify any allocation questions upon which the advice of the Designated Family Judge or the Family Division Liaison Judge is required to ensure that there is consistency of allocation, effective use of resources and the identification of specific questions, the answers to which will be used as local guidance by the gatekeepers.

Principles

12. Allocation decisions must be made in accordance with the Family Court (Composition and Distribution of Business) Rules 2014.

13. This Guidance is consistent with those Rules, the guidance issued by the President of the Family Division in accordance with PD12A (PLO 2014), and decisions of the superior courts. It is intended to reflect the wide variation in the level of experience and expertise in the Family Court. Cases should be allocated to judges (including lay justices) and case managers with the appropriate level of experience to ensure that judicial resources are used most effectively.

14. In determining allocation, the gatekeepers shall consider each application having regard to the information provided on and with the C110A application form and shall determine the appropriate level of judge of the Family Court, in accordance with the requirements of rule 20 of the Family Court (Composition and Distribution of Business) Rules 2014:

- (a) the need to make the most effective and efficient use of the local judicial resources that is appropriate, given the nature and type of application;
- (b) the need to avoid delay;
- (c) the need for judicial continuity;
- (d) the location of the parties or of any child relevant to the proceedings; and
- (e) complexity.

15. In the Family Court, no distinction is to be drawn between proceedings which may be heard by District Judges and District Judges (Magistrates Courts) ('judges of 'district judge level'). There is an expectation that judges of district judge level will assume personal responsibility for all case management hearings in proceedings allocated to them, in accordance with the President's Guidance on Judicial Continuity and Deployment (Public Law).

Allocation Guidance

16. The factors set out at paragraph (14) above, include at (a) the judicial and HMCTS resources available in each court location, at (b) the needs of the parties to ensure that cases are listed before the appropriate level of judge with the minimum of delay, so that all proceedings are heard within the Timetable for the Child and within a maximum of 26 weeks or any extended Timetable for the Proceedings, as directed by the case management judge, at (c) the President's Guidance on Judicial Continuity and Deployment (Public Law) and at (d) a location that is suitable for the parties, particularly if special requirements or circumstances exist.

17. The schedule to this Guidance sets out matters which are likely to be relevant to the consideration of the "complexity" factor referred to at paragraph (14)(e) above.

18. Subject to the guidance given below, all care, supervision and other Part IV proceedings may be heard by any judge of the Family Court (including lay justices) who has been authorised or nominated to conduct care and supervision proceedings and may be case managed by any judge or legal adviser who has likewise been authorised or nominated.

19. It is not expected that proceedings described in the schedule to this Guidance will be allocated to lay justices or the legal adviser acting as their case manager unless specifically approved by the Justices' Clerk (or his nominated deputy) in consultation with the Designated Family Judge. There is also an expectation that magistrates will not hear any contested hearing where the ELH is in excess of 3 days without the same having been approved from time to time by the Justices' Clerk (or his nominated deputy) in consultation with the Designated Family Judge.

20. It is expected that proceedings described in column 1 of the schedule to this Guidance will be allocated to a judge of district judge level.

21. It is expected that proceedings described in column 2 of the schedule to this Guidance will be allocated to a judge of circuit judge level or a judge of High Court judge level and will not be allocated to a judge of district judge level unless specifically released by the Designated Family Judge or one of his nominated deputies.

22. Proceedings described in paragraph H of column 2 of the schedule to this Guidance are to be issued in the Family Division of the High Court of Justice.

Schedule to the Allocation and Gatekeeping Guidance

Column 1	Column 2
A) Risk assessment issues	A) Risk assessment issues
(1) Allegations or risk of	(1) Allegations of physical or sexual abuse which involve any of the following features:
a) serious physical or sexual abuse causing or likely to cause significant injury to the relevant children, and/or	• Exceptional gravity in relation to the acts alleged or the nature of the harm suffered
b) serious sexual abuse of the relevant children	• Where there is, or is likely to be, conflicting expert opinion from more than two expert witnesses on any key issue
	• Shaking injuries involving retinal haemorrhage/brain injury/fractures
	• Complex medical questions involving novel issues or the determination of causation
(2) Allegations of serious domestic violence eg. causing significant injury particularly if witnessed by the child	(2) Allegations of extremely serious domestic violence or rape, particularly if witnessed by the child
	(3) Risk of serious physical or emotional harm arising from –
	• Death of another child in family, a parent or other significant person
	• A parent or other significant person who may have committed a grave crime e.g. murder, manslaughter or rape
(4) Significant disputed issues relating to psychiatric illness of a parent and/or a child	
	(5) History of suspicious death of a child in the family

(6) Significant disputed medical issues relating to the relevant child	(6) Complex medical issues, including medical causation issues and medical treatment issues including where any of the parties suffer from psychiatric illness or psychological issues or any significant disability such as profound deafness, blindness or learning disability, or which will require specialist knowledge and services in respect of parenting capacity or the needs of the children
B) Unusual/Complex issues relating to ethnicity or religion None	**B) Unusual/Complex issues relating to ethnicity or religion** (7) Significant contested issues in respect of religion, culture or ethnicity or involving medical treatment relating to the same
C) Non-subject child as a party (particularly if under 16) (8) Where a child may be required to give evidence.	**C) Non-subject child as a party (particularly if under 16)** (8) Where children (including parents who are under the age of 18) are, or may be, required to give evidence and be joined as a party
D) Capacity issues (9) Where there is a need for the Official Solicitor or another litigation friend to represent the interests of an incapacitated adult	**D) Capacity issues** (9) Where there is a need for the Official Solicitor or another litigation friend to represent the interests of more than one incapacitated party
E) Real possibility of conflict of expert evidence or difficulty in resolving conflict in the evidence of witnesses (10) Where there is an identified need for no more than two expert witnesses to report on the same key issue(s)	**E) Real possibility of conflict of expert evidence or difficulty in resolving conflict in the evidence of witnesses** (10) Where there is an identified need for more than two expert witnesses to report on the same key issue(s)

F) Novel or difficult point of law	F) Novel or difficult point of law
None	(11) Where the case involves a difficult point of law, issues of public policy or unusually complex or sensitive issues
	(12) Allegations of serious abuse where there are, or are likely to be, criminal proceedings and consideration of issues regarding disclosure of information or public interest immunity
	(13) Complex issues as to disclosure – where a party seeks leave to withhold information from another party, or where there is an issue about the release of confidential information involving a difficult point of law, or where disclosure of documentation involves a difficult or sensitive exercise of discretion or public policy issues
	(14) Where there are concurrent criminal proceedings in the Crown Court relevant to the issues between the parties and joint directions hearing(s) may be required.
	(15) Cases not in category H below, but which have significant immigration/status issues.
G) Existing proceedings relating to the child or a sibling which are proceeding before another court or have been recently completed before another court	**G) Existing proceedings relating to the child or a sibling which are proceeding before another court or have been recently completed before another court**
(16) Consideration must be given to listing the current proceedings before the judge who heard or is hearing the proceedings relating to the child or sibling in order to provide continuity.	(16) Consideration must be given to listing the current proceedings before the judge who heard or is hearing the proceedings relating to the child or sibling in order to provide continuity.

International Proceedings	**H) High Court Reserved Jurisdictions** **International Issues**
	(17) There is an issue concerning placement for adoption of the child outside the jurisdiction
(18) Cases to which Brussels II revised applies	(18) Proceedings with an international element relating to recognition or enforcement of orders, conflict or comity of laws or which have exceptional immigration/asylum status issues
(19) Cases in which placement is limited to temporary removal to a Hague Convention country.	(19) Cases in which an application is made for (a) permanent placement or (b) temporary removal from the jurisdiction to a non-Hague convention country;
	20) Cases in which a child has been brought to this jurisdiction in circumstances which might constitute a wrongful removal or retention either from a EC Member State, a Hague Convention country (a contracting State to the 1980 Hague Child Abduction Convention and/or a contracting State to the 1996 Hague Child Protection Convention) or a non-Convention country;
	(21) Cases in which a child is alleged to have been abducted overseas and applications have been made in this jurisdiction such as for a declaration that the child was habitually resident in this country prior to the abduction or for an order that the child be returned with a request for assistance etc; and
	(22) Cases in which Tipstaff Orders are applied for.

	Inherent Jurisdiction (23) Injunctions invoking the inherent jurisdiction of the court (24) Interim or substantive relief which requires the inherent jurisdiction of the High Court to be invoked.
	Other (25) Applications for Declaratory Relief (26) Applications which require the jurisdiction of the Administrative Court to be invoked (27) Issues as to publicity (identification of a child or restriction on publication or injunctions seeking to restrict the freedom of the media) (28) Applications in medical treatment cases e.g. for novel medical treatment or lifesaving procedures
I) Other case management issues (29) Where a 'split hearing' or finding of fact hearing is necessary and judicial continuity cannot otherwise be ensured	**I) Other case management issues** (29) Where a 'split hearing' or finding of fact hearing is necessary and judicial continuity before a District Judge cannot be ensured (30) Where possible local authority failures to progress plans to protect the child(ren) in the case are likely to be addressed critically by the court because it is alleged that there has been systemic failure in the proceedings and other proceedings

APPENDIX 9

STATUTORY INSTRUMENTS

ACCESS TO JUSTICE ACT 1999 (DESTINATION OF APPEALS) (FAMILY PROCEEDINGS) ORDER 2014

SI 2014/602

1 Citation, commencement and interpretation

(1) This Order may be cited as the Access to Justice Act 1999 (Destination of Appeals) (Family Proceedings) Order 2014 and comes into force on the date on which section 17(3) of the Crime and Courts Act 2013 is brought fully into force.

(2) In this Order –

"the 1984 Act" means the Matrimonial and Family Proceedings Act 1984;
"the 2007 Act" means the Tribunals, Courts and Enforcement Act 2007;
"the 2011 Order" means the Access to Justice Act 1999 (Destination of Appeals) (Family Proceedings) Order 2011;
"authorised court officer" has the meaning assigned to it by rule 44.1 of the Civil Procedure Rules 1998 as applied to family proceedings by rule 28.2(1) of the Family Procedure Rules 2010; and
"justice of the peace" means a justice of the peace who is not a District Judge (Magistrates' Courts).

2 Appeals to the family court

(1) Paragraph (3) applies to an appeal –

(a) under section 31K(1) of the 1984 Act (appeals from the family court in cases where no other right of appeal exists); or

(b) under section 13(2A) of the Administration of Justice Act 1960 (appeals in cases of contempt of court) from a decision or order of the family court.

(2) Paragraph (3) does not apply if the person, or any of the persons, who made the decision or order was when making the decision or order deployed in the family court otherwise than as the holder of an office referred to in paragraph (3).

(3) The appeal lies to the family court (instead of to the Court of Appeal) if it is from a decision or order made by –

(a) the Senior District Judge of the Family Division;

(b) a district judge of the Principal Registry of the Family Division;

(c) the Chief Taxing Master;

(d) a Taxing Master of the Senior Courts;

(e)   a person appointed to act as a deputy for any person holding an office referred to in paragraph (b) or (d), or to act as a temporary additional officer in any such office;

(f)   a district judge;

(g)   a deputy district judge appointed under section 102 of the Senior Courts Act 1981 or section 8 of the County Courts Act 1984;

(h)   a Chamber President, or a Deputy Chamber President, of a chamber of the Upper Tribunal or of a chamber of the First-tier Tribunal;

(i)   a judge of the Upper Tribunal by virtue of appointment under paragraph 1(1) of Schedule 3 to the 2007 Act;

(j)   a transferred-in judge of the Upper Tribunal (see section 31(2) of the 2007 Act);

(k)   a deputy judge of the Upper Tribunal (whether under paragraph 7 of Schedule 3 to, or section 31(2) of, the 2007 Act);

(l)   a judge of the First-tier Tribunal by virtue of appointment under paragraph 1(1) of Schedule 2 to the 2007 Act;

(m)   a transferred-in judge of the First-tier Tribunal (see section 31(2) of the 2007 Act);

(n)   a member of a panel of Employment Judges established for England and Wales or for Scotland;

(o)   a person appointed under section 30(1)(a) or (b) of the Courts-Martial (Appeals) Act 1951 (assistants to the Judge Advocate General);

(p)   a District Judge (Magistrates' Courts);

(q)   two or three justices of the peace;

(r)   a single justice of the peace;

(s)   a justices' clerk or an assistant to a justices' clerk; or

(t)   an authorised court officer.

(4) Paragraph (3) has effect subject to any requirement to obtain permission to appeal.

****

THE CHILDREN AND FAMILIES ACT 2014 (COMMENCEMENT NO 1) ORDER 2014

SI 2014/793

Citation

1 This Order may be cited as the Children and Families Act 2014 (Commencement No. 1) Order 2014.

Provisions coming into force on 22nd April 2014

2 The day appointed for the coming into force of sections 10, 13 and 17 of the Children and Families Act 2014 is 22nd April 2014.

****

THE CHILDREN AND FAMILIES ACT 2014 (COMMENCEMENT NO 2) ORDER 2014

SI 2014/889

Citation and Interpretation

1 This Order may be cited as the Children and Families Act 2014 (Commencement No. 2) Order 2014.

2 In this Order "the Act" means the Children and Families Act 2014.

Provisions coming into force on 1st April 2014

3 The following provisions of the Act come into force on 1st April 2014 for the purposes of making orders or regulations only –

    (a)   sections 30 and 31;
    (b)   section 34;
    (c)   sections 36 and 37;
    (d)   section 41;
    (e)   sections 44 to 47;
    (f)   section 49;
    (g)   sections 51 and 52;
    (h)   section 56;
    (i)   section 67;
    (j)   section 69;
    (k)   section 80;
    (l)   section 84;
    (m)   Schedule 4.

Provisions coming into force on 22nd April 2014

4 The following provisions of the Act come into force on 22nd April 2014 –

(a)   section 9;
(b)   section 12;
(c)   section 14;
(d)   section 15(1) and (3);
(e)   section 16;
(f)   Schedule 2.

Provisions coming into force on 13th May 2014

5 The following provisions of the Act come into force on 13th May 2014 –

(a)   section 4;
(b)   section 7;
(c)   section 78;
(d)   sections 85 to 89;
(e)   sections 98 and 99;
(f)   Schedule 1.

Provisions coming into force on 25th July 2014

6 The following provisions of the Act come into force on 25th July 2014 –

(a)   section 1, in relation to England only;
(b)   sections 2 and 3;
(c)   section 6;
(d)   section 8.

Provisions coming into force on 1st September 2014

7 The following provisions of the Act come into force on 1st September 2014 –

(a)   Part 3, to the extent that it is not already in force, save for –
    (i)   in section 70(1), the words "Subject to this section and sections 71 to 75,";
    (ii)   sections 70(2) to 75;
    (iii)   paragraphs 55 to 58 of Schedule 3;
(b)   section 84, to the extent that it is not already in force;
(c)   section 100;
(d)   section 106;
(e)   Schedule 4, to the extent that it is not already in force.

THE CHILDREN AND FAMILIES ACT 2014 (TRANSITIONAL PROVISIONS) ORDER 2014

SI 2014/1042

Citation and Interpretation

1 This Order may be cited as the Children and Families Act 2014 (Transitional Provisions) Order 2014 and comes into force on 22nd April 2014.

2 (1) In this Order –

"the 1989 Act" means the Children Act 1989;

"the 2014 Act" means the Children and Families Act 2014;

"a care order" has the same meaning as in the 1989 Act;

"a child arrangements order" means a child arrangements order as defined by section 8(1) of the 1989 Act;

"the commencement date" means the 22nd April 2014;

"a contact order" means a contact order as defined by section 8(1) of the 1989 Act prior to section 12 of the 2014 Act coming into force;

"a court officer" means a member of the court staff;

"residence order" means a residence order as defined by section 8(1) of the 1989 Act prior to section 12 of the 2014 Act coming into force;

"a section 31A plan" means a care plan prepared in accordance with section 31A of the 1989 Act;

"a supervision order" has the same meaning as in the 1989 Act.

(2) For the purposes of this Order, proceedings are issued on the date entered on the application form by the court officer.

Post-adoption contact orders

3 Section 51A of the Adoption and Children Act 2002, as inserted by section 9(1) of the 2014 Act, does not apply to proceedings arising out of an application for a contact order which was commenced but not disposed of prior to the commencement date.

4 The amendments made by section 9(7) of the 2014 Act do not apply in respect of family proceedings that were commenced but not disposed of prior to the commencement date.

Family mediation information and assessment meetings

5 Where a relevant family application is received but not issued by the court prior to the commencement date, that application shall be issued on or after the commencement date as if section 10 of the 2014 Act had not come into force on the commencement date.

Child arrangements orders

6 (1) This article is subject to article 7.

(2) Where, before the commencement date, there was or had been in force a contact order, then, on and after the commencement date, that contact order shall be deemed to be a child arrangements order which regulates or regulated arrangements that relate to either or both of the following –

    (a)   with whom a child is to spend time or otherwise have contact, and
    (b)   when a child is to spend time or otherwise have contact with any person.

(3) Where, before the commencement date, there was or had been in force a residence order, then, on and after the commencement date, that residence order shall be deemed to be a child arrangements order which regulates or regulated arrangements that relate to either or both of the following –

    (a)   with whom the child concerned is to live, and
    (b)   when the child is to live with any person.

(4) Where, before the commencement date, there was an application in progress for making, varying or discharging a contact order or a residence order, then, on and after the commencement date, that application shall be deemed to be an application for making, varying or discharging a child arrangements order.

(5) Nothing in this article shall be construed so as to revive a residence order or contact order that has been discharged.

7 (1) In relation to a child arrangements order that contains provisions that were in the order prior to the commencement date –

    (a)   the court may not make an enforcement order under section 11J, or an order requiring financial compensation to be paid under section 11O of the 1989 Act, in relation to any such provisions which do not regulate contact arrangements;
    (b)   to comply with section 11L(1) of the 1989 Act in relation to those provisions, the court does not need to be satisfied that the enforcement order is necessary to secure the person's compliance with those provisions which do not regulate contact arrangements.

(2) For the purposes of this article, "contact arrangements" are arrangements relating to either or both of the following –

    (a)   with whom a child is to spend time or otherwise have contact, and
    (b)   when a child is to spend time or otherwise have contact with any person.

Care, supervision and other family proceedings: time limits and timetables

8 Where proceedings to which section 32 of the 1989 Act applies –

    (a)   were commenced but not disposed of prior to the commencement date;
    (b)   were subject to a timetable drawn up by the court under section 32(1) of the 1989 Act prior to the commencement date; and
    (c)   the timetable provides for the proceedings to conclude on a date after the conclusion of a period of twenty-six weeks beginning with the day on which the application was issued,

section 32(1)(a)(ii) shall be read as if the reference to the period of within twenty-six weeks beginning with the day on which the application was issued, is a reference to the period ending with the date specified in the timetable (referred to in paragraph (b)), as the date for the disposal of the application.

Interim Orders

9 (1) Where, before the commencement date, an interim care order or an interim supervision order has been made under section 38(1) of the 1989 Act and that interim order does not specify a date on which it shall cease to have effect, it shall cease to have effect on whichever of the following events first occurs –

    (a)   the expiry of the period of eight weeks beginning with the date on which the order was made;

    (b)   if the order is the second or subsequent such order made with respect to the same child in the same proceedings, at the expiry of the relevant period.

(2) For the purposes of this article, "the relevant period" means –

    (a)   the period of four weeks beginning with the date on which the order in question was made; or

    (b)   the period of eight weeks beginning with the date on which the first order was made, if that period ends later than the period mentioned in paragraph (2)(a).

Care Plans

10 (1) Section 31(3A) and (3B) of the 1989 Act, as inserted by section 15(1) of the 2014 Act, only applies in respect of applications for care or supervision orders issued on or after the commencement date.

(2) Where a court is exercising its power under section 31(1) in relation to an application for a care or supervision order made before the commencement date, no care order may be made with respect to a child until the court has considered a section 31A plan.

Repeal of restrictions on divorce and dissolution etc where there are children

11 The repeals effected by section 17 of the 2014 Act only apply in respect of proceedings issued on or after the commencement date.

FAMILY COURT (COMPOSITION AND DISTRIBUTION OF BUSINESS) RULES 2014

SI 2014/840

PART 1
INTRODUCTORY PROVISIONS

1 Citation, commencement and interpretation

These Rules may be cited as the Family Court (Composition and Distribution of Business) Rules 2014 and come into force on 22 April 2014.

2 (1) In these Rules –

"the 1991 Act" means the Child Support Act 1991;

"appeal" includes an application seeking permission to appeal and an application in the course of the appeal proceedings;

"assistant to a justices' clerk" has the meaning given in section 27(5) of the Courts Act 2003;

"authorised", except in the context of references to an authorised court officer, means authorised by the President of the Family Division or nominated by or on behalf of the Lord Chief Justice to conduct particular business in the family court, in accordance with Part 3;

"authorised court officer" has the meaning assigned to it by rule 44.1 of the Civil Procedure Rules 1998 as applied to family proceedings by rule 28.2(1) of the Family Procedure Rules 2010;

"costs judge" means –

(a)   the Chief Taxing Master;

(b)   a taxing master of the Senior Courts; or

(c)   a person appointed to act as deputy for the person holding office referred to in paragraph (b) or to act as a temporary additional officer for any such office;

"financial remedy" has the meaning assigned to it by rule 2.3 of the Family Procedure Rules 2010;

"judge of circuit judge level" means –

(a)   a circuit judge who, where applicable, is authorised;

(b)   a Recorder who, where applicable, is authorised;

(c)   any other judge of the family court authorised to sit as a judge of circuit judge level in the family court;

"judge of district judge level" means –

(a)   the Senior District Judge of the Family Division;

(b)   a district judge of the Principal Registry of the Family Division;

(c)   a person appointed to act as deputy for the person holding office referred to in paragraph (b) or to act as a temporary additional officer for any such office;

(d)   a district judge who, where applicable, is authorised;

(e)   a deputy district judge appointed under section 102 of the Senior Courts Act 1981 or section 8 of the County Courts Act 1984 who, where applicable, is authorised;

(f)   an authorised District Judge (Magistrates' Courts);

(g)   any other judge of the family court authorised to sit as a judge of district judge level in the family court.

"judge of High Court judge level" means –

(a)   a deputy judge of the High Court;

(b)   a puisne judge of the High Court;

(c)   a person who has been a judge of the Court of Appeal or a puisne judge of the High Court who may act as a judge of the family court by virtue of section 9 of the Senior Courts Act 1981;

(d)   the Senior President of Tribunals;

(e)   the Chancellor of the High Court;

(f)   an ordinary judge of the Court of Appeal (including the vice-president, if any, of either division of that court);

(g)   the President of the Queen's Bench Division;

(h)   the President of the Family Division;

(i)   the Master of the Rolls;

(j)   the Lord Chief Justice;

"judge of the family court" means a judge referred to in section 31C(1) of the Matrimonial and Family Proceedings Act 1984;

"justices' clerk" has the meaning given in section 27(1) of the Courts Act 2003; and

"lay justice" means an authorised justice of the peace who is not a District Judge (Magistrates' Courts).

(2) In these Rules, references to provisions of the Adoption and Children Act 2002 include, as applicable, references to those provisions as modified by the Human Fertilisation and Embryology (Parental Orders) Regulations 2010.

PART 2
COMPOSITION OF THE FAMILY COURT

3 Composition: general

(1) Subject to rules in this Part, the family court shall be composed of –

(a)   one of the following –

    (i)   a judge of district judge level;

    (ii)   a judge of circuit judge level; or

    (iii)   a judge of High Court judge level; or

(b)   two or three lay justices.

(2) Where paragraph (1)(b) applies, the court shall include, so far as is practicable, both a man and a woman.

4 Composition: allocation decision

When making a decision on allocation to which rule 20 applies, the family court shall be composed of one or more of the following –

(a)   a judge of district judge level;

(b)   a judge of circuit judge level.

5 Composition: appeals heard by a judge of district judge level

(1) Subject to rule 7, the family court shall be composed of a judge of district judge level when hearing an appeal from the decision of the Secretary of State where an appeal is brought under –

- (a) regulation 25AB(1) of the Child Support (Collection and Enforcement) Regulations 1992 (Appeals);
- (b) section 20(1) (a) or (b) of the 1991 Act to a court by virtue of article 3 of the Child Support Appeals (Jurisdiction of Courts) Order 2002 (Parentage appeals to be made to courts).

(2) The family court may be composed of a judge of district judge level when hearing applications in the course of appeal proceedings against decisions of persons referred to in rule 6(2)(b) to (d) or decisions of the court referred to in rule 6(3).

(3) The family court shall be composed of a costs judge or a district judge of the High Court when hearing an appeal against the decision of an authorised court officer.

6 Composition: appeals heard by a judge of circuit judge level or a judge of High Court level

(1) Subject to rule 7, when hearing an appeal from the decisions of persons referred to in paragraph (2) or the court referred to in paragraph (3), the family court shall be composed of –

- (a) a judge of circuit judge level; or
- (b) a judge of High Court level where there is a need for such a level of judge to hear the appeal to make most effective and efficient use of local judicial resource and the resource of the High Court bench.

(2) The persons referred to in paragraph (1) are –

- (a) a judge of district judge level;
- (b) two or three lay justices;
- (c) a lay justice; or
- (d) a justices' clerk or an assistant to a justices' clerk.

(3) The court referred to in paragraph (1) is a magistrates' court where an appeal is brought under section 111A of the Magistrates' Courts Act 1980 (appeals on ground of error of law in child support proceedings).

7 Composition: appeals heard by a judge of High Court level

(1) The family court shall be composed of a judge of High Court level when hearing an appeal from the decision of –

- (a) the Senior District Judge of the Family Division in financial remedy proceedings;
- (b) a district judge of the Principal Registry of the Family Division in financial remedy proceedings or a person appointed to act as deputy or as a temporary additional officer for such a district judge in these proceedings;
- (c) a costs judge; or
- (d) the Gender Recognition Panel where an appeal is brought under section 8(1) of the Gender Recognition Act 2004 (Appeals etc.).

(2) The family court shall be composed of a judge of High Court level (instead of a judge of district judge level or a judge of circuit judge level) where there is –

(a)   an appeal against a decision referred to in rules 5 and 6; and

(b)   the Designated Family Judge or a judge of High Court level considers that the appeal would raise an important point of principle or practice.

8 Composition: matters part heard

(1) Paragraph (2) applies where a hearing –

(a)   was before two or three lay justices; and

(b)   was part heard.

(2) The court which resumes the hearing shall, wherever possible, be composed of the same lay justices as dealt with the previous part of the hearing.

PART 3
AUTHORISATIONS

9 Powers to grant authorisations

(1) Paragraph (2) applies to business in such categories as may be specified from time to time by the President of the Family Division.

(2) A judge of district judge level or a judge of circuit judge level may conduct business to which this paragraph applies in the family court only if authorised by the President of the Family Division to do so.

(3) The President of the Family Division may specify the matters referred to in paragraph (1) in directions, after consulting the Lord Chancellor.

(4) A lay justice may conduct business in the family court only if authorised by the Lord Chief Justice to do so.

PART 4
LAY JUSTICES: CHAIRMANSHIP OF THE FAMILY COURT

10 Interpretation of this Part

In this Part –

"2007 Rules" means the Justices of the Peace (Training and Development Committee) Rules 2007;

"BTDC" means the Bench Training and Development Committee established in accordance with the 2007 Rules; and

"FTDC" means the Family Training and Development Committee established in accordance with the 2007 Rules.

11 Chairman

(1) When the family court is composed of two or three lay justices, it shall sit under the chairmanship of a lay justice who is on a list of approved family court chairmen.

(2) A lay justice may preside before being included on a list of approved family court chairmen only if that lay justice is –

(a)   under the supervision of another authorised lay justice who is on the list of approved family court chairmen; and

(b)   has completed the training course required by rule 31 of the 2007 Rules.

(3) In this rule "list of approved family court chairmen" means a list kept by a FTDC or, where there is no FTDC, a BTDC in accordance with rules 32 and 35 of the 2007 Rules.

(4) This rule and rule 12 are subject to sections 18(1) and (2) of the Courts Act 2003.

12 Absence of authorised lay justice entitled to preside

(1) The lay justices present may appoint one of their number to preside in the family court to deal with any case in the absence of a lay justice entitled to preside under rule 11 if –

(a) before making such appointment the lay justices present are satisfied as to the suitability for this purpose of the lay justice proposed; and

(b) expect as mentioned in paragraph (2), the lay justice proposed has completed or is undergoing a chairman training course in accordance with rule 31(d) of the 2007 Rules.

(2) The condition in paragraph (1)(b) does not apply if by reason of illness, circumstances unforeseen when the lay justices to sit were chosen, or other emergency, no lay justice who complies with that condition is present.

PART 5
DISTRIBUTION OF BUSINESS OF THE FAMILY COURT

13 General

(1) This Part makes provision for the distribution of business of the family court among the judges of the family court.

(2) Rules 15 and 20 are subject to rule 17.

(3) Rules 15, 16, 17, 18, 19 and 20 make provision regarding the level of judge of the family court to which a matter is to be allocated initially.

> (Rule 29.19 of the Family Procedure Rules 2010 makes provision for a judge of the family court to determine that a matter should be heard by a different level of judge of the family court.)

14 Persons who may exercise jurisdiction of the family court

Subject to the provisions of this Part or of any other enactment, any jurisdiction and powers conferred by any enactment on the family court, or on a judge of the family court, may be exercised by any judge of the family court.

15 Allocation of proceedings in Schedule 1

(1) An application in a type of proceedings listed in the first column of the table in Schedule 1 shall be allocated to be heard by a judge of the level listed in the second column of that table.

(2) Paragraph (1) and the provisions of Schedule 1 are subject to the need to take into account the need to make the most effective and efficient use of local judicial resource and the resource of the High Court bench that is appropriate given the nature and type of the application.

16 Allocation of emergency applications

(1) In this rule –

"the 1986 Act" means the Family Law Act 1986;
"the 1989 Act" means the Children Act 1989; and
"the 1996 Act" means the Family Law Act 1996.

(2) An application of a type referred to in paragraph (3) shall be allocated to the first available judge of the family court who –

(a) where applicable, is authorised to conduct the type of business to which the application relates; and

(b) would not be precluded by Schedule 2 from dealing with the application.

(3) The types of applications are those –

(a) under –

(i) section 33 of the 1986 Act (disclosure of information as to the whereabouts of a child);

(ii) section 34 of the 1986 Act (order authorising the taking charge and delivery of a child);

(iii) section 44(1) of the 1989 Act (emergency protection order);

(iv) section 44(9)(b) of the 1989 Act (varying a direction in an emergency protection order given under section 44(6) of the 1989 Act);

(v) section 45(4) of the 1989 Act (extending the period during which an emergency protection order is to have effect);

(vi) section 45(8) of the 1989 Act (to discharge an emergency protection order);

(vii) section 45(8A) of the 1989 Act (to vary or discharge an emergency protection order in so far as it imposes an exclusion requirement on a person who is not entitled to apply for the order to be discharged);

(viii) section 45(8B) of the 1989 Act (to vary or discharge an emergency protection order in so far as it confers powers of arrest attached to an exclusion requirement);

(ix) section 48(9) of the 1989 Act (warrant to assist in discovery of children who may be in need of emergency protection);

(x) section 50 of the 1989 Act (recovery of abducted children);

(xi) section 102(1) of the 1989 Act (warrant for a constable to assist in the exercise of certain powers to search for children or inspect premises);

(xii) Part 4 of the 1996 Act which are made without notice, except where the applicant is under 18 or where an application for an occupation order under section 33 of that Act requires a determination of a question of property ownership;

(xiii) section 41 of the Adoption and Children Act 2002 (recovery order); or

(xiv) section 79 of the Childcare Act 2006 (warrant for a constable to assist in the exercise of powers of entry); or

(b) which are not referred to in paragraph (a) but which require the immediate attention of the court.

(4) An application of a type listed in paragraph (5) shall be allocated to the first available judge of the family court, other than lay justices, who, where applicable, is authorised to conduct the type of business to which the application relates.

(5) The types of application are those under –

(a)   Part 4 of the 1996 Act which are made without notice and where the applicant is aged under 18 or where an application for an occupation order under section 33 of that Act requires a determination of a question of property ownership;

(b)   Part 4A of the 1996 Act which are made without notice.

17 Allocation: applications in existing proceedings or in connection with proceedings that have concluded

(1) Subject to paragraphs (3) to (5), an application made within existing proceedings in the family court shall be allocated to the level of judge who is dealing with the existing proceedings to which the application relates.

(2) Subject to paragraphs (3) to (5), an application made in connection with proceedings in the family court that have concluded shall be allocated to the level of judge who last dealt with those proceedings.

(3) In Schedule 2 –

(a)   the remedies listed in tables 1, 2 and 3 may not be granted by lay justices;

(b)   the remedies listed in tables 2 and 3 may not be granted by a judge of district judge level;

(c)   the remedies listed in table 3 may not be granted by a judge of circuit judge level, subject to any exception stated in that table.

(4) Where the effect of Schedule 2 is that an application for a particular remedy may not be granted by the level of judge referred to in paragraph (1) or (2), then that application shall be allocated to a level of judge who is able to grant that remedy.

(5) Any power of the family court to make an order for committal in respect of a breach of a judgment, order or undertaking to do or abstain from doing an act may only be made by a judge of the same level as, or of a higher level than, the judge who make the judgment or order, or who accepted the undertaking, as the case may be.

18 Allocation: costs

Subject to any direction of the court, an application for detailed assessment of a bill of costs shall be allocated to an authorised court officer, a district judge or a costs judge.

19 Allocation: appeals

An appeal shall be allocated to a judge in accordance with rules 5 to 7.

20 Allocation: all other proceedings

(1) An application of a type not referred to in other rules in this Part or in Schedule 1 or Schedule 2 shall be allocated by one or more of the persons referred to in rule 4.

(2) When deciding which level of judge to allocate such an application to, the decision must be based on consideration of the relative significance of the following factors –

(a)   the need to make the most effective and efficient use of the local judicial resource and the resource of the High Court bench that is appropriate, given the nature and type of application;

(b)   the need to avoid delay;

(c)   the need for judicial continuity;

(d)   the location of the parties or of any child relevant to the proceedings; and

(e)   complexity.

PART 6
GUIDANCE

21 Guidance on distribution of business of the family court

(1) The President of the Family Division may, after consulting the Lord Chancellor, issue guidance on the application or interpretation of Part 5.

(2) Where the Lord Chancellor determines that the guidance has significant implications for resources, it may only be issued with the agreement of the Lord Chancellor.

(3) If the Lord Chancellor does not agree the guidance, the Lord Chancellor must provide the President of the Family Division with written reasons why the Lord Chancellor does not agree the guidance.

Schedule 1
Allocation

Type of proceedings	Level of judge
1. Proceedings under –	Lay justices
(a) the Maintenance Orders (Facilities for Enforcement) Act 1920;	
(b) the Marriage Act 1949;	
(c) the Maintenance Orders Act 1950;	
(d) the Maintenance Orders Act 1958;	
(e) the Maintenance Orders (Reciprocal Enforcement) Act 1972;	
(f) the Domestic Proceedings and Magistrates' Courts Act 1978;	
(g) the Civil Jurisdiction and Judgments Act 1982;	
(h) the Family Law Act 1986, section 55A (declarations of parentage);	
(i) the Child Support Act 1991, except section 32L or appeals;	
(j) the Crime and Disorder Act 1998, section 11 (child safety order);	
(k) Council Regulation (EC) No 44/2001 (known as the Judgments Regulation);	
(l) section 34 of the Children and Families (Wales) Measure 2010;	
(m) Schedule 6 to the Civil Partnership Act 2004;	
(n) the Childcare Act 2006, except section 79;	
(o) the Human Fertilisation and Embryology Act 2008, section 54, where the child's place of birth was in England and Wales and where all respondents agree to the making of the order;	

Type of proceedings	Level of judge
(p) Council Regulation (EC) No 4/2009 (known as the Maintenance Regulation).	

2. Proceedings under –
 (a) the Married Women's Property Act 1882;
 (b) the Matrimonial Causes Act 1973;
 (c) the Matrimonial and Family Proceedings Act 1984 sections 13 and 12 (permission and substantive application) where the parties consent to permission being granted and to the substantive order sought;
 (d) the Children Act 1989, Schedule 1;
 (e) the Gender Recognition Act 2004, except appeals under section 8(1) and referrals to the court under section 8(5);
 (f) the Civil Partnership Act 2004, except under –
   (i) Schedule 6 (financial provision corresponding to provision made by the Domestic Proceedings and Magistrates' Courts Act 1978); or
   (ii) Schedule 7 (financial relief after overseas dissolution), unless the parties consent to permission being granted and to the substantive order sought.
	Judge of district judge level

3. Proceedings under – (a) the Family Law Act 1986 section 55 (declarations as to marital status), 56 (declarations as to legitimacy or legitimation) or 57 (declarations as to adoptions effected overseas); (b) the Child Support Act 1991 under section 32L (orders preventing avoidance); (c) the Human Fertilisation and Embryology Act 2008, section 54, where the child's place of birth was in England and Wales but where not all respondents agree to the making of the order.	Judge of circuit judge level

4. Proceedings under –
 (a) the Matrimonial and Family Proceedings Act 1984, sections 13 and 12 (permission and substantive application) where –
   (i) the parties do not consent to permission being granted; or
   (ii) the parties consent to permission being granted but do not consent to the substantive order sought;
 (b) the Adoption and Children Act 2002, section 60(3) (order to disclose or to prevent disclosure of information to an adopted person);
 (c) the Adoption and Children Act 2002, section 79(4) (order for Registrar General to give information);
	Judge of High Court judge level

Type of proceedings	Level of judge
(d) the Civil Partnership Act 2004, paragraphs 4 and 9 of Schedule 7 (permission and substantive application) where – (i) the parties do not consent to permission being granted; or (ii) the parties consent to permission being granted but do not consent to the substantive order sought; (e) referrals to the court under section 8(5) of the Gender Recognition Act 2004; (f) the Human Fertilisation and Embryology Act 2008, section 54, where the child's place of birth was outside of England and Wales.	
5. Proceedings under the Adoption and Children Act 2002 under – (a) section 21 (placement order); (b) section 23 (order varying a placement order); (c) section 24 (order revoking a placement order); (d) section 26 (contact order); (e) section 27 (order varying or revoking a contact order); (f) section 28(2) or (3) (order permitting the child's name to be changed or the removal of the child from the United Kingdom); (g) section 46(c) (adoption order) except where – (i) a local authority is a party to the application; (ii) the application is for an overseas adoption within the meaning given in section 87 of the Adoption and Children Act 2002; or (iii) the application is for a Convention adoption within the meaning given in section 66(1)(c) of the Adoption and Children Act 2002; (h) section 51A(2)(a) or (b)(d) (post adoption contact); (i) section 55(e) (revocation of adoption on legitimation); (j) paragraph 4 of Schedule 1 (amendment of orders).	Level of judge who is dealing with, or has dealt with, proceedings relating to the same child or, if there are or were no such proceedings, to lay justices.
6. Proceedings under the Adoption and Children Act 2002 under section 46 (adoption order) where – (a) a local authority is a party to the application; (b) the application is for an overseas adoption within the meaning given in section 87 of the Adoption and Children Act 2002; or (c) the application is for a Convention adoption within the meaning given in section 66(1)(c) of the Adoption and Children Act 2002.	Level of judge who is dealing with, or dealt with, proceedings relating to the same child or, if there are or were no such proceedings, to a judge of district judge level

Schedule 2
Remedies

Table 1

Remedies which may not be granted by lay justices in the family court

---

1. Charging order.

2. Order (known as a "freezing injunction") restraining a party from:

   (a) removing from the jurisdiction assets located there;

   (b) dealing with any assets whether located in the jurisdiction or not.

3. Interim injunction.

4. Interim declaration.

5. Order under section 34 Senior Courts Act 1981 or section 53 County Courts Act 1984, as applied to the family court under section 31E Matrimonial and Family Proceedings Act 1984, for disclosure of documents or inspection of property against a non-party.

6. Order for a specified fund to be paid into court where there is a dispute over a party's right to the fund.

7. Order permitting a party seeking to recover personal property to pay money into court pending the outcome of the proceedings and directing that, if money is paid into court, the property must be given to that party.

8. Order directing a party to provide information about the location of relevant property or assets or to provide information about relevant property or assets, which are or may be the subject of an application for a freezing injunction.

9. Order directing a party to prepare and file accounts relating to the dispute.

10. Order directing an account to be taken or enquiry to be made by the court.

11. Third party debt order.

12. Order for –

    (a) detention, custody or preservation of relevant property;

    (b) inspection of relevant property;

    (c) taking of a sample of relevant property;

    (d) carrying out an experiment on or with relevant property;

    (e) sale of relevant property which is of a perishable nature or which for any other good reason it is desirable to sell quickly;

    (f) the payment of income from relevant property until an application is decided.

13. Order authorising a person to enter any land or building in the possession of a party for the purposes of carrying out an order referred to in paragraph 12.

14. Warrant of delivery.

15. Warrant of control.

16. Warrant for the possession of land.

17. Order to deliver up goods under section 4 of the Torts (Interference with Goods) Act 1977.

Table 2

Remedies which may not be granted by lay justices or judges of district judge level in the family court

---

1. Civil restraint order (limited).

Table 3

Remedies which may not be granted by lay justices, judges of district judge level or judges of circuit judge level in the family court

---

1. Civil restraint order (extended or general), except that such orders may be granted by a Designated Family Judge or a deputy Designated Family Judge.

2. Search order requiring a party to admit another party to premises for the purposes of preserving evidence etc (section 7 Civil Procedure Act 1997).

3. Claims in respect of a judicial act under the Human Rights Act 1998.

4. Action in respect of the interference with the due administration of justice.

5. Warrants of sequestration to enforce a judgment, order or undertaking in the family court.

FAMILY COURT (CONTEMPT OF COURT) (POWERS) REGULATIONS 2014

SI 2014/833

1 Citation, commencement and interpretation

These Regulations may be cited as the Family Court (Contempt of Court) (Powers) Regulations 2014 and come into force on 22 April 2014.

2 In these Regulations –

"judge of district judge level" means –
- (a) the Senior District Judge of the Family Division;
- (b) a district judge of the Principal Registry of the Family Division;
- (c) a person appointed to act as deputy for the person holding office referred to in paragraph (b) or to act as a temporary additional officer for any such office;
- (d) is a district judge (which by virtue of section 8(1C) of the Country Courts Act 1984, here includes a deputy district judge appointed under section 8 of that Act);
- (e) a deputy district judge appointed under section 102 of the Senior Courts Act 1981;
- (f) a District Judge (Magistrates' Courts); or
- (g) any other judge of the family court authorised to sit as a judge of district judge level in the family court;

"lay justice" means a justice of the peace who is not a District Judge (Magistrates' Courts);
"judge of the family court" means a judge referred to in section 31C(1) of the Matrimonial and Family Proceedings Act 1984; and
"judge of High Court judge level" means –
- (a) a deputy judge of the High Court;
- (b) a puisne judge of the High Court;
- (c) a person who has been a judge of the Court of Appeal or a puisne judge of the High Court who may act as a judge of the family court by virtue of section 9 of the Senior Courts Act 1981;
- (d) the Senior President of Tribunals;
- (e) the Chancellor of the High Court;
- (f) an ordinary judge of the Court of Appeal (including the vice-president, if any, of either division of that court);
- (g) the President of the Queen's Bench Division;
- (h) the President of the Family Division;
- (i) the Master of the Rolls; or
- (j) the Lord Chief Justice.

3 Limits on committal powers exercisable by judges of district judge level for contempt in the face of the court in the family court

The committal powers exercisable by a judge of district judge level in the family court when dealing with an individual for –

(a)   wilfully insulting a judge of the family court, or any witness, or any officer of the court during his or her sitting or attendance in court, or in going to or returning from the court; or

(b)   wilfully interrupting the proceedings of the family court or otherwise misbehaving in court,

are limited to a period not exceeding one month.

4 Limits on committal powers exercisable by lay justices for certain types of contempt of court in the family court

The committal powers exercisable by a lay justice in the family court when dealing with an individual for contempt of court in the family court are limited to a period not exceeding –

(a)   two months where any individual disobeys a judgement or an order of, or an undertaking given to, the family court that requires that individual to do anything other than the payment of money or to abstain from doing anything; and

(b)   one month where any individual –

(i)   wilfully insults a judge of the family court, or any witness, or any officer of the court during his or her sitting or attendance in court, or in going to or returning from the court; or

(ii)   wilfully interrupts the proceedings of the family court or otherwise misbehaves in court.

5 Limits on fines for contempt of court in the family court

In any case where a judge of the family court, except a judge of High Court judge level, has the power to impose a fine when dealing with a person for contempt of court in the family court, the fine must not exceed level 5 on the standard scale.

THE FAMILY PROCEDURE (AMENDMENT NO 2) RULES 2014

SI 2014/667

1. These Rules may be cited as the Family Procedure (Amendment No. 2) Rules 2014 and come into force on 22nd April 2014.

Amendments to the Family Procedure Rules 2010

2. The Family Procedure Rules 2010 are amended in accordance with rules 3 to 44.

3. In rule 2.3 –

    (a)   in paragraph (1) –
        (i)   in the definitions of "CCR" and "RSC", delete "subject to paragraph (4)";
        (ii)   after the defined term "justices' clerk" insert –

""lay justice" means a justice of the peace who is not a District Judge (Magistrates' Courts);"; and
        (iii)   for the defined term "judge" substitute –

""judge" means –
        (a)   in the High Court, a judge or a district judge of that court (including a district judge of the principal registry) or a person authorised to act as such; and
        (b)   in the family court, a person who is –
            (i)   the Lord Chief Justice;
            (ii)   the Master of the Rolls;
            (iii) the President of the Queens Bench Division;
            (iv) the President of the Family Division;
            (v)   the Chancellor of the High Court;
            (vi) an ordinary judge of the Court of Appeal (including the vice-president, if any, of either division of that court);
            (vii) the Senior President of Tribunals;
            (viii) a puisne judge of the High Court;
            (ix) a deputy judge of the High Court;
            (x)   a person who has been a judge of the Court of Appeal or a puisne judge of the High Court who may act as a judge of the family court by virtue of section 9 of the Senior Courts Act 1981;
            (xi) the Chief Taxing Master;
            (xii) a taxing master of the Senior Courts;
            (xiii) a person appointed to act as a deputy for the person holding office referred to in sub-paragraph (xiii) or to act as a temporary additional officer for any such office;
            (xiv) a circuit judge;
            (xv) a Recorder;
            (xvi) the Senior District Judge of the Family Division;
            (xvii) a district judge of the principal registry;
            (xviii) a person appointed to act as a deputy for the person holding office referred to in sub-paragraph (xvii) or to act as a temporary additional office holder for any such office;
            (xix) a district judge;
            (xx) a deputy district judge appointed under section 102 of the Senior Courts Act 1981 or section 8 of the County Courts Act 1984;
            (xxi) a District Judge (Magistrates' Courts);

(xxii) a lay justice;

(xxiii) any other judge referred to in section 31C(1) of the 1984 Act who is authorised by the President of the Family Division to conduct particular business in the family court;";

(b) in paragraph (3), for "Subject to paragraph (4), where" substitute "Where"; and

(c) omit paragraph (4).

4. For rule 2.5(1)(b) substitute –

"(b) in relation to proceedings in the family court –

(i) by the court composed in accordance with rules made under section 31D of the 1984 Act; or

(ii) where Practice Direction 2A applies, by a single lay justice who is authorised as specified in rules made under section 31D of the 1984 Act.".

5. In rule 2.6 –

(a) in paragraph (1) –

(i) for the words before sub-paragraph (a) substitute "A single lay justice who is authorised as specified in rules made under section 31D of the 1984 Act may perform the functions of the family court – "; and

(ii) omit sub-paragraph (d);

(b) in paragraph (2), for "justice of the peace" substitute "lay justice"; and

(c) in paragraph (3), for "(1)(a), (c) and (d)" substitute "(1)(a) and (c)".

6. For rule 2.7 substitute –

"Single lay justice: power to refer to the family court

2.7. Where a single lay justice –

(a) is performing a function of the family court in accordance with rule 2.5(1)(b)(ii) or rule 2.6(1) or (2); and

(b) considers, for whatever reason, that it is inappropriate to perform the function,

the single lay justice must refer the matter to the family court.".

7. Omit rule 9.2.

8. In rule 9.14, after paragraph (2) insert –

"(2ZA) Paragraph (2A) applies where the court has determined that the procedure in this Chapter should apply to an application under Article 56 of the Maintenance Regulation or Article 10 of the 2007 Hague Convention.".

9. In rule 9.18(A1)(a) –

(a) in paragraph (iii), omit "or"; and

(b) after paragraph (iii) insert –

"(iv) Article 56 of the Maintenance Regulation; or

(v) Article 10 of the 2007 Hague Convention.".

10. After rule 9.21, insert –

"Duty to make entries in the court's register

9.21A. Where a court officer receives notice of any direction made in the High Court or family court under section 28 of the 1978 Act by virtue of which an order made under that Act or the 2004 Act ceases to have effect, particulars of the direction must be noted in the court's records.".

11. After rule 9.21A, insert –

> *"Chapter 5A*
> *Certain applications".*

12. Omit rule 9.23.

13. In Chapter 6 of Part 9, after rule 9.26B, insert –

> **"Method of making periodical payments**
>
> 9.26C. (1) This rule applies where under section 1(4) or (4A) of the Maintenance Enforcement Act 1991(8) the court orders that payments under a qualifying periodical maintenance order are to be made by a particular means.
>
> (2) The court officer will record on a copy of the order the means of payment that the court has ordered.
>
> (3) The court officer will notify in writing the person liable to make payments under the order how the payments are to be made.
>
> (4) Where under section 1(4A) of the Maintenance Enforcement Act 1991 the court orders payment to the court by a method of payment under section 1(5) of that Act, the court officer will notify the person liable to make payments under the order of sufficient details of the account into which payments should be made to enable payments to be made into that account.
>
> (5) Where payments are made to the court, the court officer will give or send a receipt to any person who makes such a payment and who asks for a receipt.
>
> (6) Where payments are made to the court, the court officer will make arrangements to make the payments to –
>
> > (a)   the person entitled to them; or
> > (b)   if the person entitled to them is a child, to the child or to the person with whom the child has his or her home.
>
> (7) The Part 18 procedure applies to an application under section 1(7) of the Maintenance Enforcement Act 1991 (application from an interested party to revoke, suspend, revive or vary the method of payment).
>
> (8) Where the court makes an order under section 1(7) of the Maintenance Enforcement Act 1991 or dismisses an application for such an order, the court officer will, as far as practicable, notify in writing all interested parties of the effect of the order and will take the steps set out in paragraphs (2), (3) and (4), as appropriate.
>
> (9) In this rule, "interested party" and "qualifying periodical maintenance order" have the meanings given in section 1(10) of the Maintenance Enforcement Act 1991.
>
> **Court officer to notify subsequent marriage or formation of civil partnership of a person entitled to payments under a maintenance order**
>
> 9.26D. (1) This rule applies where –
>
> > (a)   there is an order of a type referred to in paragraph (4) which requires payments to be made to the court or to an officer of the court; and
> > (b)   the court is notified in writing by –
> > > (i)   the person entitled to receive payments under the order;
> > > (ii)   the person required to make payments under the order; or
> > > (iii)   the personal representative of such a person,
>
> that the person entitled to receive payments under the order has subsequently married or formed a civil partnership.

(2) The court officer will, where practicable, notify in writing the courts referred to in paragraph (3) of the notification of the subsequent marriage or formation of a civil partnership.

(3) The courts to be notified are –

   (a)   any other court which has made an order of a type referred to in paragraph (4);
   (b)   in the case of a provisional order made under section 3 of the 1920 Act or section 3 of the 1972 Act, the court which confirmed the order;
   (c)   if an order of a type referred to in paragraph (4) has been transmitted abroad for registration under section 2 of the 1920 Act or section 2 of the 1972 Act, the court in which the order is registered; and
   (d)   any other court in which an application to enforce the order has been made.

(4) The orders are –

   (a)   those to which the following provisions apply –
         (i)   section 38 of the 1973 Act;
         (ii)   section 4(2) of the 1978 Act;
         (iii) paragraph 65 of Schedule 5 to the 2004 Act; and
         (iv)   paragraph 26(2) of Schedule 6 to the 2004 Act; and
   (b)   an attachment of earnings order made to secure payments under an order referred to in sub-paragraph (a).

(5) In this rule –

   "the 1920 Act" means the Maintenance Orders (Facilities for Enforcement) Act 1920; and
   "the 1972 Act" means the Maintenance Orders (Reciprocal Enforcement) Act 1972.

Enforcement and apportionment where periodical payments are made under more than one order

9.26E. (1) This rule applies where periodical payments are required to be made by a payer to a payee under more than one periodical payments order.

(2) Proceedings for the recovery of payments under more than one order may be made in one application by the payee, which must indicate the payments due under each order.

(3) Paragraphs (4) and (5) apply where any sum paid to the court on any date by a payer who is liable to make payments to the court under two or more periodical payments orders is less than the total sum that the payer is required to pay to the court on that date in respect of those orders.

(4) The payment made will be apportioned between the orders in proportion to the amounts due under each order over a period of one year.

(5) If, as a result of the apportionment referred to in paragraph (4), the payments under any periodical payments order are no longer in arrears, the residue shall be applied to the amount due under the other order or, if there is more than one other order, shall be apportioned between the other orders in accordance with paragraph (4).

(6) In this rule –

   "payee" means a person entitled to receive payments under a periodical payments order; and
   "payer" means a person required to make payments under a periodical payments order.".

14. In rule 10.6(1), for sub-paragraph (b) and the words in parentheses that follow it, substitute –

   "(b)   where the order is made without notice –
         (i)   a copy of the application together with any statement supporting it; and

(ii)   where the order is made by lay justices, a copy of the written record of the reasons for the court's decision.

(Rule 27.2 makes provision in respect of lay justices giving written reasons in the family court.)".

15. For rules 10.12 and 10.13 substitute –

"Enforcement of an order: requirement for a penal notice

10.12. At the time when the order is drawn up, the court officer will –

(a)   where the order made is (or includes) a non-molestation order; or

(b)   where the order made is an occupation order and the court so directs,

issue a copy of the order, endorsed with or incorporating a notice as to the consequences of disobedience, for service in accordance with rule 10.6.

(For enforcement of an order by way of committal see Part 37 (rule 37.9 concerns the requirement for a judgment or order to do or not to do an act to contain a penal notice if it is to be enforceable by way of committal).)

Enforcement of an undertaking

10.13. Chapter 2 of Part 37 applies with the necessary modifications where an application is made to commit a person for breach of an undertaking.

(For enforcement of an undertaking by way of committal see rule 37.4(4).)".

16. For rule 11.15 substitute –

"Enforcement of orders and undertakings

11.15. (1) At the time when the order is drawn up, the court officer will, where the order made is (or includes a forced marriage protection order, issue a copy of the order, endorsed with or incorporating a notice as to the consequences of disobedience, for service in accordance with rule 11.7.

(2) Chapter 2 of Part 37 applies with the necessary modifications where an application is made to commit a person for breach of an undertaking.

(For enforcement of an order generally see Part 37 (rule 37.9 concerns the requirement for a judgment or order to do or not to do an act to contain a penal notice if it is to be enforceable by way of committal). For undertakings, see rule 37.4(4).)".

17. In rule 23.9 –

(a)   in the heading, omit "in magistrates' courts"; and

(b)   for "in a magistrates' court" substitute "in the family court before a lay justice or lay justices".

18. In rule 25.20(1), omit "or section 63 of the County Courts Act 1984".

19. In rule 27.2 –

(a)   in the heading, for "of the magistrates' courts" substitute ": proceedings before a lay justice or justices";

(b)   in paragraph (1) for "in a magistrates' court" substitute "in the family court before a lay justice or justices";

(c)   in paragraph (5) –

    (i)   in sub-paragraph (a) before "justice" insert "lay"; and

    (ii)   in sub-paragraph (b), before "justice" insert "lay";

(d)   in paragraph (7), before "justices" insert "lay"; and

(e)   omit paragraph (10).

20. After rule 29.18 insert –

"Allocation of proceedings to another level of judge

29.19. (1) Paragraphs (2) and (3) apply where there has been allocation without a hearing.

(2) A party may request the court to reconsider allocation at a hearing.

(3) Unless the court directs otherwise, a party may make a request referred to in paragraph (2) –

  (a)   at any hearing where that party first has notice of allocation; or
  (b)   in writing no later than 2 days before the first hearing in the proceedings after the party receives notice of allocation.

(4) When the party requests the court to reconsider allocation in accordance with paragraph (3)(b), the party must at the same time notify other parties of the request in writing.

(5) The court may reconsider allocation of its own initiative.

(6) Rule 4.3 does not apply to allocation without a hearing.

(7) In this rule "allocation" means allocation of proceedings other than appeal proceedings to a level of judge.".

21. In rule 30.1 –

  (a)   in paragraph 1(b), for "a county court" substitute "the family court";
  (b)   in the words in parentheses following paragraph (2), for "47.20 to 47.23" substitute "47.21 to 47.24"; and
  (c)   in paragraph (3), after the definition of "appellant" insert –

    ""costs judge" means –
      (a)   the Chief Taxing Master;
      (b)   a taxing master of the Senior Courts; or
      (c)   a person appointed to act as deputy for the person holding office referred to in paragraph (b) or to act as temporary additional officer for any such office;

    "district judge" means –
      (a)   the Senior District Judge of the Family Division
      (b)   a district judge of the Principal Registry of the Family Division;
      (c)   a person appointed to act as deputy for the person holding office referred to in paragraph (b) or to act as temporary additional officer for any such office;
      (d)   a district judge;
      (e)   a deputy district judge appointed under section 102 of the Senior Courts Act 1981 or section 8 of the County Courts Act 1984; or
      (f)   a District Judge (Magistrates' Courts);".

22. In rule 30.3 –

  (a)   in paragraph (5A), after "judge of the High Court or" insert "in the family court, a judge of the High Court or "; and
  (b)   omit paragraph (9).

23. In rule 30.4 –

  (a)   for paragraph (3) substitute –

    "(3) Where the appeal is against –

      (a)   a case management decision; or
      (b)   an order under section 38(1) of the 1989 Act,

the appellant must file the appellant's notice within 7 days beginning with the date of the decision of the lower court."; and

(b)   omit paragraph (5)(e).

24. In rule 30.5 –

(a)   in paragraph (4), for "A respondent's notice" substitute "Subject to paragraph (4A), a respondent's notice"; and

(b)   after paragraph (4) insert –

"(4A) Where the appeal is against a case management decision, a respondent's notice must be filed within –

> (a)   such period as may be directed by the lower court; or
> (b)   where the court makes no such direction, 7 days beginning with the date referred to in paragraph (5).".

25. In rule 30.13, for paragraph (2) substitute –

"(2) Paragraph (1) does not allow an application for permission to appeal to be transferred to the Court of Appeal.".

26. In rule 30.14(3), for "a county court" substitute "the family court".

27. In rule 32.10A –

(a)   in paragraph (4) –
> (i)   after "Where" insert "under section 1(4A) of the Maintenance Enforcement Act 1991"; and
> (ii)   for "section 1(5) of the Maintenance Enforcement Act 1991" substitute "section 1(5) of that Act";

(b)   in paragraph (5), for the words after "1991" substitute "(application from an interested party to revoke, suspend, revive or vary a means of payment order)";

(c)   for paragraph (6) substitute –

"(6) Where the court makes an order under section 1(7) of the Maintenance Enforcement Act 1991 or dismisses an application for such an order, the court officer will, as far as practicable, notify in writing all interested parties of the effect of the order and will take the steps set out in paragraphs (2), (3) and (4), as appropriate.

(7) In this rule, "interested party" has the meaning given in section 1(10) of the Maintenance Enforcement Act 1991.".

28. In rule 33.1 –

(a)   in paragraph (1), for "a county court" substitute "the family court"; and

(b)   in paragraph (2) –
> (i)   for "Part 50" substitute "Parts 50, 83 and 84";
> (ii)   omit the words in brackets; and
> (iii) for "a county court" substitute "the family court".

29. In rule 33.2 –

(a)   omit "and" at the end of paragraph (a); and

(b)   after paragraph (a) insert –

"(a1) in rule 70.3(1), for "County Court" there is substituted "family court"; and".

30. In rule 33.4, for "a designated county court" in all three places where it occurs substitute "the family court".

31. Omit rules 33.5 to 33.8, and insert in their place –

"Enforcement of orders by way of committal

33.5. Part 37 applies as appropriate for the enforcement by way of committal of an order made in family proceedings.".

32. In rule 33.10, for paragraph (1) substitute –

"(1) An application for the issue of a judgment summons may be made –

    (a)   in the case of an order of the High Court, to –
        (i)   the principal registry;
        (ii)   a district registry; or
        (iii)   the family court,
        whichever in the opinion of the judgment creditor is most convenient, and if to the family court, to whichever Designated Family Judge area is in the opinion of the judgment creditor most convenient; and

    (b)   in the case of an order of the family court, to whichever Designated Family Judge area is in the opinion of the judgment creditor most convenient,

having regard (in any case) to the place where the debtor resides or carries on business and irrespective of the location of the court or registry in which the order was made.

> (For the way in which information will be provided to enable Designated Family Judge areas and Designated Family Courts to be identified, see Practice Direction 34E.)".

33. In rule 33.11(3), after "court", insert "building".

34. In rule 33.14(1)(b), for "a county court" substitute "the family court".

35. In rule 33.17(5)(b), for "county court within the district of" substitute "Designated Family Judge area within".

36. Omit rule 33.18.

37. Omit rule 33.19 and insert in its place –

Application of CCR Order 27: enforcement of a judgment debt

33.19. (1) Order 27 of the CCR applies to proceedings under this Part for the enforcement of a judgment debt with the following modifications.

(2) In Order 27 rule 3 –

    (a)   in paragraph (1), for "County Court hearing centre" there is substituted "Designated Family Court for the Designated Family Judge area";
    (b)   in paragraph (2), for "County Court hearing centre in" there is substituted "Designated Family Court for the Designated Family Judge area within";
    (c)   in paragraph (3) –
        (i)   for "County Court hearing centre" there is substituted "Designated Family Court for the Designated Family Judge area";
        (ii)   for the words from "at another" to the end there is substituted "within another Designated Family Judge area, the application shall be made to the Designated Family Court for that other Designated Family Judge area."; and
    (d)   paragraph (4) is omitted.

(3) In Order 27 rule 7 –

    (a)   in paragraph (3), for "District Judge" in each place where it occurs there is substituted "court";
    (b)   in paragraph (4) –
        (i)   for "District Judge who" there is substituted "court which"; and
        (ii)   for "if the District Judge" there is substituted "if it";
    (c)   in paragraph (5) –

(i)   for "District Judge does" there is substituted "court does"; and
(ii)   for "they" there is substituted "it"; and

(d)   in paragraph (7), for "District Judge" in each place where it occurs there is substituted "court".

(4) In Order 27 rule 10 –

(a)   in paragraph (2), for "District Judge" there is substituted "court"; and
(b)   in paragraph (3) –
(i)   the words "or a magistrates' court" and "or, as the case may be, the magistrates' court" are omitted; and
(ii)   for "County Court" there is substituted "family court".

(5) In Order 27 rule 11, for "District Judge" there is substituted "court".

(6) In Order 27 rule 14, for paragraphs (1) and (2) there is substituted –

"(1) Where the question of making a consolidated attachment order falls to be considered in a Designated Family Judge area which is not the area in which an attachment of earnings order has been made to secure the payment of a judgment debt by the debtor, the family court sitting in the last-mentioned area shall, at the request of the family court sitting in the first-mentioned area, transfer to that court the matter in which the attachment of earnings order was made.

(2) Without prejudice to paragraph (1), if in the opinion of the family court sitting in a Designated Family Judge area in which an attachment of earnings order has been made the matter could more conveniently proceed in another Designated Family Judge area (whether by reason of the debtor having become resident in that other Designated Family Judge area or otherwise), the court may order the matter to be transferred to that other area."

(7) In Order 27 rule 16, in paragraph (10, for "the County Court, the District Judge" there is substituted "the family court, the court".

(8) In Order 27 rule 19, in paragraph (3D), for "District Judge who" there is substituted "court which".

Application of CCR Order 27: enforcement of a maintenance order

33.19A. (1) Order 27 of the CCR applies to proceedings under this Part for the enforcement of a maintenance order as it applies to proceedings for the enforcement of a judgment debt, subject to the following provisions of this rule –

(a)   paragraphs (2) and (3) in relation to failure by a debtor under a maintenance order to attend court and the application of section 23 of the Attachment of Earnings Act 1971; and
(b)   paragraphs (4) to (11) in relation to applications for an attachment of earnings order to secure payments under a maintenance order, the making of such attachment of earnings orders and their discharge.

(2) An order under section 23(1) of the Attachment of Earnings Act 1971 for the attendance of the debtor at an adjourned hearing for an attachment of earnings order to secure payments under a maintenance order must –

(a)   be served on the debtor personally not less than 5 days before the day fixed for the adjourned hearing; and
(b)   direct that any payments made thereafter must be paid into the court and not direct to the judgment creditor.

(3) An application by a debtor for the revocation of an order committing the debtor to prison and (if already in custody) for discharge under section 23(7) of the Attachment of Earnings Act 1971 must –

(a)   be made to court in writing without notice to any other party, stating the reasons for the debtor's failure to attend the court or refusal to be sworn or to give evidence (as the case may be) and containing an undertaking by the debtor to attend the court or to be sworn or to give evidence when next required to do so; and

(b)   if the debtor has already been lodged in prison, be attested by the governor of the prison (or any other officer of the prison not below the rank of principal officer), and in any other case be made in a witness statement or affidavit,

and before dealing with the application the court may, if it thinks fit, cause notice to be given to the judgment creditor that the application has been made and of a date and time when the judgment creditor may attend and be heard.

(4) An application for an attachment of earnings order to secure payments under a maintenance order must be made to the Designated Family Judge area within which the order was made.

(5) Any application under section 32 of the 1973 Act for permission to enforce the payment of arrears which became due more than 12 months before the application for an attachment of earnings order must be made in the application for the attachment of earnings order.

(6) Notice of the application, together with a form of reply in the appropriate form, must be served on the debtor in the manner set out in rule 6.23 and –

(a)   service of the notice must be effected not less than 21 days before the hearing, but may be effected at any time before the hearing on the applicant satisfying the court by witness statement or affidavit that the respondent is about to move from the address for service; and

(b)   rule 5(2A) of CCR Order 27 does not apply.

(7) An application by the debtor for an attachment of earnings order to secure payments under a maintenance order may be made on the making of the maintenance order or of an order varying the maintenance order, and rules 4 and 5 of CCR Order 27 do not apply in such a case.

(8) Rule 7 of CCR Order 27 has effect as if for paragraphs (1) to (8) of that rule there were substituted the following paragraph –

> "(1) An application for an attachment of earnings order to secure payments under a maintenance order shall be heard in private."

(9) Where an attachment of earnings order made by the High Court designates the court officer of the family court as the collecting officer, that officer shall, on receipt of a certified copy of the order from the court officer of the High Court, send to the person to whom the order is directed a notice as to the mode of payment.

(10) Where an attachment of earnings order made by the family court to secure payments under a maintenance order ceases to have effect and –

(a)   the related maintenance order was made by that court; or

(b)   the related maintenance order was an order of the High Court and –

(i)   the court officer of the family court has received notice of the cessation from the court officer of the High Court; or

(ii)   a committal order has been made in the family court for the enforcement of the related maintenance order, the court officer of the family court shall give notice of the cessation to the person to whom the attachment of earnings order was directed.

(11) Rule 13 of CCR Order 27 has effect as if for paragraphs (4) to (7) there were substituted the following paragraph –

> "(4) Where the family court has made an attachment of earnings order and it appears to the court that the related maintenance order has ceased to have effect (whether by virtue of the terms of the maintenance order or under section 238 of the 1973 Act or otherwise), the court may discharge or vary the attachment of earnings order."".

38. In the heading to Chapter 4 of Part 33, for "Execution" substitute "Control".

39. In rule 33.20 –

(a)   for "execution" substitute "control"; and
(b)   for "district judge" substitute "court".

40. Omit rule 33.21.

41. For rule 33.23 substitute –

"Application of the CPR

33.23. (1) Part 71 of the CPR applies to proceedings under this Part with the following modifications.

(2) In rule 71.2, for sub-paragraph (b) substitute –

> "(b)   must be –
> (i)   issued in the High Court if the High Court made the judgment or order which it is sought to enforce; or
> (ii)   made to the Designated Family Court for the Designated Family Judge area within which the judgment or order was made,
> except that if the proceedings have since been transferred to a different court or Designated Family Judge area, it must be issued in that court or made to that area."".

42. In rule 33.24 –

(a)   after paragraph (1), insert –

> "(1A) In rule 72.3, for paragraph (1)(b) there is substituted –
>
> "(b)   must be issued in the court which made the judgment or order which it is sought to enforce, or made to the Designated Family Judge area within which that judgment or order was made, except that if the proceedings have since been transferred to a different court or Designated Family Judge area, it must be issued in that court or made to that area.""; and

(b)   for paragraph (3) substitute –

> "(3) In rule 72.7 –
>
> (a)   in paragraph (2)(a), after "the Royal Courts of Justice" there is inserted "or the principal registry"; and
> (b)   in paragraph (2)(b), for "in County Court proceedings, to any County Court hearing centre" there is substituted "in family court proceedings, to any Designated Family Judge area"."

43. In rule 33.25, for paragraph (4) substitute –

> "(4) In rule 73.3, in paragraph (2) –

(a) for the words from "court" to "enforce" there is substituted "court which made the judgment or order which it is sought to enforce, or made to the Designated Family Judge area within which that judgment or order was made";

(b) in sub-paragraph (a), for the words from "different court" to the end there is substituted "different court or Designated Family Judge area, in which case the application must be issued in that court or made to that area";

(c) sub-paragraphs (b) and (c) are omitted;

(d) in sub-paragraph (d), for "County Court" there is substituted "family court"; and

(e) sub-paragraph (e) is omitted.".

44. After Part 36, insert Part 37 (Applications and proceedings in relation to contempt of court) as set out in the Schedule to these Rules.

Transitional and saving provision

45. (1) Subject to paragraphs (2) and (3), the Family Procedure Rules 2010 as amended by these Rules shall apply to any proceedings which were commenced but not disposed of before these Rules came into force.

(2) The court may in any such proceedings give any directions for the purpose of ensuring that the proceedings are dealt with fairly and, in particular, may –

(a) apply any provision in rules of court which applied to the proceedings before these Rules came into force; or

(b) disapply provisions of the Family Procedure Rules 2010 as amended by these Rules.

(3) Part 30 of the Family Procedure Rules applies to appeals or applications for permission to appeal against decisions made before these Rules come into force as if the amendments made to that Part by rule 21(c) (in so far as it refers to a District Judge (Magistrates' Courts)) and rules 23(a) and 24(a) and (b) of these Rules had not been made.

SCHEDULE

"PART 37

APPLICATIONS AND PROCEEDINGS IN RELATION TO CONTEMPT OF COURT

CONTENTS OF THIS PART

CHAPTER 1
Scope and interpretation

37.1 Scope

(1) This Part sets out the procedure in respect of –

(a) committal for breach of a judgment, order or undertaking to do or abstain from doing an act;

(b)   contempt in the face of the court;

(c)   committal for interference with the due administration of justice;

(d)   committal for making a false statement of truth;

(e)   sequestration to enforce a judgment, order or undertaking; and

(f)   the penal, contempt and disciplinary provisions of the County Courts Act 1984.

(2) So far as applicable, and with the necessary modifications, this Part applies in relation to an order requiring a person –

(a)   guilty of contempt of court; or

(b)   punishable by virtue of any enactment as if that person had been guilty of contempt of the High Court,

to pay a fine or to give security for good behaviour, as it applies in relation to an order of committal.

(3) Unless otherwise stated, this Part applies to procedure in the High Court and family court.

37.2 Saving for other powers

(1) This Part is concerned only with procedure and does not itself confer upon the court the power to make an order for –

(a)   committal;

(b)   sequestration; or

(c)   the imposition of a fine in respect of contempt of court.

(2) Nothing in this Part affects the power of the court to make an order requiring a person –

(a)   guilty of contempt of court; or

(b)   punishable by virtue of any enactment as if that person had been guilty of contempt of the High Court,

to pay a fine or to give security for good behaviour.

(3) Nothing in this Part affects any statutory or inherent power of the court to make a committal order of its own initiative against a person guilty of contempt of court.

37.3 Interpretation

In this Part –

(a)   "applicant" means a person making –

    (i)   an application for permission to make a committal application;

    (ii)   a committal application; or

    (iii)   an application for a writ of sequestration;

(b)   "committal application" means any application for an order committing a person to prison;

(c)   "judge of High Court judge level" means a person in sub-paragraphs (i) to (x) of paragraph (b) in the definition of "judge" in rule 2.3;

(d)   "respondent" means a person –

    (i)   against whom a committal application is made or is intended to be made; or

    (ii)   against whose property it is sought to issue a writ of sequestration;

(e)   "undertaking" means an undertaking to the court; and

(f)   references to a writ of sequestration are, in relation to the family court, to be read as references to a warrant containing provision corresponding to that which may be contained in a writ of sequestration.

(See section 31E of the Matrimonial and Family Proceedings Act 1984(12) (Family court has High Court and county court powers), in particular subsections (1) and (2) of that section.)

CHAPTER 2
Committal for breach of a judgment, order or undertaking to do or abstain from doing an act

37.4 Enforcement of judgment, order or undertaking to do or abstain from doing an act

(1) If a person –

(a)   required by a judgment or order to do an act does not do it within the time fixed by the judgment or order; or

(b)   disobeys a judgment or order not to do an act,

then, subject to the Debtors Acts 1869 and 1878 and to the provisions of these Rules, the judgment or order may be enforced under the court's powers by an order for committal.

(2) If the time fixed by the judgment or order for doing an act has been varied by a subsequent order, then references in paragraph (1)(a) to the time fixed are references to the time fixed by that subsequent order or agreement.

(3) If the person referred to in paragraph (1) is a company or other corporation, the committal order may be made against any director or other officer of that company or corporation.

(4) So far as applicable, and with the necessary modifications, this Chapter applies to undertakings given by a party as it applies to judgments or orders.

(Specific provision in relation to judgment summonses is contained in Chapter 2 of Part 33.)

37.5 Requirement for service of a copy of the judgment or order and time for service

(1) Unless the court dispenses with service under rule 37.8, a judgment or order may not be enforced under rule 37.4 unless a copy of it has been served on the person required to do or not do the act in question, and in the case of a judgment or order requiring a person to do an act –

(a)   the copy has been served before the end of the time fixed for doing the act, together with a copy of any order fixing that time;

(b)   where the time for doing the act has been varied by a subsequent order, a copy of that subsequent order has also been served; and

(c)   where the judgment or order was made pursuant to an earlier judgment or order requiring the act to be done, a copy of the earlier judgment or order has also been served.

(2) Where the person referred to in paragraph (1) is a company or other corporation, a copy of the judgment or order must also be served on a director or officer of the company or corporation before the end of the time fixed for doing the act.

(3) Copies of the judgment or order and any orders or agreements fixing or varying the time for doing an act must be served in accordance with rule 37.6 or 37.7, or in accordance with an order for alternative service made under rule 37.8(2)(b).

37.6 Method of service – copies of judgments or orders

Subject to rules 37.7 and 37.8, copies of judgments or orders and any orders or agreements fixing or varying the time for doing an act must be served personally.

37.7 Method of service – copies of undertakings

(1) Subject to paragraph (2) and rule 37.8, a copy of any document recording an undertaking will be delivered by the court to the person who gave the undertaking –

  (a)   by handing to that person a copy of the document before that person leaves the court building;
  (b)   by posting a copy to that person at the residence or place of business of that person where this is known; or
  (c)   by posting a copy to that person's solicitor.

(2) If delivery cannot be effected in accordance with paragraph (1), the court officer will deliver a copy of the document to the party for whose benefit the undertaking was given and that party must serve it personally on the person who gave the undertaking as soon as practicable.

(3) Where the person referred to in paragraph (1) is a company or other corporation, a copy of the judgment or order must also be served on a director or officer of the company or corporation.

37.8 Dispensation with personal service

(1) In the case of a judgment or order requiring a person not to do an act, the court may dispense with service of a copy of the judgment or order in accordance with rules 37.5 to 37.7 if it is satisfied that the person has had notice of it –

  (a)   by being present when the judgment or order was given or made; or
  (b)   by being notified of its terms by telephone, email or otherwise.

(2) In the case of any judgment or order the court may –

  (a)   dispense with service under rules 37.5 to 37.7 if the court thinks it just to do so; or
  (b)   make an order in respect of service by an alternative method or at an alternative place.

37.9 Requirement for a penal notice on judgments and orders

(1) Subject to paragraph (2), a judgment or order to do or not do an act may not be enforced under rule 37.4 unless there is prominently displayed, on the front of the copy of the judgment or order served in accordance with this Chapter, a warning to the person required to do or not do the act in question that disobedience to the order would be a contempt of court punishable by imprisonment, a fine or sequestration of assets.

(2) An undertaking to do or not do an act which is contained in a judgment or order may be enforced under rule 37.4 notwithstanding that the judgment or order does not contain the warning described in paragraph (1).

(3) In the case of –

  (a)   a section 8 order (within the meaning of section 8(2) of the Children Act 1989);
  (b)   an order under section 14A, 14B(2)(b), 14C(3)(b) or 14D of the Children Act 1989 enforceable by committal order,

the court may, on the application of the person entitled to enforce the order, direct that the court officer issue a copy of the order, endorsed with or incorporating a notice as to the consequences of disobedience, for service in accordance with this rule, and no copy of the order shall be issued with any such notice endorsed or incorporated save in accordance with such a direction.

37.10 How to make the committal application

(1) A committal application is made by an application notice using the Part 18 procedure in the proceedings in which the judgment or order was made or the undertaking was given.

(2) Where the committal application is made against a person who is not an existing party to the proceedings, it is made against that person by an application notice using the Part 18 procedure.

(3) The application notice must –

    (a)   set out in full the grounds on which the committal application is made and must identify, separately and numerically, each alleged act of contempt including, if known, the date of each of the alleged acts; and

    (b)   be supported by one or more affidavits containing all the evidence relied upon.

(4) Subject to paragraph (5), the application notice and the evidence in support must be served personally on the respondent.

(5) The court may –

    (a)   dispense with service under paragraph (4) if it considers it just to do so; or

    (b)   make an order in respect of service by an alternative method or at an alternative place.

37.11 Committal for breach of a solicitor's undertaking

(1) This rule applies where an order for committal is sought in respect of a breach by a solicitor of an undertaking given by the solicitor to the court in connection with family proceedings.

(2) The applicant must obtain permission form the court before making a committal application under this rule.

(3) The application for permission must be made by filing an application notice using the Part 18 procedure.

(4) The application for permission must be supported by an affidavit setting out –

    (a)   the name, description and address of the respondent;

    (b)   the grounds on which the committal order is sought.

(5) The application for permission may be made without notice.

(6) Rules 18.10 and 18.11 do not apply.

(7) Unless the applicant makes the committal application within 14 days after permission has been granted under this rule, the permission will lapse.

CHAPTER 3
Contempt in the face of the court

37.12 Contempt in the face of the court

Where –

    (a)   contempt has occurred in the face of the court; and
    (b)   that court has power to commit for contempt,

the court may deal with the matter of its own initiative and give such directions as it thinks fit for the disposal of the matter.

CHAPTER 4
Committal for interference with the due administration of justice

37.13 Scope

(1) This Chapter regulates committal applications in relation to interference with the due administration of justice in connection with family proceedings, except where the contempt is committed in the face of the court or consists of disobedience to an order of the court or a breach of an undertaking to the court.

(2) A committal application under this Chapter may not be made without the permission of the court.

> (The procedure for applying for permission to make a committal application is set out in rule 37.15.)

> (Rules 37.16(3) and (4) make provision for cases in which both this Chapter and Chapter 5 (Committal for making a false statement of truth) may be relevant.)

37.14 Court to which application for permission under this Chapter is to be made

(1) Where the contempt of court is committed in connection with any family proceedings, the application for permission may be made only to a single judge of the Family Division.

(2) Where the contempt of court is committed otherwise than in connection with any proceedings, Part 81 of the CPR applies.

37.15 Application for permission

(1) The application for permission to make a committal application must be made using the Part 18 procedure, and the application notice must include or be accompanied by –

    (a)   a detailed statement of the applicant's grounds for making the committal application; and
    (b)   an affidavit setting out the facts and exhibiting all documents relied upon.

(2) The application notice and the documents referred to in paragraph (1) must be served personally on the respondent unless the court otherwise directs.

(3) Within 14 days of service on the respondent of the application notice, the respondent –

    (a)   must file and serve an acknowledgment of service; and
    (b)   may file and serve evidence.

(4) The court will consider the application for permission at an oral hearing, unless it considers that such a hearing is not appropriate.

(5) If the respondent intends to appear at the permission hearing referred to in paragraph (4), the respondent must give 7 days' notice in writing of such intention to the court and any other party and at the same time provide a written summary of the submissions which the respondent proposes to make.

(6) Where permission to proceed is given, the court may give such directions as it thinks fit, and may –

    (a)   transfer the proceedings to another court; or

    (b)   direct that the application be listed for hearing before a single judge or a Divisional Court.

CHAPTER 5
Committal for making a false statement of truth (Rule 17.6)

37.16 Scope and interaction with other Chapters of this Part

(1) This Chapter contains rules about committal applications in relation to making, or causing to be made, a false statement in a document verified by a statement of truth, without an honest belief in its truth.

(2) Where the committal application relates only to a false statement of truth, this Chapter applies.

(3) Where the committal application relates to both –

    (a)   a false statement of truth; and

    (b)   breach of a judgment, order or undertaking to do or abstain from doing an act,

then Chapter 2 (Committal for breach of a judgment, order or undertaking to do or abstain from doing an act) applies, but subject to paragraph (4).

(4) To the extent that a committal application referred to in paragraph (3) relates to a false statement of truth –

    (a)   the applicant must obtain the permission of the court in accordance with rule 37.17; or

    (b)   the court may direct that the matter be referred to the Attorney General with a request that the Attorney General consider whether to bring proceedings for contempt of court.

37.17 Committal application in relation to a false statement of truth

(1) A committal application in relation a false statement of truth in connection with family proceedings in the High Court may be made only –

    (a)   with the permission of the court dealing with the proceedings in which the false statement was made; or

    (b)   by the Attorney General.

(2) A committal application in relation to a false statement of truth in connection with proceedings in the family court may be made only –

    (a)   with the permission of a single judge of the Family Division; or

    (b)   by the Attorney General.

(3) Where permission is required under paragraph (1)(a) or (2)(a), rule 37.15 applies.

(Under rule 37.15(6)(b), the court granting permission may direct that the application be listed before a single judge or a Divisional Court.)

(4) The court may direct that the matter be referred to the Attorney General with a request that the Attorney General consider whether to bring proceedings for contempt of court.

(5) Where the committal application is made by the Attorney General, the application may be made to a single judge or a Divisional Court.

CHAPTER 6
Writ of sequestration to enforce a judgment, order or undertaking

37.18 Scope

This Chapter contains rules about applications for a writ of sequestration to enforce a judgment, order or undertaking.

37.19 Writ of sequestration to enforce a judgment, order or undertaking

(1) If –

(a)   a person required by a judgment or order to do an act does not do it within the time fixed by the judgment or order; or

(b)   a person disobeys judgment or order not to do an act,

then, subject to the provisions of these Rules and if the court permits, the judgment or order may be enforced by a writ of sequestration against the property of that person.

(2) If the time fixed by the judgment or order for doing an act has been varied by a subsequent order, references in paragraph (1)(a) to the time fixed are references to the time fixed by that subsequent order.

(3) If the person referred to in paragraph (1) is a company or other corporation, the writ of sequestration may in addition be issued against the property of any director or other officer of that company or corporation.

(4) So far as applicable, and with the necessary modifications, the Chapter applies to undertakings given by a party as it applies to judgments or orders.

37.20 Requirement for service of a copy of the judgment or order and time for service

(1) Unless the court dispenses with service under rule 37.23, a judgment or order may not be enforced by writ of sequestration unless a copy of it has been served on the person required to do or not do the act in question, and in the case of a judgment or order requiring a person to act –

(a)   the copy has been served before the end of the time fixed for doing the act, together with a copy of any order fixing that time;

(b)   where the time for doing the act has been varied by a subsequent order, a copy of that subsequent order has also been served; and

(c)   where the judgment or order was made pursuant to an earlier judgment or order requiring the act to be done, a copy of the earlier judgment or order has also been served.

(2) Where the person referred to in paragraph (1) is a company or other corporation, a copy of the judgment or order must also be served on a director or officer of the company or corporation before the end of the time fixed for doing the act.

(3) Copies of the judgment or order and any orders or agreements fixing or varying the time for doing an act must be served in accordance with rule 37.21 or 37.22, or in accordance with an order for alternative service made under rule 37.23(2)(b).

37.21 Method of service – copies of judgments or orders

Subject to rules 37.22 and 37.23, copies of judgments or order and any orders or agreements fixing or varying the time for doing an act must be served personally.

37.22 Method of service – copies of undertakings

(1) Subject to paragraph (2) and rule 37.23, a copy of any document recording an undertaking will be delivered by the court to the person who gave the undertaking –

    (a)   by handing to that person a copy of the document before that person leaves the court building;

    (b)   by posting a copy to that person at the residence or place of business of that person where this is known; or

    (c)   by posting a copy to that person's solicitor.

(2) If delivery cannot be effected in accordance with paragraph (1), the court officer will deliver a copy of the document to the party for whose benefit the undertaking was given, and that party must serve it personally on the person who gave the undertaking as soon as practicable.

(3) Where the person referred to in paragraph (1) is a company or other corporation, a copy of the judgment or order must also be served on a director or officer of the company or corporation.

37.23 Dispensation with personal service

(1) In the case of a judgment or order requiring a person to do or not do an act, the court may dispense with service of a copy of the judgment or order in accordance with rules 37.20 to 37.22 if it is satisfied that the person has had notice of it –

    (a)   by being present when the judgment or order was given or made; or

    (b)   by being notified of its terms by telephone, email or otherwise.

(2) In the case of any judgment or order the court may –

    (a)   dispense with service under rules 37.20 to 37.22 if the court thinks it just to do so; or

    (b)   make an order in respect of service by an alternative method or at an alternative place.

37.24 Requirement for a penal notice on judgments and orders

(1) Subject to paragraph (2), a judgment or order to do or not do an act may not be enforced by a writ of sequestration unless there is prominently displayed, on the front of the copy of the judgment or order served in accordance with this Chapter, a warning to the person required to do or not do the act in question that disobedience to the order would be a contempt of court punishable by imprisonment, a fine or sequestration of assets.

(2) An undertaking to do or not do an act which is contained in a judgment or order may be enforced by a writ of sequestration notwithstanding that the judgment or order does not contain the warning described in paragraph (1).

37.25 How to make an application for permission to issue a writ of sequestration

(1) An application for permission to issue a writ of sequestration must be made –

    (a)   in the High Court, to a single judge of the Family Division; or

    (b)   in the family court, to a judge of High Court judge level.

(2) An application for permission to issue a writ of sequestration must be made by filing an application notice using the Part 18 procedure.

(3) The application notice must –

    (a)   set out in full the grounds on which the committal application is made and must identify, separately and numerically, each alleged act of contempt including, if known, the date of each of the alleged acts; and

    (b)   be supported by one or more affidavits containing all the evidence relied upon.

(4) Subject to paragraph (5), the application notice and the evidence in support must be served personally on the respondent.

(5) The court may –

    (a)   dispense with service under paragraph (4) if it considers it just to do so; or

    (b)   make an order in respect of service by an alternative method or at an alternative place.

37.26 Form of writ of sequestration

A writ of sequestration must be in Form No. 67 as set out in Practice Direction 5A (or, in the family court, in a form containing corresponding provision).

CHAPTER 7
General rules about committal applications, orders for committal and writs of sequestration

37.27 The hearing

(1) Unless the court hearing the committal application or application for sequestration otherwise permits, the applicant may not rely on –

    (a)   any grounds other than –
        (i)   those set out in the application notice; or
        (ii)   in relation to committal application under Chapter 4, the statement of grounds required by rule 37.15(1)(a) (where not included in the application notice);

    (b)   any evidence unless it has been served in accordance with the relevant Chapter of this Part or the Practice Direction supplementing this Part.

(2) At the hearing, the respondent is entitled –

    (a)   to give oral evidence, whether or not the respondent has filed or served written evidence, and, if doing so, may be cross-examined; and

    (b)   with the permission of the court, to call a witness to give evidence whether or not the witness has made an affidavit or witness statement.

(3) The court may require or permit any party or other person (other than the respondent) to give oral evidence at the hearing.

(4) The court may give directions requiring the attendance for cross-examination of a witness who has given written evidence.

(5) The general rule is that a committal application, application for sequestration or application for discharge from custody will be heard, and judgment given, in public, but a hearing, or any part of it, may be in private (but with the matters in paragraph (6) always stated in public) if –

(a)   publicity would defeat the object of the hearing;
(b)   it involves matters relating to national security;
(c)   it involves confidential information (including information relating to personal financial matters) and publication would damage that confidentiality;
(d)   a private hearing is necessary to protect the interests of any child or protected party;
(e)   it is a hearing of an application made without notice and it would be unjust to any respondent for there to be a public hearing; or
(f)   the court considers this to be necessary, in the interests of justice.

(6) If the court hearing an application in private decides to make a committal order against the respondent, it will in public state –

(a)   the name of the respondent;
(b)   in general terms, the nature of the contempt of court in respect of which the committal order is being made; and
(c)   the length of the period of the committal order.

(7) Where a committal order is made in the absence of the respondent, the court may on its own initiative fix a date and time when the respondent is to be brought before the court.

37.28 Power to suspend execution of a committal order

(1) The court making the committal order may also order that execution of the order will be suspended for such period or on such terms and conditions as the court may specify.

(2) Unless the court otherwise directs, the applicant must serve on the respondent a copy of any order made under paragraph (1).

37.29 Warrant of committal

(1) If a committal order is made, the order will be for the issue of a warrant of committal.

(2) Unless the court orders otherwise –

(a)   a copy of the committal order must be served on the respondent either before or at the time of the execution of the warrant of committal; or
(b)   where the warrant of committal has been signed by the judge, the committal order may be served on the respondent at any time within 36 hours after the execution of the warrant.

(3) Without further order of the court, a warrant of committal must not be enforced more than 2 years after the date on which the warrant is issued.

37.30 Discharge of a person in custody

(1) A person committed to prison for contempt of court may apply to the court to be discharged.

(2) The application must –

(a)   be in writing and attested by the governor of the prison (or any other officer of the prison not below the rank of principal officer);

(b)   show that the person committed to prison for contempt has purged, or wishes to purge, the contempt; and

(c)   be served on the person (if any) at whose instance the warrant of committal was issued at least one day before the application is made.

(3) Paragraph (2) does not apply to –

(a)   a warrant of committal to which CCR Order 27 rule 8, or CCR Order rule 4 or 14, relates;

(b)   an application made by the Official Solicitor acting with official authority for the discharge of a person in custody.

(4) If the committal order is made in the family court and –

(a)   does not direct that any application for discharge must be made to a judge; or
(b)   was made by a district judge under section 118 of the County Courts Act 1984;

the application for discharge may be made to a district judge.

(5) If the committal order is made in the High Court, the application for discharge may be made to a single judge of the Family Division.

37.31 Discharge of a person in custody where a writ of sequestration has been issued

Where –

(a)   a writ of sequestration has been issued to enforce a judgment or order;
(b)   the property is in the custody or power of the respondent;
(c)   the respondent has been committed for failing to deliver up any property or deposit it in court or elsewhere; and
(d)   the commissioners appointed by the writ of sequestration take possession of the property as if it belonged to the respondent;

then, without prejudice to rule 37.30(1) (discharge of a person in custody), the court may discharge the respondent and give such directions for dealing with the property taken by the commissioners as it thinks fit.

CHAPTER 8
Penal and disciplinary provisions under the County Courts Act 1984

37.32 Scope

(1) This Chapter applies to the family court only and contains rules in relation to the penal, contempt and disciplinary provisions of the County Courts Act 1984 as they apply to the family court.

(2) In this Chapter, "the Act" means the County Courts Act 1984.

37.33 Offences under sections 14, 92 or 118 of the Act

(1) This rule applies where it is alleged that any person has committed an offence –

(a)   under section 14 of the Act, by assaulting an officer of the court acting in the execution of the officer's duties;
(b)   under section 92 of the Act, by rescuing or attempting to rescue any goods seized in execution; or

(c)   under section 118 of the Act, by wilfully insulting a judge, juror, witness or any officer of the court or by wilfully interrupting the proceedings of the family court or otherwise misbehaving in court,

and the alleged offender has not been taken into custody and brought before the court.

(2) The court will issue a summons, which must be served on the alleged offender personally not less than 7 days before the day of the hearing stated in the summons.

(3) Rule 37.29 (warrant of committal) applies, with the necessary modifications, where an order is made under section 14, 92 or 118 of the Act committing a person to prison.

37.34 Offences under section 124 of the Act

Where a complaint is made against an officer of the court under section 124 of the Act for having lost the opportunity of levying execution, the court will issue a summons, which must be served on the alleged offender personally not less than 7 days before the date of the hearing stated in the summons.

37.35 Notice to give evidence before or after a fine is imposed under section 55 of the Act

(1) Before or after imposing a fine on any person under section 55 of the Act for disobeying a witness summons or refusing to be sworn or give evidence, the court may direct that notice be given to that person in accordance with paragraph (2).

(2) The notice must state that if the recipient of the notice can demonstrate any reason why a fine should not be or should not have been imposed, that person may give evidence –

(a)   by witness statement, affidavit or otherwise; and
(b)   on a day named in the notice.

37.36 Non-payment of fines

(1) If a fine is not paid in accordance with the order imposing it, the court officer will, as soon as reasonably possible, report the matter to a judge.

(2) Where by an order imposing a fine –

(a)   the amount of the fine is directed to be paid by instalments; and
(b)   default is made in the payment of any instalment,

the same proceedings may be taken as if default had been made in respect of the whole of the fine.

37.37 Repayment of fine

If a person pays a fine and later gives evidence to satisfy the court that, if the evidence had been given earlier, no fine or a smaller fine would have been imposed, the court may order the whole or part of the fine to be repaid.

37.38 Section 118 of the Act and the tipstaff

For the purposes of section 118 of the Act in its application to the hearing of family proceedings at the Royal Courts of Justice or the principal registry, the tipstaff is deemed to be an officer of the court."

THE FAMILY PROCEDURE (AMENDMENT NO 3) RULES 2014

SI 2014/843

Citation and commencement

1. These Rules may be cited as the Family Procedure (Amendment No. 3) Rules 2014 and come into force on 22nd April 2014.

Amendments to the Family Procedure Rules 2010

2. The Family Procedure Rules 2010(3) are amended in accordance with rules 3 to 52.

3. In rule 1.4(2)(f) for "an alternative dispute resolution" substitute "a non-court dispute resolution".

4. In rule 2.3(1) –

    (a)   after the definition of "the 2008 Act", insert –

        ""the 2014 Act" means the Children and Families Act 2014" and insert "2014 c.6" as a footnote to this definition;

    (b)   omit the definition of "alternative dispute resolution";

    (c)   after the definition of "matrimonial order" insert ""non-court dispute resolution" means methods of resolving a dispute, including mediation, other than through the normal court process;";

    (d)   after the definition of "child", insert –

        ""child arrangements order" has the meaning given to it by section 8(1) of the 1989 Act;"; and

    (e)   omit the definition of "contact order".

5. For Part 3 substitute –

"PART 3

NON-COURT DISPUTE RESOLUTION

Chapter 1
Interpretation

3.1 Interpretation

In this Part –

    "allocation" means allocation of proceedings other than appeal proceedings to a level of judge;

    "authorised family mediator" means a mediator who is –

        (a)   subject to the Family Mediation Council's code of conduct by virtue of his or her membership of a Family Mediation Council member organisation; and

(b)   certified to undertake MIAMs by the professional practice consultant who is supervising the mediator's practice and who is a member of and approved for the purpose by a Family Mediation Council member organisation;

"domestic violence" means any incident, or pattern of incidents, of controlling, coercive or threatening behaviour, violence or abuse (whether psychological, physical, sexual, financial or emotional) between the prospective applicant and another prospective party;

"family mediation information and assessment meeting" has the meaning given to it in section 10(3) of the 2014 Act.

"harm" has the meaning given to it in section 31 of the Children Act 1989;

"mediator's exemption" has the meaning given to it in Rule 3.8(2);

"MIAM" means a family mediation information and assessment meeting;

"MIAM exemption" has the meaning given to it in Rule 3.8(1);

"MIAM requirement" is the requirement in section 10(1) of the 2014 Act for a person to attend a MIAM before making a relevant family application;

"private law proceedings" has the meaning given to it in Rule 12.2;

"prospective applicant" is the person who is considering making a relevant family application;

"prospective party" is a person who would be likely to be a party to the proceedings in the relevant family application;

"prospective respondent" is a person who would be a likely respondent to the proceedings in the relevant family application; and

"relevant family application" has the meaning given to it in section 10(3) of the 2014 Act.

Chapter 2
The Court's Duty and Powers Generally

3.2 Scope of this Chapter

This Chapter contains the court's duty and powers to encourage and facilitate the use of non-court dispute resolution.

3.3 The court's duty to consider non-court dispute resolution

(1) The court must consider, at every stage in proceedings, whether non-court dispute resolution is appropriate.

(2) In considering whether non-court dispute resolution is appropriate in proceedings which were commenced by a relevant family application, the court must take into account –

(a)   whether a MIAM took place;

(b)   whether a valid MIAM exemption was claimed or mediator's exemption was confirmed; and

(c)   whether the parties attempted mediation or another form of non-court dispute resolution and the outcome of that process.

3.4 When the court will adjourn proceedings or a hearing in proceedings

(1) If the court considers that non-court dispute resolution is appropriate, it may direct that the proceedings, or a hearing in the proceedings, be adjourned for such specified period as it considers appropriate –

(a)   to enable the parties to obtain information and advice about non-court dispute resolution; and

(b)   where the parties agree, to enable non-court dispute resolution to take place.

(2) The court may give directions under this rule on an application or of its own initiative.

(3) Where the court directs an adjournment under this rule, it will give directions about the timing and method by which the parties must tell the court if any of the issues in the proceedings have been resolved.

(4) If the parties do not tell the court if any of the issues have been resolved as directed under paragraph (3), the court will give such directions as to the management of the case as it considers appropriate.

(5) The court or court officer will –

(a)   record the making of an order under this rule; and

(b)   arrange for a copy of the order to be served as soon as practicable on the parties.

(6) Where the court proposes to exercise its powers of its own initiative, the procedure set out in rule 4.3(2) to (6) applies.

Chapter 3
Family Mediation Information and Assessment Meetings (MIAMs)

3.5 Scope of this Chapter

This Chapter contains Rules about the requirement in section 10(1) of the 2014 Act to attend a MIAM.

3.6 Applications to which the MIAM requirement applies

(1) The MIAM requirement applies to any application to initiate the proceedings specified in paragraph (2), unless a MIAM exemption or a mediator's exemption applies.

(2) The specified proceedings are –

(a)   the private law proceedings relating to children specified in Practice Direction 3A; and

(b)   the proceedings for a financial remedy specified in Practice Direction 3A.

3.7 Making an application

An application to initiate any of the proceedings specified in Rule 3.8 must contain, or be accompanied by, a form containing, either –

(a)   a confirmation from an authorised family mediator that the prospective applicant has attended a MIAM;

(b)   a claim by the prospective applicant that one of the MIAM exemptions applies; or

(A list of MIAM exemptions is set out in Rule 3.8(1) below.)

(c)   a confirmation from an authorised family mediator that a mediator's exemption applies.

(A list of mediator's exemptions is set out in Rule 3.8(2) below.)

3.8 Circumstances in which the MIAM requirement does not apply (MIAM exemptions and mediator's exemptions)

The MIAM requirement does not apply if –

(1) a prospective applicant claims in the relevant form that any of the following circumstances (a "MIAM exemption") applies –

Domestic violence

    (a)   there is evidence of domestic violence, as specified in Practice Direction 3A; or

Child protection concerns

    (b)(i)   a child would be the subject of the application; and
    (ii)   that child or another child of the family who is living with that child is currently –
        (aa)   the subject of enquiries by a local authority under section 47 of the 1989 Act; or
        (ab)   the subject of a child protection plan put in place by a local authority; or

Urgency

    (c)   the application must be made urgently because –
        (i)   there is risk to the life, liberty or physical safety of the prospective applicant or his or her family or his or her home; or
        (ii)   any delay caused by attending a MIAM would cause –
            (aa)   a risk of harm to a child;
            (ab)   a risk of unlawful removal of a child from the United Kingdom, or a risk of unlawful retention of a child who is currently outside England and Wales;
            (ac)   a significant risk of a miscarriage of justice;
            (ad)   unreasonable hardship to the prospective applicant; or
            (ae)   irretrievable problems in dealing with the dispute (including the irretrievable loss of significant evidence); or
        (iii)   there is a significant risk that in the period necessary to schedule and attend a MIAM, proceedings relating to the dispute will be brought in another state in which a valid claim to jurisdiction may exist, such that a court in that other State would be seised of the dispute before a court in England and Wales; or

Previous MIAM attendance or MIAM exemption

    (d)
        (i)   in the 4 months prior to making the application, the person attended a MIAM or participated in another form of non-court dispute resolution relating to the same or substantially the same dispute; or
        (ii)   at the time of making the application, the person is participating in another form of non-court dispute resolution relating to the same or substantially the same dispute; or
    (e)
        (i)   in the 4 months prior to making the application, the person filed a relevant family application confirming that a MIAM exemption applied; and
        (ii)   that application related to the same or substantially the same dispute; or
    (f)

> (i)　　the application would be made in existing proceedings which are continuing; and
>
> (ii)　　the prospective applicant attended a MIAM before initiating those proceedings; or

(g)

> (i)　　the application would be made in existing proceedings which are continuing; and
>
> (ii)　　a MIAM exemption applied to the application for those proceedings; or

Other

(h)

> (i)　　there is evidence that the prospective applicant is bankrupt, as specified in Practice Direction 3A; and
>
> (ii)　　the proceedings would be for a financial remedy; or

(i)　　the prospective applicant does not have sufficient contact details for any of the prospective respondents to enable a family mediator to contact any of the prospective respondents for the purpose of scheduling the MIAM; or

(j)　　the application would be made without notice; or

(Paragraph 5.1 of Practice Direction 18A sets out the circumstances in which applications may be made without notice.)

(k)

> (i)　　the prospective applicant is or all of the prospective respondents are subject to a disability or other inability that would prevent attendance at a MIAM unless appropriate facilities can be offered by an authorised mediator;
>
> (i)　　the prospective applicant has contacted as many authorised family mediators as have an office within fifteen miles of his or home (or three of them if there are three or more), and all have stated that they are unable to provide such facilities; and
>
> (iii)　　the names, postal addresses and telephone numbers or e-mail addresses for such authorised family mediators, and the dates of contact, can be provided to the court if requested; or

(l)　　the prospective applicant or all of the prospective respondents cannot attend a MIAM because he or she is, or they are, as the case may be –

> (i)　　in prison or any other institution in which he or she is or they are required to be detained;
>
> (ii)　　subject to conditions of bail that prevent contact with the other person; or
>
> (iii)　　subject to a licence with a prohibited contact requirement in relation to the other person; or

(m)　　the prospective applicant or all of the prospective respondents are not habitually resident in England and Wales; or

(n)　　a child is one of the prospective parties by virtue of Rule 12.3(1); or

(o)

> (i)　　the prospective applicant has contacted as many authorised family mediators as have an office within fifteen miles of his or her home (or three of them if there are three or more), and all of them have stated that they are not available to conduct a MIAM within fifteen business days of the date of contact; and
>
> (ii)　　the names, postal addresses and telephone numbers or e-mail addresses for such authorised family mediators, and the dates of contact, can be provided to the court if requested; or

(p)   there is no authorised family mediator with an office within fifteen miles of the prospective applicant's home; or

(2) an authorised family mediator confirms in the relevant form (a "mediator's exemption") that he or she is satisfied that –

(a)   mediation is not suitable as a means of resolving the dispute because none of the respondents is willing to attend a MIAM; or

(b)   mediation is not suitable as a means of resolving the dispute because all of the respondents failed without good reason to attend a MIAM appointment; or

(c)   mediation is otherwise not suitable as a means of resolving the dispute.

3.9 Conduct of MIAMs

(1) Only an authorised family mediator may conduct a MIAM.

(2) At the MIAM, the authorised family mediator must –

(a)   provide information about the principles, process and different models of mediation, and information about other methods of non-court dispute resolution;

(b)   assess the suitability of mediation as a means of resolving the dispute;

(c)   assess whether there has been, or is a risk of, domestic violence; and

(d)   assess whether there has been, or is a risk of, harm by a prospective party to a child that would be a subject of the application.

3.10 MIAM exemption not validly claimed

(1) If a MIAM exemption has been claimed, the court will, if appropriate when making a decision on allocation, and in any event at the first hearing, inquire into whether the exemption was validly claimed.

(2) If a court finds that the MIAM exemption was not validly claimed, the court will –

(a)   direct the applicant, or direct the parties to attend a MIAM; and

(b)   if necessary, adjourn the proceedings to enable a MIAM to take place;
unless the court considers that in all the circumstances of the case, the MIAM requirement should not apply to the application in question.

(3) In making a decision under Rule 3.10(2), the court will have particular regard to –

(a)   any applicable time limits;

(b)   the reason or reasons why the MIAM exemption was not validly claimed;

(c)   the applicability of any other MIAM exemptions; and

(d)   the number and nature of issues that remain to be resolved in the proceedings."

6. In rule 7.8(2) –

(a)   at the end of sub-paragraph (a), insert "and";

(b)   in sub-paragraph (b) for "; and" substitute "."; and

(c)   omit sub-paragraph (c).

7. In rule 7.12 –

(a)   omit paragraph (7); and

(b)   in paragraph (9) omit the words after "application".

8. In rule 7.19(4) –

(a)   in sub-paragraph (a) omit the words after "application"; and

(b)   in sub-paragraph (b) omit the words from "and" to "children".

9. In rule 7.20(8) omit "(except any statement of arrangements for children)".

10. In rule 7.22 –

(a)   in paragraph (3) –
(i)   omit sub-paragraph (b); and
(ii)   in paragraph (c), omit "or (b)"; and
(b)   In the words in parentheses to paragraph (5) for "alternative dispute resolution" substitute "non-court dispute resolution".

11. Omit rule 7.25.

12. Omit rule 7.32(2)(f).

13. In rule 9.10 –

(a)   in paragraph (1) –
(i)   in paragraph (b) for the words from "in" to "family" substitute "who is named in a child arrangements order as a person with whom a child of the family is to live"; and
(ii)   in paragraph (c) for the words after "for" substitute "a child arrangements order which names that person as a person with whom a child is to live"; and
(b)   omit paragraph (2).

14. In the words in parentheses to rule 9.15(5) –

(a)   for "By rule 3.3" substitute "Under Part 3"; and
(b)   for "alternative dispute resolution" substitute "non-court dispute resolution".

15. In rule 12.2 –

(a)   after the definition of "the 2006 Act", insert –

""activity condition" has the meaning given to it by section 11C(2) of the 1989 Act;"" and
""activity direction" has the meaning given to it by section 11A(3) of the 1989 Act;";

(b)   for the definition of "Case Management Order", substitute –

""Case Management Order" means an order in the form referred to in Practice Direction 12A;";

(c)   omit the definitions of –
(i)   "contact activity condition"; and
(ii)   "contact activity direction";
(d)   after the definition of "interim order" insert –

""Part 4 proceedings" means proceedings for –
(a)   a care order, or the discharge of such an order, under section 39(1) of the 1989 Act;
(b)   an order giving permission to change a child's surname or remove a child from the United Kingdom under section 33(7) of the 1989 Act;
(c)   a supervision order, the discharge or variation of such an order under section 39(2) of the 1989 Act, or the extension of such an order under paragraph 6(3) of Schedule 3 to that Act;
(d)   an order making provision regarding contact under section 34(2) to (4) of the 1989 Act or an order varying or discharging such an order under section 34(9) of that Act;

(e)   an education supervision order, the extension of an education supervision order under paragraph 15(2) of Schedule 3 to the 1989 Act, or the discharge of such an order under paragraph 17(1) of Schedule 3 to that Act;

(f)   an order varying directions made with an interim care order or interim supervision order under section 38(8)(b) of the 1989 Act;

(g)   an order under section 39(3) of the 1989 Act varying a supervision order in so far as it affects a person with whom the child is living but who is not entitled to apply for the order to be discharged;

(h)   an order under section 39(3A) of the 1989 Act varying or discharging an interim care order in so far as it imposes an exclusion requirement on a person who is not entitled to apply for the order to be discharged;

(i)   an order under section 39(3B) of the 1989 Act varying or discharging an interim care order in so far as it confers a power of arrest attached to an exclusion requirement; or

(j)   the substitution of a supervision order for a care order under section 39(4) of the 1989 Act;"; and

(e)   in the definition of "private law proceedings" –
    (i)   for sub-paragraph (a) substitute –

"(a)   a section 8 order except a child arrangements order to which section 9(6B) of the 1989 Act applies with respect to a child who is in the care of a local authority;"; and

    (ii)   in sub-paragraph (k), for "contact order" substitute "child arrangements order"; and

(f)   in the definition of "public law proceedings" –
    (i)   after "means" insert "Part 4 proceedings and";
    (ii)   for sub-paragraph (a) substitute –

"(a)   a child arrangements order to which section 9(6B) of the 1989 Act applies with respect to a child who is in the care of a local authority;"; and

    (iii)   omit sub-paragraphs (d) to (m).

16. In rule 12.3(1) –

(a)   in the row beginning "An enforcement order" –
    (i)   for "contact order", in all four places where it occurs substitute "child arrangements order"; and
    (ii)   for "a contact activity" substitute "an activity";

(b)   in the row beginning "A financial compensation order" –
    (i)   for "contact order", in all four places, substitute "child arrangements order"; and
    (ii)   for "a contact activity", substitute "an activity";

(c)   in the row beginning "A special guardianship order", for the words "in whose favour a residence order is in force with respect to the child" substitute "who is named in a child arrangements order as a person with whom the child is to live;";

(d)   in the row beginning "Variation or discharge of a special guardianship order", for the words "in whose favour a residence order is in force with respect to the child;" substitute "who is named in a child arrangements order as a person with whom the child is to live;";

(e)   in the row beginning "An order following breach of an enforcement order" –
    (i)   for "the purposes of the contact order" substitute "the purposes of the child arrangements order";
    (ii)   for "provided for in the contact order" substitute "provided for in the child arrangements order"; and

(iii)   for "a contact activity condition imposed by a contact order;" substitute "an activity condition imposed by a child arrangements order;";

(f)   in the row beginning "An order relating to contact with the child in care (section 34(3) of the 1989 Act)", for the words "a person in whose favour there was a residence order in force with respect to the child immediately before the care order was made;" substitute "where there was a child arrangements order in force with respect to the child immediately before the care order was made, any person named in that order as a person with whom the child was to live;";

(g)   in the row beginning "An order varying a direction under section 44(6)", for "whose contact with the child" substitute "named in a child arrangements order as a person with whom the child is to spend time or otherwise have contact and who"; and

(h)   in the row beginning "A warning notice" –

    (i)   for "contact order" in all three places where it occurs substitute "child arrangements order"; and

    (ii)   for "a contact activity", substitute "an activity".

17. In rule 12.5 –

(a)   before "When" insert "(1)";

(b)   after "When" omit "the";

(c)   after "proceedings" insert "other than public law proceedings";

(d)   in subparagraph (a)(ii) after ";" insert "or"

(e)   omit subparagraph (a)(iii);

(f)   in sub-paragraph (a)(iv) omit "or an application for an interim order":

(g)   in sub-paragraph (a) for "Practice Directions 12A or 12B" substitute "Practice Direction 12B";

(h)   in sub-paragraph (c) for "Practice Directions 12A or 12B" substitute "Practice Direction 12B";

(i)   after sub-paragraph (c) insert –

"(2) When Part 4 proceedings and in so far as practicable other public law proceedings have been issued the court will –

    (a)   set a date for the Case Management Hearing in accordance with Practice Direction 12A;

    (b)   set a date for the hearing of an application for an interim order if necessary;

    (c)   give any directions listed in rule 12.12; and

    (d)   do anything else which is set out in Practice Direction 12A."; and

(j)   substitute for the words in parentheses after sub-paragraph (c) –

"(Practice Direction 12A sets out details relating to the Case Management Hearing. Practice Direction 12B supplementing this Part sets out details relating to the First Hearing Dispute Resolution Appointment.)".

18. In rule 12.6 –

(a)   omit "As" and replace with "Within a day of the issue of Part 4 proceedings or the transfer of Part 4 Proceedings to the court and as";

(b)   after "issue of" insert "other"; and

(c)   after "transfer of the" insert "other".

19. For rule 12.8 substitute –

"12.8 Service

(1) After the issue of proceedings under this Part, the documents specified in paragraph (5) must be served on the respondent or respondents.

(2) In section 8 private law proceedings, service under paragraph (1) will be effected by the court officer, unless –

    (a)   the applicant requests to do so; or

    (b)   the court directs the applicant to do so.

(3) In this Rule, "section 8 private law proceedings" are proceedings for a section 8 order except proceedings for a child arrangements order to which section 9(6B) of the 1989 Act applies with respect to a child who is in the care of a local authority.

(4) In any other proceedings to which this Part applies, service under paragraph (1) must be effected by the applicant.

(5) The documents are –

    (a)   the application together with the documents referred to in Practice Direction 12C; and

    (b)   notice of any hearing set by the court.

(6) Service under this rule must be carried out in accordance with Practice Direction 12C.

(7) The general rules about service in Part 6 apply but are subject to this rule.".

20. At the end of rule 12.8, insert the following words in parentheses, "(Practice Direction 12C (Service of Application in Children Proceedings) provides that in Part 4 proceedings (except proceedings for an interim order) the minimum number of days prior to the Case Management Hearing for service of the application and accompanying documents is 7 days. The Court has discretion to extend or shorten this time (see rule 4.1(3)(a)).".

21. In rule 12.14(9) –

    (a)   for "a contact activity" in both places where it occurs substitute "an activity"; and

    (b)   for "contact order" substitute "child arrangements order".

22. At the end of rule 12.15, insert the following words in parentheses, "(Practice Direction 12A gives guidance as to the application of this rule to Part 4 proceedings in the light of the period that is for the time being allowed under section 32(1)(a)(ii) of the 1989 Act)".

23. For rule 12.22, substitute –

"12.22 Timetable for the proceedings

In public law proceedings other than Part 4 proceedings, in so far as practicable the court will draw up the timetable for the proceedings or revise that timetable with a view to disposing of the application without delay and in any event within 26 weeks beginning with the date on which the application is issued.

> (In relation to Part 4 proceedings, section 32(1)(a) of the 1989 Act requires the court to draw up a timetable with a view to disposing of the application without delay and in any event within 26 weeks beginning with the day on which the application is issued.)".

24. For rule 12.23 substitute –

"12.23 Application of rules 12.24 to 12.26C

Rules 12.24 to 12.26C apply to Part 4 proceedings and in so far as practicable other public law proceedings.".

25. For rule 12.25, substitute –

"12.25 The Case Management Hearing and the Issues Resolution Hearing

(1) The court will conduct the Case Management Hearing with the objective of –

  (a)   confirming the level of judge to which the proceedings have been allocated;
  (b)   drawing up a timetable for the proceedings including the time within which the proceedings are to be resolved;
  (c)   identifying the issues; and
  (d)   giving directions in accordance with rule 12.12 and Practice Direction 12A to manage the proceedings.

(2) The court may hold a further Case Management Hearing only where this hearing is necessary to fulfil the objectives of the Case Management Hearing set out in paragraph (1).

(3) The court will conduct the Issues Resolution Hearing with the objective of –

  (a)   identifying the remaining issues in the proceedings;
  (b)   as far as possible resolving or narrowing those issues; and
  (c)   giving directions to manage the proceedings to the final hearing in accordance with rule 12.12 and Practice Direction 12A.

(4) Where it is possible for all the issues in the proceedings to be resolved at the Issues Resolution Hearing, the court may treat the Issues Resolution Hearing as a final hearing and make orders disposing of the proceedings.

(5) The court may set a date for the Case Management Hearing, a further Case Management Hearing and the Issues Resolution Hearing at the times referred to in Practice Direction 12A.

(6) The matters which the court will consider at the hearings referred to in this rule are set out in Practice Direction 12A.

> (Rule 25.6 (experts: when to apply for the court's permission) provides that unless the court directs otherwise, parties must apply for the court's permission as mentioned in section 13(1), (3) and (5) of the 2014 Act as soon as possible and in Part 4 proceedings and in so far as practicable other public law proceedings no later than the Case Management Hearing.)".

26. For rule 12.26, substitute –

"12.26 Discussion between advocates

(1) When setting a date for the Case Management Hearing or the Issues Resolution Hearing the court will direct a discussion between the parties' advocates to –

  (a)   discuss the provisions of a draft of the Case Management Order; and
  (b)   consider any other matter set out in Practice Direction 12A.

(2) Where there is a litigant in person the court will give directions about how that person may take part in the discussions between the parties' advocates.

(3) Unless the court directs otherwise –

  (a)   any discussion between advocates must take place no later than 2 days before the Case Management Hearing; and
  (b)   a draft of the Case Management Order must be filed with the court no later than 11a.m. on the day before the Case Management Hearing.

(4) Unless the court directs otherwise –

  (a) any discussion between advocates must take place no later than 7 days before the Issues Resolution Hearing; and

  (b) a draft of the Case Management Order must be filed with the court no later than 11a.m. on the day before the Issues Resolution Hearing.

(5) For the purposes of this rule "advocate" includes a litigant in person.".

27. After rule 12.26, insert –

"12.26A Application for extension of the time limit for disposing of the application

(1) An application requesting the court to grant an extension must state –

  (a) the reasons for the request;

  (b) the period of extension being requested; and

  (c) a short explanation of –

    (i) why it is necessary for the request to be granted to enable the court to resolve the proceedings justly;

    (ii) the impact which any ensuing timetable revision would have on the welfare of the child to whom the application relates;

    (iii) the impact which any ensuing timetable revision would have on the duration and conduct of the proceedings; and

    (iv) the reasons for the grant or refusal of any previous request for extension.

(2) Part 18 applies to an application requesting the grant of an extension.

(3) In this rule

  "ensuing timetable revision" has the meaning given to it by section 32(6) of the 1989 Act;

  "extension" means an extension of the period for the time being allowed under section 32(1)(a)(ii) of the 1989 Act which is to end no more than 8 weeks after the later of the times referred to in section 32(8) of that Act.

12.26B Disapplication of rule 4.1(3)(a) court's power to extend or shorten the time for compliance with a rule

Rule 4.1(3)(a) does not apply to any period that is for the time being allowed under section 32(1)(a)(ii) of the 1989 Act.

12.26C Extension of time limit: reasons for court's decision

(1) When refusing or granting an extension of the period that is for the time being allowed under section 32(1)(a)(ii) in the case of the application, the court will announce its decision and –

  (a) the reasons for that decision; and

  (b) where an extension is granted or refused, a short explanation of the impact which the decision would have on the welfare of the child.

(2) The court office will supply a copy of the order granting or refusing the extension including the reasons for the court's decision and the period of any extension and short explanation given under paragraph (1)(b) to –

  (a) the parties; and

  (b) any person who has actual care of the child who is the subject of the proceedings.".

28. In rule 12.33, for "contact" substitute "child arrangements".

29. In rule 12.75(1) for sub-paragraph (b) substitute –

  "(b) to attend a mediation information and assessment meeting, or to engage in mediation or other forms of non-court dispute resolution;".

30. In rule 13.1(2), for the definition of "provision for contact" substitute –

""provision for contact" means –

> (i)   contact provision contained in a child arrangements order under section 8 of the 1989 Act, or
> (ii)   an order under section 34 of the 1989 Act;"; and

""contact provision" has the meaning given to it in section 26(5A) of the 2002 Act;".

31. In rule 14.1 –

(a)   in paragraph (1)(c)(i) –

> (i)   omit "a contact" and substitute "an"; and
> (ii)   after "section 26" insert "or an order under section 51A(2)(a)";

(b)   after paragraph (1)(c)(i) insert –

> "(i)(aa)the making of an order under section 51A(2)(b) of the 2002 Act;";

(c)   in paragraph (1)(c)(ii) omit "a contact order under section 27 of the 2002 Act;" and insert –

> " –
>
> > (aa)   an order under section 27 of the 2002 Act; or
> > (bb)   an order under section 51A(2) of the 2002 Act in accordance with section 51B(1)(c);"; and

(d)   in paragraph (2), for the definition of "provision for contact" substitute –

""provision for contact" has the meaning given to it in rule 13.1(2);".

32. For rule 14.2, substitute –

"14.2 Application for a serial number

(1) This rule applies where –

(a)   any application in proceedings is made by a person who intends to adopt a child; or

(b)   an adoption order in respect of the child has been made and an application is made for –

> (i)   a contact order under section 51A(2)(a) of the 2002 Act;
> (ii)   an order prohibiting contact with the child under section 51A(2)(b) of the 2002 Act; or
> (iii)   the variation or revocation of an order under section 51A(2) of the 2002 Act in accordance with section 51B(1)(c).

(2) If, before proceedings have started, the person intending to adopt the child requests a court officer to assign a serial number to identify the person in connection with proceedings in order for the person's identity to be kept confidential in those proceedings, a serial number will be assigned.

(3) If a person in whose favour an adoption order has been made requests a court officer to assign a serial number to keep the identity of the person confidential in proceedings referred to in paragraph (1)(b), a serial number will be so assigned.

(4) The court may at any time direct that a serial number assigned to a person under paragraph (2) or (3) must be removed.

(5) If a serial number has been assigned to a person under paragraph (2) or (3) –

(a)   the court officer will ensure that any notice sent in accordance with these rules does not contain information which discloses, or is likely to disclose, the identity of that person to any other party to that application who is not already aware of that person's identity; and

(b)   the proceedings on the application will be conducted with a view to securing that the person is not seen by or made known to any party who is not already aware of the person's identity except with the person's consent.".

33. In the table in rule 14.3, after the row concerning proceedings for "An order permitting the child's name to be changed or the removal of the child from the United Kingdom (section 28(2) and (3) of the 2002 Act)." insert –

A contact order under section 51A(2)(a) of the 2002 Act.	The child; or any person who has obtained the court's leave to make the application.	A person who has applied for the adoption order or in whose favour the adoption order is or has been made; and Any adoption agency having parental responsibility for the child under section 25 of the 2002 Act.
An order prohibiting the person named in the order from having contact with the child (section 51A(2)(b) of the 2002 Act).	A person who has applied for the adoption order or in whose favour the adoption order is or has been made; the child; or any person who has obtained the court's leave to make the application.	A person against whom an application is made who – (but for the child's adoption) would be related to the child by blood (including half-blood), marriage or civil partnership; is a former guardian of the child; is a person who had parental responsibility for the child immediately before the making of the adoption order; is a person who was entitled to make an application for an order under section 26 of the 2002 Act in respect of the child (contact with children placed or to be placed for adoption) by virtue of subsection (3)(c), (d) or (e) of that section; is a person with whom the child has lived for a period of at least one year; and any adoption agency having parental responsibility for the child under section 25 of the 2002 Act.
The variation or revocation of a contact order or an order prohibiting contact under section 51A(2) of the 2002 Act (section 51B(1)(c) of that Act).	The child; a person in whose favour the adoption order was made; or a person named in the order.	The parties to the proceedings leading to the contact order or an order prohibiting contact which it is sought to have varied or revoked; and any person named in the contact order or the order prohibiting contact.

34. In the table in rule 14.3(1) –

(a)   in the row beginning "A contact order (section 26 of the 2002 Act)" –

   (i)   for "A contact order (section 26 of the 2002 Act)", substitute "An order under section 26 of the 2002 Act";

   (ii)   for "the contact order" in both places where it occurs substitute "the order"; and

   (iii)   for the words from "a person in whose favour there was a residence order" to "old", substitute "if a child arrangements order was in force immediately before the adoption agency was authorised to place the child for adoption or (as the case may be) placed the child for adoption at a time when he or she was less than six weeks old, any person named in the order as a person with whom the child was to live;"; and

(b)   in the row beginning "An order varying or revoking a contact order" –

   (i)   for "a contact order", substitute "an order under section 26 of the 2002 Act"; and

   (ii)   for "the contact order" in all three places where it occurs substitute "the order".

35. In rule 14.8 –

(a)   (1)(a), after "fix a" insert "timetable for the proceedings including a"; and
(b)   in the words in parentheses in rule 14.8(1) –
    (i)   for "By rule 3.3" substitute "Under Part 3"; and
    (ii)   for "alternative dispute resolution" substitute "non-court dispute resolution".

36. In rule 14.13(2)(a), after "rule 14.2(2)" insert "or (3)".

37. In rule 14.18(1)(c), for "allowing any person contact" substitute "containing any provision for contact".

38. In rule 14.25, insert the following words in parentheses –

> "(Rule 37.9 makes provision for the court to endorse an order prohibiting contact under section 51A(2)(b) of the 2002 Act with a penal notice on the application of the person entitled to enforce the order.)".

39. In rule 14.26 –

(a)   in paragraph (1)(e) –
    (i)   for "a copy of a contact order" substitute "a copy of an"; and
    (ii)   for "variation or revocation of a contact" substitute "variation or revocation of such"; and
(b)   in paragraph (1)(e)(iii), after ";" omit "and" and insert –

> "(ee) unless the court directs otherwise, a copy of a contact order under section 51A(2)(a) of the 2002 Act, an order prohibiting contact under section 51A(2)(b) of that Act or a variation or revocation of such orders under section 51B(1)(c) of that Act to the parties to the proceedings; and".

40. In rule 16.38(1) –

(a)   in paragraph (a)(i), for "a contact" in both places where it occurs substitute "an";
(b)   in paragraph (a)(ii), for "a contact" in both places where it occurs substitute "an"; and
(c)   in paragraph (a)(iii), for "contact" substitute "child arrangements".

41. In rule 16.38(2)(a), omit "contact" in both places where it occurs.

42. In rule 16.39(1) for "contact" substitute "child arrangements".

43. In rule 17.2 –

(a)   omit paragraph (1)(e); and
(b)   in paragraph (6)(b) omit "or statement of arrangements for children".

44. Omit rule 25.1.

45. In rule 25.2 –

(a)   omit the definition of "authorised applicant";
(b)   after the definition of "expert" insert the following words in parentheses –

> "(Section 13(8) of the 2014 Act provides for what is not included in reference to providing expert evidence or putting expert evidence before the court in children proceedings)";

(c)   omit the definition of "local authority"; and
(d)   for paragraph (2), substitute –

> "(2) The meaning of "children proceedings" in paragraph (1) is the prescribed meaning for the purposes of section 13(9) of the 2014 Act.".

46. For rule 25.4, substitute –

"25.4 Control of expert evidence in proceedings other than children proceedings

(1) This rule applies to proceedings other than children proceedings.

(2) A person may not without the permission of the court put expert evidence (in any form) before the court.

(3) The court may give permission as mentioned in paragraph (2) only if the court is of the opinion that the expert evidence is necessary to assist the court to resolve the proceedings.

> (Provision relating to the control of expert evidence in children proceedings is contained in section 13 of the 2014 Act.)".

47. In rule 25.5 –

(a)   omit paragraph (1) and replace with –

"(1) When deciding whether to give permission as mentioned in section 13(1), (3) or (5) of the 2014 Act or to give a direction under 38(6) of the 1989 Act in children proceedings, the court is to have regard in particular to any failure to comply with rule 25.6 or any direction of the court about expert evidence."; and

(b)   after paragraph (1) insert –

"(1A) The matter referred to in paragraph (1) is a prescribed matter for the purposes of section 13(7)(h) of the 2014 Act and section 38(7B) of the 1989 Act.".

48. For rule 25.6, after the heading substitute –

"**25.6.** Unless the court directs otherwise, parties must apply for the court's permission as mentioned in section 13(1), (3) or (5) of the 2014 Act or rule 25.4(2) as soon as possible and –

(a)   in Part 4 proceedings referred to in rule 12.2 and in so far as practicable other public law proceedings referred to in that rule, no later than a Case Management Hearing;

(b)   in private law proceedings referred to in rule 12.2, no later than the First Hearing Dispute Resolution Appointment;

(c)   in adoption proceedings and placement proceedings, no later than the first directions hearing;

(d)   in proceedings for a financial remedy, no later than the first appointment; and

(e)   in a defended case referred to in rule 7.1(3), no later than any Case Management Hearing directed by the court under rule 7.20.".

49. In rule 25.7 –

(a)   in paragraph (1) after "in" insert "section 13(1), (3) or (5) of the 2014 Act or" and after "rule 25.4" insert "(2)";

(b)   in paragraph (2)(a) after "in" insert "section 13(1), (3) or (5) of the 2014 Act or" and after "rule 25.4" insert "(2)"; and

(c)   in paragraph (3) omit "rule 25.4" and insert "section 13(1), (3) or (5) of the 2014 Act".

50. In rule 25.8, in paragraph (1) after "in" in the second place where it occurs insert "section 13(1), (3) or (5) of the 2014 Act or" and after "rule 25.4" insert "(2)".

51. In rule 25.19 in paragraph (2) –

(a)   after "final order" insert ", any transcript or written record of the court's decision, and its reasons for reaching its decision, within 10 business days from the date when the party received the order and any such transcript or record."; and

(b)   omit "; and" and sub-paragraphs (a) and (b).

52. In rule 37.9(3)(b), omit "," and replace with ";" and insert –

> "(c) an order prohibiting contact with a child under section 51A(2)(b) of the 2002 Act,".

JUSTICES' CLERKS AND ASSISTANTS RULES 2014

SI 2014/603

1 Citation, commencement and interpretation

(1) These Rules may be cited as the Justices' Clerks and Assistants Rules 2014 and shall come into force on the day on which section 17(3) of the Crime and Courts Act 2013 comes fully into force.

(2) In these Rules –

"the Act" means the Matrimonial and Family Proceedings Act 1984;
"assistant justices' clerk" is an assistant to a justices' clerk within the meaning of section 27(5) of the Courts Act 2003;
"CPA" means the Civil Partnership Act 2004;
"FPR" means the Family Procedure Rules 2010;
"MCA" means the Matrimonial Causes Act 1973;
"undefended case" has the meaning given in FPR rule 7.1(3);

2 Functions which may be carried out by a justices' clerk

The functions of the family court or of a judge of the court that may be carried out by a justices' clerk are the functions of the family court or of a judge of the court specified in the provisions listed in the first column of the table in the Schedule subject to the exceptions or restrictions specified in the second column in relation to particular functions.

3 Functions which may be carried out by an assistant justices' clerk

(1) An assistant justices' clerk may carry out any function that a justices' clerk may carry out pursuant to rule 2, provided that that assistant justices' clerk has been authorised by a justices' clerk to carry out that function.

(2) The functions specified in section 31O(2) of the Act may be carried out by an assistant justices' clerk.

(3) An authorisation by a justices' clerk under paragraph (1) above must be recorded in writing at the time the authorisation is given or as soon as practicable thereafter.

4 Duty to refer if inappropriate to carry out function

(1) When considering carrying out a function specified in the Schedule, a justices' clerk must consider whether in the particular circumstances it would be inappropriate to carry out the function.

(2) If a justices' clerk determines that it would be inappropriate to carry out a function specified in the Schedule, the justices' clerk must refer the matter to the court.

(3) References in this rule to a justices' clerk include a person authorised in accordance with rule 3.

Schedule

FPR rule 3.3	
FPR rule 3.4	
FPR rule 3.10	
FPR rule 4.1(3)(a)	Except any extensions in public law proceedings that would have the effect that disposal of the application would occur later than the end of twenty-six weeks beginning with the day on which the application was issued.
FPR rule 4.1(3)(b), (c), (d), (f), (h), (j), (k), (n), (o)	
FPR rule 4.3(2)	
FPR rule 4.3(5)	
FPR rule 4.7(a) and (b)	
FPR rule 6.24(2)	
FPR rule 6.26(5)	
FPR rule 6.32	
FPR rule 6.36	
MCA, section 1(3)	Only in undefended cases
MCA, sections 1(4) and 1(5)	Only in undefended cases, and only the making "absolute" of decrees of divorce
MCA, section 6(2)	Only where the parties consent to the adjournment
MCA, sections 10A(2) and (3)	Only in an application under section 10A(2) to which the other party consents
MCA, section 17(2)	Only in undefended cases
CPA, section 37(1)(a) and (d)	Only in undefended cases, and only the making "final" of such orders
CPA, section 42(3)	Only where the parties consent to the adjournment
CPA, sections 44(2) and (4)	Only in undefended cases
FPR rule 7.14(1)	Only if the parties consent to the court giving such permission
FPR rule 7.20(2)	
FPR rule 7.20(3)	
FPR rule 7.20(5)	
FPR rule 7.30(1)(d)(ii) and (3)	Only where the application under section 10A(2) was made on consent
FPR 7.32(2)	
FPR rule 8.20(4)	Only where the parties consent to the person being made a respondent and where the person is not a child
FPR rule 9.18	
FPR rule 9.20	

FPR rule 9.26	
FPR rule 10.3(1)	
FPR rule 10.6(2)	
FPR rule 10.7	
FPR rule 12.3(2)	Only where the parties consent to the person being made a respondent and where the person is not a child
FPR rule 12.3(3)	Only where the parties consent to the person being made a respondent and where the person is not a child
FPR rule 12.3(4)	Only where otherwise authorised to add or remove the person as a party
FPR rule 12.4(5)	Only where the parties consent to the person being made a respondent and where the person is not a child
FPR rule 12.5(1)	
Children Act 1989, section 32(1)	
Children Act 1989, section 32(4)	Except that the carrying out of such function must not have the direct or indirect effect of extending the timetable for the proceedings with the effect that the disposal of the application would occur later than the end of twenty-six weeks beginning with the day on which the application was issued
FPR rule 12.5(2)	Except at an Issues Resolution Hearing for which Practice Direction 12A makes provision, and except the carrying out of any function that has the direct or indirect effect of extending the timetable for the proceedings with the effect that the disposal of the application would occur later than the end of twenty-six weeks beginning with the day on which the application was issued
FPR rule 12.6(a)–(c)	
Children Act 1989, section 7(1) and FPR rule 12.6(d)	
FPR rule 12.12	Except at an Issues Resolution Hearing for which Practice Direction 12A makes provision, and except any direction in public law proceedings that has the direct or indirect effect of extending the timetable for the proceedings with the effect that the disposal of the application would occur later than the end of twenty-six weeks beginning with the day on which the application was issued
FPR rule 12.13	Except that in any public law proceedings, the carrying out of such function must not have the direct or indirect effect of extending the timetable for the proceedings with the effect that the disposal of the application would occur later than the end of twenty-six weeks beginning with the day on which the application was issued
FPR rule 12.14(3) and (4)	
FPR rule 12.15	Except any direction in a public law proceeding that has the direct or indirect effect of extending the timetable for the proceedings with the effect that the disposal of the application would occur later than the end of twenty-six weeks beginning with the day on which the application was issued
FPR rule 12.16(6)	
FPR rule 12.16(7)	
FPR rule 12.19(2) and (3)	
FPR rule 12.21(1)	

FPR rule 12.22	
FPR rule 12.73(1)(b)	
Practice Direction 12G, paragraph 1.2	
Practice Direction 12J, paragraph 6, first three bullet points only	
Practice Direction 12J, paragraph 8	
Practice Direction 12J, paragraph 15	
Practice Direction 12J, paragraph 21	
FPR rule 12.24	
FPR rule 12.25(1), (2) and (5)	
FPR rule 12.26	
FPR rule 12.29	
FPR rule 12.30	
Children Act 1989, section 41	
Children Act 1989, sections 10(1) and (2)	Only where – (a) a previous such order has been made in the same proceedings; (b) the terms of the order sought are the same as those of the last such order made; (c) the order is an order in the course of proceedings and does not dispose finally of the proceedings; and (d) a written request for such an order has been made and – (i) the other parties and any children's guardian consent to the request and they or their legal representatives have signed the request; or (ii) at least one of the other parties and any children's guardian consent to the request and they or their legal representatives have signed the request, and the remaining parties have not indicated that they either consent to or oppose the making of the order.
Children Act 1989, section 38(1)	Only where – (a) a previous such order has been made in the same proceedings; (b) the terms of the order sought are the same as those of the last such order made; and (c) a written request for such an order has been made and – (i) the other parties and any children's guardian consent to the request and they or their legal representatives have signed the request; or (ii) at least one of the other parties and any children's guardian consent to the request and they or their legal representatives have signed the request, and the remaining parties have not indicated that they either consent to or oppose the making of the order.
FPR rule 12.31	
FPR rule 13.3(3)	
FPR rule 13.3(4)	
FPR rule 13.3(5)	
FPR rule 13.5	
FPR rule 13.8	
FPR rule 13.9(1)	Except 13.9(1)(e) and (f)
FPR rule 13.9(3)	
FPR rule 13.9(6)	

FPR rule 13.9(8)	
FPR rule 13.9(9)	
FPR rule 13.11(1)	
FPR rule 13.14	
FPR rule 13.16	
FPR rule 13.17	
FPR rule 13.21(1)	
FPR rule 13.21(4)	
FPR rule 13.22(4)	
FPR rule 14.2(3)	Only where the applicant consents to the removal
FPR rule 14.3(2)	Only where the parties consent to the child being made a respondent
FPR rule 14.3(3)	Only where the parties consent to the person or body being made a respondent or to a party being removed, as the case may be, and only where the person being made a respondent or being removed as a party is not a child
FPR rule 14.3(4)	Only where such directions are consequential on directions made under FPR rule 14.3(2) or (3)
FPR rule 14.5(2)(b) and (3)	
FPR rule 14.6(1)	
FPR rule 14.6(2)(a)	
FPR rule 14.6(2)(b)	
FPR rule 14.6(3)(b)	
FPR rule 14.6(4)	
FPR rule 14.7	
Adoption and Children Act 2002, section 51B(3)	
FPR rule 14.8(1)	Except 14.8(1)(d)
FPR rule 14.8(4)	
FPR rule 14.8(6)	
FPR rule 14.8(7)	
FPR rule 14.9(4)(b)	
FPR rule 14.10(2)	
FPR rule 14.14	
FPR rule 14.16(4) and (7)	
FPR rule 14.18	
FPR rule 14.20	
FPR rule 14.26(1)	

FPR rule 14.27(2)	
Practice Direction 14E, paragraph 1.2	
FPR rule 15.6(3)	
FPR rule 15.6(5)	
FPR rule 15.8(1)(b)	
FPR rule 15.9	
Practice Direction 15B	
FPR rule 16.3(1)	
FPR rule 16.3(2), (3) and (4)	Only in relation to specified proceedings as defined in the Children Act 1989, section 41(6)
FPR rule 16.4	
FPR rule 16.11(3)	
FPR rule 16.11(5) and (6)	
FPR rule 16.21	
FPR rule 16.24	
FPR rule 16.30	
FPR rule 16.33	
FPR rule 16.34	
FPR rule 17.3(2)	
FPR rule 17.4	
FPR rule 17.5	
FPR rule 18.3(1)(c)	Only where the parties consent to the person being made a respondent and where the person being made a respondent is not a child
FPR rule 18.4(2)(b)	
FPR rule 18.5(2)(c)	
FPR rule 18.8(4)	
FPR rule 18.9(1)	Only where authorised by these Rules to deal with the application with a hearing
Practice Direction 18A, paragraph 8.1	
Practice Direction 18A, paragraph 10.1	
Practice Direction 18A, paragraph 11.2	
FPR rule 19.1(3)	
FPR rule 19.4(4)	
FPR rule 19.6(2)	
FPR rule 19.8(1)(b)	
FPR rule 19.8(3)	

FPR rule 19.9(2)	
Practice Direction 19A, paragraphs 4.1 and 4.4	
FPR rule 21.2(3)	Only where the parties consent to the application for disclosure
Practice Direction 21A, paragraph 2.4	
FPR rule 22.1(1)	
FPR rule 22.3	
FPR rule 22.5	
FPR rule 22.7(1)	
FPR rule 22.9	
FPR rule 22.10	
Practice Direction 22A, paragraph 5.3	
FPR rule 23.4(1)	
FPR rule 23.6(8)	
The Act, section 31G(2)	
FPR rule 23.9	
FPR rule 24.3	
FPR rule 24.4(2)	
FPR rule 24.7	
FPR rule 24.8	
FPR rule 24.9	
FPR rule 24.10	
FPR rule 24.11(3)	
FPR rule 24.13	
Children and Families Act 2014, section 13	
FPR rule 25.4	
FPR rule 25.8	
FPR rule 25.9	
FPR rule 25.10(2)	
FPR rule 25.10(3)	
FPR rule 25.10(4)	
FPR rule 25.11	
FPR rule 25.12	
FPR rule 25.13	
FPR rule 25.16	

FPR rule 25.17	
FPR rule 25.18	
FPR rule 25.19	
Practice Direction 25A, paragraph 2.1	
Practice Direction 25B, paragraphs 10.1 and 10.2	
Practice Direction 25E, paragraph 4.1	
FPR rule 26.3	
FPR rule 26.4	
FPR rule 27.3	
FPR rule 27.4	
FPR rule 27.7	
FPR rule 29.1	
FPR rule 29.4	
FPR rule 29.11	
FPR rule 29.14	
FPR rule 29.15	Only where the order in question is one which the justices' clerk or assistant justices' clerk made
FPR rule 29.16	Only where the order in question is one which a justices' clerk or assistant justices' clerk made
FPR rule 29.19(5)	
FPR rule 37.9(3)	
The Family Court (Composition and Distribution of Business) Rules 2014, rule 20	

APPENDIX 10

PRESIDENT'S GUIDANCE ON CONTINUITY AND DEPLOYMENT (PRIVATE LAW)

Introduction

1. This Guidance is issued by the President of the Family Division.

2. This Guidance applies to all private law proceedings under Part II of the Children Act 1989 (private children proceedings) heard in the Family Court.

3. Deployment is a judicial function which includes the patterning of judges and lay justices, the management of the workload of the court, allocation and listing.

4. The purpose of this Guidance is to ensure that family proceedings are accorded the appropriate level of priority in their listing and that they are case managed and heard by judges (including lay justices) and legal advisers who provide continuity of the conduct of the proceedings.

Continuity and Docketing

5. In accordance with the Guidance given by HMCTS on the introduction of a system for the docketing of cases (which is annexed to this Guidance) all private children proceedings are to be allocated to a case management judge in the Family Court who will be responsible for any case management hearings in the proceedings.

6. For the lay justices, the case manager is the justices' clerk or assistant justices' clerk (legal adviser) who manages the case. Continuity of the case manager for hearings before lay justices is as essential as continuity of the case management judge for other judges of the Family Court.

7. The name of the case manager(s) or case management judge must be recorded on the outside of the court file by the court staff immediately after the FHDRA or other first hearing.

8. Where possible, the case management judge or the case manager sitting with lay justices is to conduct any contested hearing including the final hearing in all proceedings allocated to them.

9. No hearing at any stage of the proceedings should conclude without a date for the next hearing having been fixed for the earliest possible date, and communicated to the parties at court.

10. It is not good practice for proceedings to have to wait until the case manager or the case management judge is available. Discussions must take place during the FHDRA, DRA or other hearings (and with HMCTS) to ensure that one of the two case managers or the case management judge is available to hear the proceedings on the date fixed for the next appointment. Legal advisers and judges must fit their availability around the

case, not the other way around. Although continuity of representation is important, lawyers will be expected to organise their diaries to ensure that cases are heard without delay.

11. The allocation of private children proceedings is to be undertaken in accordance with the President's Guidance on Allocation and Gatekeeping (Private Law), and the Family Court (Composition and Distribution of Business) Rules 2014.

Deployment

12. Circuit Judges and District Judges hearing private children proceedings should be patterned so as to be able to sit in private children proceedings with a gap of no more than a month so as to provide continuity for their allocated proceedings.

13. District Judges (Magistrates' Court) who sit on private children proceedings are identified by the Chief Magistrate and authorised by the President. The deployment of DJsMC is determined by the Chief Magistrate in consultation with Presiding Judges and the Family Division Liaison Judge (FDLJ) on each Circuit.

14. Legal advisers are generally to be patterned so that they are available to the Family Court for not less than 40% of their time. Those sitting as case managers must sit for 40% or more of their time in public and private law. Each private law application which is allocated to the lay justices must have one and not more than two allocated case managers who are legal advisers.

15. Justices' clerks will be expected to agree the deployment of their lay justices with Designated Family Judges (DFJs) and this should be done in direct meetings between the DFJ and the justices' clerk and his/her tier 4 specialists. Any disagreements are to be referred immediately to the FDLJ and the Regional Delivery Director through his/her Head of Civil, Family and Tribunals

16. The deployment of Circuit Judges and District Judges in the Family Court (i.e. their patterns and itineraries) is decided by the Presiding Judges in consultation with and on the advice of the FDLJ, and the Designated and Resident Judges. DFJs are encouraged to agree a protocol with Resident Judges for the patterning of mixed ticketed judges and their availability to provide judicial continuity.

Continuity by Lay Justices

17. The following arrangements will apply to proceedings heard by lay justices in the Family Court for case management and hearing.

18. Lay justices are patterned to sit by their justices' clerk. Continuity should be provided for in the individual case, where a decision of fact has been made which renders a case theoretically or actually part heard, in accordance with the guidance in *Re B (Children)* [2008] UKHL 35, and rule 8 of the Family Court (Composition and Distribution of Business) Rules 2014. Wherever possible, the court which resumes a hearing shall be composed of the same lay justices as dealt with the previous part of the hearing; alternatively, continuity is to be provided by at least one of the lay justices (preferably the Chairman) as well as the legal adviser who is the case manager for the proceedings.

Appeals

19. Appeals within the Family Court are to be allocated to judges in accordance with the Family Court (Composition and Distribution of Business) Rules 2014. Appeals from Circuit Judges and second appeals will continue to be heard by the Court of Appeal.

Guidance to Staff on the Introduction of a System for the Docketing of Cases

What is "Docketing"?

1. Lord Justice Jackson's Review of Civil Litigation Costs and the Family Justice Review chaired by David Norgrove both identified the need for greater docketing of cases and for more judicial continuity. The two phrases have the same meaning, although in this Guidance the word "docketing" is generally used when referring to both the civil and family jurisdictions.

2. Both the present and past Presidents of the Family Division have emphasised the need for greater judicial continuity in the handling of both public and private family law cases. With effect from 1st April 2013 the Master of the Rolls is introducing a docketing system in civil cases.

3. This Guidance is being made available to the judiciary and has been agreed with the Master of the Rolls and the President of the Family Division.

4. This Guidance is intended to apply in both the civil and family jurisdictions in all county courts and district registries in England and Wales. It does not apply to High Court work being conducted at the Royal Courts of Justice in any of the three Divisions. However, it is hoped that listing officers would be able, for instance, to ensure that a section 9 judge would be available at his/her home court to hear a consequential relief application following a sitting at the Royal Courts of Justice.

5. In relation to civil cases, the effect of a docketing system is that the interim case management of a complex case will be conducted by the one judge. In the family jurisdiction, judicial continuity will ensure the identification of the judge and/or case manager responsible for the conduct of all case management and interim hearings as well as the early identification of the judge or bench to conduct the final hearing.

6. There are many benefits to be achieved through docketing. Only one judge need read the case papers. It is easier to identify the relevant issues in the case. The judicial control exercised over a case is firmer; the case management is more consistent. Practitioners and other court users have repeatedly said that they prefer repeat interim applications to be heard by the same judge.

7. Experience has also shown that judges to whom cases are docketed accept a greater responsibility for the speedy timetabling of cases. The progress of cases is checked and urgent applications can be heard in a timely manner.

Should all cases be docketed?

8. Docketing of civil cases will only occur in the minority of defended claims. It would be very rare to docket either a small claim or a fast-track case, or a housing case. Equally, many of the more straightforward personal injury cases in the multi-track ought not to be docketed. The simple test is whether docketing "adds value" to the case management of the particular case.

9. Examples of the types of case where docketing has proven successful in the past are Chancery cases, clinical negligence cases, complex personal injury cases, mesothelioma

claims and other lengthy and involved cases. There is a suggested list at Appendix B but that should not to be applied rigidly. Local circumstances might make it desirable to docket other types of cases. Or new types of claim might arise. Similarly, it might be appropriate for a judge to docket to himself a legally simple case where the court had, by way of example, spent half a day hearing an unsuccessful application for summary judgement under CPR Part 24 which had involved consideration of many of the factual aspects of the case.

10. On the other hand, judicial continuity should apply in all public and private family law children cases.

11. There is no one-size-fits-all solution to the need for more docketing of cases. Different considerations apply as between a large civil trial centre and a one-judge court.

12. Staff at each court are encouraged to hold discussions with their local judiciary both to decide how best to implement the docketing system in their local court and to discuss whether any amendment is necessary to that court's Listing Policy. For sound constitutional reasons, Listing remains a judicial function; the local judiciary will ultimately be responsible for the docketing arrangements to apply at their court. But they will inevitably look to you to implement the system on a day-to-day basis. Questions or problems will arise from time to time: these should clearly be resolved in discussion with the local judiciary although it might be necessary, in a very few number of cases, also to involve in those conversations either the Designated Civil Judge, the Designated Family Judge or, where appropriate, a Specialist Circuit Judge.

What is the difference between docketing and reserving a case?

13. The intention behind **docketing** is that the same judge will deal with all interim hearings and possibly also the final hearing unless released in relation to family cases. However, there has to be a balance between bringing a case back before the same judge every time it needs to be listed for hearing and achieving the effective and efficient disposal of all judicial business. There may be occasions when a judge to whom a case is docketed is not available. In those circumstances the particular case ought to be considered by and, if necessary, listed for hearing before another judge.

14. **Reserving** a case to a specific judge generally means that all hearings are listed before that judge. Another judge can only hear the case if it is released to him.

What is the first step?

15. The staff and judiciary in each court need to identify the specialisms and aspirations of its judiciary. Some judges may already be considered experts in particular fields. Others may have a wish to develop a particular expertise. How this is achieved will vary from one court to another.

16. You also need to give consideration to the balance of work as between salaried judges (circuit and district judges) and fee-paid judges (Recorders and deputy district judges) as all fee-paid judges are entitled to expect a reasonable spread of work.

17. In the Court of Appeal, all new lord justices are required upon appointment to fill out a questionnaire stating their specialist areas. Whilst this might be unnecessary in a small court with only one or two judges, in larger court centres it might be beneficial to adopt a more formulaic system. By way of example, two forms (Appendices A and B) are attached which are based on forms in use at Leeds County Court; they show how it might be possible — in the civil jurisdiction — to capture judges' individual preferences and present that information on a single sheet of paper. The particular columns of the

grid should be adjusted to suit the workload and types of cases passing through the particular court. A similar grid could be used to capture specialisms and authorisations in the family jurisdiction depending on whether or not the particular court hears public law, as well as private law and ancillary relief, cases. Ultimately, however, it is for the local judiciary and staff to agree between themselves how best to capture information in relation to individual judges' specialisms and how that information is to be made available to all the staff dealing locally with allocation and case management work.

18. It would also be sensible to plan ahead of time. Cases are, as you well know, listed some time in advance. It would not be appropriate to wait until 1st April 2013 before considering with your judiciary how best to introduce a docketing system in your court. Planning for implementation should start now.

When would the docketing occur?

19. There is no simple answer. Most docketing in the civil jurisdiction will occur at the allocation stage. Based on the declared specialisms of each judge, you should refer cases falling within the particular specialism to one of the relevant judges. Care should be exercised to ensure a reasonable balance of work between the various judges at any court centre. The docketing can occur at other stages of the case such as on entry of judgment in default or on the referral of the case to a judge after the filing of a defence in a Part 8 claim.

20. In the civil context, the judge will direct 'Case management shall be by District Judge X/HH Judge Y where possible". With family cases, the judge will direct "Case management shall be by District Judge X/HH Judge Y; the final hearing, if possible, to be listed before ...".

21. In some instances, a judge might not give directions but instead indicate that the case should be considered by another judge within whose area of specialism the case more appropriately sits. Should that arise, the file should be referred directly to the second judge as quickly as possible.

22. Depending on local practice, one particular point to capture with docketing is to try to ensure that any Pre-Trial Review is listed before the trial judge where his/her identity is known. Decisions made at a PTR can very often have a profound effect on the eventual trial and are best taken by the person who is to try the case.

What do I do when the file comes back from the judge?

23. The outside cover of the file should be clearly marked with the name(s) of the judge(s) whom the file should be referred on subsequent occasions.

24. The intention is also that an upgrade will be made to CaseMan so that it will clearly record the name of the judge or judges to whom the case is docketed. Until this change is made please record the name of the judge by producing a 999 CaseMan event code.

What about listing?

25. Judges to whom particular cases are docketed will have an understandable interest in ensuring that those cases are listed as quickly as possible. You should do your best to assist in that regard, if necessary by having direct discussions with the judge concerned. How this will be achieved will obviously vary from one court another and should be discussed with your local judiciary. In essence, there needs to be frequent liaison between you and the local judiciary.

26. Whilst its use is neither mandatory nor necessary, courts may wish to consider the introduction of an own-listing system. At Leeds County Court, where docketing has been piloted, the district judges run a system of own listing under which each district judge has the opportunity him/herself to list future hearings. Each district judge has included in their sitting pattern a specified number of days each week when the judge can himself list cases. It avoids having to liaise with the listing officer but it does place on the judge the burden of finding a timeslot suitable for the needs of the particular case. That does not prohibit judges sometimes listing short matters before the commencement of the day's list proper.

How does docketing fit in with judicial profiling?

27. All staff, whether in the county courts or in the Crown Court, are encouraged to be much more flexible than hitherto has been the case in relation to judicial profiling. There needs to be greater flexibility across the various jurisdictions. If necessary, cases must follow the judge. The judge has to make him/herself available.

What about existing cases?

28. There ought to be judicial continuity already in place in all public and private family law cases. In courts where this is not occurring, arrangements need to be put in place with the local judiciary to ensure that judicial continuity is applied to all relevant family cases as a matter of urgency.

29. A different consideration will apply to civil cases issued before 1st April 2013. It is not intended that all these cases should be considered for docketing. However, and in particular where docketing would "add value" to the future conduct of a particular case, consideration should be given to docketing a case issued before 1st April 2013.

APPENDIX A
DOCKETING AND SPECIALISATION QUESTIONNAIRE

To be completed by:

> All circuit judges exercising a civil and/or family jurisdiction
> All deputy circuit judges sitting in the civil and/or family jurisdictions
> All recorders with a civil and/or family authorisation
> All district judges
> All deputy district judges (including district judges sitting in retirement)

1. What are your name and your full time or part time judicial position?

2. What are or were your areas of specialisation in practice? How many years experience do you have of practice in these areas?

3. What are or were your areas of specialisation as a judge? How many years experience do you have of judicial work in these areas? What is your order of preference for each type of work?

4. Please list any judicial authorisations which you hold

5. In what other areas would you wish to develop a specialisation?

Name

Email address

Phone number (for fee-paid judiciary only)

Signature

Date

Appendix B
Civil preferences:

Judge*	MT RTA PI	MT RTA other	MT EL PI	MT ELD PI	MT PL PI	Clinical negligence	Professional negligence	Chancery	Commercial /mercantile	Housing disrepair
Circuit Judge A										
Recorder B										
District Judge C										
D										
E										

* specify whether a Circuit Judge, Recorder, District Judge or Deputy District Judge

Glossary:

MT Multi-track
RTA PI Road Traffic personal injury
RTA other Road Traffic bent metal/credit hire etc
EL PI Employers Liability personal injury
ELD Employers Liability personal injury industrial disease
PL PI Public liability personal injury

Note: Other columns could be added, according to work done at particular court centre

APPENDIX 11

FINANCIAL PROCEEDINGS DIRECTIONS ORDER

In the Family Court   No ....

Sitting at [Place]

The Matrimonial Causes Act 1973
The Civil Partnership Act 2004
The Child Support Act 1991
Schedule 1 to the Children Act 1989
The Inheritance (Provision for Family and Dependants) Act 1975
The Matrimonial and Family Proceedings Act 1984 and Schedule 7 to the Civil Partnership Act 2004
The Trusts of Land and Appointment of Trustees Act 1996
The Married Women's Property Act 1882 and ss 67,68 and 74 of the Civil Partnership Act 2004
Delete as appropriate

The Marriage of XX and YY, or
The Civil Partnership of XX and YY, or
The Relationship of XX and YY, or
The Family of XX and YY
Adapt as necessary

After hearing *[name the advocate(s) who appeared]* ....
After consideration of the documents lodged by the parties
(In the case of an order made without notice) After reading the statements and hearing the witnesses specified in para *[insert]* of the Recitals below

ORDER MADE BY [NAME OF JUDGE] ON [DATE] SITTING IN OPEN COURT/PRIVATE AT A FIRST DIRECTIONS APPOINTMENT/FINANCIAL DISPUTE RESOLUTION APPOINTMENT/CASE MANAGEMENT HEARING

[Delete as appropriate]

WARNING: IF YOU DO NOT COMPLY WITH THIS ORDER, YOU MAY BE HELD TO BE IN CONTEMPT OF COURT AND YOU MAY BE SENT TO PRISON, BE FINED, OR HAVE YOUR ASSETS SEIZED.

The parties

1. The applicant is XX
The [*first*] respondent is YY
The [intervener]/[second] respondent is ZZ
Specify if any party acts by a litigation friend

Definitions

2. *For example*: The "family home" shall mean [*insert address including postcode*] registered at HM Land Registry with title number [*insert*].

Recitals

Recital for without notice hearings

3. (*In the case of an order made without notice*)

a. This order was made at a hearing without notice to the respondent. The reason why the order was made without notice to the respondent was [*set out*]

b. The Judge read the following affidavits/witness statements [*set out*] and heard oral testimony from [*name*].

Recital for short informal notice hearings

4. (*In the case of an order made following the giving of short informal notice*)
This order was made at a hearing without full notice having been given to the respondent. The reason why the order was made without full notice having been given to the respondent was [*set out*]

Recital as to a MIAM

5. [It is recorded that the [applicant]/[respondent]/[parties] have attended a MIAM and have sent to the court a completed Form FM1 dated [*insert*]]/[It is recorded that the [applicant has not]/[respondent has not]/[neither of the parties have] attended a MIAM; and it is further recorded that [it appears to the court that a MIAM would not be appropriate within these proceedings]/[it appears to the court that neither party has provided any reason that in the view of the court would render mediation unlikely to be effective]]

Agreements

6. (Record any agreements reached between the parties – for example: The parties have agreed the value of the family home at [insert address including postcode] at [insert value] for FDR purposes).

Undertakings to the court

7. (Record any undertakings given).

Undertaking for without notice hearings

8. By [*insert time and date*] the applicant shall [use [his]/[her] best endeavours personally to serve upon the respondent]/[serve upon the respondent, by [*insert method of service – for example posting to the respondent's usual address*]], together with this order:

a.   a copy of the application;

b.   copies of the witness statement(s) and exhibits containing the evidence relied upon by the applicant, and any other documents provided to the court on the making of the application; and

c.   a note [prepared by [his]/[her] solicitor] recording the substance of the dialogue with the court at the hearing and the reasons given by the court for making the order, which note shall include (but not be limited to) any allegation of fact made orally to the court where such allegation is not contained in the witness statement(s) or draft witness statement(s) read by the judge.

Undertaking to pay mortgage and outgoings on property

9. The [applicant]/[respondent] shall make the following payments pending [the financial dispute resolution appointment]/[the final determination of these proceedings]:- [*insert – for example* all interest and capital repayments due in respect of the mortgage secured against the family home; and all [reasonable] sums due in respect of service charge, council tax, utilities (including but not limited to gas, electricity, water and telephone accounts), and buildings and contents insurance premiums in respect of the family home].

Undertaking where a legal services order is made

10. The [applicant]/[respondent] shall repay to the [respondent]/[applicant] such part of the amounts paid under the legal services order below if, and to the extent that, the court is of the opinion, when considering costs at the conclusion of the proceedings, that (s)he ought to do so.

You may be held to be in contempt of court and imprisoned or fined, or your assets may be seized, if you break the promises that you have given to the court. If you fail to pay any sum of money which you have promised the court that you will pay, a person entitled to enforce the undertaking may apply to the court for an order. You may be sent to prison if it is proved that you-
(a) have, or have had since the date of your undertaking, the means to pay the sum; and
(b) have refused or neglected, or are refusing or neglecting, to pay that sum.
I understand the undertakings that I have given, and that if I break any of my promises to the court I may be sent to prison for contempt of court.
....

Orders

IT IS ORDERED (BY CONSENT) THAT:

Maintenance Pending Suit

11.   The [applicant]/[respondent] shall pay to the [respondent]/[applicant] maintenance pending suit until the date of decree absolute and afterwards interim periodical

payments at the rate of £[*insert*] per annum, payable [weekly]/[monthly] [in advance]/[in arrears] by standing order from [*insert date, including a date earlier than the date of the order if backdating*] until further order. [The [applicant]/[respondent] shall be given credit for the payment(s) of £[*insert*] made on [*insert dates*]].

OR

The [applicant]/[respondent] shall pay to the [respondent]/[applicant] maintenance pending suit until the date of decree absolute and afterwards interim periodical payments. Payments shall be at the rate of £[*insert*] per annum, payable [weekly]/[monthly] [in advance]/[in arrears] by standing order. Payments shall start on [*insert date, including a date earlier than the date of the order if backdating*], and shall end on the first to occur of:

a.   the death of either the applicant or the respondent;

b.   the [respondent's]/[applicant's] remarriage;

c.   the determination of the applicant's application for a financial order; or

d.   a further order.

[The [applicant]/[respondent] shall be given credit for the payment(s) of £[*insert*] made on [*insert date*]].

Legal Services Order

12.

a.   This is a legal services order made pursuant to s 22ZA of the Matrimonial Causes Act 1973/para 38A of Schedule 5 to the Civil Partnership Act 2004.

b.   The court was satisfied that without the amount specified below, the [applicant]/[respondent] would not reasonably be able to obtain appropriate legal services for the purposes of the proceedings.

c.   The [respondent/applicant] shall pay the amount of £[*insert amount*] [by *insert time and date*]/[per calendar month commencing on *insert time and date* until *insert time and date*] to [*insert name*], the legal representatives of the [applicant/respondent].

Order to attend a MIAM and to send form FM1 to the Court

13. The [applicant]/[respondent] shall attend a Mediation Information and Assessment Meeting and shall send a completed Form FM1 to the court by [*insert time and date*].

Form E/Form E1

14.

a.   The [applicant]/[respondent] shall send to the court and serve on the [respondent]/[applicant] a signed copy of [his]/[her] [Form E]/[Form E1] together with all relevant attachments and accompanying documents by [*insert time and date*].

b.   If the [applicant]/[respondent] has not been personally served with this order by [*insert date*], and the [applicant]/[respondent] has thus not completed the steps by [*insert time and date*], then [he]/[she] shall send to the court and serve on the [respondent]/[applicant] a complete signed copy of [his]/[her] [Form E]/[Form E1] together with all relevant attachments and accompanying documents by no later than 4pm on the date [*insert*] days after the date on which [he]/[she] is personally served with this order. If that date falls on a date on which the courts are closed, then [he]/[she] shall send to the court and serve on the [respondent]/[applicant] [his]/[her] [Form E]/[Form E1] by 4pm on the next day that they are open.

First appointment documents

15. The [applicant]/[respondent] shall send to the court and serve on the [respondent]/[applicant]:

a.   a chronology;

b.   a statement of issues; and

c.   a questionnaire and request for further documents [if so advised] by [*insert time and date*].

Replies to questionnaire

16. The [applicant]/[respondent]/[both parties] shall send to the court and serve on the [respondent]/[applicant]/[other party] [his]/[her]/[their respective] replies to the other's questionnaire and request for further documents [as amended by the judge]/[save for just exceptions] by [*insert time and date*].

Schedule of deficiencies and supplemental questionnaire

17. The [applicant]/[respondent] shall send to the court and serve on the [respondent]/[applicant] a schedule of deficiencies and supplemental questionnaire and request for further documents [if so advised] by [*insert time and date*].

Replies to schedule of deficiencies and supplemental questionnaire

18. The [applicant]/[respondent]/[both parties] shall send to the court and serve on the [respondent]/[applicant]/[other party] [his]/[her]/[their] respective replies to the other's schedule of deficiencies and supplemental questionnaire and request for further documents [as amended by the judge]/[save for just exceptions] by [*insert time and date*].

Statements

19.

a.   The [applicant]/[respondent]/[both parties] shall send to the court and serve on [the respondent]/[the applicant]/[the other party] a concise narrative statement [dealing with all of the relevant factors listed in [*insert the relevant section of the statute(s) or the statute(s)*]]/[dealing with [*insert*]]/[limited to dealing with [*insert*]] by [*insert time and date*].

b.   The [respondent]/[applicant] [shall]/[has permission, if so advised, to] send to the court and serve on the [applicant]/[respondent] a concise narrative statement in answer to that sent by the [applicant]/[respondent] [dealing with]/[limited to] the same issues by [*insert time and date*].

Statements dealing with conduct

20.

a.   In the event that the [applicant]/[respondent] continues to seek to advance a
     conduct case, [he]/[she] shall send to the court and serve on the
     [respondent]/[applicant] a concise statement [(limited to [*insert*] pages)] by [*insert
     time and date*], restricted to addressing the following issues:
     i.   what conduct exactly [he]/[she] is seeking to rely upon;
     ii.   the basis for [his]/[her] conduct allegations; and
     iii. what effect this alleged conduct should have on the current [financial
           remedy] application.
b.   The [respondent]/[applicant] has permission to send to the court and serve on the
     [applicant]/[respondent] a statement in answer, if so advised, by [*insert time and
     date*].

Permission regarding other evidence

21. The [applicant]/[respondent] has permission to send to the court and serve on the
[respondent]/[applicant] [evidence]/[a letter]/[a statement] from [*insert*] if so advised
[dealing with [*insert*]/limited to dealing with [*insert*]] by [*insert time and date*].

Evidence regarding mortgage raising capacity and housing needs

22.

a.   Each party shall serve on the other party copy particulars of properties they
     consider to be suitable to meet [their own] and/or [the child[ren] of the family's]
     housing needs, and the housing needs of [the other] and/or [the child[ren] of the
     family's], (limited to 5 of each) [by [*insert time and date*]]/[by [*insert time*] on the
     date [*insert*] weeks prior to the [financial dispute resolution appointment]/[final
     hearing]].
b.   Each party shall serve on the other party evidence of their mortgage raising
     capacity by [*insert time and date*]/by [*insert time*] on the date [*insert*] weeks prior
     to the [financial dispute resolution appointment]/[final hearing], [such evidence to
     be in the form of a certificate from a mortgage broker, indicating (i) the maximum
     mortgage that the broker believes [he]/[she] will be able to secure and (ii) the
     repayments that would be required on that mortgage on a repayment basis and on
     an interest only basis].
c.   Each party shall have permission to serve on the other party such evidence upon
     which they seek to rely in relation to the other's mortgage capacity within [*insert*]
     days of receipt of the other's evidence as to their own mortgage capacity.

Updating disclosure

23. Each party shall serve on the other party their updating disclosure by [*insert time
and date*]/by [*insert time*] on the date [*insert*] weeks prior to the [financial dispute
resolution appointment]/[final hearing]. Updating disclosure means the disclosure of the
following documents:-

a.   copies of all bank and building society statements relating to accounts in the
     category required by paragraph 2.3 of Form E, covering the period from the last

statement which has been disclosed to the date of updating disclosure, or covering the period from the opening of the account to the date of updating disclosure for any such accounts which have come into existence since Form E;

b.   a copy of the most up to date statement or dividend counterfoil relating to investments in the category required by paragraph 2.4 of Form E, including in respect of any investments which have come into existence since Form E;

c.   a copy of an up to date surrender value for policies in the category required by paragraph 2.5 of Form E, including in respect of any policies which have come into existence since Form E;

d.   copies of documents evidencing the up to date amount due on liabilities in the category required by paragraph 2.9 or 2.10 of Form E, including in respect of any liabilities which have come into existence since Form E;

e.   copies of any business accounts which have become available since Form E for businesses in the category required by paragraph 2.11 of Form E, including in respect of any businesses which have come into existence since Form E, identifying the expected share of business profits from these accounts;

f.   copies of an up to date statement showing the Cash Equivalent of any pension rights (or value of any PPF rights) in the category required by paragraph 2.13 of Form E, including in respect of any pension rights or PPF rights which have come into existence since Form E;

g.   copies of all P60s and P11Ds received since Form E, and all pay slips received since the last P60;

h.   copies of all tax returns sent to HMRC and tax assessments since Form E; and

i.   copies of all documents evidencing all income received since Form E in the nature of dividends, interest, rental income, state benefits or otherwise.

[Important note: paras 24 – 51 cover all possible directions concerning expert evidence. The rules differ between children and non-children cases. In financial remedy proceedings any application which relates "wholly or mainly to the maintenance of a minor" will be classified as children proceedings – see FPR 2010 rule 25.2(1). For convenience these are referred to here as Schedule 1 proceedings. Paras 22 – 27 and 34 – 44 relate to non-Schedule 1 proceedings and paras 28 – 33 and 45 – 49 relate to Schedule 1 proceedings]

Valuation of land and real property [for non-Schedule 1 cases]

Order for one party to instruct an expert [where valuer has been identified]

24.

a.   The [applicant]/[respondent] shall instruct [*insert expert*] as an expert to provide a [valuation report]/[market appraisal] in respect of the property at [*insert address and postcode*].

b.   The letter of instruction shall be drafted by the [applicant]/[respondent] by [*insert time and date*].

c.   The letter of instruction [and [*insert any other documents*]] shall be sent to the expert by [*insert time and date*].

d.   The report shall be sent to the court (in both hardcopy and electronic form) and served on the [applicant]/[respondent] by [*insert time and date*].

e. The [applicant]/[respondent] shall disclose the report to the [respondent]/ [applicant] by [*insert time and date*].

f. The costs charged by the expert for preparing the report shall be met by the [applicant]/[respondent]/[parties equally] in the first instance.

g. [Any questions shall be put to the expert by no later than 10 days after receipt of the report (in accordance with FPR 2010, rule 25.10)].

h. [The expert shall respond to those questions by [*insert time and date*]].

i. [The costs charged by the expert for answering those questions shall be met by the [applicant]/[respondent]/[parties equally]/[party raising them] in the first instance].

j. [Save as is expressly ordered by the court, the [applicant's][respondent's] expert's]/[both experts'] written report(s) shall be admissible without the attendance at court of the expert(s). However, [the applicant's expert]/[the respondent's expert]/[both experts] shall attend the final hearing to give oral evidence, unless agreement about the opinions given by the expert(s) is reached by [*insert time and date*]].

Order for one party to instruct an expert [where valuer has not been identified]

25.

a. The [applicant]/[respondent] shall instruct an [estate agent]/[chartered surveyor]/ [appropriate expert] to provide a [valuation report]/[market appraisal] in respect of the property at [*insert address and postcode*]

b. The letter of instruction shall be drafted by the [applicant]/[respondent] by [*insert time and date*].

c. The letter of instruction [and [*insert any other documents*]] shall be sent to the expert by [*insert time and date*].

d. The report shall be sent to the court (in both hardcopy and electronic form) and served on the [applicant]/[respondent] by [*insert time and date*].

e. The [applicant]/[respondent] shall disclose the report to the [respondent]/ [applicant] by [*insert time and date*].

f. The costs charged by the expert for preparing the report shall be met by the [applicant]/[respondent]/[parties equally] in the first instance.

g. [Any questions shall be put to the expert by no later than 10 days after receipt of the report (in accordance with FPR 2010, rule 25.10)].

h. [The expert shall respond to those questions by [*insert time and date*]].

i. [The costs charged by the expert for answering those questions shall be met by the [applicant]/[respondent]/[parties equally]/[party raising them] in the first instance].

j. [Save as is expressly ordered by the court, the [applicant's][respondent's] expert's]/[both experts'] written report(s) shall be admissible without the attendance at court of the expert. However, [the applicant's expert]/[the respondent's expert]/[both experts] shall attend the final hearing to give oral evidence, unless agreement about the opinions given by the expert(s) is reached by [*insert time and date*]].

Order for individually instructed experts to exchange reports/meet

26.

a. The [applicant]/[the respondent]/[the parties] shall [each] disclose [his]/[her]/[their] expert's [valuation report]/[market appraisal to [the respondent's]/[the applicant's]/ [the other's] expert by [*insert time and date*].

b. There shall be a meeting between the [applicant's]/[respondent's] expert and [respondent's]/[applicant's] expert by [*insert time and date*] to discuss:
    i.   the reasons for disagreement on any expert question and what, if any, action needs to be taken to resolve any outstanding disagreement or question;
    ii. what existing evidence or additional evidence needs to be obtained to assist the Court to determine the issues;
    iii. etc.
    At least five business days prior to this meeting, [*insert nominated professional in accordance with FPR PD 25E, para 3.1*] shall formulate an agenda including a list of questions for consideration at the meeting, and at least two business days prior to this meeting, [*insert nominated professional in accordance with FPR PD 25E, para 3.1*] shall send the agenda to both experts].

c. A statement of agreement and disagreement shall be prepared by the experts following their meeting and shall be served on both parties not later than 5 business days after the meeting has taken place.

d. [Save as is expressly ordered by the court, the [applicant's][respondent's] expert's]/[both experts'] written report(s) shall be admissible without the attendance at court of the expert(s). However, [the applicant's expert]/[the respondent's expert]/[both experts] shall attend the final hearing to give oral evidence, unless agreement about the opinions given by the expert(s) is reached by [*insert time and date*]].

Order to instruct a single joint expert [where valuer has been identified]

27.

The parties shall jointly instruct [*insert expert*] as a single joint expert to provide a [valuation report]/[market appraisal] in respect of the property at [*insert address and postcode*], in accordance with the attached letter of instruction, and the following consequential provisions shall apply:

a. The letter of instruction [and [*insert any other documents*]] shall be sent to the expert by [*insert time and date*].

b. The report shall be sent to the court (in both hardcopy and electronic format) and served on the parties simultaneously by [*insert time and date*].

c. The costs charged by the expert for preparing the report shall be met by the [applicant]/[respondent]/[parties equally] in the first instance.

d. [Any questions shall be put to the expert by no later than 10 days after receipt of the report (in accordance with FPR 2010, rule 25.10)].

e. [The expert shall respond to those questions by [*insert time and date*]].

f. [The costs charged by the expert for answering those questions shall be met by the [applicant]/[respondent]/[parties equally]/[party raising them] in the first instance].

g. [Save as is expressly ordered by the court, the expert's written report shall be admissible without the attendance at court of the expert. However, the expert shall attend the final hearing to give oral evidence, unless agreement about the opinions given by the expert is reached by [*insert time and date*]].

OR

The parties [shall] jointly instruct [*insert expert*] as a single joint expert to provide a [valuation report]/[market appraisal] in respect of the property at [*insert address and postcode*], and the following consequential provisions shall apply:

a. The letter of instruction shall be drafted by the [applicant]/[respondent] and agreed with the [respondent]/[applicant] by [*insert time and date*], or determined by the court in default of agreement.

b. The letter of instruction [and [*insert any other documents*]] shall be sent to the expert by [*insert time and date*];

c. The report shall be sent to the court (in both hardcopy and electronic format) and served on the parties simultaneously by [*insert time and date*].

d. The costs charged by the expert for preparing the report shall be met by the [applicant]/[respondent]/[parties equally] in the first instance.

e. [Any questions shall be put to the expert by no later than 10 days after receipt of the report (in accordance with FPR 2010, rule 25.10)].

f. [The expert shall respond to those questions by [*insert time and date*]].

g. [The costs charged by the expert for answering those questions shall be met by the [applicant]/[respondent]/[parties equally]/[party raising them] in the first instance].

h. [Save as is expressly ordered by the court, the expert's written report shall be admissible without the attendance at court of the expert. However, the expert shall attend the final hearing to give oral evidence, unless agreement about the opinions given by the expert is reached by [*insert time and date*]].

Order to instruct a single joint expert [where valuer has not been identified]

28. The value of the property at [*insert address and postcode*] shall be agreed if possible. In default of agreement by [*insert time and date*], the parties shall jointly instruct an [estate agent]/[chartered surveyor]/[appropriate expert] to act as a single joint expert and to provide a [valuation report]/[market appraisal] in respect of the property at [*insert address and postcode*] and the following consequential provisions shall apply:

a. [The parties shall agree the identity of the single joint expert by [*insert time and date*]. If the parties cannot agree the identity of the single joint expert, [the President of the Royal Institution of Chartered Surveyors shall nominate an [estate agent]/[surveyor]]/[the [applicant]/[respondent] shall provide the [respondent]/[applicant] with a list of three appropriate experts by [*insert date and time*], and the [respondent]/[applicant] shall select one of the experts from the list by [*insert time and date*].

b. The letter of instruction shall be drafted by the [applicant]/[respondent] and agreed with the [respondent]/[applicant] by [*insert time and date*], or determined by the court in default of agreement.

c. The letter of instruction [and [*insert any other documents*]] shall be sent to the expert by [*insert time and date*].

d. The report shall be sent to the court (in both hardcopy and electronic format) and served on the parties simultaneously by [*insert time and date*].

e. The costs charged by the expert for preparing the report shall be met by the [applicant]/[respondent]/[parties equally] in the first instance.

f. [Any questions shall be put to the expert by no later than 10 days after receipt of the report (in accordance with FPR 2010, rule 25.10)].

g. [The expert shall respond to those questions by [*insert time and date*]].

h. [The costs charged by the expert for answering those questions shall be met by the [applicant]/[respondent]/[parties equally]/[party raising them] in the first instance].

i. [Save as is expressly ordered by the court, the expert's written report shall be admissible without the attendance at court of the expert. However, the expert shall attend the final hearing to give oral evidence, unless agreement about the opinions given by the expert is reached by [*insert time and date*]].

Other

29. [The valuation of the property at [*insert address and postcode*] prepared by [*insert name*] and dated [*insert date*] shall be the valuation to be used for the purposes of the [financial dispute resolution appointment]/[final hearing]/[*as appropriate.*]

OR

[The parties have]/[The applicant has]/[The respondent has] permission to rely on the valuation of the property at [*insert address and postcode*] prepared by [*insert name*] and dated [*insert date*], and this shall be the valuation to be used, for the purposes of the [financial dispute resolution appointment]/[final hearing]/[*as appropriate.*]

Valuation of land and real property [for Schedule 1 cases]

Permission to one party to instruct an expert [where valuer has been identified]

30.

a. The [applicant]/[respondent] has permission to instruct [*insert expert*] as an expert to provide a [valuation report]/[market appraisal] in respect of the property at [*insert address and postcode*].

b. The question(s) which the [applicant]/[respondent] shall ask of [*insert expert*] shall be as follows:
    i.   set out the estimated amount which a willing buyer could be expected to pay a willing seller for the property in an arms-length transaction after proper marketing of the property on the open market, where both the buyer and the seller have acted knowledgably, prudently and without compulsion;
    ii. etc

c. The letter of instruction shall be drafted by the [applicant]/[respondent] by [*insert time and date*].

d. The letter of instruction [and [*insert any other documents*]] shall be sent to the expert by [*insert time and date*].

e. The report shall be sent to the court (in both hardcopy and electronic form) and served on the [applicant]/[respondent] by [*insert time and date*].

f. The [applicant]/[respondent] shall disclose the report to the [respondent]/[applicant] by [*insert time and date*].

g. The costs charged by the expert for preparing the report shall be met by the [applicant]/[respondent]/[parties equally] in the first instance.

h. [Any questions shall be put to the expert by no later than 10 days after receipt of the report (in accordance with FPR 2010, rule 25.10)].

i. [The expert shall respond to those questions by [*insert time and date*]].

j.   [The costs charged by the expert for answering those questions shall be met by the [applicant]/[respondent]/[parties equally]/[party raising them] in the first instance].

k.   [Save as is expressly ordered by the court, the [applicant's][respondent's] expert's]/[both experts'] written report(s) shall be admissible without the attendance at court of the expert(s). However, [the applicant's expert]/[the respondent's expert]/[both experts] shall attend the final hearing to give oral evidence, unless agreement about the opinions given by the expert(s) is reached by [*insert time and date*]].

Permission to one party to instruct an expert [where valuer has not been identified]

31.

a.   The [applicant]/[respondent] has permission to instruct an [estate agent]/[chartered surveyor]/[appropriate expert] to provide a [valuation report]/[market appraisal] in respect of the property at [*insert address and postcode*]

b.   The question(s) which the [applicant]/[respondent] shall ask of the expert shall be as follows:
   i.   set out the estimated amount which a willing buyer could be expected to pay a willing seller for the property in an arms-length transaction after proper marketing of the property on the open market, where both the buyer and the seller have acted knowledgably, prudently and without compulsion;
   ii.   etc

c.   The letter of instruction shall be drafted by the [applicant]/[respondent] by [*insert time and date*].

d.   The letter of instruction [and [*insert any other documents*]] shall be sent to the expert by [*insert time and date*].

e.   The report shall be sent to the court (in both hardcopy and electronic form) and served on the [applicant]/[respondent] by [*insert time and date*].

f.   The [applicant]/[respondent] shall disclose the report to the [respondent]/[applicant] by [*insert time and date*].

g.   The costs charged by the expert for preparing the report shall be met by the [applicant]/[respondent]/[parties equally] in the first instance.

h.   [Any questions shall be put to the expert by no later than 10 days after receipt of the report (in accordance with FPR 2010, rule 25.10)].

i.   [The expert shall respond to those questions by [*insert time and date*]].

j.   [The costs charged by the expert for answering those questions shall be met by the [applicant]/[respondent]/[parties equally]/[party raising them] in the first instance].

k.   [Save as is expressly ordered by the court, the [applicant's][respondent's] expert's]/[both experts'] written report(s) shall be admissible without the attendance at court of the expert(s). However, [the applicant's expert]/[the respondent's expert]/[both experts] shall attend the final hearing to give oral evidence, unless agreement about the opinions given by the expert(s) is reached by [*insert time and date*]].

Order for individually instructed experts to exchange reports/meet

32.

a. [The applicant]/[the respondent]/[the parties] shall [each] disclose [his]/[her]/[their] expert's [valuation report]/[market appraisal to [the respondent's]/[the applicant's]/ [the other's] expert by [*insert time and date*.

b. There shall be a meeting between the [applicant's]/[respondent's] expert and [respondent's]/[applicant's] expert by [*insert time and date*] to discuss:
   i. the reasons for disagreement on any expert question and what, if any, action needs to be taken to resolve any outstanding disagreement or question;
   ii. what existing evidence or additional evidence needs to be obtained to assist the Court to determine the issues;
   iii. etc.
   At least five business days prior to this meeting, [*insert nominated professional in accordance with FPR PD 25E, para 3.1*] shall formulate an agenda including a list of questions for consideration at the meeting, and at least two business days prior to this meeting, [*insert nominated professional in accordance with FPR PD 25E, para 3.1*] shall send the agenda to both experts].

c. A statement of agreement and disagreement shall be prepared by the experts following their meeting and shall be served on both parties not later than 5 business days after the meeting has taken place.

d. [Save as is expressly ordered by the court, the [applicant's][respondent's] expert's]/[both experts'] written report(s) shall be admissible without the attendance at court of the expert(s). However, [the applicant's expert]/[the respondent's expert]/[both experts] shall attend the final hearing to give oral evidence, unless agreement about the opinions given by the expert(s) is reached by [*insert time and date*]].

Permission to instruct a single joint expert [where valuer has been identified]

33. The parties have permission to jointly instruct [*insert expert*] as a single joint expert to provide a [valuation report]/[market appraisal] in respect of the property at [*insert address and postcode*], in accordance with the attached letter of instruction, and the following consequential provisions shall apply:

a. The question(s) which the parties shall ask of the expert shall be as follows:
   i. set out the estimated amount which a willing buyer could be expected to pay a willing seller for the property in an arms-length transaction after proper marketing of the property on the open market, where both the buyer and the seller have acted knowledgably, prudently and without compulsion; and
   ii. etc

b. The letter of instruction [and [*insert any other documents*]] shall be sent to the expert by [*insert time and date*].

c. The report shall be sent to the court (in both hardcopy and electronic format) and served on the parties simultaneously by [*insert time and date*].

d. The costs charged by the expert for preparing the report shall be met by the [applicant]/[respondent]/[parties equally] in the first instance.

e. [Any questions shall be put to the expert by no later than 10 days after receipt of the report (in accordance with FPR 2010, rule 25.10)].

f. [The expert shall respond to those questions by [*insert time and date*]].

g. [The costs charged by the expert for answering those questions shall be met by the [applicant]/[respondent]/[parties equally]/[party raising them] in the first instance].

h. [Save as is expressly ordered by the court, the expert's written report shall be admissible without the attendance at court of the expert. However, the expert shall attend the final hearing to give oral evidence, unless agreement about the opinions given by the expert is reached by [*insert time and date*]].

OR

The parties have permission to jointly instruct [*insert expert*] as a single joint expert to provide a [valuation report]/[market appraisal] in respect of the property at [*insert address and postcode*], and the following consequential provisions shall apply:

a.   The question(s) which the parties shall ask of the expert shall be as follows:
 i. set out the estimated amount which a willing buyer could be expected to pay a willing seller for the property in an arms-length transaction after proper marketing of the property on the open market, where both the buyer and the seller have acted knowledgably, prudently and without compulsion; and
 ii. etc.

b.   The letter of instruction shall be drafted by the [applicant]/[respondent] and agreed with the [respondent]/[applicant] by [*insert time and date*], or determined by the court in default of agreement.

c.   The letter of instruction [and [*insert any other documents*]] shall be sent to the expert by [*insert time and date*];

d.   The report shall be sent to the court (in both hardcopy and electronic format) and served on the parties simultaneously by [*insert time and date*].

e.   The costs charged by the expert for preparing the report shall be met by the [applicant]/[respondent]/[parties equally] in the first instance.

f.   [Any questions shall be put to the expert by no later than 10 days after receipt of the report (in accordance with FPR 2010, rule 25.10)].

g.   [The expert shall respond to those questions by [*insert time and date*]].

h.   [The costs charged by the expert for answering those questions shall be met by the [applicant]/[respondent]/[parties equally]/[party raising them] in the first instance].

i.   [Save as is expressly ordered by the court, the expert's written report shall be admissible without the attendance at court of the expert. However, the expert shall attend the final hearing to give oral evidence, unless agreement about the opinions given by the expert is reached by [*insert time and date*]].

Permission to instruct a single joint expert [where valuer has not been identified]

34. The value of the property at [insert address and postcode] shall be agreed if possible. In default of agreement by [insert time and date], the parties have permission to jointly instruct an [estate agent]/[chartered surveyor]/[appropriate expert] to act as a single joint expert and to provide a [valuation report]/[market appraisal] in respect of the property at [insert address and postcode] the following consequential provisions shall apply:

a.   The question(s) which the parties shall ask of the expert shall be as follows:
 i. set out the estimated amount which a willing buyer could be expected to pay a willing seller for the property in an arms-length transaction after proper marketing of the property on the open market, where both the buyer and the seller have acted knowledgably, prudently and without compulsion;
 ii. etc

b.   [The parties shall agree the identity of the single joint expert by [*insert time and date*]. If the parties cannot agree the identity of the single joint expert, [the President of the Royal Institution of Chartered Surveyors shall nominate an [estate agent]/[surveyor]/[the [applicant]/[respondent] shall provide the [respondent]/[applicant] with a list of three appropriate experts by [*insert date and time*], and the [respondent]/[applicant] shall select one of the experts from the list by [*insert time and date*]].

c. The letter of instruction shall be drafted by the [applicant]/[respondent] and agreed with the [respondent]/[applicant] by [*insert time and date*], or determined by the court in default of agreement.

d. The letter of instruction [and [*insert any other documents*]] shall be sent to the expert by [*insert time and date*].

e. The report shall be sent to the court (in both hardcopy and electronic format) and served on the parties simultaneously by [*insert time and date*].

f. The costs charged by the expert for preparing the report shall be met by the [applicant]/[respondent]/[parties equally] in the first instance.

g. [Any questions shall be put to the expert by no later than 10 days after receipt of the report (in accordance with FPR 2010, rule 25.10)].

h. [The expert shall respond to those questions by [*insert time and date*]].

i. [The costs charged by the expert for answering those questions shall be met by the [applicant]/[respondent]/[parties equally]/[party raising them] in the first instance].

j. [Save as is expressly ordered by the court, the expert's written report shall be admissible without the attendance at court of the expert. However, the expert shall attend the final hearing to give oral evidence, unless agreement about the opinions given by the expert is reached by [*insert time and date*]].

Other

35. [The valuation of the property at [insert address and postcode] prepared by [insert name] and dated [insert date] shall be the valuation to be used for the purposes of the [financial dispute resolution appointment]/[final hearing]/[as appropriate.]]/[The parties have]/[The applicant has]/[The respondent has] permission to rely on the valuation of the property at [insert address and postcode] prepared by [insert name] and dated [insert date], and this shall be the valuation to be used, for the purposes of the [financial dispute resolution appointment]/[final hearing]/[as appropriate.]]

Updating property valuations for final hearing

36. In relation to any real property valued prior to the financial dispute resolution appointment and in relation to which either party wishes to assert that the value has significantly changed since that valuation was undertaken, the parties shall instruct (by way of an agreed joint letter of instruction) the single joint expert to express a view on whether there has been any change in value since the initial report and, if so, what is the current value. The costs of this exercise shall be met by the parties equally in the first instance.

Other expert reports – pensions report [for non-Schedule 1 cases]

Pensions information

37. The [pension provider]/[pension scheme] shall [complete, send to the court and serve on the parties a copy of the Form P1 (pension inquiry form)]/[provide the information

required by Regulations 2, 3 and 4 of the Pensions on Divorce etc (Provision of Information Regulations) 2000] by [insert date and time].

Order for one party to instruct an expert [where expert has been identified]

38.

a. The [applicant]/[respondent] shall instruct [*insert actuary/pensions expert*] as an expert to provide a report, addressing:
   i. the most cost-effective way to divide the pension provision available to [the applicant]/[the respondent]/[both parties] between the parties so as to provide equality of pension income [now]/[when the [applicant]/[respondent] reaches the age of 60, 65 or as appropriate];
   ii. an estimate of the pension income that would be receivable by the [applicant]/[respondent] in each of the scenarios in paragraph (ii) above;
   iii. the most cost-effective way to divide the pension provision available to [the applicant]/[the respondent]/[both parties] between the parties so as to achieve equality of [capital value]/[CE] of those pensions;
   iv. etc

b. The letter of instruction shall be drafted by the [applicant]/[respondent] by [*insert time and date*].

c. The letter of instruction [and [*insert any other documents*]] shall be sent to the expert by [*insert time and date*].

d. The report shall be sent to the court (in both hardcopy and electronic form) and served on the [applicant]/[respondent] by [*insert time and date*].

e. The [applicant]/[respondent] shall disclose the report to the [respondent]/[applicant] by [*insert time and date*].

f. The costs charged by the expert for preparing the report shall be met by the [applicant]/[respondent]/[parties equally] in the first instance.

g. [Any questions shall be put to the expert by no later than 10 days after receipt of the report (in accordance with FPR 2010, rule 25.10)].

h. [The expert shall respond to those questions by [*insert time and date*]].

i. [The costs charged by the expert for answering those questions shall be met by the [applicant]/[respondent]/[parties equally]/[party raising them] in the first instance].

j. [Save as is expressly ordered by the court, the [applicant's][respondent's] expert's]/[both experts'] written report(s) shall be admissible without the attendance at court of the expert(s). However, [the applicant's expert]/[the respondent's expert]/[both experts] shall attend the final hearing to give oral evidence, unless agreement about the opinions given by the expert(s) is reached by [*insert time and date*]].

Order for one party to instruct an expert [where expert has not been identified]

39.

a. The [applicant]/[respondent] shall instruct an [actuary]/[pensions expert]/ [appropriate expert] to provide a report, addressing:
   i. the most cost-effective way to divide the pension provision available to [the applicant]/[the respondent]/[both parties] between the parties so as to provide equality of pension income [now]/[when the [applicant]/[respondent] reaches the age of 60, 65 or as appropriate];

ii. an estimate of the pension income that would be receivable by the [applicant]/[respondent] in each of the scenarios in paragraph (ii) above;

iii. the most cost-effective way to divide the pension provision available to [the applicant]/[the respondent]/[both parties] between the parties so as to achieve equality of [capital value]/[CE] of those pensions;

iv. etc

b. The letter of instruction shall be drafted by the [applicant]/[respondent] by [*insert time and date*].

c. The letter of instruction [and [*insert any other documents*]] shall be sent to the expert by [*insert time and date*].

d. The report shall be sent to the court (in both hardcopy and electronic form) and served on the [applicant]/[respondent] by [*insert time and date*].

e. The [applicant]/[respondent] shall disclose the report to the [respondent]/[applicant] by [*insert time and date*].

f. The costs charged by the expert for preparing the report shall be met by the [applicant]/[respondent]/[parties equally] in the first instance.

g. [Any questions shall be put to the expert by no later than 10 days after receipt of the report (in accordance with FPR 2010, rule 25.10)].

h. [The expert shall respond to those questions by [*insert time and date*]].

i. [The costs charged by the expert for answering those questions shall be met by the [applicant]/[respondent]/[parties equally]/[party raising them] in the first instance].

j. [Save as is expressly ordered by the court, the [applicant's][respondent's] expert's]/[both experts'] written report(s) shall be admissible without the attendance at court of the expert(s). However, [the applicant's expert]/[the respondent's expert]/[both experts] shall attend the final hearing to give oral evidence, unless agreement about the opinions given by the expert(s) is reached by [*insert time and date*]].

Order for individually instructed experts to exchange reports/meet

40.

a. [The applicant]/[the respondent]/[the parties] shall [each] disclose [his]/[her]/[their] expert's report to [the respondent's]/[the applicant's]/[the other's] expert by [*insert time and date.*

b. There shall be a meeting between the [applicant's]/[respondent's] expert and [respondent's]/[applicant's] expert by [*insert time and date*] to discuss:

i. the reasons for disagreement on any expert question and what, if any, action needs to be taken to resolve any outstanding disagreement or question;

ii. what existing evidence or additional evidence needs to be obtained to assist the Court to determine the issues;

iii. etc.

At least five business days prior to this meeting, [*insert nominated professional in accordance with FPR PD 25E, para 3.1*] shall formulate an agenda including a list of questions for consideration at the meeting, and at least two business days prior to this meeting, [*insert nominated professional in accordance with FPR PD 25E, para 3.1*] shall send the agenda to both experts].

c. A statement of agreement and disagreement shall be prepared by the experts following their meeting and shall be served on both parties not later than 5 business days after the meeting has taken place.

d. [Save as is expressly ordered by the court, the [applicant's][respondent's] expert's]/[both experts'] written report(s) shall be admissible without the attendance at court of the expert(s). However, [the applicant's expert]/[the respondent's expert]/[both experts] shall attend the final hearing to give oral evidence, unless agreement about the opinions given by the expert(s) is reached by [*insert time and date*]].

Order to instruct a single joint expert [where expert has been identified]

41.

a. The parties shall jointly instruct [*insert actuary/pensions expert*] as a single joint expert to provide a report in accordance with the attached letter of instruction, addressing

    i.   the most cost-effective way to divide the pension provision available to [the applicant]/[the respondent]/[both parties] between the parties so as to provide equality of pension income [now]/[when the [applicant]/[respondent] reaches the age of 60, 65 or as appropriate];

    ii. an estimate of the pension income that would be receivable by the [applicant]/[respondent] in each of the scenarios in paragraph (ii) above;

    iii. the most cost-effective way to divide the pension provision available to [the applicant]/[the respondent]/[both parties] between the parties so as to achieve equality of [capital value]/[CE] of those pensions;

    iv. etc

b. The letter of instruction [and [*insert any other documents*]] shall be sent to the expert by [*insert time and date*].

c. The report shall be sent to the court (in both hardcopy and electronic format) and served on the parties simultaneously by [*insert time and date*].

d. The costs charged by the expert for preparing the report shall be met by the [applicant]/[respondent]/[parties equally] in the first instance.

e. [Any questions shall be put to the expert by no later than 10 days after receipt of the report (in accordance with FPR 2010, rule 25.10)].

f. [The expert shall respond to those questions by [*insert time and date*]].

g. [The costs charged by the expert for answering those questions shall be met by the [applicant]/[respondent]/[parties equally]/[party raising them] in the first instance].

h. [Save as is expressly ordered by the court, the expert's written report shall be admissible without the attendance at court of the expert. However, the expert shall attend the final hearing to give oral evidence, unless agreement about the opinions given by the expert is reached by [*insert time and date*]].

OR

The parties shall jointly instruct [*insert actuary/pensions expert*] as a single joint expert to provide a report, addressing the following matters:

a. the most cost-effective way to divide the pension provision available to [the applicant]/[the respondent]/[both parties] between the parties so as to provide equality of pension income [now]/[when the [applicant]/[respondent] reaches the age of 60, 65 or as appropriate];

b. an estimate of the pension income that would be receivable by the [applicant]/[respondent] in each of the scenarios in paragraph (a) above;

c. the most cost-effective way to divide the pension provision available to [the applicant]/[the respondent]/[both parties] between the parties so as to achieve equality of [capital value]/[CETV] of those pensions;

d. ...

and the following consequential provisions shall apply:

e. The letter of instruction shall be drafted by the [applicant]/[respondent] and agreed with the [respondent]/[applicant] by [*insert time and date*], or determined by the court in default of agreement.

f. The letter of instruction [and [*insert any other documents*]] shall be sent to the expert by [*insert time and date*].

g. The report shall be sent to the court (in both hardcopy and electronic format) and served on the parties simultaneously by [*insert time and date*].

h. The costs charged by the expert for preparing the report shall be met by the [applicant]/[respondent]/[parties equally] in the first instance.

i. [Any questions shall be put to the expert by no later than 10 days after receipt of the report (in accordance with FPR 2010, rule 25.10)].

j. [The expert shall respond to those questions by [*insert time and date*]].

k. [The costs charged by the expert for answering those questions shall be met by the [applicant]/[respondent]/[parties equally]/[party raising them] in the first instance].

l. [Save as is expressly ordered by the court, the expert's written report shall be admissible without the attendance at court of the expert. However, the expert shall attend the final hearing to give oral evidence, unless agreement about the opinions given by the expert is reached by [*insert time and date*]].

Order to instruct a single joint expert [where expert has not been identified]

42.

The parties shall jointly instruct an [actuary]/[pensions expert]/[appropriate expert] to act as a single joint expert and to provide a report, addressing the following matters:

a. the most cost-effective way to divide the pension provision available to [the applicant]/[the respondent]/[both parties] between the parties so as to provide equality of pension income [now]/[when the [applicant]/[respondent] reaches the age of 60, 65 *or as appropriate*];

b. an estimate of the pension income that would be receivable by the [applicant]/[respondent] in each of the scenarios in paragraph (a) above;

c. the most cost-effective way to divide the pension provision available to [the applicant]/[the respondent]/[both parties] between the parties so as to achieve equality of [capital value]/[CE] of those pensions;

d. ...

and the following consequential provisions shall apply:

e. The [applicant]/[respondent] shall provide the [respondent]/[applicant] with a list of three appropriate experts by [*insert date and time*].

f. The [respondent]/[applicant] shall select one of the experts from the list by [*insert time and date*].

g. The letter of instruction shall be drafted by the [applicant]/[respondent] and agreed with the [respondent]/[applicant] by [*insert time and date*], or determined by the court in default of agreement.

h.   The letter of instruction [and [*insert any other documents*]] shall be sent to the expert by [*insert time and date*].

i.   The report shall be sent to the court (in both hardcopy and electronic form) and served on the parties simultaneously by [*insert time and date*].

j.   The costs charged by the expert for preparing the report shall be met by the [applicant]/[respondent]/[parties equally] in the first instance.

k.   [Any questions shall be put to the expert by no later than 10 days after receipt of the report (in accordance with FPR 2010, rule 25.10)].

l.   [The expert shall respond to those questions by [*insert time and date*]].

m.   [The costs charged by the expert for answering those questions shall be met by the [applicant]/[respondent]/[parties equally]/[party raising them] in the first instance].

n.   [Save as is expressly ordered by the court, the expert's written report shall be admissible without the attendance at court of the expert. However, the expert shall attend the final hearing to give oral evidence, unless agreement about the opinions given by the expert is reached by [*insert time and date*]].

Other expert reports – tax report [for non-Schedule 1 cases]

Order to one party to instruct an expert [where expert has been identified]

43.

a.   The [applicant]/[respondent] shall instruct [*insert expert*] as an expert to provide a report, addressing the tax liabilities, if any, and date(s) for payment, which would arise whether in the UK or elsewhere in each of the following scenarios:
   i.   the disposal by [the applicant]/[the respondent] of [his]/[her] interest in [*insert property*];
   ii.   the transfer by [the applicant]/[the respondent] of [his]/[her] interest in [*insert property*] to [the respondent]/[the applicant];
   iii. the settling by [the applicant]/[the respondent] of [his]/[her] interest in [*insert property*] on [the respondent]/[the applicant];
   iv.   the disposal by either party of any of their other assets, including the [applicant's]/[respondent's] offshore assets;
   v.   the transfer by either party of any of their other assets to the other, including the [applicant's]/[respondent's] offshore assets;
   vi.   the repatriation of any of the [applicant's]/[respondent's] offshore assets;
   vii. the possible methods of mitigating the amount of tax due in any of the above scenarios, and the likely effects of such mitigation on the amounts of tax due;
   viii. etc

b.   The letter of instruction shall be drafted by the [applicant]/[respondent] by [*insert time and date*].

c.   The letter of instruction [and [*insert any other documents*]] shall be sent to the expert by [*insert time and date*].

d.   The report shall be sent to the court (in both hardcopy and electronic form) and served on the [applicant]/[respondent] by [*insert time and date*].

e.   The [applicant]/[respondent] shall disclose the report to the [respondent]/[applicant] by [*insert time and date*].

f.   The costs charged by the expert for preparing the report shall be met by the [applicant]/[respondent]/[parties equally] in the first instance.

g.   The [applicant]/[respondent]/[both parties] shall provide the expert with any reasonable assistance requested in compiling the report, including providing any necessary information and documentation within a reasonable timeframe of the request.

h.   [Any questions shall be put to the expert by no later than 10 days after receipt of the report (in accordance with FPR 2010, rule 25.10)].

i.   [The expert shall respond to those questions by [*insert time and date*]].

j.   [The costs charged by the expert for answering those questions shall be met by the [applicant]/[respondent]/[parties equally]/[party raising them] in the first instance].

k.   [Save as is expressly ordered by the court, the [applicant's][respondent's] expert's]/[both experts'] written report(s) shall be admissible without the attendance at court of the expert(s). However, [the applicant's expert]/[the respondent's expert]/[both experts] shall attend the final hearing to give oral evidence, unless agreement about the opinions given by the expert(s) is reached by [*insert time and date*]].

Order to one party to instruct an expert [where expert has not been identified]

44.

a.   The [applicant]/[respondent] shall instruct an [accountant]/[appropriate expert] to provide a report, addressing the tax liabilities, if any, and date(s) for payment, which would arise whether in the UK or elsewhere in each of the following scenarios:

    i.   the disposal by [the applicant]/[the respondent] of [his]/[her] interest in [*insert property*];

    ii.   the transfer by [the applicant]/[the respondent] of [his]/[her] interest in [*insert property*] to [the respondent]/[the applicant];

    iii.   the settling by [the applicant]/[the respondent] of [his]/[her] interest in [*insert property*] on [the respondent]/[the applicant];

    iv.   the disposal by either party of any of their other assets, including the [applicant's]/[respondent's] offshore assets;

    v.   the transfer by either party of any of their other assets to the other, including the [applicant's]/[respondent's] offshore assets;

    vi.   the repatriation of any of the [applicant's]/[respondent's] offshore assets;

    vii.   the possible methods of mitigating the amount of tax due in any of the above scenarios, and the likely effects of such mitigation on the amounts of tax due;

    viii. etc

b.   The letter of instruction shall be drafted by the [applicant]/[respondent] by [*insert time and date*].

c.   The letter of instruction [and [*insert any other documents*]] shall be sent to the expert by [*insert time and date*].

d.   The report shall be sent to the court (in both hardcopy and electronic form) and served on the [applicant]/[respondent] by [*insert time and date*].

e.   The [applicant]/[respondent] shall disclose the report to the [respondent]/[applicant] by [*insert time and date*].

f.   The costs charged by the expert for preparing the report shall be met by the [applicant]/[respondent]/[parties equally] in the first instance.

g. The [applicant]/[respondent]/[both parties] shall provide the expert with any reasonable assistance requested in compiling the report, including providing any necessary information and documentation within a reasonable timeframe of the request.

h. [Any questions shall be put to the expert by no later than 10 days after receipt of the report (in accordance with FPR 2010, rule 25.10)].

i. [The expert shall respond to those questions by [*insert time and date*]].

j. [The costs charged by the expert for answering those questions shall be met by the [applicant]/[respondent]/[parties equally]/[party raising them] in the first instance].

k. [Save as is expressly ordered by the court, the [applicant's][respondent's] expert's]/[both experts'] written report(s) shall be admissible without the attendance at court of the expert(s). However, [the applicant's expert]/[the respondent's expert]/[both experts] shall attend the final hearing to give oral evidence, unless agreement about the opinions given by the expert(s) is reached by [*insert time and date*]].

Order for individually instructed experts to exchange reports/meet

45.

a. [The applicant]/[the respondent]/[the parties] shall [each] disclose [his]/[her]/[their] expert's [valuation report]/[market appraisal to [the respondent's]/[the applicant's]/ [the other's] expert by [*insert time and date*.

b. There shall be a meeting between the [applicant's]/[respondent's] expert and [respondent's]/[applicant's] expert by [*insert time and date*] to discuss:
    i.   the reasons for disagreement on any expert question and what, if any, action needs to be taken to resolve any outstanding disagreement or question;
    ii. what existing evidence or additional evidence needs to be obtained to assist the Court to determine the issues;
    iii. etc.
    At least five business days prior to this meeting, [*insert nominated professional in accordance with FPR PD 25E, para 3.1*] shall formulate an agenda including a list of questions for consideration at the meeting, and at least two business days prior to this meeting, [*insert nominated professional in accordance with FPR PD 25E, para 3.1*] shall send the agenda to both experts].

c. A statement of agreement and disagreement shall be prepared by the experts following their meeting and shall be served on both parties not later than 5 business days after the meeting has taken place.

d. [Save as is expressly ordered by the court, the [applicant's][respondent's] expert's]/[both experts'] written report(s) shall be admissible without the attendance at court of the expert(s). However, [the applicant's expert]/[the respondent's expert]/[both experts] shall attend the final hearing to give oral evidence, unless agreement about the opinions given by the expert(s) is reached by [*insert time and date*]].

Order to instruct a single joint expert [where expert has been identified]

46.

a. The parties shall jointly instruct [*insert accountant*] as a single joint expert to provide a report, in accordance with the attached letter of instruction, addressing the tax liabilities, if any, and date(s) for payment, which would arise whether in the UK or elsewhere in each of the following scenarios:

    i.   the disposal by [either party]/[the applicant]/[the respondent] of [any of their interests in their real property]/[[his]/[her] interest in [*insert property*];

    ii.   the transfer by [either party]/[the applicant]/[the respondent] of [any of their interests in their real property to the other]/[of [his]/[her] interest in [*insert property*] to [the respondent]/[the applicant]];

    iii.   the settling by [the applicant]/[the respondent] of [his]/[her] interest in [*insert property*] on [the respondent]/[the applicant];

    iv.   the disposal by either party of any of their other assets, including the [applicant's]/[respondent's] offshore assets;

    v.   the transfer by either party of any of their other assets to the other, including the [applicant's]/[respondent's] offshore assets;

    vi.   the repatriation of any of the [applicant's]/[respondent's] offshore assets;

    vii.   the possible methods of mitigating the amount of tax due in any of the above scenarios, and the likely effects of such mitigation on the amounts of tax due;

    viii.   etc

b.   The letter of instruction [and [*insert any other documents*]] shall be sent to the expert by [*insert time and date*].

c.   The report shall be sent to the court (in both hardcopy and electronic format) and served on the parties simultaneously by [*insert time and date*].

d.   The costs charged by the expert for preparing the report shall be met by the [applicant]/[respondent]/[parties equally] in the first instance.

e.   The [applicant]/[respondent]/[both parties] shall provide the expert with any reasonable assistance requested in compiling the report, including providing any necessary information and documentation within a reasonable timeframe of the request.

f.   [Any questions shall be put to the expert by no later than 10 days after receipt of the report (in accordance with FPR 2010, rule 25.10)].

g.   [The expert shall respond to those questions by [*insert time and date*]].

h.   [The costs charged by the expert for answering those questions shall be met by the [applicant]/[respondent]/[parties equally]/[party raising them] in the first instance].

i.   [Save as is expressly ordered by the court, the expert's written report shall be admissible without the attendance at court of the expert. However, the expert shall attend the final hearing to give oral evidence, unless agreement about the opinions given by the expert is reached by [*insert time and date*]].

OR

a.   The parties shall jointly instruct [*insert accountant*] as a single joint expert to provide a report, addressing the tax liabilities, if any, and date(s) for payment, which would arise whether in the UK or elsewhere in each of the following scenarios:

    i.   the disposal by [either party]/[the applicant]/[the respondent] of [any of their interests in their real property]/[[his]/[her] interest in [*insert property*];

    ii.   the transfer by [either party]/[the applicant]/[the respondent] of [any of their interests in their real property to the other]/[of [his]/[her] interest in [*insert property*] to [the respondent]/[the applicant]];

    iii.   the settling by [the applicant]/[the respondent] of [his]/[her] interest in [*insert property*] on [the respondent]/[the applicant];

    iv.   the disposal by either party of any of their other assets, including the [applicant's]/[respondent's] offshore assets;

v.   the transfer by either party of any of their other assets to the other, including the [applicant's]/[respondent's] offshore assets;

vi.   the repatriation of any of the [applicant's]/[respondent's] offshore assets; and

vii. the possible methods of mitigating the amount of tax due in any of the above scenarios, and the likely effects of such mitigation on the amounts of tax due.

b.   The letter of instruction shall be drafted by the [applicant]/[respondent] and agreed with the [respondent]/[applicant] by [*insert time and date*], or determined by the court in default of agreement.

c.   The letter of instruction [and [*insert any other documents*]] shall be sent to the expert by [*insert time and date*].

d.   The report shall be sent to the court (in both hardcopy and electronic format) and served on the parties simultaneously by [*insert time and date*].

e.   The costs charged by the expert for preparing the report shall be met by the [applicant]/[respondent]/[parties equally] in the first instance.

f.   The [applicant]/[respondent]/[both parties] shall provide the expert with any reasonable assistance requested in compiling the report, including providing any necessary information and documentation within a reasonable timeframe of the request.

g.   [Any questions shall be put to the expert by no later than 10 days after receipt of the report (in accordance with FPR 2010, rule 25.10)].

h.   [The expert shall respond to those questions by [*insert time and date*]].

i.   [The costs charged by the expert for answering those questions shall be met by the [applicant]/[respondent]/[parties equally]/[party raising them] in the first instance].

j.   [Save as is expressly ordered by the court, the expert's written report shall be admissible without the attendance at court of the expert. However, the expert shall attend the final hearing to give oral evidence, unless agreement about the opinions given by the expert is reached by [*insert time and date*]].

Order to instruct a single joint expert [where expert has not been identified]

47.

a.   The parties shall jointly instruct an [accountant]/[appropriate expert] to act as a single joint expert and to provide a report, addressing the tax liabilities, if any, and date(s) for payment, which would arise whether in the UK or elsewhere in each of the following scenarios:

i.   the disposal by [either party]/[the applicant]/[the respondent] of [any of their interests in their real property]/[[his]/[her] interest in [*insert property*]];

ii.   the transfer by [either party]/[the applicant]/[the respondent] of [any of their interests in their real property to the other]/[of [his]/[her] interest in [*insert property*] to [the respondent]/[the applicant]]];

iii. the settling by [the applicant]/[the respondent] of [his]/[her] interest in [*insert property*] on [the respondent]/[the applicant];

iv.   the disposal by either party of any of their other assets, including the [applicant's]/[respondent's] offshore assets;

v.   the transfer by either party of any of their other assets to the other, including the [applicant's]/[respondent's] offshore assets;

vi.   the repatriation of any of the [applicant's]/[respondent's] offshore assets; and

vii. the possible methods of mitigating the amount of tax due in any of the above scenarios, and the likely effects of such mitigation on the amounts of tax due

b. The [applicant]/[respondent] shall provide the [respondent]/[applicant] with a list of three appropriate experts by [*insert date and time*].

c. The [respondent]/[applicant] shall select one of the experts from the list by [*insert time and date*].

d. The letter of instruction shall be drafted by the [applicant]/[respondent] and agreed with the [respondent]/[applicant] by [*insert time and date*], or determined by the court in default of agreement.

e. The letter of instruction [and [*insert any other documents*]] shall be sent to the expert by [*insert time and date*].

f. The report shall be sent to the court (in both hardcopy and electronic form) and served on the parties simultaneously by [*insert time and date*].

g. The costs charged by the expert for preparing the report shall be met by the [applicant]/[respondent]/[parties equally] in the first instance.

h. [Any questions shall be put to the expert by no later than 10 days after receipt of the report (in accordance with FPR 2010, rule 25.10)].

i. [The expert shall respond to those questions by [*insert time and date*]].

j. [The costs charged by the expert for answering those questions shall be met by the [applicant]/[respondent]/[parties equally]/[party raising them] in the first instance].

k. [Save as is expressly ordered by the court, the expert's written report shall be admissible without the attendance at court of the expert. However, the expert shall attend the final hearing to give oral evidence, unless agreement about the opinions given by the expert is reached by [*insert time and date*]].

Other expert reports – tax report [for Schedule 1 cases]

***Permission to one party to instruct an expert* [where expert has been identified]**

48.

a. The [applicant]/[respondent] has permission to instruct [*insert expert*] as an expert to provide a report, going to the following issue in these proceedings: [*insert*].

b. The question(s) which the report shall address shall be the tax liabilities, if any, and date(s) for payment, which would arise whether in the UK or elsewhere in each of the following scenarios:
    i.   the disposal by [the applicant]/[the respondent] of [his]/[her] interest in [*insert property*];
    ii. the transfer by [the applicant]/[the respondent] of [his]/[her] interest in [*insert property*] to [the respondent]/[the applicant];
    iii. the settling by [the applicant]/[the respondent] of [his]/[her] interest in [*insert property*] on [the respondent]/[the applicant];
    iv. the possible methods of mitigating the amount of tax due in any of the above scenarios, and the likely effects of such mitigation on the amounts of tax due;
    v.   etc

c. The letter of instruction shall be drafted by the [applicant]/[respondent] by [*insert time and date*].

d. The letter of instruction [and [*insert any other documents*]] shall be sent to the expert by [*insert time and date*].

e. The report shall be sent to the court (in both hardcopy and electronic form) and served on the [applicant]/[respondent] by [*insert time and date*].

f.　The [applicant]/[respondent] shall disclose the report to the [respondent]/ [applicant] by [*insert time and date*].

g.　The costs charged by the expert for preparing the report shall be met by the [applicant]/[respondent]/[parties equally] in the first instance.

h.　The [applicant]/[respondent]/[both parties] shall provide the expert with any reasonable assistance requested in compiling the report, including providing any necessary information and documentation within a reasonable timeframe of the request.

i.　[Any questions shall be put to the expert by no later than 10 days after receipt of the report (in accordance with FPR 2010, rule 25.10)].

j.　[The expert shall respond to those questions by [*insert time and date*]].

k.　[The costs charged by the expert for answering those questions shall be met by the [applicant]/[respondent]/[parties equally]/[party raising them] in the first instance].

l.　[Save as is expressly ordered by the court, the [applicant's][respondent's] expert's]/[both experts'] written report(s) shall be admissible without the attendance at court of the expert(s). However, [the applicant's expert]/[the respondent's expert]/[both experts] shall attend the final hearing to give oral evidence, unless agreement about the opinions given by the expert(s) is reached by [*insert time and date*]].

Permission to one party to instruct an expert [where expert has not been identified]

49.

a.　The [applicant]/[respondent] has permission to instruct an [accountant]/ [appropriate expert] to provide a report, going to the following issue in these proceedings: [*insert*].

b.　The question(s) which the report shall address shall be the tax liabilities, if any, and date(s) for payment, which would arise whether in the UK or elsewhere in each of the following scenarios:
  i.　the disposal by [the applicant]/[the respondent] of [his]/[her] interest in [*insert property*];
  ii.　the transfer by [the applicant]/[the respondent] of [his]/[her] interest in [*insert property*] to [the respondent]/[the applicant];
  iii.　the settling by [the applicant]/[the respondent] of [his]/[her] interest in [*insert property*] on [the respondent]/[the applicant];
  iv.　the possible methods of mitigating the amount of tax due in any of the above scenarios, and the likely effects of such mitigation on the amounts of tax due;
  v.　etc

c.　The letter of instruction shall be drafted by the [applicant]/[respondent] by [*insert time and date*].

d.　The letter of instruction [and [*insert any other documents*]] shall be sent to the expert by [*insert time and date*].

e.　The report shall be sent to the court (in both hardcopy and electronic form) and served on the [applicant]/[respondent] by [*insert time and date*].

f.　The [applicant]/[respondent] shall disclose the report to the [respondent]/ [applicant] by [*insert time and date*].

g.　The costs charged by the expert for preparing the report shall be met by the [applicant]/[respondent]/[parties equally] in the first instance.

h. The [applicant]/[respondent]/[both parties] shall provide the expert with any reasonable assistance requested in compiling the report, including providing any necessary information and documentation within a reasonable timeframe of the request.

i. [Any questions shall be put to the expert by no later than 10 days after receipt of the report (in accordance with FPR 2010, rule 25.10)].

j. [The expert shall respond to those questions by [*insert time and date*]].

k. [The costs charged by the expert for answering those questions shall be met by the [applicant]/[respondent]/[parties equally]/[party raising them] in the first instance].

l. [Save as is expressly ordered by the court, the [applicant's][respondent's] expert's]/[both experts'] written report(s) shall be admissible without the attendance at court of the expert(s). However, [the applicant's expert]/[the respondent's expert]/[both experts] shall attend the final hearing to give oral evidence, unless agreement about the opinions given by the expert(s) is reached by [*insert time and date*]].

Order for individually instructed experts to exchange reports/meet

50.

a. [The applicant]/[the respondent]/[the parties] shall [each] disclose [his]/[her]/[their] expert's [valuation report]/[market appraisal to [the respondent's]/[the applicant's]/[the other's] expert by [*insert time and date*.

b. There shall be a meeting between the [applicant's]/[respondent's] expert and [respondent's]/[applicant's] expert by [*insert time and date*] to discuss:
    i.   the reasons for disagreement on any expert question and what, if any, action needs to be taken to resolve any outstanding disagreement or question;
    ii. what existing evidence or additional evidence needs to be obtained to assist the Court to determine the issues;
    iii. etc.
    At least five business days prior to this meeting, [*insert nominated professional in accordance with FPR PD 25E, para 3.1*] shall formulate an agenda including a list of questions for consideration at the meeting, and at least two business days prior to this meeting, [*insert nominated professional in accordance with FPR PD 25E, para 3.1*] shall send the agenda to both experts].

c. A statement of agreement and disagreement shall be prepared by the experts following their meeting and shall be served on both parties not later than 5 business days after the meeting has taken place.

d. [Save as is expressly ordered by the court, the [applicant's][respondent's] expert's]/[both experts'] written report(s) shall be admissible without the attendance at court of the expert(s). However, [the applicant's expert]/[the respondent's expert]/[both experts] shall attend the final hearing to give oral evidence, unless agreement about the opinions given by the expert(s) is reached by [*insert time and date*]].

Permission to instruct a single joint expert [where expert has been identified]

51.

a. The parties have permission to jointly instruct [*insert accountant*] as a single joint expert to provide a report, in accordance with the attached letter of instruction, going to the following issue in these proceedings: [*insert*].

b. The question(s) which the report shall address shall be the tax liabilities, if any, and date(s) for payment, which would arise whether in the UK or elsewhere in each of the following scenarios:

    i. the disposal by [either party]/[the applicant]/[the respondent] of [any of their interests in their real property]/[[his]/[her] interest in [*insert property*];

    ii. the transfer by [either party]/[the applicant]/[the respondent] of [any of their interests in their real property to the other]/[of [his]/[her] interest in [*insert property*] to [the respondent]/[the applicant]];

    iii. the settling by [the applicant]/[the respondent] of [his]/[her] interest in [*insert property*] on [the respondent]/[the applicant];

    iv. the possible methods of mitigating the amount of tax due in any of the above scenarios, and the likely effects of such mitigation on the amounts of tax due;

    v. etc

c. The letter of instruction [and [*insert any other documents*]] shall be sent to the expert by [*insert time and date*].

d. The report shall be sent to the court (in both hardcopy and electronic format) and served on the parties simultaneously by [*insert time and date*].

e. The costs charged by the expert for preparing the report shall be met by the [applicant]/[respondent]/[parties equally] in the first instance.

f. The [applicant]/[respondent]/[both parties] shall provide the expert with any reasonable assistance requested in compiling the report, including providing any necessary information and documentation within a reasonable timeframe of the request.

g. [Any questions shall be put to the expert by no later than 10 days after receipt of the report (in accordance with FPR 2010, rule 25.10)].

h. [The expert shall respond to those questions by [*insert time and date*]].

i. [The costs charged by the expert for answering those questions shall be met by the [applicant]/[respondent]/[parties equally]/[party raising them] in the first instance].

j. [Save as is expressly ordered by the court, the expert's written report shall be admissible without the attendance at court of the expert. However, the expert shall attend the final hearing to give oral evidence, unless agreement about the opinions given by the expert is reached by [*insert time and date*]].

OR

a. The parties have permission to jointly instruct [*insert accountant*] as a single joint expert to provide a report, going to the following issue in these proceedings: [*insert*].

b. The question(s) which the report shall address shall be the tax liabilities, if any, and date(s) for payment, which would arise whether in the UK or elsewhere in each of the following scenarios:

    i. the disposal by [either party]/[the applicant]/[the respondent] of [any of their interests in their real property]/[[his]/[her] interest in [*insert property*];

    ii.   the transfer by [either party]/[the applicant]/[the respondent] of [any of their interests in their real property to the other]/[of [his]/[her] interest in [*insert property*] to [the respondent]/[the applicant]];

    iii.   the settling by [the applicant]/[the respondent] of [his]/[her] interest in [*insert property*] on [the respondent]/[the applicant];

    iv.   the possible methods of mitigating the amount of tax due in any of the above scenarios, and the likely effects of such mitigation on the amounts of tax due;

    v.   etc

c.   The letter of instruction shall be drafted by the [applicant]/[respondent] and agreed with the [respondent]/[applicant] by [*insert time and date*], or determined by the court in default of agreement.

d.   The letter of instruction [and [*insert any other documents*]] shall be sent to the expert by [*insert time and date*].

e.   The report shall be sent to the court (in both hardcopy and electronic format) and served on the parties simultaneously by [*insert time and date*].

f.   The costs charged by the expert for preparing the report shall be met by the [applicant]/[respondent]/[parties equally] in the first instance.

g.   The [applicant]/[respondent]/[both parties] shall provide the expert with any reasonable assistance requested in compiling the report, including providing any necessary information and documentation within a reasonable timeframe of the request.

h.   [Any questions shall be put to the expert by no later than 10 days after receipt of the report (in accordance with FPR 2010, rule 25.10)].

i.   [The expert shall respond to those questions by [*insert time and date*]].

j.   [The costs charged by the expert for answering those questions shall be met by the [applicant]/[respondent]/[parties equally]/[party raising them] in the first instance].

k.   [Save as is expressly ordered by the court, the expert's written report shall be admissible without the attendance at court of the expert. However, the expert shall attend the final hearing to give oral evidence, unless agreement about the opinions given by the expert is reached by [*insert time and date*]].

Permission to instruct a single joint expert [where expert has not been identified]

52.

a.   The parties have permission to jointly instruct an [accountant]/[appropriate expert] to act as a single joint expert and to provide a report, going to the following issue in these proceedings: [*insert*].

b.   The question(s) which the report shall address shall be the tax liabilities, if any, and date(s) for payment, which would arise whether in the UK or elsewhere in each of the following scenarios:

    i.   the disposal by [either party]/[the applicant]/[the respondent] of [any of their interests in their real property]/[[his]/[her] interest in [*insert property*]];

    ii.   the transfer by [either party]/[the applicant]/[the respondent] of [any of their interests in their real property to the other]/[of [his]/[her] interest in [*insert property*] to [the respondent]/[the applicant]];

    iii.   the settling by [the applicant]/[the respondent] of [his]/[her] interest in [*insert property*] on [the respondent]/[the applicant];

    iv.   the possible methods of mitigating the amount of tax due in any of the above scenarios, and the likely effects of such mitigation on the amounts of tax du;

    v.   etc

c. The [applicant]/[respondent] shall provide the [respondent]/[applicant] with a list of three appropriate experts by [*insert date and time*].

d. The [respondent]/[applicant] shall select one of the experts from the list by [*insert time and date*].

e. The letter of instruction shall be drafted by the [applicant]/[respondent] and agreed with the [respondent]/[applicant] by [*insert time and date*], or determined by the court in default of agreement.

f. The letter of instruction [and [*insert any other documents*]] shall be sent to the expert by [*insert time and date*].

g. The report shall be sent to the court (in both hardcopy and electronic form) and served on the parties simultaneously by [*insert time and date*].

h. The costs charged by the expert for preparing the report shall be met by the [applicant]/[respondent]/[parties equally] in the first instance.

i. The [applicant]/[respondent]/[both parties] shall provide the expert with any reasonable assistance requested in compiling the report, including providing any necessary information and documentation within a reasonable timeframe of the request.

j. [Any questions shall be put to the expert by no later than 10 days after receipt of the report (in accordance with FPR 2010, rule 25.10)].

k. [The expert shall respond to those questions by [*insert time and date*]].

l. [The costs charged by the expert for answering those questions shall be met by the [applicant]/[respondent]/[parties equally]/[party raising them] in the first instance].

m. [Save as is expressly ordered by the court, the expert's written report shall be admissible without the attendance at court of the expert. However, the expert shall attend the final hearing to give oral evidence, unless agreement about the opinions given by the expert is reached by [*insert time and date*]].

No other expert evidence without the court's permission

53. Save as is expressly ordered by the court, no further expert evidence shall be admissible before the court.

Variation of settlement

54.

a. A copy of the applicant's application for variation of the [*insert*] marriage settlement [and a copy of [*insert other documents to be served*]] shall be served on the following beneficiaries under the settlement [*insert beneficiaries*] by [*insert time and date*].

b. The beneficiaries have permission leave to send to the court and serve signed statements in answer or otherwise in response to the application [by [*insert time and date*]]/[within [*insert*] days after service on them].

Consolidation of proceedings

55.

a.   The [applicant's] [and]/[or] [first respondent's]/[second respondent's] [respective] applications under [*insert statutes – e.g. the Matrimonial Causes Act 1973, Schedule 1 to the Children Act 1989, Trust of Land and Appointment of Trustee Act 1996*] are consolidated.

b.   The applicant's application under [*insert statute*] shall become the lead application, and the consolidated applications shall proceed under case number [*insert*].

c.   The [applicant]/[first respondent]/[second respondent] shall serve on the [first respondent]/[second respondent] etc copies of the following documents in relation to the [applicant's]/[first respondent's]/[second respondent's] application(s) under [*insert statutes – e.g. the Matrimonial Causes Act 1973, Schedule 1 to the Children Act 1989, Trust of Land and Appointment of Trustee Act 1996*]: [*insert documents*]

Intervener(s)

56. [*Insert name*] is given permission to intervene in these proceedings.

Joinder of parties

57. [*Insert name*] and [*insert name*] are joined as [second]/[third] [*etc as appropriate*] respondents to these proceedings.

Evidence to be served on intervener(s)/additional parties

58. The [applicant's]/[respondent's] [solicitors] shall by [*insert time and date*] serve upon the [intervenor]/[second]/[third etc respondent] copies of the following documents:

a. [*Insert*]

Evidence of intervener(s)/additional parties

59. The parties shall identify the basis of the dispute between them by complying with the following directions:

a.   The [applicant]/[respondent]/[intervener]/[second respondent] shall by [*insert time and date*] send to the court and serve on the other parties points of claim, [setting out [his]/[her]/[their] case as to [*insert*] fully]/[dealing with [*insert*]/limited to dealing with [*insert*]] by [*insert date and time*]].

b.   The [applicant]/[respondent]/[intervener]/[second respondent] shall by [*insert time and date*] send to the court and serve on the other parties [points of dispute]/[a defence], [setting out [his]/[her]/[their] case in reply by [*insert time and date*]].

c.   The [applicant]/[respondent]/[intervener]/[second respondent] shall by [*insert time and date*] send to the court and serve on the other parties any witness statements upon which [he]/[she]/[they] intend to rely.

d.   There be the following additional directions for disclosure: [*insert*].

Documents to be produced by trustees

60. The [second] [third etc] respondent shall by [*insert time and date*] send to the court and serve on the applicant and the respondent the following information and documents in respect of the [*insert*] settlement:

a. copies of the deed of trust and all subsequent deeds of variation and appointment;
b. copies of the completed and approved trust accounts for the last [*insert*] years;
c. copies of any letter of wishes;
d. confirmation as to the identity of the present trustees [and protector] of the trust;
e. confirmation as to the identity of the present beneficiaries of the trust;
f. a schedule authenticated by the trustees setting out all distributions and appointments made to or on behalf of the [applicant]/[respondent]/[*insert*] since [*insert date*];
g. a short narrative statement setting out the trustees anticipated position in respect of any further distributions to or on behalf of the [applicant]/[respondent]/[*insert as appropriate*];
h. …

Preliminary issue hearing

61. The issue of the [*insert*] interest in [*insert*] be listed for determination by way of a preliminary issue before a District Judge sitting at [*insert*] court at [*insert*] on [*insert*] with a time estimate of [*insert*].

Scott schedule

62. The [applicant]/[respondent][parties] shall [each] prepare a Scott Schedule, stating in relation to each item of property in dispute [their]/[each party's] case as to:

a. the party by whom it was acquired;
b. how and from whom it was acquired [purchase/inheritance/gift etc] with documentary evidence in support;
c. its current value with documentary evidence in support;
d. what order is sought and the justification for seeking it;
e. …

by [*insert time and date*].

63. [The parties shall send to the court and serve their schedules on each other by [*insert time and date*]]/[The [applicant]/[respondent] shall send to the court and serve on the [respondent]/[applicant] [his]/[her] schedule by [insert time and date], and the [respondent]/[applicant] shall send to the court and serve on the [applicant]/[respondent] [his]/[her] response to the schedule by [*insert time and date*]].

Permission to disclose order to CMS

64.

a.   There be permission to the [applicant]/[respondent] under FPR 2010, rule 12.73(1)(b) to produce to the CMS a copy of the [respondent's]/[applicant's] [Form E]/[Form E1] and Replies to Questionnaire if so advised.

b.   The [applicant]/[respondent] shall send the [respondent]/[applicant] a copy of any letter and supporting documentation sent to the CMS forthwith after sending it.

Further hearing(s)

65. The application shall be listed for a [mention hearing]/[further directions appointment]/[financial dispute resolution appointment]/[case management appointment]/[pre-trial review]/[final hearing] before [*insert name or level of judge*] at the [*insert court*] on [*insert date and time*]/[on the first open day after [*insert date*] [suitable to counsel for both parties]/[on a date to be fixed in consultation with counsel's clerks] with a time estimate of [*insert*]. [The parties and their legal advisors shall send to court their dates to avoid by [*insert time and date*]. [The parties and their legal advisers shall attend the court building at least one hour prior to the listing time of the financial dispute resolution appointment to negotiate and attempt to narrow the issues].

Adjournment

66. This hearing is adjourned until [*insert time and date*] on the following terms [*set out directions to prevail*].

Adjournment for settlement negotiations/mediation/arbitration/private financial dispute resolution appointment

67. This application is adjourned until [*insert time and date*] to enable the parties to attempt to resolve the matters in dispute by means of [negotiation]/[mediation *(details of mediator and start date could be inserted here if useful and available)*]/[arbitration *(insert details if available)*]/[a private financial dispute resolution appointment [arranged in front of [*insert*]]/[to be arranged in front of [*insert*]]/[*other*] Note: *if an adjournment for arbitration is made then give consideration to the available orders in the arbitration section.*

Evidence at the financial dispute resolution appointment

68.

a.   The [applicant]/[respondent] shall prepare a bundle containing:
    i.   an [agreed] chronology;
    ii.   an [agreed] summary of the history of the case;
    iii.   an [agreed] summary of the issues to be determined;
    iv.   an [agreed] schedule of assets. Where the schedule cannot be agreed then the bundle should include the schedule of assets contended for by each party which should identify which items are not agreed between the parties;

v. [*list other documents to be included* – for example [all applications and orders made in these proceedings], [the parties' narrative Forms E], [the parties' narrative replies to questionnaire], [the parties' etc narrative witness statements], [the expert reports].

b. The bundle shall be agreed [if possible] by both parties. The [applicant]/[respondent] shall send the [respondent]/[applicant] a draft index for the bundle by [[*insert time and date*]/[not later than [*insert*] days before the financial dispute resolution appointment]], and the [respondent]/[applicant] shall send the [applicant]/[respondent] any comments on the index by [[*insert time and date*]/[not later than [*insert*] days before the financial dispute resolution appointment]].

c. The bundle must be paginated and the documents shall be in chronological order within each section.

d. The [applicant]/[respondent] shall send the bundle to the court by [[*insert time and date*]/[not later than [*insert*] days before the financial dispute resolution appointment]], and shall provide a copy of the bundle to the [respondent]/[applicant] by [[*insert time and date*]/[not later than [*insert*] days before the financial dispute resolution appointment]] provided that the [respondent]/[applicant] agrees to discharge [his]/[her] reasonable costs of photocopying the bundle. If [he]/[she] does not do so, the [applicant]/[respondent] shall provide an index for the bundle to the [respondent]/[applicant] by [[*insert time and date*]/[not later than [*insert*] days before the financial dispute resolution appointment]].

Evidence at final hearing

69.

a. Both parties shall attend the final hearing to give oral evidence.

b. Any witness [swearing an affidavit]/[sending to the court and serving on the parties a witness statement] shall attend the final hearing to give oral evidence [unless their evidence is not disputed].

c. The hearing shall not be before [District/Circuit/High Court] Judge [*insert*].

d. The [applicant]/[respondent] shall prepare a bundle containing:
   i.   an [agreed] chronology;
   ii. an [agreed] summary of the history of the case;
   iii. an [agreed] summary of the issues to be determined;
   iv. an [agreed] schedule of assets. Where the schedule cannot be agreed then the bundle should include the schedule of assets contended for by each party which should identify which items are not agreed between the parties;
   v.   [*list other documents to be included* – for example [all applications and orders made in these proceedings], [the parties' Forms E], [the parties' Replies to Questionnaire], [the parties' etc witness statements], [the expert reports].

e. The bundle shall be agreed [if possible] by both parties. The [applicant]/[respondent] shall send the [respondent]/[applicant] a draft index for the bundle by [[*insert time and date*]/[not later than [*insert*] days before the final hearing]], and the [respondent]/[applicant] shall send the [applicant]/[respondent] any comments on the index by [[*insert time and date*]/[not later than [*insert*] days before the final hearing]].

f. The bundle must be paginated and the documents shall be in chronological order within each section.

g.   The [applicant]/[respondent] shall send the bundle to court by [[*insert time and date*]/[not later than [*insert*] days before the final hearing]], and shall provide a copy of the bundle to the [respondent]/[applicant] by [[*insert time and date*]/[not later than [*insert*] days before the final hearing]] provided that the [respondent]/[applicant] agrees to discharge [his]/[her] reasonable costs of photocopying the bundle. If [he]/[she] does not do so, the [applicant]/[respondent] shall provide an index for the bundle to the [respondent]/[applicant] by [[*insert time and date*]/[not later than [*insert*] days before the final hearing]],

Costs Estimates

70.

a.   [The [applicant]/[respondent]/[second respondent]/[third respondent] etc shall send to the court and serve on the other parties costs estimates in Form H not later than [*insert*] days before the [adjourned directions appointment]/[financial dispute resolution appointment]/[case management hearing]].

b.   [The [applicant]/[respondent]/[second respondent]/[third respondent] etc shall send to the court and serve on the other parties costs estimates in Form H1 not later than [*insert*] days before the final hearing].

Offers for financial dispute resolution appointment

71.

a.   [The parties shall exchange without prejudice proposals for the resolution of the matters in dispute [by [*insert date and time*]]/[not later than [*insert*] days before the financial dispute resolution appointment].]

b.   [The [applicant]/[respondent] shall serve [his]/[her] without prejudice proposals for the resolution of the matters in dispute on the [respondent]/[applicant] by [*insert date and time*]/[not later than [*insert*] days before the financial dispute resolution appointment], and the [respondent]/[applicant] shall serve [his]/[her] without prejudice proposals on the [applicant]/[respondent] for the resolution of the matters in dispute in reply by [*insert date and time*]/[not later than [*insert*] days before the financial dispute resolution appointment].]

c.   The [applicant]/[respondent] shall send to the court a schedule of the without prejudice and open proposals made by each party for the resolution of the matters in dispute by [*insert date and time*]/[not later than [*insert*] days before the financial dispute resolution appointment].

d.   The [applicant]/[respondent]/[both parties] may, if so advised, decline to send to the court and serve on the [respondent]/[applicant]/[other party] without prejudice proposals for the resolution of the matters in dispute. If [he]/[she] decides not to send to the court such proposals [he]/[she] shall notify the [respondent]/[applicant] by [*insert time and date*]/[not later than [*insert*] days before the financial dispute resolution appointment].

Offers for other hearings

72.

a. [The parties shall exchange open proposals for the resolution of the matters in dispute [by [*insert date and time*]]/[not later than [*insert*] days before the [adjourned directions appointment]/[case management hearing]/[final hearing]].]

b. [The [applicant]/[respondent] shall serve [his]/[her] open proposals for the resolution of the matters in dispute on the [respondent]/[applicant] [by [*insert date and time*]]/[not later than [*insert*] days before the [adjourned directions appointment]/[case management hearing]/[final hearing]], and the [respondent]/[applicant] shall serve [his]/[her] open proposals for the resolution of the matters in dispute in reply on the [applicant]/[respondent] [by [*insert date and time*]]/[not later than [*insert*] days before the [adjourned directions appointment]/[case management hearing]/[final hearing]].]

c. The [applicant]/[respondent] shall send to the court a schedule of the open proposals made by each party for the resolution of the matters in dispute [by [*insert date and time*]]/[not later than [*insert*] days before the [adjourned directions appointment]/[case management hearing]/[final hearing]].

d. The [applicant]/[respondent]/[both parties] may, if so advised, decline to send to the court and serve on the [respondent]/[applicant]/[other party] open proposals for the resolution of the matters in dispute. If [he]/[she] decides not to send to the court such proposals [he]/[she] shall notify the [respondent]/[applicant]/[other party] [by [*insert time and date*]]/[not later than [*insert*] days before the [adjourned directions appointment]/[case management hearing]/[final hearing]].

Costs

73. [Costs in the application]/[No order as to costs]/[The [applicant]/[respondent] shall pay £[*insert*] towards the [respondent's]/[applicant's] costs of and relating to this hearing by [*insert date*], [summarily assessed at [£ *insert amount*]]/[subject to detailed assessment if not agreed]]/[The [applicant]/[respondent] shall pay the [respondent's]/[applicant's] costs of and relating to this hearing by [*insert date*] [including the costs reserved by the order(s) made on [*insert date(s)*], [summarily assessed at [£ *insert amount*]]/[subject to detailed assessment if not agreed].]

APPENDIX 12

FINANCIAL REMEDY ORDER

In the Family Court   No ....

Sitting at [Place]

The Matrimonial Causes Act 1973
The Civil Partnership Act 2004
The Child Support Act 1991
The Inheritance (Provision for Family and Dependents) Act 1975
Adapt as necessary

The Marriage of XX and YY, or
The Civil Partnership of XX and YY
Adapt as necessary

After hearing *[name the advocate(s) who appeared]*....
After consideration of the documents lodged by the parties
(In the case of an order made without notice) After reading the statements and hearing
the witnesses specified in para x of the Recitals below

ORDER MADE BY [NAME OF JUDGE] ON [DATE] SITTING IN OPEN
COURT/PRIVATE [FOLLOWING A [RESERVED]/[WRITTEN]/[EX TEMPORE]
JUDGMENT GIVEN ON [DATE]

> WARNING: IF YOU DO NOT COMPLY WITH THIS ORDER, YOU MAY BE
> HELD TO BE IN CONTEMPT OF COURT AND YOU MAY BE SENT TO
> PRISON, BE FINED, OR HAVE YOUR ASSETS SEIZED.

The parties

1. The applicant is XX
The respondent is YY
The second respondent is ZZ
Specify if any party acts by a litigation friend

Definitions

2. Children of the Family

The "children of the family" are:

a.   *[forename and surname]* born on *[date]*;

b.   [*forename and surname*] born on [*date*]; and

c.   etc

3. Family Home

The "family home" shall mean [*insert address including postcode*] registered at HM Land Registry with title number [*insert*].

4. Other properties

[*for example*] "Blackacre" shall mean [*insert address including postcode*] registered at HM Land Registry with title number [*insert*].

5. "The mortgage" shall mean the mortgage secured upon [*insert property*] in favour of [*insert name of mortgagee*].

6. "The net proceeds of sale" shall mean the actual sale price of the property concerned (including any sum paid for fixtures and fittings) less the amount outstanding on the mortgage, the solicitors' conveyancing costs, estate agents' costs and any other costs in connection with the sale which have been agreed by the parties.

7. "The policy" shall mean the policy or policies issued by [*insert company*] and numbered [*insert*].

8. "The [*insert bank*] bank account" shall mean the account in [the [applicant's]/ [respondent's] name]/[the parties' joint names] with [*insert name of bank/building society*], with account number and sort code [*insert*];

9. "The bank accounts" shall mean the following:

a.   the account in [the [applicant's]/[respondent's] name]/[the parties' joint names] with [*insert name of bank/building society*], with account number and sort code [*insert*];

b.   the account in [the [applicant's]/[respondent's] name]/[the parties' joint names] with [*insert name of bank/building society*], with account number and sort code [*insert*]; and

c.   etc

10. "The joint bank accounts" shall mean the following:

a.   the account in the parties' joint names with [insert name of bank/building society], with account number [insert] and sort code [insert];

b.   the account in the parties' joint names with [insert name of bank/building society], with account number [insert] and sort code; and

c.   etc

11. "CMS" shall mean the Child Support Agency, the Child Maintenance Enforcement Commission, the Child Maintenance Service, or such other state appointed agency operating within the United Kingdom as may from time to time replace any of them.

12. "CMS calculation" shall mean the assessment or calculation or periodic demand by the CMS.

13. "The [*insert company name*] pension arrangement" shall mean the pension arrangement/plan held by [*insert party*] with [*insert name of scheme/plan provider*] with reference number [*insert*]; and

14. "The pension arrangements" shall mean the following:

a.   the pension arrangement/plan held by [*insert party*] with [*insert name of scheme/plan provider*] with reference number [*insert*]; and

b.   the pension arrangement/plan held by [*insert party*] with [*insert name of scheme/plan provider*] with reference number [*insert*]; and

c.   etc

15. "PPF" shall mean the Pension Protection Fund.

16. "PRPA" shall mean the person responsible for the pension arrangement.

Recitals

17. (*In the case of an order made without notice*)

a.   This order was made at a hearing without notice to the respondent. The reason why the order was made without notice to the respondent was [*set out*].

b.   The Judge read the following affidavits/witness statements [*set out*] and heard oral testimony from [*name*].

18. (*In the case of an order made following the giving of short informal notice*)

This order was made at a hearing without full notice having been given to the respondent. The reason why the order was made without full notice having been given to the respondent was [set out].

Arbitration award recital

19.

a.   The documents lodged in relation to this application include the parties' arbitration agreement (Form ARB1), their Form(s) D81, a copy of the arbitrator's award, and a draft of the order which the court is requested to make.

b.   *Either:*
[By their Form ARB1 the parties agreed to refer to arbitration the issues described in it which include some or all of the financial remedies for which applications are pending in this court. The issues were referred to [*insert arbitrator*] under the IFLA scheme, who made an arbitral award on [*insert date*]. The parties have invited the court to make an order in agreed terms, which reflects the arbitrator's award.]
or
[Although by their Form ARB1 the parties agreed to refer to arbitration the issues described in it which include some or all of the financial remedies for which applications are pending in this court. The issues were referred to [*insert*

arbitrator] under the IFLA scheme, who made an arbitral award on [*insert date*]. There has been no agreement between the parties as to the form of an order to give effect to the arbitrator's award. The [applicant]/[respondent] has applied for the other party to show why an order should not be made in the terms of the draft proposed; and the court having considered the representations made by each party has directed that an order be made in the terms of this order.]

Mediation recital

20. The parties attended mediation with [*insert mediator*]. They have now invited the court to make this order in agreed terms, reflecting the agreement reached at mediation.

Collaborative recital

21.

a. The parties have reached agreement as to the contents of this order under the collaborative family law process.

b. The parties agree and acknowledge that their respective solicitors have placed themselves on the court record for the sole purpose of representation in respect of undefended divorce/dissolution of civil partnership proceedings; the taking of all steps as may be necessary to seek the approval of the court to the agreed terms; to secure their incorporation into a consent order; and where necessary to implement the terms of the consent order. In the event of any subsequent dispute arising from the proceedings, the parties agree that their solicitors shall be immediately removed from the court record.

c. On [*insert date*] the parties attended a final meeting held under the collaborative family law process at which the terms set out in this order were agreed and recorded and in respect of which the parties acknowledge that they both had independent legal advice.

Introductory recital

22. The parties agree that the terms set out in this order are accepted in full and final satisfaction of:

a. All claims for income;

b. All claims for capital, that is payments of lump sums, transfers of property and variations of settlements;

c. All claims in respect of each other's pensions;

d. All claims in respect of the contents of the family home/[*insert*] and personal belongings including but not limited to furniture, art work, jewellery and motor vehicles;

e. All claims in respect of legal costs including those of the divorce/dissolution proceedings;

f. All claims against each other's estate on death;

g. All other claims of any nature which one may have against the other as a result of their marriage/civil partnership howsoever arising either in England and Wales or in any other jurisdiction.

General Agreements/Declarations

23. The parties agree that neither of them has any legal or equitable interest in the property or assets [currently in the sole name or possession of the other]/[owned by the other], and neither of them has any liability for the debts of the other, except as provided for in this order.

24. The parties agree that neither of them shall institute proceedings against the other under [the Married Women's Property Act 1882]/[the Law of Property Act 1925]/[the Trusts of Land and Appointment of Trustees Act 1996].

25. The parties agree that the contents of the [family home] and/or [the property/ies] known as [*as in definition above*] shall [remain the absolute property of the person in whose possession they now are]/[shall be divided in accordance with schedule[s] [*insert number or letter*] attached to this order]/[shall be divided between the parties by agreement by [*insert date*] and in the event that the parties cannot reach agreement by then either of them shall be free to make an application to the court for it to decide the issue, save that it is recorded that in the event that there has been no agreement, order or further application made to the court by [*insert*] all claims in respect of the contents of the [family home] and/or [the property/ies] shall be dismissed and such contents shall remain the absolute property of the person in whose possession they are as at that date]/[shall remain the absolute property of the [applicant]/[respondent] except for [*insert*]/[the items attached at schedule [*insert*] attached to this order which are to be retained by the [respondent]/[applicant] and shall be made available by the [applicant]/[respondent] for collection on or before [*insert date*]/on the date of completion of the sale of the property/or other specified event]]. The [applicant]/ [respondent] agrees to give the [respondent]/[applicant] access to the [property] to collect such items on receiving [*insert*] days' notice from him/her of his/her wish to do so.

Declaration regarding lump sum order(s)

26. The parties agree and declare that the lump sum order set out in paragraph [*insert*] below should be considered to be [a series of lump sum orders]/[a lump sum order payable by instalments].

Declaration as to true presentation of assets

27.

a. The [applicant]/[respondent] declares that [he]/[she] signed as true the attached Statement of Information for a Consent Order at the same time as signing this order; and

b. The [applicant]/[respondent] undertakes that should there be any material changes to the Statement of Information between the date of [his]/[her] signing this order and the date upon which this order shall take effect, [he]/[she] shall notify the [respondent]/[applicant] in writing of such changes within five working days of learning of them.

Declaration as to solvency

28.

a.   The [applicant]/[respondent] declares that [he]/[she] is solvent as at the date of [his]/[her] signing this order in that: (i) [he]/[she] is able to pay [his]/[her] debts as they fall due; and (ii) the value of [his]/[her] assets equals or exceeds the amount of [his]/[her] liabilities, including contingent and prospective liabilities;

b.   The [applicant]/[respondent] declares that [he]/[she] signed as true the attached Statement of Information for a Consent Order at the same time as signing this order; and

c.   The [applicant]/[respondent] undertakes that should there be any material changes to the Statement of Information between the date of [his]/[her] signing this order and the date upon which this order shall take effect, [he]/[she] shall notify the [respondent]/[applicant] in writing of such changes within five working days of learning of them.

Declaration of intention not to seek a variation of a periodical payments order (*receiving party*)

29. The [applicant]/[respondent] declares that it is not their intention to seek an increase of the order for periodical payments at paragraph [*insert*] below for themselves [and the children of the family] [for a period of at least [*insert*] years from the date of this order]/[for so long as the [respondent]/[applicant] does not [earn]/[become entitled to drawings] in excess of £[*insert*] gross [per annum] [RPI index-linked]/except [in exceptional circumstances]/[in the event that [he]/[she] becomes unintentionally unemployed through no action or fault of their own]/[in the event that [he]/[she] suffers from severe illness or disability rendering them unable to work].

Declaration of intention not to seek a variation of a periodical payments order (*paying party*)

30. The [respondent]/[applicant] declares that it is not their intention to seek a decrease of the order for periodical payments at paragraph [*insert*] below in favour of the [applicant]/[respondent] [and the children of the family] [for a period of at least [*insert*] years from the date of this order]/[for so long as the [respondent]/[applicant] does not [earn]/[become entitled to drawings of] in excess of £[*insert*] gross [per annum] [RPI index-linked]/[for so long as the [applicant]/[respondent] does not [earn]/[become entitled to drawings of] less than £[*insert*] gross [per annum] [RPI index-linked]/except [in exceptional circumstances]/[unless there has been a material change in their or the [applicant's]/[respondent's] financial circumstances.

Declaration of intention to limit claims under the Inheritance (Provision for Family and Dependants) Act 1975

31. The [applicant]/[respondent] acknowledges that, if the [respondent]/[applicant] predeceases him/her, any claim that [he]/[she] may make against the [respondent's]/[applicant's] estate under the Inheritance (Provision for Family and Dependants) Act 1975 shall be limited to seeking a sum to compensate them for the loss of the periodical payments the [respondent]/[applicant] was ordered to pay them at paragraph [*insert*] below for themselves [and the children of the family].

Declaration of intention not to apply to the CMS

32. Although the parties accept that the jurisdiction of the CMS cannot be excluded for more than one year, neither party has any intention of applying to the CMS for a CMS calculation in substitution of the periodical payments payable under paragraph [*insert*] below.

Declaration of interim payments made by the [respondent]/[applicant] intended to count against CMS arrears

33. The parties declare that the [respondent]/[applicant] has made payments totalling £[*insert*] to the [applicant]/[respondent], that they intend that those payments should count towards the arrears of maintenance due under the CMS calculation, and that they shall take all reasonable steps to ensure that the CMS takes these payments into account when calculating the arrears of maintenance due under that calculation.

Undertakings to the court

> You may be held to be in contempt of court and imprisoned or fined, or your assets may be seized, if you break the promises that you have given to the court. If you fail to pay any sum of money which you have promised the court that you will pay, a person entitled to enforce the undertaking may apply to the court for an order. You may be sent to prison if it is proved that you-
> (a) have, or have had since the date of your undertaking, the means to pay the sum; and
> (b) have refused or neglected, or are refusing or neglecting, to pay that sum.
> I understand the undertakings that I have given, and that if I break any of my promises to the court I may be sent to prison for contempt of court.
> ....

Undertaking to stand as guarantor

34.

a.   [The [applicant]/[respondent] shall stand as guarantor in relation to the mortgage secured upon [*insert full address including postcode*] in favour of [*insert company*] [for a term of [*insert*] years]]/[The [applicant]/[respondent] shall, [if and only if it shall be necessary to enable the [respondent]/[applicant] to obtain borrowing on reasonable terms], guarantee a mortgage of up to £[*insert*] to be taken out by the [respondent]/[applicant] on [his]/[her] purchase of [*insert property*] or such property [within England and Wales] as [he]/[she] shall [within one year of the date of this order offer to] purchase as [his]/[her] principal residence provided that, if the [respondent]/[applicant] shall default in making any of the payments due under the mortgage and the [applicant]/[respondent] shall be called upon to make any payments under the guarantee, the [respondent]/[applicant] shall indemnify [him]/[her] in respect of that liability and any consequential interest or charges [and shall repay the sum due immediately upon written request from the [respondent]/[applicant] and in default of such payment, the [respondent]/[applicant] shall be entitled to deduct the same from the periodical payments due to the [applicant]/[respondent] under the terms of this order]].

b.   The [respondent]/[applicant] shall forthwith in the event of [her]/[his] remarriage [or in the event that [she]/[he] shall have cohabited with another person [for a [continuous] period of more than [*insert period*]]]/[for a period of [*insert*] months in any [*insert*] month period]] take all such steps as shall be necessary to procure the release of the [applicant]/[respondent] from all liability under the guarantee.

Undertaking to discharge liabilities

35. The [applicant]/[respondent] shall discharge as when each payment becomes due, be solely responsible for and in any event indemnify the [respondent]/[applicant] against:

a.   the premiums in respect of the [policy]/[endowment policy]/[pension policy] with [*insert name of company*] numbered [*insert*];

b.   the [monthly] repayments to [*insert name of company*] in respect of the hire purchase agreement with them numbered [*insert*] in respect of the [family car]/[*insert car make and model*] with registration number [*insert*];

c.   the [*monthly*] repayments [*insert name of company*] in respect of the loan agreement with them numbered [*insert*] in respect of [*insert*];

d.   etc
The payments shall start on [*insert date*] and shall end on the first to occur of:
i.   [*insert date*];
ii.   the sale of the family home;
iii.   the youngest surviving [of the] child[ren] of the family attaining the age of 18 years or ceasing [his]/[her]/[their] full-time [secondary]/[tertiary] education [to first degree level] [including/excluding a gap year], or [permanently] ceasing to live with the [applicant]/[respondent], whichever is the later;
iv.   the [respondent's]/[applicant's] remarriage;
v.   the death of either party;
vi.   the retirement of the [applicant]/[respondent]; or
vii.   a court order discharging this obligation.
[as appropriate]

Undertaking to discharge arrears

36. The [applicant]/[respondent] shall discharge by [*insert date*], be solely responsible for and in any event indemnify the [respondent]/[applicant] against:

a.   the arrears which have accrued in respect of the [policy]/[endowment policy]/[pension policy] with [*insert name of company*] numbered [*insert*];

b.   the arrears which have accrued in respect of the hire purchase agreement with [*insert name of company*] numbered [*insert*] in respect of the [*insert car make and model*] with registration number [*insert*];

c.   the arrears which have accrued in respect of the loan agreement with [*insert name of company*] numbered [*insert*] in respect of [*insert*];

d.   etc

Undertaking to use best endeavours to secure release from liabilities

37. The [applicant]/[respondent] shall use [his]/[her] best endeavours to obtain the consent of each creditor to release the [respondent]/[applicant] from any liability in respect of the following:

a.   the hire purchase agreement with [*insert name of company*] numbered [*insert*] in respect of the [family car]/[*insert car make and model*] with registration number [*insert*];

b.   the loan agreement with [*insert name of company*] numbered [*insert*] in respect of [*insert*];

c.   etc

Undertaking to mitigate capital gains tax liability

38. The [applicant]/[respondent] shall take the following steps to mitigate any liability for capital gains tax or any other tax consequent upon the implementation of paragraph(s) [*insert*] of this order:

a.   [*set out as appropriate*];

Undertaking to maintain medical insurance cover

39.

a.   The [applicant]/[respondent] shall maintain the existing medical insurance cover, including paying promptly any premiums due, with [*insert company*] or any successor company for the [applicant]/[respondent] [until [he]/[she] shall remarry]/[for so long as the order for periodical payments at paragraph [*insert*] below in the [applicant's]/[respondent's] favour shall subsist] and/or for the child[ren] of the family [until [he]/[she][they] shall [respectively] attain the age of 18 or cease [his]/[her]/[their] full-time secondary education]/[for so long as the order for periodical payments at paragraph [*insert*] below in respect of [him]/[her][them] shall subsist] at [*specify scale of cover – e.g. at the same level of cover currently provided*].

b.   If the [applicant]/[respondent] and/or the child[ren] of the family cannot remain part of the existing medical insurance cover, the [respondent]/[applicant] shall pay for separate medical insurance cover with [the same insurance company]/[a reputable United Kingdom insurance company] for the [applicant]/[respondent] [until [he]/[she] shall remarry]/[for so long as the order for periodical payments at paragraph [*insert*] below in the [applicant's]/[respondent's] favour shall subsist] and/or for the child[ren] of the until [he]/[she][they] shall [respectively] attain the age of 18 or cease [his]/[her]/[their] full-time secondary education]/[for so long as the order for periodical payments at paragraph [*insert*] below in respect of [him]/[her]/[them] shall subsist] at [*specify scale of cover – e.g. at the same level of cover currently provided*].

c.   The [respondent]/[applicant] shall provide the [applicant]/[respondent] with written evidence within 14 days of the date of this order that this medical insurance cover is in place, and shall provide the [applicant]/[respondent] with written evidence within 14 days of the date of renewal each year that this medical insurance cover remains in place.

d.   When the order for periodical payments at paragraph [*insert*] below in the [applicant's]/[respondent's] favour comes to an end such that the [respondent]/[applicant] is no longer obliged to provide medical insurance cover for the [applicant]/[respondent] and/or when the child[ren] of the family [[respectively] attain the age of 18 or cease their full-time secondary education]/[when the order for periodical payments at paragraph [*insert*] below in respect of the child[ren] of the family comes to an end] such that the [respondent]/[applicant] is no longer obliged to provide medical insurance cover for [him]/[her]/[them], the [respondent]/[applicant] shall use [his]/[her] best endeavours to ensure that the [applicant]/[respondent] is able to take over the medical insurance cover at [her]/[his] own cost should [she]/[he] wish to do so.

Undertaking to maintain medical insurance cover with employers

40.

a.   The [respondent]/[applicant] shall ensure that the [applicant]/[respondent] and/or the child[ren] of the family are covered by such medical insurance scheme as [his]/[her] employers shall from time to time arrange [until the [applicant]/ [respondent] shall remarry]/[for so long as the order for periodical payments at paragraph [*insert*] below in the [applicant's]/[respondent's] favour shall subsist] and/or [until the child[ren] of the family shall respectively attain the age of 18 or cease [his]/[her]/[their] full-time secondary education]/[for so long as the order for periodical payments at paragraph [*insert*] below in respect of [him]/[her]/[them] shall subsist] at [*specify scale of cover – e.g. at the same level of cover currently provided*] [provided that such cover shall be at no cost to the [respondent]/ [applicant], save for any additional charge to income tax].

b.   If the [respondent]/[applicant] leaves [*insert name of employer*] but has the benefit of medical insurance in [his]/[her] new employment, the [respondent]/[applicant] shall use [his]/[her] best endeavours to ensure that the [applicant]/[respondent] and/or the child[ren] of the family are covered by such medical insurance scheme as [his]/[her] new employers shall from time to time arrange [until the [applicant]/[respondent] shall remarry]/[for so long as the order for periodical payments at paragraph [*insert*] below in the [applicant's]/[respondent's] favour shall subsist] and/or [until the child[ren] of the family shall [respectively] attain the age of 18 or cease [his]/[her]/[their] full-time secondary education]/[for so long as the order for periodical payments at paragraph [*insert*] below in respect of [him]/[her]/[them shall] subsist] at [*specify scale of cover – e.g. at the same level of cover currently provided*] [provided that such cover shall be at no cost to the [respondent]/[applicant], save for any additional charge to income tax].

c.   If the [applicant]/[respondent] and/or the child[ren] of the family cannot remain part of the existing medical insurance cover, the [respondent]/[applicant] shall pay for separate medical insurance cover with a reputable United Kingdom insurance company for the [applicant]/[respondent] [until [he]/[she] shall remarry]/[for so long as the order for periodical payments at paragraph [*insert*] below in the [applicant's]/[respondent's] favour shall subsist] and/or for the child[ren] of the family [until [he]/she]/[they] shall [respectively] attain the age of 18 or cease [his]/[her]/[their] full-time secondary education]/[for so long as the order for periodical payments at paragraph [*insert*] below in respect of [him]/[her]/[them] shall subsist] at [*specify scale of cover – e.g. at the same level of cover currently provided*].

d.   The [respondent]/[applicant] shall provide the [applicant]/[respondent] with written evidence within 14 days of the date of this order that this medical insurance cover is in place, and shall provide the [applicant]/[respondent] with written evidence within 14 days of the date of renewal each year that this medical insurance cover remains in place.

e.   When the order for periodical payments at paragraph [*insert*] below in the [applicant's]/[respondent's] favour comes to an end such that the [respondent]/ [applicant] is no longer obliged to provide medical insurance cover for the [applicant]/[respondent] and/or when the child[ren] of the family [[respectively] attain the age of 18 or cease their full-time secondary education]/[when the order for periodical payments at paragraph [*insert*] below in respect of the child[ren] of the family comes to an end] such that the [respondent]/[applicant] is no longer obliged to provide medical insurance cover for [him]/[her]/[them], the [respondent]/[applicant] shall use [his]/[her] best endeavours to ensure that the [applicant]/[respondent] is able to take over the medical insurance cover at [her]/[his] own cost should [she]/[he] wish to do so.

Undertaking to pay for medical insurance cover

41.

a. The [respondent]/[applicant] shall pay for medical insurance cover with a reputable United Kingdom insurance company for the [applicant]/[respondent] [until [he]/[she] shall remarry]/[for so long as the order for periodical payments at paragraph [*insert*] below in the [applicant's]/[respondent's] favour shall subsist] and/or for the child[ren] of the family [until [he]/[she]/[they] shall [respectively] attain the age of 18 or cease [his]/[her]/[their] full-time secondary education]/[for so long as the order for periodical payments at paragraph [*insert*] below in respect of [him]/[her]/[them] shall subsist] at [*specify scale of cover*].

b. The [respondent]/[applicant] shall provide the [applicant]/[respondent] with written evidence within 14 days of the date of this order that this medical insurance cover is in place, and shall provide the [applicant]/[respondent] with written evidence within 14 days of the date of renewal each year that this medical insurance cover remains in place.

c. When the order for periodical payments at paragraph [*insert*] below in the [applicant's]/[respondent's] favour comes to an end such that the [respondent]/[applicant] is no longer obliged to provide medical insurance cover for the [applicant]/[respondent] and/or when the child[ren] of the family [[respectively] attain the age of 18 or cease their full-time secondary education]/[when the order for periodical payments at paragraph [*insert*] below in respect of the child[ren] of the family comes to an end] such that the [respondent]/[applicant] is no longer obliged to provide medical insurance cover for [him]/[her]/[them], the [respondent]/[applicant] shall use [his]/[her] best endeavours to ensure that the [applicant]/[respondent] is able to take over the medical insurance cover at [her]/[his] own cost should [she]/[he] wish to do so.

Undertaking to take out and maintain a life assurance policy

42.

a. The [respondent]/[applicant] shall [forthwith]/[by [*insert time*] on the date [*insert*] days from the date of this order] [use [his]/[her] best endeavours to] take out with [*insert company*]/[a reputable United Kingdom insurance company] a policy of assurance on [his]/[her] life in the sum of [*insert sum*] [with/without profits] [for a term of [*insert*] years]/[for the whole of [his]/[her] life]/[to mature on [*insert*]] for the benefit of the [applicant]/[respondent] and/or the child[ren] of the family/[for the duration of the subsistence of the order[s] for periodical payments at paragraph [*insert*] below in respect of [the applicant]/[respondent] and/or the child[ren] of the family] in the sum of [*insert sum*] [with/without profits]/in the sum of [*insert sum*] [reducing on a straight line basis by annual increments to £0 by the end of the term]/[in such sum as shall pay out £[*insert*] per annum, [RPI]/[CPI]-index-linked, from the date of his death until the cessation of the order for periodical payments at paragraph [*insert*] below in respect of [the applicant]/[respondent] and/or the child[ren] of the family, and shall provide the [applicant]/[respondent] with written evidence that [he]/[she] has done so.

b. The [respondent]/[applicant] shall promptly pay all premiums due and take all necessary steps to ensure that the policy shall remain in full force, [until the [applicant's]/[respondent's] death or remarriage, whichever shall be the earlier]/[for so long as the order for periodical payments at paragraph [*insert*] below in the [applicant's]/[respondent's] favour shall subsist] and/or [until the child[ren] of the family shall [respectively] attain the age of 18 or cease [his]/[her]/[their] full-time secondary education]/[for so long as the order for periodical payments at paragraph [*insert*] below in respect of the child[ren] of the family shall subsist], and shall provide the [applicant]/[respondent] with written evidence that [he]/[she] has done so if [he]/[she] requests it; [*in the case, for example of a policy capable of acquiring a surrender value:* the applicant and the respondent having agreed that all of the benefits under the policy shall be paid to the [applicant]/[respondent] and/or the child[ren] of the family [or the [applicant's]/[respondent's] estate] and that the [respondent]/[applicant] shall have no beneficial interest in the policy or its proceeds at any time, [except that if the [applicant]/[respondent] remarries or predeceases the [respondent]/[applicant], the [respondent]/[applicant] and/or the child[ren] of the family shall be entitled to all of the benefits under the policy].

Undertaking to take out and assign a life assurance policy

43. The [respondent]/[applicant] shall [forthwith]/[by [*insert time*] on the date [*insert*] days from the date of this order] [use [his]/[her] best endeavours to] take out with [*insert company*]/[a reputable United Kingdom insurance company] a policy of assurance on [his]/[her] life in the sum of [*insert sum*] [with/without profits] [for a term of [*insert*] years]/[for the whole of [his]/[her] life]/[to mature on [*insert*]/[for the duration of the subsistence of the order for periodical payments at paragraph [*insert*] below in respect of the [applicant]/[respondent] and/or the child[ren] of the family] in the sum of [*insert sum*] [with/without profits]/in the sum of [*insert sum*] [reducing on a straight line basis by annual increments to zero by the end of the term]/[in such sum as shall pay out £[*insert*] per annum, [RPI]/[CPI]-index-linked, from the date of his death until the cessation of the order for periodical payments at paragraph [*insert*] below in respect of the child[ren] of the family], and shall forthwith assign it absolutely to the [applicant]/[respondent], who shall be responsible for the payment of all premiums.

Undertaking to give authority to insurance company to divulge information

44. The [respondent]/[applicant] shall forthwith [upon taking out the policy referred to in recital [*insert*] above] irrevocably authorise [*insert company*]/[the company with whom the policy is taken out] to disclose to the [applicant]/[respondent], for so long as the applicant is entitled to the benefits under the policy, such information as [he]/[she] may from time to time request relating to the policy [numbered [*insert*]] [at the cost of the [applicant]/[respondent]].

Undertaking to undergo medical examination

45. The [respondent]/[applicant] shall, within [*insert*] days of being asked to do so, undergo such medical examination [and provide such information] as may be required by [*insert company*]/[the company with whom the assurance policy is to be taken out] to enable the [applicant]/[respondent] to insure [his]/[her] life [and/or against [his]/[her] ill

health and/or against [his]/[her] redundancy] in the sum of [*insert sum*]/[in such sum as the [applicant]/[respondent] may reasonably require].

Undertaking to surrender life assurance policy

46. The applicant [and]/[or] the respondent shall [by [*insert time*] on the date [*insert*] days from the date of this order]/[upon completion of the sale of [*insert*] referred to at paragraph [*insert*] below] [surrender]/[sell for not less than the surrender value] the insurance policy with [*insert company*] numbered [*insert*], and shall divide the proceeds [net of any tax and costs of sale] [between the applicant and the respondent equally]/[as to [*insert*] % to the applicant and as to [*insert*] % to the respondent], but if the sale is not completed [by [*insert time*] on the date [*insert*] days from the date of this order]/[within [*insert*] days of the date of the completion of the sale of [*insert*] referred to at paragraph [*insert*] below] the applicant [and]/[or] the respondent shall surrender the policy within [*insert*] days afterwards.

Undertaking to retain and continue paying life assurance policy premiums until maturity

47.

a.   The applicant [and]/[or] the respondent shall retain and continue the insurance policy with [*insert company*] numbered [*insert*] until its maturity, shall take all necessary steps to ensure that the policy shall remain in full force until its maturity, and shall do nothing which might prejudice or invalidate the policy until its maturity.

b.   The applicant [and]/[or] the respondent shall pay promptly all of the premiums [equally]/[as to [*insert*] % by the applicant and as to [*insert*] % by the respondent]. Upon the maturity of the policy, the applicant [and]/[or] the respondent shall divide the proceeds [net of any tax and costs of sale] [between the applicant and the respondent equally]/[as to [*insert*] % to the applicant and as to [*insert*] % to the respondent].

Undertaking to leave by Will/make financial arrangements on death

48.

a.   The [respondent]/[applicant] shall [forthwith]/[by [*insert time*] on the date [*insert*] days from the date of this order] enter into an irrevocable deed of covenant with the [applicant]/[respondent], which shall be binding on the executors and trustees of [his]/[her] estate/will, that in the event of his death during the subsistence of order(s) for periodical payments at paragraph(s) [*insert*] below in respect of the [applicant]/[respondent] and/or the child[ren] of the family, he shall make arrangements [that shall continue the financial provision made in those paragraph(s) for the [applicant]/[respondent] and/or the child[ren] of the family until the order(s) shall cease]/[such that in the event of [his]/[her] death on or before [*insert date*] in the year appearing in the left hand of the table below, then the sum in the right hand of the table below shall be paid to the [applicant]/[respondent] for [his]/[her] benefit and/or for the benefit of the child[ren] of the family:

b.   The [respondent]/[applicant] shall provide the [applicant]/[respondent] with written evidence that he has entered into the deed of covenant [and]/[or] a certified copy of the deed [forthwith after]/[within [*insert*] days of] doing so.

c. The parties agree that provided that the [respondent]/[applicant] enters into the deed of covenant and provided that the sums under the deed of covenant

Year	Sum
2013	[*insert*]
2014	[*insert*]
2015	[*insert*]
	Etc

are paid to the [applicant]/[respondent] for [his]/[her] benefit and/or for the benefit of the child[ren] of the family in the event of the [respondent's]/[applicant's] death, then this should be regarded by the Court as a sufficient discharge of the [applicant's]/[respondent's] claims [his]/[her] behalf and/or on behalf of the child[ren] of the family and/or the child[ren's] claims against the [respondent's]/[applicant's] estate under the Inheritance (Provision for Family and Dependants) Act 1975.

Undertaking to obtain a Get

49. [The [applicant]/[respondent] shall take all steps necessary to obtain a Get. The [applicant]/[respondent] shall apply for the Get [by *insert date and time*]/[within [*insert*] days of the date of this order], and the Get shall be concluded [by *insert date and time*]/[within [*insert*] days of the date of this order]. All expenses in connection with this shall be paid by the [applicant]/[respondent]/[jointly][as agreed].]

[The decree nisi/conditional order made in these proceedings on [*insert date*] shall not be made absolute until a declaration has been filed at court signed by both parties that they have taken such steps as are necessary to dissolve their [marriage]/[civil partnership] dated [*insert*] in accordance with the customs of the Jewish faith [and have filed such other documents [*insert*]].]

Undertaking not to disclose information

50. The [applicant] and/or [respondent] shall not:

a. reveal to any third party unconnected with these proceedings (excluding any person to whom it is necessary to disclose [relevant parts of] this order for the purposes of implementation or professional advice: (i) the terms of this order, and (ii) any of the financial particulars disclosed in these proceedings;

b. cause or facilitate publication in any form of the terms or particulars;

c. take any steps as a result of which the terms or particulars are likely to become public knowledge or are reasonably foreseeable as being likely to become public knowledge; and

d. [fail to take any steps which either party may reasonably be expected to take to prevent the said terms or particulars from being public knowledge in circumstances in which they would otherwise be likely to do so].

Orders

IT IS ORDERED (BY CONSENT) (with effect from Decree Absolute):

Lump sum order

51.

a. The [applicant]/[respondent] shall pay to the [respondent]/[applicant] a lump sum of £[*insert*] by [*insert time*] on [*insert date*]/[by [*insert time*] on the date [*insert*] days after the date of this order]/[by [*insert time*] on the date [[*insert*] days after the date] of completion of the sale of [*insert*] referred to at paragraph [*insert*] above/below].

b. [*If the lump sum is more than £5,000*: If the [applicant]/[respondent] fails to pay all or any part of this lump sum [by [*insert date for payment*]]/[within [*insert*] days of [*insert date for payment*]] simple interest shall accrue on the remaining balance of the lump sum at [the rate applicable for the time being to a High Court judgment debt]/[the rate of [*insert*] % per annum]].

c. [*If the lump sum is less than £5,000*: If the [applicant]/[respondent] fails to pay all or any part of this lump sum [by [*insert date for payment*]]/[within [*insert*] days of [*insert date for payment*]], the [applicant]/[respondent] shall pay to the [respondent]/[applicant] a further lump sum calculated as follows: £[*insert*] per day from [*insert date for payment*] until the lump sum payment referred to at paragraph [*insert* (a)] above is paid in full].

Series of lump sum orders

52.

The [applicant]/[respondent] shall pay to the [respondent]/[applicant] the following lump sums:

a. £[*insert*] by [*insert time*] on [*insert date*];

b. £[*insert*] by [*insert time*] on [*insert date*]; and

c. £[*insert*] by [*insert time*] on [*insert date*].

Lump sum order by instalments

53. The [applicant]/[respondent] shall pay to the [respondent]/[applicant] a lump sum of £[*insert*] payable by instalments as follows:

a. as to £[*insert*] by [*insert time*] on [*insert date*];

b. as to £[*insert*] by [*insert time*] on [*insert date*]; and

c. as to the balance by [*insert time*] on [*insert date*].

And it is directed that if the [applicant]/[respondent] fails to pay all or any part of any instalment to the [respondent]/[applicant] [on]/[within [*insert*] days of] the due date for the instalment, the whole of the balance remaining of the lump sum of £[*insert*] shall become immediately payable to the [respondent]/[applicant] [and that in default of payment there shall be an order for sale of [*insert property*] pursuant to paragraph [*insert*] below]. And it is [further] directed that simple interest shall be payable by the [applicant]/[respondent] at [the rate applicable for the time being to a High Court judgment debt]/[the rate of [*insert*] % per annum], on the [remaining balance of each of the] instalments from [*insert date – date to be no earlier than the date of the order*] until the dates on which the instalments are respectively due to be paid].

And it is [further] directed that the instalments totalling £[*insert*] be secured upon [*insert property*]/[security to be agreed or in default of agreement determined by a District Judge] [and in default of agreement as to the form of instrument for the security, the matter shall be referred to conveyancing counsel of the court to settle the instrument].

Transfers of property

54. The [applicant]/[respondent] shall transfer to the [respondent]/[applicant] all [his]/[her] legal estate and beneficial interest in the [family home]/[property/ies] [*as in definition above*], [subject to the mortgage(s) [*as in definition above*] secured against the property], [on [*insert date*]]/[within [*insert*] days of [the date of this order]/[the date of decree absolute]]/[upon [*insert condition e.g. upon payment of the lump sum ordered in paragraph [insert]*]].

Order for sale

55. The [family home]/[property/ies] [*as in definition above*] shall be sold forthwith on the open market for sale and the following conditions will apply:

a. the property shall be placed on the open market for sale immediately by [*insert*] for [*insert price*]/[such price as may be agreed between the parties or in default of agreement determined by the court];

b. the property shall be sold for [a price in excess of [*insert*]]/[such price as may be agreed between the parties [in excess of [*insert*]] or in default of agreement determined by the court;

c. [both parties]/[the applicant]/[the respondent] shall have conduct of the sale;

d. [the [applicant's]/[respondent's] solicitors]/[*insert name of solicitors*]/[such solicitors as may be agreed between the parties or in default of agreement determined by the court] shall have the conduct of the conveyancing work relating to the sale;

e. [*insert name of estate agents*]/[such estate agents as may be agreed between the parties or in default of agreement determined by the court] shall offer the property for sale; and

f. the proceeds of sale shall be applied as follows:
    i.   to discharge the mortgage [*as in definitions*];
    ii.   in payment of the solicitors' conveyancing costs and disbursements in connection with the sale;
    iii. in payment of the estate agents' charges;
    iv.   [in payment of any capital gains tax payable upon the sale];
    v.   [in payment to the [applicant]/[respondent] of the lump sum of [*insert*] and in payment of the balance to the [respondent]/[applicant]]/[in payment of the balance as to [*insert*]% to the applicant and as to [*insert*]% to the respondent.

Trust of land

56. With effect from [the making of this order]/[the date of decree absolute or final order dissolving the civil partnership (*if decree absolute has not already been made or the civil partnership has not been dissolved*)] the [family home]/[property [*as in definition above*] shall be held by the applicant and the respondent upon a trust of land for themselves as beneficial tenants in common in [equal shares/as to [*insert*]% to the applicant and as to [*insert*]% to the respondent] upon the following terms:

a.   the [applicant]/[respondent] shall be entitled to occupy the property rent free to the exclusion of the [respondent]/[applicant] until the determining event as defined below;

b.   the property shall not be sold without the prior written consent of both parties or further order until the first to happen of the following events ("the determining event");

   i.   the youngest surviving [of the] child[ren] of the family attaining the age of 18 years or ceasing [his]/[her]/their full-time [secondary]/[tertiary] education [to first degree level] [including/excluding a gap year], or permanently ceasing to live with the [applicant]/[respondent], whichever is the later;

   ii.   the death of the last surviving [of the] child[ren] of the family;

   iii. the death of the [applicant]/[respondent]; or

   iv.   the [applicant's]/[respondent's] remarriage or cohabitation with another person [as man and wife] [for a [continuous] period of more than [*insert period*]]/[for a period of [*insert*] months in any [*insert*] month period];

   v.   the [applicant's]/[respondent's] failure to occupy the property for a period of *insert*] months in any [*insert*] month period];

   vi.   the [applicant's]/[respondent's] failure to occupy the property as [his]/[her] primary residence; or

   vii. further order of the court; provided that in any event the property shall not be sold without the permission of the court while any child of the family in occupation of the property is still a minor or of full age but receiving full time education or training.

c.   the [applicant]/[respondent] shall [from the date of this order]/[*insert*] be [solely]/[jointly]/[*insert*] responsible for all payments of capital and interest on the mortgage [and the [respondent]/[applicant] shall on the sale of the property repay to the [applicant]/[respondent] from [his]/[her] share of the net proceeds of sale one half of the element of repayment of capital comprised in such payments made by [him]/[her] to the date of sale of the property];

d.   the [applicant]/[respondent] shall be responsible for all [routine] maintenance and [decorative] repairs to the property;

e.   the cost of insuring the property and of carrying out structural repairs [defined as *insert*] shall be [the responsibility of the [applicant]/[respondent]]/[shared equally]/[*insert*], provided that no works of structural repair shall be carried out to the property unless agreed by the parties or ordered by the court;

f.   if the [applicant]/[respondent] wishes to spend money on the property to improve its amenities then the parties shall enter into a deed recording their interests in the [net]/[gross] proceeds of the sale of the property. The [applicant]/[respondent] shall acquire such further share in the [net]/[gross] proceeds of the property as may be agreed between the parties or in default of agreement as shall be determined by the court as reflecting the likely increase in the sale price (when [the family home]/[*insert property*] is eventually sold) referable to [her]/[his] outlay. The [applicant]/[respondent] shall be responsible for the costs of preparing and executing the deed of trust.

g.   in the event of the [applicant]/[respondent] wishing to move to another property during the subsistence of this trust with the agreement of the [respondent]/ [applicant] such agreement not to be unreasonably withheld:

   i.   the [applicant]/[respondent] shall be entitled to direct the trustees to sell the property and to apply the proceeds in the purchase of such other freehold or leasehold property ("the new home") as [he]/[she] shall direct for [his]/[her] occupation;

   ii.   the costs of the sale and purchase shall be borne by the [applicant]/[respondent]/[*insert*];

   iii. the new home shall be held upon the same trusts, terms and conditions as the property and the trustees shall have full power as if they were beneficial owners thereof to execute such mortgage deed as may be necessary to enable the purchase thereof to be completed;

   iv. if the purchase price excluding stamp duty, Land Registry fees and conveyancing costs of the new home shall be less than the net proceeds of sale of the property the difference shall be [divided equally between the applicant and the respondent]/[paid to the [applicant]/[respondent] on account of [his]/[her] entitlement under this order [and]/[or] if the purchase price excluding stamp duty, Land Registry fees and conveyancing costs of the property purchased shall be more than the net proceeds of sale of the property the difference shall be met by the [applicant]/[respondent]. The parties shall then enter into a written deed recording their interests in the [net]/[gross] proceeds of sale of the property purchased as proportionate to their contributions towards the purchase price [or such other arrangement as may be agreed between them]. The [applicant]/[respondent] shall be responsible for the costs of preparing and executing the deed of trust;

h.   if the [applicant]/[respondent] shall remain in occupation of the property for more than [*insert*] months after the determining event, [he]/[she] shall pay to the [respondent]/[applicant] from that date such sum by way of occupation rent as may be agreed or in default of agreement determined by the court;

i.   on or before the determining event the [applicant]/[respondent] shall have the right to purchase the [respondent's]/[applicant's] interest in the property at an open market valuation to be agreed, or in default of agreement to be determined by [a valuer nominated by the President of the Royal Institution of Chartered Surveyors who shall act as an expert and not as an arbitrator]/[the court]; and

j.   if either the applicant or the respondent shall die during the currency of the trust, the power of appointing a substitute trustee shall be exercised by his or her personal representatives.

Transfer with charge back

57.

a.   The [applicant]/[respondent] shall [on or before [*insert date*]]/[within [*insert*] days [of the date of this order [*if decree absolute already made*]]/[of the date of decree absolute]] transfer to the [applicant]/[respondent] all [his]/[her] legal and beneficial interest in the [family home]/[property] [*as in definition above*] [subject to the mortgage(s) [*as in definition above*] secured against the property], on condition that as from the date of the said transfer the property shall be charged by way of legal charge as security for the payment to the [respondent]/[applicant] of a lump sum [of £[*insert*]]/[equal to [*insert*]% of the [gross]/[net] proceeds of sale], such charge to be in the form annexed to this Order ("the Charge").

b.   But this charge shall not become enforceable/exerciseable without the permission of the court or the consent of the parties until:

   i.   the youngest surviving of the children of the family attains the age of 18 years or ceases [his]/[her]/[their] full-time [secondary]/[tertiary] education [to first degree level] [including/excluding a gap year], or ceases to live with the [applicant]/[respondent], whichever is the later;

   ii. the death of the last surviving [of the] child[ren] of the family;

iii.   the death of the [applicant]/[respondent];

iv.   the [applicant's]/[respondent's] remarriage or cohabitation with another person [as man and wife] [for a [continuous] period of more than [insert period]]/[for a period of [insert] months in any [insert] month period];

v.   the [applicant's]/[respondent's] failure to occupy the property for a period of insert] months in any [insert] month period];

vi.   the [applicant's]/[respondent's] failure to occupy the property as [his]/[her] primary residence; or

vii.   any [dealing with]/[sale of] the property by the [applicant]/[respondent] whichever shall first occur or further order of the court provided that in any event the said legal charge shall not be exercisable without the leave of the court while any child of the family in occupation of the property is still a minor or of full age but receiving full time education or training.

c.   And the [applicant]/[respondent] shall not increase the sum presently owing in respect of the mortgage by arrears or by further advances under it and the [respondent]/[applicant] shall give credit to the [applicant]/[respondent] for such capital repayments as [he]/[she] shall have made in respect of the mortgage between the date of this order and redemption of the charge.

d.   And so long as the [applicant]/[respondent] remains entitled to occupy the property under the terms set out above, the [respondent]/[applicant] shall not seek to exercise [his]/[her] power of leasing under the charge.

Procure release from mortgage and to indemnify

58. The [applicant]/[respondent] shall use [his]/[her] best endeavours to procure the release of the [respondent]/[applicant] from any liability under the mortgage [as in definition above] [by [insert date]]/[on or before completion of the transfer provided for by paragraph [insert]/[within [insert] days of the date of this order], and shall in any event indemnify the [applicant]/[respondent] against all such liability.

Payment of mortgage and outgoings on property

59. The [applicant]/[respondent] shall discharge as and when each payment becomes due, be solely responsible for and in any event indemnify the [respondent]/[applicant] against:

a.   all interest and capital repayments due in respect of the mortgage [as in definition above];

b.   all [reasonable] sums due in respect of service charge, council tax, utilities (including but not limited to gas, electricity, water and telephone accounts), and buildings and contents insurance premiums in respect of [the family home] and/or [insert property/ies as in definition above]; and

c.   etc

The payments shall start on [insert date] and shall end on the first to occur of:

i.   [insert date];

ii.   the sale of the family home;

iii.   the youngest surviving [of the] child[ren] of the family attaining the age of 18 years or ceasing [his]/[her]/[their] full-time [secondary]/[tertiary] education [to first degree level] [including/excluding a gap year], or ceasing to live with the [applicant]/[respondent], whichever is the later;

iv.   the death of the last surviving [of the] child[ren] of the family;

v.   the death of the [applicant]/[respondent];

vi.   the [respondent's]/[applicant's] remarriage or cohabitation with another
       person [as man and wife] [for a [continuous] period of more than [insert
       period]]/[for a period of [insert] months in any [insert] month period];
vii.   the [applicant's]/[respondent's] failure to occupy the property for a period of
       insert] months in any [insert] month period];
viii. the [applicant's]/[respondent's] failure to occupy the property as [his]/[her]
       primary residence;
ix.   the retirement of the [applicant]/[respondent]; or
x.   a court order discharging this obligation.
             [as appropriate].

Payment of arrears of mortgage and outgoings on property

60. The [applicant]/[respondent] shall discharge by [*insert date*], be solely responsible for
and in any event indemnify the [respondent]/[applicant] against:

a.   the arrears which have accrued under the mortgage [*as in definition above*];
b.   the arrears which have accrued in respect of service charge, council tax, utilities
      (including but not limited to gas, electricity, water and telephone accounts), and
      buildings and contents insurance premiums in respect of [the family home] and/or
      [*insert property/ies as in definition above*];
c.   etc

Payment of and indemnity in respect of CGT/other tax

61. The [applicant]/[respondent] shall:

a.   discharge any liability for capital gains tax [or any other tax] consequent upon the
      implementation of paragraph(s) [*insert*] of this order promptly and in any event
      within 28 days of receiving any demand from HM Revenue and Customs; and
b.   in any event indemnify the [respondent]/[applicant] [and [his]/[her] estate] as to
      any such liability for capital gains tax [or any other tax] consequent upon the
      implementation of paragraph(s) [*insert*] of this order.

Transfer of tenancy

62. [*In the case of protected or secure tenancy*]

The [applicant]/[respondent] shall transfer to the [respondent]/[applicant] any estate or
interest which the [applicant]/[respondent] has in [the family home]/[the property] [*as in
definition*] with effect from [*insert date*]/[the date [*insert*] days from the date of this
order] and without further assurance transferred to and vested in the [respondent]/
[applicant].

[*In the case of a statutory tenancy*]

The [applicant]/[respondent] shall with effect from [*insert date*]/[the date [*insert*] days
from the date of this order] cease by virtue of [his]/[her] statutory tenancy of [the family
home]/[the property] [*as in definition*] to be entitled to occupy the same and the
[respondent]/[applicant] shall be deemed to be the sole tenant under the said tenancy.

Indemnity in respect of leasehold property

63. The [applicant]/[respondent] shall:

a.   comply with the terms of the lease [*give particulars*];

b.   promptly discharge any claims arising from the lease after [*insert date*]/[the date of assignment of the lease];

c.   in any event indemnify the [respondent]/[applicant] in respect of any claims arising from the lease after [*insert date*]/[the date of assignment of the lease]; and

d.   use his/her best endeavours to procure the [respondent's]/[applicant's] release from any liability under the lease by [*insert date*]/[within [*insert*] days of the date of this order.

Variation of Settlement

64. The ante/post-nuptial settlement dated [*insert date*] and made between [*insert*] and [*insert*] be varied so as to [e.g. extinguish the interest of the [applicant]/[respondent] in the settlement/settle all of the interest of the [applicant]/[respondent] on [*insert*] etc]. [The settlement to be in the form of the draft deed attached marked [*insert*]]/[The parties shall agree the form of the settlement by [*insert date*]. In default of agreement by that date, the matter shall be referred to conveyancing Counsel of the Court to settle. And it is directed that the Decree Nisi shall not be made Absolute until the necessary instrument or instruments have been executed].

Company resignation and transfer of shares

65.

a.   The [applicant]/[respondent] shall resign on or before [*insert date*] as director/company secretary of [*insert name of company/ies*].

b.   The [applicant]/[respondent] shall transfer to the [respondent]/[applicant] all/[*insert*]% of [his]/[her] [preference]/[ordinary] shares in [*insert name of company/ies*] by [*insert date*]/[within [*insert*] days of the date of this order.

c.   The [applicant]/[respondent] acknowledges that [he]/[she] has no claim against [*insert name of company/ies*] [arising out of the termination of [his]/[her] employment or otherwise].

d.   The [applicant]/[respondent] shall indemnify the [respondent]/[applicant] and [his]/[her] estate in respect of any losses, claims, demands or other liabilities arising from her involvement with [*insert name of company/ies*], including but not limited to any capital gains tax liability or other tax liability, fees or other professional fees arising on the transfer by the [applicant]/[respondent] of [his]/[her] shareholding in [*insert name of company/ies*] to the [respondent]/[applicant] which are incurred by the [applicant]/[respondent] as a result of this order, [save in relation to personal income tax and national insurance which shall remain the sole responsibility of the [respondent]/[applicant]].

Company non-disclosure

66. The [applicant]/[respondent] shall not reveal to any third party unconnected with [*insert name of company/ies*] or these proceedings any information concerning the company/ies unless authorised to do by the [respondent]/[applicant] or an authorised officer of the company/ies.

Transfer of car

67. The [applicant]/[respondent] shall transfer to the [respondent]/[applicant] all [his]/[her] interest in the family car [on [*insert date*]]/[within [*insert*] days of [the date of this order] [by [*insert time*] on the date [*insert*] days after the date of this order]. The [respondent]/[applicant] shall be responsible for the costs of running and maintaining the family car.

Transfer of life policy

68. The [applicant]/[respondent] shall transfer by [*insert time*] on [*insert date*]/[by [*insert time*] on the date [*insert*] days after the date of this order]/[by [*insert time*] on the date [[*insert*] days after the date] of completion of the sale of [*insert*] referred to at paragraph [*insert*] above/below], by [assigning]/[joining in an assignment to the [respondent]/[applicant] [his]/[her] interest in the life assurance policy with [*insert company*] numbered [*insert*].

Maintenance pending suit/interim periodical payments

69. The [applicant]/[respondent] shall pay to the [respondent]/[applicant] maintenance pending suit until the date of decree absolute and afterwards interim periodical payments at the rate of £[*insert*] per annum, payable [weekly]/[monthly] [in advance]/[in arrears] by standing order from [*insert date, including a date earlier than the date of the order if backdating*] until further order. [The [applicant]/[respondent] shall be given credit for the payment(s) of £[*insert*] made on [*insert dates*]].

OR

The [applicant]/[respondent] shall pay to the [respondent]/[applicant] maintenance pending suit until the date of decree absolute and afterwards interim periodical payments. Payments shall be at the rate of £[*insert*] per annum, payable [weekly]/[monthly] [in advance]/[in arrears] by standing order. Payments shall start on [*insert date, including a date earlier than the date of the order if backdating*], and shall end on the first to occur of:

a. the death of either the applicant or the respondent;
b. the [respondent's]/[applicant's] remarriage;
c. the determination of the applicant's application for a financial order; or
d. a further order.

[The [applicant]/[respondent] shall be given credit for the payment(s) of £[*insert*] made on [*insert date*]].

Spousal periodical payments order without a term

70. The [applicant]/[respondent] shall pay to the [respondent]/[applicant] maintenance pending suit until the date of decree absolute and afterwards periodical payments. Payments shall be at the rate of £[*insert*] per annum, payable [weekly]/[monthly] [in advance]/[in arrears] by standing order. Payments shall start on [*insert date*], and shall end on the first to occur of:

a.   the death of either the applicant or the respondent;

b.   the [respondent's]/[applicant's] remarriage; or

c.   a further order.

Spousal periodical payments order with an extendable/non-extendable term

71. The [applicant]/[respondent] shall pay to the [respondent]/[applicant] maintenance pending suit until the date of decree absolute and afterwards periodical payments. Payments shall be at the rate of £[*insert*] per annum, payable [weekly]/[monthly] [in advance]/[in arrears] by standing order. Payments shall start on [*insert date*], and shall end on the first to occur of:

a.   the death of either the applicant or the respondent;

b.   the [respondent's]/[applicant's] remarriage;

c.   a further order; or
     [*Extendable Term*:]

d.   [*insert date*]/[*e.g.* the youngest surviving child of the family attaining the age of 18 or ceasing full-time [secondary]/[tertiary] education [to first degree level] [including/excluding a gap year]] after which the [respondent's]/[applicant's] claims for periodical payments and secured periodical payments shall be dismissed, and it is directed that upon the expiry of the term:
     i.   the [respondent]/[applicant] shall not be entitled to make any further application in relation to the marriage for an order under the Matrimonial Causes Act 1973 section 23(1)(a) or (b) for periodical payments or secured periodical payments; and
     ii.   the [respondent]/[applicant] shall not be entitled on the [applicant's]/[respondent's] death to apply for an order under the Inheritance (Provision for Family and Dependants) Act 1975, section 2. However, the [respondent]/[applicant] may apply for an order to extend this term, provided the application is made before the term expires.
     [*Non-Extendable Term*:]

e.   [*insert date*]/[*e.g.* the youngest surviving child of the family attaining the age of 18 or ceasing full-time [secondary]/[tertiary] education [to first degree level] [including/excluding a gap year]] after which the [respondent's]/[applicant's] claims for periodical payments and secured periodical payments shall be dismissed, and it is directed that:
     i.   upon the expiry of the term, the [respondent]/[applicant] shall not be entitled to make any further application in relation to the marriage for an order under the Matrimonial Causes Act 1973 section 23(1)(a) or (b) for periodical payments or secured periodical payments;
     ii.   pursuant to the Matrimonial Causes Act 1973 section 28(1A), the [respondent]/[applicant] may not apply for an order to extend this term;

iii.   upon the expiry of the term, the [respondent]/[applicant] shall not be entitled on the [applicant's]/[respondent's] death to apply for an order under the Inheritance (Provision for Family and Dependants) Act 1975, section 2.

For the avoidance of doubt, the [respondent]/[applicant] may not apply for an order to extend this term.

Secured spousal periodical payments order

72.

a.   The [applicant]/[respondent] shall by [*insert time*] on [*insert date*]/[by [*insert time*] on the date [*insert*] days after the date of this order] secure periodical payments to be made to the [respondent]/[applicant] at the rate of £[*insert*] per annum. Such payments shall be made from [*insert date*] and continue until the first to occur of:
    i.   the death of the [respondent]/[applicant];
    ii.   the [respondent's]/[applicant's] remarriage;
    iii. [*insert date*]; or
    iv.   further order.

b.   Such payments shall be secured by the sum of £[*insert*]/[such security to be agreed between the parties or in default of agreement referred to the district judge] and shall be security for the [applicant's]/[respondent's] obligation to pay periodical payments provided for in paragraph [*insert*] above.

c.   The security shall be used to meet the [applicant's]/[respondent's] obligation to pay periodical payments to the extent that this obligation is not met by the [applicant]/[respondent].

d.   The applicant and the respondent shall by [*insert time*] on [*insert date*]/[by [*insert time*] on the date [*insert*] days after the date of this order] enter into a deed of security [and in default of agreement as to the form of the deed, the matter shall be referred to conveyancing counsel of the court to settle the deed].

Child periodical payments order – Interim order pending CMS calculation

73. [By agreement between the parties] the [respondent]/[applicant] shall pay to the [applicant]/[respondent] periodical payments for benefit of the child[ren] of the family. Payments shall be at the rate of £[*insert*] per annum [per child], payable [weekly]/[monthly] [in advance]/[in arrears] by standing order. Payments shall start on [*insert date*], and shall end on the issue of a CMS calculation. [Payments made under this paragraph shall be received by the [applicant]/[respondent] on account of any payments that may be due under the CMS calculation].

Child periodical payments order

74. [By agreement between the parties] the [applicant]/[respondent] shall pay to the [respondent]/[applicant] periodical payments for benefit of the child[ren] of the family. Payments shall be at the rate of £[*insert*] per annum per child, payable [weekly]/[monthly] [in advance]/[in arrears] by standing order. Payments shall start on [*insert date*], and shall end on:

a.   each child respectively attaining the age of 18 years or ceasing their fulltime [secondary]/[tertiary] education [to first degree level] [including/excluding a gap year], whichever shall be the later; or

b.   a further order.

The court may (prior to the expiry of the term or subsequently) order a longer period of payment. [In the event of a CMS calculation being carried out, from the effective date of any CMS calculation, periodical payments made under this paragraph for the benefit of the children shall be received by the [respondent]/[applicant] on account of any sums falling due under the CMS calculation].

Child periodical payments order whilst in tertiary education

75. [By agreement between the parties] the [applicant]/[respondent] shall pay to the [respondent]/[applicant] periodical payments for benefit of the child[ren] of the family at the rate of £[*insert*] per annum per child, payable [weekly]/[monthly] [in advance]/[in arrears] by standing order. Payments shall start on [*insert date*], and shall end on each child respectively attaining the age of 18 or ceasing their full-time tertiary education [to first degree level] [including/excluding a gap year], whichever shall be the later, or a further order.

OR

[By agreement between the parties] the [applicant]/[respondent] shall pay to the respective children of the family periodical payments at the rate of £[*insert*] per annum per child, payable [weekly]/[monthly] [in advance]/[in arrears] by standing order. Payments shall start on [*insert date*], and shall end on each child respectively attaining the age of 18 or ceasing their full-time tertiary education [to first degree level] [including/excluding a gap year], whichever shall be the later, or a further order.

Child periodical payments order for costs of disability

76. The [applicant]/[respondent] shall pay to the [respondent]/[applicant] periodical payments for benefit of [*insert name*] at the rate of £[*insert*] per annum to meet the costs of [his]/[her] disability. Payments shall start on [*insert date*], and shall end on:

a.   [*insert name*] attaining the age of 18 years or ceasing [his]/[her] full-time [secondary]/[tertiary] education [to first degree level] [including/excluding a gap year], whichever shall be the later; or

b.   a further order.

The court may (prior to the expiry of the term or subsequently) order a longer period of payment. This order is made pursuant to the Child Support Act 1991 section 8(8).

Child periodical payments order – top-up order

77.

a.   In circumstances where (a) the CMS has made a CMS calculation in respect of the child[ren] of the family; and (b) the court is satisfied that the circumstances of the case make it appropriate for the [applicant]/[respondent] to make periodical payments as ordered in paragraph [*insert*] below in addition to the child maintenance payable in accordance with the CMS calculation, the [applicant]/[respondent] shall pay to the [respondent]/[applicant] periodical payments for benefit of the child[ren] of the family.

b.   Payments shall be [at the rate of £[*insert*] per annum per child]/[in the sum which, when added to the payments (if any) made by the [applicant]/[respondent] to the CMS pursuant to a CMS calculation, total £[*insert*] per annum whilst both children are provided for under the CMS calculation or £[*insert*] per annum whilst only one such child is provided for under the CMS calculation], payable [weekly]/[monthly] [in advance]/[in arrears] by standing order. Payments shall start on [*insert date*], and shall end on:
  i.   each child respectively attaining the age of 18 years or ceasing their full-time [secondary]/[tertiary] education [to first degree level] [including/excluding a gap year], whichever shall be the later; or
  ii.   a further order.

The court may (prior to the expiry of the term or subsequently) order a longer period of payment.

Delayed Commencement Orders

78. The order in paragraph [*insert*] above shall only start to have effect when the CMS ceases to have jurisdiction for the child[ren] of the family because:

a.   [he]/[she]/[they] [is]/[are] no longer in full-time, non-advanced education as set out in s 55 Child Support Act 1991; or

b.   [he]/[she]/[they] or either party are no longer habitually resident within the jurisdiction of England and Wales.

Global order

79. The [applicant]/[respondent] shall pay to the [respondent]/[applicant] maintenance pending suit until the date of decree absolute and afterwards periodical payments for the benefit of herself and the children of the family. Payments shall be at the rate of £[*insert*] per annum less any payments) made by the [applicant]/[respondent] to the CMS pursuant to a CMS calculation. Payments shall start on [*insert date*], and shall end on the first to occur of:

a.   the death of either the applicant or the respondent;

b.   the [respondent's]/[applicant's] remarriage; or

c.   a further order.
       OR

a.   The [applicant]/[respondent] shall pay to the [respondent]/[applicant] maintenance pending suit until the date of decree absolute and afterwards periodical payments. Payments shall be at the rate of £[*insert*] per annum less any payments made by the [applicant]/[respondent] to the CMS pursuant to a CMS calculation and the payments made by the [applicant]/[respondent] in accordance with paragraph (b). Payments shall start on [*insert date*], and shall end on the first to occur of: (i) the death of either the applicant or the respondent; (ii) the [respondent's]/[applicant's] remarriage; or (iii) a further order.

b.   The [applicant]/[respondent] shall pay to the [respondent]/[applicant] maintenance pending suit until the date of decree absolute and afterwards periodical payments for the benefit the child[ren] of the family. Payments shall be at the rate of £[*insert*] per annum per child, payable [weekly]/[monthly] [in advance]/[in arrears] by standing order. Payments shall start on [*insert date – same date as in (a)*], and shall end on: (i) each child respectively attaining the age of 18 years or ceasing their full-time [secondary]/[tertiary] education [to first degree level] [including/excluding a gap year], whichever shall be the later; or (ii) a further order. The court may (prior to the expiry of the term or subsequently) order a longer period of payment.

School fees order – nursery education

80. The [respondent]/[applicant] shall pay [further] periodical payments for benefit of the child[ren] of the family in such sum as shall be equivalent to the child[ren]'s nursery fees [but not the extras on the nursery bill]/[and all reasonable extras appearing on the nursery bill [and all exceptional extras appearing on the nursery bill agreed between the parties in advance]]/[and all extras appearing on the nursery bill up to a total of £[*insert*] [per child] per term or such greater sum as is agreed in advance in writing between the parties] at such nurseries as the child[ren] of the family shall from time to time attend by agreement between the parties or in default of agreement by order of the court [provided that the [respondent]/[applicant] is at liberty to avail [himself]/[herself] if possible of free non-means tested state-funded provision at any such nursery]. Payments shall be made in three instalments paid on [*insert*]/[not less than one month before the beginning of the term to which they relate] directly to the nursery bursar or other person indicated on the bill as recipient for the nursery. The [respondent]/[applicant] shall produce to the [applicant]/[respondent] documentary evidence that he has discharged each payment by no later than the due date for each payment.

School fees order – primary/secondary education

81. The [applicant]/[respondent] shall pay [further] periodical payments for benefit of the child[ren] of the family in such sum as shall be equivalent to the child[ren]'s school fees [but not the extras on the school bill]/[and all reasonable extras appearing on the school bill [and all exceptional extras appearing on the school bill agreed between the parties in advance]]/[and all extras appearing on the school bill up to a total of £[*insert*] [per child] per term or such greater sum as is agreed in advance in writing between the parties] at such schools as the child[ren] of the family shall from time to time attend by agreement between the parties or in default of agreement by order of the court. Payments shall be made in three instalments paid on [*insert*]/[not less than one month before the beginning of the term to which they relate] directly to the school bursar or other person indicated on the bill as recipient for the school. The [respondent]/[applicant] shall produce to the [applicant]/[respondent] documentary evidence that he has discharged each payment by no later than the due date for each payment. This order is made pursuant to the Child Support Act 1991 section 8(7).

School fees order – tertiary education

82. The [applicant]/[respondent] shall pay [further] periodical payments for benefit of the child[ren] of the family in such sum as shall be equivalent to the child[ren]'s college and/or university fees and [all reasonable extras appearing on the [college]/[university] bill [and all exceptional extras appearing on the [college]/[university] bill agreed between the parties and the relevant child in advance]] for a first undergraduate degree course of tertiary education at such [college]/[university] as the child[ren] of the family shall from time to time attend by agreement between the parties and the relevant child. Payments shall be made as and when they become due directly to the [college]/[university] bursar or other person indicated on the bill as recipient for the [college]/[university]. The

[respondent]/[applicant] shall produce to the [applicant]/[respondent]/[the relevant child] documentary evidence that he has discharged each payment by no later than the due date for each payment.

Child Support Act 1991 clawback: charge or lump sum

83. [The property known as [*insert property*] shall be charged with payment to the [applicant]/[respondent] of]/[the [respondent]/[applicant] shall pay to the [applicant]/[respondent] a lump sum of] an amount equal to the total of the following sums paid by the [applicant]/[respondent]:

a.   any sums paid under any CMS calculation to the [respondent]/[applicant] in respect of the child[ren] of the family [inasmuch as such sums exceed the monthly equivalent of £[*insert*] [for each child] [(automatically varied on [*insert date*] each year ("the variation date") by the percentage [change]/[increase], if any, in the [retail prices index]/[consumer prices index] during the most recent 12 month period preceding the variation date for which index data has been published; and

b.   any sums paid under sections 106 and 108 of the Social Security Administration Act 1992. [together with simple interest on these sums at the rate applicable for the time being to a High Court judgment debt]/[the rate of [*insert*] % per annum] from [*insert date*], [the payment to be due and the charge to be enforceable]/[the lump sum to be payable] on the first to occur of:
       i.   the death of the [respondent]/[applicant];
       ii.   the [respondent's]/[applicant's] remarriage;
       iii.   the youngest surviving [of the] child[ren] of the family attaining the age of 18 years or ceasing [his]/[her]/[their] full-time [secondary]/[tertiary] education [to first degree level] [including/excluding a gap year], or [permanently] ceasing to live with the [applicant]/[respondent], whichever is the later;
       iv.   [the sale of the family home/property]; or
       v.   a further order of the court, for which both parties shall be at liberty to apply to the court [provided that the amount as to which the property shall be charged shall not exceed [e.g. one half of the gross proceeds of sale of the property, or if it shall not have been sold, one half of the gross value, any dispute as to such value to be settled by a surveyor agreed between the parties or in default of agreement appointed by the President for the time being of the Royal Institution of Chartered Surveyors].

Child Support Act 1991 clawback: adjournment of capital claims

84.

a.   In circumstances where the parties have agreed that (i) the provision made by this order fulfils the [applicant's]/[respondent's] responsibilities to the child[ren] of the family; (ii) the [respondent]/[applicant] does not intend to seek any [further] financial provision for the maintenance of the child[ren] of the family [including school fees and/or any other extras for the child[ren], whether through the court, the CMS or otherwise; and (iii) in the event that the [applicant]/[respondent] becomes liable to make any [further] financial provision for the child[ren] of the family, the [respondent]/[applicant] will indemnify [him]/[her] against any liability, and in default of the [respondent]/[applicant] performing [her]/[his] agreement to indemnify the [applicant]/[respondent], the [applicant]/[respondent] shall be entitled to make a claim for a [lump sum order]/[property adjustment order [in respect of [*insert*]]] for the purpose of recompensing [him]/[her], the [applicant's]/[respondent's] claims for a [lump sum order]/[property adjustment order in respect of [*insert*]] shall be adjourned generally with liberty to the [applicant]/[respondent] to restore.

b.   In the event of the [applicant]/[respondent] not having restored his claim(s) by [*insert date* – e.g. by the date three months after the date on which the youngest surviving child of the family attains the age of 18 or ceases fulltime secondary education], his claims shall be dismissed.

c.   The [respondent]/[applicant] shall indemnify the [applicant]/[respondent] against [his]/[her] liability to make any [further] financial provision for the child[ren] of the family.

Annual variation in periodical payments

85. The periodical payments set out in paragraph [*insert*] [and paragraph [*insert*] above] shall be varied automatically on the "variation date", which shall be on the date of the payment due in [*insert month*] and at yearly intervals afterwards. The change in the payments shall be the percentage [change]/[increase], if any, between the [retail prices index]/[consumer prices index] during the most recent 12 month period preceding the variation date for which index data has been published.

OR

The periodical payments set out in paragraph [*insert*] [and paragraph [*insert*] above] shall be varied automatically on the "variation date", which shall be on the date of the payment due in [*insert month*] and at yearly intervals afterwards. The change in payments shall be the [greater]/[lesser] of: a. the percentage [change]/[increase], if any, between the [retail prices index]/[consumer prices index] for the month 15 months before the variation date (i.e. [*insert month*] in the first instance) and the [retail prices index]/[consumer prices index] for the month 3 months before the variation date (i.e. [*insert month*] in the first instance); and

b.   the percentage by which the [applicant's]/[respondent's] total [earned] income [including bonus and commission] after deduction of income tax and national insurance contributions [and car allowance and pension contributions] shall have increased between the date 15 months before the variation date (i.e. [*insert month*] in the first instance) and the date 3 months before the variation date (i.e. [*insert month*] in the first instance). The [applicant]/[respondent] shall produce their P60 and last three payslips to the [respondent]/[applicant] by [*insert date*] each year, and production of these documents shall be sufficient evidence of the [applicant's]/[respondent's] total income and the income tax and national insurance contributions payable on it.

Payment of periodical payments by standing order

86. The [applicant]/[respondent] shall make payment of the sums due under paragraph [*insert*] [and paragraph [*insert*]] above by standing order into the [respondent's]/[applicant's] following account:

Name of Bank/Building Society: [*insert*]

Sort Code: [*insert*]

Account Number: [*insert*]

Name of account holder: [*insert*]

or such other account as the [respondent]/[applicant] may from time to time nominate in writing.

Permission to disclose order to CMS

87. There be permission under FPR 2010, rule 12.73(1)(b) to produce a copy of this order to the CMS.

Variation: periodical payments

88.

a. Paragraph [*insert*] of the order in this matter dated [*insert date*] shall be varied to provide that the [applicant]/[respondent] shall pay to the [respondent]/[applicant] periodical payments. Payments shall be at the rate of £[*insert*] per annum, payable [weekly]/[monthly] [in advance]/[in arrears] by standing order. Payments shall start on [*insert date*], and shall end on the first to occur of: (i) the death of either the applicant or the respondent; (ii) the [respondent's]/[applicant's] remarriage; or (iii) a further order [*and, if appropriate an extendable/non-extendable term as above*].

b. [The [applicant]/[respondent] shall be released from his/her undertaking to [*insert*] in paragraph [*insert*] of the order in this matter dated [*insert date*]].

c. [The arrears under paragraph [*insert*] of the order in this matter dated [*insert date*] accrued to [*insert date*] shall be remitted.]

Variation: lump sum or pension sharing in lieu of periodical payments

89. The order in this matter dated [*insert date*] shall be varied as follows:

a. Paragraph [*insert*] of the order, providing for the [applicant]/[respondent] to pay periodical payments to the [respondent]/[applicant], shall be discharged with effect from the date on which [the [applicant]/[respondent] pays the lump sum provided for in paragraph (b) below in full] and/or [the pension share provided for in paragraph (b)/(c) below is implemented], after which the [respondent's]/[applicant's] claims for periodical payments and secured periodical payments shall be dismissed and it is directed that:
    i.   the [respondent]/[applicant] shall not be entitled to make any further application in relation to the marriage for an order under the Matrimonial Causes Act 1973 section 23(1)(a) or (b) for periodical payments or secured periodical payments;
    ii. pursuant to the Matrimonial Causes Act 1973 section 28(1A), the [respondent]/[applicant] may not apply for an order to extend the term;
    iii. the [respondent]/[applicant] shall not be entitled on the [applicant's]/[respondent's] death to apply for an order under the Inheritance (Provision for Family and Dependants) Act 1975, section 2.

b. Pursuant to the Matrimonial Causes Act 1973, section 31, [the [applicant]/[respondent] shall pay to the [respondent]/[applicant] a lump sum of £[*insert*] by [*insert time*] on [*insert date*]] and/or [there be provision by way of a pension sharing order in favour of the [respondent]/[applicant] in respect of the [applicant's]/[respondent's] rights in the [*insert*] pension arrangement(s) with [*insert company*] in accordance with the annexe(s) to this order it being agreed between the parties that in the event of [applicant]/[respondent] predeceasing the [respondent]/[applicant] after this order has taken effect but before its implementation the [respondent]/[applicant] shall have the [applicant's]/ [respondent's] personal representative's consent to an application for leave to appeal out of time against the terms of this order].

c.   [The arrears under paragraph [*insert*] of the order in this matter dated [*insert date*] accrued to [*insert date*] shall be remitted.]

Pension sharing order

90. There shall be provision by way of a pension sharing order in favour of the [applicant]/[respondent] in respect of the [respondent's]/[applicant's] rights under [his]/[her] pension arrangement[s] [*as in definition*] in accordance with the annex[es] to this order, it being agreed between the parties that in the event of the [applicant]/[respondent] predeceasing the [respondent]/[applicant] after this order has taken effect but before its implementation the [respondent]/[applicant] shall have the [applicant's]/[respondent's] personal representative's consent to an application for leave to appeal out of time against the terms of this order.

Nomination of death in service benefit

91. The [applicant]/[respondent] shall forthwith nominate the [respondent]/[applicant] to receive [not less than [*insert*]% of the death in service benefit payable under such pension scheme(s) as he shall from time to time be a member of [subject to a sum not greater than [*insert*] times the annual amount of the periodical payments due to her]/[£[*insert*]]. The [applicant]/[respondent] shall only be required to make such nomination until the earlier/later of the following:

a.   the death of the [respondent]/[applicant];

b.   the remarriage of the [respondent]/[applicant]; or

c.   an order terminating the [respondent's]/[applicant's] maintenance payments.

Pension attachment order

92. There shall be provision by way of a pension attachment order in favour of the [applicant]/[respondent] in respect of the [respondent's]/[applicant's] rights under [his]/[her] pension arrangement[s] [*as in definition*] under the Matrimonial Causes Act 1973 section 25B by way of periodical payments in accordance with the annex(es) to this order. Any such payment by the PRPA shall be treated for all purposes as a payment made by the [respondent]/[applicant] as the party with pension rights in or towards [his]/[her] liability under this order.

Declaration under the EU Maintenance Regulation

93. The provisions under paragraphs [insert] of this order represent "maintenance" for the purposes of the Council Regulation (EC) No 4/2009 of 18 December 2008 on jurisdiction, applicable law, recognition and enforcement of decisions and cooperation in matters relating to maintenance obligations.

Clean break: capital

94. Except as provided for in this order, the [applicant's]/[respondent's] claims for lump sum orders, property adjustment orders, pension sharing orders and pension attachment orders shall be dismissed.

Clean break: capital and income

95. Except as provided for in this order, the [applicant's]/[respondent's] claims for periodical payments orders, secured periodical payments orders, lump sum orders, property adjustment orders, pension sharing orders and pension attachment orders shall be dismissed, and [he]/[she] shall not be entitled to make any further application in relation to the marriage for an order under the Matrimonial Causes Act 1973 section 23(1)(a) or (b) and [he]/[she] shall not be entitled on the [respondent's]/[applicant's] death to apply for an order under the Inheritance (Provision for Family and Dependants) Act 1975, section 2.

Costs

96. [There shall be no order as to costs]/[The [applicant]/[respondent] shall pay £[*insert*] towards the [respondent's]/[applicant's] costs by [*insert date*]]/[The [applicant]/ [respondent] shall pay the [respondent's]/[applicant's] costs by [*insert date*] [including the costs reserved by the order(s) made on [*insert date(s)*], and if the costs are not agreed they shall be assessed/subject to detailed assessment in accordance with the Civil Procedure Rules 1998 Part 47].

Costs – no order save for detailed assessment of a party's publicly funded costs

97. There shall be no order as to costs save for detailed assessment of the [applicant's]/[respondent's] publicly funded costs in accordance with the Civil Procedure Rules 1998 Part 47.17.

Costs – order against a publicly funded party

98. The [applicant]/[respondent] shall pay [the [respondent's]/[applicant's] costs]/[[*insert* %] of the [respondent's]/[applicant's] costs], [summarily assessed at £[*insert*]]/[to be subject to detailed assessment in default of agreement between the parties], by [*insert time*] on [*insert date*], subject to there being a determination pursuant to section 11 of the Access to Justice Act 1999 that it is reasonable for the [applicant]/[respondent] to do so. [This order for costs shall not be enforced without the court's permission].

Delayed costs order

99. The time for commencement of proceedings for the assessment of the costs under the Community Legal Services (Financial) Regulations 2000 shall not start until the date of completion of the [transfer]/[sale] of the [family home]/[property] referred to in paragraph [*insert*] of this order.

INDEX

References are to paragraph numbers.